Moral Discourse and Practice

Moral Discourse and Practice
Some Philosophical Approaches

Stephen Darwall
Allan Gibbard
Peter Railton

New York   Oxford
OXFORD UNIVERSITY PRESS
1997

OXFORD UNIVERSITY PRESS

Oxford   New York
Athens   Auckland   Bangkok   Bogota   Bombay
Buenos Aires   Calcutta   Cape Town   Dar es Salaam
Delhi   Florence   Hong Kong   Istanbul   Karachi
Kuala Lumpur   Madras   Madrid   Melbourne
Mexico City   Nairobi   Paris   Singapore
Taipei   Tokyo   Toronto

and associated companies in
Berlin   Ibadan

Published by Oxford University Press, Inc.
198 Madison Avenue, New York, New York 10016

Oxford is a registered trademark of Oxford University Press

Library of Congress Cataloging-in-Publication Data
Darwall, Stephen L., 1946–
Moral discourse and practice : some philosophical approaches /
Stephen Darwall, Allan Gibbard, Peter Railton.
p.   cm.
Includes bibliographical references.
ISBN 0-19-510749-7   ISBN 0-19-509669-X (pbk.)
1. Ethics.   I. Gibbard, Allan.   II. Railton, Peter Albert.
III. Title.
BJ1012.D325   1997
170—dc20   95-51121

3 5 7 9 8 6 4 2

Printed in the United States of America
on acid-free paper

Acknowledgments

We would like to thank our colleagues at Michigan, both students and faculty, for a stimulating moral philosophical community; Angela Blackburn, Robert Miller, and reviewers for Oxford University Press, for their helpful advice; Frederick Courtright, for his work in arranging permissions; Dr. Thomas Skrentny, for his gift of *Philosophers' Index* on CD ROM to the Tanner Philosophy Library, which greatly aided bibliographical work; the staff of the Michigan Philosophy Department, for general support; and Dawn Pointer, for her invaluable help in compiling the bibliography and preparing the manuscript.

Simon Blackburn, "How to Be an Ethical Antirealist," *Midwest Studies in Philosophy* 12 (1988): 361–375. Copyright © 1988 by Regents of the University of Minnesota. Reprinted with the permission of Midwest Studies in Philosophy, Inc.

Allan Gibbard, excerpts from *Wise Choices, Apt Feelings* (Cambridge, Mass.: Harvard University Press, 1990). Copyright © 1990 by Allan Gibbard. Reprinted with permission of the author.

John McDowell, "Values and Secondary Qualities," from *Morality and Objectivity: A Tribute to J. L. Mackie*, edited by Ted Honderich (London: Routledge & Kegan Paul, 1985). Copyright © 1985 by Routledge & Kegan Paul. Reprinted with the permission of the author and the publishers.

John McDowell, "Projection and Truth in Ethics," The Lindley Lecture, The University of Kansas, 1987. Copyright © 1987 by the Department of Philosophy, University of Kansas. Reprinted with the permission of the publishers.

David Wiggins, "A Sensible Subjectivism?" from *Needs, Values, Truth: Essays in the Philosophy of Value* (Oxford: Blackwell, 1991). Reprinted with the permission of the author and Blackwell Publishers, Ltd.

John Rawls, "Kantian Constructivism in Moral Theory," *The Journal of Philosophy* 77 (1980): 515–572. Revised as part of *Political Liberalism* (New York: Columbia University Press, 1993). Copyright © 1980, 1993 by Columbia University Press. Reprinted with the permission of the author and publisher.

T. M. Scanlon, "Contractualism and Utilitarianism," from *Utilitarianism and Beyond*, edited by Amartya Sen and Bernard Williams (Cambridge: Cambridge University Press, 1982). Copyright © 1982 by Maisons des Sciences de l'Homme and Cambridge University Press. Reprinted with the permission of the author and Cambridge University Press.

Jürgen Habermas, "Discourse Ethics: Notes on a Program of Philosophical Justification," in *Moral Consciousness and Communicative Action,* translated by Christian Lenhardt and Shierry Weber Nicholsen. Copyright © 1990 by the Massachusetts Institute of Technology. Reprinted with the permission of MIT Press.

Philippa Foot, "Morality as a System of Hypothetical Imperatives," from *Virtues and Vices and Other Essays in Moral Philosophy* (Berkeley: University of California Press, 1978). Originally in *The Philosophical Review* 81 (1972): 305–316. Copyright © 1978 by Philippa Foot. Reprinted with the permission of the author.

Thomas Nagel, excerpts from *The Possibility of Altruism* (Princeton: Princeton University Press, 1978). Copyright © 1970 by Princeton University Press. Reprinted with the permission of the publishers.

David Gauthier, excerpts from *Morals by Agreement* (Oxford: Oxford University Press, 1986). Copyright © 1986 by David Gauthier. Reprinted with the permission of Oxford University Press.

Bernard Williams, "Internal and External Reasons," from *Moral Luck* (New York: Cambridge University Press, 1981). Copyright © 1981 by Cambridge University Press. Reprinted with the permission of the author and Cambridge University Press.

Christine Korsgaard, "Skepticism About Practical Reason," *The Journal of Philosophy* 83 (1986): 5–26. Copyright © 1986 by the Journal of Philosophy, Inc. Reprinted with the permission of the author and The Journal of Philosophy.

Christine Korsgaard, "The Sources of Normativity," *The Tanner Lectures on Human Values,* vol. 15, edited by Grethe B. Peterson (Salt Lake City: University of Utah Press, 1994). Copyright © 1994 by the University of Utah. Reprinted with the permission of the University of Utah Press.

Contents

IV. REASONS, MOTIVES, AND THE DEMANDS OF MORALITY

I

Introduction

1

Toward *Fin de siècle* Ethics: Some Trends

STEPHEN DARWALL, ALLAN GIBBARD, AND PETER RAILTON

1. SETTING THE STAGE

Principia's Revenge

The *Philosophical Review* is a century old; so too—nearly enough—is a certain controversy in moral philosophy, a controversy initiated by G. E. Moore's *Principia Ethica*.[1] Both centenarians are still full of life. This we celebrate without reserve in the case of the *Review*; should we be equally happy about the continuing vitality of the other?

After all, the controversy began with Moore's charge that previous moral philosophy had been disfigured by a fallacy—the fallacy of defining Good in either naturalistic or metaphysical terms. Yet it has been known for the last fifty years that Moore discovered no *fallacy* at all. Moreover, Moore's accident-prone deployment of his famous "open question argument" in defending his claims made appeal to a now defunct intuitionistic Platonism, and involved assumptions about the transparency of concepts and obviousness

of analytic truth that were seen (eventually, by Moore himself) to lead inescapably to the "paradox of analysis." To grant Moore all of the resources he deploys or assumes in his official presentation of the open question argument would suffice to bring the whole enterprise of conceptual analysis to a standstill, and show nothing about Good in particular.[2] One contemporary philosopher concludes that "as it stands the open question argument is invalid," since it purports to refute all definitional analyses of 'good', but relies upon an arbitrarily narrowed conception of philosophical or scientific definition.[3]

Why, then, isn't Moore's argument a mere period piece? However readily we now reject as antiquated his views in semantics and epistemology, it seems impossible to deny that Moore was on to something.

The Heyday of Analytic Metaethics

Moore had discovered not a proof of a fallacy, but rather an argumentive device that

3

implicitly but effectively brings to the fore certain characteristic features of 'good'—and of other normative vocabulary—that seem to stand in the way of our accepting any known naturalistic or metaphysical definition as unquestionably right, as definitions, at least when fully understood, seemingly should be. Dissociated from Moorean thought experiments that call Platonic concepts before the mind's eye, the open question argument can do its job case by case. One asks of any purported account identifying some descriptive property or state P as the meaning of 'good' whether on careful reflection we do not in fact find that we understand the question, "*Is P really good?*" If this question is intelligible—even, it seems, to those who hold that having or being P is a good thing (perhaps the only good thing) and who are moved to give nonlinguistic reasons in defense of a positive answer to the question—then, absent some further story, P could hardly just be what we *mean* by 'good'. If this argumentative device is to succeed conclusively, we must be utterly convinced that the intelligibility of this question does not arise from ignorance of logical implication, or of factual or linguistic information. Here is where the qualification 'absent some further story' comes into play: How can one claim utter conviction that no logical, factual, or linguistic oversight is involved without simply begging the question?

The best response comes in two parts. First, one should not claim utter conviction, but merely observe that the open question argument *is* compelling for otherwise competent, reflective speakers of English, who appear to have no difficulty imagining what it would be like to dispute whether P is good.

Second, one should articulate a philosophical explanation of why this might be so. Here is one such explanation. Attributions of goodness appear to have a conceptual link with the guidance of action, a link exploited whenever we gloss the open question 'Is P really good?' as 'Is it clear that, other things equal, we really ought to, or must, devote

ourselves to bringing about P?' Our confidence that the openness of the open question does not depend upon any error or oversight may stem from our seeming ability to imagine, for any naturalistic property R, clearheaded beings who would fail to find appropriate reason or motive to action in the mere fact that R obtains (or is seen to be in the offing). Given this imaginative possibility, it has not been *logically* secured that P is action-guiding (even if, as a matter of fact, we all do find R psychologically compelling).[4] And this absence of a logical or conceptual link to action shows us exactly where there is room to ask, intelligibly, whether R really is good.

This explanation would permit us to see why the open question argument, which has bulked so large in ethics, has had little if any explicitly recognized influence in other areas of philosophy in which reductive naturalistic accounts have been proposed—for these areas have (perhaps wrongly) not been thought to have this conceptual tie to action-guidingness.[5] Moreover, this explanation would permit us to understand how the argument could have come to be seen as convincing against the entire range of reductive naturalisms, not just those considered to date and not just those narrowly definitional. Finally, this explanation would enable us to understand how the argument came to bite the hand that first fed it, and, eventually, to count Intuitionism among its victims. For, it appears no easier to see how an appropriate link to motivation or action could be logically secured if we were to substitute—in the conditional considered in the previous paragraph—'*sui generis*, simple, nonnatural property Q' for 'naturalistic property R'. The response of Prichard, namely, that seeing the relevant nonnatural property just *is* seeing a binding obligation to act, with no further explanation or incentive, merely deepens the mystery of the nature of this alleged property and what it would be like to see it clearly or find it normative.[6]

Wittgenstein, for one, could see something else quite clearly—"as it were in a flash of light," he says—namely, that "no description that I can think of would do to describe what I mean by absolute value, [and] I would reject every significant description anybody could suggest, *ab initio*, on the [very] ground of its significance."[7] Description, he concludes, could not be the essential semantic role of a vocabulary with action-guidingness logically built into it.[8]

Yet moral discourse unquestionably has the surface form of a descriptive, property-attributing language. One might at this point be tempted toward the conclusion that moral discourse therefore is systematically misleading. But a potentially more illuminating and less revisionist alternative suggests itself. If we interpret sincere acceptance of a moral judgment as the (noncognitive) expression of an attitude of categorical endorsement, we can dispense with the need to find some indescribable property that moral judgments descry. Categorical endorsement *is* logically tied to the action-tendencies or normative posture of the person making the judgment—categorical endorsement being a *pro-attitude* toward the object of assessment. This account of what is going on in moral judgment thus is not vulnerable to the open question argument as stated above, and, indeed, can take advantage of whatever force this argument may have to help eliminate competitors.

Thus we are led to see noncognitivism as the real historical beneficiary of the open question argument. Of course, it will be able fully to enjoy this benefit only if a noncognitivist reconstruction is possible for the seemingly cognitive aspects of moral discourse, including the phenomena of moral disagreement, and this has proved no easy task. If such reconstruction is possible, then noncognitivism will afford a compact explanation of why such seemingly cognitive disagreement actually proves so resistant (in basic cases) to cognitive—that is, deductive or inductive—resolution.[9] Then too, an appropriately developed noncognitivism could afford considerable insight into the *dynamic social character* of moral discourse.[10] In a social setting we find ourselves with differences in interest and opinion, but also with a need for common principles and practices. Thus we need our subjective expressions on matters of feeling and conduct to have an "objective purport," so that they can be used to apply pressure on others (and even on oneself) to draw toward consensus and compliance even in the presence of conflicting interests.[11]

The capacity of noncognitivism to use the open question argument to its advantage while promising to render morality intelligible and defensible became better understood and more obvious as noncognitivism developed in the 1930s and 1940s. Eventually noncognitivism bested the competition and dominated the scene of analytic metaethics;[12] even Moore found himself half inclined to concede defeat.[13] Stasis—the less charitable would say *rigor mortis*—set in. Why, then, do we say that the controversy Moore began is lively today?

The Great Expansion

The 1950s witnessed increasing challenges to the adequacy or inevitability of noncognitivism. In England, a number of philosophers urged on broadly Wittgensteinian grounds that we question the picture of language they saw as underlying the noncognitivists' version of the fact/value distinction.[14] Elizabeth Anscombe and Philippa Foot began to force reconsideration of the idea that substantive, even naturalistic, content might be conceptually tied to moral evaluation.[15] At the same time, Peter Geach argued that such linguistic phenomena as embedding moral expressions within conditionals could not be handled by extant noncognitivist accounts, intensifying worries about whether a noncognitivist reconstruction of the cognitive grammar of moral discourse could succeed.[16]

In the United States, W. V. Quine had undermined confidence in the analytic/synthetic distinction, and, with Nelson Goodman, had urged a conception of the task of philosophy in which theory, metatheory, evidence, and inferential norm, or, alternatively, content and framework, were not sharply distinguished.[17] This removed some of the pressure to identify either prescriptive or descriptive content as "primary," permitting the relation between them to depend upon general features of our going scheme and circumstances rather than insisting that it be a "conceptual truth" sustained come what may in every corner of logical space. The "ideal observer" and "qualified attitude" theories of Roderick Firth and Richard Brandt explored ways of capturing normativity within a cognitivist account through the *idealization* of dispositions to respond; in a somewhat similar vein, John Rawls suggested a "decision procedure" for ethics.[18] William Frankena identified the centrality of internalism to debates in metaethics, and wondered aloud whether the phenomena of moral discourse and experience really support the sort of internalism that underwrote the move to noncognitivism.[19] Kurt Baier, Stephen Toulmin, and G. H. Von Wright, among others, revived a conception of objectivity in ethics based upon principles of practical reason.[20] Slowly, the landscape of moral philosophy, which had become stark, even dessicated, during the final years of the reign of analytic metaethics, was being populated by a richer variety of views, many of which placed substantive and normative questions at the fore.

In the United States in particular, one such view became the reference point for all others, thanks in part to its systematic character and normative attractiveness: John Rawls's *Theory of Justice,* with its method of "reflective equilibrium."[21] The narrowly language-oriented agenda of analytic metaethics was fully displaced, not so much because of a refutation of, say, noncognitivism, but because of an uneasiness about the notions of "meaning" or "analytic truth," and because reflective equilibrium arguments, which tended to set aside metaethical questions, promised to shed much greater light on substantive—and in many cases socially pressing—moral questions. A period that might be called "the Great Expansion" had begun in ethics.

In the Great Expansion a sense of liberation came to ethics. Moral philosophers shed the obsessions of analytic metaethics, and saw—or thought they saw—ways of exploring normative morality as a cognitive domain, without a bad philosophical conscience. The result was an unprecedented pouring of philosophical effort and personnel into ethics, which in turn spread out into the most diverse issues and applications. There is no prospect of summarizing these events here, and no point in trying. What is of chief interest from the standpoint of the present essay is the way that the Great Expansion partly contributed to the contemporary revival of metaethics.

During the Great Expansion, moral intuitions (not Moorean insights into the Forms but substantive moral responses that strike us as compelling) flowed abundantly—occasionally urged on by a bit of pumping. Competing normative theories were "tested" dialectically against these intuitions in a procedure that appeared to be licensed by reflective equilibrium. Over time this reflective equilibrium widened to include a broad range of empirical and philosophical questions.[22] Moral philosophers and their critics grew increasingly aware that a host of questions about the semantic, epistemic, metaphysical, or practical status of morality arose in full force about new normative methods and theories. Working in somewhat different ways, Gilbert Harman and John Mackie made these questions hard to ignore.[23]

Metaethics has come back to life, though the terms in which its questions can be posed or answered have been changed by the philosophy that has taken place since the heyday of analytic metaethics. New forms of naturalism and nonnaturalism have once again become competitive with noncognitivism, which itself has been significantly refocused, for example, to encompass rationality as well as ethics. And postwar work in game theory and rational choice theory has opened the way to rethinking and sharpening questions of practical justification, bringing them into a prominence they had not enjoyed under analytic metaethics. Finally, as we approach the *fin de siècle*, self-consciousness leaves little untouched; philosophy, including metaethics, has become reflective both about the limitations of the notion of meaning and about the point or prospects of philosophical inquiry itself.

Caveat Lector

In this way, as we see it, the stage has been set for the contemporary scene in moral philosophy. This scene is remarkably rich and diverse, and our account of it is necessarily selective—emphasis has been placed in order to create coherence. In what follows, we will be concerned largely with (what unblushingly used to be called) metaethical issues, sketching how these issues look, for now, from our three separate but mutually regarding philosophical perspectives.[24,25] We have tried to keep to issues we think important, but we could not keep to all important issues. Our sketch is judgmental in other ways as well. Without judgment there would be neither plot nor moral; but judgmental sketches—cartoons are another example—make their points in part by exaggerating and oversimplifying.

2. THE REVIVAL OF METAETHICS

Back to Basics

The method of reflective equilibrium accorded a cognitive and evidential status to moral intuitions or "considered moral judgments," particular and general alike. As the Great Expansion wore on, philosophers increasingly questioned whether this status was deserved.[26] At the same time, partly in response to developments in the philosophy of

language, of science, and of mathematics, new conceptions (and new critiques) of objectivity and value were emerging on both sides of the Atlantic. These stirrings induced a widespread philosophical response and ushered in a genuinely new period in twentieth-century ethics, the vigorous revival of metaethics coincidentally with the emergence on several fronts of a criticism of the enterprise of moral theory itself.

Let us postpone discussion of the critique of moral theory for now (see Section 3, below), and turn instead to the revival of "metaethics." We use this term broadly, not assuming that one can avoid normative commitments in doing metaethics and not restricting metaethics to the analysis of moral language; we include under "metaethics" studies of the justification and justifiability of ethical claims as well as their meaning, and also the metaphysics and epistemology of morals, and like matters.[27] Indeed, it would be misleading to attempt to draw a clear distinction between the revival of metaethics in recent years and what broad reflective equilibrium was becoming during the Great Expansion. For what does broad reflective equilibrium demand if not that we bring morality into some congruence with whatever else we hold in our going view of the world?

But what is our going view of the world? Perhaps most contemporary philosophers would agree that our going view treats empirical science as the paradigm of synthetic knowledge, and that an acceptable account of ethics must "place" it with respect to this paradigm, either by effecting some sort of methodological (and perhaps also substantive) assimilation (which might include a correction of some stereotypes of empirical science), or by establishing a convincing contrast.[28] Such "placement" would enable us to see how much of morality remains in order. Without some such placement, one might well ask what business philosophers had in pronouncing or systematizing normative moral judgments as if they were operating in an area of objective knowledge.[29] Even those philosophers who have insisted that ethics stands in no need of underpinnings in order to be an area of objective knowledge have tended to *explain* how this could be so by giving a theoretical account of what morality is, and how this compares or contrasts with other areas of thought and practice.

The task set for the revival of metaethics thus has two elements. Put most simply, we can distinguish, first, the need for an account of what existing moral discourse and practice commits us to, and, second, the need for an answer as to how nearly these commitments can be made good. The second question implicitly involves a third, namely, if the commitments can be made good only to an approximation, how good an approximation is needed in order to vindicate moral discourse and practice (or some recognizable successor to them)? To understand the commitments of existing moral discourse and practice, then, is to separate apparent from real commitments (as, for example, the noncognitivist does when he distinguishes the superficially cognitive form of moral discourse from its underlying expressivist character; or, as the externalist does when he denies that "intrinsic reason giving" is a genuine feature of moral experience), and to determine which of the real commitments are most central to the nature and function of morality (as, for example, certain revisionists do when they claim their reforming account permits us to address all the practically significant questions that pre-revised morality was used to pose).

Understanding the commitments of ordinary moral or value discourse and practice would appear to involve accounts of at least the following: the semantics of the language of morals and value; the apparent metaphysical status of moral properties or values; the putative epistemology of morality or value theory; and the relation of morality or values to practical reasoning. These questions are interconnected, since the question of what, for example, values might *be* would appear to be inseparable from the question of how values are supposed to furnish practical reasons or engage us affectively or conatively. No account of the semantics or ontology of moral discourse could vindicate the objectivity of morality without showing either that a suitable relation between moral evaluation and action can be sustained, or that the appearance of such a special relation can be explained away without undue revisionism.[30] Similarly, any account of the epistemology of moral understanding and attribution must reckon with the practical character of morality, for example, by showing either that moral knowledge as explicated by the account would not run afoul of constraints against "esoteric morality," or that principled reasons can be given for weakening or rejecting such constraints.

We can distinguish two broad trends in contemporary moral theory depending upon how "the problem of placing ethics" is identified and faced, and the implications drawn. The first starts out from the idea that the "problem" is a product not of ethics, but of the wrong-headed notion of seeking to understand the objectivity of moral judgments on the model of the objectivity of empirical science. This approach depends upon finding some substantial contrast or discontinuity between facts (at least, facts of the paradigm sort treated of in natural science) and norms or values. Perhaps most philosophers find such a contrast *prima facie* plausible; more controversial, and thus the focus of the most urgent dialectical task of this first trend, is the claim that a *bona fide* form of objectivity[31] can be elaborated and defended for the ethical side of this contrast. As we will see, philosophers advocating discontinuity have attempted to carry out this task in various ways; perhaps the principal distinction among them turns on whether moral judgment is held to be cognitive (despite the discontinuity with a certain paradigm of factual judgment) or noncognitive (and so objective in some sense that does not involve aptness for—literal—truth evaluation).[32]

The second broad trend in response to "the problem of placing ethics" accepts the challenge of showing that moral judgments are factual in the paradigm sense afforded by empirical or theoretical judgments in the natural sciences.[33] Views in this second broad trend can also, in principle, be further divided as between cognitivist and noncognitivist. However, despite the readiness with which it may be admitted that assertoric scientific discourse typically involves some noncognitive elements, few, if any, philosophers seem to occupy the position that "paradigm factual" judgments are primarily noncognitive.[34] The chief dialectical task for those in this second trend, it would seem, is to show how a paradigm factual area of discourse could have—or could convincingly provide the appearance of—the peculiar characteristics of the discourse of value or morality, for example, normativity and contestability.

Let us begin our comparative investigation with the first-mentioned, and by far best-represented, trend: the view that there is a discontinuity between ethics and science. For brevity, call this view Discontinuity; its opposite, Continuity.

Discontinuity

Nonnaturalistic intuitionists, such as Moore, famously insisted that morality is a genuine and objective area of inquiry, but that it is discontinuous in an important sense with empirical science. On the contemporary scene, the four most active forms of discontinuity are practical reasoning theories (as represented by, e.g., Thomas Nagel, Alan Donagan, Alan Gewirth, Stephen Darwall, and others); constructivism (e.g., John Rawls); noncognitivism (e.g., Simon Blackburn and Allan Gibbard); and (what we will call) sensibility theories (e.g., John McDowell and David Wiggins). Various other forms of discontinuity have their adherents, but we will somewhat arbitrarily confine our discussion to these four groups, discussing them in the order just given.

Moreover, some who defend discontinuity *deny*—perhaps partly because of discontinuity—that ethics is in some special sense an area of genuine and objective inquiry; these views, too, will largely be passed over in what follows.[35] While we will discuss some of the particular advantages and disadvantages of various approaches to the question of objectivity, it should be clear in advance that the plausibility of any one of these positions is best assessed comparatively, in light of the philosophical or explanatory power of its competitors. Within the confines of the present project, we can attempt little more than to identify what strike us as areas of comparative strength and weakness, and therefore will say little about overall plausibility.

Practical Reasoning Theories

One way of trying to take a broadly cognitivist view of ethics, while stressing discontinuities with science, has been to argue that what is needed in ethics is the idea of a valid reason *for acting*, as opposed to that of a reason for belief as it operates in theoretical disciplines. Unlike the intuitionisms of Section 1, the rationalisms that have taken on new life have been those of *practical* reason. Objectivity, for such a view, consists not in accurate representation of an independent metaphysical order, but in universal demands imposed within an agent's practical reasoning. By insisting, on the one hand, that morality must be grounded in practical rather than theoretical reason, these views have stressed a discontinuity with science. It is ethics' intrinsically practical character, its hold on us *as agents*, that explains the open question and, they say, marks ethics off from science.[36] By arguing, on the other hand, that there is such a thing as practical *reason* in which ethics can be grounded, they have tried to assure its objectivity. Recent versions of this approach can be distinguished into those with Hobbesian affinities and those that are broadly Kantian. The first group is typified by Baier and Gauthier, the second by Nagel, Korsgaard, Donagan, Darwall, and Gewirth.

Hobbesian views take the agent's interests or aims as the touchstone of practical reasons and attempt to argue that the standing of morals can be secured by the fact that moral reasons can be adequately based in these. For most recent Hobbesians, the idea is not that moral reasons are a kind of prudential reason. Rather, morality as a system of practical reasoning is in each person's interests; each gains by using it since this is necessary for mutually advantageous cooperation.

Recent versions of this view have their roots in ideas advanced by Kurt Baier in the late fifties, and they attempt to address a significant problem faced by Baier's early view.[37] While it may be in the interest of each that *all* accept interest-trumping, moral reasons, rather than face a mutually disadvantageous war of interests resulting from universal unconstrained prudence, it is not clear how this shows that any individual agent should reason morally rather than prudentially.[38] For each agent, *her* acting contrary to moral reasons will still be most in her interest, when morality and self-interest conflict.

One way of dealing with this problem has been to argue, as Baier has recently, that there is an independent constraint of *universal acceptability* on any theory of practical reasons. No such theory can be correct if the grounds for holding it would be undermined by everyone's accepting it.[39] Since the consequences of everyone's being guided by unconstrained self-interest can hardly be accepted, the theory that practical reasons are exhausted by prudence violates this condition. But what exactly is the argument for thinking that a correct theory of practical reasons cannot be collectively self-defeating?[40]

A second Hobbesian approach, taken by Gauthier, is to hold that collective self-defeat does not rule out a theory of practical reasons, but to insist that individual self-defeat does. Practical reasons consist of whatever considerations inform the practical reasoning

of an ideally rational agent, where an agent is ideally rational just in case she reasons in the way likeliest to achieve her interests. So long as agents have enough evidence about each others' motivations, and are unwilling to cooperate with others whom they believe to be disposed not to constrain self-interest when that is necessary for mutual advantage, it will be in the interest of each agent that *she* deliberate with interest-trumping, moral reasons.[41]

Individual or collective self-defeatingness may be grounds for doubting the advisability of acting on or accepting a theory in certain practical contexts, but don't we distinguish between the practical advisability of using or accepting a theory, on the one hand, and the conditions of its epistemic credibility or truth, on the other? Presumably, any cognitivist attempt to defend either of these conditions must show why this distinction, so central in our thinking about theoretical reason, does not hold when it comes to theories of practical reason.[42] Practical reasoning theorists will insist that this is exactly what one should expect, and that it mirrors the difference between objectivity and knowledge in science and objectivity and knowledge in ethics.

But even if this challenge can be met, both Gauthier's and Baier's theories may face further problems, since they appear to combine a material condition for rationality (connection to the agent's interests) with a formal one (playing the right role in the agent's—or all agents'—deliberation). The rationales for these conditions have different philosophical affinities—Hobbesian versus Kantian, respectively—and perhaps for good reason.[43] And although combining them may suggest a powerful synthetic theory, it also loads rationality with conditions that appear to be, absent some demonstration to the contrary, potentially in conflict. What guarantees that there is available to us any policy for living that will satisfy both conditions at once? If there is none, then perhaps this calls into question one or the other of these conditions as constituents of our notion of rationality, or, then again, perhaps the notion of rationality pulls us in two incompatible directions, and affords morality a shaky foundation.[44]

This brings us to the other major practical reason view: Kantian rationalism. The first steps in this direction in recent years were taken by Nagel in *The Possibility of Altruism*. This work can be (and was) read as having both a modest and a more ambitious agenda. Nagel's more modest goal, suggested by his title, was to show how such "objective" (or, as he later called them, "agent-neutral") considerations as "that acting would relieve *someone's* pain" can be genuine reasons to act. A consideration can be rationally motivating, he argued, even if the agent lacks any "unmotivated desire" to explain her acting as the reason recommends. The only implicated present desire may be attributable as a consequence of motivation, and not necessary, therefore, to explain her being motivated by the consideration itself. A person may be moved in this way, he argued, by considering long-term interests. And if motivation at a distance is possible with prudence, there is no reason why it cannot happen with altruism as well. Altruistic (and other agent-neutral) considerations may be no less *rationally* motivating.[45]

Nagel's more ambitious agenda was to show that practical reasoning is subject to a formal constraint which effectively requires that *any* genuine reason to act be agent-neutral. Stressing what he termed the "motivational content" of genuine practical judgments, he argued that a kind of solipsism can be avoided only if an agent is able to make the same practical judgment of himself from an impersonal standpoint as he does from an egocentric point of view. Accepting practical judgments from one's own point of view normally motivates, so, Nagel maintained, making the same judgment of oneself from an impersonal standpoint should normally motivate also. And this can be so only if the reasons that ground the practical judgment are agent-neutral, formulable without a "free agent variable." It follows that such considerations as that an act will advance *his own* (or *the agent's*) interests cannot be ultimate reasons for acting; at best they are incomplete specifications of some underlying agent-neutral reason, for example, that the act will advance someone's interests.

Were this argument to work it would establish a purely formal conclusion: no ultimate reason for acting can have a free agent variable. By this test, some central moral considerations have the right form to be genuine reasons, while many of those which have been traditionally opposed to morality, for example, self-interest and instrumental rationality, do not. The latter considerations can be reasons only when subsumed under the former. On the other hand, as perhaps became apparent only later, much of commonsense morality is also not of the proper form. Such agent-relative considerations as that an act would keep *one's* promise or provide support for one's child could not be genuine reasons either.[46]

In the end, Nagel rejected the more ambitious agenda as well as the argument designed to secure it. The modest agenda, however, has had a continuing influence.[47] In his more recent writings Nagel has pressed it further, stressing both the phenomenology of moral and deliberative experience, and an autonomous agent's need to endorse her life from perspectives more objective than her own.[48]

Although in some ways Nagel's more ambitious agenda recalled Moorean intrinsic (if not nonnatural) value, it also drew from, and was identified with, the Kantian program in ethics. A number of other philosophers also sought resources in Kant's ideas to mount arguments with similar (some would say "vaulting") ambitions. Like Nagel, each argued that morality can be grounded in *practical* reason—in reason as it is employed in *agency*. Gewirth maintained, for example, that a claim to a right to goods critical to achieving his ends is intrinsic to the rational agent's perspective in *acting*, and that fundamental moral obligations follow from this claim.[49] In addition to these efforts to bring Kantian rationalistic themes explicitly into contemporary debates, a flourishing scholarly literature on Kant's own writings also contributed substantially to our understanding of the resources available to a rationalism of practical reason.[50]

No doubt the attraction of Kantian theories is that they aim to give some account of the way morality appears to confront agents with objective, categorical demands, which, nonetheless, ultimately issue from deep within the moral agent. As theories of discontinuity, Kantian rationalisms insist that morality's normative grip must be understood practically, as imposed within the practical reasoning of moral agents. And as a version of cognitivism, they aim to ground a notion of validity through the idea of universal norms that practical reason prescribes. However, these twin aims make Kantian rationalism vulnerable from two directions. Noncognitivist discontinuity theorists will agree that any adequate account of morality must stress normative grip, but insist that, just for this reason, cognitivist aims must be abandoned. And cognitivists will second the Kantian rationalist's aim to secure genuine truth and knowledge for morality, but argue that successfully placing it in this way requires continuity, not discontinuity. If Kantian rationalism is attractive because it at least tries to combine these two aspects of a quite common view of morality, it may be unstable precisely because these two aspects resist being combined.

Constructivism

The views we have been discussing treat morality as a demand of practical rationality as such. Moral reasons are reasons whatever one's concerns and desires may be, and this result falls out of a theory of practical reason that does not presuppose morality—so these rationalists claim. Recently there has been another trend in moral theory, also claiming

Kantian roots: the family of programs John Rawls labels "constructivism." Constructivism resembles Kantian rationalism on a number of counts: It claims a kind of objectivity for morality, and at the same time holds that this objectivity is sharply different from the objectivity of empirical judgments. It looks to the nature of practical choice as a basis for moral judgment. Still, in most of its versions, it avoids the daunting rationalist claim that morality is demanded by practical reason independently of even the broadest, deepest contingent features of one's concerns.

Rawls calls his theory a form of "Kantian constructivism." Like other broad Kantians, he rejects a picture of reason as discovering independent moral facts. "Moral objectivity is to be understood in terms of a suitably constructed social point of view that all can accept. Apart from the procedure of constructing the principles of justice, there are no moral facts."[51] He speaks of "the search for reasonable grounds for reaching agreement rooted in our conception of ourselves and our relation to society." Out goes any "search for moral truth interpreted as fixed by a prior and independent order of objects and relations, . . . an order apart and distinct from how we conceive of ourselves." It is best to endorse moral principles not as true but as "reasonable for us."[52]

Words like these might be read to suggest that as theorists we must step aside, to await the outcome of a social procedure. In the meantime we must regard ourselves not as theorists, each able, in principle, to reach conclusions himself, but as participants in the social construction of reasonable moral standards. This would be a sharp departure from the usual conception of moral justification.

Such an interpretation, though, would raise a grave worry, for social procedures can be horrendous. In that case, principles may be constructed through an actual social procedure, but we ought not to accept those principles as a reasonable morality—reasonable for us. Reasonable principles must emerge from social procedures that are, in some sense, *suitable*. That gives the moral theorist a job: to say what social procedures would be thus suitable, what procedures count as yielding reasonable principles. And indeed if the theorist can answer that, he may have a further job. We in our society, after all, have never completed a fully suitable procedure. Still, we want to say now what principles of morality are reasonable for us. Perhaps the theorist can settle what principles we would construct if we did engage in a suitable procedure.[53]

It may be in this spirit that Rawls is working, addressing the hypothetical question, How would a suitable procedure for the social construction of moral rules come out? Construction then enters at two points: the theorist constructs a social point of view, a hypothetical circumstance for the choice of moral principles, and hypothetical choosers construct the moral principles that best serve their ends. The hypothetical choosers are "agents of construction" in both senses: the theorist constructs them and they construct principles.

What, then, is constructivism in general? We might read it as another term for what Rawls earlier called "hypothetical contractarianism." Brian Barry proposes a nutshell characterization along these lines, speaking of theories of justice in particular.[54] Constructivism, he says, is "the doctrine that what would be agreed on in some specified kind of situation constitutes justice."[55] This is to treat justice as purely procedural at base. The choice situation is not designed to yield outcomes that are just by some independent standard—as cutting and choosing leads selfish people to equal division of a cake. Rather, the very fact that something would be agreed upon in the specified situation is what makes it constitute justice. As for the agreement situation itself, it "is specified by a description of the actors in it (including their knowledge and objectives) and the norms governing their pursuit of their objectives: what moves are to be legitimate. And the 'emergence' is

to be a particular kind of emergence, namely, the result of the actors in the situation pursuing their given objectives within the given constraints."[56]

This suggests an even wider reading of the term constructivism: the constructivist is a hypothetical proceduralist. He endorses some hypothetical procedure as determining which principles constitute valid standards of morality. The procedure might be one of coming to agreement on a social contract, or it might be, say, one of deciding which moral code to support for one's society. A proceduralist, then, maintains there are no moral facts independent of the finding that a certain hypothetical procedure would have such and such an upshot.[57]

So understood, constructivism is not a metaethical position in the old sense. Hypothetical proceduralism does not pronounce on whether moral thinking is, at base, continuous or discontinuous with scientific thinking, or what kind of objectivity moral judgments can claim. Rather, it is a family of substantive normative theories—including hypothetical contractarian theories. A hypothetical contractarian with regard to justice maintains that justice is whatever would be agreed to in a certain hypothetical position. This is not a theory of the meaning of moral statements, and it is not a full theory of their justification. We can ask standard metaethical questions about a contractarian's claims: What do they mean? What would constitute justifying them? Two contractarians might embrace different hypothetical situations for agreement. What, then, would be at issue between them? The answer might be naturalistic, intuitionistic, noncognitivistic, or reformist. What would it be to justify one claim as opposed to the other? Again, different traditional answers might be given.[58]

Rawls sounds metaethical when he renounces talk of moral truth, but this might be misleading. He says only that there is no moral truth "apart and distinct from how we conceive of ourselves." This would allow for a moral truth somehow dependent on our self-conception.[59] Old-fashioned moral theorists would then want this claim of dependence to be spelled out, and would proceed to ask what this claim means and how it could be justified.

Still, with Rawls's talk of rooting matters "in our conception of ourselves and our relation to society," he moves beyond the bare tenets of hypothetical proceduralism. Consider a hypothetical contractarian: He formulates a particular hypothetical circumstance in which parties are to agree on principles to govern themselves. He needs, though, to justify his choice of this circumstance, to justify the claim that the principles parties would choose in this particular circumstance are valid principles of justice. Constructivism, as Rawls thinks of it, might be a special view of what would constitute this justification. A constructivist theory might explain why some specific form of hypothetical contractarianism is the one that succeeds in identifying what is reasonable for us.[60]

How would it do this? Rawls has not offered detail about how his own form of contractarianism is to be justified, or what it has to do with the older frameworks in which the nature of moral judgment was debated. His words suggest, though, that he takes morals and science to have sharply different goals, and hopes that the right insights into the nature of morality will allow us to sidestep traditional metaethics.

Ethics is to be "the search for reasonable grounds for reaching agreement rooted in our conception of ourselves and our relation to society." These words may bear many interpretations. One is both Kantian and conceptually reformist.

Rawls declares himself broadly Kantian; he sees in constructivism a way of elucidating Kant's core insights. Morality is an aspect of practical reason; the search for moral principles consists in reasoning practically, not in tracking independent moral facts. What we validly decide is right or wrong is determined by the nature of our practical reason—in Rawls's case, by what he calls the "rational" and the "reasonable."

How might a construction express this? A constructivist, we might venture, begins with a source of moral concern, a vision of why morality matters to us. In Scanlon's version, it is "the desire to be able to justify one's actions to others on grounds they could not reasonably reject."[61] Rawls himself starts with two ideals: an ideal ("conception") of the person, and an ideal of the social role of morality (a "well-ordered society"). What, he asks, "would free and equal moral persons themselves agree upon, if they were fairly represented solely as such persons and thought of themselves as citizens living a complete life in an on-going society?"[62] Now if we can settle fully on a source of moral concern, perhaps we can find a hypothetical circumstance for agreement that fully speaks to it. Perhaps once we knew what would be agreed to in that circumstance, this knowledge would satisfy all the felt needs that bring us to ethical theory. Then we might no longer care what our moral questions originally meant, or what would have constituted justifying an answer to them. We might have sidestepped traditional metaethics.

In specifying a source of moral concern, though, a constructivist may face a dilemma. On one horn, he can specify the concern in broad, morally laden language. He can speak of "reasonable" circumstances for agreement, of people "fairly represented solely as free and equal moral beings," of grounds a person "could not reasonably reject." The import of these terms then needs to be specified. It is fine to start with suggestive motivations, but eventually implications must be spelled out, and that can give rise to interpretive problems and disputes. Suppose two people both want to abide by whatever contract they would negotiate in reasonable circumstances—but they fail to agree on which circumstances would be reasonable. Perhaps they simply want different things, and their discord is masked by vague language. Then the theorist can do no more than identify the content of their clashing wants. Perhaps, though, they are in genuine disagreement about what circumstances would be reasonable. If so, old metaethical questions return in new guise. What is at issue in disputes over what is reasonable? What would justify accepting one answer and rejecting another?

On the other horn, the constructivist might stipulate a source of moral concern quite precisely. Concern with justice, he might specify, is concern to abide by the agreement that would be framed in such and such exact circumstances. We listeners, though, may not be at all sure that this concern is precisely the one we have. And if we are told that this, at any rate, is the concern that would constitute a concern with justice, we shall find this claim disputable. It amounts to dogmatically claiming that some specific version of hypothetical contractarianism is correct: that the valid principles of justice are the ones we would have framed in such and such circumstances. Adherents of rival versions of hypothetical contractarianism will dispute this claim, and then, again, old metaethical issues reappear. What is at issue between the disputants, and how would either claim be justified?

A constructivist might sidestep these questions if he could articulate a concern we all found, on consideration, to be all we want from morality. This concern would have to be put in exact terms, and to hold our allegiance even when so put. This is the achievement that might render traditional metaethics obsolete. Or at least it might cause us to find the old metaethical questions less pressing—though we might still ask whether the root concern we found so unproblematic was really justified, and why. In any case, if constructivism is to be metaethically ambitious, its hope must be to find such a specification.

Few constructivists so far would claim any such full success, and it may not be in the offing. Perhaps no constructivist has held such lofty metaethical ambitions. Constructivists have been mostly silent on the old

metaethical questions, with not much explanation why. We have explored one possible rationale, but not the only one. Constructivists may simply not think they know what to say on these questions, and think that other questions can fruitfully be pursued in the meantime.[63]

A metaethically modest constructivism would try for important insights into the nature of morality, without claiming to preempt traditional metaethics. The prospects for such a modest constructivism may be brilliant, for anything we have argued. Going versions are so far of limited scope: they tend to deal specifically with social justice, and conceive of the principles of justice as governing a system of mutual benefit. Within this sphere at least, a modest constructivism may hold real promise. It envisions large parts of morality as justified by the social role morality can play, by the mutual appeal of the fruits of moral agreement. It elucidates prime sources of moral concern, and founds morality on the broad social agreement it would be reasonable to make.

Noncognitivism

If moral theorists cannot long evade questions of meaning, they may find their way back to variants of earlier metaethical theories. Recent years have seen new stirrings of noncognitivism. Noncognitivists claim that moral and scientific meanings differ sharply. Recent noncognitivists, though, have stressed similarities as well as differences. They have sought out aspects of objectivity that they can claim for morality, ways moral judgments mimic strict factual judgments.

A half-century ago, Moore's tests seemed to force anyone to noncognitivism, even kicking and screaming. Subsequent philosophical developments open up better alternatives—or so many philosophers think. Noncognitivists deny this, and so in part their work has been to attack the proffered alternatives. Old problems beset new cognitivisms, they insist.

In addition, though, new problems beset old noncognitivisms, and so noncognitivism has had to develop or die. The new problems come in three clusters. One concerns meaning, objectivity, and the sense in which moral judgments could be noncognitive. A second concerns the state of mind a moral statement expresses. Finally, there is the problem of moral terms in complex grammatical contexts.

First, then, meaning and objectivity: Quine's attacks on a philosophically useful analytic/synthetic distinction, along with new Wittgensteinian treatments of language, not only made alternatives to noncognitivism seem newly eligible; they left it unclear whether noncognitivism itself constitutes a distinct position. Once old theories of cognitive content fall, what is the noncognitivist denying?

Current noncognitivists, then, navigate precariously between two shoals. A classic problem for noncognitivists is that moral judgments have so many earmarks of claims to objective truth. A successful noncognitivism must explain away these earmarks. At the same time, if noncognitivism is to be distinct from cognitivism, it must insist that some judgments are cognitive in contrast with moral judgments. Noncognitivism is threatened not only by hardening values to make them like the hard facts of old; it is threatened by softening facts to make them more like emotive values. Often opponents of noncognitivism work at bridging the fact/value gap from both ends.

Finally, noncognitivists may find themselves losing an exchange with reforming cognitivists. The reformer debunks: he thinks our old concepts are confused, or perhaps even rooted in error. Still, they serve a valuable purpose, he thinks, and a reform will serve that purpose without error or confusion. Now the noncognitivist has a hard time avoiding a stance that is likewise debunking, at least to a degree. Is there nothing to the ordinary sense that right and wrong are properties? If the noncognitivist thinks ordinary

thought is confused on this score, he must admit that his too is something of a reform. He then faces a challenge: A naturalistic reformer can retort, "Why not take my reform instead? Mine, after all, gives moral terms a meaning in the usual sense."

A noncognitivist will then have to argue that his is the better reform. We need a kind of language, he must say, that we come close to having already, but which until now has confused us. The naturalistic reformer, he must claim, beckons us to an overly stark linguistic world. In it we may still have overtly emotive language like "Yea!" and "Boo!" and "Yech!" Moral terms, though, are now like nonmoral terms: thanks to reforming definitions, they now have clear naturalistic criteria. The noncognitivist must say that the old, confused language had virtues this reform loses—virtues that can be preserved in his own reform, and without loss of clarity.

Blackburn argues that if objective-looking emotive predicates did not exist, we would have to invent them. Start with a language with interjections like "Hurrah!" and "Boo!" but no moral predicates like "right" and "wrong." This language does let us express attitudes. But what we need is "an instrument of serious, reflective evaluative practice, able to express concern for improvements, clashes, implications, and coherence of attitudes." To get this, we could "invent a predicate answering to the attitude, and treat commitments as if they were judgements, and then use all the natural devices for debating truth."[64] Blackburn gives this as his cashing out of a Hume-like metaphor, "projecting attitudes onto the world."[65]

Gibbard stresses coordination in a broad game-theoretic sense: narrowly moral judgments, along with normative judgments of other kinds, serve to coordinate actions and feelings. Such coordination is crucial to peaceful and cooperative life together. Appearances of objectivity—the various ways normative judgments mimic judgments of fact—promote this coordination. In evolutionary terms, a coordinating function helps explain why we have the dispositions to normative thought and language that we do. In evaluative terms, the goods that stem from social coordination give us reason to be glad we think and speak in these ways. They give us reason not to reform away the expressive, objective-like aspects of moral language.[66]

Current noncognitivists, then, stress the various ways in which a motivation-laden state of mind—an emotive disposition, a universal preference, or the acceptance of a system of norms—might mimic strict factual belief. For convenience, call any such state of mind an "attitude." In the first place, an attitude may be unconditional, applying even to situations where everyone lacks it.[67] In addition, a person's higher-order attitudes may require a given attitude, and require it of everyone.[68] Conversational demands may be made on behalf of an attitude, and other attitudes may sanction those demands.[69]

These features, we might say, "quasi-objectivize" attitudes.[70] A reforming noncognitivist must establish the need for attitudes of some sort that are quasi-objectivized frankly: for motivation-laden states that are not strict factual beliefs, but are treated in many ways as if they were. He claims that what goes on roughly with moral language—and overtly if his reform is accepted—is quasi-objectivizing thought about how to conduct ourselves, and perhaps how to feel about various aspects of life. The noncognitivist will claim that our rough tendencies to do this explain familiar features of moral discourse: the broad action-guidingness of this factual-seeming discourse. It also explains what has been called the "essential contestability" of moral concepts:[71] If a moral term is tied by its very meaning to questions of how to live, any stipulation of a factual property it is to stand for forecloses some questions of how to live—questions we may need to treat quasi-objectively.

All this leaves the question, Is any contrast left between value and fact? Once we are using all the usual devices for debating the truth of moral judgments, does this quasi-truth differ from a real truth we can seriously accept in other realms of language? A "noncognitivist" and a "moral realist" might agree about how moral language works, and disagree only about whether some other kinds of language—scientific language in particular—are descriptive in a way that moral language is not.

This has been one of the most active areas of contention between noncognitivists and those who deny a contrast between moral and "factual" concepts. Those maintaining the contrast claim that on our best, naturalistic view of the universe, factual concepts play an explanatory role that moral concepts do not.[72] Opponents find moral concepts explanatory in the same ways as the concepts used in psychosociological explanation, or they liken moral qualities to secondary quality concepts, factual though not ultimately explanatory.[73] One noncognitivist, Blackburn, argues for another contrast: moral properties are peculiarly supervenient, in a way that is explained if they are quasi-objectivized sentiments.[74] Crispin Wright distinguishes a "thin" truth that moral statements can attain from a substantial truth with various marks of objectivity. To claim substantial truth, one must explain how we have a cognitive capacity to detect the property in question, so that absent any impediment to proper functioning of this capacity, one gets the property right.[75]

Turn now to the second cluster of problems current noncognitivists must sort through: the problem of complex contexts. Most noncognitivists are *expressivists*: they explain moral language as expressing moral judgments, and explain moral judgments as something other than beliefs.[76] As for what special kind of state of mind a moral judgment is, different expressivists say different things, and each account has its problems.

Emotivists hold that a moral judgment consists in a feeling—or better, in a disposition to have certain feelings. It seems, though, that a person can judge something wrong even if he has lost all disposition to feelings about it. As Ewing and Brandt had suggested decades earlier, moral judgments seem not to be moral sentiments or dispositions to certain moral sentiments, but judgments of what moral sentiments are fitting or justified.[77]

Moreover, if moral judgments are dispositions to feelings, will any old feeling do? What, then, differentiates moral judgments from any other kind of standing like or dislike? Perhaps there are special feelings of moral disapproval, and calling something "wrong," say, expresses such a special feeling—or the corresponding attitude. What, then, is this feeling of moral disapproval? Among theorists of emotion, cognitivists predominate. Emotional "cognitivism" is different from metaethical cognitivism: an emotional cognitivist thinks that having a given emotion, such as anger, involves making some special kind of cognitive judgment. Now in the case of moral disapproval, the only plausible candidate is a cognitive judgment that the thing in question is morally wrong. If so, we need to understand judgments of wrongness before we can understand moral disapproval. We cannot *explain* the judgment that something is wrong as an attitude of moral disapproval.

The sensibility theorists discussed below hold that both directions of explanation are correct: Disapproving something must be explained as feeling that it is wrong, and conversely, to judge something wrong is to judge that it merits disapproval. If this is right, then although moral concepts are to some degree explained in terms of feelings, the explanations are not of the broadly reductive kind an emotivist seeks: they do not explain moral concepts in terms that could be fully understood prior to grasping moral concepts.

Hare sets out to avoid the emotivists' pitfalls. A moral judgment, he says, is a special state of preference—a preference that is "overriding" and "universal." It is a preference all told and not merely one preference tendency among others. It is uninfluenced by who is who in the situation to which it applies.[78] Now one consequence is that a person can never want wrong things done—things he judges wrong, that is. If he thinks it would be wrong for the governor to pardon a murderer, then he must want not to be pardoned himself in the hypothetical case of being the murderer. Hare embraces this consequence; many others find it implausible.[79]

Gibbard rejects emotivism, and adopts a part of Ewing's rival view: moral judgments concern which moral sentiments are warranted or justified. Whereas Ewing was a nonnaturalist about warrant, though, Gibbard remains expressivist: he gives an expressivistic account of judgments of warrant. To call a feeling warranted, he says, is (roughly) to express one's acceptance of norms that permit the feeling. Moral judgments, then, express a state of mind that is not, in the strictest sense, belief in a moral fact. Neither, though, is it a feeling or a disposition to feelings. Rather, it is a complex state of mind that consists in accepting certain norms. His problem, then, is to explain, in psychological terms, what it is to accept norms.[80]

Moral judgments are "normative," everyone agrees, but there is great disagreement among philosophers as to what this normativity consists in. According to Gibbard, it consists in a tie to warrant, and the concept of warrant is *sui generis*. Making a judgment of warrant consists in being in a special, motivation-laden state—namely, accepting a system of norms. Feelings, then, are not treated as normative judgments in themselves. Rather, the special normative judgments that constitute moral convictions consist in accepting norms to govern certain feelings. Norms are motivation-laden, and at the same time, they are crucially discursive and subject to reasoning. They can bear the full weight of quasi-objectivization as discussed above—so Gibbard claims.

Still, like the emotivists, Gibbard holds that moral feelings help explain moral judgments. Moral judgments are judgments about whether guilt and impartial anger are warranted. Gibbard, then, must reject emotional cognitivism. Along with the emotivists, he owes an explanation of specially moral feelings—guilt and impartial anger, in his book—in terms that do not require a prior understanding of moral judgments. Emotional cognitivism has its problems: on the surface, it seems quite possible to feel guilty, say, and yet reject the (purportedly cognitive) claim that one has done wrong. One may think one's guilt irrational. Gibbard surveys lines of psychological explanation of emotions that could fit a Ewing-like theory.[81]

Turn finally to the charge that expressivism fails with "embedded contexts." When a person calls something "wrong," expressivists say, he is not stating a purported fact; he is expressing a special state of mind—a feeling or attitude, say. Now at best, such an account works for simple ascriptions of rightness or wrongness. It does not extend to more elaborate uses of moral language, as in "He did something wrong," or "If taking bribes is wrong, then so is offering them."[82]

Blackburn and Gibbard both take up this problem. Blackburn adopts a strategy of separate explanations for various different grammatical constructions; he works on conjunctions and on conditionals. "If lying is wrong, then so is getting your little brother to lie" expresses rejection of a kind of sensibility: one that condemns lying and yet condones getting little brother to lie.[83] Gibbard attempts a more uniform explanation of normative terms in embedded contexts: Complex normative judgments are to be explained by their inferential ties to simple normative ascriptions, and to factual judgments. A special class of simple normative ascription—judgments of what is warranted for oneself right now—has a special tie to the world: these judgments tend to motivate. All this makes for a radical modification of expressivism.[84]

Perhaps noncognitivism is obsolete—because it fails with embedded contexts, or because it clings to a bad theory of meaning, or because all refinements that could matter were worked out some time ago. It can seem

a theory to beat or fall back on, but not to develop. A handful of authors now see it as full of unrealized possibilities. Some opponents, on the other hand, find the whole list of traditional metaethical possibilities unappetizing, and look for sharply new alternatives. To some of these we now turn.

Sensibility Theories

Several of the most influential contemporary writers on the nature of ethics and value, notably John McDowell and David Wiggins, have drawn inspiration from the idea that normative or evaluative judgments might bear some analogy with judgments of secondary qualities, or other judgments essentially tied to the exercise of certain human sensibilities.[85] This analogy holds out the possibility of a cognitivist version of discontinuity, since the judgments tied to the exercise of these sensibilities might be seen as straightforwardly cognitive[86] while yet concerning properties that are neither part of the fundamental causal/explanatory structure of the world in their own right nor reducible to properties that are. That is, even though such properties would not meet the most ambitious naturalistic strictures, their place in cognition could nonetheless be secure in virtue of their presence to experience and the existence of a fairly well-articulated "space of reasons" regulating their application.[87]

For example, physical science has moved away from color as a significant dimension of similarity in its classification of substances or entities, so that its fundamental explanations are "colorless"; nonetheless, color is a definite feature of our experience, and our attribution of color is an exercise of a perceptual faculty regulated by standards for appraising judgers as better- or worse-situated (e.g., with regard to "standard conditions of viewing") for the detection of color properties, and for appraising judgments as better or worse-supported by evidence. We clearly recognize greater or lesser degrees of refinement in capacities accurately to discern color, and this possibility of *corrected* judgments and *improved* discernment is manifest in a practice in which we give reasons and make arguments in ways by no means arbitrary or idiosyncratic, but rather capable of yielding considerable interpersonal convergence in judgment. All of this is compatible with the fact that color attribution is, at bottom, dependent upon human subjectivity. So, even though it has turned out that the properties discerned by this practice do not have (what Crispin Wright has called) a "wide cosmological role" akin to primary qualities,[88] and that they depend for their presence in experience upon "rationally optional" sensibilities, this need not undermine their cognitive, even objective, standing—unless, that is, one presupposes a "scientistic" or "cosmological" conception of cognitivity and objectivity.[89]

Thus, sensibility theorists present their approach as a significant improvement over both noncognitivism and Intuitionism. Noncognitivism has, in their view, rightly stressed the contribution of sentiment to moral judgment, but wrongly forced such judgments into the mold of expressive projection. Intuitionism has, again in their view, rightly stressed the cognitive aspects of value judgment, but wrongly forced such judgments into the mold of detecting a special realm of independently existing properties. The sensibility theorist sees neither moral sentiment nor moral properties as able to do without—or to explain away—the other.[90] As noted earlier, the resulting view embraces both "directions of explanation," and is claimed to do greater justice to the cognitive grammar of evaluative and normative discourse and to the phenomenology of moral experience.

But what of the supposed internal connection between moral judgment and motivation or will, a connection that has done so much to account for the appeal of noncognitivism in this century? McDowell made possible a significant innovation within the contemporary English tradition of nonreduc-

tionist cognitivism by showing the availability of an alternative explanation of this connection: the very sensibility that gives individuals the capacity to discern these sensibility-tied properties could, he urged, necessarily involve possession of certain affective or conative propensities.

Humor, for example, is a sense that also is affective; a person with no sense of humor is not someone who discerns the humor in comic situations but simply fails to be amused. Rather, he misses their humorousness altogether. He may, it is said, fully grasp the primary, causal/explanatory qualities of the situations in question; yet there is something about these situations to which he is blind. This blindness stems in part from the absence of a sensibility. This is not akin to the mere absence of a "laugh reflex": it involves a lack of appreciation of reasons for amusement. There may—although this has yet to be shown—be no way of explaining the nature of these reasons, or the nature of the property humorousness, itself, except by depending upon the notion of finding things funny. A circular relation between the sensibility and the property would explain why humorousness seems *sui generis* and unanalyzable, on the one hand, while on the other hand being, for those with a sense of humor, "action-guiding" (so to speak) in a familiar way. If our humorless person were to develop a sense of humor, he would both see the comic features of the world around him (and thus overcome his cognitive lack) and find that they *are* amusing (and thus overcome his affective lack).

Obligation and value might similarly involve a matched pair of sensibility and property.[91] To take the case of obligation: Suppose that a child has accidentally become separated from his parents and is wandering down the sidewalk, lost and distressed. A passing individual lacking in moral sensibility might observe this scene and see it as merely curious or annoying, but not as *calling for* intervention. Such a person would not be someone who perceived the *needfulness* of the child's situation but simply failed to feel moved to help. Rather, he would be blind to the needfulness itself.[92] Were the defects in our pedestrian's moral character overcome, he would both see the situation in a way that inherently involves a claim for remedy and find himself motivated to help (or, at least, to feel a certain remorse should he fail to do so).

In this way a sensibility theorist seeks to reconcile cognitivism with the "action-guiding" character of moral judgment that has been thought to tell decisively for noncognitivism: appropriate motivational tendencies are part of the sensibility necessary for the cognitive discernment of certain *sui generis*, but nonetheless genuine, properties. Further, this could contribute to our understanding of the "thickness" of concepts like need, their seemingly inextricable and symmetric fusion of descriptive content and action-guidingness. Speakers who possess authority about the extension of thick concepts to novel cases will be led both by the affective force of their sensibility and by the descriptive features of the world to which this sensibility is attuned.[93]

The sensibility theorist's account would also help explain why (according to a long tradition) moral demands are experienced by those who recognize them as categorical rather than hypothetical.[94] A person with a well-developed moral sensibility will not see the needfulness of the child's situation and then require, as a further condition for rational action, awareness of a desire or interest on her own part that aiding the child would satisfy. Rather, her very recognition of the needfulness depends upon her being so constituted as to be disposed both to meet it and to find competing *desires* or *interests* inappropriate or overridden or less compelling than they otherwise would have been.[95] (Though, of course, the agent might also recognize—and have to weigh—other *moral* requirements or claims of need.)

However, it is important to emphasize that this account captures only part of what Kant intended by the notion of a categorical imperative, since it does not follow from what has been said that it would be a defect in rationality or autonomy for someone to lack a sensibility that would permit him to descry moral properties. And McDowell apparently does not suppose that such a lack must be a *rational* defect.[96] This is one way one might be led to raise questions about the capacity of sensibility theories to capture the normative force of moral discourse or provide justification or objectivity for morality.

Indeed, for all that we have said thus far, a moral sensibility and a sense of humor are on a par, with perhaps this difference: it appears to be part of a moral sensibility that (at least a subclass of) the properties it enables one to discern have the effect, when recognized, of silencing or outweighing or making less compelling other sorts of reasons or motives in practical deliberation. Could this feature of moral judgments be used to distinguish morality or to justify its special deliberative weight? This seems doubtful, since many alternative schemes of normative regulation will support sensibilities that constitutively involve claims of precedence in practical deliberation. Perhaps, for example, only those truly devout really experience the sanctity of certain objects, places, and rites, and for such individuals the sacred *will* call for precedence over appetite or interest. Similarly, *mutatis mutandis*, for those genuinely diabolical, or for the true aesthete. A circular account identifies a structural relationship between a sensibility and its matched property, but since neither is independently characterized, we do not as yet have a way of distinguishing one such sensibility from another[97]—much less of showing one to have a different normative or objective status from another. A peg that fits a round hole has a particular shape; so does a hole that fits a square peg; but what shape in particular do an otherwise unspecified peg and hole have thanks to the fact that they fit each other?

Circular characterizations are not entirely

uninformative. For example, if the following circular characterization of *good* is held to be *a priori:*

(1) *x* is good if and only if *x* is such as to elicit in us (in "normal circumstances") a sentiment of moral approbation,

then an *a priori* link is being claimed between the property of goodness and a human sentiment, and this might be challenged.[98] Now, if the sentiment of moral approbation had a robust and distinctive phenomenology—the way, for example, redness does—then a circular *a priori* equation might simply be a way of saying that the domain of this property is determined by reference to a *sui generis* qualitative state. Thanks to the distinctive character of such a qualitative state, the circular equation would afford a way of *distinguishing* the property (though not of *analyzing* it reductively). But no such robust and distinctive phenomenology exists—or so it seems to us—in the case of moral judgments.[99]

Alternatively, if there were *a priori* ties radiating out from moral approbation—for example, to a *substantively* characterized "space of reasons" that regulates moral approval—then the circular equation would effect a linkage between moral properties and a distinctive class of reasons. These reasons would not need to support anything so strong as an analysis or reduction of moral judgments in order to contribute materially to distinguishing a moral sensibility from others structurally similar, and to open the possibility of a nonreductive "placing" or vindication of morality.[100] However, when McDowell raises the question whether the standing of morality can be defended against "the idea that there is nothing to ethical thinking but rationally arbitrary subjective stances," he concludes that "the necessary scrutiny does not involve stepping outside the point of view constituted by an ethical sensibility."[101] This suggests that appeal to the "space of reasons" linked to a moral sensibility might not im-

prove our grip on the content or normative standing of moral judgments after all.

Perhaps it is misguided to seek a better grip on the content or standing of moral judgment—explication and justification do have to come to an end somewhere. Yet it would seem to matter a good deal where. Many rationally optional "subjective stances" with the same structure as morality would appear to be candidates for our allegiance—and some have been in real social competition with morality. Yet we tend to think something more can be said on behalf of morality. McDowell rightly points out that the appeal to internal reasons permits deployment of the full critical resources of our moral thinking, so that it will not be true that anything goes.[102] At the same time, however, this will not distinguish or justify the seeking and following of internal reasons within a moral scheme from the seeking and following of internal reasons within structurally similar alternative schemes.

Wiggins appears to have taken the question of "objective justification," as he calls it, somewhat further. He asks us to suppose that our moral practices are "off the ground" already, so there is no problem of trying to see how they might raise themselves by their own bootstraps. Then, he urges, we might be objectively justified in "simple acceptance" of the dictates of our moral sensibility if at least two further conditions are met: (i) the sensibility and practices with which moral judgment is bound up are important to our identities as individuals, so that life is "scarcely conceivable without them"; and (ii) these practices are not "manifestly unjust."[103] The first condition will strike some as overly strong on the point of psychic investment; the second, either as an internal condition once again—if, that is, justice is understood by the lights of the sensibility itself—or as a restatement of the problem of objective justification.

It is important to distinguish questions about objective justification from the question whether moral or evaluative discourse, when circularly characterized, is inevitably relativistic. As Wiggins notes, relativism can be avoided if our (circular) characterizations contain an expression that rigidly designates our actual dispositions to respond, following a strategy that does in some respects clearly fit our color discourse.[104] The property of redness is plausibly seen as tied down *a priori* to the features that elicit a red response in humans as they actually are. To imagine humans with a different color sensibility is not to imagine that blood, say, would have had a different color, but only that humans might have seen red things differently. This would, if granted, suffice to rule out a kind of color relativism, and a similar rigidification would rule out certain forms of evaluative or deliberative relativism.

But does rigidification contribute to "objective justication"? It, in effect, guarantees *a priori* that the names 'goodness' and 'rightness', say, belong to properties tracked by *our* sensibilities.[105] Would that tend to show that we are justified in regulating our choices accordingly? Proprietary labeling seems to remove the threat of relativism from our evaluative language without addressing underlying worries about the possible arbitrariness of our evaluative practices, since the feature seized upon to privilege our practices is simply that they *are* our practices. This is not the sort of thing that carries much justificatory weight even within our moral scheme. Not only is it hard to imagine appealing to this feature in an attempted justification aimed at outsiders; it is hard to imagine it succeeding very far in showing nonarbitrariness to ourselves. Thus, we might be led to wonder whether such rigidification does fit a nonrevisionist account of our moral discourse: it might, for example, block expression in that discourse of certain serious, seemingly moral questions.

Sensibility theorists may well be right both about the cognitive character of moral discourse and about the cognitive—even *sui generis*—character of the distinctive sentiments morality engages. The special interest of sensibility theory in morality is that it may afford a way of understand how some form of action-guidingness might—without the demands of a Kantian theory of agency—be "built into" our moral discourse consistently with its possessing cognitivity and objectivity (at least in the sense of intersubjective convergence among "people of a certain culture who have what it takes to understand [the relevant] sort of judgment").[106]

However, sensibility theorists have also noted an important disanalogy between secondary qualities such as color and evaluative properties such as good. Suppose that we accept the following *a priori* equation for *red*, suspending for now any reservations we might have about its circularity:

> (2) x is red if and only if x is such as to elicit in normal humans as they now are (and in "normal circumstances") the visual impression of redness.

Still, there remains a contrast with *good*. Consider now (a paraphrase of) Wiggins's suggested *a priori* equation for *good*, which involves a revision of (1) that introduces the disanalogy:

> (3) x is good if and only if x is such as to make appropriate normal humans as they now are (and in "normal circumstances") a sentiment of moral approval.[107]

A noncognitivist would be quick to point out that the analogy with color (even if it otherwise were sound) breaks down precisely at the point one would expect were recognition of goodness fundamentally different from experiential knowledge, the point signaled by the replacement of the perceptual/explanatory expression 'elicit in' in (2) by the normative expression 'make appropriate for' in (3). Of course, once we have (2), it is clear why we are entitled to claim that exposure to normally-red-response-eliciting properties "makes appropriate" a red response (at least, in "normal circumstances" for normal human observers), and this epistemic certification does not require any reductive analysis of redness. The difficulty in the case of good, however, is that we are given nothing like (2) to underwrite the justificatory idiom—we instead are proffered the justificatory idiom itself, namely (3). In the absence both of a robust phenomenology and of a dispositional grounding on the model of (2), it becomes harder to say what the distinctive import of the secondary-quality model is, or whether it can serve to license cognitivism or objectivity about goodness (or rightness).

It is worth asking how much of the insight of sensibility theories could be preserved if one were to downplay the analogy to secondary qualities[108] and instead try to develop further the idea that various properties may depend in part on human sensibilities, but nonetheless have conditions of correctness and improvement and, thereby, cognitive (or objective) status.[109] Seen as examples of this general idea, sensibility theories could be very attractive indeed if the worries expressed above could be overcome, or explained away. Such theories would afford a cognitivist interpretation of morality able to supply a version of the internal connection between judgment and motivation that makes expressivism or projectivism attractive.[110] Moreover, they would manage to do so without noncognitivism's complex semantics and purportedly imperfect fit with the phenomenology of moral experience. And sensibility theories could appeal to their diagnosis of an underlying, circular involvement with our sentiments both to explain the often-claimed impossibility of analyzing moral predicates and to locate moral properties within our reach, thus reviving the prospects of a nonreductive moral realism without the dubious epistemology of turn-of-the-century Intuitionism. In these respects, these complex and fascinating theories pose the most important contemporary challenge to the terms of the standard, and perhaps stalemated, dialectic between noncognitivism and naturalistic cognitivism.

The excitement and promise of sensibility theories is that they seek to possess each of two usually-contrasted "directions of explanation"; their risk, however—like the risk of Aesop's fox, who sought to possess both his bunch of grapes and (what turned out to be) their reflection—is that of genuinely possessing neither.

Continuity

Cognitivism has its attractions, affording by far the most straightforward account of the surface grammar of moral discourse, and promising to avoid revisionism about moral experience and argument. It also has its costs. Sensibility theories seek to provide the attractions at reduced cost, though they may get what they pay for. Perhaps what is needed is a revival of substantive naturalism?[111] Such a revival *is* underway, but surely one is entitled to ask: Must the history of twentieth-century metaethics now be recapitulated?

Perhaps not. The first cycle of criticism of naturalism in this century was directed only at narrowly analytic naturalism; philosophy of language has moved on, and the prospects of naturalisms based on a more expansive view of analyticity, or on views of meaning that do not ask the analytic/synthetic distinction to do much work, are not well known. Thus, the possibility remains that a naturalistic account will emerge able to accommodate all the normative characteristics and uses of moral discourse; or, at least, all such characteristics and uses as survive critical scrutiny.

With this possibility in mind, let us consider three contemporary naturalisms—neo-Aristotelian, postpositivist nonreductionist, and reductionist.[112]

Neo-Aristotelian. Philippa Foot argued, in a series of influential articles,[113] that it would manifest a kind of incompetence with the moral vocabulary to fail to see the inappropriateness of applying moral terms strictly as a function of pro- or con-attitudes (even when the attitudes have certain "formal" features, such as prescribing universally). For example, suppose there were a community of speakers whose language by and large went smoothly into the English tongue and whose beliefs in general seemed reassuringly familiar, and yet who used a term, 'glim', which in all respects appeared to have the same expressive force as 'morally good' but which they readily applied only to those who demonstrated the physical strength and dexterity to crack a walnut in a bare fist. 'Morally good' would not, it seems, be a happy translation of 'glim' into English—what they are praising, finding admirable, and treating as action-guiding seems to be something other than a person's moral character. One way or another, a connection with certain things—for example, intrinsic concern with effects on human well-being, such as the avoidance of cruelty—seems as intimately a part of our moral usage as, say, universalizability.[114]

This would be a recipe for a potentially unstable "mixed view" of the meaning of moral terms if it combined a claim that possession of certain substantive properties (such as promotion of well-being) is logically sufficient for something to be good with a claim that (correctly) accepting that something is good logically requires endorsing it. For, if Foot is right, there will be no conceptually guaranteed connection between any particular substantive phenomena and such endorsement. Noncognitivists have sought to avoid this instability by insisting that whatever descriptive meaning might accrue to such terms, the prescriptive content is primary.[115] Foot takes the other tack, building the substantive conditions into the meaning of moral terms and ultimately denying that their purported "action-guidingness" is "automatic," claiming instead that it depends hypothetically upon the presence in the population of agents motivated to take the well-being of others seriously.[116] Yet aren't moral requirements categorical?

The existence of etiquette shows that norms can be nonhypothetical without being categorically motivating: one can sincerely and correctly judge that such requirements apply to oneself (for example) without endorsing compliance or otherwise feeling motivated to comply. Morality, Foot reasoned, could be like that. If morality is more important than etiquette, then the appropriate explanation is that, to us, the promotion of human well-being and the prevention of cruelty are more important than simply giving no offense to conventional expectations. This would dispel the seeming mystery surrounding moral assessment while enabling us to understand how morality might have gotten off the ground—for we can understand how it would be important for a community to evolve and support practices and standards that tend to prevent mutual cruelty and promote mutual well-being, standards that are applied largely independently of (or even in the face of) the particular inclinations of the individuals on whom they are brought to bear by the community, that are reflected at the level of individual moral development in the stringency and priority of moral training, and that are by and large, though not perfectly, internalized.

Such a resolution of the problem of instability seems to do justice to the uncontroversial components of the substantive content of moral expressions in a way that noncognitivism does not. It also might appear to fit better some of the evidence of common sense concerning the somewhat spotty relation between moral evaluation and motivation.[117] Of course, concepts such as cruelty and well-being are not on their face strictly naturalistic. So perhaps the uncontroversiality of the claim that morality is concerned with the prevention of cruelty (for example) trades on a normatively loaded, prescriptive reading of 'cruelty'. But Foot has argued quite generally that prescriptive readings devoid of primary descriptive content cannot do justice to our linguistic practices, at least in the case of evaluative expressions like 'a good *x*'. And it perhaps is plausible that the notion of well-being contains no normative component other than "a good life for the person who leads it"—in contrast, say, to the imperatival notions of obligation or duty. One might attempt an account of this normative component along Aristotelian lines, although a difficulty would arise: 'good' in its various evaluative uses typically is anchored by attachment to characteristic functions or roles—*a good pitch pipe*, *a good dentist*, and so on; Aristotelian theory would in principle permit one to carry this functionally anchored use forward into broader-ranging evaluations such as *a good life*, because Aristotle's underlying teleology affords to humans essential functions and roles; but this essentialist teleology is precisely the element of Aristotle's ethics that now seems least likely to be refurbished.[118] The *neo*-Aristotelian can reply that a cosmic teleology would be needed only if one sought to capture the idea of *a cosmically good life*. All that is needed for the idea of *a humanly good life* is the teleology inherent in the psychology of interest and desire, as realized in species-typical human beings. This latter view would nonetheless confront the familiar difficulties attending attempts to capture the normative in terms of the typical.[119]

Postpositivist Nonreductionist. Accounts of ethics that are more self-consciously naturalistic have multiplied in recent years, encouraged in part by work in epistemology, philosophy of science, and philosophy of language.

One important group of continuity theories of this kind starts out from the claim that reflective equilibrium is the method of the sciences as well as ethics.[120] In both cases, use of this method in critically evaluating our beliefs is seen as inevitably involving some appeal both to the evidence of experience and to currently held substantive theory—for example, application of a principle of inference to the best explanation requires recourse to our going theory as well as experience in assessing the plausibility of competing explanatory claims. Thus, the fact that moral epistemology cannot dispense with an appeal to existing moral judgments or "intuitions," and can subject such judgments to criticism

and revision only in broadly coherentist ways, does not show a fundamental difference or discontinuity between moral and scientific epistemology. Since, according to such views, we arrive at belief in the reality of moral properties as part of an inference to the best explanation of human conduct and its history, it has become a central issue for them whether so-called "moral explanations" are genuine—and good—explanations.

Harman has denied that *irreducible* moral properties could have a genuine explanatory role, but Nicholas Sturgeon, Richard Boyd, David Brink, and others have pursued analogies with natural and social science to argue that moral properties might be both irreducible and explanatorily efficacious.[121] One might, for example, argue that various chemical or biological "natural kinds"—acid, catalyst, gene, organism—are not obviously type-reducible to the natural kinds of physics, and yet play a role in good scientific explanations.

Moral properties might behave like natural kinds, on this view, because they might effect a theoretical unification of physiochemically and psychosociologically diverse phenomena in ways that would throw into relief common causal-explanatory roles: in light of the diverse physiochemical or psychosociological ways in which cruelty or injustice can be instantiated, there could be an illuminating unifying effect of explanations that successfully attribute various social or behavioral outcomes to cruelty or injustice. Like natural kinds, these moral properties would owe their explanatory capacity in part to their location within a constellation of law-governed—or at least counterfactual-supporting—properties that displays some structural or functional coherence.

For example, the notion of social justice might pick out an array of conditions that enhance the possibility of psychologically self-respecting and attractive individual lives while at the same time promoting social cooperation, stability, and prosperity. Such conditions would, in a sense, be mutually supporting. This would not suffice to secure any very strict form of internalism at the individual level, but it would help to explain how justice, and just social arrangements, might attract and retain public support, leading to the inculcation of norms of justice in individuals. And this in turn would help us to see how justice—or injustice—could have a causal-explanatory role.[122]

Of course, nonreductionists must supply a convincing answer to critics of the application of "inference to the *best* explanation" to the moral case, given the alleged availability of alternative, more minimal, and more obviously naturalistic explanations. It has, for example, been argued that supervenient properties should be expunged from good explanations, since the "real explanatory work" is being done by the supervenience base. However, this standard of "best explanation" seems unduly restrictive even for natural science, where theory development is not typically a minimalist enterprise and virtues such as depth, unification, and scope are also sought in explanations, and where there may emerge at a supervenient level lawlike regularities that seem genuinely to contribute to explanatory understanding. For example, explanations citing genes and natural selection afford a distinctive and worthwhile insight into the distribution of amino acids over the world's surface, even if this distribution could also be explained in purely physical terms, and even if the biological types are not (neatly) reducible to physical types, but merely supervene upon them. Since no standard account exists of what makes for "the best explanation," even in paradigm natural sciences, it is unlikely that definitive refutation—or vindication—of nonreductive naturalism will come from this quarter.

If moral properties are to be viewed as irreducible natural properties akin to natural kinds, then this sort of naturalism would run afoul of no Moorean argument: no *a priori* analysis is being offered, and full respect is being paid to Moore's Butlerian motto, "Everything is what it is, and not another thing."[123] It would perhaps seem extravagant to admit irreducible moral properties into the domain of natural properties if one did not allow, as the postpositivists do, that moral natural properties supervene (in roughly the sense Moore seems to have had in mind)[124] upon nonmoral natural properties. However, one might wonder whether in this setting supervenience is genuinely distinct from (messy) reducibility. For these accounts operate at the level of properties, not concepts, and advance supervenience as a metaphysical, not normative, doctrine.[125] And supervenience between two seemingly disparate classes of properties is in some respects a quite strong and surprising relation; it is the kind of relation that would appear to call out for explanation. If the postpositivist held that nonmoral properties wholly and exclusively *constitute* moral properties, that would afford some explanation, but it would also make it more difficult to contrast such a view with some species of reductionism.

On the epistemological side, the nonreductionist naturalisms we have been considering must defend the view that reflective equilibrium is the method of natural science as well as ethics, and must explain the sense in which this method, despite its extensive use of intuition and nonconfirmatory desiderata of theory choice such as simplicity and explanatory coherence, genuinely warrants belief in the truth of its conclusions (since the postpositivists under discussion reject coherentism about truth). Now not all postpositivist nonreductionist naturalisms accept reflective equilibrium as an adequate account of justified claims in the sciences or ethics. Richard Miller, for example, insists that justification must involve a nontrivial claim that one's beliefs are the result of a reliable process for detection. Such a claim must itself be justified, on Miller's view, but regress is avoided by bringing such claims to ground in topic-specific principles that are part of the believer's framework, principles whose truth cannot be established by further, topic-neutral justifications. Such a procedure need not be merely self-congratulatory: it could turn out that the actual processes of belief formation that we have employed in morality, say, are not as they would have to be in order to satisfy our fundamental principles concerning moral detection.[126]

Despite their differences, these nonreductionist views do face common opposition from those who question the granting of initial epistemic standing to irreducible moral beliefs, even when they happen to be *our* beliefs. Such criticism is usually countered by noting that theory development in general begins with according *prima facie* standing to some existing beliefs—and indeed there seems to be scant alternative. But critics will reply by citing many differences in the actual *accomplishments* of theory development in science as opposed to ethics, differences that might be thought to cast light back on the reasonableness of the original supposition of epistemic standing. Just as, in the case of religion, it has eventually come to count against the reasonableness of taking "religious experience" as possessing *prima facie* epistemic standing that religious theory has proven so persistently controversial and unreliable in its claims about the details of nature and history, so might it be held that the lack of consensus and accomplishment in ethics counts against what would otherwise be a reasonable willingness to assign *prima facie* epistemic weight to moral beliefs. There would of course be little left of ethics, or ethical inquiry, as a cognitive domain were no initial weight given to going moral beliefs; but critics might not find this skeptical result wholly uncongenial.

An effective reply to such critics would involve giving an explanation of moral controversy that competes favorably with the skeptical alternative and, more importantly, would involve developing nonreductionist ethical theory itself, showing it to have (or to make possible) some worthwhile theoretical accomplishments. Accomplishing this task would involve articulating the connections between *sui generis* moral or evaluative

properties, on the one hand, and judgment, motivation, behavior, and other elements of social or psychological theory, on the other, in ways adequate both to illustrate the explanatory gains secured by appeal to such properties and to explicate (and in some suitable sense capture) their normativity.[127]

Reductionist. A more direct, but also riskier, way of attempting to answer a number of the questions raised above—about normativity, about which explanations "do all the work," about epistemic standing, and about supervenience—is to pursue reductionism. Reductionist proposals with regard to moral rightness or nonmoral good have in recent years been broached by, among others, Richard Brandt, Gilbert Harman, Peter Railton, and David Lewis.[128] The reduction might be in the form of a putative analytic truth (of a kind more complex than any envisaged by Moore), a reforming definition, or a synthetic identity statement.[129] By exhibiting which *bona fide* natural properties value discourse can be construed as being about, it is possible to exploit the features of these properties to answer questions about the motivational or normative force of evaluation, to give an unmysterious account of the epistemology of value, and to account for the supervenience of value.[130]

Depending upon the nature of the reduction, it might turn out that relativism about value or morality is vindicated (Brandt, Harman, Lewis)[131] or not (Railton).[132] Moreover, all of these accounts are dispositional in the sense that they make matters of value depend upon the affective dispositions of agents. Most, though not all, seek to capture the component of normativity that consists in the possibility of criticizing our existing affective dispositions by providing for some sort of *idealization* of the familiar epistemology that underwrites so much of our evaluative discourse. The criticism of our desires and ends typically proceeds by, for example, asking whether satisfying them would interfere with other ends, or showing that we have misconceived their origins or objects, or convincing us that, if we knew what it would be like to satisfy them, we would no longer want to be guided by them, and so on. More generally, we believe that one knows better what one's good is, or what is right, the more comprehensive or vivid one's awareness of what living out various possibilities would be like for oneself, or for all affected, a view whose ancestry reaches back to Hume on taste, Mill on utility, and, more recently, Firth on the "Ideal Observer."[133] The component of normativity that consists in "action-guidingness" is, in turn, sought by appeal to the motivational force of our affective dispositions (again, perhaps as they are when our circumstances are in certain ways improved or idealized—since motivation when benighted might not be *normative* for us), and including perhaps characteristic desires to see our values or choices as defensible, or to make them part of a coherent and effective life.[134]

These views locate the ultimate ground of normativity in the affective dispositions of agents, and this immediately raises the question whether suitable "objectivity" can be secured for ethics by such reductive naturalisms. If it is essential to the genuineness of value or moral judgments that they not be relational in certain ways—not be tied, for example, to contingent dispositions of creatures like us to be drawn to some things rather than others—then a validation as "objective" would not be forthcoming from the reduction. We will have something better described as "subjectivity objectified" than as objectivity *tout court*. Yet it may be a strength of "idealized response" views that there seems nothing for value to be, on deepest reflection, wholly apart from what moves, or could move, valuers—agents for whom something can matter. Indeed, one way to defend idealized response views (naturalistic or otherwise) is to observe that there appears to be no alternative in critical discussion of value to a process of asking how things might strike us on reflection. It would, accordingly, be an

intolerably reified conception of value or morality to insist that "objective" value must be "absolute" in the sense of possessing independence from all facts about motivation (even, should there be such a thing, "rational motivation").[135]

But even if the specter of absolute value can be laid to rest, and even if such accounts can avoid direct collision with the open question argument in virtue of advancing their claims via reforming definitions, property identities, or non-obvious analytic equivalences, they nonetheless cannot avoid eventual confrontation with something very much like the open question argument. With regard to whatever explication they offer of good in terms of some (possibly complex) property P, it still seems coherent to ask, "Yes, I see that x is P, but isn't there still room for me to wonder whether x is genuinely good, whether I ought to regulate my life accordingly?" This question's intelligibility appears to call for some meaning of 'good' other than the reductionist proposal. Even reductionist proposals set forward as reforming definitions face a similar challenge, since they purport to provide an account of 'good', say, that gives it a clear meaning but also enables us to pose all the significant questions that the pre-reformed term permitted.[136] Yet isn't the question "Yes, I see that x is P, but isn't there still room for me to wonder. . . ?" a significant one? And how could we use the reformed term to state it?

Reductionists will have to convince us better than they have that their proposals make this question less than pressing, at least with respect to, say, a person's own good. (It need not be the ambition of an account of nonmoral good to tell us *how to lead our lives*, for example, in cases where morality, or friendship, or aesthetics point in ways other than toward promotion of one's own good.)[137] Of course, none of the naturalistic reductionist proposals are free of revisionism, and so none could possibly fit all aspects of English usage. We probably do not suppose that our intuitive notions of value or rightness are free of confusion or ambiguity, and so can hardly expect that any philosophical account of them that is not itself confused and ambiguous will have just the right intuitive "fit."

In this area as in many others, intellectual developments may lead us to a view that differs from common sense, and yet helps us both to understand what common sense does believe, and to correct it in certain ways, consistent with preserving core elements of the function of common sense—whether the area be explanation of the natural world or evaluation of the human world. Even so, the fact that these accounts seem inevitably to be led from some fairly uncontroversial repudiation of reification to some much more controversial account of the conditions of idealization, or of the relation of idealization to actual motivation, indicates the depth of the problems they face—whether they are proposed as linguistic analyses or as reforming definitions.

Questions of revisionism and controversy also inevitably bring us back to the issue of the contestability of questions of morality and value. Reductionist accounts can explain the difficulty in resolving conflicts over these questions in various ways: the intense and inevitable involvement of competing interests; the apparent plurality of values and lack of determinacy about assessment and trade-offs;[138] the inherent complexity of the issues, and the relatively underdeveloped state both of social and psychological theory and of moral theory and theory of value; and so on.[139] But even if such explanations are granted some standing, they may seem to fall well short of taking full measure of the depth of contestability and the issues it raises.

Questions of revisionism and controversy also inevitably bring us back to issues about how a reductionist account might claim to capture the "peculiar connection to action" of morality. Can an account that makes moral motivation other than rationally mandatory yield an adequate explanation—one that is at most tolerably revisionist—of the phenomena of moral experience or of the seeming truisms of commonsense moral thought? Perhaps such features of our ordinary conception of morality as the nonhypothetical scope and content of moral requirements, which the idea of automatic rational authority has been invoked to explain, can be otherwise accommodated, or shown to be less central or indispensable to commonsense moral thought than Kantians have imagined. But reductionists have not gone far in showing any such thing; despite their protestations, they might turn out to be error theorists after all.

3. MODERN MORALITY, MODERN MORAL THEORY

Even the most abbreviated account of recent developments in ethics must record the strenuous criticisms some modern philosophers writing on morality have lodged against modern moral philosophy, and, at times, against modern morality itself.[140]

There surely is a sense in which contemporary "Western" society finds itself without a sufficiently rich shared cosmology or theology, or a sufficiently rich constellation of vigorous, uncontroversial, and unselfconscious collective practices, to be able to escape a certain anxiety about morality, or to be able to articulate crucial moral questions without reaching for a high level of abstraction or generality, a level that seems at times unrelated to the conditions and motivations characteristic of actual lives and their particular sources of interest. Given the diversity of large societies, the tenuousness of many of the connections that bind together their members, the pressures toward rationalization exerted by large and seemingly inevitable institutions, and the universalist aspiration of modern thought in general, there may be little for philosophers out of sympathy with modern morality and modern moral philosophy to do but bemoan this condition. Indeed, discomforted philosophers have typically claimed to find modern philosophy in general to be unhelpful in this predicament—either because, as a child of secular, rationalizing, universalizing impulses itself, it is part of the problem, or because it simply lacks the kind of insight necessary to diagnose the real problems besetting morality and moral philosophy or the kind of power sufficient to affect these problems' real causes.

For the most part, criticisms of morality and moral theory have been set out in bold outline, in somewhat deliberate defiance of the complexities of history, society, and philosophy. So there is no end of possible rejoinders to such critiques of the mincing, "yes, but . . ." form. Certainly this is not the place to present these critiques of morality and moral theory more fully or to ask how much of their force would remain were they made more responsive to the historical record and more nuanced philosophically. However, since we have been up to our necks in moral theory in this essay, it behooves us to make some general sort of reply to these critiques, even if it must be much more schematic than the criticisms themselves.

One can discern at least two aspects of modern moral theory—as opposed to modern morality proper—that have especially been called into question: normative theory (the effort to bring some system or unity to the multiplicity of particular moral assessments and commonsense moral principles by developing—some might say discovering—a highly general set of normative principles or procedures to organize them) and metatheory (understood broadly as the effort to develop—or discover—a systematic understanding of what morality is, or purports to be). Let us take these up in order.

This essay has had little to say about normative theory in its own right.[141] Those who write in a critical vein about normative theory as an enterprise typically find themselves somewhat torn. Existing moral conceptions are, after all, the product of diverse historical forces, and it would be surprising indeed for them to fall into one neat pattern, as perhaps Kantian or utilitarian normative theories

might seem to claim. Yet one cannot without qualm call for "fidelity to existing conceptions in all their particularity" as an alternative. Not only are "existing conceptions" in flux, but it would also appear that we owe much of what seems most admirable in modern societies—movements for political democracy and universal suffrage, for the emancipation of slaves and women, for the elimination of racial, ethnic, and religious discrimination, for universal social provision of basic needs, and for international law and human rights—in significant measure to universalizing and generalizing pressures that have precisely gone against the grain of some entrenched (and still powerful) particularistic moral conceptions and individual or group commitments. One might hope for a better reconciliation of universalizing ethics and the particularity of individual lives and communities than either Kantian or utilitarian normative theories have thus far effected. More dramatically, one might insist that this "better reconciliation" will yield something that looks less like a *theory* than either Kantianism or utilitarianism. But pronouncing on this latter question would seem to us premature, given the remarkable development of Kantian and utilitarian theories in recent decades and the fact that some alternative theories, such as hybrid theories and ethics of virtue, have only begun to receive sustained discussion.[142]

About metatheorizing, critics typically manifest a different kind of ambivalence. It is less that they admire the effects of some of its well-known products than that they find themselves hard-working practitioners of the trade. Alisdair MacIntyre, in *After Virtue*, devotes substantial effort to a philosophical investigation of the conceptual presuppositions of morality and to a discussion of the adequacy of noncognitivism as a theory of the meaning of moral terms.[143] And Bernard Williams, in *Ethics and the Limits of Philosophy*, defines 'ethical theory' in a way that exempts a systematic attempt to explain what is going on in moral language and thought—including an attempt to "place" ethics with respect to scientific inquiry—if it implies that a given "test" of normative correctness *sometimes* (but not always or never) applies; that is, he defines the term in a way that exempts his own quite interesting metatheorizing.[144] Unable as we are to locate any deep distinction between the sorts of investigations we have been carrying out and those pursued by *les théoriciens malgré eux*, we prefer to see our efforts as animated by a common desire to understand morality, its preconditions, and its prospects, however much our substantive conclusions might differ from theirs.

4. IN LIEU OF A CONCLUSION

Metaethics as revived today differs in a number of ways from metaethics during its analytic heyday, but no difference is more striking than the multiplicity of now active positions and questions. No view currently enjoys the predominance noncognitivism once did, and questions about meaning have been forced to make room for a range of metaphysical, epistemological, and practical questions as well. Such philosophical progress as has been made in metaethics has come not from simplifying the debate or reducing the number of viable alternatives, but from bringing greater sophistication to the discussion of well-known positions and from exploring heretofore disregarded possibilities and interconnections. Indeed, debate has now extended even to the metaphilosophical level, as philosophers have asked with increasing force and urgency whether, or in what ways, theorizing is appropriate to morality. Since there appears to be no immediate danger of things returning to a staid consensus, we will end by making a few observations without attempting anything so grand as a conclusion. Somewhat perversely, perhaps, our observations will be concerned in part with whether some of the distinctions upon which current debates have fastened may be of less ultimate

significance, or (more respectfully) of much greater subtlety, than they now appear. Here follow six examples, not all quite in dead earnest, of areas where genuine issues exist, but where current debates have exaggerated contrasts for effect, somewhat masking the issues themselves.

1. A contemporary noncognitivist, still impressed that the open question argument reveals something about the meaning of moral terms, might claim that a naturalistic realism about ethics or value founded on reforming definitions or property identities should not be seen as really in competition with his view. The noncognitivist aims to capture (something roughly equivalent to) the senses expressed by our evaluative terms, made evident by the possibility of using the words 'good', 'right', to conduct meaningful debate over competing naturalistic views. The word 'good', for example, is used to bring something—quite possibly a naturalistic something—forward in a certain mode of presentation, *as* evaluatively appropriate. The naturalistic realist may by contrast see herself as aiming to locate those properties that discourse about goodness can—or could within the limits of tolerable revisionism, or should when we have cleared away various confusions—be construed as tracking, or as settling upon as we grow in knowledge and experience. Something like a division of labor between sense and reference might therefore be in the offing—made possible in part by the fact that the "sense" which the noncognitivist assigns to the moral vocabulary is expressive, and so *a fortiori* not logically reference-fixing. To adapt a Moorean distinction: the noncognitivist is seeking the concept "Good" while the naturalistic cognitivist is seeking "good-making features"; and the latter may stand in a metaphysical, or nomological, or practical—without insisting upon a logical or conceptual—relation to the attitude 'good' expresses. The noncognitivist thus can say what he wants to say about the peculiar, dynamic function of evaluative or moral vocabulary, and the naturalist can say

what she wants to say about what makes something good, or right, and why these are "hard facts."

Those impressed by Quine's critique of analyticity or by the Wittgensteinian dictum that "meaning is use" may find this way of dividing things up altogether too nice. We might well agree whenever the pattern of use of 'good' or 'right' shows wide consensus on the good- or right-making features. Post-Quine and post-Wittgenstein, the distinction between the concept "Good" and "good-making features," between subject matter and doctrine, may thus be seen to be negotiable, though not in just any way one pleases. To the extent that certain good-making features are truistically so, or certain substantive constraints on dialectical uses of 'good' such that they cannot be violated by speakers without gross anomaly, these features or constraints lay claim to be part of the meaning of 'good' that competent speakers acquire.[145] Where disagreement persists, however, or even seems sensible (as reflected in the possibility of a nongratuitous open question argument), the noncognitivist can plausibly urge that there is a point in trying to capture a distinctive sense of evaluative terms that enables us to understand how the competing accounts could be expressing contending views on something held constant and in common. Presumably, the noncognitivist's claim will be strongest for those terms of most general evaluation—'good', 'right', 'rational'—although all of these appear to have some substance, and so are unlikely to be *purely* expressive. Is anything left? Just the all-important, all-inclusive, almost certainly not substantive, seemingly endlessly contentious, but plainly action-guiding phrase 'the thing to do'.

Of course, our speculation here is oversimple. Suffice it to say that the relation between a noncognitivist and a naturalistic cognitivist could stand some rethinking, perhaps more along the lines of a dynamic oligopoly than over-ambitious efforts toward static monopoly.

2. Despite the tendency of holders of various views to brand competitors as revisionist, the term cannot be a definitive criticism since virtually every participant in contemporary metaethical debates is willing to entertain some or other degree of revisionism. Noncognitivists try to conserve certain practical aspects of ordinary moral discourse, but perhaps at the expense of semantic revisionism and of rejection of the claims of existence internalism.[146] Kantians also try to conserve features of the practical realm, though in a form that may not capture some of the motivational point of judgment internalism. Moreover, their account of reasons for action, though originating in an appeal to commonsense morality, may go beyond anything actually contained in common sense. As a result, they may find themselves facing an unwanted need to reject important elements of commonsense morality in order to insure the required connection to appropriate reasons for action. Naturalists may be prepared to accept some revision in the matter of practicality (at least as neo-Kantian philosophers have conceived it) in order to incur less revision in recognized moral substance. Since we can hardly single out any particular position with the charge of "revisionism of moral common sense," the real issues concern the balances that are struck between revisionism and conservatism, and what purposes a revision can or should serve.

Similarly, the distinction between revisionist accounts and error theories is itself a subtle matter, and may have to do with two little-understood questions: Would the best philosophical clarification of the nature of morality lead us to accept or reject morality so characterized? And, what metaethical relevance does such a "critical reflection" test have?

3. Although the debate over internalism versus externalism remains central to understanding the divisions in ethical theory, there is no uncontroversial understanding of how much internalism, and what sort of internalism, commonsense or reflective morality re-

quires. Indeed, most views embody internalism at some point, so that all-purpose attacks on "externalism" too often are set pieces. Another set piece debate contrasts corresponding internalist and externalist views with respect to how much they are prepared to leave to contingency. An externalist, for example, typically seeks a contingent or nomological connection between moral judgment or moral obligation and motivation, while an internalist insists that the connection is necessary or conceptual. But any appearance that internalists leave less to contingency is misleading. The more conceptual pre-commitments are built into notions such as agency, morality, and reason, the more chancy it becomes whether we humans possess agency, a morality, or reasons.

4. Now that Platonic ethical intuitionism has lost its following, the distinctions among forms of moral "realism," "constructivism," "quasi-realism," and so on can no longer be understood as turning upon commitment to (or rejection of) a domain of moral facts "independent of human capacities and interests." Moral realists, constructivists, and quasi-realists alike look to the responses and reasons of persons, rather than some self-subsistent realm, to ground moral practice. Such claims are complicated by the fact that "realism" itself bears no agreed-upon significance, that the role or nature of a theory of truth is so much in dispute in philosophy generally, and that "constructivism" as it now stands seems still to embody non-"constructed" normative notions of rationality or reasonableness. It will be some time before these issues are sorted out, and their significance, such as it might be, firmly identified.

5. There have been, running more or less simultaneously but without notable mutual regard, at least two seemingly independent debates about the justification of morality. The first debate has focused on such matters as the nature of morality, and the objectivity (or lack of it) of the reasons it offers for action. The second debate has focused on the question, Why be moral?, taking the content

of morality as given (e.g., by common sense) and requiring that any satisfactory answer show that individuals enjoy advantages for conducting themselves in accord with moral demands. Yet it has become increasingly difficult to see how these two debates might be kept apart, in some measure because the conditions under which the question, Why be moral?, is asked are often restricted or idealized—and not inappropriately, since some otherwise quite impressive ways of making morality advantageous (such as devising a reliable scheme of coercion) are thought to be beside the point. The question of what we are asking for when we seek a rational justification for morality, and what would count as an answer, remains as urgent as ever.

6. The increasing criticism of ethical theory has itself largely been based upon a theoretical understanding of ethics, or of how ethics differs from other areas of inquiry. Often these criticisms therefore seem less to be suggesting how we might content ourselves with less by way of ethical theory, than to be suggesting how ethical theorizing might be improved, either by adding variables or complexity or (theoretically motivated and systematic) relativity at the normative level, or by altering some of our views (again, for theoretically motivated and systematic reasons) about what must be done in order to "place" ethics satisfactorily.

As contemporary metaethics moves ahead and positions gain in sophistication and complexity, victories, or even clear advantages, may become harder to achieve or consolidate. That is a kind of progress, but only if a clearer articulation of the surviving issues emerges as a result.

Finally, in the effervescent discussion of the desirability of moral theory, various camps express agreement that more careful and empirically informed work on the nature or history or function of morality is needed. Perhaps unsurprisingly, very little such work has been done even by some of those who have recommended it most firmly.[147] Too many moral philosophers and commentators on moral philosophy—we do not exempt ourselves—have been content to invent their psychology or anthropology from scratch and do their history on the strength of selective reading of texts rather than more comprehensive research into contexts. Change is underway in this regard, especially, perhaps, in the emergence of less ahistorical approaches to the history of philosophy. But any real revolution in ethics stemming from the infusion of a more empirically informed understanding of psychology, anthropology, or history must hurry if it is to arrive in time to be part of *fin de siècle* ethics.

NOTES

1. Cambridge: Cambridge University Press, 1903.

2. John Maynard Keynes is said to have thought Moore's *Principia* "better than Plato," but subsequent writers have been more reserved. W. K. Frankena noted Moore's failure to locate a fallacy of any sort, in "The Naturalistic Fallacy," *Mind* 48 (1939): 464–77. Casimir Lewy points out some of Moore's missteps in stating the open question argument—but also tries to put the argument aright—in "G. E. Moore on the Naturalistic Fallacy," *Proceedings of the British Academy* 50 (1964): 251–62. Pressed by critics later in life to state his criteria of analysis, Moore laid down conditions that left him unable to identify any successful analyses. An open question argument that relies upon these conditions establishes an 'is'/'ought' gap only in the sense that it also establishes a 'brother'/'male sibling' gap. See his "Reply to My Critics," in *The Philosophy of G. E. Moore*, ed. P. A. Schilpp (La Salle, Ill.: Open Court, 1942), pp. 660–66.

3. See Gilbert Harman, *The Nature of Morality* (New York: Oxford University Press. 1977), pp. 19–20. He remarks, "There are . . . various kinds of definitions and the open question argument is not relevant to most of them" (p. 19).

4. By contrast, Harman claims that if certain tendencies of approval and disapproval were "wired in" in humans, along with associated "automatic" action-tendencies, then "the open question fails" (ibid., p. 29). Noncognitivists have assumed that the connection must be logically rather than nomologically secured—a matter of meaning, not of fact. Such an assumption rests at bottom on the possibility of drawing an interesting analytic/synthetic distinction. As Quine writes: "My rejection of the analyticity notion just means drawing no line between what goes into the mere understanding of the sentences of a language and what else the community sees eye-to-eye on." ("Epistemology Naturalized," in *Ontological Relativity and Other Essays* [New York: Columbia University Press, 1969], p. 86.) For more discussion, see below, and Sec. 4.

5. This impression may of course be in error. Some recent work has emphasized the normativity of epistemic and semantic concepts. Predictably, this had in turn led to a questioning of the very possibility of naturalistic reductions of these concepts as well. See, for example, Saul Kripke, *Wittgenstein on Rules and Private Language* (Cambridge: Harvard University Press, 1982); Paul Boghossian, "The Rule-Following Considerations," *Mind* 98 (1989): 507–49; and Jaegwon Kim, "What is 'Naturalized Epistemology'?" *Philosophical Perspectives* 2 (1988): 381–405. Whether there is the basis for a non-naturalistic approach to meaning, say, that avoids the difficulties of Platonism that naturalism was conceived in order to circumvent (compare the discussion of Intuitionism that follows) remains to be seen.

6. H. A. Prichard, "Does Moral Philosophy Rest on a Mistake?" *Mind* 21 (1912): 21–37. For a similar criticism, see P. H. Nowell-Smith, *Ethics* (London: Penguin, 1945), p. 41: "A new world is revealed for our inspection [by "rational intuition" of nonnatural properties] . . . it is mapped and described in elaborate detail. No doubt it is all very interesting. If I happen to have a thirst for knowledge, I shall read on. . . . But what if I am not interested? Why should I do anything about these newly-revealed objects?" Moreover, as Nowell-Smith goes on to claim and as Prichard would agree, even discovering a (mere) *interest* in these properties would not show they could constitute *moral obligations*.

7. L. Wittgenstein, "Lecture on Ethics," *Philosophical Review* 74 (1965): 11. We are indebted to David Wiggins for drawing our attention to Wittgenstein's "Lecture" as a *locus classicus* for the view

of normativity under discussion here, as well as to Casimir Lewy's discussion of Moore, cited in note 2, above.

8. See also Moore's "Reply to My Critics," pp. 590–91.

9. Cf. Ayer's defense of emotivism on grounds of the impossibility of resolving basic value conflicts, and also Stevenson's view that it is a condition of any adequate account of goodness that it explain why questions of good and bad cannot be settled by science alone. See A. J. Ayer, *Language, Truth, and Logic* (London: Gollancz, 1946), chap. 6; and C. L. Stevenson, "The Emotive Meaning of Ethical Terms," *Mind* 46 (1937): 14–31, especially pp. 16–17.

10. Stevenson in particular demonstrated the potential power of noncognitivism in this connection by stressing the persuasive, rather than merely expressive, role of the invocation of moral terminology. See his *Ethics and Language* (New Haven: Yale University Press, 1944) and *Facts and Values* (New Haven: Yale University Press. 1963).

11. This objective purport need not be seen simply to be a matter of the (noncognitive) "magnetism" of the moral vocabulary; for it also is manifest in the (cognitive) considerations we take as persuasive in moral discussion, considerations which must be capable of supplying substantive answers to the questions people raise when wondering together about how it makes sense to act. Thus arise both a noncognitivist version of the supervenience of the moral upon the natural—understood as a normative constraint upon admissible moral argumentation rather than as a principle of metaphysics—and also the possibility that some *secondary* descriptive content might accrue to moral terms. In this way noncognitivism would be able to capture for moral discourse not only a conceptual link to action-guidingness, but also its *a priori* supervenience and its descriptive informativeness whenever relatively uncontroversial "standards" or evaluations are in play.

12. A possible exception was the theory of value, where naturalism had greater staying power. See especially C. I. Lewis, *An Analysis of Knowledge and Valuation* (La Salle, Ill.: Open Court, 1947); and R. B. Perry, *Realms of Value* (Cambridge, Mass.: Harvard University Press, 1954).

13. "[I]f you ask me to which of these incompatible views [cognitivism vs. noncognitivism] I have the *stronger* inclination, I can only answer that I simply do not know, whether I am more strongly inclined to take the one than to take the other.—I think this is at least an honest statement of my present attitude," Moore wrote in his "Reply to My Critics" (p. 545).

14. Such work drew inspiration not from Wittgenstein's "Lecture on Ethics" (first published in 1965) or related work, but from a general approach to meaning and use attributed to the later Wittgenstein, especially in *Philosophical Investigations*, trans. G. E. M. Anscombe (London: Macmillan, 1953). The "Lecture," and perhaps Stevenson's work as well, suggests that there need not be a natural affinity between a Wittgensteinian position and cognitivism. For discussion of the influence of postwar English moral philosophy on the United States, see W. K. Frankena's account of "The Latest Invasion from Britain," in R. M. Chisholm et al., *Philosophy: The Princeton Studies* (Englewood Cliffs, N.J.: Prentice Hall, 1964), pp. 409–15.

15. See G. E. M. Anscombe, "On Brute Facts," *Analysis* 18 (1958): 69–72, and "Modern Moral Philosophy," *Philosophy* 33 (1958): 1–19 (where Anscombe announces that "the 'naturalistic fallacy' . . . does not impress me, because I do not find accounts of it coherent" [p. 3]); and Philippa Foot, "Moral Arguments," *Mind* 67 (1958): 502–13, and "Moral Beliefs," *Proceedings of the Aristotelian Society* 59 (1958–59): 83–104.

16. P. T. Geach, "Ascriptivism," *Philosophical Review* 69 (1960): 221–25.

17. W. V. Quine, "Two Dogmas of Empiricism," *Philosophical Review* 60 (1951): 20–43 (see also H. Putnam, "The Analytic and the Synthetic," in *Minnesota Studies in the Philosophy of Science*, vol. 3, ed. H. Feigl and G. Maxwell [Minneapolis: University of Minnesota Press, (1962)]; N. Goodman, *Fact, Fiction, and Forecast* (Cambridge, Mass.: Harvard University Press, 1955).

18. See R. M. Firth, "Ethical Absolutism and the Ideal Observer." *Philosophy and Phenomenological Research* 12 (1952): 317–45; R. B. Brandt, "The Status of Empirical Assertion Theories in Ethics," *Mind* 61 (1952): 458–79, and *Ethical Theory* (Englewood Cliffs, N.J.: Prentice-Hall, 1959); and J. Rawls, "Outline of a Decision Procedure for Ethics," *Philosophical Review* 60 (1951): 177–97.

19. W. K. Frankena, "Obligation and Motivation in Recent Moral Philosophy," in *Essays on Moral Philosophy*, ed. A. I. Melden (Seattle: University of Washington Press, 1958). Frankena also noted a shift in moral philosophy—within metaethics, increasing attention was being paid to the effort to identify morality substantively—in "Recent Conceptions of Morality," in *Morality and the Language of Conduct*, ed. H.-N. Castañeda and G. Nakhnikian (Detroit: Wayne State University Press, 1965).

20. See Kurt Baier, *The Moral Point of View* (Ithaca, N.Y.: Cornell University Press, 1958); S. Toulmin, *The Place of Reason in Ethics* (Cambridge: Cambridge University Press, 1961); and G. H. von Wright, *The Varieties of Goodness* (London: Routledge & Kegan Paul, 1963).

21. Cambridge, Mass.: Harvard University Press, 1971.

22. See, esp. Norman Daniels, "Wide Reflective Equilibrium and Theory Acceptance in Ethics," *Journal of Philosophy* 76 (1979): 256–82. The work of Derek Parfit greatly influenced the broadening of reflective equilibrium by displaying sharply the relevance of metaphysical questions about personal identity. See his "Later Selves and Moral Principles," in *Philosophy and Personal Relations*, ed. A. Montefiore (London: Routledge & Kegan Paul, 1973), and also his *Reasons and Persons* (Oxford: Oxford University Press/Clarendon, 1984).

23. G. Harman, *The Nature of Morality*, and J. L. Mackie, *Ethics: Inventing Right and Wrong* (New York: Penguin, 1977).

24. Among the notable phenomena in contemporary ethics that will receive scant or no attention below are the greatly increased articulation and range of normative ethics, including the emergence of a variety of Kantianisms and virtue theories to challenge consequentialism, as well as the proliferation of more sophisticated forms of consequentialism; the increase in interest and scholarliness in the history of ethics; the dramatic development of applied ethics; feminist critiques of contemporary moral philosophy (but see Section 3 for some discussion of the critique of "moral theory"); the growing literature on moral emotions and moral psychology generally, including (but not wholly overlapping with) recent phenomenological or "continental" studies in ethics; and approaches to metaethics based on blanket irrealism or antirealism.

25. Various colleagues have tried—persistently, but with mixed results—to enlarge these perspectives, and we would like to express thanks to them, and to Richard B. Brandt and William K. Frankena in particular, for many and continuing conversations.

26. Various philosophers, notably Brandt and Hare, had long raised questions of this kind. See R. B. Brandt, *A Theory of the Good and the Right* (New York: Oxford University Press, 1979);1 and R. M. Hare, *Moral Thinking* (New York: Oxford University Press, 1981). For a forceful expression of this concern, see Gilbert Harman, *The Nature of Morality.*

27. It remains true—and one might well ask how it could be otherwise—that an approach to the semantic interpretation of moral language typically plays a central role in current discussions of metaphysics and justification.

28. The term "placing" is due to Simon Blackburn. See his "Errors and the Phenomenology of Value," in *Morality and Objectivity*, ed. Ted Honderich (London: Routledge & Kegan Paul, 1985), though we may not be using it in exactly the sense he intends.

29. One cannot, of course, assume that 'objective knowledge' has any definite, well-understood and articulated meaning. Especially, one cannot simply assume that it amounts to "knowledge as attained in the empirical sciences," since that would beg the question straight off (as Thomas Nagel points out—see *The View from Nowhere* [New York: Oxford University Press, 1987], esp. p. 144). We use the term 'objective' as an abbreviation for "of a kind consistent with a respectable resolution of a range of issues—epistemological, metaphysical, semantic—that in philosophical common sense are characteristically bundled together in the idea of objectivity."

One of the great hopes one might have for ethical philosophy is that it would shed some light on this characteristic bundle of issues and ideas. The development of ethical theory might, for example, permit one to see the possibility of philosophically respectable conceptions of objectivity other than those modeled on mathematics of the empirical sciences. Or, one might find that a notion of objectivity developed for ethics could provide an unorthodox, but superior, understanding of objectivity in mathematics and science.

30. David Copp has coined the term 'confirmationalism' for the view (which he imputes to some naturalists) that one can rest a case for the objectivity of ethics simply on a showing that the instantiation of properties one identifies as moral can be confirmed by scientific means. See D. Copp, "Explanation and Justification in Ethics," *Ethics* 100 (1990): 237–58. In the end, confirmationalism is not a genuine alternative to the position urged in the text—without a suitable account of the normativity of these purported moral properties, one could not identify them as *moral* properties. Thus, confirmation of their existence as moral properties necessarily involves showing that they satisfy relevant constraints of normativity (whatever these might be). For further discussion, see P. Railton, "Moral Realism," *Philosophical Review* 95 (1986): 163–207, esp. p. 188–89, 204–5.

31. Compare Blackburn's discussion of "earning truth" in ethics (e.g., in *Spreading the Word* [Oxford: Oxford University Press/Clarendon, 1984]). At the heart of these issues is a concern about truth or correctness conditions. Clearly, it would *not* do to explain truth or correctness as a matter of "whatever now happens to strike us as right." What appears to be wanted is a notion of a domain of inquiry which not only *purports* to be apt for truth evaluation, but in which one can also distinguish between *improvement* and *mere change* of opinion, where improvement is suitably represented as in the direction of correctness (as opposed, say, to mere increase in internal coherence). One way of expressing this has been to ask whether the best explanation of our belief that *p* would attribute some appropriate role to *p* itself; this would then contrast with a "purely internal" or "merely subjective" explanation of belief that *p*. Part of the source of vagueness here is that there is no agreed upon model of what it would be for *p* to play an appropriate explanatory role. Harman, for example, concludes that "[t]here does not ever seem to be, even in practice, any point to explaining someone's moral observations by appeal to what is actually right or wrong, just or injust, good or bad" (*The Nature of Morality*, 22). (Unless, of course, we could reduce these evaluative terms to some explanatorily efficacious natural property or properties.) This causal-explanatory test has been challenged as too narrow, since we may have good, nonsubjective *reasons* for belief that *p* even in areas where it seems implausible to claim a causal-explanatory role for *p*, for example, in logic and mathematics. (Although some philosophers have thought that mathematics, too, needs a causal-explanatory credential, and have claimed to find it in the alleged "indispensability" of mathematics for science or in the reducibility of those elements of mathematics genuinely needed for science, and the eliminability of the rest. Here we find various parallels to debates in metaethics.)

32. This distinction can appear to lose its interest under a minimalist conception of truth. For example, if it suffices for a mode of discourse to qualify as truth-evaluable that it bear all the characteristic syntactic features of assertoric discourse, then moral discourse clearly qualifies even before any interesting question of "placing" ethics has been raised, much less settled. Still, though (minimal) truth would not need to be "earned" by ethics, other important contrasts between ethics and, say, empirical science or mathematics might remain. For there will be differences in the kinds of features of the world that figure in the (minimal) *truth conditions* of sentences in various domains, and differences, too, in the *methods* available for establishing (minimal) truth and in the amount of *rational consensus* such methods can bring about. These contrasts might shed a good deal of light on the distinctive nature of ethics. Cf. Crispin Wright, "Realism: The Contemporary Debate—Whither Now?" in J. Haldane and C. Wright, *Reality, Representation and Projection* (Oxford: Oxford University Press, 1993).

33. This may, but need not, be combined with the view that the scientific model is the *only* available model of objectivity or factuality. Moreover, such a position might involve challenging various aspects of orthodox views of science.

34. *Noncognitive* here and elsewhere is contrasted not with *realist* but with *cognitivist*. Irrealist and antirealist accounts of scientific language that nonetheless treat such language as apt for literal truth evaluation thus are placed on the cognitivist side. Instrumentalism, by contrast, is both antirealist and a form of noncognitivism about scientific language. But few instrumentalists have adopted this attitude toward science as a whole, preferring instead to distinguish (allegedly instrumental) theoretical language from (paradigm factual) observation language. Similarly, those philosophers who have urged that the contrast between "scientific law" and "accidental generalization" be understood along noncognitivist lines (e.g., as involving a special kind of commitment in the case of laws; cf. A. J. Ayer, "What Is a Law of Nature?" *Review internationale de philosophie* 36 [1956]), have characteristically held that (bare) empirical generalizations are to be interpreted as literally true or false. Thus, examples of continuity founded on a thoroughly noncognitivist interpretation of both scientific and ethical language are scarce. (Dewey's "instrumentalism" about science, for, example, is to be distinguished from logical empiricist varieties, and went along with a distinctive conception of cognitive inquiry and truth.)

35. This sort of line is available to those who use noncognitivism as part of an argument that no claims to objective knowledge are part of ethics, or those error theorists who believe that such claims *are* part of ethics, but are systematically mistaken, for example, Mackie, *Ethics: Inventing Right and Wrong*.

36. Thus, Nagel writes that "it is really an unrecognized assumption of internalism that underlies" Moore's open question argument (*The Possibility of Altruism* [Oxford: Oxford University Press/Clarendon, 1970], p. 8).

37. K. Baier, *The Moral Point of View*.

38. See, for example, David Gauthier, "Morality and Advantage," *Philosophical Review* 76 (1967): 460–75.

39. Baier calls this a principle of *"universalizability"*; without this constraint, he says, "it might not be a good thing if everyone were perfectly rational. But that seems absurd." See Kurt Baier, "The Social Source of Reason, "*Proceedings and Addresses of the American Philosophical Association* 51 (1978): 719; see, also, K. Baier, "Moral Reasons and Reasons to be Moral," in *Value and Morals*, ed. A. I. Goldman and J. Kim (Dordrecht, Netherlands: Reidel, 1978).

40. The term is due to Derek Parfit, who uses it to raise this question in *Reasons and Persons* (Oxford: Oxford University Press/Clarendon, 1984), pp. 87–92.

41. "Reason and Maximization," *Canadian Journal of Philosophy* 4 (1975): 411–34; and *Morals by Agreement* (Oxford: Oxford University Press/Clarendon, 1986), pp. 157–89.

42. This relates to the need to show that truth (or objectivity) can be combined with discontinuity. For a brief discussion of this point in connection with Kantian rationalism, see below.

43. Thus Gauthier originally gave the following rationale for thinking a conception of practical rationality should be (individually) self-supporting: "A person who is unable to submit his conception of rationality to critical assessment, indeed to the critical assessment which must arise from the conception itself, is rational in only a restricted and mechanical sense.... [W]e must agree, with Kant, that in a deeper sense, reason is freedom" ("Reason and Maximization," p. 431).

44. For further discussion of such worries in connection with Gauthier's views, see Stephen Darwall, "Rational Agent, Rational Act," *Philosophical Topics* 14 (1986): 33–57.

45. John McDowell later pursued this same line of thought in his critique of Foot's claim that morality can be regarded as a "system of hypothetical imperatives": "Why should the reasons which move people to virtuous behavior not be similar to the reasons which move them to prudent behavior?" ("Are Moral Requirements Hypothetical Imperatives?" *Proceedings of the Aristotelian Society* 52 [suppl.] [1978]: 15). If, as Nagel had argued and Foot agreed, prudential considerations can cast a "favorable light" on alternatives that does not derive from an unmotivated present desire, then so might moral considerations. Their recommending force, for the agent, will then apparently be independent of their relation to present desire.

46. Nagel discusses this phenomenon in *The View from Nowhere*, pp. 164–88. It is also discussed in Samuel Scheffler, *The Rejection of Consequentialism* (Oxford: Oxford University Press/Clarendon, 1982); and in Derek Parfit, *Reasons and Persons*.

47. For example, on Foot and McDowell.

48. Especially in *The View From Nowhere*, pp. 113–20, 134–37, 149–63.

49. In *Reason and Morality* (Chicago: University of Chicago Press, 1978). Also, Alan Donagan took the view that, while no argument could establish it, insight into the essence of practical reason reveals that practical reasoning imposes a demand to respect rational agents as ends-in-themselves. If this was a kind of intuitionism, it was a sort different from the variety discussed in Section 1; the fundamental moral norm is itself imposed by practical reason, and intuition reveals that fact (Donagan, *The Theory of Morality* [Chicago: University of Chicago Press, 1977]). Finally, Stephen Darwall argued that the normativity of practical reason is itself best understood through the idea of impartial endorsement of principle (Darwall, *Impartial Reason* [Ithaca, N.Y.: Cornell University Press, 1983]).

50. See especially Christine Korsgaard, "Morality as Freedom," in *Kant's Practical Philosophy Reconsidered*, ed. Y. Yovel (Dordrecht, Netherlands: Kluwer Academic Publishers, 1989), pp. 23–48; Henry Allison, "Morality and Freedom: Kant's Reciprocity Thesis," *Philosophical Review* 95 (1986): 393–425; and Thomas E. Hill, Jr., "Kant's Argument for the Rationality of Moral Conduct," *Pacific Philosophical Quarterly* 66 (1985): 3–23.

51. John Rawls, "Kantian Constructivism in Moral Theory," *Journal of Philosophy* 77 (1980): 519.

52. Ibid.

53. See, also, Rawls, "Justice as Fairness: Political not Metaphysical," *Philosophy and Public Affairs* 14 (1985): 223–51, esp. pp. 226–31 and 235–39. Rawls again rejects truth as a goal, and substitutes finding a conception of justice "that can serve as a basis of informed and willing political agreement between citizens viewed as free and equal persons" (p. 230). This might seem to suggest that the only test for proposed principles of justice is an actual procedure eventuating in "informed and willing agreement" to those principles. In this article too, though, Rawls moves to a hypothetical agreement. Appropriate conditions "must situate free and equal citizens fairly" (p. 235).

54. Rawls himself has mostly confined his theorizing to justice, and in "Justice as Fairness: Political not Metaphysical" he seeks a rationale for principles of justice that will not be dependent on any one comprehensive moral doctrine, but rather can attract an overlapping consensus (pp. 246–47).

55. Brian Barry, *Theories of Justice* (Berkeley: University of California Press, 1989), p. 268.

56. Ibid., p. 266.

57. Rawls speaks of "pure procedural justice" as the basis for his theory (A *Theory of Justice*, p. 136). We take the term "proceduralism" from David M. Anderson, "Reconstructing the Justice Dispute in America" (Ph.D. diss., University of Michigan, 1990). Anderson gives an extended analysis and critique of what we are calling hypothetical proceduralism.

58. Rawls has his own answer: we seek broad reflective equilibrium (*A Theory of Justice*, pp. 46–53). But that is not part of contractarianism; it is a metaethical position in the old sense.

59. This would still be a rejection of Platonism in ethics, which says we are equipped to apprehend ethical truths that hold independently of what we ourselves are like. In rejecting ethical Platonism, hypothetical proceduralists would not be alone; ethical Platonism these days has few defenders. (There are still live issues concerning Platonism, to be sure: how far ordinary moral thought is committed to it, how it goes wrong, and how alternatives are to cope with apparently Platonistic aspects of ordinary moral thought—accommodating or rejecting them.)

60. Indeed, Rawls, in *A Theory of Justice*, suggests that the formulation of his theory in terms of a hypothetical choice is dispensable. The idea "is simply to make vivid to ourselves the restrictions that it seems reasonable to impose on arguments for principles of justice" (p. 18). We could look at the original position as "an expository device" (p. 21).

61. T. M. Scanlon, "Contractualism and Utilitarianism," in *Utilitarianism and Beyond*, ed. Amartya Sen and Bernard Williams (Cambridge: Cambridge University Press, 1982), p. 116.

62. Rawls, "Kantian Constructivism in Moral Theory," p. 517.

63. Rawls took a view like this in *A Theory of Justice*; see pp. 51–52.

64. Simon Blackburn, *Spreading the Word* (Oxford: Oxford University Press/Clarendon, 1984), p. 195.

65. Ibid., pp. 170–71, 195.

66. Allan Gibbard, *Wise Choices, Apt Feelings* (Cambridge, Mass.: Harvard University Press, 1990), esp. pp. 64–80, 293–300.

67. R. M. Hare, *Moral Thinking*, pp. 208–9; Simon Blackburn, *Spreading the Word*, p. 11; Gibbard, *Wise Choices*, pp. 164–66.

68. Harry Frankfurt invokes higher-order desires in "Freedom of the Will and the Concept of a Person," *Journal of Philosophy* 68 (1971): 5–25. Blackburn, in *Spreading the Word*, speaks of how admirable one finds a moral sensibility. Gibbard, in *Wise Choices*, develops a theory of higher-order norms (pp. 168–250).

69. C. L. Stevenson proposed that to call something good is to say, "I like it; do so as well." See "The Emotive Theory of Ethical Terms," *Mind* 46 (1937): 21–25. Gibbard calls this "do so as well" a conversational demand, and develops a theory of norms for conversational demands. See Gibbard, *Wise Choices*, pp. 172–208.

70. Blackburn speaks of "quasi-realism" (*Spreading the Word*, p. 171 and elsewhere).

71. W. B. Gallie, "Essentially Contested Concepts," *Proceedings of the Aristotelian Society* 56 (1955–56): 167–98.

72. Gilbert Harman, *The Nature of Morality*, pp. 6–7; Blackburn, *Spreading the Word*, pp. 164–65, 185–86; Gibbard, *Wise Choices*, pp. 107–25.

73. Respectively, among others, Nicholas Sturgeon, "Moral Explanations," in *Morality, Reason, and Truth*, ed. David Copp and David Zimmerman (Totowa, N.J.: Rowman and Allanheld, 1985), pp. 49–78; John McDowell, "Values and Secondary Properties," in *Morality and Objectivity*, ed. Ted Honderich (London: Routledge & Kegan Paul, 1985), pp. 110–29.

74. Blackburn, *Spreading the Word*, pp. 182–89.

75. A rough gloss of Crispin Wright, "Realism, Antirealism, Irrealism Quasi-Realism," in *Midwest Studies in Philosophy*, vol. 12, ed. Peter French, Theodore Uehling, and Howard Wettstein (Minneapolis: University of Minnesota Press, 1988), pp. 25–49.

76. According to Ayer, for instance, moral judgments are emotions; according to Hare, they are universal, overriding preferences. Stevenson stands out among classical noncognitivists as a nonexpressivist:

in his analysis of "Is it good" as "I like it, do so as well," the noncognitive element is the demand "do so as well." Wright, in "Realism, Antirealism," rejects expressivism. Moral assertions aim to be assertions of truths, not expressions of a state of mind—though the truths are thin.

77. A. C. Ewing, *The Definition of Good* (New York: Macmillan, 1947), esp. pp. 168–69; R. B. Brandt, "Moral Valuation," *Ethics* 56 (1946): 106–21.

78. See, among other places, R. M. Hare, *Moral Thinking*, pp. 20–24, 107–16.

79. Hare, *Freedom and Reason* (Oxford: Oxford University Press, 1963), pp. 67–85; *Moral Thinking*, pp. 57–60.

80. Gibbard, *Wise Choices*, esp. pp. 45–80.

81. Gibbard, *Wise Choices*, pp. 129–47.

82. Peter Geach, "Imperative and Deontic Logic," *Analysis* 18 (1958): 49–56, at 54n.; John Searle, "Meaning and Speech Acts," *Philosophical Review* 71 (1962): 423–32; Geach, "Assertion," *Philosophical Review* 74 (1965): 449–65. Geach attributes the point to Frege.

83. Blackburn, *Spreading the Word*, pp. 189–96.

84. Gibbard, *Wise Choices*, pp. 92–102.

85. See especially J. McDowell, "Values and Secondary Qualities," and "Projection and Truth in Ethics," Lindley Lecture (University of Kansas, 1987); and D. Wiggins, "Truth, Invention, and the Meaning of Life," "Truth, and Truth as Predicated of Moral Judgments," and "A Sensible Subjectivism?" reprinted in his *Needs, Values, and Truth: Essays in the Philosophy of Value* (Oxford: Basil Blackwell, 1987). For expository purposes, we will not always distinguish normative (deliberative) and evaluative (value-appreciating) judgments, although sensibility theorists have noticed that they may need different treatment. Wiggins, for example, develops his view for "particular pure valuations," and finds "more questionable" its extension to moral judgments in general ("Truth as Predicated of Moral Judgments," p. 161).

86. 'Cognitive' both in the sense of "being apt for truth evaluation" and "being the exercise of a cognitive faculty," on analogy, for example, with perception. Wiggins is careful to distinguish the "cognitive aspiration" of evaluative or normative discourse from success in meeting this aspiration; for both areas of discourse, he appears to hold, a "cognitive underdetermination" exists and helps explain their (claimed) "essential contestability." See his "Truth, Invention, and the Meaning of Life." It should be mentioned here that Wiggins prefers to call his position "subjectivism," whereas McDowell sees his view as a form of "moral realism."

87. It is somewhat problematic to characterize sensibility theories as versions of "discontinuity," for an advocate of this sort of view can also soften up the "fact" side of the traditional fact/value dichotomy by insisting that in science, too, the notion of truth is *constitutively* tied to the idea of good reasons and arguments, so that we cannot think of Facts of Nature, ready-made, without the help of our going evaluative practices. McDowell appears to be advocating such a softening of the notion of scientific fact in his critical notice of Bernard Williams's *Ethics and the Limits of Philosophy* in *Mind* 95 (1986): 377–86. However, since the relevant notions of "good reasons and arguments" can be thought of as importantly different in science versus morality, discontinuity can still be upheld.

88. See Crispin Wright, "Moral Values, Projection, and Secondary Qualities." *Proceedings of the Aristotelian Society* 62 (supp.) (1988), for related discussion.

89. For the dual character of such concepts as objective and subjective, see Wiggins, "A Sensible Subjectivism?" esp. pp. 201–2. There is, of course, a long tradition of viewing secondary qualities-as suspect, and secondary-quality attributions as erroneous, albeit perhaps cognitive. A sensibility theorist will argue that this view of secondary qualities is wrong. See McDowell, "Values and Secondary Qualities." For discussion of "scientism," see McDowell, "Aesthetic Value, Objectivity, and the Fabric of the World," in *Pleasure, Preference, and Value: Studies in Philosophical Aesthetics*, ed. Eva Schaper (Cambridge: Cambridge University Press, 1983), esp. pp. 14–16.

90. McDowell remarks that "the sentiments [need not] be regarded as parents of apparent features; it may be pairs of sentiments and features reciprocally related—siblings rather than parents and children." See "Projection and Truth in Ethics," p. 12.

91. Once again, a more careful account would attend to relevant differences between obligation and value. For example, the phenomenology of value might be thought to turn on some notion of "attraction," the phenomenology of obligation upon a "must." The general picture suggested by Wiggins in "Truth, Invention, and the Meaning of Life"—in which the relevant "secondary quality" is a kind of attractive highlighting of the landscape of choice brought about by the agent (cf. p. 137)—is more apt for the former; the picture suggested by McDowell in "Are Moral Requirements Hypothetical Imperatives?"—in which the phenomenology seems to be more than a matter of seeing an option "in a favorable light," since it involves the silencing of various competing considerations—is more apt for the latter. The distinction between value and obligation are reflected in an older phenomenological tradition, and also, more empirically, in Gestalt psychology. Wiggins and McDowell have attempted to ward off the confusions that have beset recent debates over "moral realism" when the categories of value and obligation are not appropriately distinguished.

92. Needfulness involves a lack, but not a mere lack: a lack that merits or requires attention. Compare the Pittsburghese idiom, "This needs fixed."

93. On the idea of a "thick concept," see Bernard Williams, *Ethics and the Limits of Philosophy* (Cambridge, Mass.: Harvard University Press, 1985), pp. 129, 143–45. In his critical notice of Williams's book, McDowell suggests why, on a view like his, reflection need not emerge as the sort of threat to moral knowledge it does in Williams's account (pp. 382–83).

94. See McDowell, "Are Moral Requirements Hypothetical Imperatives?"

95. McDowell favors the view that recognition of a moral requirement by a virtuous person silences competing desires: "If a situation in which a virtue imposes a requirement is genuinely conceived as such, according to this view, then considerations which, in the absence of this requirement, would have constituted reasons for acting otherwise are silenced altogether—not overridden—by the requirement" (ibid., p. 26). Wiggins appears content with the weaker position that the *content* of judgments of moral requirement is categorical—in the sense that it "carries no reference whatever to my inclinations"—though its *motivational force* is simply that of a "good reason," not always a "better reason" than any stemming from my interests. (See his "Reply to Peter Railton," in J. Haldane and C. Wright, *Reality, Representation, and Projection*.)

96. "Are Moral Requirements Hypothetical Imperatives?" p. 13. As mentioned in the previous note, Wiggins departs further from Kant in allowing that other, noncategorical reasons might (rationally) outweigh moral requirements.

97. For related criticism of circular accounts of color as accounts of content, see Paul A. Boghossian and J. David Velleman, "Colour as a Secondary Quality," *Mind* 98 (1989): 81–103, esp. 89–90. Their discussion turns on a more subtle point. A sensibility theorist might urge that we not take over-literally the idea that value or obligation is like redness in being a content of experience, but one can hardly say the same about redness itself. Yet a circular account makes it unclear how redness *could* be a content of experience. To the extent that the sensibility theorist's account of the tie between judgment and motivation does depend upon taking this analogy with the experience of redness seriously (see note 110, below), sensibility theories would inherit this more subtle difficulty as well.

98. Wiggins writes: "Circularity as such is no objection to it, provided that the offending formulation is also *true*. But what use (I shall be asked) is such a circular formulation? My answer is that, by tracing out such a circle, the subjectivist hopes to elucidate the concept of value by displaying it in its actual involvement with the sentiments" ("A Sensible Subjectivism?" p. 189). Of course, one could read (1) in such a way as to make even "involvement with the sentiments" uninformative—if "normal circumstances" were specified to mean "whatever circumstances are necessary in order to guarantee that moral judgments are correct." The interest of (1), then, depends upon avoiding such a trivialization of "normal circumstances" (or, for that matter, of "us").

99. For example, the convergence of color judgments among ordinary human observers speaking a given language but holding otherwise diverse opinions is a noteworthy difference from the moral case. Moreover, though there may be something to the idea of a "Gestalt" of value or obligatoriness when we experience certain simple and familiar cases, when we face more complex and novel moral questions—for example, questions about distributive justice—where multiple trade-offs and aggregation are involved, it looks as if any experienced "attraction" or "must" will be the result of a complex deliberation, not something that straightforwardly guides judgment. A complex blending of colors still strikes us irresistibly as a color, and close attention to its qualitative character typically guides our classificatory response; the blending of moral considerations may yet yield a *judgment* that a certain policy or course of action is best, or most just, but not thanks to any irresistible qualitative state to which one can attend closely and that guides judgment (at least, not if the authors' moral experience is typical).

100. Wiggins might be broaching the idea of such a development of sensibility theory when he notes (in "A Sensible Subjectivism?" p. 188) that there in fact are *two* elements in a characterization of moral approval, not one: "Surely a sentiment of approbation cannot be identified except by its association [a] with the thought or feeling that *x* is good (or right or beautiful) and [b] with the various considerations in which that thought can be grounded, given some particular item and context, *in situ*." Care is needed here. Any account of (b) that went as far as stating logically sufficient "ground" would create the risk of affording epistemic access to moral facts on the part of those without proper moral character, spoiling the sensibility theorist's account of the tie between judgment and motivation.

101. McDowell, "Projection and Truth in Ethics," pp. 4–5, 9.

102. Ibid., p. 9.

103. "Reply to Peter Railton." Wiggins also mentions—in a somewhat different connection—the condition that an individual seeking justification not be "on the margins of society . . . [or] systematically disadvantaged by the workings or practices of [the prevailing] morality."

104. "A Sensible Subjectivism?" p. 206. For discussion, see the contributions of Michael Smith and Mark Johnston to the symposium "Dispositional Theories of Value," *Proceedings of the Aristotelian Society* 63 (supp.) (1989). Such a rigidifying strategy was suggested by Martin Davies and Lloyd Humberstone, "Two Notions of Necessity," *Philosophical Studies* 38 (1980): 1–30.

105. Of course, other societies may have homonyms for 'good' and 'right', linked *a priori* to *their* dispositions. What looks like a disagreement with them over what is good or right might therefore actually be equivocation. See Johnston, "Dispositional Theories," pp. 166–70.

106. Wiggins, "Truth as Predicated of Moral Judgments," in *Needs, Values, and Truth*, p. 160. See, also, McDowell, "Aesthetic Value, Objectivity, and the Fabric of the World," 16n., and Wiggins, "What Would Be a Substantial Theory of Truth?" in *Philosophical Subjects: Essays Presented to P. F. Strawson*, ed. Zak van Straaten (Oxford: Oxford University Press/Clarendon, 1980), pp. 218–19

107. "Hume could have said that *x* is good/right/beautiful if and only if *x* is such as to make a certain sentiment of approbation *appropriate*" (Wiggins, "A Sensible Subjectivism?" p. 187; see, also, 189). McDowell makes this contrast with the case of color in "Values and Secondary Qualities," pp. 117–20.

108. Wiggins at one point remarks that value does not so much appear to be one other part of the world that impinges upon the individual as it seems to be an aspect of the world that is *lit up* by the perspective of the agent. See his "Truth, Invention, and the Meaning of Life," p. 137. For would-be value realists, this image may (if it is faithful to the phenomenology of value) be an improvement over Hume's suggestion that the agent's sensibilities "gild and stain" the world, since the latter seems to make inevitable a view of values as mere projections. Wiggins's image, however, also illustrates one other way in which the analogy with secondary qualities breaks down. For secondary qualities are examples *par excellence* of what presents itself in experience as a part of the world that impinges upon the individual.

109. Giving a nontrivial account of "correction and improvement" is a crucial part of this task. For related discussion, see Crispin Wright, "Moral Values, Projection, and Secondary Qualities." *Proceedings of the Aristotelian Society* 62 (supp.) (1988), and Mark Johnston, "Dispositional Theories of Value" and "Objectivity Refigured" to appear in Haldane and Wright, *Reality, Representation and Projection*, along with a reply by Crispin Wright).

110. Of course, on sensibility theories the connection is effected by the claim that a properly developed moral sensibility is a precondition for cognitive access to moral or value properties. This view may strike some as too limited—or, alternatively, as genuinely sublime—because it addresses itself so thoroughly to the condition of the virtuous. The view does seem most plausible when cognitive access to moral or value properties is viewed as conforming rather closely to the model of perceptual experience of seemingly ineffable secondary qualities, perhaps along the lines of our discussion above of humorlessness as a kind of "humor-blindness." Further argument would be needed to establish the ineffability of the humorous, the moral, or the evaluative, or to show why one might not be capable of judging correctly—by indirect means, to be sure—that some act *warrants* amusement or moral disapproval even if one oneself lacks the relevant sensibilities.

111. For a brief, and hardly unproblematic, characterization of the distinction between substantive and methodological naturalism, see P. Railton, "Naturalism and Prescriptivity," *Social Philosophy and Policy* 7 (1989): 151–74, at pp. 155–57. A noncognitivist—such as Gibbard—can be methodologically naturalistic, but substantively anti- (or non-) naturalistic.

112. Obviously these categories are not mutually exclusive or jointly exhaustive—they serve here only to organize some competing positions for expository purposes.

113. See in particular "Moral Arguments," "Moral Beliefs," "Goodness and Choice," and "Morality as a System of Hypothetical Imperatives," all reprinted in *Virtues and Vices*.

114. "One way or another. . . ." Indeed; but *which* way, of course, is the crux of the matter. Is it to be interpreted as a matter of *meaning* (analytic) or *doctrine* (synthetic), or are we doubtful about whether there is a fact of the matter? (See Sect. 4, below.)

115. See, for example, R. M. Hare, *The Language of Morals.*

116. See, especially, "Morality as a System of Hypothetical Imperatives."

117. Compare William Frankena's remark that "the record of human conduct is not such as to make it obvious that human beings always do have some tendency to do what they regard as their duty. The contention that our common moral consciousness supposes that there is no gap [between obligation and motivation] will be met by conflicting evidence . . ." ("Obligation and Motivation in Recent Moral Philosophy," p. 79). See, also, his essays "Recent Conceptions of Moral Philosophy" and "Three Questions about Morality," *Monist* 63 (1980): 3–68. Frankena distinguishes the moral point of view in part substantively (as involving, for example, a degree of intrinsic interest in the well-being of others). Over time, however, Frankena's views have become friendlier to internalism.

118. Compare Bernard Williams's comment—in *Ethics and the Limits of Philosophy*—that an Aristotelian ethical objectivism is the only sort that might work, though, in his view, even Aristotle fails to deploy his teleology effectively in securing the objective underwriting needed (p. 44). We are making no claim here that this "functionalist" view of Aristotle's ethics is historically correct or adequate; we simply wish to note that one could be quite comfortable with a function-based naturalism for various evaluative uses of 'good' but still resist extending such an account to *a good human life*—perhaps because one cannot see one's way to a view about what a human life (as opposed to a pitch pipe or even a dentist) is *for*.

119. See Moore, *Principia*, pp. 44–45. A possible response, though one that might make the neo-Aristotelian position less distinct from a number of recent naturalisms, would be to introduce an idealization of the species-typical in order better to capture normativity, developing an account of *ideal-typical* human desires and interests.

120. See Nicholas Sturgeon, "Moral Explanations"; Richard Boyd" "How to Be a Moral Realist," in *Moral Realism*, ed. G. Sayre-McCord (Ithaca, N.Y.: Cornell University Press, 1988); and David O. Brink, *Moral Realism and the Foundations of Ethics* (Cambridge: Cambridge University Press, 1989).

121. See Harman, *The Nature of Morality*, chaps. 1 and 2; Sturgeon, "Moral Explanations"; Harman, "Moral Explanations of Natural Facts—Can Moral Claims Be Tested against Moral Reality?" and Sturgeon, "Harman on Moral Explanations of Natural Facts" and "What Difference Does It Make Whether Moral Realism Is True?" all in *Moral Realism: Proceedings of the 1985 Spindel Conference*, ed. N. Gillespie *Southern Journal of Philosophy* 4 (supp.) (1986); Brink, *Moral Realism and the Foundations of Ethics*; and Boyd, "How to Be a Moral Realist." See, also, Richard Miller, "Reason and Commitment in the Social Sciences," *Philosophy and Public Affairs* 8 (1979): 241–66, esp. pp. 252–55; and G. Sayre-McCord, "Moral Theory and Explanatory Impotence," in G. Sayre-McCord, ed., *Moral Realism*.

122. Boyd has given the best developed version of this view, according to which moral properties—like relevant natural kinds in science—pick out "homeostatic clusters." See his "How to Be a Moral Realist." Note that the sort of explanatory role under discussion could not be replaced without loss by explanations in terms of the beliefs about justice of those involved (as has been suggested by Harman. *The Nature of Morality*, p. 22)—for we can appeal to actual injustice to explain how these beliefs about injustice came about. On this point, see P. Railton, "Moral Realism," p. 192

123. See the epigram opposite the title page of *Principia*. One question that cannot be entered into in detail here is whether one can overcome various apparent obstacles to application of the semantics of natural kind terms to our evaluative vocabulary. On the view favored by postpositivist nonreductionists, natural kind terms function like proper names contributing to propositions primarily by serving up a referent rather than providing an essential of identificatory description. According to this account, it is left to the course of science to provide us true descriptions that reveal the essence of the kind in question, and our linguistic usage shows us this pattern of deference to theory and expertise, present and future. But our evaluative vocabulary seems to put its putative referents forward under a rather particular mode of presentation (see Sect. 4), and patterns of deference in contemporary evaluative usage are, to say the least, less straightforward. (The normativity of conditions of idealization, discussed below in connection with reductionist accounts, might be one such pattern of deference—we tend to think our current moral or evaluative responses could be misguided in various ways if based upon ignorance, and tend to take our more informed responses as more authoritative, other things equal.)

124. For Moore's view, see his "Reply to My Critics," p. 588.

125. Normative theses of supervenience state *commitments concerning the invocation of certain concepts* rather than metaphysical relations among properties. For a noncognitivist, supervenience is a commitment to the effect that nothing can aptly be deemed good except in virtue of some nonnormative features it possesses; thus, if two things are judged different with respect to goodness, one is committed to finding them different in their nonnormative features as well. Theses of supervenience of this ilk carry no special metaphysical implications.

126. See R. Miller, "Ways of Moral Learning," *Philosophical Review* 94 (1985): 507–56, and *Fact and Method: Explanation, Confirmation, and Reality in the Natural and Social Sciences* (Princeton: Princeton University Press, 1987).

127. For example, appeal to homeostatic equilibria will not afford an approach to explanation or normativity for those areas where severe or contentious trade-offs are inevitable. It is open to the postpositivist nonreductionist either to show how some suitable internalist constraint can be met, or to show why internalism is the wrong account of normativity (even while explaining how it has seemed to many philosophers obviously right).

128. See R. B. Brandt, *A Theory of the Good and the Right*; G. Harman, "Moral Explanations of Natural Facts," pp. 66–67, and *The Nature of Morality*, pp. 125–36; P. Railton, "Moral Realism," "Facts and Values," and "Naturalism and Prescriptivity"; and D. Lewis, "Dispositional Theories of Value," *Proceedings of the Aristotelian Society* 63 (supp.) (1989). John Rawls, in *A Theory of Justice* (secs. 60–63), offers an account of nonmoral good that shows many affinities with those just mentioned, and he cites a long list of historical and contemporary antecedents. Some of the accounts mentioned above are of moral rightness, others of nonmoral value. For convenience, though at some cost to accuracy and coherence, in what follows we still often speak simply of "value" to cover both.

129. Reservations expressed above (note 123) about employing a natural kinds semantics for evaluative vocabulary remain in force. For an example of a semantics based upon complex analytic truth, see D. Lewis, "Dispositional Theories of Value." The "putative analytic truth" escapes Moorean refutation by showing that the reduction "scores best" in an overall account of the meaning of the terms, where it is part of the meaning of terms that they apply to whatever fits their associated truisms, or does so near enough. The proposal would identify that which "best deserves" the name 'value', say, and then note that it comes quite close to that which would "perfectly deserve" the name. See also Lewis, "Score-keeping in a Language Game," reprinted in *Philosophical Papers*, vol. 1 (New York: Oxford University Press, 1983). How genuine a difference exists among these three approaches—via putative analytic truth, reforming definition, or synthetic property identity? Functionally, at any rate, they may come to much the same thing when fully developed and suitably hedged.

130. The account of supervenience is not, perhaps, *a priori*, since it may rely upon a principle such as "same cause, same effect." Critics of reductionist accounts have argued that the supervenience of the moral upon the nonmoral is a conceptual matter. See, for example, S. Blackburn, *Spreading the Word*, and Mark Johnston, "Dispositional Theories of Value." However, if we think of value as given by what we are *stably* disposed to want to want, say, then it will follow *a priori* that nothing could be a value unless the dispositions exhibited the requisite stability. In any event, it perhaps is in the normative rather than metaphysical form that supervenience is *a priori*, and the reductionist is not blocked from viewing supervenience in this sense as one of the normative commitments that come with *use* of moral language.

131. For the moral case, see Brandt, *A Theory of the Good and the Right*, chap. 10; and Harman, "Moral Relativism Defended," *Philosophical Review* 84 (1975): 3–22, "Relativistic Ethics: Morality as Politics," *Midwest Studies in Philosophy* 3 (1978): 109–21, and "Is There a Single True Morality?" in *Morality, Reason, and Truth*. For the case of nonmoral intrinsic value, see Lewis, "Dispositional Theories of Value."

132. For the case of intrinsic nonmoral good, the account is relational, rather than relativistic; see Railton, "Facts and Values," pp. 10 ff. Contrast Lewis's relativistic use of the second-person plural in "Dispositional Theories of Value," pp. 132 ff. For an example of nonrelativism about the moral case, see Railton, "Moral Realism," sec. 4.

133. D. Hume, "Of the Standard of Taste," reprinted in *Of the Standard of Taste and Other Essays*, ed. J. W. Lenz (Indianapolis: Bobbs-Merrill, 1965); J. S. Mill, *Utilitarianism*, ed. George Sher (Indianapolis: Hackett, 1979), chap. 4; R. Firth, "Ethical Absolutism and the Ideal Observer," *Philosophy and Phenomenological Research* 12 (1952): 317–45.

134. On the various actual desires engaged by idealized-desire accounts of intrinsic nonmoral value, see Brandt, *A Theory of the Good and the Right*, chap. 8; and Railton, "Facts and Values," pp. 14–17. It is important to notice the diversity of positions available here. Harman, in *The Nature of Morality*, claims that 'ought' judgments cannot sensibly be applied to individuals who are not motivated to comply. The result is a kind of internalism about 'ought' judgments—as distinguished from judgments about what is, from a moral point of view, better or worse. By contrast, Brandt and Railton insist upon a kind of internalism for judgments of intrinsic nonmoral good, and make concessions to the externalist conception of obligation that Harman means to exclude. Harman, in "Moral Relativism Defended" and "Relativistic Ethics: Morality as Politics," seems concerned with actual, nonidealized motivations (though compare his "ideal reasoner" naturalistic account of reasons in *The Nature of Morality*), whereas Brandt is concerned with what moral code one would support in idealized circumstances.

135. Note that there can be "idealized response" views that do not presuppose all moral motivation to be liable to independent characterization such as a reductive naturalist seeks. Such views might be realist, and they would share with the naturalistic view under discussion a criticism of "absolute value" as incoherent. See, for example, Mark Johnston, "Dispositional Theories of Value."

136. On reforming definitions, see, for example, Brandt, *A Theory of the Good and the Right*, chap. 1.

137. Indeed, even an account of moral rightness need not have the ambition of "deciding for us" what place moral considerations will have in our deliberations. Compare here Mill's distinguishing of the moral, aesthetic, and sympathetic "modes of viewing," in his essay on Bentham, reprinted in J. S. Mill, *Utilitarianism and Other Essays*, ed. M. Warnock (New York: Meridian, 1962), pp. 121 f. Mill thought the moral point of view ought to be "paramount," though one can accept his distinctions without—or without always—accepting this further claim.

138. It need not be an obstacle to realism about value, or to the continuity thesis, that value's boundaries or magnitudes might involve some vagueness or indeterminacy. Consider, for comparison, the question, What is the surface area of Iceland? Do we take the coastline at high or low water, neap or spring tide? How short a "measuring stick" do we use to gauge the coastline's edge? And so on. Iceland's surface area may be indeterminate in these respects, but it also is determinate enough to be clearly greater than Tobago's and less than Great Britain's. The thesis that ethics or value theory is substantively or methodologically continuous with empirical inquiry would hardly be in grave peril if, for example, value turned out to be "no more determinate than the surface area of Iceland." The real difficulty in the case of value is not with vagueness or indeterminacy as such, but with our unhappiness at the idea of resolving vagueness or indeterminacy via any sort of linguistic reform of regimentation. Cartographers may be happy to adopt conventions to resolve indeterminacy about surface area, but merely conventional resolutions seem inappropriate in the case of value: owing to the connection between value and action, such resolutions may strike us as substantive in a way that begs controversial questions about how to live. How we should respond theoretically or practically to this situation is, of course, a central question. One theoretical response would be to show that a purported reduction of value preserves whatever indeterminacy survives critical reflection.

139. These same considerations suggest that some areas of morality and value should be less controversial than others. A plausible reductionist account should help us to explain which are which. For relevant discussion, see Railton, "Moral Realism," pp. 197–200.

140. See E. Anscombe, "Modern Moral Philosophy"; P. Foot, "Virtues and Vices"; Alasdair MacIntyre, *After Virtue* (Notre Dame, Ind.: University of Notre Dame Press, 1981); M. Stocker, "The Schizophrenia of Modern Ethical Theories," and *Plural and Conflicting Values* (New York: Oxford University Press, 1990); B. Williams, *Ethics and the Limits of Philosophy*; A. Baier, "Theory and Reflective Practices" and "Doing Without Moral Theory?" reprinted in *Postures of the Mind* (Minneapolis: University of Minnesota Press, 1985); James Wallace, *Moral Relevance and Moral Conflict* (Ithaca, N.Y.: Cornell University Press, 1988); and Stanley G. Clarke and Evan Simpson, eds., *Anti-Theory in Ethics and Moral Conservatism* (Albany: State University of New York Press, 1989).

141. Annette Baier has usefully identified the goal of developing a normative theory as the best-defined target for a range of criticisms often leveled at "moral theory" without qualification. See her "Doing Without Moral Theory?"

142. Among the interesting recent works in a broadly Kantian tradition that might have more to say about particularity are Rawls, "Justice as Fairness: Political Not Metaphysical," and Scanlon,

"Contractualism and Utilitarianism"; within the utilitarian tradition, recent approaches that may make more room for various sorts of social or individual particularity include David Lyons, "Human Rights and the General Welfare," *Philosophy and Public Affairs* 6 (1977): 113–29; and Michael Slote, *Commonsense Morality and Consequentialism* (London: Routledge & Kegan Paul, 1985). A hybrid theory is discussed in S. Scheffler, *The Rejection of Consequentialism*. See also W. K. Frankena's "mixed deontological theory," in his *Ethics*, 2d ed. (Englewood Cliffs, N.J.: Prentice-Hall, 1973), pp. 43–54. Some advocates of virtue-based approaches to ethics have seen this as part of a movement against normative theorizing; yet one could very well think that a plausible virtue-based approach will call for a normative theory of the various virtues.

143. See *After Virtue*, esp. chaps. 2–5. Cf. also W. K. Frankena's review essay, "MacIntyre and Modern Morality," *Ethics* 93 (1983): 579–87, esp. pp. 582–83.

144. See *Ethics and the Limits of Philosophy*, p. 72. Moreover, it may be unclear whether one has a single, relativistic test, or multiple, relative tests.

145. Of course, we may for various purposes also find it helpful to distinguish broader versus narrower senses of a term. Compare Stevenson's distinction between "first" and "second pattern" analysis of normative language, in *Ethics and Language*, chap. 4.

146. For the distinction between *judgment internalism* and *existence internalism*, see S. Darwall, *Impartial Reason*, pp. 54–55. Existence internalism may have been the more important form in shaping the historical evolution of ethics from Hume (and perhaps before) to Kant and Kantianism, although elements of judgment internalism can also be found in Hume. For a related distinction, see D. Brink, *Moral Realism*, on "agent" versus "appraiser internalism" (p. 40).

147. There are some exceptions. Empirical psychology plays an important role in Brandt's *Theory of the Good and the Right*, and others have paid significant attention to psychology and social theory in their work; see, for example, Lawrence Blum, *Friendship, Altruism and Morality* (London: Routledge & Kegan Paul, 1980); Richard Miller, "Ways of Moral Learning"; Owen Flanagan, *Varieties of Moral Personality: Ethics and Psychological Realism* (Cambridge, Mass.: Harvard University Press, 1991); and some of the essays in Owen Flanagan and Amelie Rorty, eds., *Identity, Character, and Morality: Essays in Moral Psychology* (Cambridge, Mass.: MIT Press, Bradford Books, 1990). We should not suppose, however, that there is a well-developed literature in the social sciences simply awaiting philosophical discovery and exploitation. Social psychologists, for example, can be heard to complain that, apart from certain phenomena of moral development, little empirical work has been done on moral deliberation and decision. For examples of some preliminary experiments involving "framing effects" on relatively mature judgments of prudence and fairness—experiments that might be seen as affording philosophers a caution against over-ready reliance on moral intuitions—see A. Tversky and D. Kahneman, "Rational Choice and the Framing of Decisions," and D. Kahneman, J. L. Knetsch, and R. H. Thaler, "Fairness and the Assumptions of Economics," both in *Journal of Business* 59 (1986): 251–78 and 285–300, respectively. Issues about the role of personality, emotions, identity, and self-concept in deliberation have also begun to receive increasing attention.

II

Problems

2

From *Principia Ethica*

G. E. MOORE

5. [O]ur question "What is good?" may have still another meaning. We may, in the third place, mean to ask, not what thing or things are good, but how "good" is to be defined. This is an enquiry which belongs only to Ethics, not to Casuistry; and this is the enquiry which will occupy us first.

It is an enquiry to which most special attention should be directed; since this question, how "good" is to be defined, is the most fundamental question in all Ethics. That which is meant by "good" is, in fact, except its converse "bad," the *only* simple object of thought which is peculiar to Ethics. Its definition is, therefore, the most essential point in the definition of Ethics; and moreover a mistake with regard to it entails a far larger number of erroneous ethical judgments than any other. Unless this first question be fully understood, and its true answer clearly recognised, the rest of Ethics is as good as useless from the point of view of systematic knowledge. True ethical judgments, of the two kinds last dealt with, may indeed be made by those who do not know the answer to this question as well as by those who do; and it goes without saying that the two classes of people may lead equally good lives. But it is extremely unlikely that the *most general* ethical judgments will be equally valid, in the absence of a true answer to this question: I shall presently try to shew that the gravest errors have been largely due to beliefs in a false answer. And, in any case, it is impossible that, till the answer to this question be known, any one should know *what is the evidence* for any ethical judgment whatsoever. But the main object of Ethics, as a systematic science, is to give correct *reasons* for thinking that this or that is good; and, unless this question be answered, such reasons cannot be given. Even, therefore, apart from the fact that a false answer leads to false conclusions, the present enquiry is a most necessary and important part of the science of Ethics.

6. What, then, is good? How is good to be defined? Now, it may be thought that this is

51

a verbal question. A definition does indeed often mean the expressing of one word's meaning in other words. But this is not the sort of definition I am asking for. Such a definition can never be of ultimate importance in any study except lexicography. If I wanted that kind of definition I should have to consider in the first place how people generally used the word "good"; but my business is not with its proper usage, as established by custom. I should, indeed, be foolish, if I tried to use it for something which it did not usually denote: if, for instance, I were to announce that, whenever I used the word "good," I must be understood to be thinking of that object which is usually denoted by the word "table." I shall, therefore, use the word in the sense in which I think it is ordinarily used; but at the same time I am not anxious to discuss whether I am right in thinking that it is so used. My business is solely with that object or idea, which I hold, rightly or wrongly, that the word is generally used to stand for. What I want to discover is the nature of that object or idea, and about this I am extremely anxious to arrive at an agreement.

But, if we understand the question in this sense, my answer to it may seem a very disappointing one. If I am asked "What is good?" my answer is that good is good, and that is the end of the matter. Or if I am asked "How is good to be defined ?" my answer is that it cannot be defined, and that is all I have to say about it. But disappointing as these answers may appear, they are of the very last importance. To readers who are familiar with philosophic terminology, I can express their importance by saying that they amount to this: That propositions about the good are all of them synthetic and never analytic; and that is plainly no trivial matter. And the same thing may be expressed more popularly, by saying that, if I am right, then nobody can foist upon us such an axiom as that "Pleasure is the only good" or that "The good is the desired" on the pretense that this is "the very meaning of the word."

7. Let us, then, consider this position. My point is that "good" is a simple notion, just as "yellow" is a simple notion; that, just as you cannot, by any manner of means, explain to any one who does not already know it, what yellow is, so you cannot explain what good is. Definitions of the kind that I was asking for, definitions which describe the real nature of the object or notion denoted by a word, and which do not merely tell us what the word is used to mean, are only possible when the object or notion in question is something complex. You can give a definition of a horse, because a horse has many different properties and qualities, all of which you can enumerate. But when you have enumerated them all, when you have reduced a horse to his simplest terms, then you can no longer define those terms. They are simply something which you think of or perceive, and to any one who cannot think of or perceive them, you can never, by any definition, make their nature known. It may perhaps be objected to this that we are able to describe to others, objects which they have never seen or thought of. We can, for instance, make a man understand what a chimaera is, although he has never heard of one or seen one. You can tell him that it is an animal with a lioness's head and body, with a goat's head growing from the middle of its back, and with a snake in place of a tail. But here the object which you are describing is a complex object; it is entirely composed of parts, with which we are all perfectly familiar—a snake, a goat, a lioness; and we know, too, the manner in which those parts are to be put together, because we know what is meant by the middle of a lioness's back, and where her tail is wont to grow. And so it is with all objects, not previously known, which we are able to define: they are all complex; all composed of parts, which may themselves, in the first instance, be capable of similar definition, but which must in the end be reducible to simplest parts, which can no longer be defined. But yellow and good, we say, are not complex: they are notions of that simple kind, out of which de-

finitions are composed and with which the power of further defining ceases.

8. When we say, as Webster says, "The definition of horse is 'A hoofed quadruped of the genus Equus,' " we may, in fact, mean three different things. (1) We may mean merely: "When I say 'horse,' you are to understand that I am talking about a hoofed quadruped of the genus Equus." This might be called the arbitrary verbal definition: and I do not mean that good is indefinable in that sense. (2) We may mean, as Webster ought to mean: "When most English people say 'horse,' they mean a hoofed quadruped of the genus Equus." This may be called the verbal definition proper, and I do not say that good is indefinable in this sense either; for it is certainly possible to discover how people use a word: otherwise, we could never have known that "good" may be translated by "gut" in German and by "bon" in French. But (3) we may, when we define horse, mean something much more important. We may mean that a certain object, which we all of us know, is composed in a certain manner: that it has four legs, a head, a heart, a liver, etc., etc., all of them arranged in definite relations to one another. It is in this sense that I deny good to be definable. I say that it is not composed of any parts, which we can substitute for it in our minds when we are thinking of it. We might think just as clearly and correctly about a horse, if we thought of all its parts and their arrangement instead of thinking of the whole: we could, I say, think how a horse differed from a donkey just as well, just as truly, in this way, as now we do, only not so easily; but there is nothing whatsoever which we could so substitute for good; and that is what I mean, when I say that good is indefinable.

9. But I am afraid I have still not removed the chief difficulty which may prevent acceptance of the proposition that good is indefinable. I do not mean to say that *the* good, that which is good, is thus indefinable; if I did think so, I should not be writing on

Ethics, for my main object is to help towards discovering that definition. It is just because I think there will be less risk of error in our search for a definition of "the good," that I am now insisting that *good* is indefinable. I must try to explain the difference between these two. I suppose it may be granted that "good" is an adjective. Well "the good," "that which is good," must therefore be the substantive to which the adjective "good" will apply: it must be the whole of that to which the adjective will apply, and the adjective must *always* truly apply to it. But if it is that to which the adjective will apply, it must be something different from that adjective itself; and the whole of that something different, whatever it is, will be our definition of *the* good. Now it may be that this something will have other adjectives, beside "good," that will apply to it. It may be full of pleasure, for example; it may be intelligent: and if these two adjectives are really part of its definition, then it will certainly be true, that pleasure and intelligence are good. And many people appear to think that, if we say "Pleasure and intelligence are good," or if we say "Only pleasure and intelligence are good," we are defining "good." Well, I cannot deny that propositions of this nature may sometimes be called definitions; I do not know well enough how the word is generally used to decide upon this point. I only wish it to be understood that that is not what I mean when I say there is no possible definition of good, and that I shall not mean this if I use the word again. I do most fully believe that some true proposition of the form "Intelligence is good and intelligence alone is good" can be found; if none could be found, our definition of *the* good would be impossible. As it is, I believe *the* good to be definable; and yet I still say that good itself is indefinable.

10. "Good," then, if we mean by it that quality which we assert to belong to a thing, when we say that the thing is good, is incapable of any definition, in the most important sense of that word. The most important sense of "definition" is that in which a definition states what are the parts which invariably compose a certain whole; and in this sense "good" has no definition because it is simple and has no parts. It is one of those innumerable objects of thought which are themselves incapable of definition, because they are the ultimate terms by reference to which whatever *is* capable of definition must be defined. That there must be an indefinite number of such terms is obvious, on reflection; since we cannot define anything except by an analysis, which, when carried as far as it will go, refers us to something, which is simply different from anything else, and which by that ultimate difference explains the peculiarity of the whole which we are defining: for every whole contains some parts which are common to other wholes also. There is, therefore, no intrinsic difficulty in the contention that "good" denotes a simple and indefinable quality. There are many other instances of such qualities.

Consider yellow, for example. We may try to define it, by describing its physical equivalent; we may state what kind of light-vibrations must stimulate the normal eye, in order that we may perceive it. But a moment's reflection is sufficient to show that those light-vibrations are not themselves what we mean by yellow. *They* are not what we perceive. Indeed we should never have been able to discover their existence, unless we had first been struck by the patent difference of quality between the different colours. The most we can be entitled to say of those vibrations is that they are what corresponds in space to the yellow which we actually perceive.

Yet a mistake of this simple kind has commonly been made about "good." It may be true that all things which are good are *also* something else, just as it is true that all things which are yellow produce a certain kind of vibration in the light. And it is a fact, that Ethics aims at discovering what are those other properties belonging to all things which are good. But far too many philosophers have

thought that when they named those other properties they were actually defining good; that these properties, in fact, were simply not "other," but absolutely and entirely the same with goodness. This view I propose to call the "naturalistic fallacy" and of it I shall now endeavour to dispose.

11. Let us consider what it is such philosophers say. And first it is to be noticed that they do not agree among themselves. They not only say that they are right as to what good is, but they endeavour to prove that other people who say that it is something else, are wrong. One, for instance, will affirm that good is pleasure, another, perhaps, that good is that which is desired; and each of these will argue eagerly to prove that the other is wrong. But how is that possible? One of them says that good is nothing but the object of desire, and at the same time tries to prove that it is not pleasure. But from his first assertion, that good just means the object of desire, one of two things must follow as regards his proof:

(1) He may be trying to prove that the object of desire is not pleasure. But, if this be all, where is his Ethics? The position he is maintaining is merely a psychological one. Desire is something which occurs in our minds, and pleasure is something else which so occurs; and our would-be ethical philosopher is merely holding that the latter is not the object of the former. But what has that to do with the question in dispute? His opponent held the ethical proposition that pleasure was the good, and although he should prove a million times over the psychological proposition that pleasure is not the object of desire, he is no nearer proving his opponent to be wrong. The position is like this. One man says a triangle is a circle: another replies "A triangle is a straight line, and I will prove to you that I am right: *for*" (this is the only argument) "a straight line is not a circle." "That is quite true," the other may reply; "but nevertheless a triangle is a circle, and you have said nothing whatever to prove the contrary. What is proved is that one of us is wrong, for

we agree that a triangle cannot be both a straight line and a circle: but which is wrong, there can be no earthly means of proving, since you define triangle as straight line and I define it as circle."—Well, that is one alternative which any naturalistic Ethics has to face; if good is *defined* as something else, it is then impossible either to prove that any other definition is wrong or even to deny such definition.

(2) The other alternative will scarcely be more welcome. It is that the discussion is after all a verbal one. When *A* says "Good means pleasant" and *B* says "Good means desired," they may merely wish to assert that most people have used the word for what is pleasant and for what is desired respectively. And this is quite an interesting subject for discussion: only it is not a whit more an ethical discussion than the last was. Nor do I think that any exponent of naturalistic Ethics would be willing to allow that this was all he meant. They are all so anxious to persuade us that what they call the good is what we really ought to do. "Do, pray, act so, because the word 'good' is generally used to denote actions of this nature": such, on this view, would be the substance of their teaching. And in so far as they tell us how we ought to act, their teaching is truly ethical, as they mean it to be. But how perfectly absurd is the reason they would give for it! "You are to do this, because most people use a certain word to denote conduct such as this." "You are to say the thing which is not, because most people call it lying." That is an argument just as good!—My dear sirs, what we want to know from you as ethical teachers, is not how people use a word; it is not even, what kind of actions they approve, which the use of this word "good" may certainly imply: what we want to know is simply what *is* good. We may indeed agree that what most people do think good, is actually so; we shall at all events be glad to know their opinions: but when we say their opinions about what *is* good, we do mean what we say; we do not care whether they call that thing which they

mean "horse" or "table" or "chair," "gut" or "bon" or "ἀγαθός"; we want to know what it is that they so call. When they say "Pleasure is good," we cannot believe that they merely mean "Pleasure is pleasure" and nothing more than that.

12. Suppose a man says "I am pleased"; and suppose that is not a lie or a mistake but the truth. Well, if it is true, what does that mean? It means that his mind, a certain definite mind, distinguished by certain definite marks from all others, has at this moment a certain definite feeling called pleasure. "Pleased" *means* nothing but having pleasure, and though we may be more pleased or less pleased, and even, we may admit for the present, have one or another kind of pleasure; yet in so far as it is pleasure we have, whether there be more or less of it, and whether it be of one kind or another, what we have is one definite thing, absolutely indefinable, some one thing that is the same in all the various degrees and in all the various kinds of it that there may be. We may be able to say how it is related to other things: that, for example, it is in the mind, that it causes desire, that we are conscious of it, etc., etc. We can, I say, describe its relations to other things, but define it we can *not*. And if anybody tried to define pleasure for us as being any other natural object; if anybody were to say, for instance, that pleasure *means* the sensation of red, and were to proceed to deduce from that that pleasure is a colour, we should be entitled to laugh at him and to distrust his future statements about pleasure. Well, that would be the same fallacy which I have called the naturalistic fallacy. That "pleased" does not mean "having the sensation of red," or anything else whatever, does not prevent us from understanding what it does mean. It is enough for us to know that "pleased" does mean "having the sensation of pleasure," and though pleasure is absolutely indefinable, though pleasure is pleasure and nothing else whatever, yet we feel no difficulty in saying that we are pleased. The reason is, of course,

that when I say "I am pleased," I do *not* mean that "I" am the same thing as "having pleasure." And similarly no difficulty need be found in my saying that "pleasure is good" and yet not meaning that "pleasure" is the same thing as "good," that pleasure *means* good, and that good *means* pleasure. If I were to imagine that when I said "I am pleased," I meant that I was exactly the same thing as "pleased," I should not indeed call that a naturalistic fallacy, although it would be the same fallacy as I have called naturalistic with reference to Ethics. The reason of this is obvious enough. When a man confuses two natural objects with one another, defining the one by the other, if for instance, he confuses himself, who is one natural object, with "pleased" or with "pleasure" which are others, then there is no reason to call the fallacy naturalistic. But if he confuses "good," which is not in the same sense a natural object, with any natural object whatever, then there is a reason for calling that a naturalistic fallacy; its being made with regard to "good" marks it as something quite specific, and this specific mistake deserves a name because it is so common. As for the reasons why good is not to be considered a natural object, they may be reserved for discussion in another place. But, for the present, it is sufficient to notice this: Even if it were a natural object, that would not alter the nature of the fallacy nor diminish its importance one whit. All that I have said about it would remain quite equally true: only the name which I have called it would not be so appropriate as I think it is. And I do not care about the name: what I do care about is the fallacy. It does not matter what we call it, provided we recognise it when we meet with it. It is to be met with in almost every book on Ethics; and yet it is not recognised: and that is why it is necessary to multiply illustrations of it, and convenient to give it a name. It is a very simple fallacy indeed. When we say that an orange is yellow, we do not think our statement binds us to hold that "orange" means nothing else than "yellow," or that nothing can be yellow

but an orange. Supposing the orange is also sweet! Does that bind us to say that "sweet" is exactly the same thing as "yellow," that "sweet" must be defined as "yellow"? And supposing it be recognised that "yellow" just means "yellow" and nothing else whatever, does that make it any more difficult to hold that oranges are yellow? Most certainly it does not: on the contrary, it would be absolutely meaningless to say that oranges were yellow, unless yellow did in the end mean just "yellow" and nothing else whatever— unless it was absolutely indefinable. We should not get any very clear notion about things, which are yellow—we should not get very far with our science, if we were bound to hold that everything which was yellow, *meant* exactly the same thing as yellow. We should find we had to hold that an orange was exactly the same thing as a stool, a piece of paper, a lemon, anything you like. We could prove any number of absurdities; but should we be the nearer to the truth? Why, then, should it be different with "good"? Why, if good is good and indefinable, should I be held to deny that pleasure is good? Is there any difficulty in holding both to be true at once? On the contrary, there is no meaning in saying that pleasure is good, unless good is something different from pleasure. It is absolutely useless, so far as Ethics is concerned, to prove, as Mr. Spencer tries to do, that increase of pleasure coincides with increase of life, unless good *means* something different from either life or pleasure. He might just as well try to prove that an orange is yellow by shewing that it always is wrapped up in paper.

13. In fact, if it is not the case that "good" denotes something simple and indefinable, only two alternatives are possible: either it is a complex, a given whole, about the correct analysis of which there may be disagreement; or else it means nothing at all, and there is no such subject as Ethics. In general, however, ethical philosophers have attempted to define good, without recognising what such an attempt must mean. They actually use arguments which involve one or both of the absurdities considered in Section 11. We are, therefore, justified in concluding that the attempt to define good is chiefly due to want of clearness as to the possible nature of definition. There are, in fact, only two serious alternatives to be considered, in order to establish the conclusion that "good" does denote a simple and indefinable notion. It might possibly denote a complex, as "horse" does; or it might have no meaning at all. Neither of these possibilities has, however, been clearly conceived and seriously maintained, as such, by those who presume to define good; and both may be dismissed by a simple appeal to facts.

(1) The hypothesis that disagreement about the meaning of good is disagreement with regard to the correct analysis of a given whole, may be most plainly seen to be incorrect by consideration of the fact that, whatever definition be offered, it may be always asked, with significance, of the complex so defined, whether it is itself good. To take, for instance, one of the more plausible, because one of the more complicated, of such proposed definitions, it may easily be thought, at first sight, that to be good may mean to be that which we desire to desire. Thus if we apply this definition to a particular instance and say "When we think that *A* is good, we are thinking that *A* is one of the things which we desire to desire," our proposition may seem quite plausible. But, if we carry the investigation further, and ask ourselves "Is it good to desire to desire *A*?" it is apparent, on a little reflection, that this question is itself as intelligible, as the original question "Is *A* good?"—that we are, in fact, now asking for exactly the same information about the desire to desire *A,* for which we formerly asked with regard to A itself. But it is also apparent that the meaning of this second question cannot be correctly analysed into "Is the desire to desire *A* one of the things which we desire to desire?": we have not before our minds anything so complicated as the question "Do we desire to desire to desire to desire *A*?" Moreover anyone can easily convince himself by inspection that the predicate of this proposition—"good"—is positively different from the notion of "desiring to desire" which enters into its subject: "That we should desire to desire *A* is good" is *not* merely equivalent to "That *A* should be good is good." It may indeed be true that what we desire to desire is always also good; perhaps, even the converse may be true: but it is very doubtful whether this is the case, and the mere fact that we understand very well what is meant by doubting it, shews clearly that we have two different notions before our minds.

(2) And the same consideration is sufficient to dismiss the hypothesis that "good" has no meaning whatsoever. It is very natural to make the mistake of supposing that what is universally true is of such a nature that its negation would be self-contradictory: the importance which has been assigned to analytic propositions in the history of philosophy shews how easy such a mistake is. And thus it is very easy to conclude that what seems to be a universal ethical principle is in fact an identical proposition; that, if, for example, whatever is called "good" seems to be pleasant, the proposition "Pleasure is the good" does not assert a connection between two different notions, but involves only one, that of pleasure, which is easily recognised as a distinct entity. But whoever will attentively consider with himself what is actually before his mind when he asks the question "Is pleasure (or whatever it may be) after all good?" can easily satisfy himself that he is not merely wondering whether pleasure is pleasant. And if he will try this experiment with each suggested definition in succession, he may become expert enough to recognise that in every case he has before his mind a unique object, with regard to the connection of which with any other object, a distinct question may be asked. Every one does in fact understand the question "Is this good?" When he thinks of it, his state of mind is different from what

it would be, were he asked "Is this pleasant, or desired, or approved?" It has a distinct meaning for him, even though he may not recognise in what respect it is distinct. Whenever he thinks of "intrinsic value," or "intrinsic worth," or says that a thing "ought to exist," he has before his mind the unique object—the unique property of things— which I mean by "good." Everybody is constantly aware of this notion, although he may never become aware at all that it is different from other notions of which he is also aware. But, for correct ethical reasoning, it is extremely important that he should become aware of this fact; and, as soon as the nature of the problem is clearly understood, there should be little difficulty in advancing so far in analysis.

14. "Good," then, is indefinable; and yet, so far as I know, there is only one ethical writer, Prof. Henry Sidgwick, who has clearly recognised and stated this fact. We shall see, indeed, how far many of the most reputed ethical systems fall short of drawing the conclusions which follow from such a recognition. At present I will only quote one instance, which will serve to illustrate the meaning and importance of this principle that "good" is indefinable, or, as Prof. Sidgwick says, an "unanalysable notion." It is an instance to which Prof. Sidgwick himself refers in a note on the passage, in which he argues that "ought" is unanalysable.[1]

"Bentham," says Sidgwick, "explains that his fundamental principle 'states the greatest happiness of all those whose interest is in question as being the right and proper end of human action' "; and yet "his language in other passages of the same chapter would seem to imply" that he *means* by the word "right" "conducive to the general happiness." Prof. Sidgwick sees that, if you take these two statements together, you get the absurd result that "greatest happiness is the end of human action, which is conducive to the general happiness"; and so absurd does it seem to him to call this result, as Bentham calls it,

"the fundamental principle of a moral system," that he suggests that Bentham cannot have meant it. Yet Prof. Sidgwick himself states elsewhere[2] that Psychological Hedonism is "not seldom confounded with Egoistic Hedonism"; and that confusion, as we shall see, rests chiefly on that same fallacy, the naturalistic fallacy, which is implied in Bentham's statements. Prof. Sidgwick admits therefore that this fallacy is sometimes committed, absurd as it is; and I am inclined to think that Bentham may really have been one of those who committed it. Mill, as we shall see, certainly did commit it. In any case, whether Bentham committed it or not, his doctrine, as above quoted, will serve as a very good illustration of this fallacy, and of the importance of the contrary proposition that good is indefinable.

Let us consider this doctrine. Bentham seems to imply, so Prof. Sidgwick says, that the word "right" *means* "conducive to general happiness." Now this, by itself, need not necessarily involve the naturalistic fallacy. For the word "right" is very commonly appropriated to actions which lead to the attainment of what is good; which are regarded as *means* to the ideal and not as ends-in-themselves. This use of "right," as denoting what is good as a means, whether or not it be also good as an end, is indeed the use to which I shall confine the word. Had Bentham been using "right" in this sense, it might be perfectly consistent for him to *define* right as "conducive to the general happiness," *provided only* (and notice this proviso) he had already proved, or laid down as an axiom, that general happiness was *the* good, or (what is equivalent to this) that general happiness alone was good. For in that case he would have already defined *the* good as general happiness (a position perfectly consistent, as we have seen, with the contention that "good" is indefinable), and, since right was to be defined as "conducive to *the* good," it would actually *mean* "conducive to general happiness." But this method of escape from the charge of having committed the naturalistic fallacy has been closed by Bentham himself For his fundamental principle is, we see, that the greatest happiness of all concerned is the *right* and proper *end* of human action. He applies the word "right," therefore, to the end, as such, not only to the means which are conducive to it; and, that being so, right can no longer be defined as "conducive to the general happiness," without involving the fallacy in question. For now it is obvious that the definition of right as conducive to general happiness can be used by him in support of the fundamental principle that general happiness is the right end; instead of being itself derived from that principle. If right, by definition, means conducive to general happiness, then it is obvious that general happiness is the right end. It is not necessary now first to prove or assert that general happiness is the right end, before right is defined as conducive to general happiness—a perfectly valid procedure; but on the contrary the definition of right as conducive to general happiness proves general happiness to be the right end—a perfectly invalid procedure, since in this case the statement that "general happiness is the right end of human action" is not an ethical principle at all, but either, as we have seen, a proposition about the meaning of words, or else a proposition about the *nature* of general happiness, not about its rightness or goodness.

Now, I do not wish the importance I assign to this fallacy to be misunderstood. The discovery of it does not at all refute Bentham's contention that greatest happiness is the proper end of human action, if that be understood as an ethical proposition, as he undoubtedly intended it. That principle may be true all the same; we shall consider whether it is so in succeeding chapters. Bentham might have maintained it, as Prof. Sidgwick does, even if the fallacy had been pointed out to him. What I am maintaining is that the *reasons* which he actually gives for his ethical proposition are fallacious ones so far as they consist in a definition of right. What I suggest is that he did not perceive

them to be fallacious; that, if he had done so, he would have been led to seek for other reasons in support of his Utilitarianism; and that, had he sought for other reasons, he *might* have found none which he thought to be sufficient. In that case he would have changed his whole system—a most important consequence. It is undoubtedly also possible that he would have thought other reasons to be sufficient, and in that case his ethical system, in its main results, would still have stood. But, even in this latter case, his use of the fallacy would be a serious objection to him as an ethical philosopher. For it is the business of Ethics, I must insist, not only to obtain true results, but also to find valid reasons for them. The direct object of Ethics is knowledge and not practice; and any one who uses the naturalistic fallacy has certainly not fulfilled this first object, however correct his practical principles may be.

My objections to Naturalism are then, in the first place, that it offers no reason at all, far less any valid reason, for any ethical principle whatever; and in this it already fails to satisfy the requirements of Ethics, as a scientific study. But in the second place I contend that, though it gives a reason for no ethical principle, it is a *cause* of the acceptance of false principles—it deludes the mind into accepting ethical principles, which are false; and in this it is contrary to every aim of Ethics. It is easy to see that if we start with a definition of right conduct as conduct conducive to general happiness; then, knowing that right conduct is universally conduct conducive to the good, we very easily arrive at the result that the good is general happiness. If, on the other hand, we once recognise that we must start our Ethics without a definition, we shall be much more apt to look about us, before we adopt any ethical principle whatever; and the more we look about us, the less likely are we to adopt a false one. It may be replied to this: Yes, but we shall look about us just as much, before we settle on our definition, and are therefore just as likely to be right. But I will try to shew that this is not the case. If we start with the conviction that a definition of good can be found, we start with the conviction that good *can mean* nothing else than some one property of things; and our only business will then be to discover what that property is. But if we recognise that, so far as the meaning of good goes, anything whatever may be good, we start with a much more open mind. Moreover, apart from the fact that, when we think we have a definition, we cannot logically defend our ethical principles in any way whatever, we shall also be much less apt to defend them well, even if illogically. For we shall start with the conviction that good must mean so and so, and shall therefore be inclined either to misunderstand our opponent's arguments or to cut them short with the reply, "This is not an open question: the very meaning of the word decides it; no one can think otherwise except through confusion."

15. Our first conclusion as to the subject-matter of Ethics is, then, that there is a simple, indefinable, unanalysable object of thought by reference to which it must be defined. By what name we call this unique object is a matter of indifference, so long as we clearly recognise what it is and that it does differ from other objects. The words which are commonly taken as the signs of ethical judgments all do refer to it; and they are expressions of ethical judgments solely because they do so refer. But they may refer to it in two different ways, which it is very important to distinguish, if we are to have a complete definition of the range of ethical judgments. Before I proceeded to argue that there was such an indefinable notion involved in ethical notions, I stated (Sec. 4) that it was necessary for Ethics to enumerate all true universal judgments, asserting that such and such a thing was good, whenever it occurred. But, although all such judgments do refer to that unique notion which I have called "good," they do not all refer to it in the same way. They may either assert that this unique property does always attach to the thing in

question, or else they may assert only that the thing in question is *a cause or necessary condition* for the existence of other things to which this unique property does attach. The nature of these two species of universal ethical judgments is extremely different; and a great part of the difficulties, which are met with in ordinary ethical speculation, are due to the failure to distinguish them clearly. Their difference has, indeed, received expression in ordinary language by the contrast between the terms "good as means" and "good in itself," "value as a means" and "intrinsic value." But these terms are apt to be applied correctly only in the more obvious instances; and this seems to be due to the fact that the distinction between the conceptions which they denote has not been made a separate object of investigation. This distinction may be briefly pointed out as follows.

16. Whenever we judge that a thing is "good as a means," we are making a judgment with regard to its causal relations: we judge *both* that it will have a particular kind of effect, *and* that that effect will be good in itself. But to find causal judgments that are universally true is notoriously a matter of extreme difficulty. The late date at which most of the physical sciences became exact, and the comparative fewness of the laws which they have succeeded in establishing even now, are sufficient proofs of this difficulty. With regard, then, to what are the most frequent objects of ethical judgments, namely actions, it is obvious that we cannot be satisfied that any of our universal causal judgments are true, even in the sense in which scientific laws are so. We cannot even discover hypothetical laws of the form "Exactly this action will always, under these conditions, produce exactly that effect." But for a correct ethical judgment with regard to the effects of certain actions we require more than this in two respects. (1) We require to know that a given action will produce a certain effect, *under whatever circumstances it occurs.* But this is certainly impossible. It is certain that in different circumstances the same action may produce effects which are utterly different in all respects upon which the value of the effects depends. Hence we can never be entitled to more than a *generalization*—to a proposition of the form "This result *generally* follows this kind of action"; and even this generalization will only be true, if the circumstances under which the action occurs are generally the same. This is in fact the case, to a great extent, within any one particular age and state of society. But, when we take other ages into account, in many most important cases the normal circumstances of a given kind of action will be so different, that the generalization which is true for one will not be true for another. With regard then to ethical judgments which assert that a certain kind of action is good as a means to a certain kind of effect, none will be *universally* true; and many, though *generally* true at one period, will be generally false at others. But (2) we require to know not only that *one* good effect will be produced, but that, among all subsequent events affected by the action in question, the balance of good will be greater than if any other possible action had been performed. In other words, to judge that an action is generally a means to good is to judge not only that it generally does *some* good, but that it generally does the greatest good of which the circumstances admit. In this respect ethical judgments about the effects of action involve a difficulty and a complication far greater than that involved in the establishment of scientific laws. For the latter we need only consider a single effect; for the former it is essential to consider not only this, but the effects of that effect, and so on as far as our view into the future can reach. It is, indeed, obvious that our view can never reach far enough for us to be certain that any action will produce the best possible effects. We must be content, if the greatest possible balance of good seems to be produced within a limited period. But it is important to notice that the whole series of effects within a period of considerable length is actually taken

account of in our common judgments that an action is good as a means; and that hence this additional complication, which makes ethical generalisations so far more difficult to establish than scientific laws, is one which is involved in actual ethical discussions, and is of practical importance. The commonest rules of conduct involve such considerations as the balancing of future bad health against immediate gains; and even if we can never settle with any certainty how we shall secure the greatest possible total of good, we try at least to assure ourselves that probable future evils will not be greater than the immediate good.

17. There are, then, judgments which state that certain kinds of things have good effects; and such judgments, for the reasons just given, have the important characteristics (1) that they are unlikely to be true, if they state that the kind of thing in question *always* has good effects, and (2) that, even if they only state that it *generally* has good effects, many of them will only be true of certain periods in the world's history. On the other hand there are judgments which state that certain kinds of things are themselves good; and these differ from the last in that, if true at all, they are all of them universally true. It is, therefore, extremely important to distinguish these two kinds of possible judgments. Both may be expressed in the same language: in both cases we commonly say "Such and such a thing is good." But in the one case "good" will mean "good as means," that is, merely that the thing is a means to good—will have good effects: in the other case it will mean "good as end"—we shall be judging that the thing itself has the property which, in the first case, we asserted only to belong to its effects. It is plain that these are very different assertions to make about a thing; it is plain that either or both of them may be made, both truly and falsely, about all manner of things; and it is certain that unless we are clear as to which of the two we mean to assert, we shall have a very poor chance of deciding rightly whether our assertion is true or false It is precisely this clearness as to the meaning of the question asked which has hitherto been almost entirely lacking in ethical speculation. Ethics has always been predominantly concerned with the investigation of a limited class of actions. With regard to these we may ask *both* how far they are good in themselves *and* how far they have a general tendency to produce good results. And the arguments brought forward in ethical discussion have always been of both classes—both such as would prove the conduct in question to be good in itself and such as would prove it to be good as a means. But that these are the only questions which any ethical discussion can have to settle, and that to settle the one is *not* the same thing as to settle the other— these two fundamental facts have in general escaped the notice of ethical philosophers. Ethical questions are commonly asked in an ambiguous form. It is asked "What is a man's duty under these circumstances?" or "Is it right to act in this way?" or "What ought we to aim at securing?" But all these questions are capable of further analysis; a correct answer to any of them involves both judgments of what is good in itself and causal judgments. This is implied even by those who maintain that we have a direct and immediate judgment of absolute rights and duties. Such a judgment can only mean that the course of action in question is *the* best thing to do; that, by acting so, every good that *can* be secured will have been secured. Now we are not concerned with the question whether such a judgment will ever be true. The question is: What does it imply, if it is true? And the only possible answer is that, whether true or false, it implies both a proposition as to the degree of goodness of the action in question, as compared with other things, and a number of causal propositions. For it cannot be denied that the action will have consequences: and to deny that the consequences matter is to make a judgment of their intrinsic value, as compared with the action itself. In asserting that the action is *the* best thing to do, we assert that it together with its con-

sequences presents a greater sum of intrinsic value than any possible alternative. And this condition may be realised by any of the three cases:—(a) If the action itself has greater intrinsic value than any alternative, whereas both its consequences and those of the alternatives are absolutely devoid either of intrinsic merit or intrinsic demerit; or (b) if, though its consequences are intrinsically bad, the balance of intrinsic value is greater than would be produced by any alternative; or (c) if, its consequences being intrinsically good, the degree of value belonging to them and it conjointly is greater than that of any alternative series. In short, to assert that a certain line of conduct is, at a given time, absolutely right or obligatory, is obviously to assert that more good or less evil will exist in the world, if it be adopted than if anything else be done instead. But this implies a judgment as to the value both of its own consequences and of those of any possible alternative. And that an action will have such and such consequences involves a number of causal judgments.

Similarly, in answering the question "What ought we to aim at securing?" causal judgments are again involved, but in a somewhat different way We are liable to forget, because it is so obvious, that this question can never be answered correctly except by naming something which *can* be secured. Not everything can be secured; and, even if we judge that nothing which cannot be obtained would be of equal value with that which can, the possibility of the latter, as well as its value, is essential to its being a proper end of action. Accordingly neither our judgments as to what actions we ought to perform, nor even our judgments as to the ends which they ought to produce, are pure judgments of intrinsic value. With regard to the former, an action which is absolutely obligatory *may* have no intrinsic value whatsoever; that it is perfectly virtuous may mean merely that it causes the best possible effects. And with regard to the latter, these best possible results which justify our action can, in any case, have only so much of intrinsic value as the laws of nature allow us to secure; and they in their turn *may* have no intrinsic value whatsoever, but may merely be a means to the attainment (in a still further future) of something that has such value. Whenever, therefore, we ask "What ought we to do?" or "What ought we to try to get?" we are asking questions which involve a correct answer to two others, completely different in kind from one another. We must know *both* what degree of intrinsic value different things have, *and* how these different things may be obtained. But the vast majority of questions which have actually been discussed in Ethics—*all* practical questions, indeed—involve this double knowledge; and they have been discussed without any clear separation of the two distinct questions involved. A great part of the vast disagreements prevalent in Ethics is to be attributed to this failure in analysis. By the use of conceptions which involve both that of intrinsic value and that of causal relation, as if they involved intrinsic value only, two different errors have been rendered almost universal.

Either it is assumed that nothing has intrinsic value which is not possible, or else it is assumed that what is necessary must have intrinsic value. Hence the primary and peculiar business of Ethics, the determination what things have intrinsic value and in what degrees, has received no adequate treatment at all. And on the other hand a *thorough* discussion of means has been also largely neglected, owing to an obscure perception of the truth that it is perfectly irrelevant to the question of intrinsic values. But however this may be, and however strongly any particular reader may be convinced that some one of the mutually contradictory systems which hold the field has given a correct answer either to the question what has intrinsic value, or to the question what we ought to do, or to both, it must at least be admitted that the questions what is best in itself and what will bring about the best possible, are utterly distinct; that both belong to the actual subject-matter of Ethics; and that the more clearly distinct questions are distinguished, the better is our chance of answering both correctly.

NOTES

1. *Methods of Ethics*, bk. I, chap. iii, sec. 1 (6th ed.).
2. *Methods of Ethics*, bk. I, chap. iv, sec. 1.

3

Lecture on Ethics

LUDWIG WITTGENSTEIN

The following lecture was prepared by Wittgenstein for delivery in Cambridge sometime between September 1929 and December 1930. It was probably read to the society known as "The Heretics," to which Wittgenstein gave an address at that time. The manuscript bears no title. So far as is known, this was the only popular lecture ever composed or delivered by Wittgenstein.

Before I begin to speak about my subject proper let me make a few introductory remarks. I feel I shall have great difficulties in communicating my thoughts to you and I think some of them may be diminished by mentioning them to you beforehand. The first one, which almost I need not mention, is that English is not my native tongue and my expression therefore often lacks that precision and subtlety which would be desirable if one talks about a difficult subject. All I can do is to ask you to make my task easier by trying to get at my meaning in spite of the faults which I will constantly be committing against the English grammar. The second difficulty I will mention is this, that probably many of you come up to this lecture of mine with slightly wrong expectations. And to set you right in this point I will say a few words about the reason for choosing the subject I have chosen: When your former secretary honoured me by asking me to read a paper to your society, my first thought was that I would certainly do it and my second thought was that if I was to have the opportunity to speak to you I should speak about something which I am keen on communicating to you and that I should not misuse this opportunity to give you a lecture about, say, logic. I call this a misuse, for to explain a scientific matter to you it would need a course of lectures and not an hour's paper. Another alternative would have been to give you what's called a popular-scientific lecture, that is a lecture intended to make you believe that you understand a thing which actually you don't understand, and to gratify what I believe to be one of the lowest desires of modern people, namely the superficial curiosity about the latest discoveries of science. I rejected these alternatives and decided to talk to you about a subject which seems to me to be of general importance, hoping that it may help to clear up your thoughts about this subject (even if you should entirely disagree with what I will say about it). My third and last difficulty is one which, in fact, adheres to most lengthy philosophical lectures and it is this, that the hearer is incapable of seeing both the road he is led and the goal which it leads to. That is to say: he either thinks: "I understand all he says, but what on earth is he driving at" or else he thinks "I see what he's driving at, but how on earth is he going to get there." All I can do is again to ask you to be patient and to hope that in the end you may see both the way and where it leads to.

I will now begin. My subject, as you know, is Ethics and I will adopt the explanation of that term which Professor Moore has given in his book *Principia Ethica*. He says: "Ethics is the general enquiry into what is good." Now I am going to use the term Ethics in a slightly wider sense, in a sense in fact which includes what I believe to be the most essential part of what is generally called Aesthetics. And to make you see as clearly as possible what I take to be the subject matter of Ethics I will put before you a number of more or less synonymous expressions each of which could be substituted for the above definition, and by enumerating them I want to produce the same sort of effect which Galton produced when he took a number of photos of different faces on the same photographic plate in order to get the picture of the typical features they all had in common. And as by showing to you such a collective photo I could make you see what is the typical—say—Chinese face; so if you look through the row of synonyms which I will put before you, you will, I hope, be able to see the characteristic features they all have in common and these are the characteristic features of Ethics. Now instead of saying "Ethics is the enquiry into what is good" I could have said Ethics

is the enquiry into what is valuable, or, into what is really important, or I could have said Ethics is the enquiry into the meaning of life, or into what makes life worth living, or into the right way of living. I believe if you look at all these phrases you will get a rough idea as to what it is that Ethics is concerned with. Now the first thing that strikes one about all these expressions is that each of them is actually used in two very different senses. I will call them the trivial or relative sense on the one hand and the ethical or absolute sense on the other. If for instance I say that this is a *good* chair this means that the chair serves a certain predetermined purpose and the word good here has only meaning so far as this purpose has been previously fixed upon. In fact the word good in the relative sense simply means coming up to a certain predetermined standard. Thus when we say that this man is a good pianist we mean that he can play pieces of a certain degree of difficulty with a certain degree of dexterity. And similarly if I say that it is *important* for me not to catch cold I mean that catching a cold produces certain describable disturbances in my life and if I say that this is the *right* road I mean that it's the right road relative to a certain goal. Used in this way these expressions don't present any difficult or deep problems. But this is not how Ethics uses them. Supposing that I could play tennis and one of you saw me playing and said "Well, you play pretty badly" and suppose I answered "I know, I'm playing badly but I don't want to play any better," all the other man could say would be "Ah then that's all right." But suppose I had told one of you a preposterous lie and he came up to me and said "You're behaving like a beast" and then I were to say "I know I behave badly, but then I don't want to behave any better," could he then say "Ah, then that's all right"? Certainly not; he would say "Well, you *ought* to want to behave better." Here you have an absolute judgment of value, whereas the first instance was one of a relative judgment The essence of this difference seems to be obviously this: Every judgment of relative value is a mere statement of facts and can therefore be put in such a form that it loses all the appearance of a judgment of value: Instead of saying "This is the right way to Granchester," I could equally well have said, "This is the right way you have to go if you want to get to Granchester in the shortest time"; "This man is a good runner" simply means that he runs a certain number of miles in a certain number of minutes, etc. Now what I wish to contend is that, although all judgments of relative value can be shown to be mere statements of facts, no statement of fact can ever be, or imply, a judgment of absolute value. Let me explain this: Suppose one of you were an omniscient person and therefore knew all the movements of all the bodies in the world dead or alive and that he also knew all the states of mind of all human beings that ever lived, and suppose this man wrote all he knew in a big book, then this book would contain the whole description of the world; and what I want to say is, that this book would contain nothing that we would call an *ethical* judgment or anything that would logically imply such a judgment. It would of course contain all relative judgments of value and all true scientific propositions and in fact all true propositions that can be made. But all the facts described would, as it were, stand on the same level and in the same way all propositions stand on the same level. There are no propositions which, in any absolute sense, are sublime, important, or trivial. Now perhaps some of you will agree to that and be reminded of Hamlet's words: "Nothing is either good or bad, but thinking makes it so." But this again could lead to a misunderstanding. What Hamlet says seems to imply that good and bad, though not qualities of the world outside us, are attributes to our states of mind. But what I mean is that a state of mind, so far as we mean by that a fact which we can describe, is in no ethical sense good or bad. If for instance in our world-book we read the description of a murder with all its details physical and psychological, the mere description

of these facts will contain nothing which we could call an *ethical* proposition. The murder will be on exactly the same level as any other event, for instance the falling of a stone. Certainly the reading of this description might cause us pain or rage or any other emotion, or we might read about the pain or rage caused by this murder in other people when they heard of it, but there will simply be facts, facts, and facts but no Ethics. And now I must say that if I contemplate what Ethics really would have to be if there were such a science, this result seems to me quite obvious. It seems to me obvious that nothing we could ever think or say should be *the* thing. That we cannot write a scientific book, the subject matter of which could be intrinsically sublime and above all other subject matters. I can only describe my feeling by the metaphor, that, if a man could write a book on Ethics which really was a book on Ethics, this book would, with an explosion, destroy all the other books in the world. Our words used as we use them in science, are vessels capable only of containing and conveying meaning and sense, *natural* meaning and sense. Ethics, if it is anything, is supernatural and our words will only express facts; as a teacup will only hold a teacup full of water and if I were to pour out a gallon over it. I said that so far as facts and propositions are concerned there is only relative value and relative good, right, etc. And let me, before I go on, illustrate this by a rather obvious example. The right road is the road which leads to an arbitrarily predetermined end and it is quite clear to us all that there is no sense in talking about the right road apart from such a predetermined goal. Now let us see what we could possibly mean by the expression, "*the* absolutely right road." I think it would be the road which *everybody* on seeing it would, *with logical necessity*, have to go, or be ashamed for not going. And similarly the *absolute good*, if it is a describable state of affairs, would be one which everybody, independent of his tastes and inclinations, would *necessarily* bring about or feel guilty for not bringing about. And I want to say that such a state of affairs is a chimera. No state of affairs has, in itself, what I would like to call the coercive power of an absolute judge. Then what have all of us who, like myself, are still tempted to use such expressions as "absolute good," "absolute value," etc., what have we in mind and what do we try to express? Now whenever I try to make this clear to myself it is natural that I should recall cases in which I would certainly use these expressions and I am then in the situation in which you would be if, for instance, I were to give you a lecture on the psychology of pleasure. What you would do then would be to try and recall some typical situation in which you always felt pleasure. For, bearing this situation in mind, all I should say to you would become concrete and, as it were, controllable. One man would perhaps choose as his stock example the sensation when taking a walk on a fine summer's day. Now in this situation I am, if I want to fix my mind on what I mean by absolute or ethical value. And there, in my case, it always happens that the idea of one particular experience presents itself to me which therefore is, in a sense, my experience *par excellence* and this is the reason why, in talking to you now, I will use this experience as my first and foremost example. (As I have said before, this is an entirely personal matter and others would find other examples more striking.) I will describe this experience in order, if possible, to make you recall the same or similar experiences, so that we may have a common ground for our investigation. I believe the best way of describing it is to say that when I have it *I wonder at the existence of the world*. And I am then inclined to use such phrases as "how extraordinary that anything should exist" or "how extraordinary that the world should exist." I will mention another experience straight away which I also know and which others of you might be acquainted with: it is, what one might call, the experience of feeling *absolutely* safe. I mean the state of mind in which one is inclined to say "I am safe,

nothing can injure me whatever happens." Now let me consider these experiences, for, I believe, they exhibit the very characteristics we try to get clear about. And there the first thing I have to say is, that the verbal expression which we give to these experiences is nonsense! If I say "I wonder at the existence of the world" I am misusing language. Let me explain this: It has a perfectly good and clear sense to say that I wonder at something being the case, we all understand what it means to say that I wonder at the size of a dog which is bigger than anyone I have ever seen before or at any thing which, in the common sense of the word, is extraordinary. In every such case I wonder at something being the case which I *could* conceive *not* to be the case. I wonder at the size of this dog because I could conceive of a dog of another, namely the ordinary size, at which I should not wonder. To say "I wonder at such and such being the case" has only sense if I can imagine it not to be the case. In this sense one can wonder at the existence of, say, a house when one sees it and has not visited it for a long time and has imagined that it had been pulled down in the meantime. But it is nonsense to say that I wonder at the existence of the world, because I cannot imagine it not existing. I could of course wonder at the world round me being as it is. If for instance I had this experience while looking into the blue sky, I could wonder at the sky being blue as opposed to the case when it's clouded. But that's not what I mean. I am wondering at the sky being *whatever it is*. One might be tempted to say that what I am wondering at is a tautology, namely at the sky being blue or not blue. But then it's just nonsense to say that one is wondering at a tautology. Now the same applies to the other experience which I have mentioned, the experience of absolute safety. We all know what it means in ordinary life to be safe. I am safe in my room, when I cannot be run over by an omnibus. I am safe if I have had whooping cough and cannot therefore get it again. To be safe essentially means that it is physically impossible that certain things should happen to me and therefore it's nonsense to say that I am safe *whatever* happens. Again this is a misuse of the word "safe" as the other example was of a misuse of the word "existence" or "wondering." Now I want to impress on you that a certain characteristic misuse of our language runs through *all* ethical and religious expressions. All these expressions *seem*, *prima facie*, to be just *similes*. Thus it seems that when we are using the word *right* in an ethical sense, although, what we mean, is not right in its trivial sense, it's something similar, and when we say "This is a good fellow," although the word good here doesn't mean what it means in the sentence "This is a good football player" there seems to be some similarity. And when we say "This man's life was valuable" we don't mean it in the same sense in which we would speak of some valuable jewelry but there seems to be some sort of analogy. Now all religious terms seem in this sense to be used as similes or allegorically. For when we speak of God and that he sees everything and when we kneel and pray to him all our terms and actions seem to be parts of a great and elaborate allegory which represents him as a human being of great power whose grace we try to win, etc, etc. But this allegory also describes the experience which I have just referred to. For the first of them is, I believe, exactly what people were referring to when they said that God had created the world; and the experience of absolute safety has been described by saying that we feel safe in the hands of God. A third experience of the same kind is that of feeling guilty and again this was described by the phrase that God disapproves of our conduct. Thus in ethical and religious language we seem constantly to be using similes. But a simile must be the simile for *something*. And if I can describe a fact by means of a simile I must also be able to drop the simile and to describe the facts without it. Now in our case as soon as we try to drop the simile and simply to state the facts which stand behind it, we find that there are no such facts. And so,

what at first appeared to be a simile now seems to be mere nonsense. Now the three experiences which I have mentioned to you (and I could have added others) seem to those who have experienced them, for instance to me, to have in some sense an intrinsic, absolute value. But when I say they are experiences, surely, they are facts; they have taken place then and there, lasted a certain definite time and consequently are describable. And so from what I have said some minutes ago I must admit it is nonsense to say that they have absolute value. And I will make my point still more acute by saying "It is the paradox that an experience, a fact, should seem to have supernatural value." Now there is a way in which I would be tempted to meet this paradox. Let me first consider, again, our first experience of wondering at the existence of the world and let me describe it in a slightly different way; we all know what in ordinary life would be called a miracle. It obviously is simply an event the like of which we have never yet seen. Now suppose such an event happened. Take the case that one of you suddenly grew a lion's head and began to roar. Certainly that would be as extraordinary a thing as I can imagine. Now whenever we should have recovered from our surprise, what I would suggest would be to fetch a doctor and have the case scientifically investigated and if it were not for hurting him I would have him vivisected. And where would the miracle have got to ? For it is clear that when we look at it in this way everything miraculous has disappeared; unless what we mean by this term is merely that a fact has not yet been explained by science which again means that we have hitherto failed to group this fact with others in a scientific system. This shows that it is absurd to say "Science has proved that there are no miracles." The truth is that the scientific way of looking at a fact is not the way to look at it as a miracle. For imagine whatever fact you may, it is not in itself miraculous in the absolute sense of that term. For we see now that we have been using the word "miracle" in a relative and an absolute sense. And I will now describe the experience of wondering at the existence of the world by saying: it is the experience of seeing the world as a miracle. Now I am tempted to say that the right expression in language for the miracle of the existence of the world, though it is not any proposition *in* language, is the existence of language itself. But what then does it mean to be aware of this miracle at some times and not at other times? For all I have said by shifting the expression of the miraculous from an expression *by means of* language to the expression *by the existence* of language, all I have said is again that we cannot express what we want to express and that all we *say* about the absolute miraculous remains nonsense. Now the answer to all this will seem perfectly clear to many of you. You will say: Well, if certain experiences constantly tempt us to attribute a quality to them which we call absolute or ethical value and importance, this simply shows that by these words we *don't* mean nonsense, that after all what we mean by saying that an experience has absolute value *is just a fact like other facts* and that all it comes to is that we have not yet succeeded in finding the correct logical analysis of what we mean by our eth-

ical and religious expressions. Now when this is urged against me I at once see clearly, as it were in a flash of light, not only that no description that I can think of would do to describe what I mean by absolute value, but that I would reject every significant description that anybody could possibly suggest, *ab initio*, on the ground of its significance. That is to say: I see now that these nonsensical expressions were not nonsensical because I had not yet found the correct expressions, but that their nonsensicality was their very essence. For all I wanted to do with them was just *to go beyond* the world and that is to say beyond significant language. My whole tendency and I believe the tendency of all men who ever tried to write or talk Ethics or Religion was to run against the boundaries of language. This running against the walls of our cage is perfectly, absolutely hopeless. Ethics so far as it springs from the desire to say something about the ultimate meaning of life, the absolute good, the absolute valuable, can be no science. What it says does not add to our knowledge in any sense. But it is a document of a tendency in the human mind which I personally cannot help respecting deeply and I would not for my life ridicule it.

4

The Emotive Meaning of Ethical Terms

CHARLES STEVENSON

I

Ethical questions first arise in the form "Is so and so good?" or "Is this alternative better than that?" These questions are difficult partly because we don't quite know what we are seeking. We are asking, "Is there a needle in that haystack?" without even knowing just what a needle is. So the first thing to do is to examine the questions themselves. We must try to make them clearer, either by defining the terms in which they are expressed, or by any other method that is available.

The present paper is concerned wholly with this preliminary step of making ethical questions clear. In order to help answer the question "Is X good?" we must *substitute* for it a question which is free from ambiguity and confusion.

It is obvious that in substituting a clearer question we must not introduce some utterly different kind of question. It won't do (to take an extreme instance of a prevalent fallacy) to substitute for "Is X good?" the question "Is X pink with yellow trimmings?" and then point out how easy the question really is. This would beg the original question, not help answer it. On the other hand, we must not expect the substituted question to be strictly "identical" with the original one. The original question may embody hypostatization, anthropomorphism, vagueness, and all the other ills to which our ordinary discourse is subject. If our substituted question is to be clearer, it must remove these ills. The questions will be identical only in the sense that a child is identical with the man he later becomes. Hence we must not demand that the substitution strike us, on immediate introspection, as making no change in meaning.

Just how, then, must the substituted question be related to the original? Let us assume (inaccurately) that it must result from replacing "good" by some set of terms which define it. The question then resolves itself to this: How must the defined meaning of "good" be related to its original meaning?

I answer that it must be *relevant*. A defined meaning will be called "relevant" to the original meaning under these circumstances: Those who have understood the definition must be able to say all that they then want to say by using the term in the defined way. They must never have occasion to use the term in the old, unclear sense. (If a person did have to go on using the word in the old sense, then to this extent his meaning would not be clarified, and the philosophical task would not be completed.) It frequently happens that a word is used so confusedly and ambiguously that we must give it *several* defined meanings, rather than one. In this case only the whole set of defined meanings will be called "relevant," and any one of them will be called "partially relevant." This is not a rigorous treatment of *relevance*, by any means; but it will serve for the present purposes.

Let us now turn to our particular task—that of giving a relevant definition of "good." Let us first examine some of the ways in which others have attempted to do this.

The word "good" has often been defined in terms of *approval*, or similar psychological attitudes. We may take as typical examples: "good" means *desired by me* (Hobbes); and "good" means *approved by most people* (Hume, in effect). It will be convenient to refer to definitions of this sort as "interest theories," following Mr. R. B. Perry, although neither "interest" nor "theory" is used in the most usual way.

Are definitions of this sort relevant?

It is idle to deny their *partial* relevance. The most superficial inquiry will reveal that "good" is exceedingly ambiguous. To maintain that "good" is *never* used in Hobbes's sense, and never in Hume's, is only to manifest an insensitivity to the complexities of language. We must recognize, perhaps, not only these senses, but a variety of similar ones, differing both with regard to the kind of interest in question, and with regard to the people who are said to have the interest.

But this is a minor matter. The essential question is not whether interest theories are *partially* relevant, but whether they are *wholly* relevant. This is the only point for intelligent dispute. Briefly: Granted that some senses of "good" may relevantly be defined in terms of interest, is there some *other* sense which is *not* relevantly so defined? We must give this question careful attention. For it is quite possible that when philosophers (and many others) have found the question "Is *X* good?" so difficult, they have been grasping for this *other* sense of "good," and not any sense relevantly defined in terms of interest. If we insist on defining "good" in terms of interest, and answer the question when thus interpreted, we may be begging *their* question entirely. Of course this *other* sense of "good" may not exist, or it may be a complete confusion; but that is what we must discover.

Now many have maintained that interest theories are *far* from being completely relevant. They have argued that such theories neglect the very sense of "good" which is most vital. And certainly, their arguments are not without plausibility. Only . . . what *is* this "vital" sense of "good"? The answers have been so vague, and so beset with difficulties, that one can scarcely determine.

There are certain requirements, however, with which this "vital" sense has been expected to comply—requirements which appeal strongly to our common sense. It will be helpful to summarize these, showing how they exclude the interest theories:

In the first place, we must be able sensibly to *disagree* about whether something is "good." This condition rules out Hobbes's definition. For consider the following argument: "This is good." "That isn't so; it's not good." As translated by Hobbes, this becomes: "I desire this." "That isn't so, for *I* don't." The speakers are not contradicting one another, and think they are, only because of an elementary confusion in the use of pronouns. The definition, "good" means *desired by my community*, is also excluded, for how could people from different communities disagree?[1]

In the second place, "goodness" must have, so to speak, a magnetism. A person who recognizes X to be "good" must *ipso facto* acquire a stronger tendency to act in its favour than he otherwise would have had. This rules out the Humian type of definition. For according to Hume, to recognize that something is "good" is simply to recognize that the majority approve of it. Clearly, a man may see that the majority approve of X without having, himself, a stronger tendency to favour it. This requirement excludes any attempt to define "good" in terms of the interest of people *other* than the speaker.[2]

In the third place, the "goodness" of anything must not be verifiable solely by use of the scientific method. "Ethics must not be psychology." This restriction rules out all of the traditional interest theories, without exception. It is so sweeping a restriction that we must examine its plausibility. What are the methodological implications of interest theories which are here rejected?

According to Hobbes's definition, a person can prove his ethical judgments, with finality, by showing that he is not making an introspective error about his desires. According to Hume's definition, one may prove ethical judgments (roughly speaking) by taking a vote. *This* use of the empirical method, at any rate, seems highly remote from what we usually accept as proof, and reflects on the complete relevance of the definitions which imply it.

But aren't there more complicated interest theories which are immune from such methodological implications? No, for the same factors appear; they are only put off for a while. Consider, for example, the definition: "X is good" means *most people would approve of X if they knew its nature and consequences*. How, according to this definition, could we prove that a certain X was good? We should first have to find out, empirically, just what X was like, and what its consequences would be. To this extent the empirical method, as required by the definition, seems beyond intelligent objection. But what

remains? We should next have to discover whether most people would approve of the sort of thing we had discovered X to be. This couldn't be determined by popular vote—but only because it would be too difficult to explain to the voters, beforehand, what the nature and consequences of X really were. Apart from this, voting would be a pertinent method. We are again reduced to counting noses, as a *perfectly final* appeal.

Now we need not scorn voting entirely. A man who rejected interest theories as irrelevant might readily make the following statement: "If I believed that X would be approved by the majority, when they knew all about it, I should be strongly *led* to say that X was good." But he would continue: "*Need* I say that X was good, under the circumstances? Wouldn't my acceptance of the alleged 'final proof' result simply from my being democratic? What about the more aristocratic people? They would simply say that the approval of most people, even when they knew all about the object of their approval, simply had nothing to do with the goodness of anything, and they would probably add a few remarks about the low state of people's interests." It would indeed seem, from these considerations, that the definition we have been considering has presupposed democratic ideals from the start; it has dressed up democratic propaganda in the guise of a definition.

The omnipotence of the empirical method, as implied by interest theories and others, may be shown unacceptable in a somewhat different way. Mr. G. E. Moore's familiar objection about the open question is chiefly pertinent in this regard. No matter what set of scientifically knowable properties a thing may have (says Moore, in effect), you will find, on careful introspection, that it is an open question to ask whether anything having these properties is *good*. It is difficult to believe that this recurrent question is a totally confused one, or that it seems open only because of the ambiguity of "good." Rather, we must be using some sense of "good" which is not definable, relevantly, in terms of any-thing scientifically knowable. That is, the sci-entific method is not sufficient for ethics.[3]

These, then, are the requirements with which the "vital" sense of "good" is expected to comply: (1) goodness must be a topic for intelligent disagreement; (2) it must be "mag-netic"; and (3) it must not be discoverable solely through the scientific method.

II

Let us now turn to my own analysis of ethi-cal judgments. First let me present my posi-tion dogmatically, showing to what extent I vary from tradition.

I believe that the three requirements, given above, are perfectly sensible; that there is some *one* sense of "good" which satisfies all three requirements; and that no traditional in-terest theory satisfies them all. But this does not imply that "good" must be explained in terms of a Platonic Idea, or of a Categorical Imperative, or of an unique, unanalyzable property. On the contrary, the three require-ments can be met by a *kind* of interest the-ory. *But we must give up a presupposition which all the traditional interest theories have made.*

Traditional interest theories hold that eth-ical statements are *descriptive* of the existing state of interests—that they simply *give in-formation* about interests. (More accurately, ethical judgments are said to describe what the state of interests is, was, or will be, or to indicate what the state of interests *would* be under specified circumstances.) It is this emphasis on description, on information, which leads to their incomplete relevance. Doubtless there is always *some* element of description in ethical judgments, but this is by no means all. Their major use is not to in-dicate facts, but to *create an influence.* Instead of merely describing people's inter-ests, they *change* or *intensify* them. They *rec-ommend* an interest in an object, rather than state that the interest already exists.

For instance: When you tell a man that he oughtn't to steal, your object isn't merely to let him know that people disapprove of steal-ing. You are attempting, rather, to get *him* to disapprove of it. Your ethical judgment has a quasi-imperative force which, operating through suggestion, and intensified by your tone of voice, readily permits you to begin to *influence*, to *modify*, his interests. If in the end you do not succeed in getting *him* to dis-approve of stealing, you will feel that you've failed to convince him that stealing is wrong. You will continue to feel this, even though he fully acknowledges that you disapprove of it, and that almost everyone else does. When you point out to him the consequences of his actions—consequences which you suspect he already disapproves of—these *reasons* which support your ethical judgment are simply a means of facilitating your influence. If you think you can change his interests by making vivid to him how others will disapprove of him, you will do so; otherwise not. So the consideration about other people's interest is just an additional means you may employ, in order to move him, and is not a part of the ethical judgment itself. Your ethical judg-ment doesn't merely describe interests to him, it directs his very interests. The differ-ence between the traditional interest theories and my view is like the difference between describing a desert and irrigating it.

Another example: A munition maker de-clares that war is a good thing. If he merely meant that he approved of it, he would not have to insist so strongly, nor grow so ex-cited in his argument. People would be quite easily convinced that he approved of it. If he merely meant that most people approved of war, or that most people would approve of it if they knew the consequences, he would have to yield his point if it were proved that this wasn't so. But he wouldn't do this, nor does consistency require it. He is not *de-scribing* the state of people's approval; he is trying to *change* it by his influence. If he found that few people approved of war, he might insist all the more strongly that it was good, for there would be more changing to be done.

This example illustrates how "good" may be used for what most of us would call bad purposes. Such cases are as pertinent as any others. I am not indicating the *good* way of using "good." I am not influencing people, but am describing the way this influence sometimes goes on. If the reader wishes to say that the munition maker's influence is bad—that is, if the reader wishes to awaken people's disapproval of the man, and to make him disapprove of his own actions—I should at another time be willing to join in this undertaking. But this is not the present concern. I am not using ethical terms, but am indicating how they *are* used. The munition maker, in his use of "good," illustrates the persuasive character of the word just as well as does the unselfish man who, eager to encourage in each of us a desire for the happiness of all, contends that the supreme good is peace.

Thus ethical terms are *instruments* used in the complicated interplay and readjustment of human interests. This can be seen plainly from more general observations. People from widely separated communities have different moral attitudes. Why? To a great extent because they have been subject to different social influences. Now clearly this influence doesn't operate through sticks and stones alone; words play a great part. People praise one another, to encourage certain inclinations, and blame one another, to discourage others. Those of forceful personalities issue commands which weaker people, for complicated instinctive reasons, find it difficult to disobey, quite apart from fears of consequences. Further influence is brought to bear by writers and orators. Thus social influence is exerted, to an enormous extent, by means that have nothing to do with physical force or material reward. The ethical terms facilitate such influence. Being suited for use in *suggestion*, they are a means by which men's attitudes may be led this way or that. The reason, then, that we find a greater similarity in the moral attitudes of one community than in

those of different communities is largely this: ethical judgments propagate themselves. One man says "This is good"; this may influence the approval of another person, who then makes the same ethical judgment, which in turn influences another person, and so on. In the end, by a process of mutual influence, people take up more or less the same attitudes. Between people of widely separated communities, of course, the influence is less strong; hence different communities have different attitudes.

These remarks will serve to give a general idea of my point of view. We must now go into more detail. There are several questions which must be answered: How does an ethical sentence acquire its power of influencing people—why is it suited to suggestion? Again, what has this influence to do with the *meaning* of ethical terms? And finally, do these considerations really lead us to a sense of "good" which meets the requirements mentioned in the preceding section?

Let us deal first with the question about *meaning*. This is far from an easy question, so we must enter into a preliminary inquiry about meaning in general. Although a seeming digression, this will prove indispensable.

III

Broadly speaking, there are two different *purposes* which lead us to use language. On the one hand we use words (as in science) to record, clarify, and communicate *beliefs*. On the other hand we use words to give vent to our feelings (interjections), or to create moods (poetry), or to incite people to actions or attitudes (oratory).

The first use of words I shall call "descriptive"; the second, "dynamic." Note that the distinction depends solely upon the *purpose* of the *speaker*.

When a person says "Hydrogen is the lightest known gas," his purpose *may* be simply to lead the hearer to believe this, or to believe that the speaker believes it. In that case the words are used descriptively. When a person cuts himself and says "Damn," his purpose is not ordinarily to record, clarify, or communicate any belief. The word is used dynamically. The two ways of using words, however, are by no means mutually exclusive. This is obvious from the fact that our purposes are often complex. Thus when one says "I want you to close the door," part of his purpose, ordinarily, is to lead the hearer to believe that he has this want. To that extent the words are used descriptively. But the major part of one's purpose is to lead the hearer to *satisfy* the want. To that extent the words are used dynamically.

It very frequently happens that the same sentence may have a dynamic use on one occasion, and may not have a dynamic use on another; and that it may have different dynamic uses on different occasions. For instance: A man says to a visiting neighbour, "I am loaded down with work." His purpose may be to let the neighbour know how life is going with him. This would *not* be a dynamic use of words. He may make the remark, however, in order to drop a hint. This *would* be dynamic usage (as well as descriptive). Again, he may make the remark to arouse the neighbour's sympathy. This would be a *different* dynamic usage from that of hinting.

Or again, when we say to a man, "Of course you won't make those mistakes any more," we *may* simply be making a prediction. But we are more likely to be using "suggestion," in order to encourage him and hence *keep* him from making mistakes. The first use would be descriptive; the second, mainly dynamic.

From these examples it will be clear that we can't determine whether words are used dynamically or not, merely by reading the dictionary—even assuming that everyone is faithful to dictionary meanings. Indeed, to know whether a person is using a word dynamically, we must note his tone of voice, his gestures, the general circumstances under which he is speaking, and so on.

We must now proceed to an important question: What has the dynamic use of words to do with their *meaning*? One thing is clear—we must not define "meaning" in a way that would make meaning vary with dynamic usage. If we did, we should have no use for the term. All that we could say about such "meaning" would be that it is very complicated, and subject to constant change. So we must certainly distinguish between the dynamic use of words and their meaning.

It doesn't follow, however, that we must define "meaning" in some non-psychological fashion. We must simply restrict the psychological field. Instead of identifying meaning with *all* the psychological causes and effects that attend a word's utterance, we must identify it with those that it has a *tendency* (causal property, dispositional property) to be connected with. The tendency must be of a particular kind, moreover. It must exist for all who speak the language; it must be persistent; and must be realizable more or less independently of determinate circumstances attending the word's utterance. There will be further restrictions dealing with the interrelation of words in different contexts. Moreover, we must include, under the psychological responses which the words tend to produce, not only immediately introspectable experiences, but *dispositions* to react in a given way with appropriate stimuli. I hope to go into these matters in a subsequent paper. Suffice it now to say that I think "meaning" may be thus defined in a way to include "propositional" meaning as an important kind. Now a word may *tend* to have causal relations which in fact it sometimes doesn't; and it may sometimes have causal relations which it *doesn't tend* to have. And since the tendency of words which constitutes their meaning must be of a particular kind, and may include, as responses, dispositions to reactions, of which any of *several* immediate experiences may be a sign, then there is nothing surprising in the fact that words have a permanent meaning, in spite of the fact that the immediately introspectable experiences which attend their usage are so highly varied.

When "meaning" is defined in this way, meaning will not include dynamic use. For although words are sometimes accompanied by dynamic purposes, they do not *tend* to be accompanied by them in the way above mentioned. For example, there is no tendency realizable independently of the determinate circumstances under which the words are uttered.

There will be a kind of meaning, however, in the sense above defined, which has an intimate relation to dynamic usage. I refer to "emotive" meaning (in a sense roughly like that employed by Ogden and Richards).[4] The emotive meaning of a word is a tendency of a word, arising through the history of its usage, to produce (result from) *affective* responses in people. It is the immediate aura of feeling which hovers about a word. Such tendencies to produce affective responses cling to words very tenaciously. It would be difficult, for instance, to express merriment by using the interjection "alas." Because of the persistence of such affective tendencies (among other reasons) it becomes feasible to classify them as "meanings."

Just *what* is the relation between emotive meaning and the dynamic use of words? Let us take an example. Suppose that a man is talking with a group of people which includes Miss Jones, aged fifty-nine. He refers to her, without thinking, as an "old maid." Now even if his purposes are perfectly innocent—even if he is using the words purely descriptively—Miss Jones won't think so. She will think he is encouraging the others to have contempt for her, and will draw in her skirts, defensively. The man might have done better if instead of saying "old maid" he had said "elderly spinster." The latter words could have been put to the same descriptive use, and would not so readily have caused suspicions about the dynamic use.

"Old maid" and "elderly spinster" differ, to be sure, only in emotive meaning. From the example it will be clear that certain words, because of their emotive meaning, are suited to a certain kind of dynamic use—so

well suited, in fact, that the hearer is likely to be misled when we use them in any other way. The more pronounced a word's emotive meaning is, the less likely people are to use it purely descriptively. Some words are suited to encourage people, some to discourage them, some to quiet them, and so on.

Even in these cases, of course, the dynamic purposes are not to be identified with any sort of meaning; for the emotive meaning accompanies a word much more persistently than do the dynamic purposes. But there is an important contingent relation between emotive meaning and dynamic purpose: the former assists the latter. Hence if we define emotively laden terms in a way that neglects their emotive meaning, we are likely to be confusing. *We lead people to think that the terms defined are used dynamically less often than they are.*

IV

Let us now apply these remarks in defining "good." This word may be used morally or non-morally. I shall deal with the non-moral usage almost entirely, but only because it is simpler. The main points of the analysis will apply equally well to either usage.

As a preliminary definition, let us take an inaccurate approximation. It may be more misleading than helpful, but will do to begin with. Roughly, then, the sentence "X is good" means *We like* X. ("We" includes the hearer or hearers.)

At first glance this definition sounds absurd. If used, we should expect to find the following sort of conversation: A. "This is good." B. " But I *don't* like it. What led you to believe that I did?" The unnaturalness of B's reply, judged by ordinary word-usage, would seem to cast doubt on the relevance of my definition.

B's unnaturalness, however, lies simply in this: he is assuming that "We like it" (as would occur implicitly in the use of "good") is being used descriptively. This won't do.

When "We like it" is to take the place of "This is good," the former sentence must be used not purely descriptively, but dynamically. More specifically, it must be used to promote a very subtle (and for the non-moral sense in question, a very easily resisted) kind of *suggestion*. To the extent that "we" refers to the hearer, it must have the dynamic use, essential to suggestion, of leading the hearer to *make* true what is said, rather than merely to believe it. And to the extent that "we" refers to the speaker, the sentence must have not only the descriptive use of indicating belief about the speaker's interest, but the quasi-interjectory, dynamic function of giving direct expression to the interest. (This immediate expression of feelings assists in the process of suggestion. It is difficult to disapprove in the face of another's enthusiasm.)

For an example of a case where "We like this" is used in the dynamic way that "This is good" is used, consider the case of a mother who says to her several children, "One thing is certain, *we all like to be neat*." If she really believed this, she wouldn't bother to say so. But she is not using the words descriptively. She is *encouraging* the children to like neatness. By telling them that they like neatness, she will lead them to *make* her statement true, so to speak. If, instead of saying "We all like to be neat" in this way, she had said "It's a good thing to be neat," the effect would have been approximately the same.

But these remarks are still misleading. Even when "We like it" is used for suggestion, it isn't quite like "This is good." The latter is more subtle. With such a sentence as "This is a good book," for example, it would be practically impossible to use instead "We like this book." When the latter is used, it must be accompanied by so exaggerated an intonation, to prevent its becoming confused with a descriptive statement, that the force of suggestion becomes stronger, and ludicrously more overt, than when "good" is used.

The definition is inadequate, further, in that the definiens has been restricted to dynamic usage. Having said that dynamic us-age was different from meaning, I should not have to mention it in giving the *meaning* of "good."

It is in connection with this last point that we must return to emotive meaning. The word "good" has a pleasing emotive meaning which fits it especially for the dynamic use of suggesting favourable interest. But the sentence "We like it" has no such emotive meaning. Hence my definition has neglected emotive meaning entirely. Now to neglect emotive meaning is likely to lead to endless confusions, as we shall presently see; so I have sought to make up for the inadequacy of the definition by letting the restriction about dynamic usage take the place of emotive meaning. What I should do, of course, is to find a definiens whose emotive meaning, like that of "good," simply does *lead* to dynamic usage.

Why didn't I do this? I answer that it isn't possible, if the definition is to afford us increased clarity. No two words, in the first place, have quite the same emotive meaning. The most we can hope for is a rough approximation. But if we seek for such an approximation for "good," we shall find nothing more than synonyms, such as "desirable" or "valuable"; and these are profitless because they do not clear up the connection between "good" and favourable interest. If we reject such synonyms, in favour of non-ethical terms, we shall be highly misleading. For instance "This is good" has something like the meaning of "I *do* like this; do so as well." But this is certainly not accurate. For the imperative makes an appeal to the conscious efforts of the hearer. Of course he can't like something just by trying. He must be led to like it through suggestion. Hence an ethical sentence differs from an imperative in that it enables one to make changes in a much more subtle, less fully conscious way. Note that the ethical sentence centres the hearer's attention not on his interests, but on the object of interest, and thereby facilitates suggestion. Because of its subtlety, moreover, an ethical sentence readily permits counter-suggestion, and leads to the give and take situation which is so characteristic of arguments about values.

Strictly speaking, then, it is impossible to define "good" in terms of favourable interest if emotive meaning is not to be distorted. Yet it is possible to say that "This is good" is *about* the favourable interest of the speaker and the hearer or hearers, and that it has a pleasing emotive meaning which fits the words for use in suggestion. This is a rough description of meaning, not a definition. But it serves the same clarifying function that a definition ordinarily does; and that, after all, is enough.

A word must be added about the moral use of "good." This differs from the above in that it is about a different kind of interest. Instead of being about what the hearer and speaker *like*, it is about a stronger sort of approval. When a person *likes* something, he is pleased when it prospers, and disappointed when it doesn't. When a person *morally approves* of something, he experiences a rich feeling of security when it prospers, and is indignant, or "shocked" when it doesn't. These are rough and inaccurate examples of the many factors which one would have to mention in distinguishing the two kinds of interest. In the moral usage, as well as in the non-moral, "good" has an emotive meaning which adapts it to suggestion.

And now, are these considerations of any importance? Why do I stress emotive meanings in this fashion? Does the omission of them really lead people into errors? I think, indeed, that the errors resulting from such omissions are enormous. In order to see this, however, we must return to the restrictions, mentioned in Section 1, with which the "vital" sense of "good" has been expected to comply.

V

The first restriction, it will be remembered, had to do with disagreement. Now there is clearly some sense in which people disagree on ethical points; but we must not rashly assume that all disagreement is modelled after the sort that occurs in the natural sciences. We must distinguish between "disagreement in belief" (typical of the sciences) and "disagreement in interest." Disagreement in belief occurs when A believes p and B disbelieves it. Disagreement in interest occurs when A has a favourable interest in X, when B has an unfavourable one in it, and when neither is content to let the other's interest remain unchanged.

Let me give an example of disagreement in interest. A. "Let's go to a cinema to-night." B. "I don't want to do that. Let's go to the symphony." A continues to insist on the cinema, B on the symphony. This is disagreement in a perfectly conventional sense. They can't agree on where they want to go, and each is trying to redirect the other's interest. (Note that imperatives are used in the example.)

It is disagreement in *interest* which takes place in ethics. When C says "This is good," and D says "No, it's bad," we have a case of suggestion and counter-suggestion. Each man is trying to redirect the other's interest. There obviously need be no domineering, since each may be willing to give ear to the other's influence; but each is trying to move the other none the less. It is in this sense that they disagree. Those who argue that certain interest theories make no provision for disagreement have been misled, I believe, simply because the traditional theories, in leaving out emotive meaning, give the impression that ethical judgments are used descriptively only; and of course when judgments are used purely descriptively, the only disagreement that can arise is disagreement *in belief*. Such disagreement may be disagreement in belief *about* interests; but this is not the same as disagreement *in* interest. My definition doesn't provide for disagreement in belief about interests, any more than does Hobbes's; but that is no matter, for there is no reason to believe, at least on commonsense grounds, that this kind of disagreement exists. There is only disagreement *in* interest. (We shall see in a moment that disagreement in interest does not remove ethics from sober argument—that this kind of disagreement may often be resolved through empirical means.)

The second restriction, about "magnetism," or the connection between goodness and actions, requires only a word. This rules out *only* those interest theories which do *not* include the interest of the speaker, in defining "good." My account does include the speaker's interest; hence is immune.

The third restriction, about the empirical method, may be met in a way that springs naturally from the above account of disagreement. Let us put the question in this way: When two people disagree over an ethical matter, can they completely resolve the disagreement through empirical considerations, assuming that each applies the empirical method exhaustively, consistently, and without error?

I answer that sometimes they can, and sometimes they cannot: and that at any rate, even when they can, the relation between empirical knowledge and ethical judgments is quite different from the one which traditional interest theories seem to imply.

This can best be seen from an analogy. Let's return to the example where *A* and *B* couldn't agree on a cinema or a symphony. The example differed from an ethical argument in that imperatives were used, rather than ethical judgments; but was analogous to the extent that each person was endeavouring to modify the other's interest. Now how would these people argue the case, assuming that they were too intelligent just to shout at one another?

Clearly, they would give "reasons" to support their imperatives. *A* might say, "But you know, Garbo is at the Bijou." His hope is that *B*, who admires Garbo, will acquire a desire to go to the cinema when he knows what play will be there. *B* may counter, "But Toscanini is guest conductor to-night, in an all-

Beethoven programme." And so on. Each supports his imperative ("*Let's* do so and so") by reasons which may be empirically established.

To generalize from this: disagreement in interest may be rooted in disagreement in belief. That is to say, people who disagree in interest would often cease to do so if they knew the precise nature and consequences of the object of their interest. To this extent disagreement in interest may be resolved by securing agreement in belief, which in turn may be secured empirically.

This generalization holds for ethics. If *A* and *B*, instead of using imperatives, had said, respectively, "It would be *better* to go to the cinema," and "It would be better to go to the symphony," the reasons which they would advance would be roughly the same. They would each give a more thorough account of the object of interest, with the purpose of completing the redirection of interest which was begun by the suggestive force of the ethical sentence. On the whole, of course, the suggestive force of the ethical statement merely exerts enough pressure to start such trains of reasons, since the reasons are much more essential in resolving disagreement in interest than the persuasive effect of the ethical judgment itself.

Thus the empirical method is relevant to ethics simply because our knowledge of the world is a determining factor to our interests. But note that empirical facts are not inductive grounds from which the ethical judgment problematically follows. (This is what traditional interest theories imply.) If someone said "Close the door," and added the reason "We'll catch cold," the latter would scarcely be called an inductive ground of the former. Now imperatives are related to the reasons which support them in the same way that ethical judgments are related to reasons.

Is the empirical method *sufficient* for attaining ethical agreement? Clearly not. For empirical knowledge resolves disagreement in interest only to the extent that such disagreement is rooted in disagreement in belief. Not all disagreement in interest is of this sort. For instance: *A* is of a sympathetic nature, and *B* isn't. They are arguing about whether a public dole would be good. Suppose that they discovered all the consequences of the dole. Isn't it possible, even so, that *A* will say that it's good, and *B* that it's bad? The disagreement in interest may arise not from limited factual knowledge, but simply from *A*'s sympathy and *B*'s coldness. Or again, suppose, in the above argument, that *A* was poor and unemployed, and that *B* was rich. Here again the disagreement might not be due to different factual knowledge. It would be due to the different social positions of the men, together with their predominant self-interest.

When ethical disagreement is not rooted in disagreement in belief, is there *any* method by which it may be settled? If one means by "method" a *rational* method, then there is no method. But in any case there is a "way." Let's consider the above example, again, where disagreement was due to *A*'s sympathy and *B*'s coldness. Must they end by saying, "Well, it's just a matter of our having different temperaments"? Not necessarily. *A*, for instance, may try to *change* the temperament of his opponent. He may pour out his enthusiasms in such a moving way—present the sufferings of the poor with such appeal—that he will lead his opponent to see life through different eyes. He may build up, by the contagion of his feelings, an influence which will modify *B*'s temperament, and create in him a sympathy for the poor which didn't previously exist. This is often the only way to obtain ethical agreement, if there is any way at all. It is persuasive, not empirical or rational; but that is no reason for neglecting it. There is no reason to scorn it, either for it is only by such means that our personalities are able to grow, through our contact with others.

The point I wish to stress, however, is simply that the empirical method is instrumental to ethical agreement only to the extent that disagreement in interest is rooted in dis-agreement in belief. There is little reason to believe that all disagreement is of this sort. Hence the empirical method is not sufficient for ethics. In any case, ethics is not psychology, since psychology doesn't endeavour to *direct* our interests; it discovers facts about the ways in which interests are or can be directed, but that's quite another matter.

To summarize this section: my analysis of ethical judgments meets the three requirements for the "vital" sense of "good" that were mentioned in Section I. The traditional interest theories fail to meet these requirements simply because they neglect emotive meaning. This neglect leads them to neglect dynamic usage, and the sort of disagreement that results from such usage, together with the method of resolving the disagreement. I may add that my analysis answers Moore's objection about the open question. Whatever scientifically knowable properties a thing may have, it *is* always open to question whether a thing having these (enumerated) qualities is good. For to ask whether it is good is to ask for *influence*. And whatever I may know about an object, I can still ask, quite pertinently, to be influenced with regard to my interest in it.

VI

And now, have I really pointed out the "vital" sense of "good"?

I suppose that many will still say "No," claiming that I have simply failed to set down *enough* requirements which this sense must meet, and that my analysis, like all others given in terms of interest, is a way of begging the issue. They will say: "When we ask 'Is *X* good?' we don't want mere influence, mere advice. We decidedly don't want to be influenced through persuasion, nor are we fully content when the influence is supported by a wide scientific knowledge of *X*. The answer to our question will, of course, modify our interests. But this is only because an unique sort of *truth* will be revealed to us—

a truth which must be apprehended *a priori*. We want our interests to be guided by this truth, and by nothing else. To substitute for such a truth mere emotive meaning and suggestion is to conceal from us the very object of our search."

I can only answer that I do not understand. What is this truth to be *about*? For I recollect no Platonic Idea, nor do I know what to *try* to recollect. I find no indefinable property, nor do I know what to look for. And the "self-evident" deliverances of reason, which so many philosophers have claimed, seem, on examination, to be deliverances of their respective reasons only (if of anyone's) and not of mine.

I strongly suspect, indeed, that any sense of "good" which is expected both to unite itself in synthetic *a priori* fashion with other concepts, and to influence interests as well, is really a great confusion. I extract from this meaning the power of influence alone, which I find the only intelligible part. If the rest is confusion, however, then it certainly de-serves more than the shrug of one's shoulders. What I should like to do is to *account* for the confusion—to examine the psychological needs which have given rise to it, and to show how these needs may be satisfied in another way. This is *the* problem, if confusion is to be stopped at its source. But it is an enormous problem, and my reflections on it, which are at present worked out only roughly, must be reserved until some later time.

I may add that if "*X* is good" is essentially a vehicle for suggestion, it is scarcely a statement which philosophers, any more than many other men, are called upon to make. To the extent that ethics predicates the ethical terms of anything, rather than explains their meaning, it ceases to be a reflective study. Ethical statements are social instruments. They are used in a cooperative enterprise in which we are mutually adjusting ourselves to the interests of others. Philosophers have a part in this, as do all men, but not the major part.

NOTES

1. See G. E. Moore's *Philosophical Studies* [Boston: Routledge & Kegan Paul, 1922], pp. 332–34.

2. See G. C. Field's *Moral Theory*, [London: Methuen & Co., 1932], pp. 52, 56–57.

3. See G. E. Moore's *Principia Ethica*, [Cambridge: Cambridge University Press, 1903], chap. i. I am simply trying to preserve the spirit of Moore's objection, and not the exact form of it.

4. See *The Meaning of Meaning*, by C. K. Ogden and I. A. Richards [London: Routledge & Kegan Paul, 1949]. On p. 125, 2d ed., there is a passage on ethics which was the source of the ideas embodied in this paper.

5

Ethics and Observation

GILBERT HARMAN

1. THE BASIC ISSUE

Can moral principles be tested and confirmed in the way scientific principles can? Consider the principle that, if you are given a choice between five people alive and one dead or five people dead and one alive, you should always choose to have five people alive and one dead rather than the other way round. We can easily imagine examples that appear to confirm this principle. Here is one:

You are a doctor in a hospital's emergency room when six accident victims are brought in. All six are in danger of dying but one is much worse off than the others. You can just barely save that person if you devote all of your resources to him and let the others die. Alternatively, you can save the other five if you are willing to ignore the most seriously injured person.

It would seem that in this case you, the doctor, would be right to save the five and let the other person die. So this example, taken by itself, confirms the principle under consideration. Next, consider the following case:

You have five patients in the hospital who are dying, each in need of a separate organ. One needs a kidney, another a lung, a third a heart, and so forth. You can save all five if you take a single healthy person and remove his heart, lungs, kidneys, and so forth, to distribute to these five patients. Just such a healthy person is in Room 306. He is in the hospital for routine tests. Having seen his test results, you know that he is perfectly healthy and of the right tissue compatibility. If you do nothing, he will survive without incident; the other patients will die, however. The other five patients can be saved only if the person in Room 306 is cut up and his organs distributed. In that case, there would be one dead but five saved.

The principle in question tells us that you should cut up the patient in Room 306. But in this case, surely you must not sacrifice this innocent bystander, even to save the five other patients. Here a moral principle has been tested and disconfirmed in what may seem to be a surprising way.

This, of course, was a "thought experiment." We did not really compare a hypothesis with the world. We compared an explicit principle with our feelings about certain imagined examples. In the same way, a physicist performs thought experiments in order to compare explicit hypotheses with his "sense" of what should happen in certain situations, a "sense" that he has acquired as a result of his long working familiarity with current theory. But scientific hypotheses can also be tested in real experiments, out in the world.

Can moral principles be tested in the same way, out in the world? You can observe someone do something, but can you ever perceive the rightness or wrongness of what he does? If you round a corner and see a group of young hoodlums pour gasoline on a cat and ignite it, you do not need to *conclude* that what they are doing is wrong; you do not need to figure anything out; you can *see* that it is wrong. But is your reaction due to the actual wrongness of what you see or is it simply a reflection of your moral "sense," a "sense" that you have acquired perhaps as a result of your moral upbringing?

2. OBSERVATION

The issue is complicated. There are no pure observations. Observations are always "theory laden." What you perceive depends to some extent on the theory you hold, consciously or unconsciously. You see some children pour gasoline on a cat and ignite it. To really see that, you have to possess a great deal of knowledge, know about a considerable number of objects, know about people: that people pass through the life stages infant, baby, child, adolescent, adult. You must know what flesh and blood animals are, and in particular, cats. You must have some idea of life. You must know what gasoline is, what burning is, and much more. In one sense,

what you "see" is a pattern of light on your retina, a shifting array of splotches, although even that is theory, and you could never adequately describe what you see in that sense. In another sense, you see what you do because of the theories you hold. Change those theories and you would see something else, given the same pattern of light.

Similarly, if you hold a moral view, whether it is held consciously or unconsciously, you will be able to perceive rightness or wrongness, goodness or badness, justice or injustice. There is no difference in this respect between moral propositions and other theoretical propositions. If there is a difference, it must be found elsewhere.

Observation depends on theory because perception involves forming a belief as a fairly direct result of observing something; you can form a belief only if you understand the relevant concepts and a concept is what it is by virtue of its role in some theory or system of beliefs. To recognize a child as a child is to employ, consciously or unconsciously, a concept that is defined by its place in a framework of the stages of human life. Similarly, burning is an empty concept apart from its theoretical connections to the concepts of heat, destruction, smoke, and fire.

Moral concepts—Right and Wrong, Good and Bad, Justice and Injustice—also have a place in your theory or system of beliefs and are the concepts they are because of their context. If we say that observation has occurred whenever an opinion is a direct result of perception, we must allow that there is moral observation, because such an opinion can be a moral opinion as easily as any other sort. In this sense, observation may be used to confirm or disconfirm moral theories. The observational opinions that, in this sense, you find yourself with can be in either agreement or conflict with your consciously explicit moral principles. When they are in conflict, you must choose between your explicit theory and observation. In ethics, as in science, you sometimes opt for theory, and say that you made an error in observation or were biased or whatever, or you sometimes opt for observation, and modify your theory.

In other words, in both science and ethics, general principles are invoked to explain particular cases and, therefore, in both science and ethics, the general principles you accept can be tested by appealing to particular judgments that certain things are right or wrong, just or unjust, and so forth; and these judgments are analogous to direct perceptual judgments about facts.

3. OBSERVATIONAL EVIDENCE

Nevertheless, observation plays a role in science that it does not seem to play in ethics. The difference is that you need to make assumptions about certain physical facts to explain the occurrence of the observations that support a scientific theory, but you do not seem to need to make assumptions about any moral facts to explain the occurrence of the so-called moral observations I have been talking about. In the moral case, it would seem that you need only make assumptions about the psychology or moral sensibility of the person making the moral observation. In the scientific case, theory is tested against the world.

The point is subtle but important. Consider a physicist making an observation to test a scientific theory. Seeing a vapor trail in a cloud chamber, he thinks, "There goes a proton." Let us suppose that this is an observation in the relevant sense, namely, an immediate judgment made in response to the situation without any conscious reasoning having taken place. Let us also suppose that his observation confirms his theory, a theory that helps give meaning to the very term "proton" as it occurs in his observational judgment. Such a confirmation rests on inferring an explanation. He can count his making the observation as confirming evidence for his theory only to the extent that it is reasonable to explain his making the observation by assuming that, not only is he in a certain psy-

chological "set," given the theory he accepts and his beliefs about the experimental apparatus, but furthermore, there really was a proton going through the cloud chamber, causing the vapor trail, which he saw as a proton. (This is evidence for the theory to the extent that the theory can explain the proton's being there better than competing theories can.) But, if his having made that observation could have been equally well explained by his psychological set alone, without the need for any assumption about a proton, then the observation would not have been evidence for the existence of that proton and therefore would not have been evidence for the theory. His making the observation supports the theory only because, in order to explain his making the observation, it is reasonable to assume something about the world over and above the assumptions made about the observer's psychology. In particular, it is reasonable to assume that there was a proton going through the cloud chamber, causing the vapor trail.

Compare this case with one in which you make a moral judgment immediately and without conscious reasoning, say, that the children are wrong to set the cat on fire or that the doctor would be wrong to cut up one healthy patient to save five dying patients. In order to explain your making the first of these judgments, it would be reasonable to assume, perhaps, that the children really are pouring gasoline on a cat and you are seeing them do it. But, in neither case is there any obvious reason to assume anything about "moral facts," such as that it really is wrong to set the cat on fire or to cut up the patient in Room 306. Indeed, an assumption about moral facts would seem to be totally irrelevant to the explanation of your making the judgment you make. It would seem that all we need assume is that you have certain more or less articulated moral principles that are reflected in the judgments you make, based on your moral sensibility. It seems to be completely irrelevant to our explanation whether your intuitive immediate judgment is true or false.

The observation of an event can provide

observational evidence for or against a scientific theory in the sense that the truth of that observation can be relevant to a reasonable explanation of why that observation was made. A moral observation does not seem, in the same sense, to be observational evidence for or against any moral theory, since the truth or falsity of the moral observation seems to be completely irrelevant to any reasonable explanation of why that observation was made. The fact that an observation of an event was made at the time it was made is evidence not only about the observer but also about the physical facts. The fact that you made a particular moral observation when you did does not seem to be evidence about moral facts, only evidence about you and your moral sensibility. Facts about protons can affect what you observe, since a proton passing through the cloud chamber can cause a vapor trail that reflects light to your eye in a way that, given your scientific training and psychological set, leads you to judge that what you see is a proton. But there does not seem to be any way in which the actual rightness or wrongness of a given situation can have any effect on your perceptual apparatus. In this respect, ethics seems to differ from science.

In considering whether moral principles can help explain observations, it is therefore important to note an ambiguity in the word "observation." You see the children set the cat on fire and immediately think, "That's wrong." In one sense, your observation is that what the children are doing is wrong. In another sense, your observation is your thinking that thought. Moral principles might explain observations in the first sense but not in the second sense. Certain moral principles might help to explain why it was *wrong* of the children to set the cat on fire, but moral principles seem to be of no help in explaining *your thinking* that that is wrong. In the first sense of "observation," moral principles can be tested by observation—"That this act is wrong is evidence that causing unnecessary suffering is wrong." But in the second

sense of "observation," moral principles cannot clearly be tested by observation, since they do not appear to help explain observations in this second sense of "observation." Moral principles do not seem to help explain your observing what you observe.

Of course, if you are already given the moral principle that it is wrong to cause unnecessary suffering, you can take your seeing the children setting the cat on fire as observational evidence that they are doing something wrong. Similarly, you can suppose that your seeing the vapor trail is observational evidence that a proton is going through the cloud chamber, if you are given the relevant physical theory. But there is an important apparent difference between the two cases. In the scientific case, your making that observation is itself evidence for the physical theory because the physical theory explains the proton, which explains the trail, which explains your observation. In the moral case, your making your observation does not seem to be evidence for the relevant moral principle because that principle does not seem to help explain your observation. The explanatory chain from principle to observation seems to be broken in morality. The moral principle may "explain" why it is wrong for the children to set the cat on fire. But the wrongness of that act does not appear to help explain the act, which you observe, itself. The explanatory chain appears to be broken in such a way that neither the moral principle nor the wrongness of the act can help explain why you observe what you observe.

A qualification may seem to be needed here. Perhaps the children perversely set the cat on fire simply "because it is wrong." Here it may seem at first that the actual wrongness of the act does help explain why they do it and therefore indirectly helps explain why you observe what you observe just as a physical theory, by explaining why the proton is producing a vapor trail, indirectly helps explain why the observer observes what he observes. But on reflection we must agree that this is probably an illusion. What explains the children's act is not clearly the actual wrongness of the act but, rather, their belief that the act is wrong. The actual rightness or wrongness of their act seems to have nothing to do with why they do it.

Observational evidence plays a part in science it does not appear to play in ethics, because scientific principles can be justified ultimately by their role in explaining observations, in the second sense of observation— by their explanatory role. Apparently, moral principles cannot be justified in the same way. It appears to be true that there can be no explanatory chain between moral principles and particular observings in the way that there can be such a chain between scientific principles and particular observings. Conceived as an explanatory theory, morality, unlike science, seems to be cut off from observation.

Not that every legitimate scientific hypothesis is susceptible to direct observational testing. Certain hypothesis about "black holes" in space cannot be directly tested, for example, because no signal is emitted from within a black hole. The connection with observation in such a case is indirect. And there are many similar examples. Nevertheless, seen in the large, there is the apparent difference between science and ethics we have noted. The scientific realm is accessible to observation in a way the moral realm is not.

4. ETHICS AND MATHEMATICS

Perhaps ethics is to be compared, not with physics, but with mathematics. Perhaps such a moral principle as "You ought to keep your promises" is confirmed or disconfirmed in the way (whatever it is) in which such a mathematical principle as "$5 + 7 = 12$" is. Observation does not seem to play the role in mathematics it plays in physics. We do not and cannot perceive numbers, for example, since we cannot be in causal contact with them. We do not even understand what it would be like to be in causal contact with the number 12, say. Relations among numbers cannot have any more of an effect on our perceptual apparatus than moral facts can.

Observation, however, *is* relevant to mathematics. In explaining the observations that support a physical theory, scientists typically appeal to mathematical principles. On the other hand, one never seems to need to appeal in this way to moral principles. Since an observation is evidence for what best explains it, and since mathematics often figures in the explanations of scientific observations, there is indirect observational evidence for mathematics. There does not seem to be observational evidence, even indirectly, for basic moral principles. In explaining why certain observations have been made, we never seem to use purely moral assumptions. In this respect, then, ethics appears to differ not only from physics but also from mathematics.

In what follows [in the *Nature of Morality*], we will be considering a number of possible responses to the apparent fact that ethics is cut off from observational testing in a way that science is not. Some of these responses claim that there is a distinction of this sort between science and ethics and try to say what its implications are. Others deny that there is a distinction of this sort between science and ethics and argue that ethics is not really exempt from observational testing in the way it appears to be.

A NOTE ON FURTHER READING

For a brief argument distinguishing the role of observational evidence in ethics and in science, see R. M. Hare, *Freedom and Reason* (Oxford: Oxford University Press, 1963), pp. 1–3.

Alan Gewirth notes some complications in "Positive 'Ethics' and Normative 'Science,' "*Philosophical Review* 69 (1960).

On the "theory ladenness" of observation, see Norwood Russell Hanson, *Patterns of Discovery* (Cambridge: Cambridge University Press, 1958), chap. 1.

The role of explanation in inference is discussed in Gilbert Harman, "Inference to the Best Explanation," *Philosophical Review* 74 (1965).

The suggestions that there can be intuitive knowledge of moral truths is examined in P.F. Strawson, "Ethical Intuitionism," *Philosophy* 24 (1949).

Paul Benacerraf discusses problems about mathematical knowledge in "Mathematical Truth," *Journal of Philosophy* 70 (1973).

6

From *Ethics: Inventing Right and Wrong*

J. L. MACKIE

The Subjectivity of Values

1. MORAL SCEPTICISM

There are no objective values. This is a bald statement of the thesis of this chapter, but before arguing for it I shall try to clarify and restrict it in ways that may meet some objections and prevent some misunderstanding.

The statement of this thesis is liable to provoke one of three very different reactions. Some will think it not merely false but pernicious; they will see it as a threat to morality and to everything else that is worthwhile, and they will find the presenting of such a thesis in what purports to be a book on ethics paradoxical or even outrageous. Others will regard it as a trivial truth, almost too obvious to be worth mentioning, and certainly too plain to be worth much argument. Others again will say that it is meaningless or empty, that no real issue is raised by the question whether values are or are not part of the fabric of the world. But, precisely because there

can be these three different reactions, much more needs to be said.

The claim that values are not objective, are not part of the fabric of the world, is meant to include not only moral goodness, which might be most naturally equated with moral value, but also other things that could be more loosely called moral values or disvalues—rightness and wrongness, duty, obligation, an action's being rotten and contemptible, and so on. It also includes nonmoral values, notably aesthetic ones, beauty and various kinds of artistic merit. I shall not discuss these explicitly, but clearly much the same considerations apply to aesthetic and to moral values, and there would be at least some initial implausibility in a view that gave the one a different status from the other.

Since it is with moral values that I am primarily concerned, the view I am adopting may be called moral scepticism. But this name is likely to be misunderstood: "moral scepticism" might also be used as a name for either of two first order views, or perhaps for an incoherent mixture of the two. A moral sceptic might be the sort of person who says "All this talk of morality is tripe," who rejects morality and will take no notice of it. Such a person may be literally rejecting all moral judgements; he is more likely to be making moral judgements of his own, expressing a positive moral condemnation of all that conventionally passes for morality; or he may be confusing these two logically incompatible views, and saying that he rejects all morality, while he is in fact rejecting only a particular morality that is current in the society in which he has grown up. But I am not at present concerned with the merits or faults of such a position. These are first order moral views, positive or negative: the person who adopts either of them is taking a certain practical, normative, stand. By contrast, what I am discussing is a second order view, a view about the status of moral values and the nature of moral valuing, about where and how they fit into the world. These first and second order views are not merely distinct but completely independent: one could be a second order moral sceptic without being a first order one, or again the other way round. A man could hold strong moral views, and indeed ones whose content was thoroughly conventional, while believing that they were simply attitudes and policies with regard to conduct that he and other people held. Conversely, a man could reject all established morality while believing it to be an objective truth that it was evil or corrupt.

With another sort of misunderstanding moral scepticism would seem not so much pernicious as absurd. How could anyone deny that there is a difference between a kind action and a cruel one, or that a coward and a brave man behave differently in the face of danger? Of course, this is undeniable; but it is not to the point. The kinds of behaviour to which moral values and disvalues are ascribed are indeed part of the furniture of the world, and so are the natural, descriptive, differences between them; but not, perhaps, their differences in value. It is a hard fact that cruel actions differ from kind ones, and hence that we can learn, as in fact we all do, to distinguish them fairly well in practice, and to use the words "cruel" and "kind" with fairly clear descriptive meanings; but is it an equally hard fact that actions which are cruel in such a descriptive sense are to be condemned? The present issue is with regard to the objectivity specifically of value, not with regard to the objectivity of those natural, factual, differences on the basis of which differing values are assigned.

2. SUBJECTIVISM

Another name often used, as an alternative to "moral scepticism," for the view I am discussing is "subjectivism." But this too has more than one meaning. Moral subjectivism too could be a first order, normative, view, namely that everyone really ought to do whatever he thinks he should. This plainly is a (systematic) first order view; on examination it soon ceases to be plausible, but that is beside the point, for it is quite independent of the second order thesis at present under consideration. What is more confusing is that different second order views compete for the name "subjectivism." Several of these are doctrines about the meaning of moral terms and moral statements. What is often called moral subjectivism is the doctrine that, for example, "This action is right" *means* "I approve of this action," or more generally that moral judgements are equivalent to reports of the speaker's own feelings or attitudes. But the view I am now discussing is to be distinguished in two vital respects from any such doctrine as this. First, what I have called moral scepticism is a negative doctrine, not a positive one: it says what there isn't, not what there is. It says that there do not exist entities or relations of a certain kind, objective values or requirements, which many people have believed to exist. Of course, the moral sceptic cannot leave it at that. If his position is to be at all plausible, he must give some account of how other people have fallen into what he regards as an error, and this account will have to include some positive suggestions about how values fail to be objective, about what has been mistaken for, or has led to false beliefs about, objective values. But this will be a development of his theory, not its core: its core is the negation. Secondly, what I have called moral scepticism is an ontological thesis, not a linguistic or conceptual one. It is not, like the other doctrine often called moral subjectivism, a view about the meanings of moral statements. Again, no doubt, if it is to be at all plausible, it will have to give some account of their meanings, and I shall say something about this in Section 7 of this chapter and again [later in *Ethics: Inventing Right and Wrong*]. But this too will be a development of the theory, not its core.

It is true that those who have accepted the moral subjectivism which is the doctrine that moral judgements are equivalent to reports of the speaker's own feelings or attitudes have usually presupposed what I am calling moral scepticism. It is because they have assumed that there are no objective values that they have looked elsewhere for an analysis of what moral statements might mean, and have settled upon subjective reports. Indeed, if all our moral statements were such subjective reports, it would follow that, at least so far as we are aware, there are no objective moral values. If we were aware of them, we would say something about them. In this sense this sort of subjectivism entails moral scepticism. But the converse entailment does not hold. The denial that there are objective values does not commit one to any particular view about what moral statements mean, and certainly not to the view that they are equivalent to subjective reports. No doubt if moral values are not objective they are in some very broad sense subjective, and for this reason I would accept "moral subjectivism" as an alternative name to "moral scepticism." But subjectivism in this broad sense must be distinguished from the specific doctrine about meaning referred to above. Neither name is altogether satisfactory: we simply have to guard against the (different) misinterpretations which each may suggest. . . .

7. THE CLAIM TO OBJECTIVITY

If I have succeeded in specifying precisely enough the moral values whose objectivity I am denying, my thesis may now seem to be trivially true. Of course, some will say, valuing, preferring, choosing, recommending, rejecting, condemning, and so on, are human activities, and there is no need to look for values that are prior to and logically independent of all such activities. There may be widespread agreement in valuing, and particular value-judgements are not in general arbitrary or isolated: they typically cohere with others, or can be criticized if they do not, reasons can be given for them, and so on: but if all that the subjectivist is maintaining is that desires, ends, purposes, and the like figure somewhere in the system of reasons, and that no ends or purposes are objective as opposed to being merely intersubjective, then this may be conceded without much fuss.

But I do not think that this should be conceded so easily. As I have said, the main tradition of European moral philosophy includes the contrary claim, that there are objective values of just the sort I have denied. I have referred already to Plato, Kant, and Sidgwick. Kant in particular holds that the categorical imperative is not only categorical and imperative but objectively so: though a rational being gives the moral law to himself, the law that he thus makes is determinate and necessary. Aristotle begins the *Nicomachean Ethics* by saying that the good is that at which all things aim, and that ethics is part of a science which he calls "politics," whose goal is not knowledge but practice; yet he does not doubt that there can be *knowledge* of what is the good for man, nor, once he has identified this as well-being or happiness, *eudaimonia*, that it can be known, rationally determined, in what happiness consists; and it is plain that he thinks that this happiness is intrinsically desirable, not good simply because it is desired. The rationalist Samuel Clarke holds that

> these eternal and necessary differences of things make it *fit and reasonable* for creatures so to act ... even separate from the consideration of these rules being the *positive will* or *command of God*; and also antecedent to any respect or regard, expectation or apprehension, of any *particular private and personal advantage or disadvantage, reward or punishment*, either present or future. ...

Even the sentimentalist Hutcheson defines moral goodness as "some quality apprehended in actions, which procures approbation. ...," while saying that the moral sense by which we perceive virtue and vice has been given to us (by the Author of nature) to direct our actions. Hume indeed was on the other side, but he is still a witness to the dominance of the objectivist tradition, since he claims that when we "see that the distinction of vice and virtue is not founded merely on the relations of objects, nor is perceiv'd by reason," this "wou'd subvert all the vulgar systems of morality." And Richard Price insists that right and wrong are "real characters of actions," not "qualities of our minds," and are perceived by the understanding; he criticizes the notion of moral sense on the ground that it would make virtue an affair of taste, and moral right and wrong "nothing in the objects themselves"; he rejects Hutcheson's view because (perhaps mistakenly) he sees it as collapsing into Hume's.

But this objectivism about values is not only a feature of the philosophical tradition. It has also a firm basis in ordinary thought, and even in the meanings of moral terms. No doubt it was an extravagance for Moore to say that "good" is the name of a non-natural quality, but it would not be so far wrong to say that in moral contexts it is used as if it were the name of a supposed non-natural quality, where the description "nonnatural"

leaves room for the peculiar evaluative, prescriptive, intrinsically action-guiding aspects of this supposed quality. This point can be illustrated by reflection on the conflicts and swings of opinion in recent years between noncognitivist and naturalist views about the central, basic, meanings of ethical terms. If we reject the view that it is the function of such terms to introduce objective values into discourse about conduct and choices of action, there seem to be two main alternative types of account. One (which has importantly different subdivisions) is that they conventionally express either attitudes which the speaker purports to adopt towards whatever it is that he characterizes morally, or prescriptions or recommendations, subject perhaps to the logical constraint of universalizability. Different views of this type share the central thesis that ethical terms have, at least partly and primarily, some sort of noncognitive, non-descriptive, meaning. Views of the other type hold that they are descriptive in meaning, but descriptive of natural features, partly of such features as everyone, even the non-cognitivist, would recognize as distinguishing kind actions from cruel ones, courage from cowardice, politeness from rudeness, and so on, and partly (though these two overlap) of relations between the actions and some human wants, satisfactions, and the like. I believe that views of both these types capture part of the truth. Each approach can account for the fact that moral judgements are action-guiding or practical. Yet each gains much of its plausibility from the felt inadequacy of the other. It is a very natural reaction to any non-cognitive analysis of ethical terms to protest that there is more to ethics than this, something more external to the maker of moral judgements, more authoritative over both him and those of or to whom he speaks, and this reaction is likely to persist even when full allowance has been made for the logical, formal, constraints of full-blooded prescriptivity and universalizability. Ethics, we are inclined to believe, is more a matter of knowledge and less a matter of decision than any non-cognitive analysis allows. And of course naturalism satisfies this demand. It will not be a matter of choice or decision whether an action is cruel or unjust or imprudent or whether it is likely to produce more distress than pleasure. But in satisfying this demand, it introduces a converse deficiency. On a naturalist analysis, moral judgements can be practical, but their practicality is wholly relative to desires or possible satisfactions of the person or persons whose actions are to be guided; but moral judgements seem to say more than this. This view leaves out the categorical quality of moral requirements. In fact both naturalist and noncognitive analyses leave out the apparent authority of ethics, the one by excluding the categorically imperative aspect, the other the claim to objective validity or truth. The ordinary user of moral language means to say something about whatever it is that he characterizes morally, for example a possible action, as it is in itself, or would be if it were realized, and not about, or even simply expressive of, his, or anyone else's, attitude or relation to it. But the something he wants to say is not purely descriptive, certainly not inert, but something that involves a call for action or for the refraining from action, and one that is absolute, not contingent upon any desire or preference or policy or choice, his own or anyone else's. Someone in a state of moral perplexity, wondering whether it would be wrong for him to engage, say, in research related to bacteriological warfare, wants to arrive at some judgment about this concrete case, his doing this work at this time in these actual circumstances; his relevant characteristics will be part of the subject of the judgement, but no relation between him and the proposed action will be part of the predicate. The question is not, for example, whether he really wants to do this work, whether it will satisfy or dissatisfy him, whether he will in the long run have a pro-attitude towards it, or even whether this is an action of a sort that he can happily and sincerely recommend in all relevantly similar

cases. Nor is he even wondering just whether to recommend such action in all relevantly similar cases. He wants to know whether this course of action would be wrong in itself. Something like this is the everyday objectivist concept of which talk about non-natural qualities is a philosopher's reconstruction.

The prevalence of this tendency to objectify values—and not only moral ones—is confirmed by a pattern of thinking that we find in existentialists and those influenced by them. The denial of objective values can carry with it an extreme emotional reaction, a feeling that nothing matters at all, that life has lost its purpose. Of course this does not follow; the lack of objective values is not a good reason for abandoning subjective concern or for ceasing to want anything. But the abandonment of a belief in objective values can cause, at least temporarily, a decay of subjective concern and sense of purpose. That it does so is evidence that the people in whom this reaction occurs have been tending to objectify their concerns and purposes, have been giving them a fictitious external authority. A claim to objectivity has been so strongly associated with their subjective concerns and purposes that the collapse of the former seems to undermine the latter as well.

This view, that conceptual analysis would reveal a claim to objectivity, is sometimes dramatically confirmed by philosophers who are officially on the other side. Bertrand Russell, for example, says that "ethical propositions should be expressed in the optative mood, not in the indicative"; he defends himself effectively against the charge of inconsistency in both holding ultimate ethical valuations to be subjective and expressing emphatic opinions on ethical questions. Yet at the end he admits:

> Certainly there *seems* to be something more. Suppose, for example, that some one were to advocate the introduction of bullfighting in this country. In opposing the proposal, I should *feel*, not only that I was expressing my desires, but that my desires in the matter are *right*, whatever that may mean. As a matter of argu-

ment, I can, I think, show that I am not guilty of any logical inconsistency in holding to the above interpretation of ethics and at the same time expressing strong ethical preferences. But in feeling I am not satisfied.

But he concludes, reasonably enough, with the remark: "I can only say that, while my own opinions as to ethics do not satisfy me, other people's satisfy me still less."

I conclude, then, that ordinary moral judgements include a claim to objectivity, an assumption that there are objective values in just the sense in which I am concerned to deny this. And I do not think it is going too far to say that this assumption has been incorporated in the basic, conventional, meanings of moral terms. Any analysis of the meanings of moral terms which omits this claim to objective, intrinsic, prescriptivity is to that extent incomplete; and this is true of any non-cognitive analysis, any naturalist one, and any combination of the two.

If second order ethics were confined, then, to linguistic and conceptual analysis, it ought to conclude that moral values at least are objective: that they are so is part of what our ordinary moral statements mean: the traditional moral concepts of the ordinary man as well as of the main line of western philosophers are concepts of objective value. But it is precisely for this reason that linguistic and conceptual analysis is not enough. The claim to objectivity, however ingrained in our language and thought, is not self-validating. It can and should be questioned. But the denial of objective values will have to be put forward not as the result of an analytic approach, but as an "error theory," a theory that although most people in making moral judgements implicitly claim, among other things, to be pointing to something objectively prescriptive, these claims are all false. It is this that makes the name "moral scepticism" appropriate.

But since this is an error theory, since it goes against assumptions ingrained in our thought and built into some of the ways in which language is used, since it conflicts with what is sometimes called common sense, it needs very solid support. It is not something we can accept lightly or casually and then quietly pass on. If we are to adopt this view, we must argue explicitly for it. Traditionally it has been supported by arguments of two main kinds, which I shall call the argument from relativity and the argument from queerness, but these can, as I shall show, be supplemented in several ways.

8. THE ARGUMENT FROM RELATIVITY

The argument from relativity has as its premiss the well-known variation in moral codes from one society to another and from one period to another, and also the differences in moral belief between different groups and classes within a complex community. Such variation is in itself merely a truth of descriptive morality, a fact of anthropology which entails neither first order nor second order ethical views Yet it may indirectly support second order subjectivism: radical differences between first order moral judgements make it difficult to treat those judgements as apprehensions of objective truths. But it is not the mere occurrence of disagreements that tells against the objectivity of values. Disagreement on questions in history or biology or cosmology does not show that there are no objective issues in these fields for investigation to disagree about. But such scientific disagreement results from speculative inferences or explanatory hypotheses based on inadequate evidence, and it is hardly plausible to interpret moral disagreement in the same way. Disagreement about moral codes seems to reflect people's adherence to and participation in different ways of life. The causal connection seems to be mainly that way round: it is that people approve of monogamy because they participate in a monogamous way of life rather than that they participate in a monogamous way of life because they approve of monogamy. Of course, the standards may be an idealization of the way of life from which they arise: the monogamy in which people participate may be less complete, less rigid, than that of which it leads them to approve. This is not to say that moral judgements are purely conventional. Of course there have been and are moral heretics and moral reformers, people who have turned against the established rules and practices of their own communities for moral reasons, and often for moral reasons that we would endorse. But this can usually be understood as the extension, in ways which, though new and unconventional, seemed to them to be required for consistency, of rules to which they already adhered as arising out of an existing way of life. In short, the argument from relativity has some force simply because the actual variations in the moral codes are more readily explained by the hypothesis that they reflect ways of life than by the hypothesis that they express perceptions, most of them seriously inadequate and badly distorted, of objective values.

But there is a well-known counter to this argument from relativity, namely to say that the items for which objective validity is in the first place to be claimed are not specific moral rules or codes but very general basic principles which are recognized at least implicitly to some extent in all society—such principles as provide the foundations of what Sidgwick has called different methods of ethics: the principle of universalizability, perhaps, or the rule that one ought to conform to the specific rules of any way of life in which one takes part, from which one profits, and on which one relies, or some utilitarian principle of doing what tends, or seems likely, to promote the general happiness. It is easy to show that such general principles, married with differing concrete circumstances, different existing social patterns or different preferences, will beget different specific moral rules, and there is some plausibility in the claim that the specific rules thus generated will vary from community to com-

munity or from group to group in close agreement with the actual variations in accepted codes.

The argument from relativity can be only partly countered in this way. To take this line the moral objectivist has to say that it is only in these principles that the objective moral character attaches immediately to its descriptively specified ground or subject: other moral judgements are objectively valid or true, but only derivatively and contingently—if things had been otherwise, quite different sorts of actions would have been right. And despite the prominence in recent philosophical ethics of universalization, utilitarian principles, and the like, these are very far from constituting the whole of what is actually affirmed as basic in ordinary moral thought. Much of this is concerned rather with what Hare calls "ideals" or, less kindly, "fanaticism." That is, people judge that some things are good or right, and others are bad or wrong, not because—or at any rate not only because—they exemplify some general principle for which widespread implicit acceptance could be claimed, but because something about those things arouses certain responses immediately in them, though they would arouse radically and irresolvably different responses in others. "Moral sense" or "intuition" is an initially more plausible description of what supplies many of our basic moral judgements than "reason." With regard to all these starting points of moral thinking the argument from relativity remains in full force.

9. THE ARGUMENT FROM QUEERNESS

Even more important, however, and certainly more generally applicable, is the argument from queerness. This has two parts, one metaphysical, the other epistemological. If there were objective values, then they would be entities or qualities or relations of a very strange sort, utterly different from anything else in the universe. Correspondingly, if we were aware of them, it would have to be by some special faculty of moral perception or intuition, utterly different from our ordinary ways of knowing everything else. These points were recognized by Moore when he spoke of non-natural qualities, and by the intuitionists in their talk about a "faculty of moral intuition." Intuitionism has long been out of favour, and it is indeed easy to point out its implausibilities. What is not so often stressed, but is more important, is that the central thesis of intuitionism is one to which any objectivist view of values is in the end committed: intuitionism merely makes unpalatably plain what other forms of objectivism wrap up. Of course the suggestion that moral judgements are made or moral problems solved by just sitting down and having an ethical intuition is a travesty of actual moral thinking. But, however complex the real process, it will require (if it is to yield authoritatively prescriptive conclusions) some input of this distinctive sort, either premisses or forms of argument or both. When we ask the awkward question, how we can be aware of this authoritative prescriptivity, of the truth of these distinctively ethical premises or of the cogency of this distinctively ethical pattern of reasoning, none of our ordinary accounts of sensory perception or introspection or the framing and confirming of explanatory hypotheses or inference or logical construction or conceptual analysis, or any combination of these, will provide a satisfactory answer; "a special sort of intuition" is a lame answer, but it is the one to which the clearheaded objectivist is compelled to resort.

Indeed, the best move for the moral objectivist is not to evade this issue, but to look for companions in guilt. For example, Richard Price argues that it is not moral knowledge alone that such an empiricism as those of Locke and Hume is unable to account for, but also our knowledge and even our ideas of essence, number, identity, diversity, solidity, inertia, substance, the necessary existence and infinite extension of time and space, necessity and possibility in general, power, and causation. If the understanding, which Price defines as the faculty within us that discerns truth, is also a source of new simple ideas of so many other sorts, may it not also be a power of immediately perceiving right and wrong, which yet are real characters of actions?

This is an important counter to the argument from queerness. The only adequate reply to it would be to show how, on empiricist foundations, we can construct an account of the ideas and beliefs and knowledge that we have of all these matters. I cannot even begin to do that here, though I have undertaken some parts of the task elsewhere. I can only state my belief that satisfactory accounts of most of these can be given in empirical terms. If some supposed metaphysical necessities or essences resist such treatment, then they too should be included, along with objective values, among the targets of the argument from queerness.

This queerness does not consist simply in the fact that ethical statements are "unverifiable." Although logical positivism with its verifiability theory of descriptive meaning gave an impetus to non-cognitive accounts of ethics, it is not only logical positivists but also empiricists of a much more liberal sort who should find objective values hard to accommodate. Indeed, I would not only reject the verifiability principle but also deny the conclusion commonly drawn from it, that moral judgements lack descriptive meaning. The assertion that there are objective values or intrinsically prescriptive entities or features of some kind, which ordinary moral judgements presuppose, is, I hold, not meaningless but false.

Plato's Forms give a dramatic picture of what objective values would have to be. The Form of the Good is such that knowledge of it provides the knower with both a direction and an overriding motive; something's being good both tells the person who knows this to pursue it and make him pursue it. An objective good would be sought by anyone who was acquainted with it, not because of any contingent fact that this person, or every person, is so constituted that he desires this end, but just because the end has to-be-pursued-ness somehow built into it. Similarly, if there were objective principles of right and wrong, any wrong (possible) course of action would have not-to-be-doneness somehow built into it. Or we should have something like Clarke's necessary relations of fitness between situations and actions, so that a situation would have a demand for such-and-such an action somehow built into it.

The need for an argument of this sort can be brought out by reflection on Hume's argument that "reason"—in which at this stage he includes all sorts of knowing as well as reasoning—can never be an "influencing motive of the will." Someone might object that Hume has argued unfairly from the lack of influencing power (not contingent upon desires) in ordinary objects of knowledge and ordinary reasoning, and might maintain that values differ from natural objects precisely in their power, when known, automatically to influence the will. To this Hume could, and would need to, reply that this objection involves the postulating of value-entities or value-features of quite a different order from anything else with which we are acquainted, and of a corresponding faculty with which to detect them. That is, he would have to supplement his explicit argument with what I have called the argument from queerness.

Another way of bringing out this queerness is to ask, about anything that is supposed to have some objective moral quality, how this is linked with its natural features. What is the connection between the natural fact that an action is a piece of deliberate cruelty—say, causing pain just for fun—and the moral fact that it is wrong? It cannot be an entailment, a logical or semantic necessity. Yet it is not merely that the two features occur together. The wrongness must somehow be "consequential" or "supervenient"; it is wrong because it is a piece of deliberate cruelty. But just what *in the world* is signified by this "because"? And how do we know the relation that it signifies, if this is something more than such actions being socially condemned, and condemned by us too, perhaps through our having absorbed attitudes from our social environment? It is not even sufficient to postulate a faculty which "sees" the wrongness: something must be postulated which can see at once the natural features that constitute the cruelty, and the wrongness, and the mysterious consequential link between the two. Alternatively, the intuition required might be the perception that wrongness is a higher order property belonging to certain natural properties; but what is this belonging of properties to other properties, and how can we discern it? How much simpler and more comprehensible the situation would be if we could replace the moral quality with some sort of subjective response which could be causally related to the detection of the natural features on which the supposed quality is said to be consequential.

It may be thought that the argument from queerness is given an unfair start if we thus relate it to what are admittedly among the wilder products of philosophical fancy—Platonic Forms, non-natural qualities, self-evident relations of fitness, faculties of intuition, and the like. Is it equally forceful if applied to the terms in which everyday moral judgements are more likely to be expressed—though still, as has been argued in Section 7, with a claim to objectivity—"you must do this," "you can't do that," "obligation," "unjust," "rotten," "disgraceful," "mean," or talk about good reasons for or against possible actions? Admittedly not; but that is because the objective prescriptivity, the element a claim for whose authoritativeness is embedded in ordinary moral thought and language, is not yet isolated in these forms of speech, but is presented along with relations to desires and feelings, reasoning about the means to desired ends, interpersonal demands, the injustice which consists in the violation of what are in the context the accepted standards of merit, the psychological constituents of meanness, and so on. There is nothing queer about any of these, and under cover of them the claim for moral authority may pass unnoticed. But if I am right in arguing that it is ordinarily there, and is therefore very likely to be incorporated almost automatically in philosophical accounts of ethics which systematize our ordinary thought even in such apparently innocent terms as these, it needs to be examined, and for this purpose it needs to be isolated and exposed as it is by the less cautious philosophical reconstructions.

10. PATTERNS OF OBJECTIFICATION

Considerations of these kinds suggest that it is in the end less paradoxical to reject than to retain the common-sense belief in the objectivity of moral values, provided that we can explain how this belief, if it is false, has become established and is so resistant to criticisms. This proviso is not difficult to satisfy.

On a subjectivist view, the supposedly objective values will be based in fact upon attitudes which the person has who takes himself to be recognizing and responding to those values. If we admit what Hume calls the mind's "propensity to spread itself on external objects," we can understand the supposed objectivity of moral qualities as arising from what we can call the projection or objectification of moral attitudes. This would be analogous to what is called the "pathetic fallacy," the tendency to read our feelings into their objects. If a fungus, say, fills us with disgust, we may be inclined to ascribe to the fungus itself a non-natural quality of foulness. But in moral contexts there is more than this propensity at work. Moral attitudes themselves are at least partly social in origin: socially established—and socially necessary—patterns of behaviour put pressure on individuals, and each individual tends to internalize these pressures and to join in requiring these patterns of behaviour of himself and of others. The attitudes that are objectified into moral values have indeed an

external source, though not the one assigned to them by the belief in their absolute authority. Moreover, there are motives that would support objectification. We need morality to regulate interpersonal relations, to control some of the ways in which people behave towards one another, often in opposition to contrary inclinations. We therefore want our moral judgements to be authoritative for other agents as well as for ourselves: objective validity would give them the authority required. Aesthetic values are logically in the same position as moral ones; much the same metaphysical and epistemological considerations apply to them. But aesthetic values are less strongly objectified than moral ones; their subjective status, and an "error theory" with regard to such claims to objectivity as are incorporated in aesthetic judgements, will be more readily accepted, just because the motives for their objectification are less compelling.

But it would be misleading to think of the objectification of moral values as primarily the projection of feelings, as in the pathetic fallacy. More important are wants and demands. As Hobbes says, "whatsoever is the object of any man's Appetite or Desire, that is it, which he for his part calleth *Good*"; and certainly both the adjective "good" and the noun "goods" are used in non-moral contexts of things because they are such as to satisfy desires. We get the notion of something's being objectively good, or having intrinsic value, by reversing the direction of dependence here, by making the desire depend upon the goodness, instead of the goodness on the desire. And this is aided by the fact that the desired thing will indeed have features that make it desired, that enable it to arouse a desire or that make it such as to satisfy some desire that is already there. It is fairly easy to confuse the way in which a thing's desirability is indeed objective with its having in our sense objective value. The fact that the word "good" serves as one of our main moral terms is a trace of this pattern of objectification.

Similarly related uses of words are covered by the distinction between hypothetical and categorical imperatives. The statement that someone "ought to" or, more strongly, "must" do such-and-such may be backed up explicitly or implicitly by reference to what he wants or to what his purposes and objects are. Again, there may be a reference to the purposes of someone else, perhaps the speaker: "You must do this"—"Why?"—"Because I want such-and-such." The moral categorical imperative which could be expressed in the same words can be seen as resulting from the suppression of the conditional clause in a hypothetical imperative without its being replaced by any such reference to the speaker's wants. The action in question is still required in something like the way in which it would be if it were appropriately related to a want, but it is no longer admitted that there is any contingent want upon which its being required depends. Again this move can be understood when we remember that at least our central and basic moral judgements represent social demands, where the source of the demand is indeterminate and diffuse. Whose demands or wants are in question, the agent's, or the speaker's, or those of an indefinite multitude of other people? All of these in a way, but there are advantages in not specifying them precisely. The speaker is expressing demands which he makes as a member of a community, which he has developed in and by participation in a joint way of life; also, what is required of this particular agent would be required of any other in a relevantly similar situation; but the agent too is expected to have internalized the relevant demands, to act as if the ends for which the action is required were his own. By suppressing any explicit reference to demands and making the imperatives categorical we facilitate conceptual moves from one such demand relation to another. The moral uses of such words as "must" and "ought" and "should," all of which are used also to express hypothetical imperatives, are traces of this pattern of objectification.

It may be objected that this explanation links normative ethics too closely with descriptive morality, with the mores or socially enforced patterns of behaviour that anthropologists record. But it can hardly be denied that moral thinking starts from the enforcement of social codes. Of course it is not confined to that. But even when moral judgements are detached from the mores of any actual society they are liable to be framed with reference to an ideal community of moral agents, such as Kant's kingdom of ends, which but for the need to give God a special place in it would have been better called a commonwealth of ends.

Another way of explaining the objectification of moral values is to say that ethics is a system of law from which the legislator has been removed. This might have been derived either from the positive law of a state or from a supposed system of divine law. There can be no doubt that some features of modern European moral concepts are traceable to the theological ethics of Christianity. The stress on quasi-imperative notions, on what ought to be done or on what is wrong in a sense that is close to that of "forbidden," are surely relics of divine commands. Admittedly, the central ethical concepts for Plato and Aristotle also are in a broad sense prescriptive or intrinsically action-guiding, but in concentrating rather on "good" than on "ought" they show that their moral thought is an objectification of the desired and the satisfying rather than of the commanded. Elizabeth Anscombe has argued that modern, non-Aristotelian, concepts of *moral* obligation, *moral* duty, of what is *morally* right and wrong, and of the *moral* sense of "ought" are survivals outside the framework of thought that made them really intelligible, namely the belief in divine law. She infers that "ought" has "become a word of mere mesmeric force," with only a "delusive appearance of content," and that we would do better to discard such terms and concepts altogether, and go back to Aristotelian ones.

There is much to be said for this view. But

while we can explain some distinctive features of modern moral philosophy in this way, it would be a mistake to see the whole problem of the claim to objective prescriptivity as merely local and unnecessary, as a post-operative complication of a society from which a dominant system of theistic belief has recently been rather hastily excised. As Cudworth and Clarke and Price, for example, show, even those who still admit divine commands, or the positive law of God, may believe moral values to have an independent objective but still action-guiding authority. Responding to Plato's *Euthyphro* dilemma, they believe that God commands what he commands because it is in itself good or right, not that it is good or right merely because and in that he commands it. Otherwise God himself could not be called good. Price asks, "What can be more preposterous, than to make the Deity nothing but will; and to exalt this on the ruins of all his attributes?" The apparent objectivity of moral value is a widespread phenomenon which has more than one source: the persistence of a belief in something like divine law when the belief in the divine legislator has faded out is only one factor among others. There are several different patterns of objectification, all of which have left characteristic traces in our actual moral concepts and moral language. . . .

12. CONCLUSION

I have maintained that there is a real issue about the status of values, including moral values. Moral scepticism, the denial of objective moral values, is not to be confused with any one of several first order normative views, or

with any linguistic or conceptual analysis. Indeed, ordinary moral judgements involve a claim to objectivity which both non-cognitive and naturalist analyses fail to capture. Moral scepticism must, therefore, take the form of an error theory, admitting that a belief in objective values is built into ordinary moral thought and language, but holding that this ingrained belief is false. As such, it needs arguments to support it against "common sense." But solid arguments can be found. The considerations that favour moral scepticism are: first, the relativity or variability of some important starting points of moral thinking and their apparent dependence on actual ways of life; secondly, the metaphysical peculiarity of the supposed objective values, in that they would have to be intrinsically action-guiding and motivating; thirdly, the problem of how such values could be consequential or supervenient upon natural features; fourthly, the corresponding epistemological difficulty of accounting for our knowledge of value entities or features and of their links with the features on which they would be consequential; fifthly, the possibility of explaining, in terms of several different patterns of objectification, traces of which remain in moral language and moral concepts, how even if there were no such objective values people not only might have come to suppose that there are but also might persist firmly in that belief. These five points sum up the case for moral scepticism; but of almost equal importance are the preliminary removal of misunderstandings that often prevent this thesis from being considered fairly and explicitly, and the isolation of those items about which the moral sceptic is sceptical from many associated qualities and relations whose objective status is not in dispute.

III

Metaethics

A
REALISM

7

How To Be a Moral Realist

RICHARD BOYD

1. INTRODUCTION

1.1. Moral Realism

Scientific realism is the doctrine that scientific theories should be understood as putative descriptions of real phenomena, that ordinary scientific methods constitute a reliable procedure for obtaining and improving (approximate) knowledge of the real phenomena which scientific theories describe, and that the reality described by scientific theories is largely independent of our theorizing. Scientific theories describe reality and reality is "prior to thought" (see Boyd 1982).

By "moral realism" I intend the analogous doctrine about moral judgments, moral statements, and moral theories. According to moral realism:

1. Moral statements are the sorts of statements which are (or which express propositions which are) true or false (or approximately true, largely false, etc.);

2. The truth or falsity (approximate truth . . .) of moral statements is largely independent of our moral opinions, theories, etc.;

3. Ordinary canons of moral reasoning—together with ordinary canons of scientific and everyday factual reasoning—constitute, under many circumstances at least, a reliable method for obtaining and improving (approximate) moral knowledge.

It follows from moral realism that such moral terms as 'good', 'fair', 'just', 'obligatory' usually correspond to real properties or relations and that our ordinary standards for moral reasoning and moral disputation—together with reliable standards for scientific and everyday reasoning—constitute a fairly reliable way of finding out which events, persons, policies, social arrangements, etc., have these properties and enter into these relations. It is *not* a consequence of moral realism that our ordinary procedures are "best possible" for this purpose—just as it is not a consequence of scientific realism that our existing scientific methods are best possible. In the scientific case, improvements in knowledge can be expected to produce improvements in method (Boyd 1980, 1982, 1983, 1985a, 1985b, 1985c), and there is no reason to exclude this possibility in the moral case.

Scientific realism contrasts with instrumentalism and its variants and with views like that of Kuhn (1970) according to which the reality which scientists study is largely constituted by the theories they adopt. Moral realism contrasts with non-cognitivist metaethical theories like emotivism and with views according to which moral principles are largely a reflection of social constructs or conventions.

What I want to do in this essay is to explore the ways in which recent developments in realist philosophy of science, together with related "naturalistic" developments in epistemology and philosophy of language, can be employed in the articulation and defense of moral realism. It will not be my aim here to establish that moral realism is true. Indeed, if moral realism is to be defended along the lines I will indicate here then a thoroughgoing defense of moral realism would be beyond the scope of a single essay. Fortunately a number of extremely important defenses of moral realism have recently been published (see, e.g., Brink 1984, 1989; Gilbert 1981b, 1982, 1984b, 1986b, forthcoming; Miller 1984b; Railton 1986; Sturgeon 1984a, 1984b). What I hope to demonstrate in the present essay is that moral realism can be shown to be a more attractive and plausible philosophical position if recent developments in realist philosophy of science are brought to bear in its defense. I intend the general defense of moral realism offered here as a proposal regarding the metaphysical, epistemological, and semantic framework within which arguments for moral realism are best formulated and best understood.

In addition, I am concerned to make an indirect contribution to an important recent debate among Marxist philosophers and Marx scholars concerning the Marxist analysis of moral discourse (see, e.g. Gilbert 1981a, 1981b, 1982, 1984b, 1986a, 1986b; Miller 1979, 1981, 1982, 1983, 1984a, 1984b; Wood 1972, 1979). Two questions are central in this debate: the question of what metaethical views Marx and other Marxist figures actually held or practiced and the question of what metaethical views are appropriate to a Marxist analysis of history and in particular to a Marxist analysis of the role of class ideology in the determination of the content of moral conceptions. I have nothing to contribute to the efforts to answer the first question, which lies outside my competence. About the second, I am convinced that Marxists should be moral realists and that the admirably motivated decision by many anti-revisionist Marxists to adopt a nonrealist relativist stance in metaethics represents a sectarian (if nonculpable) error. I intend the defense of moral realism presented here to be fully compatible with the recognition of the operation in the history of moral inquiry of just the sort of ideological forces which Marxist historians (among others) have emphasized. A thoroughgoing defense of this compatibility claim is not attempted in the present essay; I develop it in a forthcoming essay.

1.2. Scientific Knowledge and Moral Skepticism

One of the characteristic motivations for anti-realistic metaethical positions—either for non-cognitivist views or for views according to which moral knowledge has a strong constructive or conventional component—lies in a presumed epistemological contrast between ethics, on the one hand, and the sciences, on the other. Scientific methods and theories appear to have properties—objectivity, value-neutrality, empirical testability, for example—which are either absent altogether or, at any rate, much less significant in the case of moral beliefs and the procedures by which we form and criticize them. These differences make the methods of science (and of every-day empirical knowledge) seem apt for the *discovery* of facts while the 'methods' of moral reasoning seem, at best, to be appropriate for the rationalization, articulation, and application of preexisting social conventions or individual preferences.

Many philosophers would like to explore the possibility that scientific beliefs and moral beliefs are not so differently situated as this presumed epistemological contrast suggests. We may think of this task as the search for a conception of 'unified knowledge' which will bring scientific and moral knowledge together within the same analytical framework in much the same way as the positivists' conception of 'unified science' sought to provide an integrated treatment of knowledge within the various special sciences. There are, roughly, two plausible general strategies for unifying scientific and moral knowledge and minimizing the apparent epistemological contrast between scientific and moral inquiry:

1. Show that our scientific beliefs and methods actually possess many of the features (e.g., dependence on nonobjective 'values' or upon social conventions) which form the core of our current picture of moral beliefs and methods of moral reasoning.

2. Show that moral beliefs and methods are much more like our current conception of scientific beliefs and methods (more 'objective', 'external', 'empirical', 'intersubjective', for example) than we now think.

The first of these options has already been explored by philosophers who subscribe to a 'constructivist' or neo-Kantian conception of scientific theorizing (see, e.g., Hanson 1958; Kuhn 1970). The aim of the present essay will be to articulate and defend the second alternative. In recent papers (Boyd 1979, 1982, 1983, 1985a, 1985b, 1985c) I have argued that scientific realism is correct, but that its adequate defense requires the systematic

adoption of a distinctly naturalistic and realistic conception of knowledge, of natural kinds, and of reference. What I hope to show here is that once such a distinctly naturalistic and realistic conception is adopted, it is possible to offer a corresponding defense of moral realism which has considerable force and plausibility.

My argumentative strategy will be to offer a list of several challenges to moral realism which will, I hope, be representative of those considerations which make it plausible that there is the sort of epistemological contrast between science and ethics which we have been discussing. Next, I will present a summary of some recent work in realistic philosophy of science and related "naturalistic" theories in epistemology and the philosophy of language. Finally, I will indicate how the results of this recent realistic and naturalistic work can be applied to rebut the arguments against moral realism and to sketch the broad outlines of an alternative realistic conception of moral knowledge and of moral language.

2. SOME CHALLENGES TO MORAL REALISM

2.1. Moral Intuitions and Empirical Observations

In the sciences, we decide between theories on the basis of observations, which have an important degree of objectivity. It appears that in moral reasoning, moral intuitions play the same role which observations do in science: we test general moral principles and moral theories by seeing how their consequences conform (or fail to conform) to our moral intuitions about particular cases. It appears that it is the foundational role of observations in science which makes scientific objectivity possible. How could moral intuitions possibly play the same sort of foundational role in ethics, especially given the known diversity of moral judgments between people? Even if moral intuitions do provide a 'foundation' for moral inquiry, wouldn't the fact that moral 'knowledge' is grounded in intuitions rather than in observation be exactly the sort of fundamental epistemological contrast which the received view postulates, especially since peoples' moral intuitions typically reflect the particular moral theories or traditions which they already accept, or their culture, or their upbringing? Doesn't the role of moral intuitions in moral reasoning call out for a 'constructivist' metaethics? If moral intuitions don't play a foundational role in ethics and if morality is supposed to be epistemologically like science, *then what plays, in moral reasoning, the role played by observation in science?*

2.2. The Role of "Reflective Equilibrium" in Moral Reasoning

We have already seen that moral intuitions play a role in moral reasoning which appears to threaten any attempt to assimilate moral reasoning to the model of objective empirical scientific methodology. Worse yet, as Rawls (1971) has reminded us, what we do with our moral intuitions, our general moral principles, and our moral theories, in order to achieve a coherent moral position, is to engage in 'trading-off' between these various categories of moral belief in order to achieve a harmonious 'equilibrium'. Moral reasoning *begins* with moral *presuppositions*, general as well as particular, and proceeds by negotiating between conflicting *presuppositions*. It is easy to see how this could be a procedure for rationalization of individual or social norms or, to put it in more elevated terms, a procedure for the 'construction' of moral or ethical systems. But if ethical beliefs and ethical reasoning are supposed to be like scientific beliefs and methods, then this procedure would have to be a procedure for *discovering* moral facts! How could any procedure so presupposition-dependent be a *discovery* procedure rather than a *construction procedure*? (See Dworkin 1973.)

2.3. Moral Progress and Cultural Variability

If moral judgments are a species of factual judgment, then one would expect to see moral progress, analogous to progress in science. Moreover, one of the characteristics of factual inquiry in science is its relative independence from cultural distortions: scientists with quite different cultural backgrounds can typically agree in assessing scientific evidence. If moral reasoning is reasoning about objective moral *facts*, then what explains our lack of progress in ethics and the persistence of cultural variability in moral beliefs?

2.4 Hard Cases

If goodness, fairness, etc., are real and objective properties, then what should one say about the sorts of hard cases in ethics which we can't seem *ever* to resolve? Our experience in science seems to be that hard scientific questions are only *temporarily* rather than permanently unanswerable. Permanent disagreement seems to be very rare indeed. Hard ethical questions seem often to be permanent rather than temporary.

In such hard ethical cases, is there a fact of the matter inaccessible to moral inquiry? If so, then doesn't the existence of such facts constitute a significant epistemological difference between science and ethics? If not, if there are not facts of the matter, then isn't moral realism simply refuted by such indeterminacy?

2.5. Naturalism and Naturalistic Definitions

If goodness, for example, is a real property, then wouldn't it be a *natural* property? If not, then isn't moral realism committed to some unscientific and superstitious belief in the existence of non-natural properties? If goodness would be a natural property, then isn't moral realism committed to the extremely implausible claim that moral terms like good' possess naturalistic definitions?

2.6. Morality, Motivation, and Rationality

Ordinary factual judgments often provide us with reasons for action: they serve as constraints on rational choice. But they do so only because of our antecedent interests or desires. If moral judgments are merely factual judgments, as moral realism requires, then the relation of moral judgments to motivation and rationality must be the same. It would be possible in principle for someone, or some thinking thing, to be entirely rational while finding moral judgments motivationally neutral and irrelevant to choices of action.

If this consequence follows from moral realism, how can the moral realist account for the particularly close connection between moral judgments and judgments about what to do? What about the truism that moral judgments have commendatory force as a matter of their meaning or the plausible claim that the moral preferability of a course of action always provides a reason (even if not an overriding one) for choosing it?

2.7 The Semantics of Moral Terms

Moral realism is an anti-subjectivist position. There is, for example, supposed to be a single objective property which we're all talking about when we use the term 'good' in moral contexts. But people's moral concepts differ profoundly. How can it be maintained that our radically different concepts of 'good' are really concepts of one and the same property? Why not a different property for each significantly different conception of the good? Don't the radical differences in our conceptions of the good suggest either a non-cognitivist or a constructivist conception of the semantics of ethical terms?

2.8. Verificationism and Anti-Realism in Ethics

Anti-realism in ethics, like the rejection of theoretical realism in science, is a standard positivist position. In the case of science, there is a straightforward verificationist objection to realism about alleged "theoretical entities": they are unobservables; statements about them lie beyond the scope of empirical investigation and are thus unverifiable in principle. (See Boyd 1982 for a discussion of various formulations of this key verificationist argument.)

It is interesting to note that the challenges to moral realism rehearsed in 2.1–2.7 do not take the form of so direct an appeal to verificationism. Only in the case of the concern about non-natural moral properties (2.5) might the issue of verifiability be directly relevant, and then only if the objection to non-natural properties is that they would be unobservable. Instead, the arguments in 2.1–2.7 constitute an *indirect* argument against moral realism: they point to features of moral beliefs or of moral reasoning for which, it is suggested, the best explanation would be one which entailed the rejection of moral realism. Moreover, what is true of the challenges to moral realism rehearsed above is typical: by and large positivists, and philosophers influenced by positivism, did not argue directly for the unverifiability of moral statements: they did not make an appeal to the unobservability of alleged moral properties or deny that moral theories had observational consequences. Instead, they seemed to take a non-cognitivist view of ethics to be established by an "inductive inference to the best explanation" of the sort of facts cited in 2.1–2.7.

In this regard, then, the standard arguments against moral realism are more closely analogous to Kuhnian objections to scientific realism than they are to the standard verificationist arguments against the possibility of knowledge of "theoretical entities." Sections 2.1, 2.2, 2.3, and 2.7 rehearse arguments which are importantly similar to Kuhn's arguments from the paradigm dependence of scientific concepts and methods to a constructivist and anti-realistic conception of science. I have argued elsewhere (Boyd 1979, 1982, 1983, 1985a) that a systematic rebuttal to the verificationist epistemology and philosophy of language which form the foundations of logical positivism can in fact be extended to a defense of scientific realism against the more constructivist and neo-Kantian considerations represented by Kuhn's work. If the arguments of the present essay are successful, then this conclusion can be generalized: a realist and anti-empiricist account in the philosophy of science can be extended to a defense of *moral* realism as well, even though the challenges to moral realism are apparently only indirectly verificationist.

3. REALIST PHILOSOPHY OF SCIENCE

3.1. The Primacy of Reality

By "scientific realism" philosophers mean the doctrine that the methods of science are capable of providing (partial or approximate) knowledge of unobservable ('theoretical') entities, such as atoms or electromagnetic fields, in addition to knowledge about the behavior of observable phenomena (and of course, that the properties of these and other entities studied by scientists are largely theory-independent).

Over the past three decades or so, philosophers of science within the empiricist tradition have been increasingly sympathetic toward scientific realism and increasingly inclined to alter their views of science in a realist direction. The reasons for this realist tendency lie largely in the recognition of the extraordinary role which theoretical considerations play in actual (and patently successful) scientific practice. To take the most striking example, scientists routinely modify or extend operational 'measurement' or 'detection' procedures for 'theoretical' magnitudes or entities on the basis of new theoretical developments. This sort of methodology is perfectly explicable on the realist assumption that the operational procedures in question really are procedures for the measurement or

detection of unobservable entities and that the relevant theoretical developments reflect increasingly accurate knowledge of such "theoretical" entities. Accounts of the revisability of operational procedures which are compatible with a non-realist position appear inadequate to explain the way in which theory-dependent revisions of 'measurement' and 'detection' procedures make a positive methodological contribution to the progress of science.

This pattern is quite typical: The methodological contribution made by theoretical considerations in scientific methodology is inexplicable on a non-realist conception but easily explicable on the realist assumption that such considerations are a reflection of the growth of *theoretical* knowledge. (For a discussion of this point see Boyd l982, 1983, 1985a, 1985b.) Systematic development of this realist theme has produced developments in epistemology, metaphysics, and the philosophy of language which go far beyond the mere rejection of verificationism and which point the way toward a distinctly realist conception of the central issues in the philosophy of science. These developments include the articulation of causal or naturalistic theories of reference (Kripke 1971, 1972; Putnam 1975a; Boyd 1979, 1982), of measurement (Byerly and Lazara 1973) of 'natural kinds' and scientific categories (Quine 1969a; Putnam 1975a; Boyd 1979, 1982, 1983, 1985b), of scientific epistemology generally (Boyd 1972, 1979, 1982, 1983, 1985a, 1985b, 1985c), and of causation (Mackie 1974; Shoemaker 1980; Boyd 1982, 1985b).

Closely related to these developments has been the articulation of causal or naturalistic theories of knowledge (see, e.g., Armstrong 1973; Goldman 1967, 1976; Quine 1969b). Such theories represent generalizations of causal theories of perception and reflect a quite distinctly realist stance with respect to the issue of our knowledge of the external world. What all these developments—both within the philosophy of science and in epistemology generally—have in common is that they portray as *a posteriori* and contingent various matters (such as the operational 'definitions' of theoretical terms, the 'definitions' of natural kinds, or the reliability of the senses) which philosophers in the modern tradition have typically sought to portray as *a priori*. In an important sense, these developments represent the fuller working out of the philosophical implications of the realist doctrine that reality is prior to thought. (For a further development of this theme see Boyd 1982, 1983, 1985a, 1985b.) It is just this *a posteriority* and contingency in philosophical matters, l shall argue, which will make possible a plausible defense of moral realism against the challenges outlined in Part 2.

In the remaining sections of Part 3 I will describe some of the relevant features of these naturalistic and realistic developments. These 'results' in recent realistic philosophy are not, of course, uncontroversial, and it is beyond the scope of this essay to defend them. But however much controversy they may occasion, unlike moral realism, they do not occasion incredulity: they represent a plausible and defensible philosophical position. The aim of this essay is to indicate that, if we understand the relevance of these recent developments to issues in moral philosophy, then moral realism should, though controversial, be equally credible.

3.2. Objective Knowledge from Theory-Dependent Methods

I suggested in the preceding section that the explanation for the movement toward realism in the philosophy of science during the past two or three decades lies in the recognition of the extraordinarily theory-dependent character of scientific methodology and in the inability of any but a realist conception of science to explain why so theory-dependent a methodology should be reliable. The theoretical revisability of measurement and detection procedures, I claimed, played a crucial role in establishing the plausibility of a realist philosophy of science.

If we look more closely at this example, we can recognize two features of scientific methodology which are, in fact, quite general. In the first place, the realist's account of the theoretical revisability of measurement and detection procedures rests upon a conception of scientific research as *cumulative by successive approximations to the truth.*

Second, this cumulative development is possible because *there is a dialectical relationship between current theory and the methodology for its improvement.* The approximate truth of current theories explains why our existing measurement procedures are (approximately) reliable. That reliability, in turn, helps to explain why our experimental or observational investigations are successful in uncovering new theoretical knowledge, which, in turn, may produce improvements in experimental techniques, etc.

These features of scientific methodology are *entirely* general. Not only measurement and detection procedures but all aspects of scientific methodology—principles of experimental design, choices of research problems, standards for the assessment of experimental evidence, principles governing theory choice, and rules for the use of theoretical language—are highly dependent upon current theoretical commitments (Boyd 1972, 1973, 1979, 1980, 1982, 1983, 1985a, 1985b; Kuhn 1970; van Fraassen 1980). No aspect of scientific method involves the 'presupposition-free' testing of individual laws or theories. Moreover, the theory dependence of scientific methodology *contributes* to its reliability rather than detracting from it.

The only scientifically plausible explanation for the reliability of a scientific methodology which is so theory-dependent is a thoroughgoingly realistic explanation: Scientific methodology, dictated by currently accepted theories, is reliable at producing further knowledge precisely *because, and to the extent that, currently accepted theories are relevantly approximately true.* For example, it is because our current theories are approximately true that the canons of experimental design which they dictate are appropriate for the rigorous testing of new (and potentially more accurate) theories. What the scientific method provides is a paradigm-dependent paradigm-modification strategy: a strategy for modifying or amending our existing theories in the light of further research, which is such that its methodological principles at any given time will themselves depend upon the theoretical picture provided by the currently accepted theories. If the body of accepted theories is itself relevantly sufficiently approximately true, then this methodology operates to produce a subsequent dialectical improvement both in our knowledge of the world and in our methodology itself. Both our new theories and the methodology by which we develop and test them depend upon previously acquired theoretical knowledge. It is not possible to explain even the instrumental reliability of actual scientific practice without invoking this explanation and without adopting a realistic conception of scientific knowledge (Boyd 1972, 1973, 1979, 1982, 1983, 1985a, 1985b, 1985c).

The way in which scientific methodology is theory-dependent dictates that we have a strong methodological preference for new theories which are plausible in the light of our existing theoretical commitments: this means that we prefer new theories which relevantly resemble our existing theories (where the determination of the relevant respects of resemblance is itself a theoretical issue). The reliability of such a methodology is explained by the approximate truth of existing theories, and one consequence of this explanation is that *judgments of theoretical plausibility are evidential.* The fact that a proposed theory is itself plausible in the light of previously confirmed theories is evidence for its (approximate) truth (Boyd 1972, 1973, 1979, 1982, 1983, 1985a, 1985b, 1985c). A purely conventionalistic account of the methodological role of considerations of theoretical plausibility cannot be adequate because it cannot explain the contribution which such considerations make to the instrumental reliability of scientific methodology (Boyd 1979, 1982, 1983).

The upshot is this: The theory-dependent conservatism of scientific methodology is *essential* to the rigorous and reliable testing and development of new scientific theories; on balance, theoretical 'presuppositions' play neither a destructive nor a conventionalistic role in scientific methodology. They are essential to its reliability. If by the 'objectivity' of scientific methodology we mean its capacity to lead to the discovery of *theory-independent reality*, then scientific methodology is objective precisely because it *is theory-dependent* (Boyd 1979, 1982, 1983, 1985a, 1985b, 1985c).

3.3. Naturalism and Radical Contingency in Epistemology

Modern epistemology has been largely dominated by positions which can be characterized as 'foundationalist': all knowledge is seen as ultimately grounded in certain foundational beliefs which have an epistemically privileged position—they are a priori or self-warranting, incorrigible, or something of the sort. Other true beliefs are instances of knowledge only if they can be justified by appeals to foundational knowledge. Whatever the nature of the foundational beliefs, or whatever their epistemic privilege is suppose to consist in, it is an a priori question which beliefs fall in the privileged class. Similarly, the basic inferential principles which are legitimate for justifying non-foundational knowledge claims, given foundational premises, are such that they can be identified a priori and it can be shown a priori that they are rational principles of inference. We may fruitfully think of foundationalism as consisting of two parts, *premise foundationalism*, which holds that all knowledge is justifiable from an a priori specifiable core of foundational beliefs, and *inference foundationalism*, which holds that the principles of justifiable inference are ultimately reducible to inferential principles which can be shown a priori to be rational.

Recent work in "naturalistic epistemology" or "causal theories of knowing" (see e.g., Armstrong 1973; Goldman 1967, 1976; Quine 1969b) strongly suggest that the foundationalist conception of knowledge is fundamentally mistaken. For the crucial case of perceptual knowledge, there seem to be (in typical cases at least) neither premises (foundational or otherwise) nor inferences; instead, perceptual knowledge obtains when perceptual beliefs are produced by epistemically reliable mechanisms. For a variety of other cases, even where premises and inferences occur, it seems to be the reliable production of belief that distinguishes cases of knowledge from other cases of true belief. A variety of naturalistic considerations suggests that there are no beliefs which are epistemically privileged in the way foundationalism seems to require.

I have argued (see Boyd 1982, 1983, 1985a, 1985b, 1985c) that the defense of scientific realism requires an even more thoroughgoing naturalism in epistemology and, consequently, an even more thoroughgoing rejection of foundationalism. In the first place, the fact that scientific knowledge grows cumulatively by successive approximation and the fact that the evaluation of theories is an ongoing social phenomenon require that we take the crucial causal notion in epistemology to be reliable *regulation* of belief rather than reliable belief *production*. The relevant conception of belief regulation must reflect the approximate social and dialectical character of the growth of scientific knowledge. It will thus be true that the causal mechanisms relevant to knowledge will include mechanisms, social and technical as well as psychological, for the criticism, testing, acceptance, modification, and transmission of scientific theories and doctrines. For that reason, an understanding of the role of social factors in science may be relevant not only for the sociology and history of science but for the epistemology of sciences as well. The epistemology of science is in this respect dependent upon empirical knowledge.

There is an even more dramatic respect in which the epistemology of science rests upon empirical foundations. All the significant methodological principles of scientific inquiry (except, perhaps, the rules of deductive logic, but see Boyd 1985c) are profoundly theory-dependent. They are a reliable guide to the truth *only* because, and to the extent that, the body of background theories which determines their application is relevantly approximately true. The rules of rational scientific inference are not reducible to some more basic rules whose reliability as a guide to the truth is independent of the truth of background theories. Since it is a contingent empirical matter which background theories are approximately true, the rationality of scientific principles of inference ultimately rests on a contingent matter of empirical fact, just as the epistemic role of the senses rests upon the contingent empirical fact that the senses are reliable detectors of external phenomena. Thus inference foundationalism is radically false; there are no a priori justifiable rules of nondeductive inference. The epistemology of empirical science is an empirical science (Boyd 1982, 1983, 1985a, 1985b, 1985c).

One consequence of this radical contingency of scientific methods is that the emergence of scientific rationality as we know it depended upon the logically, epistemically, and historically contingent emergence of a relevantly approximately true theoretical tradition. It is not possible to understand the initial emergence of such a tradition as the consequence of some more abstractly conceived scientific or rational methodology which itself is theory-independent. There is no such methodology. We must think of the establishment of the corpuscular theory of matter in the seventeenth century as the beginning of rational methodology in chemistry, not as a consequence of it (for a further discussion see Boyd 1982).

3.4. Scientific Intuitions and Trained Judgment

Both noninferential perceptual judgments and elaborately argued explicit inferential judgments in theoretical science have a purely contingent a posteriori foundation.

Once this is recognized, it is easy to see that there are methodologically important features of scientific practice which are intermediate between noninferential perception and explicit inference. One example is provided by what science textbook authors often refer to as 'physical intuition', 'scientific maturity', or the like. One of the intended consequences of professional training in a scientific discipline (and other disciplines as well) is that the student acquire a "feel" for the issues and the actual physical materials which the science studies. As Kuhn (1970) points out, part of the role of experimental work in the training of professional scientists is to provide such a feel for the paradigms or 'worked examples' of good scientific practice. There is very good reason to believe that having good physical (or biological or psychological) intuitions is important to epistemically reliable scientific practice. It is also quite clear both that the acquisition of good scientific intuitions depends on learning explicit theory, as well as on other sorts of training and practice, *and* that scientists are almost never able to make fully explicit the considerations which play a role in their intuitive judgments. The legitimate role of such 'tacit' factors in science has often been taken (especially by philosophically inclined scientists) to be an especially puzzling feature of scientific methodology.

From the perspective of the naturalistic epistemology of science, there need be no puzzle. It is, of course, a question of the very greatest psychological interest just how intuitive judgments in science work and how they are related to explicit theory, on the one hand, and to experimental practice, on the other. But it seems overwhelmingly likely that scientific intuitions should be thought of as trained judgments which resemble perceptual judgments in not involving (or at least not being fully accounted for by) explicit inferences, but which resemble explicit inferences in science in depending for their reliability upon the relevant approximate truth of the explicit theories which help to determine them.

This dependence upon the approximate truth of the relevant background theories will obtain even in those cases (which may be typical) in which the tacit judgments reflect a deeper understanding than that currently captured in explicit theory. It is an important and exciting fact that some scientific knowledge can be represented tacitly before it can be represented explicitly, but this fact poses no difficulty for a naturalistic treatment of scientific knowledge. Tacit or intuitive judgments in science are reliable because they are grounded in a theoretical tradition (itself partly tacit) which is, as a matter of contingent empirical fact, relevantly approximately true.

3.5. Non-Humean Conceptions of Causation and Reduction

The Humean conception of causal relations according to which they are analyzable in terms of regularity, correlation, or deductive subsumability under laws is defensible only from a verificationist position. If verificationist criticisms of talk about unobservables are rejected—as they should be—then there is nothing more problematical about talk of causal powers than there is about talk of electrons or electromagnetic fields. There is no reason to believe that causal terms have definitions (analytic or natural) in noncausal terms. Instead, 'cause' and its cognates refer to natural phenomena whose analysis is a matter for physicists, chemists, psychologists, historians, etc., rather than a matter of conceptual analysis. In particular, it is perfectly legitimate—as a naturalistic conception of epistemology requires—to employ unreduced causal notions in philosophical analysis (Boyd, 1982, 1985b, Shoemaker 1980).

One crucial example of the philosophical application of such notions lies in the analysis of 'reductionism'. If a materialist perspective is sound, then *in some sense* all natural phenomena are 'reducible' to basic physical phenomena. The (prephilosophically) natural way of expressing the relevant sort of reduction is to say that all substances are composed of purely physical substances, all forces are composed of physical forces, all causal powers or potentialities are realized in physical substances and their causal powers, etc. This sort of analysis freely employs unreduced causal notions. If it is 'rationally reconstructed' according to the Humean analysis of such notions, we get the classic analysis of reduction in terms of the syntactic reducibility of the theories in the special sciences to the laws of physics, which in turn dictates the conclusion that all natural properties must be definable in the vocabulary of physics. Such an analysis is entirely without justification from the realistic and natural istic perspective we are considering. Unreduced causal notions are philosophically acceptable, and the Humean reduction of them mistaken. The prephilosophically natural analysis of reduction is also the philosophically appropriate one. In particular, purely physical objects, states, properties, etc. need not have definitions in "the vocabulary of physics" or in any other reductive vocabulary (see Boyd 1982).

3.6. Natural Definitions

Locke speculates at several places in Book IV of the *Essay* (see, e.g., IV, iii, 25) that when kinds of substances are defined by 'nominal essences', as he thinks they must be, it will be impossible to have a general science of, say, chemistry. The reason is this: nominal essences define kinds of substance in terms of sensible properties, but the factors which govern the behavior (even the observable behavior) of substances are insensible corpuscular real essences. Since there is no reason to suppose that our nominal essences will correspond to categories which reflect uniformities in microstructure, there is no reason to believe that kinds defined by nominal essences provide a basis for obtaining general knowledge of substances. Only if we could sort substances according to their hidden real essences would systematic general knowledge of substances be possible.

Locke was right. Only when kinds are defined by natural rather than conventional definitions is it possible to obtain sound scientific explanations (Putnam 1975a; Boyd 1985b) or sound solutions to the problem of 'projectibility' in inductive inference in science (Quine 1969a; Boyd 1979, 1982, 1983, 1985a, 1985b, 1985c). Indeed this is true not only for the definitions of natural kinds but also for the definitions of the properties, relations, magnitudes, etc., to which we must refer in sound scientific reasoning. In particular, a wide variety of terms do not possess analytic or stipulative definitions and are instead defined in terms of properties, relations, etc., which render them appropriate to particular sorts of scientific or practical reasoning. In the case of such terms, proposed definitions are always in principle revisable in the light of new evidence or new theoretical developments. Similarly, the fact that two people or two linguistic communities apply different definitions in using a term is not, by itself, sufficient to show that they are using the term to refer to different kinds, properties, etc.

3.7. Reference and Epistemic Access

If the traditional empiricist account of definition by nominal essences (or 'operational definitions' or 'criterial attributes') is to be abandoned in favor of a naturalistic account of definitions (at least for some terms) then a naturalistic conception of reference is required for those cases in which the traditional empiricist semantics has been abandoned. Such a naturalistic account is provided by recent causal theories of reference (see, e.g., Feigl 1956; Kripke 1972; Putnam 1975a). The reference of a term is established by causal connections of the right sort between the use of the term and (instances of) its referent.

The connection between causal theories of reference and naturalistic theories of knowledge and of definitions is quite intimate: reference is itself an epistemic notion and the sorts of causal connections which are relevant to reference are just those which are involved in the reliable regulation of belief (Boyd 1979, 1982). *Roughly*, and for nondegenerate cases, a term *t* refers to a kind (property, relation, etc.) *k* just in case there exist causal mechanisms whose tendency is to bring it about, over time, that what is predicated of the term *t* will be approximately true of *k* (excuse the blurring of the use-mention distinction). Such mechanisms will typically include the existence of procedures which are approximately accurate for recognizing members or instances of *k* (at least for easy cases) and which relevantly govern the use of *t*, the social transmission of certain relevantly approximately true beliefs regarding *k*, formulated as claims about *t* (again excuse the slight to the use-mention distinction), a pattern of deference to experts on *k* with respect to the use of *t*, etc. (for a fuller discussion see Boyd 1979, 1982). When relations of this sort obtain, we may think of the properties of *k* as regulating the use of *t* (via such causal relations), and we may think of what is said using *t* as providing us with socially coordinated *epistemic access* to *k*; *t* refers to *k* (in nondegenerate cases) just in case the socially coordinated use of *t* provides significant epistemic access to *k*, and not to other kinds (properties, etc.) (Boyd 1979, 1982).

3.8. Homeostatic Property-Cluster Definitions

The sort of natural definition[1] in terms of corpuscular real essences anticipated by Locke is reflected in the natural definitions of chemical kinds by molecular formulas; 'water = H_2O' is by now the standard example (Putnam 1975a). Natural definitions of this sort specify necessary and sufficient conditions for membership in the kind in question. Recent *non*-naturalistic semantic theories in the ordinary language tradition have examined the possibility of definitions which do not provide necessary and sufficient conditions in this way. According to various property-cluster or criterial attribute theories, some terms have definitions which are provided by a collection of properties such that the possession of an adequate number of these properties is sufficient for falling within the extension of the term. It is supposed to be a conceptual (and thus an a priori) matter what properties belong in the cluster and which combinations of them are sufficient for falling under the term. Insofar as different properties in the cluster are differently "weighted" in such judgments, the weighting is determined by our concept of the kind or property being defined. It is characteristically insisted, however, that our concepts of such kinds are 'open textured' so that there is some indeterminacy in extension *legitimately* associated with property-cluster or criterial attribute definitions. The 'imprecision' or 'vagueness' of such definitions is seen as a perfectly appropriate feature of ordinary linguistic usage, in contrast to the artificial precision suggested by rigidly formalistic positivist conceptions of proper language use.

I shall argue (briefly) that—despite the philistine antiscientism often associated with 'ordinary language' philosophy—the property-cluster conception of definitions provides an extremely deep insight into the possible form of *natural* definitions. I shall argue that there are a number of scientifically important kinds, properties, etc., whose natural definitions are very much like the property-cluster definitions postulated by ordinary-language philosophers (for the record, I doubt that there are any terms whose definitions actually fit the ordinary-language model, because I doubt that there are any significant 'conceptual truths' at all). There are natural kinds, properties, etc., whose natural definitions involve a kind of property cluster *together with* an associated indeterminacy in extension. Both the property-cluster form of such definitions and the associated indeterminacy are dictated by the scientific task of employing categories which correspond to inductively and explanatorily relevant causal structures. In particular, the indeterminacy in extension of such natural definitions could not be remedied without rendering the definitions *un*natural in the sense of being scientifically misleading. What I believe is that the following sort of situation is commonplace in the special sciences which study complex structurally or functionally characterized phenomena:

1. There is a family F of properties which are 'contingently clustered' in nature in the sense that they co-occur in an important number of cases.

2. Their co-occurrence is not, at least typically, a statistical artifact, but rather the result of what may be metaphorically (sometimes literally) described as a sort of *homeostasis*. Either the presence of some of the properties in F tends (under appropriate conditions) to favor the presence of the others, or there are underlying mechanisms or processes which tend to maintain the presence of the properties in F, or both.

3. The homeostatic clustering of the properties in F is causally important: there are (theoretically or practically) important effects which are produced by a conjoint occurrence of (many of) the properties in F together with (some or all of) the underlying mechanisms in question.

4. There is a kind term t which is applied to things in which the homeostatic clustering of most of the properties in F occurs.

5. This t has no analytic definition; rather all or part of the homeostatic cluster F together with some or all of the mechanisms which underlie it provides the natural definition of t. The question of just which properties and mechanisms belong in the definition of t is an a posteriori question—often a difficult theoretical one.

6. Imperfect homeostasis is nomologically possible or actual: some thing may dis-

play some but not all of the properties in F; some but not all of the relevant underlying homeostatic mechanisms may be present.

7. In such cases, the relative importance of the various properties in F and of the various mechanisms in determining whether the thing falls under t—if it can be determined at all—is a theoretical rather than an conceptual issue.

8. In cases in which such a determination is possible, the outcome will typically depend upon quite particular facts about the actual operation of the relevant homeostatic mechanisms, about the relevant background conditions and about the causal efficacy of the partial cluster of properties from F. For this reason the outcome, if any, will typically be different in different possible worlds, even when the partial property cluster is the same and even when it is unproblematical that the kind referred to by t in the actual world exists.

9. Moreover, there will be many cases of extensional vagueness which are such that they are not resolvable, even given all the relevant facts and all the true theories. There will be things which display some but not all of the properties in F (and/or in which some but not all of the relevant homeostatic mechanisms operate) such that no rational considerations dictate whether or not they are to be classed under t, assuming that a dichotomous choice is to be made.

10. The causal importance of the homeostatic property cluster F together with the relevant underlying homeostatic mechanisms is such that the kind or property denoted by t is a natural kind in the sense discussed earlier.

11. No refinement of usage which replaces t by a significantly less extensionally vague term will preserve the naturalness of the kind referred to. Any such refinement would either require that we treat

as important distinctions which are ir-relevant to causal explanation or to in-duction or that we ignore similarities which are important in just these ways.

The reader is invited to assure herself that I through 11 hold, for example, for the terms 'healthy' and 'is healthier than'. Whether these are taken to be full-blown cases of nat-ural property (relation) terms is not crucial here. They do illustrate almost perfectly the notion of a homeostatic property cluster and the correlative notion of a homeostatic clus-ter term. It is especially important to see *both* that a posteriori theoretical considerations in medicine can sometimes decide problemati-cal cases of healthiness or of relative health-iness, often in initially counterintuitive ways *and* that nevertheless only highly artificial modifications of the notions of health and rel-ative health could eliminate most or all of the extensional vagueness which they possess. One way to see the latter point is to consider what we would do if, for some statistical study of various medical practices, we were obliged to eliminate most of the vagueness in the notion of relative healthiness even where medical theory was silent. What we would strive to do would be to resolve the vague-ness in such a way as not to bias the results of the study—not to favor one finding about the efficacy of medical practices over an-other. The role of natural kinds is, by con-trast, precisely to *bias* (in the pejoratively neutral sense of the term) inductive general-ization (Quine 1969a; Boyd 1979, 1981, 1983, 1985a, 1985b). Our concern not to bias the findings reflects our recognition that the resolution of vagueness in question would be *un*natural in the sense relevant to this inquiry.

The paradigm cases of natural kinds—bi-ological species—are examples of homeo-static cluster kinds in this sense. The ap-propriateness of any particular biological species for induction and explanation in bi-ology depends upon the *imperfectly* shared and homeostatically related morphological,

physiological, and behavioral features which characterize its members. The defi-nitional role of mechanisms of homeostasis is reflected in the role of interbreeding in the modern species concept; for sexually re-producing species, the exchange of genetic material between populations is thought by some evolutionary biologists to be essential to the homeostatic unity of the other prop-erties characteristic of the species and it is thus reflected in the species definition which they propose (see Mayr 1970). The *neces-sary* indeterminacy in extension of species terms is a consequence of evolutionary the-ory, as Darwin observed: speciation depends on the existence of populations which are intermediate between the parent species and the emerging one. Any 'refinement' of clas-sification which artificially eliminated the resulting indeterminacy in classification would obscure the central fact about herita-ble variations in phenotype upon which biological evolution depends. More deter-minate species categories would be scien-tifically inappropriate and misleading.

It follows that a consistently developed scientific realism *predicts* indeterminacy for those natural kind or property terms which refer to complex phenomena; such indeter-minacy is a necessary consequence of "cut-ting the world at its (largely theory-indepen-dent) joints." Thus consistently developed scientific realism *predicts* that there will be some failures of bivalence for statements which refer to complex homeostatic phe-nomena (contrast, e.g., Putnam 1983 on 'metaphysical realism' and vagueness). Precision in describing indeterminate or 'bor-derline' cases of homeostatic cluster kinds (properties, etc.) consists not in the introduc-tion of artificial precision in the definitions of such kinds but rather in a detailed de-scription of the ways in which the indeter-minate cases are like and unlike typical mem-bers of the kind (see Boyd 1982 on borderline cases of knowledge, which are themselves homeostatic cluster phenomena).

4. HOW TO BE A MORAL REALIST

4.1. Moral Semantics, Intuitions, Reflective Equilibrium, and Hard Cases

Some philosophical opportunities are too good to pass up. For many of the more abstract challenges to moral realism, recent realistic and naturalistic work in the philosophy of science is suggestive of possible responses in its defense. Thus for example, it has occurred to many philosophers (see, e.g., Putnam 1975b) that naturalistic theories of reference and of definitions might be extended to the analysis of moral language. *If* this could be done successfully *and if* the results were favorable to a realist conception of morals, then it would be possible to reply to several anti-realist arguments. For example, against the objection that wide divergence of moral concepts or opinions between traditions or cultures indicates that, at best, a constructivist analysis of morals is possible, the moral realist might reply that differences in conception or in working definitions need not indicate the absence of shared causally fixed referents for moral terms.

Similarly, consider the objection that a moral realist must hold that goodness is a natural property, and thus commit the "naturalistic fallacy" of maintaining that moral terms possess analytic definitions in, say, physical terms. The moral realist may choose to agree that goodness is probably a physical property but deny that it has any analytic definition whatsoever. If the realist's critique of the syntactic analysis of reductionism in science is also accepted, then the moral realist can deny that it follows from the premise that goodness is a physical property or that goodness has any physical definition, analytic or otherwise.

If the moral realist takes advantage of naturalistic and realistic conceptions in epistemology as well as in semantic theory, other rebuttals to anti-realist challenges are suggested. The extent of the potential for rebuttals of this sort can best be recognized if we consider the objection that the role of reflective equilibrium in moral reasoning dictates a constructivist rather than a realist conception of morals. The moral realist might reply that the dialectical interplay of observations, theory, and methodology which, according to the realist, constitutes the *discovery* procedure for scientific inquiry *just is* the method of reflective equilibrium, so that the prevalence of that method in moral reasoning cannot by *itself* dictate a non-realist conception of morals.

If the response just envisioned to the concern over reflective equilibrium is successful, then the defender of moral realism will have established that—in moral reasoning as in scientific reasoning—the role of culturally transmitted presuppositions in reasoning does not necessitate a constructivist (or noncognitivist) rather than a realist analysis of the subject matter. *If* that is established, then the moral realist might defend the epistemic role of culturally determined intuitions in ethics by treating ethical intuitions on the model of theory-determined intuitions in science, which the scientific realist takes to be examples of epistemically reliable trained judgments.

Finally, if the moral realist is inclined to accept the antirealist's claim that the existence of hard cases in ethics provides a reason to doubt that there is a moral fact of the matter which determines the answer in such cases (more on this later), then the scientific realist's conclusion that bivalence fails for some statements involving homeostatic cluster kind terms *might* permit the moral realist to reason that similar failures of bivalence for some ethical statements need not be fatal to moral realism.

In fact, I propose to employ just these rebuttals to the various challenges to moral realism I have been discussing. They represent the application of a coherent naturalistic conception of semantics and of knowledge against the challenges raised by the critic of moral realism. But they do not stand any chance of rebutting moral anti-realism unless they are incorporated into a broader conception of morals and of moral knowledge which meets certain very strong constraints. These constraints are the subject of the next section.

4.2. Constraints on a Realist Conception of Moral Knowledge

Suppose that a defense of moral realism is to be undertaken along the lines just indicated. What constraints does that particular defensive strategy place on a moral realist's conception of morals and of moral knowledge? Several important constraints are suggested by a careful examination of the realist doctrines in the philosophy of science whose extension to moral philosophy is contemplated.

In the first place, the scientific realist is able to argue that 'reflective equilibrium' in science and a reliance on theory-dependent scientific intuitions are epistemically reliable *only* on the assumption that the theoretical tradition which governs these methodological practices contains theories which are relevantly approximately true. Indeed, the most striking feature of the consistently realistic epistemology of science is the insistence that the epistemic reliability of scientific methodology is contingent upon the establishment of such a theoretical tradition. Moreover, the possibility of offering a realist rather than a constructivist interpretation of reflective equilibrium and of intuition in science rests upon the realist's claim that observations and theory-mediated measurement and detection of 'unobservables' in science represent epistemically relevant causal interactions between scientists and a theory-independent reality. Were the realist unable to treat observation and measurement as providing 'epistemic access' to reality in this way, a constructivist treatment of scientific knowledge would be almost unavoidable.

Similarly, the scientific realist is able to employ a naturalistic conception of definitions and of reference only because (I) it is arguable that the nature of the subject matter of science dictates that kinds, properties, etc., be defined by nonconventional definitions and (2) it is arguable that actual scientific practices result in the establishment of 'epistemic access' to the various 'theoretical entities' which, the realist maintains, are (part of) the subject matter of scientific inquiry.

Finally, the realist can insist that realism not only can tolerate but implies certain failures of bivalence only because it can be argued that homeostatic cluster kinds (properties, etc.) must have indeterminacy in extension in order for reference to them to be scientifically fruitful. These considerations suggest that the following constraints must be satisfied by an account of moral knowledge if it is to be the basis for the proposed defense of moral realism:

1. It must be possible to explain how our moral reasoning *started out* with a stock of relevantly approximately true moral beliefs so that reflective equilibrium in moral reasoning can be treated in a fashion analogous to the scientific realist's treatment of reflective equilibrium in scientific reasoning. Note that this constraint does not require that it be possible to argue that we started out with close approximations to the truth (seventeenth-century corpuscular theory was quite far from the truth). What is required is that the respects of approximation be such that it is possible to see how continued approximations would be forthcoming as a result of subsequent moral and nonmoral reasoning.

2. There must be an answer to the question "What plays, in moral reasoning, the role played by observation in science?" which can form the basis for a realist rather than a constructivist conception of the foundations of reflective equilibrium in moral reasoning.

3. It must be possible to explain why moral properties, say goodness, would require

natural rather than conventional definitions.

4. It must be possible to show that our ordinary use of moral terms provides us with epistemic access to moral properties. Moral goodness must, to some extent, regulate the use of the word 'good' in moral reasoning. Here again examination of the corresponding constraint in the philosophy of science indicates that the regulation need not be nearly perfect, but it must be possible to show that sufficient epistemic access is provided to form the basis for the growth of moral knowledge.

5. It must be possible to portray occasional indeterminacy in the extension of moral terms as rationally dictated by the nature of the subject matter in a way analogous to the scientific realist's treatment of such indeterminacy in the case of homeostatic cluster terms.

In the work of scientific realists, the case that the analogous constraints are satisfied has depended upon examination of the substantive findings of various of the sciences (such as, e.g., the atomic theory of matter or the Darwinian conception of speciation). It is very unlikely that an argument could be mounted in favor of the view that moral knowledge meets the constraints we are considering which does not rely in a similar way on substantive doctrines about the foundations of morals. What I propose to do instead is to *describe* one account of the nature of morals which almost ideally satisfies the constraints in question and to indicate how a defense of moral realism would proceed on the basis of this account.

It will not be my aim here to defend this account of morals against morally plausible rivals. In fact, I am inclined to think—*partly* because of the way in which it allows the constraints we are considering to be satisfied—that *if* there is a truth of the matter about morals (that is, if moral realism is true), then the account I will be offering is close to

the truth. But my aim in this paper is merely to establish that moral realism is plausible and defensible. The substantive moral position I will consider is a plausible version of nonutilitarian consequentialism, one which—I believe—captures many of the features which make consequentialism *one* of the standard and plausible positions in moral philosophy. If moral realism is defensible on the basis of a plausible version of consequentialism, then it is a philosophically defensible position which must be taken seriously in metaethics; and that's all I'm trying to establish here.

It is, moreover, pretty clear that a variety of plausible alternative conceptions of the foundations of morals satisfy the constraints we are discussing. If I am successful here in mounting a plausible defense of moral realism, given the substantive conception I will propose, then it is quite likely that the very powerful semantic and epistemic resources of recent realist philosophy of science could be effectively employed to defend moral realism on the basis of many of the alternative conceptions. I leave it to the defenders of alternative conceptions to explore these possibilities. The defense of moral realism offered here is to be thought of as (the outline of) a 'worked example' of the application of the general strategy proposed in 4.1.

One more thing should be said about the substantive conception of morals offered here. Like any naturalistic account, it rests upon potentially controversial empirical claims about human psychology and about social theory. It is a commonplace, I think, that moral realism is an optimistic position (or, perhaps, that it is typically an optimist's position). One nice feature of the substantive analysis of morals upon which my defense of moral realism will be based is that it quite obviously rests upon optimistic claims about human potential. Perhaps in that respect it is well suited to serve as a representative example of the variety of substantive moral views which would satisfy the constraints in question.

4.3 Homeostatic Consequentialism

In broad outline, the conception of morals upon which the sample defense of moral realism will rest goes like this:

1. There are a number of important human goods, things which satisfy important human needs. Some of these needs are physical or medical. Others are psychological or social; these (probably) include the need for love and friendship, the need to engage in cooperative efforts, the need to exercise control over one's own life, the need for intellectual and artistic appreciation and expression, the need for physical recreation, etc. The question of just which important human needs there are is a potentially difficult and complex empirical question.

2. Under a wide variety of (actual and possible) circumstances these human goods (or rather instances of the satisfaction of them) are homeostatically clustered. In part they are clustered because these goods themselves are—when present in balance or moderation—mutually supporting. There are in addition psychological and social mechanisms which when, and to the extent to which, they are present contribute to the homeostasis. They probably include cultivated attitudes of mutual respect, political democracy, egalitarian social relations, various rituals, customs, and rules of courtesy, ready access to education and information, etc. It is a complex and difficult question in psychology and social theory just what these mechanisms are and how they work.

3. Moral goodness is defined by this cluster of goods and the homeostatic mechanisms which unify them. Actions, policies, character traits, etc. are morally good to the extent to which they tend to foster the realization of these goods or to develop and sustain the homeostatic mechanisms upon which their unity depends.

4. In actual practice, a concern for moral goodness can be a guide to action for the morally concerned because the homeostatic unity of moral goodness tends to mitigate possible conflicts between various individual goods. In part, the possible conflicts are mitigated just because various of the important human goods are mutually reinforcing. Moreover, since the existence of effective homeostatic unity among important human goods is part of the moral good, morally concerned choice is constrained by the imperative to balance potentially competing goods in such a way that homeostasis is maintained or strengthened. Finally, the improvement of the psychological and social mechanisms of homeostasis themselves is a moral good whose successful pursuit tends to further mitigate conflicts of the sort in question. In this regard, moral practice resembles good engineering practice in product design. In designing, say, automobiles there are a number of different desiderata (economy, performance, handling, comfort, durability, . . .) which are potentially conflicting but which enjoy a kind of homeostatic unity if developed in moderation. One feature of good automotive design is that it promotes these desiderata within the limits of homeostasis. The other feature of good automotive design (or, perhaps, of good automotive engineering) is that it produces technological advances which permit that homeostatic unity to be preserved at higher levels of the various individual desiderata. So it is with good moral practice as well.[2]

I should say something about how the claim that the nature of the constituents of moral goodness is an empirical matter should be understood. I mean the analogy between moral inquiry and scientific inquiry to be taken *very* seriously. It is a commonplace in the history of science that major advances often depend on appropriate social conditions, technological advances, and prior scientific discoveries. Thus, for example, much of eighteenth-century physics and chemistry was possible only because there had developed (a) the social conditions in which work in the physical sciences was economically supported, (b) a technology sufficiently advanced to make the relevant instrumentation possible, and (c) the theoretical legacy of seventeenth-century Newtonian physics and corpuscular chemistry.

Via somewhat different mechanisms the same sort of dependence obtains in the growth of our knowledge of the good. Knowledge of fundamental human goods and their homeostasis represents basic knowledge about human psychological and social potential. Much of this knowledge is genuinely *experimental* knowledge and the relevant experiments are ('naturally' occurring) political and social experiments whose occurrence and whose interpretation depends both on 'external' factors and upon the current state of our moral understanding. Thus, for example, we would not have been able to explore the dimensions of our needs for artistic expression and appreciation had not social and technological developments made possible cultures in which, for some classes at least, there was the leisure to produce and consume art. We would not have understood the role of political democracy in the homeostasis of the good had the conditions not arisen in which the first limited democracies developed. Only after the moral insights gained from the first democratic experiments were in hand, were we equipped to see the depth of the moral peculiarity of slavery. Only since the establishment of the first socialist societies are we even beginning to obtain the data necessary to assess the role of egalitarian social practices in fostering the good.

It is also true of moral knowledge, as it is in case of knowledge in other 'special sciences', that the improvement of knowledge may depend upon theoretical advances in related disciplines. It is hard, for example, to see how deeper understanding in history or economic theory could fail to add to our understanding of human potential and of the mechanisms underlying the homeostatic unity of the good.

Let us now consider the application of the particular theory of the good presented here as a part of the strategy for the defense of moral realism indicated in the preceding section. I shall be primarily concerned to defend the realist position that moral goodness is a real property of actions, policies, states of affairs, etc., and that our moral judgments are, often enough, reflections of truths about the good. A complete realist treatment of the semantics of moral terms would of course require examining notions like obligation and justice as well. I will not attempt this examination here, in part because the aim of this essay is merely to indicate briefly how a plausible defense of moral realism might be carried out rather than to carry out the defense in detail. Moreover, on a consequentialist conception of morals such notions as obligation and justice are derivative ones, and it is doubtful if the details of the derivations are relevant to the defense of moral realism in the way that the defense of a realist conception of the good is.

In the remaining sections of the essay I shall offer a defense of homeostatic consequentialist moral realism against the representative anti-realist challenges discussed in Part 2. The claim that the term 'good' in its moral uses refers to the homeostatic cluster property just described (or even the claim that there is such a property) represents a complex and controversial philosophical and empirical hypothesis. For each of the responses to anti-realist challenges which I will present, there are a variety of possible anti-realist rebuttals, both empirical and philosophical. It is beyond the scope of this essay to explore these rebuttals and possible moral realist responses to them in any detail. Instead, I shall merely indicate how plausible realist rebuttals to the relevant challenges can be defended. Once again, the aim of the present paper is not to establish moral realism but merely to establish its plausibility and to offer a general framework within which further defenses of moral realism might be understood.

4.4. Observations, Intuitions, and Reflective Equilibrium

Of the challenges to moral realism we are considering, two are straightforwardly epistemological. They suggest that the role of moral intuitions and of reflective equilibrium in moral reasoning dictate (at best) a constructivist interpretation of morals. As we saw in Section 4.2. it would be possible for the moral realist to respond by assimilating the role of moral intuitions and reflective equilibrium to the role of scientific intuitions and theory-dependent methodological factors in the realist account of scientific knowledge, but this response is viable only if it is possible to portray many of our background moral beliefs and judgments as relevantly approximately true and only if there is a satisfactory answer to the question: "What plays, in moral reasoning, the role played in science by observation?" Let us turn first to the latter question.

I propose the answer: 'Observation'.

According to the homeostatic consequentialist conception of morals (indeed, according to any naturalistic conception) goodness is an ordinary natural property, and it would be odd indeed if observations didn't play the same role in the study of this property that they play in the study of all the others. According to the homeostatic consequentialist conception, goodness is a property quite similar to the other properties studied by psychologists, historians, and social scientists, and observations will play the same role in moral inquiry that they play in the other kinds of empirical inquiry about people.

It is worth remarking that in the case of any of the human sciences *some* of what must count as observation is observation of oneself, and *some* is the sort of self-observation involved in introspection. Moreover, *some* of our observations of other people will involve

trained judgment and the operation of sympathy. No reasonable naturalistic account of the foundations of psychological or social knowledge *or* of our technical knowledge in psychology or the social sciences will fail to treat such sources of belief—when they are generally reliable—as cases of observation in the relevant sense.

It is true, of course, that both the content and the evidential assessment of observations of this sort will be influenced by theoretical considerations, but this does not distinguish observations in the human sciences from those in other branches of empirical inquiry. The theory dependence of observations and their interpretation is simply one aspect of the pervasive theory dependence of methodology in science which the scientific realist cheerfully acknowledges (since it plays a crucial role in arguments for scientific realism). It is possible to defend a realist interpretation of the human sciences because it is possible to argue that actual features in the world constrain the findings in those sciences sufficiently that the relevant background theories will be approximately true enough for theory-dependent observations to play a reliable epistemic role.

In the case of moral reasoning, observations and their interpretation will be subject to just the same sort of theory-dependent influences. This theory dependence is one aspect of the general phenomenon of theory dependence of methodology in moral reasoning which we, following Rawls, have been describing as reflective equilibrium. We will be able to follow the example of scientific realists and to treat the observations which play a role in moral reasoning as sufficiently reliable for the defense of moral realism just in case we are able to portray the theories upon which they and their interpretation depend as relevantly approximately true—that is, just in case we are able to carry out the other part of the moral realist's response to epistemic challenges and to argue that our background moral beliefs are sufficiently near the truth to form the foundations for a reliable empirical investigation of moral matters. Let us turn now to that issue.

What we need to know is whether it is reasonable to suppose that, for quite some time, we have had background moral beliefs sufficiently near the truth that they could form the basis for subsequent improvement of moral knowledge in the light of further experience and further historical developments. Assuming, as we shall, a homeostatic consequentialist conception of morals, this amounts to the question whether our background beliefs about human goods and the psychological and social mechanisms which unite them have been good enough to guide the gradual process of expansion of moral knowledge envisioned in that conception. Have our beliefs about our own needs and capacities been good enough—since, say the emergence of moral and political philosophy in ancient Greece—that we have been able to respond to new evidence and to the results of new social developments by expanding and improving our understanding of those needs and capacities even when doing so required rejecting some of our earlier views in favor of new ones? It is hard to escape the conclusion that this is simply the question "Has the rational empirical study of human kind proven to be possible?" Pretty plainly the answer is that such study has proven to be possible, though difficult. In particular we have improved our understanding of our own needs and our individual and social capacities by just the sort of historically complex process envisioned in the homeostatic consequentialist conception. I conclude therefore that there is no reason to think that reflective equilibrium—which is just the standard methodology of any empirical inquiry, social or otherwise—raises any epistemological problems for the defense of moral realism.

Similarly, we may now treat moral intuitions exactly on a par with scientific intuitions, as a species of trained judgment. Such intuitions are *not* assigned a foundational role in moral inquiry; in particular they do not substitute for observations. Moral intuitions

are simply one cognitive manifestation of our moral understanding, just as physical intuitions, say, are a cognitive manifestation of physicists' understanding of their subject matter. Moral intuitions, like physical intuitions, play a limited but legitimate role in empirical inquiry *precisely because* they are linked to theory *and* to observations in a generally reliable process of reflective equilibrium.

It may be useful by way of explaining the epistemic points made here to consider very briefly how the moral realist might respond to one of the many possible anti-realist rebuttals to what has just been said. Consider the following objection: The realist treatment of reflective equilibrium requires that our background moral beliefs have been for some time relevantly approximately true. As a matter of fact, the overwhelming majority of people have probably always believed in some sort of theistic foundation of morals: moral laws are God's laws; the psychological capacities which underlie moral practice are a reflection of God's design; etc. According to the homeostatic consequentialism which we are supposed to accept for the sake of argument, moral facts are mere natural facts. Therefore, according to homeostatic consequentialism, most people have always had profoundly mistaken moral beliefs. How then can it be claimed that our background beliefs have been relevantly approximately true?

I reply that—assuming that people have typically held theistic beliefs of the sort in question—it does follow from homeostatic consequentialism that they have been *in that respect* very wrong indeed. But being wrong in that respect does not preclude their moral judgments having been relatively reliable reflections of facts about the homeostatic cluster of fundamental human goods, according to the model of the development of moral knowledge discussed earlier. Until Darwin, essentially all biologists attributed the organization and the adaptive features of the physiology, anatomy, and behavior of plants and animals to God's direct planning. That attribution did not prevent biologists from accumulating the truly astonishing body of knowledge about anatomy, physiology, and animal behavior upon which Darwin's discovery of evolution by natural selection depended; nor did it prevent their recognizing the profound biological insights of Darwin's theory. Similarly, seventeenth-century corpuscular chemistry did provide the basis for the development of modern chemistry in a way that earlier quasi-animistic renaissance naturalism' in chemistry could not. Early corpuscular theory was right that the chemical properties of substances are determined by the fundamental properties of stable 'corpuscles': it was wrong about almost everything else, but what it got right was enough to point chemistry in a fruitful direction. I understand the analogy between the development of scientific knowledge and the development of moral knowledge to be very nearly exact.

There may indeed be one important respect in which the analogy between the development of scientific knowledge and the development of moral knowledge is *in*exact, but oddly, this respect of disanalogy makes the case for moral realism stronger. One of the striking consequences of a full-blown naturalistic and realistic conception of knowledge is that our knowledge, even our most basic knowledge, rests upon logically contingent 'foundations'. Our perceptual knowledge, for example, rests upon the logically contingent *a posteriori* fact that our senses are reliable detectors of certain sorts of external objects. In the case of perceptual knowledge, however, there is a sense in which it is nonaccidental, noncontingent, that our senses are reliable detectors. The approximate reliability of our senses (with respect to some applications) is explained by evolutionary theory in a quite fundamental way (Quine l969a). By contrast, the reliability of our methodology in chemistry is much more dramatically contingent. As a matter of fact, early thinkers tried to explain features of the natural world by analogy to sorts of order they already partly understood: mathe-

matical, psychological, and mechanical. The atomic theory of matter represents one such attempt to assimilate chemical order to the better-understood mechanical order. In several important senses it was highly contingent that the microstructure of matter turned out to be particulate and mechanical enough that the atomic (or 'corpuscular') *guess* could provide the foundation for epistemically reliable research in chemistry. The accuracy of our guess in this regard is not, for example, explained by either evolutionary necessity or by deep facts about our psychology. In an important sense, the seventeenth century belief in the corpuscular theory of matter was not reliably produced. It was not produced by an antecedent generally reliable methodology: reasoning by analogy is *not* generally reliable except in contexts where a rich and approximately accurate body of theory *already* exists to guide us in finding the right respects of analogy (see Boyd 1982).

By contrast, the emergence of relevantly approximately true beliefs about the homeostatic cluster of fundamental human goods—although logically contingent—was much less strikingly 'accidental'. From the point of view either of evolutionary theory or of basic human psychology it is hardly accidental that we are able to recognize many of our own and others' fundamental needs. Moreover, it is probably not accidental from an evolutionary point of view that we were able to recognize some features of the homeostasis of these needs. Our initial relevantly approximately accurate beliefs about the good may well have been produced by generally reliable psychological and perceptual mechanisms and thus may have been clear instances of knowledge in a way in which our initial corpuscular beliefs were not (for a discussion of the latter point see Boyd 1982). It is *easier*, not *harder*, to explain how moral knowledge is possible than it is to explain how scientific knowledge is possible. Locke was right that we are fitted by nature for moral knowledge (in both the seventeenth- and the twentieth-century senses of the term) in a way that we are not so fitted for scientific knowledge of other sorts.

4.5. Moral Semantics

We have earlier considered two objections to the moral realist's account of the semantics of moral terms. According to the first, the observed diversity of moral concepts—between cultures as well as between individuals and groups within a culture—suggests that it will not be possible to assign a single objective subject matter to their moral disputes. The divergence of concepts suggests divergence of reference of a sort which constructivist relativism is best suited to explain. According to the second objection, moral realism is committed to the absurd position that moral terms possess definitions in the vocabulary of the natural sciences. We have seen that a moral realist rebuttal to these challenges is possible which assimilates moral terms to naturalistically and nonreductively definable terms in the sciences. Such a response can be successful only if (1) there are good reasons to think that moral terms must possess natural rather than stipulative definitions and (2) there are good reasons to think that ordinary uses of moral terms provides us with epistemic access to moral properties, so that, for example, moral goodness to some extent regulates our use of the word 'good' in moral contexts.

The homeostatic consequentialist conception of morals provides a justification for the first of these claims. If the good is defined by a homeostatic phenomenon the details of which we still do not entirely know, then it is a paradigm case of a property whose 'essence' is given by a natural rather than a stipulative definition.

Is it plausible that the homeostatic cluster of fundamental human goods has, to a significant extent, regulated the use of the term 'good' so that there is a general tendency, of the sort indicated by the homeostatic consequentialist conception of the growth of moral knowledge, for what we say about the good to be true of that cluster? If what I have already said about the possibility of defending a realist conception of reflective equilibrium in moral reasoning is right, the answer must be "yes." Such a tendency is guaranteed by basic evolutionary and psychological facts, and it is just such a tendency which we can observe in the ways in which our conception of the good has changed in the light of new evidence concerning human needs and potential. Indeed, the way we ('preanalytically') recognize moral uses of the term 'good' and the way we identify moral terms in other languages are precisely by recourse to the idea that moral terms are those involved in discussions of human goods and harms. We tacitly assume *something like* the proposed natural definition of 'good' in the practice of translation of moral discourse. I think it will help to clarify this realist response if we consider two possible objections to it. The first objection reflects the same concern about the relation between moral and theological reasoning that we examined in the preceding section. It goes like this: How is it possible for the moral realist who adopts homeostatic consequentialism to hold that there is a general tendency for our beliefs about the good to get truer? After all, the error of thinking of the good as being defined by God's will persists unabated and is—according to the homeostatic consequentialist's conception—a very important falsehood.

I reply, first, that the sort of tendency to the truth required by the epistemic access account of reference is not such that it must preclude serious errors. Newtonians were talking about mass, energy, momentum, etc., all along, even though they were massively wrong about the structure of space-time. We might be irretrievably wrong about some other issue in physics and still use the terms of physical theory to refer to real entities, magnitudes, etc. All that is required is a significant epistemically relevant causal connection between the use of a term and its referent.

Moreover, as I suggested earlier, it is characteristic of what we recognize as moral discourse (whether in English or in some other language) that considerations of human well-being play a significant role in determining what is said to be 'good'. The moral realist need not deny that other considerations—perhaps profoundly false ones—also influence what we say is good. After all, the historian of biology need not deny that the term 'species' has relatively constant reference throughout the nineteenth century, even though, prior to Darwin, religious considerations injected profound errors into biologists' conception of species. Remember that we do not ordinarily treat a theological theory as a theory *of* moral goodness at all unless it says something about what we independently recognize as human well-being. The role of religious considerations in moral reasoning provides a challenge for moral realists, but exactly the same challenge faces a realist interpretation of biological or psychological theorizing before the twentieth century, and it can surely be met.

The second objection I want to consider represents a criticism of moral realism often attributed to Marx (see, e.g., Wood 1972; for the record I believe that Marx's position on this matter was confused and that he vacillated between an explicit commitment to the relativist position, which Wood discusses, and a tacit commitment to a position whose reconstruction would look something like the position defended here). The objection goes like this: The moral realist—in the guise of the homeostatic consequentialist, say—holds that what regulate the use of moral terms are facts about human well-being. But this is simply not so. Consider, for example, sixteenth-century discussions of rights. One widely acknowledged 'right' was the divine right of kings. Something surely regulated the use of the language of rights in the sixteenth century, but it clearly wasn't human well-being construed in the way the moral realist intends. Instead, it was the well-being of kings and of the aristocratic class of which they were a part.

I agree with the analysis of the origin of the doctrine of the divine right of kings; indeed, I believe that such class determination of moral beliefs is a commonplace phenomenon. But I do not believe that this analysis undermines the claim that moral terms refer to aspects of human well-being. Consider, for example, the psychology of thinking and intelligence. It is extremely well documented (see, e.g., Gould 1981; Kamin 1974) that the content of much of the literature in this area is determined by class interests rather than by the facts. Nevertheless, the psychological terms occurring in the most egregiously prejudiced papers refer to real features of human psychology; this is so because, in other contexts, their use is relevantly regulated by such features. Indeed—and this is the important point—if there were not such an epistemic (and thus referential) connection to real psychological phenomena, the ideological rationalization of class structures represented by the class-distorted literature would be ineffective. It's only when people come to believe, for example, that Blacks lack a trait, *familiar in other contexts as 'intelligence'*, that racist theories can serve to rationalize the socioeconomic role to which Blacks are largely confined.

Similarly, I argue, in order for the doctrine of the divine right of kings to serve a class function, it had to be the case that moral language was often enough connected to issues regarding the satisfaction of real human needs. Otherwise, an appeal to such a supposed right would be ideologically ineffective. Only when rights-talk has *some* real connection to the satisfaction of the needs of nonaristocrats could this instance of rights-talk be useful to kings and their allies.

Once again, when the analogy between moral inquiry and scientific inquiry is fully exploited, it becomes possible to defend the doctrines upon which moral realism rests.

4.6. Hard Cases and Divergent Views

Two of the challenges to moral realism we are considering are grounded in the recognition that some moral issues seem very hard to resolve. On the one hand, there seem to be moral dilemmas which resist resolution even for people who share a common moral culture. Especially with respect to the sort of possible cases often considered by moral philosophers, there often seems to be no rational way of deciding between morally quite distinct courses of action. Our difficulty in resolving moral issues appears even greater when we consider the divergence in moral views that exists between people from different backgrounds or cultures. The anti-realist proposes to explain the difficulties involved by denying that there is a common objective subject matter which determines answers to moral questions.

We have seen that—to the extent that she chooses to take the difficulties in resolving moral issues as evidence for the existence of moral statements for which bivalence fails— the moral realist can try to assimilate such failures to the failures of bivalence which realist philosophy *predicts* in the case, for example, of some statements involving homeostatic cluster terms. Such a response will work only to the extent that moral terms can be shown to possess natural definitions relevantly like homeostatic cluster definitions. Of course, according to homeostatic consequentialism, moral terms (or 'good' at any rate) just are homeostatic cluster terms, so this constraint is satisfied. What I want to emphasize is that a moral realist *need not* invoke failures of bivalence in every case in which difficulties arise in resolving moral disputes.

Recall that on the conception we are considering moral inquiry is about a complex and difficult subject matter, proceeds often by the analysis of complex and "messy" naturally occurring social experiments, and is subject to a very high level of social distortion by the influence of class interests and other cultural factors. In this regard moral inquiry resembles inquiry in any of the complex and politically controversial social sciences. In such cases, even where there is no reason to expect failures of bivalence, one would predict that the resolution of some issues will prove

difficult or, in some particular social setting, impossible. Thus the moral realist can point to the fact that moral inquiry is a species of social inquiry to explain much of the observed divergence in moral views and the apparent intractability of many moral issues.

Similarly, the complexity and controversiality of moral issues can be invoked to explain the especially sharp divergence of moral views often taken to obtain between different cultures. For the homeostatic consequentialist version of moral realism to be true it must be the case that in each culture in which moral inquiry takes place the homeostatically clustered human goods epistemically regulate moral discourse to an appreciable extent. On the realistic and naturalistic conception of the growth of knowledge, this will in turn require that the moral tradition of the culture in question embody some significant approximations to the truth about moral matters. It is, however, by no means required that two such cultural traditions have started with initial views which approximated the truth to the same extent or along the same dimensions, nor is it required that they have been subjected to the same sorts of social distortion, nor that they have embodied the same sorts of naturally occurring social experimentation. It would thus be entirely unsurprising if two such traditions of moral inquiry should have, about some important moral questions, reached conclusions so divergent that no resolution of their disagreement will be possible within the theoretical and methodological framework which the two traditions *currently* have in common, even though these issues may possess objective answers eventually discoverable from within either tradition or from within a broader tradition which incorporates insights from both.

In this regard it is useful to remember the plausibility with which it can be argued that, if there were agreement on all the nonmoral issues (including theological ones), then there would be no moral disagreements. I'm not sure that this is exactly right. For one thing, the sort of moral agreement which philosophers typically have in mind when they say this sort of thing probably does not include agreement that some question has an indeterminate answer, which is something predicted by homeostatic consequentialism. Nevertheless, careful philosophical examination will reveal. I believe, that agreement on nonmoral issues would eliminate *almost all* disagreement about the sorts of moral issues which arise in ordinary moral practice. Moral realism of the homeostatic consequentialist variety provides a quite plausible explanation for this phenomenon.

It is nevertheless true that, for some few real-world cases and for *lots* of the contrived cases so prevalent in the philosophical literature, there does appear to be serious difficulty in finding rational resolutions—assuming as we typically do that an appeal to indeterminacy of the extension of 'good' doesn't count as a resolution. In such cases the strategy available to the moral realist *is* to insist that failures of bivalence do occur just as a homeostatic consequentialist moral realist predicts.

Philosophers often suggest that the major normative ethical theories will yield the same evaluations in almost all actual cases. Often it is suggested that this fact supports the claim that there is some sort of objectivity in ethics, but it is very difficult to see just why this should be so. Homeostatic consequentialist moral realism provides the basis for a satisfactory treatment of this question. Major theories in normative ethics have almost always sought to provide definitions for moral terms with almost completely definite extensions. This is, of course, in fact a mistake; moral terms possess homeostatic cluster definitions instead. The appearance of sharp divergence between major normative theories, with respect to the variety of possible cases considered by philosophers, arises from the fact that they offer different putative resolutions to issues which lack any resolution *at all* of the sort anticipated in those theories. The general agreement of major normative theories on almost all actual cases is explained both by the fact that the actual features of the good regulate the use of the term 'good' in philosophical discourse *and* by the homeostatic character of the good: when different normative theories put different weight on different components of the good, the fact that such components are—in actual cases— linked by reliable homeostatic mechanisms tends to mitigate, in real-world cases, the effects of the differences in the weights assigned. Homeostatic consequentialism represents the common grain of truth in other normative theories.

4.7. Morality, Motivation, and Rationality

There remains but one of the challenges to moral realism which we are here considering. It has often been objected against moral realism that there is some sort of logical connection between moral judgments and reasons for action which a moral realist cannot account for. It might be held, for example, that the recognition that one course of action is morally preferable to another *necessarily* provides a reason (even if not a decisive one) to prefer the morally better course of action. Mere facts (especially mere *natural* facts) cannot have this sort of logical connection to rational choice or reasons for action. Therefore, so the objection goes, there cannot be moral facts; moral realism (or at least naturalistic moral realism) is impossible.

It is of course true that the naturalistic moral realist must deny that moral judgments necessarily provide reasons for action; surely, for example, there could be nonhuman cognizing systems which could understand the natural facts about moral goodness but be entirely indifferent to them in choosing how to act. Moral judgments might provide for them no reasons for action whatsoever. Moreover, it is hard to see how the naturalistic moral realist can escape the conclusion that it would be *logically possible* for there to be a human being for whom moral judgments provided no reasons for action.

The moral realist must therefore deny that the connection between morality and reasons for action is so strong as the objection we are considering maintains. The appearance of an especially intimate connection must be explained in some other way.

The standard naturalist response is to explain the apparent intimacy of the connection by arguing that the natural property moral goodness is one such that for psychologically normal humans, the fact that one of two choices is morally preferable will in fact provide some reason for preferring it. The homeostatic consequentialist conception of the good is especially well suited to this response since it defines the good in terms of the homeostatic unity of fundamental human needs. It seems to me that this explanation of the close connection between moral judgments and reasons for action is basically right, but it ignores—it seems to me—one important source of the anti-realist's intuition that the connection between moral judgments and rational choice must be a necessary one. What I have in mind is the very strong intuition which many philosophers share that the person for whom moral judgments are motivationally indifferent would not only be psychologically atypical but would have some sort of *cognitive* deficit with respect to moral reasoning as well. The anti-realist diagnoses this deficit as a failure to recognize a definitional or otherwise necessary connection between moral goodness and reasons for action.

I think that there is a deep insight in the view that people for whom questions of moral goodness are irrelevant to how they would choose to act suffer a cognitive deficit. I propose that the deficit is not—as the anti-realist would have it—a failure to recognize a necessary connection between moral judgments and reasons for action. Instead, I suggest, if we adopt a naturalistic conception of moral knowledge we can diagnose in such people a deficit in the capacity to make moral judgments somewhat akin to a perceptual deficit. What I have in mind is the application of a causal theory of moral knowledge to the examination of a feature of moral reasoning which has been well understood in the empiricist tradition since Hume, that is, the role of sympathy in moral understanding.

It is extremely plausible that for normal human beings the capacity to access human goods and harms—the capacity to *recognize* the extent to which others are well or poorly off with respect to the homeostatic cluster of moral goods and the capacity to *anticipate correctly* the probable effect on others' well-being of various counterfactual circumstances—depends upon their capacity for sympathy, their capacity to imagine themselves in the situation of others or even to find themselves involuntarily doing so in cases in which others are especially well or badly off. The idea that sympathy plays this sort of cognitive role is a truism of nineteenth-century faculty psychology, and it is very probably right.

It is also very probably right, as Hume insists, that the operation of sympathy is *motivationally* important: as a matter of contingent psychological fact, when we put ourselves in the place of others in imagination, the effects of our doing so include our taking pleasure in others' pleasures and our feeling distress at their misfortune, and we are thus motivated to care for the well-being of others. The psychological mechanisms by which all this takes place may be more complicated than Hume imagined, but the fact remains that one and the same psychological mechanism—sympathy—plays *both* a cognitive *and* a motivational role in normal human beings. We are now in a position to see why the morally unconcerned person, the person for whom moral facts are motivationally irrelevant, probably suffers a *cognitive* deficit with respect to moral reasoning. Such a person would have to be deficient in sympathy, because the motivational role of sympathy is precisely to make moral facts motivationally relevant. In consequence, she or he would be deficient with respect to a cognitive capacity (sympathy) which is ordinarily important for the correct assessment of moral facts. The motivational deficiency would, as a matter of contingent fact about human psychology, be a cognitive deficiency as well.

Of course it does not follow that there could not be cognizing systems which are quite capable of assessing moral facts without recourse to anything like sympathy; they might, for example, rely on the application of a powerful tacit or explicit theory of human psychology instead. Indeed it does not follow that there are not actual people—some sociopaths and con artists, for example—who rely on such theories instead of sympathy. But it is true, just as the critic of moral realism insists, that there is generally a cognitive deficit associated with moral indifference. The full resources of naturalistic epistemology permit the moral realist to acknowledge and explain this important insight of moral anti-realists.

4.8. Conclusion

I have argued that if the full resources of naturalistic and realistic conceptions of scientific knowledge and scientific language are deployed and if the right sort of positive theory of the good is advanced, then it is possible to make a plausible case for moral realism in response to typical anti-realist challenges. Two methodological remarks about the arguments I have offered may be useful. In the first place, the rebuttals I have offered to challenges to moral realism really do depend strongly upon the naturalistic and nonfoundational aspects of current (scientific) realist philosophy of science. They depend, roughly, upon the aspects of the scientific realist's program which make it plausible for the scientific realist to claim that philosophy is an empirical inquiry continuous with the sciences and with, for example, history and empirical social theory. I have argued elsewhere (Boyd 1981, 1982, 1983, 1985a, 1985b, 1985c) that these aspects of scientific realism are essential to the defense of scientific realism against powerful empiricist and constructivist arguments.

If we now ask how one should decide between scientific realism and its rivals, I am inclined to think that the answer is that the details of particular technical arguments will not be sufficient to decide the question rationally; instead, one must assess the overall conceptions of knowledge, language, and understanding which go with the rival conceptions of science (I argue for this claim in Boyd 1983). *One* important constraint on an acceptable philosophical conception in these areas is that it permit us to understand the obvious fact that moral reasoning is not nearly so different from scientific or other factual reasoning as logical positivists have led us to believe. It is initially plausible, I think, that a constructivist conception of science is favored over both empiricist and realist conceptions insofar as we confine our attention to this constraint. If what I have said here is correct, this may well not be so. Thus the successful development of the arguments presented here may be relevant not only to our assessment of moral realism but to our assessment of scientific realism as well. Here is a kind of methodological unity of philosophy analogous to (whatever it was which positivists called) 'unity of science'.

My second methodological point is that the arguments for moral realism presented here depend upon optimistic empirical claims both about the organic unity of human goods and about the possibility of reliable knowledge in the 'human sciences' generally. Although I have not argued for this claim here, I believe strongly that any plausible defense of naturalistic moral realism would require similarly optimistic empirical assumptions. I am also inclined to believe that insofar as moral anti-realism is plausible its plausibility rests not only upon technical philosophical arguments but also upon relatively pessimistic empirical beliefs about the same issues. I suggest, therefore, that our philosophical examination of the issues of moral realism should include, in addition to the examination of technical arguments on both sides, the careful examination of empirical claims about the unity and diversity of human goods and about our capacity for knowledge of ourselves. That much of philosophy ought surely to be at least partly empirical.

NOTES

An early version of this paper, incorporating the naturalistic treatments of the roles of reflective equilibrium and moral intuitions in moral reasoning and a naturalistic conception of the semantics of moral terms (but not the homeostatic property cluster formulation of consequentialism), was presented to the Philosophy Colloquium at Case-Western Reserve University in 1977. I am grateful to the audience at that colloquium for helpful criticisms which greatly influenced my formulation of later versions.

In approximately the version published here, the paper was presented at the University of North Carolina, the University of Chicago, Cornell University, the Universities of California at Berkeley and at Los Angeles, the University of Washington, Dartmouth College, and Tufts University. Papers defending the general homeostatic property cluster account of natural definitions were presented at Oberlin, Cornell, and Stanford. Extremely valuable criticisms from the audiences at these universities helped me in developing the more elaborate defense of moral realism presented in *Realism and the Moral Sciences* and summarized in Part 5 [not included in this anthology].

My interest in the question of moral realism initially arose from my involvement in the anti-Vietnam War movement of the late 1960s and was sustained in significant measure by my participation in subsequent progressive movements. I have long been interested in whether or not moral relativism played a progressive or a reactionary role in such movements; the present essay begins an effort to defend the latter alternative. I wish to acknowledge the important influence on my views of the Students for a Democratic Society (especially its Worker-Student Alliance Caucus), the International Committee against Racism, and the Progressive Labor party. Their optimism about the possibility of social progress and about the rational capacity of ordinary people have played an important role in the development of my views.

I have benefited from discussions with many people about various of the views presented here. I want especially to thank David Brink, Norman Daniels, Philip Gasper, Paul Gomberg, Kristen Guyot, Terence Irwin, Barbara Koslowski, David Lyons, Christopher McMahon, Richard Miller, Milton Rosen, Sydney Shoemaker, Robert Stalnaker, Stephen Sullivan, Milton Wachsberg, Thomas Weston, and David Whitehouse. My thinking about homeostatic property cluster definitions owes much to conversations with Philip Gasper, David Whitehouse, and especially Kristin Guyot. I am likewise indebted to Richard Miller for discussions about the foundations of non-utilitarian consequentialism. My greatest debt is to Alan Gilbert and Nicholas Sturgeon. I wish to thank the Society for the Humanities at Cornell University for supporting much of the work reflected in Part 5.

1. This is the only section of Part 3 which advances naturalistic and realistic positions not already presented in the published literature. It represents a summary of work in progress. For some further developments see Section 5.2 [not printed in this anthology].

2. Two points of clarification about the proposed homeostatic consequentialist definition of the good are in order. In the first place, I understand the homeostatic cluster which defines moral goodness to be social rather than individual. The properties in homeostasis are to be thought of as instances of the satisfaction of particular human needs among people generally, rather than within the life of a single individual. Thus, the homeostatic consequentialist holds not (or at any rate not merely) that the satisfaction of each of the various human needs within the life of an individual contributes (given relevant homeostatic mechanisms) to the satisfaction of the others in the life of that same individual. Instead, she claims that, given the relevant homeostatic mechanisms, the satisfaction of those needs for one individual tends to be conducive to their satisfaction for others, and it is to the homeostatic unity of human need satisfaction in the society generally that she or he appeals in proposing a definition of the good.

Homeostatic consequentialism as I present it here is, thus, not a version of ethical egoism. I am inclined to think that individual well-being has a homeostatic property cluster definition and thus that a homeostatic property cluster conception of the definition of the good would be appropriate to the formulation of the most plausible versions of egoism, but I do not find even those versions very plausible and it is certainly not a version of egoism to which I mean to appeal in illustrating the proposed strategy for defending moral realism.

Second, I owe to Judith Jarvis Thomson the observation that, strictly speaking, the homeostatic consequentialist conception of the good does not conform to the more abstract account of homeostatic property cluster definitions presented in Section 3.8. According to that account, the homeostatically united properties and the definitionally relevant properties associated with the relevant mechanisms of homeostasis are all properties of the same kind of thing: organisms, let us say, in the case of the homeostatic property cluster definition of a particular biological species.

By contrast, some of the properties which characterize human well-being and the mechanisms upon which its homeostatic unity depends are (on the homeostatic consequentialist conception) in the first instance properties of individuals, whereas others are properties of personal relations between individuals and still others are properties of large-scale social arrangements. Homeostatic unity is postulated between instances of the realization of the relevant properties in objects of different logical type.

It should be obvious that the additional logical complexity of the proposed homeostatic property cluster definition of the good does not vitiate the rebuttals offered here to anti-realist arguments. For the record, it seems to me that Professor Thomson's observation in fact applies to the actual case of species definitions as well: some of the homeostatically united properties and homeostatic mechanisms which define a species are in the first instance properties of individual organisms, some properties of small groups of organisms, some of larger populations (in the standard sense of that term), and some of the relations between such populations.

BIBLIOGRAPHY

Armstrong, D. M. 1973. *Belief, Truth and Knowledge*. Cambridge: Cambridge University Press.

Boyd, R. 1972. "Determinism, Laws and Predictability in Principle." *Philosophy of Science* 39: 431–50.

———. 1973. "Realism, Underdetermination and a Causal Theory of Evidence." *Nous* 7: 1–12.

———. 1979. "Metaphor and Theory Change." In A. Ortony, ed., *Metaphor and Thought*. Cambridge: Cambridge University Press.

———. 1980. "Materialism without Reductionism: What Physicalism Does Not Entail." In N. Block, ed., *Readings in Philosophy of Psychology*, vol. 1. Cambridge, Mass.: Harvard University Press.

———. 1982. "Scientific Realism and Naturalistic Epistemology." In P. D. Asquith and R. N. Giere, eds., *PSA 1980*, vol. 2. East Lansing: Philosophy of Science Association.

———. 1983. "On the Current Status of the Issue of Scientific Realism." *Erkenntnis* 19: 45–90.

———. 1985a. "Lex Orendi Est Lex Credendi." In Paul Churchland and Clifford Hooker, eds., *Images of Science: Scientific Realism Versus Constructive Empiricism*. Chicago: University of Chicago Press.

———. 1985b. "Observations, Explanatory Power, and Simplicity." In P. Achinstein and O. Hannaway, eds. *Observation, Experiment, and Hypothesis in Modern Physical Science*. Cambridge, Mass.: MIT Press.

———. 1985c. "The Logician's Dilemma: Deductive Logic, Inductive Inference and Logical Empiricism." *Erkenntnis* 22: 197–252.

———. Forthcoming. *Realism and the Moral Sciences* (unpublished manuscript).

Brink, D. 1984. "Moral Realism and the Skeptical Arguments from Disagreement and Queerness." *Australasian Journal of Philosophy* 62.2: 111–25.

———. 1989. *Moral Realism and the Foundation of Ethics*. Cambridge: Cambridge University Press.

Byerly, H., and V. Lazara. 1973. "Realist Foundations of Measurement." *Philosophy of Science* 40: 10–28.

Carnap, R. 1934. *The Unity of Science*. Trans. M. Black. London: Kegan Paul.

Dworkin, R. 1973. "The Original Position." *University of Chicago Law Review* 40: 500–33.

Feigl, H. 1956. "Some Major Issues and Developments in the Philosophy of Science of Logical Empiricism." In H. Feigl and M. Scriven. eds., *Minnesota Studies in the Philosophy of Science*, vol. I. Minneapolis: University of Minnesota Press.

Field, H. 1973. "Theory Change and the Indeterminacy of Reference." *Journal of Philosophy* 70: 462–81.

Gilbert, A. 1981a. *Marx's Politics: Communists and Citizens*. New Brunswick, N.J.: Rutgers University Press.

———. 1981b. "Historical Theory and the Structure of Moral Argument in Marx," *Political Theory* 9: 173–205.

———. 1982. "An Ambiguity in Marx's and Engel's Account of Justice and Equality," *American Political Science Review* 76: 328–46.

———. 1984a. "The Storming of Heaven: Capital and Marx's Politics." In J. R. Pennock, ed., *Marxism Today*, Nomos 26. New York: New York University Press.

———. 1984b. "Marx's Moral Realism: Eudaimonism and Moral Progress." In J. Farr and T. Ball, eds., *After Marx*, Cambridge: Cambridge University Press.

———. 1986a. "Moral Realism, Individuality and Justice in War," *Political Theory* 14: 105–35.

———. 1986b. "Democracy and Individuality," *Social Philosophy and Policy* 3: 19–58.

———. Forthcoming. *Equality and Objectivity*.

Goldman, A. 1967. "A Causal Theory of Knowing." *Journal of Philosophy* 64: 357–72.

———. 1976. "Discrimination and Perceptual Knowledge." *Journal of Philosophy* 73: 771–91.

Goodman, N. 1973. *Fact, Fiction, and Forecast*. 3d ed. Indianapolis: Bobbs-Merrill.

Gould, S. J. 1981. *The Mismeasure of Man*. New York: W. W. Norton.

Hanson, N. R. 1958. *Patterns of Discovery*. Cambridge: Cambridge University Press.

Kamin, L. J. 1974. *The Science and Politics of I.Q.* Potomac, Md.: Lawrence Erlbaum Associates.

Kripke, S. A. 1971. "Identity and Necessity." In M. K. Munitz, ed., *Identity and Individuation*. New York: New York University Press.

———. 1972. "Naming and Necessity." In D. Davidson and G. Harman, eds., *The Semantics of Natural Language*. Dordrecht, Netherlands: D. Reidel.

Kuhn, T. 1970. *The Structure of Scientific Revolutions*. 2d ed. Chicago: University of Chicago Press.

Mackie, J. L. 1974. *The Cement of the Universe*. Oxford: Oxford University Press.

Mayr, E. 1970. *Populations. Species and Evolution*. Cambridge: Harvard University Press.

Miller, R. 1978. "Methodological Individualism and Social Explanation." *Philosophy of Science* 45: 387–414.

———. 1979. "Reason and Commitment in the Social Sciences." *Philosophy and Public Affairs* 8: 241–66.

———. 1981. "Rights and Reality." *Philosophical Review* 90: 383–407.

———. 1982. "Rights and Consequences." *Midwest Studies in Philosophy* 7: 151–74.

———. 1983. "Marx and Morality." *Nomos* 26: 3–32.

———. 1984a. *Analyzing Marx*. Princeton: Princeton University Press.

———. 1984b. "Ways of Moral Learning." *Philosophical Review* 94: 507–56.

Putnam, H. 1975a. "The Meaning of 'Meaning'." In H. Putnam, *Mind, Language and Reality*. Cambridge: Cambridge University Press.

———. 1975b. "Language and Reality." In H. Putnam. *Mind, Language and Reality*. Cambridge: Cambridge University Press.

———. 1983. "Vagueness and Alternative Logic." In H. Putnam. *Realism and Reason*. Cambridge: Cambridge University Press.

Quine, W. V. O. 1969a. "Natural Kinds." In W. V. O. Quine. *Ontological Relativity and Other Essays*. New York: Columbia University Press.

———. 1969b. "Epistemology Naturalized." In W. V. O. Quine, *Ontological Relativity and Other Essays*. New York: Columbia University Press.

Railton, P. 1986. "Moral Realism." *Philosophical Review* 95: 163–207.

Rawls, J. 1971. *A Theory of Justice*. Cambridge, Mass.: Harvard University Press.

Shoemaker, S. 1980. "Causality and Properties." In P. van Inwagen. ed., *Time and Cause*. Dordecht, Netherlands: D. Reidel.

Sturgeon, N. 1984a. "Moral Explanations." In D. Copp and D. Zimmerman, eds., *Morality, Reason and Truth*. Totowa, N.J.: Rowman and Allanheld. Reprinted in this volume.

———. 1984b. "Review of P. Foot, *Moral Relativism and Virtues and Vices*." *Journal of Philosophy* 81: 326–33.

van Fraassen, B. 1980. *The Scientific Image*. Oxford: Oxford University Press.

Wood, A. 1972. "The Marxian Critique of Justice." *Philosophy and Public Affairs* 1: 244–82.

———. 1979. "Marx on Right and Justice: A reply to Husami." *Philosophy and Public Affairs* 8: 267–95.

———. 1984. "A Marxian Approach to 'The Problem of Justice.' " *Philosophica* 33: 9–32.

8

Moral Realism

PETER RAILTON

Among contemporary philosophers, even those who have not found skepticism about empirical science at all compelling have tended to find skepticism about morality irresistible. For various reasons, among them an understandable suspicion of moral absolutism, it has been thought a mark of good sense to explain away any appearance of objectivity in moral discourse. So common has it become in secular intellectual culture to treat morality as subjective or conventional that most of us now have difficulty imagining what it might be like for there to be facts to which moral judgments answer.

Undaunted, some philosophers have attempted to establish the objectivity of morality by arguing that reason, or science, affords a foundation for ethics. The history of such attempts hardly inspires confidence. Although rationalism in ethics has retained adherents long after other rationalisms have been abandoned, the powerful philosophical currents that have worn away at the idea that unaided reason might afford a standpoint from which to derive substantive conclusions show no signs of slackening. And ethical naturalism has yet to find a plausible synthesis of the empirical and the normative: the more it has given itself over to descriptive accounts of the origin of norms, the less has it retained recognizably moral force; the more it has undertaken to provide a recognizable basis for moral criticism or reconstruction, the less has it retained a firm connection with descriptive social or psychological theory.[1]

In what follows, I will present in a programmatic way a form of ethical naturalism that owes much to earlier theorists, but that seeks to effect a more satisfactory linkage of the normative to the empirical. The link cannot, I believe, be effected by proof. It is no more my aim to refute moral skepticism than it is the aim of contemporary epistemic naturalists to refute Cartesian skepticism. The naturalist in either case has more modest aspirations. First, he seeks to provide an analysis of epistemology or ethics that permits us to see how the central evaluative functions of this domain could be carried out within existing (or prospective) empirical theories. Second, he attempts to show how traditional non-naturalist accounts rely upon assumptions that are in some way incoherent, or that fit in with existing science. And third, he presents to the skeptic a certain challenge, namely, to show how a skeptical account of our epistemic or moral practices could be as plausible, useful, or interesting as the account the naturalist offers, and how a skeptical reconstruction of such practices—should the skeptic, as often he does, attempt one—could succeed in preserving their distinctive place and function in human affairs. I will primarily be occupied with the first of these three aspirations.

One thing should be said at the outset. Some may be drawn to, or repelled by, moral realism out of a sense that it is the view of ethics that best expresses high moral earnestness. Yet one can be serious about morality, even to a fault, without being a moral realist. Indeed, a possible objection to the sort of moral realism I will defend here is that it may not make morality serious enough.

I. SPECIES OF MORAL REALISM

Such diverse views have claimed to be—or have been accused of being—realist about morality, that an initial characterization of the position I will defend is needed before proceeding further. Claims—and accusations—of moral realism typically extend along some or all of the following dimensions. Roughly put: (1) Cognitivism—Are moral judgments capable of truth and falsity? (2) Theories of truth—If moral judgments do have truth values, in what sense? (3) Objectivity—In what ways, if any, does the existence of moral properties depend upon the actual or possible states of mind of intelligent beings? (4) Reductionism—Are moral properties reducible to, or do they in some weaker sense supervene upon, non-moral properties? (5) Naturalism—Are moral properties natural

properties? (6) Empiricism—Do we come to know moral facts in the same way we come to know the facts of empirical science, or are they revealed by reason or by some special mode of apprehension? (7) Bivalence—Does the principle of the excluded middle apply to moral judgments? (8) Determinateness—Given whatever procedures we have for assessing moral judgments, how much of morality is likely to be determinable? (9) Categoricity—Do all rational agents necessarily have some reason to obey moral imperatives? (10) Universality—Are moral imperatives applicable to all rational agents, even (should such exist) those who lack a reason to comply with them? (11) Assessment of existing moralities—Are present moral beliefs approximately true, or do prevailing moral intuitions in some other sense constitute privileged data? (12) Relativism—Does the truth or warrant of moral judgments depend directly upon individually- or socially-adopted norms or practices? (13) Pluralism—Is there a uniquely good form of life or a uniquely right moral code, or could different forms of life or moral codes be appropriate in different circumstances?

Here, then, are the approximate coordinates of my own view in this multidimensional conceptual space. I will argue for a form of moral realism which holds that moral judgments can bear truth values in a fundamentally non-epistemic sense of truth; that moral properties are objective, though relational; that moral properties supervene upon natural properties, and may be reducible to them; that moral inquiry is of a piece with empirical inquiry; that it cannot be known *a priori* whether bivalence holds for moral judgments or how determinately such judgments can be assessed; that there is reason to think we know a fair amount about morality, but also reason to think that current moralities are wrong in certain ways and could be wrong in quite general ways; that a rational agent may fail to have a reason for obeying moral imperatives, although they may nonetheless be applicable to him; and that, while there are perfectly general criteria of moral assessment, nonetheless, by the nature of these criteria no one kind of life is likely to be appropriate for all individuals and no one set of norms appropriate for all societies and all times. The position thus described might well be called 'stark, raving moral realism', but for the sake of syntax, I will colorlessly call it 'moral realism'. This usage is not proprietary. Other positions, occupying more or less different coordinates, may have equal claim to either name.

II. THE FACT/VALUE DISTINCTION

Any attempt to argue for a naturalistic moral realism runs headlong into the fact/value distinction. Philosophers have given various accounts of this distinction, and of the arguments for it, but for present purposes I will focus upon several issues concerning the epistemic and ontological status of judgments of value as opposed to judgments of fact.

Perhaps the most frequently heard argument for the fact/value distinction is epistemic: it is claimed that disputes over questions of value can persist even after all rational or scientific means of adjudication have been deployed, hence, value judgments cannot be cognitive in the sense that factual or logical judgments are. This claim is defended in part by appeal to the instrumental (hypothetical) character of reason, which prevents reason from dictating ultimate values. In principle, the argument runs, two individuals who differ in ultimate values could, without manifesting any rational defect, hold fast to their conflicting values in the face of any amount of argumentation or evidence. As Ayer puts it, "we find that argument is possible on moral questions only if some system of values is presupposed."[2]

One might attempt to block this conclusion by challenging the instrumental conception of rationality. But for all its faults and for all that it needs to be developed, the instrumental conception seems to me the clear-

est notion we have of what it is for an agent to have reasons to act. Moreover, it captures a central normative feature of reason-giving, since we can readily see the commending force for an agent of the claim that a given act would advance his ends. It would be hard to make much sense of someone who sincerely claimed to have certain ends and yet at the same time insisted that they could not provide him even *prima facie* grounds for action. (Of course, he might also believe that he has other, perhaps countervailing, grounds.)

Yet this version of the epistemic argument for the fact/value distinction is in difficulty even granting the instrumental conception of rationality. From the standpoint of instrumental reason, belief-formation is but one activity among others: to the extent that we have reasons for engaging in it, or for doing it one way rather than another, these are at bottom a matter of its contribution to our ends.[3] What it would be rational for an individual to believe on the basis of a given experience will vary not only with respect to his other beliefs, but also with respect to what he desires.[4] From this it follows that no amount of mere argumentation or experience could force one on pain of irrationality to accept even the factual claims of empirical science. The long-running debate over inductive logic well illustrates that rational choice among competing hypotheses requires much richer and more controversial criteria of theory choice than can be squeezed from instrumental reason alone. Unfortunately for the contrast Ayer wished to make, we find that argument is possible on scientific questions only if some system of values is presupposed.

However, Hume had much earlier found a way of marking the distinction between facts and values without appeal to the idea that induction—or even deduction—could require a rational agent to adopt certain beliefs rather than others when this would conflict with his contingent ends.[5] For Hume held the thesis that morality is practical, by which he meant that if moral facts existed, they would necessarily provide a reason (although perhaps not an overriding reason) for moral action to all rational beings, regardless of their particular desires. Given this thesis as a premise, the instrumental conception of rationality can clinch the argument after all, for it excludes the possibility of categorical reasons of this kind. By contrast, Hume did not suppose it to be constitutive of logic or science that the facts revealed by these forms of inquiry have categorical force for rational agents, so the existence of logical and scientific facts, unlike the existence of moral facts, is compatible with the instrumental character of reason.

Yet this way of drawing the fact/value distinction is only as compelling as the claim that morality is essentially practical in Hume's sense.[6] Hume is surely right in claiming there to be an intrinsic connection, no doubt complex, between valuing something and having some sort of positive attitude toward it that provides one with an instrumental reason for action. We simply would disbelieve someone who claimed to value honesty and yet never showed the slightest urge to act honestly when given an easy opportunity. But this is a fact about the connection between the values *embraced by* an individual and his reasons for action, not a fact showing a connection between moral evaluation and rational motivation.

Suppose for example that we accept Hume's characterization of justice as an artificial virtue directed at the general welfare. This is in a recognizable sense an evaluative or normative notion—"a value" in the loose sense in which this term is used in such debates—yet it certainly does not follow from its definition that every rational being, no matter what his desires, who believes that some or other act is just in this sense will have an instrumental reason to perform it. A rational individual may fail to value justice for its own sake, and may have ends contrary to it. In Hume's discussion of our "interested obligation" to be just, he seems to recognize

that in the end it may not be possible to show that a "sensible knave" has a reason to be just. Of course, Hume held that the rest of us—whose hearts rebel at Sensible Knave's attitude that he may break his word, cheat, or steal whenever it suits his purposes—have reason to be just, to deem Knave's attitude unjust, and to try to protect ourselves from his predations.[7]

Yet Knave himself could say, perhaps because he accepts Hume's analysis of justice, "Yes, my attitude is unjust." And by Hume's own account of the relation of reason and passion, Knave could add "But what is that to me?" without failing to grasp the content of his previous assertion. Knave, let us suppose, has no doubts about the intelligibility or reality of "the general welfare," and thinks it quite comprehensible that people attach great significance in public life to the associated notion of justice. He also realizes that for the bulk of mankind, whose passions differ from his, being just is a source and a condition of much that is most worthwhile in life. He thus understands that appeals to justice typically have motivating force. Moreover, he himself uses the category of justice in analyzing the social world, and he recognizes—indeed, his knavish calculations take into account—the distinction between those individuals and institutions that truly are just, and those that merely appear just or are commonly regarded as just. Knave does view a number of concepts with wide currency—religious ones, for example—as mere fictions that prey on weak minds, but he does not view justice in this way. Weak minds and moralists have, he thinks, surrounded justice with certain myths—that justice is its own reward, that once one sees what is just one will automatically have a reason to do it, and so on. But then, he thinks that weak minds and moralists have likewise surrounded wealth and power with myths—that the wealthy are not truly happy, that the powerful inevitably ride for a fall, and so on—and he does not on this account doubt whether there are such things as wealth and power. Knave is glad to be free of prevailing myths about wealth, power, and justice; glad, too, that he is free in his own mind to pay as much or as little attention to any of these attributes as his desires and circumstances warrant. He might, for example, find Mae West's advice convincing: diamonds are very much worth acquiring, and "goodness ha[s] nothing to do with it."

We therefore must distinguish the business of saying what an individual values from the business of saying what it is for him to make measurements against the criteria of a species of evaluation that he recognizes to be genuine.[8]

To deny Hume's thesis of the practicality of moral judgment, and so remove the ground of his contrast between facts and values, is not to deny that morality has an action-guiding character. Morality surely can remain prescriptive within an instrumental framework, and can recommend itself to us in much the same way that, say, epistemology does: various significant and enduring—though perhaps not universal—human ends can be advanced if we apply certain evaluative criteria to our actions. That may be enough to justify to ourselves our abiding concern with the epistemic or moral status of what we do.[9]

By arguing that reason does not compel us to adopt particular beliefs or practices apart from our contingent, and variable, ends, I may seem to have failed to negotiate my way past epistemic relativism, and thus to have wrecked the argument for moral realism before it has even left port. Rationality does go relative when it goes instrumental, but epistemology need not follow. The epistemic warrant of an individual's belief may be disentangled from the rationality of his holding it, for epistemic warrant may be tied to an external criterion—as it is for example by causal or reliabilist theories of knowledge.[10] It is part of the naturalistic realism that informs this essay to adopt such a criterion of warrant. We should not confuse the obvious fact that in general our ends are well served by reliable causal mechanisms of belief-formation with an internalist claim to the effect that reason requires us to adopt such means. Reliable mechanisms have costs as well as benefits, and successful pursuit of some ends—Knave would point to religious ones, and to those of certain moralists—may in some respects be incompatible with adoption of reliable means of inquiry.

This rebuttal of the charge of relativism invites the defender of the fact/value distinction to shift to ontological ground. Perhaps facts and values cannot be placed on opposite sides of an epistemological divide marked off by what reason and experience can compel us to accept. Still, the idea of reliable causal mechanisms for moral learning, and of moral facts "in the world" upon which they operate, is arguably so bizarre that I may have done no more than increase my difficulties.

III. VALUE REALISM

The idea of causal interaction with moral reality certainly would be intolerably odd if moral facts were held to be *sui generis*;[11] but there need be nothing odd about causal mechanisms for learning moral facts if these facts are constituted by natural facts, and that is the view under consideration. This response will remain unconvincing, however, until some positive argument for realism about moral facts is given. So let us turn to that task.

What might be called 'the generic stratagem of naturalistic realism' is to postulate a realm of facts in virtue of the contribution they would make to the *a posteriori* explanation of certain features of our experience. For example, an external world is posited to explain the coherence, stability, and intersubjectivity of sense-experience. A moral realist who would avail himself of this stratagem must show that the postulation of moral facts similarly can have an explanatory function. The stratagem can succeed in either case only if the reality postulated has these two characteristics:

1. *independence:* it exists and has certain determinate features independent of whether we think it exists or has those features, independent, even, of whether we have good reason to think this;
2. *feedback:* it is such—and we are such—that we are able to interact with it, and this interaction exerts the relevant sort of shaping influence or control upon our perceptions, thought, and action.

These two characteristics enable the realist's posit to play a role in the explanation of our experience that cannot be replaced without loss by our mere *conception* of ourselves or our world. For although our conceptual scheme mediates even our most basic perceptual experiences, an experience-transcendent reality has ways of making itself felt without the permission of our conceptual scheme—causally. The success or failure of our plans and projects famously is not determined by expectation alone. By resisting or yielding to our worldly efforts in ways not anticipated by our going conceptual scheme, an external reality that is never directly revealed in perception may nonetheless significantly influence the subsequent evolution of that scheme.

The realist's use of an external world to explain sensory experience has often been criticized as no more than a picture. But do we even have a picture of what a realist explanation might look like in the case of values?[12] I will try to sketch one, filling in first a realist account of non-moral value—the notion of something being desirable for someone, or good for him.[13]

Consider first the notion of someone's *subjective interests*—his wants or desires, conscious or unconscious. Subjective interest can be seen as a secondary quality, akin to taste. For me to take a subjective interest in something is to say that it has a positive *valence* for me, that is, that in ordinary circumstances it

excites a positive attitude or inclination (not necessarily conscious) in me. Similarly, for me to say that I find sugar sweet is to say that in ordinary circumstances sugar excites a certain gustatory sensation in me. As secondary qualities, subjective interest and perceived sweetness supervene upon primary qualities of the perceiver, the object (or other phenomenon) perceived, and the surrounding context: the perceiver is so constituted that this sort of object in this sort of context will excite that sort of sensation. Call this complex set of relational, dispositional, primary qualities the *reduction basis* of the secondary quality.

We have in this reduction basis an objective notion that corresponds to, and helps explain, subjective interests. But it is not a plausible foundation for the notion of non-moral goodness, since the subjective interests it grounds have insufficient normative force to capture the idea of desirableness. My subjective interests frequently reflect ignorance, confusion, or lack of consideration, as hindsight attests. The fact that I am now so constituted that I desire something which, had I better knowledge of it, I would wish I had never sought, does not seem to recommend it to me as part of my good.

To remedy this defect, let us introduce the notion of an *objectified subjective interest* for an individual A, as follows.[14] Give to an actual individual A unqualified cognitive and imaginative powers, and full factual and nomological information about his physical and psychological constitution, capacities, circumstances, history, and so on. A will have become A+, who has complete and vivid knowledge of himself and his environment, and whose instrumental rationality is in no way defective. We now ask A+ to tell us not what *he* currently wants, but what he would want his non-idealized self A to want—or, more generally, to seek—were he to find himself in the actual condition and circumstances of A.[15] Just as we assumed there to be a reduction basis for an individual A's actual subjective interests, we may assume there to be a reduction basis for his objectified subjective interests, namely, those facts about A and his circumstances that $A+$ would combine with his general knowledge in arriving at his views about what he would want to want were he to step into A's shoes.

For example, Lonnie, a traveler in a foreign country, is feeling miserable. He very much wishes to overcome his malaise and to settle his stomach, and finds he has a craving for the familiar: a tall glass of milk. The milk is desired by Lonnie, but is it also desirable for him? Lonnie-Plus can see that what is wrong with Lonnie, in addition to homesickness, is dehydration, a common affliction of tourists, but one often not detectable from introspective evidence. The effect of drinking hard-to-digest milk would be to further unsettle Lonnie's stomach and worsen his dehydration. By contrast, Lonnie-Plus can see that abundant clear fluids would quickly improve Lonnie's physical condition—which, incidentally, would help with his homesickness as well. Lonnie-Plus can also see just how distasteful Lonnie would find it to drink clear liquids, just what would happen were Lonnie to continue to suffer dehydration, and so on. As a result of this information, Lonnie-Plus might then come to desire that were he to assume Lonnie's place, he would want to drink clear liquids rather than milk, or at least want to act in such a way that a want of this kind would be satisfied. The reduction basis of this objectified interest includes facts about Lonnie's circumstances and constitution, which determine, among other things, his existing tastes and his ability to acquire certain new tastes, the consequences of continued dehydration, the effects and availability of various sorts of liquids, and so on.

Let us say that this reduction basis is the constellation of primary qualities that make it be the case that the Lonnie has a certain *objective interest*.[16] That is, we will say that Lonnie has an objective interest in drinking clear liquids in virtue of this complex, relational, dispositional set of facts. Put another way, we can say that the reduction basis, not the fact that Lonnie-Plus would have certain

wants, is the truth-maker for the claim that this is an objective interest of Lonnie's. The objective interest thus explains why there is a certain objectified interest, not the other way around.[17]

Let us now say that X is *non-morally good for A* if and only if X would satisfy an objective interest of A.[18] We may think of $A+$'s views about what he would want to want were he in A's place as generating a ranking of potential objective interests of A, a ranking that will reflect what is better or worse for A and will allow us to speak of A's actual wants as better or worse approximations of what is best for him. We may also decompose $A+$'s views into *prima facie* as opposed to "on balance" objective interests of A, the former yielding the notion of '*a good for A*', the latter, of '*the good for A*'.[19]

This seems to me an intuitively plausible account of what someone's non-moral good consists in: roughly, what he would want himself to seek if he knew what he were doing.[20]

Moreover, this account preserves what seems to me an appropriate link between non-moral value and motivation. Suppose that one desires X, but wonders whether X really is part of one's good. This puzzlement typically arises because one feels that one knows too little about X, oneself, or one's world, or because one senses that one is not being adequately rational or reflective in assessing the information one has—perhaps one suspects that one has been captivated by a few salient features of X (or repelled by a few salient features of its alternatives). If one were to learn that one would still want oneself to want X in the circumstances were one to view things with full information and rationality, this presumably would reduce the force of the original worry. By contrast, were one to learn that when fully informed and rational one would want oneself *not* to want X in the circumstances, this presumably would add force to it. Desires being what they are, a reinforced worry might not be sufficient to remove the desire for X. But if one were to become genuinely and vividly convinced that one's desire for X is in this sense not supported by full reflection upon the facts, one presumably would feel this to be a count against acting upon the desire. This adjustment of desire to belief might not in a given case be required by reason or logic; it might be "merely psychological." But it is precisely such psychological phenomena that naturalistic theories of value take as basic.

In what follows, we will need the notion of intrinsic goodness, so let us say that X is *intrinsically non-morally good for A* just in case X is in A's objective interest without reference to any other objective interest of A. We can in an obvious way use the notion of objective intrinsic interest to account for all other objective interests. Since individuals and their environments differ in many respects, we need not assume that everyone has the same objective intrinsic interests. *A fortiori*, we need not assume that they have the same objective instrumental interests. We should, however, expect that when personal and situational similarities exist across individuals—that is, when there are similarities in reduction bases—there will to that extent be corresponding similarities in their interests.

It is now possible to see how the notion of non-moral goodness can have explanatory uses. For a start, it can explain why one's actual desires have certain counterfactual features, for example, why one would have certain hypothetical desires rather than others were one to become fully informed and aware. Yet this sort of explanatory use—following as it does directly from the definition of objective interest—might well be thought unimpressive unless some other explanatory functions can be found.

Consider, then, the difference between Lonnie and Tad, another traveler in the same straits, but one who, unlike Lonnie, wants to drink clear liquids, and proceeds to do so. Tad will perk up while Lonnie remains listless. We can explain this difference by noting that although both Lonnie and Tad acted upon their wants, Tad's wants better reflected his interests. The congruence of Tad's wants with his interests may be fortuitous, or it may be that Tad knows he is dehydrated and knows the standard treatment. In the latter case we would ordinarily say that the explanation of the difference in their condition is that Tad, but not Lonnie, "knew what was good for him."

Generally, we can expect that what $A+$ would want to want were he in A's place will correlate well with what would permit A to experience physical or psychological well-being or to escape physical or psychological ill-being. Surely our well- or ill-being are among the things that matter to us most, and most reliably, even on reflection.[21] Appeal to degrees of congruence between A's wants and his interests thus will often help to explain facts about how satisfactory he finds his life. Explanation would not be preserved were we to substitute 'believed to be congruent' for 'are (to such-and-such a degree) congruent', since, as cases like Lonnie's show, even if one were to convince oneself that one's wants accurately reflected one's interests, acting on these wants might fail to yield much satisfaction.

In virtue of the correlation to be expected between acting upon motives that congrue with one's interests and achieving a degree of satisfaction or avoiding a degree of distress, one's objective interests may also play an explanatory role in the *evolution* of one's desires. Consider what I will call the *wants/interests mechanism*, which permits individuals to achieve self-conscious and unselfconscious learning about their interests through experience. In the simplest sorts of cases, trial and error leads to the selective retention of wants that are satisfiable and lead to satisfactory results for the agent.

For example, suppose that Lonnie gives in to his craving and drinks the milk. Soon afterwards, he feels much worse. Still unable to identify the source of his malaise and still in the grips of a desire for the familiar, his attention is caught by a green-and-red sign in the window of a small shop he is moping past: "7-Up," it says. He rushes inside and buys a bottle. Although it is lukewarm, he drinks it eagerly. "Mmm," he thinks, "I'll have another." He buys a second bottle, and drains it to the bottom. By now he has had his fill of tepid soda, and carries on. Within a few hours, his mood is improving. When he passes the store again on the way back to his hotel, his pleasant association with drinking 7-Up leads him to buy some more and carry it along with him. That night, in the dim solitude of his room, he finds the soda's reassuringly familiar taste consoling, and so downs another few bottles before finally finding sleep. When he wakes up the next morning, he feels very much better. To make a dull story short: the next time Lonnie is laid low abroad, he may have some conscious or unconscious, reasoned or superstitious, tendency to seek out 7-Up. Unable to find that, he might seek something quite like it, say, a local lime-flavored soda or perhaps even the *agua mineral con gaz* he had previously scorned. Over time, as Lonnie travels more and suffers similar malaise, he regularly drinks clearish liquids and regularly feels better, eventually developing an actual desire for such liquids—and an aversion to other drinks, such as milk—in such circumstances.

Thus have Lonnie's desires evolved through experience to conform more closely to what is good for him, in the naturalistic sense intended here. The process was not one of an ideally rational response to the receipt of ideal information, but rather of largely unreflective experimentation, accompanied by positive and negative associations and reinforcements. There is no guarantee that the desires "learned" through such feedback will accurately or completely reflect an individual's good. Still less is there any guarantee that, even when an appropriate adjustment in desire occurs, the agent will comprehend the origin of his new desires or be able to represent to himself the nature the interests they reflect. But then, it is a quite general feature of the various means by which we learn about the world that they may fail to provide accu-

rate or comprehending representations of it. My ability to perceive and understand my surroundings coexists with, indeed draws upon the same mechanisms as, my liability to deception by illusion, expectation, or surface appearance.

There are some broad theoretical grounds for thinking that something like the wants/interests mechanism exists and has an important role in desire-formation. Humans are creatures motivated primarily by wants rather than instincts. If such creatures were unable through experience to conform their wants at all closely to their essential interests—perhaps because they were no more likely to experience positive internal states when their essential interests are met than when they are not—we could not expect long or fruitful futures for them. Thus, if humans in general did not come to want to eat the kinds of food necessary to maintain some degree of physical well-being, or to engage in the sorts of activities or relations necessary to maintain their sanity, we would not be around today to worry whether we can know what is good for us. Since creatures as sophisticated and complex as humans have evolved through encounters with a variety of environments, and indeed have made it their habit to modify their environments, we should expect considerable flexibility in our capacity through experience to adapt our wants to our interests. However, this very flexibility makes the mechanism unreliable: our wants may at any time differ arbitrarily much from our interests; moreover, we may fail to have experiences that would cause us to notice this, or to undergo sufficient feedback to have much chance of developing new wants that more nearly approximate our interests. It is entirely possible, and hardly infrequent, that an individual live out the course of a normal life without ever recognizing or adjusting to some of his most fundamental interests. Individual limitations are partly remedied by cultural want-acquiring mechanisms, which permit learning and even theorizing over multiple lives and life-spans, but these same mechanisms also create a vast potential for the inculcation of wants at variance with interests.

The argument for the wants/interests mechanism has about the same status, and the same breezy plausibility, as the more narrowly biological argument that we should expect the human eye to be capable of detecting objects the size and shape of our predators or prey. It is not necessary to assume anything approaching infallibility, only enough functional success to hold our own in an often inhospitable world.[22]

Thus far the argument has concerned only those objective interests that might be classified as needs, but the wants/interests mechanism can operate with respect to any interest—even interests related to an individual's particular aptitudes or social role—whose frustration is attended even indirectly by consciously or unconsciously unsatisfactory results for him. (To be sure, the more indirect the association the more unlikely that the mechanism will be reliable.) For example, the experience of taking courses in both mathematics and philosophy may lead an undergraduate who thought himself cut out to be a mathematician to come to prefer a career in philosophy, which would in fact better suit his aptitudes and attitudes. And a worker recently promoted to management from the shop floor may find himself less inclined to respond to employee grievances than he had previously wanted managers to be, while his former co-workers may find themselves less inclined to confide in him than before.

If a wants/interests mechanism is postulated, and if what is non-morally good for someone is a matter of what is in his objective interest, then we can say that objective value is able to play a role in the explanation of subjective value of the sort the naturalistic realist about value needs. These explanations even support some qualified predictions: for example, that, other things equal, individuals will ordinarily be better judges of their own interests than third parties; that

knowledge of one's interests will tend to increase with increased experience and general knowledge; that people with similar personal and social characteristics will tend to have similar values; and that there will be greater general consensus upon what is desirable in those areas of life where individuals are most alike in other regards (e.g., at the level of basic motives), and where trial-and-error mechanisms can be expected to work well (e.g., where esoteric knowledge is not required). I am in no position to pronounce these predictions correct, but it may be to their credit that they accord with widely-held views.

It should perhaps be emphasized that although I speak of the objectivity of value, the value in question is human value, and exists only because humans do. In the sense of old-fashioned theory of value, this is a relational rather than absolute notion of goodness. Although relational, the relevant facts about humans and their world are objective in the same sense that such non-relational entities as stones are: they do not depend for their existence or nature merely upon our conception of them.[23]

Thus understood, objective interests are supervenient upon natural and social facts. Does this mean that they cannot contribute to explanation after all, since it should always be possible in principle to account for any particular fact that they purport to explain by reference to the supervenience basis alone? If mere supervenience were grounds for denying an explanatory role to a given set of concepts, then we would have to say that chemistry, biology, and electrical engineering, which clearly supervene upon physics, lack explanatory power. Indeed, even outright reducibility is no ground for doubting explanatoriness. To establish a relation of reduction between, for example, a chemical phenomenon such as valence and a physical model of the atom does nothing to suggest that there is no such thing as valence, or that generalizations involving valence cannot support explanations. There can be no issue here of ontological economy or eschewing unnecessary entities, as might be the case if valence were held to be something *sui generis*, over and above any constellation of physical properties. The facts described in principles of chemical valence are genuine, and permit a powerful and explanatory systematization of chemical combination; the existence of a successful reduction to atomic physics only bolsters these claims.

We are confident that the notion of chemical valence is explanatory because proffered explanations in terms of chemical valence insert explananda into a distinctive and well-articulated nomic nexus, in an obvious way increasing our understanding of them. But what comparably powerful and illuminating theory exists concerning the notion of objective interest to give us reason to think—whether or not strict reduction is possible—that proffered explanations using this notion are genuinely informative?

I would find the sort of value realism sketched here uninteresting if it seemed to me that no theory of any consequence could be developed using the category of objective value. But in describing the wants/interests mechanism I have already tried to indicate that such a theory may be possible. When we seek to explain why people act as they do, why they have certain values or desires, and why sometimes they are led into conflict and other times into cooperation, it comes naturally to common sense and social science alike to talk in terms of people's interests. Such explanations will be incomplete and superficial if we remain wholly at the level of subjective interests, since these, too, must be accounted for.[24]

IV. NORMATIVE REALISM

Suppose everything said thus far to have been granted generously. Still, I would as yet have no right to speak of *moral* realism, for I have done no more than to exhibit the possibility of a kind of realism with regard to non-moral goodness, a notion that perfect moral skep-

tics can admit. To be entitled to speak of moral realism I would have to show realism to be possible about distinctively moral value, or moral norms. I will concentrate on moral norms—that is, matters of moral rightness and wrongness—although the argument I give may, by extension, be applied to moral value. In part, my reason is that normative realism seems much less plausible intuitively than value realism. It therefore is not surprising that many current proposals for moral realism focus essentially upon value—and sometimes only upon what is in effect nonmoral value. Yet on virtually any conception of morality, a moral theory must yield an account of rightness.

Normative moral realism is implausible on various grounds, but within the framework of this essay, the most relevant is that it seems impossible to extend the generic strategy of naturalistic realism to moral norms. Where is the place in explanation for facts about what *ought* to be the case—don't facts about the way things are do all the explaining there is to be done? Of course they do. But then, my naturalistic moral realism commits me to the view that facts about what ought to be the case are facts of a special kind about the way things are. As a result, it may be possible for them to have a function within an explanatory theory. To see how this could be, let me first give some examples of explanations outside the realm of morality that involve naturalized norms.

"Why did the roof collapse?—For a house that gets the sort of snow loads that one did, the rafters ought to have been 2×8's at least, not 2×6's." This explanation is quite acceptable, as far as it goes, yet it contains an 'ought'. Of course, we can remove this 'ought' as follows: "If a roof of that design is to withstand the snow load that one bore, then it must be framed with rafters at least 2×8 in cross-section." An architectural 'ought' is replaced by an engineering 'if . . . then . . .'. This is possible because the 'ought' clearly is hypothetical, reflecting the universal architectural goal of making roofs strong enough not to collapse. Because the goal is contextually fixed, and because there are more or less definite answers to the question of how to meet it, and moreover because the explanandum phenomenon is the result of a process that selects against instances that do not attain that goal, the 'ought'-containing account conveys explanatory information.[25] I will call this sort of explanation *criterial*: we explain why something happened by reference to a relevant criterion, given the existence of a process that in effect selects for (or against) phenomena that more (or less) closely approximate this criterion. Although the criterion is defined naturalistically, it may at the same time be of a kind to have a regulative role in human practice—in this case, in house-building.

A more familiar sort of criterial explanation involves norms of individual rationality. Consider the use of an instrumental theory of rationality to explain an individual's behavior in light of his beliefs and desires, or to account for the way an individual's beliefs change with experience.[26] Bobby Shaftoe went to sea because he believed it was the best way to make his fortune, and he wanted above all to make his fortune. Crewmate Reuben Ramsoe came to believe that he wasn't liked by the other deckhands because he saw that they taunted him and greeted his frequent lashings at the hands of the First Mate with unconcealed pleasure. These explanations work because the action or belief in question was quite rational for the agent in the circumstances, and because we correctly suppose both Shaftoe and Ramsoe to have been quite rational.

Facts about degrees of instrumental rationality enter into explanations in other ways as well. First, consider the question why Bobby Shaftoe has had more success than most like-minded individuals in achieving his goals. We may lay his success to the fact that Shaftoe is more instrumentally rational than most—perhaps he has greater-than-average acumen in estimating the probabilities of outcomes, or is more-reliable-than-average at deductive inference, or is more-imaginative-than-average in surveying alternatives.

Second, although we are all imperfect deliberators, our behavior may come to embody habits or strategies that enable us to approximate optimal rationality more closely than our deliberative defects would lead one to expect. The mechanism is simple. Patterns of beliefs and behaviors that do not exhibit much instrumental rationality will tend to be to some degree self-defeating, an incentive to change them, whereas patterns that exhibit greater instrumental rationality will tend to be to some degree rewarding, an incentive to continue them. These incentives may affect our beliefs and behaviors even though the drawbacks or advantages of the patterns in question do not receive conscious deliberation. In such cases we may be said to acquire these habits or strategies because they *are* more rational, without the intermediation of any *belief* on our part that they are. Thus, cognitive psychologists have mapped some of the unconscious strategies or heuristics we employ to enable our limited intellects to sift more data and make quicker and more consistent judgments than would be possible using more standard forms of explicit reasoning.[27] We unwittingly come to rely upon heuristics in part because they are selectively reinforced as a result of their instrumental advantages over standard, explicit reasoning, that is, in part because of their greater rationality. Similarly, we may, without realizing it or even being able to admit it to ourselves, develop patterns of behavior that encourage or discourage specific behaviors in others, such as the unconscious means by which we cause those whose company we do not enjoy not to enjoy our company. Finally, as children we may have been virtually incapable of making rational assessments when a distant gain required a proximate loss. Yet somehow over time we managed in largely nondeliberative ways to acquire various interesting habits, such as putting certain vivid thoughts about the immediate future at the periphery of our attention, which enable us as adults to march ourselves off to the dentist without a push from behind. Criterial explanation in terms of individual rationality thus extends to behaviors beyond the realm of deliberate action. And, as with the wants/interests mechanism, it is possible to see in the emergence of such behaviors something we can without distortion call learning.

Indeed, our tendency through experience to develop rational habits and strategies may cooperate with the wants/interests mechanism to provide the basis for an *extended* form of criterial explanation, in which an individual's rationality is assessed not relative to his occurrent beliefs and desires, but relative to his objective interests. The examples considered earlier of the wants/interests mechanism in fact involved elements of this sort of explanation, for they showed not only wants being adjusted to interests, but also behavior being adjusted to newly adjusted wants. Without appropriate alteration of behavior to reflect changing wants, the feedback necessary for learning about wants would not occur. With such alteration, the behavior itself may become more rational in the extended sense. An individual who is instrumentally rational is disposed to adjust means to ends; but one result of his undertaking a means—electing a course of study, or accepting a new job—may be a more informed assessment, and perhaps a reconsideration, of his ends.

The theory of individual rationality—in either its simple or its extended form—thus affords an instance of the sort needed to provide an example of normative realism. Evaluations of degrees of instrumental rationality play a prominent role in our explanations of individual behavior, but they simultaneously have normative force for the agent. Whatever other concerns an agent might have, it surely counts for him as a positive feature of an action that it is efficient relative to his beliefs and desires or, in the extended sense, efficient relative to beliefs and desires that would appropriately reflect his condition and circumstances.

The normative force of these theories of individual rationality does not, however, merely derive from their explanatory use. One can employ a theory of instrumental rationality to explain behavior while rejecting it as a normative theory of reasons, just as one can explain an action as due to irrationality without thereby endorsing unreason.[28] Instead, the connection between the normative and explanatory roles of the instrumental conception of rationality is traceable to their common ground: the human motivational system. It is a fact about us that we have ends and have the capacity for both deliberate action relative to our ends and nondeliberate adjustment of behavior to our ends. As a result, we face options among pathways across a landscape of possibilities variously valenced for us. Both when we explain the reasons for people's choices and the causes of their behavior and when we appeal to their intuitions about what it would be rational to decide or to do, we work this territory, for we make what use we can of facts about what does-in-fact or can-in-principle motivate agents.

Thus emerges the possibility of saying that facts exist about what individuals have reason to do, facts that may be substantially independent of, and more normatively compelling than, an agent's occurrent conception of his reasons. The argument for such realism about individual rationality is no stronger than the arguments for the double claim that the relevant conception of instrumental individual rationality has both explanatory power and the sort of commendatory force a theory of *reasons* must possess, but (although I will not discuss them further here) these arguments seem to me quite strong.

Passing now beyond the theory of individual rationality, let us ask what criterial explanations involving distinctively moral norms might look like. To ask this, we need to know what distinguishes moral norms from other criteria of assessment. Moral evaluation seems to be concerned most centrally with the assessment of conduct or character where the interests of more than one individual are at stake. Further, moral evaluation assesses actions or outcomes in a peculiar way: the interests of the strongest or most prestigious party do not always prevail, purely prudential reasons may be subordinated, and so on. More generally, moral resolutions are thought to be determined by criteria of choice that are *non-indexical* and in some sense *comprehensive* This has led a number of philosophers to seek to capture the special character of moral evaluation by identifying a *moral point of view* that is impartial, but equally concerned with all those potentially affected. Other ethical theorists have come to a similar conclusion by investigating the sorts of reasons we characteristically treat as relevant or irrelevant in moral discourse. Let us follow these trends. We thus may say that moral norms reflect a certain kind of rationality, rationality not from the point of view of any particular individual, but from what might be called a social point of view.[29]

By itself, the equation of moral rightness with rationality from a social point of view is not terribly restrictive, for, depending upon what one takes rationality to be, this equation could be made by a utilitarian, a Kantian, or even a non-cognitivist. That is as it should be, for if it is to capture what is distinctive about moral norms, it should be compatible with the broadest possible range of recognized moral theories. However, once one opts for a particular conception of rationality— such as the conception of rationality as efficient pursuit of the non-morally good, or as autonomous and universal self-legislation, or as a noncognitive expression of hypothetical endorsement—this schematic characterization begins to assume particular moral content. Here I have adopted an instrumentalist conception of rationality, and this—along with the account given of non-moral goodness—means that the argument for moral realism given below is an argument that pre-

supposes and purports to defend a particular substantive moral theory.[30]

What is this theory? Let me introduce an idealization of the notion of social rationality by considering what would be rationally approved of were the interests of all potentially affected individuals counted equally under circumstances of full and vivid information.[31] Because of the assumption of full and vivid information, the interests in question will be objective interests. Given the account of goodness proposed in Section III, this idealization is equivalent to what is rational from a social point of view with regard to the realization of intrinsic non-moral goodness. This seems to me to be a recognizable and intuitively plausible—if hardly uncontroversial—criterion of moral rightness. Relative moral rightness is a matter of relative degree of approximation to this criterion.

The question that now arises is whether the notion of degrees of moral rightness could participate in explanations of behavior or in processes of moral learning that parallel explanatory uses of the notion of degrees of individual rationality—especially, in the extended sense. I will try to suggest several ways in which it might.

Just as an individual who significantly discounts some of his interests will be liable to certain sorts of dissatisfaction, so will a social arrangement—for example, a form of production, a social or political hierarchy— that departs from social rationality by significantly discounting the interests of a particular group have a potential for dissatisfaction and unrest. Whether or not this potential will be realized depends upon a great many circumstances. Owing to socialization, or to other limitations on the experience or knowledge of members of this group, the wants/interests mechanism may not have operated in such a way that the wants of its members reflect their interests. As a result they may experience no direct frustration of their desires despite the discounting of their interests. Or, the group may be too scattered or too weak to mobilize effectively. Or, it may face overawing repression. On the other hand, certain social and historical circumstances favor the realization of this potential for unrest, for example, by providing members of this group with experiences that make them more likely to develop interest-congruent wants, by weakening the existing repressive apparatus, by giving them new access to resources or new opportunities for mobilization, or merely by dispelling the illusion that change is impossible. In such circumstances, one can expect the potential for unrest to manifest itself.

Just as explanations involving assessments of individual rationality were not always replaceable by explanations involving individual *beliefs about* what would be rational, so, too, explanations involving assessments of social rationality cannot be replaced by explanations involving *beliefs about* what would be morally right. For example, discontent may arise because a society departs from social rationality, but not as a result of a belief that this is the case. Suppose that a given society is believed by all constituents to be just. This belief may help to stabilize it, but if in fact the interests of certain groups are being discounted, there will be a potential for unrest that may manifest itself in various ways—in alienation, loss of morale, decline in the effectiveness of authority, and so on—well before any changes in belief about the society's justness occur, and that will help explain why members of certain groups come to believe it to be unjust, if in fact they do.

In addition to possessing a certain sort of potential for unrest, societies that fail to approximate social rationality may share other features as well: they may exhibit a tendency toward certain religious or ideological doctrines, or toward certain sorts of repressive apparatus; they may be less productive in some ways (e.g., by failing to develop certain human resources) and more productive in others (e.g., by extracting greater labor from some groups at less cost), and thus may

be differentially economically successful depending upon the conditions of production they face, and so on.

If a notion of social rationality is to be a legitimate part of empirical explanations of such phenomena, an informative characterization of the circumstances under which departures from, or approximations to, social rationality could be expected to lead to particular social outcomes—especially, of the conditions under which groups whose interests are sacrificed could be expected to exhibit or mobilize discontent—must be available. Although it cannot be known *a priori* whether an account of this kind is possible, one can see emerging in some recent work in social history and historical sociology various elements of a theory of when, and how, a persisting potential for social discontent due to persistently sacrificed interests comes to be manifested.[32]

An individual whose wants do not reflect his interests or who fails to be instrumentally rational may, I argued, experience feedback of a kind that promotes learning about his good and development of more rational strategies. Similarly, the discontent produced by departures from social rationality may produce feedback that, at a social level, promotes the development of norms that better approximate social rationality. The potential for unrest that exists when the interests of a group are discounted is potential for pressure from that group—and its allies—to accord fuller recognition to their interests in social decision-making and in the socially-instilled norms that govern individual decision-making. It therefore is pressure to push the resolution of conflicts further in the direction required by social rationality, since it is pressure to give fuller weight to the interests of more of those affected. Such pressure may of course be more or less forceful or coherent; it may find the most diverse ideological expression; and it may produce outcomes more or less advantageous in the end to those exerting it.[33] Striking historical examples of the mobilization of excluded groups to promote greater representation of their interests include the rebellions against the system of feudal estates, and more recent social movements against restrictions on religious practices, on suffrage and other civil rights, and on collective bargaining.[34]

Of course, other mechanisms have been at work influencing the evolution of social practices and norms at the same time, some with the reverse effect.[35] Whether mechanisms working on behalf of the inclusion of excluded interests will predominate depends upon a complex array of social and historical factors. It would be silly to think either that the norms of any actual society will at any given stage of history closely approximate social rationality, or that there will be a univocal trend toward greater social rationality. Like the mechanisms of biological evolution or market economics, the mechanisms described here operate in an "open system" alongside other mechanisms, and do not guarantee optimality or even a monotonic approach to equilibrium. Human societies do not appear to have begun at or near equilibrium in the relevant sense, and so the strongest available claim might be that in the long haul, barring certain exogenous effects, one could expect an uneven secular trend toward the inclusion of the interests of (or interests represented by) social groups that are capable of some degree of mobilization. But under other circumstances, even in the long run, one could expect the opposite. New World plantation slavery, surely one of the most brutally exclusionary social arrangements ever to have existed, emerged late in world history and lasted for hundreds of years. Other brutally exclusionary social arrangements of ancient or recent vintage persist yet.

One need not, therefore, embrace a theory of moral progress in order to see that the feedback mechanism just described can give an explanatory role to the notion of social rationality. Among the most puzzling, yet most common, objections to moral realism is that there has not been uniform historical progress

toward worldwide consensus on moral norms. But it has not to my knowledge been advanced as an argument against *scientific* realism that, for example, some contemporary cultures and subcultures do not accept, and do not seem to be moving in the direction of accepting, the scientific world view. Surely realists are in both cases entitled to say that only certain practices in certain circumstances will tend to produce theories more congruent with reality, especially when the subject matter is so complex and so far removed from anything like direct inspection. They need not subscribe to the quaint idea that "the truth will out" come what may. The extended theory of individual rationality, for example, leads us to expect that in societies where there are large conflicts of interest people will develop large normative disagreements, and that, when (as they usually do) these large conflicts of interest parallel large differences in power, the dominant normative views are unlikely to embody social rationality. What is at issue here, and in criterial explanations generally, is the explanation of certain patterns among others, not necessarily the existence of a single overall trend. We may, however, point to the existence of the feedback mechanisms described here as grounds for belief that we can make qualified use of historical experience as something like experimental evidence about what kinds of practices in what ranges of circumstances might better satisfy a criterion of social rationality. That is, we may assign this mechanism a role in a qualified process of moral learning.

The mechanisms of learning about individual rationality, weak or extended, involved similar qualifications. For although we expect that, under favorable circumstances, individuals may become better at acting in an instrumentally rational fashion as their experience grows, we are also painfully aware that there are powerful mechanisms promoting the opposite result. We certainly do not think that an individual must display exceptionless rationality, or even show ever-increasing rationality over his life-time, in order to apply reason-giving explanations to many of his actions. Nor do we think that the inevitable persistence of areas of irrationality in individuals is grounds for denying that they can, through experience, acquire areas of greater rationality.

The comparison with individual rationality should not, however, be overdrawn. First, while the inclusion-generating mechanisms for social rationality operate through the behavior of individuals, interpersonal dynamics enter ineliminably in such a way that the criteria selected for are not reducible to those of disaggregated individual rationality. Both social and biological evolution involve selection mechanisms that favor behaviors satisfying criteria of relative optimality that are collective (as in prisoner's dilemma cases) or genotypic (which may also be collective, as in kin selection) as well as individual or phenotypic. Were this not so, it is hardly possible that moral norms could ever have emerged or come to have the hold upon us they do.

Second, there are rather extreme differences of degree between the individual and the social cases. Most strikingly, the mechanisms whereby individual wants and behaviors are brought into some congruence with individual interests and reasons operate in more direct and reliable ways than comparable mechanisms nudging social practices or norms in the direction of what is socially rational. Not only are the information demands less formidable in the individual case—that is the least of it, one might say—but the ways in which feedback is achieved are more likely in the individual case to serve as a prod for change and less likely to be distorted by social asymmetries.

Nonetheless, we do have the skeleton of an explanatory theory that uses the notion of what is more or less rational from a social point of view and that parallels in an obvious way uses of assessments of rationality from the agent's point of view in explanations of individual beliefs and behaviors.

Like the individual theory, it suggests prediction- and counterfactual-supporting generalizations of the following kind: over time, and in some circumstances more than others, we should expect pressure to be exerted on behalf of practices that more adequately satisfy a criterion of rationality.

Well, if this is a potentially predictive and explanatory theory, how good is it? That is a very large question, one beyond my competence to answer. But let me note briefly three patterns in the evolution of moral norms that seem to me to bear out the predictions of this theory, subject to the sorts of qualifications that the existence of imperfections and competing mechanisms would lead one to expect. I do so with trepidation, however, for although the patterns I will discuss are gross historical trends, it is not essential to the theory that history show such trends, and it certainly is not part of the theory to endorse a set of practices or norms merely because it is a result of them.

Generality. It is a commonplace of anthropology that tribal peoples often have only one word to name both their tribe and "the people" or "humanity." Those beyond the tribe are not deemed full-fledged people, and the sorts of obligations one has toward people do not apply fully with regard to outsiders. Over the span of history, through processes that have involved numerous reversals, people have accumulated into larger social units—from the familial band to the tribe to the "people" to the nation-state—and the scope of moral categories has enlarged to follow these expanding boundaries. Needless to say, this has not been a matter of the contagious spread of enlightenment. Expanding social entities frequently subjugate those incorporated within their new boundaries, and the means by which those thus oppressed have secured greater recognition of their interests have been highly conflictual, and remain—perhaps, will always remain—incomplete. Nonetheless, contemporary moral theory, and to a surprising degree contemporary moral discourse, have come to reject any limitation short of the species.[36]

Humanization. Moral principles have been assigned various origins and natures: as commandments of supernatural origin, grounded in the will or character of a deity, to be interpreted by a priesthood; as formalistic demands of a caste-based code of honor; as cosmic principles of order; as dictates of reason or conscience that make no appeal to human inclinations or well-being; and so on. While vestiges of these views survive in contemporary moral theory, it is typical of almost the entire range of such theory, and of much of contemporary moral discourse, to make some sort of intrinsic connection between normative principles and effects on human interests. Indeed, the very emergence of morality as a distinctive subject matter apart from religion is an instance of this pattern.

Patterns of Variation. In addition to seeing patterns that reflect some pressure toward the approximation of social rationality, we should expect to see greater approximation in those areas of normative regulation where the mechanisms postulated here work best, for example, in areas where almost everyone has importantly similar or mutually satisfiable interests, where almost everyone has some substantial potential to infringe upon the interests of others, where the advantages of certain forms of constraint or cooperation are highly salient even in the dynamics of small groups, and where individuals can significantly influence the likelihood of norm-following behavior on the part of others by themselves following norms. The clearest examples have to do with prohibitions of aggression and theft, and of the violation of promises.[37] By contrast, moral questions that concern matters where there are no solutions compatible with protecting the most basic interests of all, where there exist very large asymmetries in the capacity to infringe upon interests, where the gains or losses from particular forms of cooperation or constraint are difficult to per-

ceive, and where individual compliance will little affect general compliance, are less likely to achieve early or stable approximation to social rationality. Clear examples here have to do with such matters as social hierarchy—for example, the permissibility of slavery, of authoritarian government, of caste or gender inequalities—and social responsibility—for example, what is the nature of our individual or collective obligation to promote the well-being of unrelated others?

Given a suitable characterization of the conditions that prevailed during the processes of normative evolution described by these patterns, the present theory claims not only that these changes could have been expected, but that an essential part of the explanation of their occurrence is a mechanism whereby individuals whose interests are denied are led to form common values and make common cause along lines of shared interests, thereby placing pressure on social practices to approximate more closely to social rationality.

These descriptions and explanations of certain prominent features of the evolution of moral norms will no doubt strike some as naive at best, plainly—perhaps even dangerously—false at worst. I thoroughly understand this. I have given impossibly sketchy, one-sided, simple-minded accounts of a very complex reality.[38] I can only hope that these accounts will seem as believable as one could expect sketchy, one-sided, simple-minded accounts to be, and that this will make the story I have tried to tell about mechanisms and explanation more plausible.

Needless to say, the upshot is not a complacent functionalism or an overall endorsement of current moral practice or norms. Instead, the account of morality sketched here emphasizes conflict rather than equilibrium, and provides means for criticizing certain contemporary moral practices and intuitions by asking about their historical genesis. For example, if we come to think that the explanation of a common moral intuition assigns no significant role to mechanisms that could be expected to exert pressure toward socially rational outcomes, then this is grounds for questioning the intuition, however firmly we may hold it. In the spirit of a naturalized moral epistemology, we may ask whether the explanation of why we make certain moral judgments is an example of a reliable process for discovering moral facts.

V. LIMITATIONS

Thus far I have spoken of what is morally best as a matter of what is instrumentally rational from a social point of view. But I have also characterized a genuinely moral point of view as one impartial with respect to the interests of all potentially affected, and that is not a socially-bounded notion. In fact, I have claimed that a trend away from social specificity is among the patterns visible in the evolution of moral norms. Part of the explanation of this pattern—and part, therefore, of the explanatory role of degrees of impartial rationality—is that the mechanisms appealed to above are not socially-bounded, either. Societies, and individuals on opposite sides of social boundaries, constrain one another in various ways, much as groups and individuals constrain one another within societies: they can threaten aggression, mobilize resistance to external control, withhold cooperation, and obstruct one another's plans; and they are prone to resort to such constraining activities when their interests are denied or at risk. As with intrasocial morality, so in intersocial morality, the best-established and most nearly impartially rational elements are those where the mechanisms we have discussed work most reliably: prohibitions on aggression are stronger and more widely accepted than principles of equity or redistribution. Of course, many factors make intersocietal dynamics unlike intrasocietal ones. . . . But the reader will for once be spared more armchair social science. Still, what results is a form of moral realism that is essentially tied to a limited point of view,

an impartial yet human one. Is this too limited for genuine moral realism?

A teacher of mine once remarked that the question of moral realism seemed to him to be the question whether the universe cares what we do. Since we have long since given up believing that the cosmos pays us any mind, he thought we should long since have given up moral realism. I can only agree that if this were what moral realism involved, it should—with relief rather than sorrow—be let go. However, the account offered here gives us a way of understanding how moral values or imperatives might be objective without being cosmic. They need be grounded in nothing more transcendental than facts about man and his environment, facts about what sorts of things matter to us, and how the ways we live affect these things.

Yet the present account is limited in another way, which may be of greater concern from the standpoint of contemporary moral theory: it does not yield moral imperatives that are categorical in the sense of providing a reason for action to all rational agents regardless of their contingent desires. Although troubling, this limitation is not tantamount to relativism, since on the present account rational motivation is not a precondition of moral obligation. For example, it could truthfully be said that I ought to be more generous even though greater generosity would not help me to promote my existing ends, or even to satisfy my objective interests. This could be so because what it would be morally right for me to do depends upon what is rational from a point of view that includes, but is not exhausted by, my own.

In a similar way, it could be said that I logically ought not to believe both a proposition p and a proposition that implies not-p. However, it may not be the case that every rational agent will have an instrumental reason to purge all logical contradictions from his thought. It would require vast amounts of cogitation for anyone to test all of his existing beliefs for consistency, and to insure that every newly acquired belief preserves it.

Suppose someone to be so fortunate that the only contradictions among his beliefs lie deep in the much-sedimented swamp of factual trivia. Perhaps his memories of two past acquaintances have become confused in such a way that somewhere in the muck there are separate beliefs which, taken together, attribute to one individual logically incompatible properties. Until such a contradiction rears its head in practice, he may have no more reason to lay down his present concerns and wade in after it than he has to leave his home in suburban New Jersey to hunt alligators in the Okefenokee on the off chance that he might one day find himself stranded and unarmed in the backwaters of southeast Georgia.[39] What an individual rationally ought to do thus may differ from what logic requires of him. Still, we may say that logical evaluation is not subjective or arbitrary, and that good grounds of a perfectly general kind are available for being logical, namely, that logical contradictions are necessarily false and logical inferences are truth-preserving. Since in public discourse and private reflection we are often concerned with whether our thinking is warranted in a sense that is more intimately connected with its truth-conduciveness than with its instrumentality to our peculiar personal goals, it therefore is far from arbitrary that we attach so much importance to logic as a standard of criticism and self-criticism.

By parallel, if we adopt the account of moral rightness proposed above we may say that moral evaluation is not subjective or arbitrary, and that good, general grounds are available for following moral 'ought's', namely, that moral conduct is rational from an impartial point of view. Since in public discourse and private reflection we are often concerned with whether our conduct is justifiable from a general rather than merely personal standpoint, it therefore is far from arbitrary that we attach so much importance to morality as a standard of criticism and self-criticism.

The existence of such phenomena as reli-gion and ideology is evidence for the pervasiveness and seriousness of our concern for impartial justification. Throughout history individuals have sacrificed their interests, even their lives, to meet the demands of religions or ideologies that were compelling for them in part because they purported to express a universal—*the* universal—justificatory standpoint. La Rochefoucauld wrote that hypocrisy is the tribute vice pays to virtue,[40] but 'hypocrisy' suggests cynicism. We might better say that ideology is the respect partisans show to impartiality. Morality, then, is not ideology made sincere and general—ideology is intrinsically given to heart-felt generalization. Morality is ideology that has faced the facts.

I suspect the idea that moral evaluations must have categorical force for rational agents owes some of its support to a fear that were this to be denied, the authority of morality would be lost. That would be so if one held onto the claim that moral imperatives cannot exist for someone who would not have a reason to obey them, for then an individual could escape moral duties by the simple expedient of having knavish desires. But if we give up this claim about the applicability of moral judgment, then variations in personal desires cannot license exemption from moral obligation.[41]

Thus, while it certainly is a limitation of the argument made here that it does not yield a conception of moral imperatives as categorical, that may be a limitation we can live with and still accord morality the scope and dignity it traditionally has enjoyed. Moreover, it may be a limitation we must live with. For how many among us can convince ourselves that reason is other than hypothetical? Need it also be asked: How many of us would find our sense of the significance of morality or the importance of moral conduct enhanced by a demonstration that even a person with the most thoroughly repugnant ends would find that moral conduct advanced them?

One implication of what has been said is

that if we want morality to be taken seriously and to have an important place in people's lives—and not merely as the result of illusion or the threat of repression—we should be vitally concerned with the ways in which social arrangements produce conflicts of interest and asymmetries of power that affect the nature and size of the gap between what is individually and socially rational. Rather than attempt to portray morality as something that it cannot be, as "rationally compelling no matter what one's ends," we should ask how we might change the ways we live so that moral conduct would more regularly be rational given the ends we actually will have.

VI. SUMMARY AND CONCLUSION

I have outlined a form of moral realism, and given some indication of how it might be defended against certain objections. Neither a full characterization of this view, nor full answers to the many objections it faces, can be given within the present essay. Perhaps then I should stop trying to say just a bit more, and close by indicating roughly what I have, and have not, attempted to show.

I have proposed what are in effect reforming naturalistic definitions of non-moral goodness and moral rightness. It is possible to respond: "Yes, I can see that such-and-such an end is an objective interest of the agent in your sense, or that such-and-such a practice is rational from an impartial point of view, but can't I still ask whether the end is good for him or the practice right?" Such "open questions" cannot by their nature be closed, since definitions are not subject to proof or disproof. But open questions may be more or less disturbing, for although definitional proposals cannot be demonstrated, they can fare better or worse at meeting various desiderata.

I have assumed throughout that the drawing up of definitions is part of theory-construction, and so is to be assessed by asking (1) whether the analyses given satisfy appro-

priate constraints of intelligibility and function, and (2) whether the terms as analyzed contribute to the formulation and testing of worthwhile theories. How do my proposals fit with these criteria?

(1) Beyond constraints of intelligibility, such as clarity and non-circularity, specifically naturalistic definitions of evaluative terms should satisfy two further analytic constraints arising from their intended function. (a) They should insofar as possible capture the normative force of these terms by providing analyses that permit these terms to play their central evaluative roles. In the present setting, this involves showing that although the definitions proposed may not fit with all of our linguistic or moral intuitions, they nonetheless express recognizable notions of goodness and rightness. Further, it involves showing that the definitions permit plausible connections to be drawn between, on the one hand, what is good or right and, on the other, what characteristically would motivate individuals who are prepared to submit themselves to relevant sorts of scrutiny. (b) The naturalistic definitions should permit the evaluative concepts to participate in their own right in genuinely empirical theories. Part of this consists in showing that we have appropriate epistemic access to these concepts. Part, too, (and a related part) consists in showing that generalizations employing these concepts, among others, can figure in potentially explanatory accounts. I have tried to offer reasonably clear definitions and to show in a preliminary way how they might meet constraints (a) and (b).

(2) However, a good deal more must be done, for it remains to show that the empirical theories constructed with the help of these definitions are reasonably good theories, that is, theories for which we have substantial evidence and which provide plausible explanations. I have tried in the most preliminary way imaginable to suggest this. If I have been wholly unpersuasive on empirical matters, then I can expect that the definitions I have offered will be equally unpersuasive.

It is an attraction for me of naturalism in ethics and epistemology alike that it thus is constrained in several significant dimensions at once. One has such ample opportunities to be shown wrong or found unconvincing if one's account must be responsive to empirical demands as well as normative intuitions. Theorizing in general is more productive when suitably constrained; in ethics especially, constraints are needed if we are to have a clearer idea of how we might make progress toward the resolution of theoretical disputes. Of course, not just any constraints will do. A proposed set of constraints must present itself as both appropriate and useful. Let me say something about (1) the utility of the constraints adopted here, and then a final word about (2) their appropriateness.

(1) Consider three classes of competitors to the substantive moral theory endorsed above, and notice how criticisms of them *naturally* intertwine concerns about normative justification and empirical explanation. *Kantian* conceptions of morality are widely viewed as having captured certain intuitively compelling normative characteristics of such notions as rationality and moral rightness, but it seems they have done so partly at the expense of affording a plausible way of integrating these notions into an empirical account of our reasons and motives in action. Moreover, this descriptive difficulty finds direct expression on the normative side. Not only must any normative 'ought' be within the scope of an empirical 'can', but a normatively compelling 'ought' must—as recent criticisms of Kantianism have stressed—reach to the real springs of human action and concern. *Intuitionist* moral theories also enjoyed some success in capturing normative features of morality, but they have largely been abandoned for want of a credible account of the nature or operation of a faculty of moral intuition. It is too easy for us to give a nonjustifying psychological explanation of the existence in certain English gentlemen of something which they identified upon introspection as a faculty of moral insight, an ex-

planation that ties this purported faculty more closely to the rigidity of prevailing social conventions than to anything that looks as if it could be a source of universal truth. *Social choice theories* that take occurrent subjective interests or revealed preferences as given fit more readily than Kantian or intuitionist theories with empirical accounts of behavior, and, unlike them, have found a place in contemporary social science. But they suffer well-known limitations as normative theories, some of which turn out to be bound up with their limitations as explanatory theories: they lack an account of the origin or evolution of preferences, and partly for that reason are unable to capture the ways in which we evaluate purportedly rational or moral conduct by criticizing ends as well as means.

(2) However, the issues at stake when we evaluate competing approaches to morality involve not only this sort of assessment of largish theories, but also questions about which criteria of assessment appropriately apply to definitions and theories in ethics, and about whether definitional systematization and largish theorizing are even appropriate for ethics. I am drawn to the view that the development of theory in ethics is not an artificial contrivance of philosophers but an organic result of the personal and social uses of moral evaluation: time and again individuals and groups have faced difficult questions to which common sense gave conflicting or otherwise unsatisfactory answers, and so they have pressed their questions further and pursued their inquiry more systematically. The felt need for theory in ethics thus parallels the felt need for theory in natural or social science.[42] It does not follow from this alone that ethical theorizing must run parallel to or be integrable with theorizing in the natural and social sciences. Ethics might be deeply different. Although initially plausible and ultimately irrefutable, the view that ethics stands thus apart is one that in the end I reject. We are natural and social creatures, and I know of nowhere else to look for ethics than in this rich conjunction of facts. I have tried to suggest that we might indeed find it there.[43]

NOTES

1. Nineteenth-century evolutionary naturalism affords an example of the former, Dewey—and, on at least one reading, perhaps Mill as well—an example of the latter.

2. A. J. Ayer, *Language, Truth, and Logic* (New York: Dover, 1952), p. 111.

3. In saying this, I am insisting that questions about what it would be rational to believe belong to practical rather than theoretical reason. While results of theoretical reason—for example, conclusions of deductive inferences—are in general relevant to questions about rational belief, they are not determinative apart from the agent's practical reasons.

4. Of course, individual belief-formation is not typically governed by explicit means-end reasoning, but rather by habits of belief-formation and tendencies to invest varying degrees of confidence in particular kinds of beliefs. If we accept an instrumental account of rationality, then we can call such habits rational from the standpoint of the individual to the extent that they fit into a constellation of attitudes and tendencies that promote his ends. This matter will arise again in Section IV.

5. Neither these remarks, nor those in subsequent paragraphs, are meant to be a serious exegesis of Hume's arguments, which admit of interpretations other than the one suggested here. I mean only to capture certain features of what I take Hume's arguments to be, e.g., in Bk. III, pt. I, sec. I of *A Treatise of Human Nature*, ed. L. A. Selby-Bigge (Oxford: Clarendon, 1973), esp. pp. 465–66, and in App. I of *An Inquiry Concerning the Principles of Morals*, ed. C. W. Hendel (Indianapolis: Bobbs-Merrill, 1957), esp. pp. 111–12.

6. Philippa Foot has questioned this thesis, although her way of posing and arguing the question differs enough from mine that I cannot judge whether she would be in agreement with the argument that follows. See her *Virtues and Vices* (Berkeley: University of California Press, 1978), esp. Essay XI. The presentation of the issues here owes its main inspiration to William K. Frankena's distinction between the rational and the moral points of view.

7. See the *Inquiry Concerning the Principles of Morals*, Sec. IX, Pt. II, pp. 102–3.

8. The ancient criticism of non-cognitivism that it has difficulty accounting for the difference between moral value and other sorts of desirability (so that Hume can speak in one breath of our approval of a man's "good offices" and his "well-contrived apartment"), gains some vitality in the present context. To account for such differences it is necessary to have a contentful way of characterizing criteria of moral assessment so that moral approval does not reduce to "is valued by the agent." (Such a characterization will be offered in Section IV.) Value *sans phrase* is a generic, and not necessarily moral, notion. One sometimes hears it said that generic value becomes moral in character when we reach that which the agent prizes above all else. But this would invest pets and mementos with moral value, and have the peculiar effect of making amoralism a virtual conceptual impossibility. It seems more plausible to say that not all value is moral value, and that the highest values for an individual need not be, nor need they even seem to him to be, moral values. Once we turn to questions of duty, the situation should be clearer still: moral theorists have proposed quite different relations among the categories of moral rightness, moral goodness, and non-moral goodness, and it seems implausible to say that deeming an act or class of actions morally right is necessarily equivalent to viewing it personally as valuable *sans phrase*.

9. The character of moral imperatives receives further discussion in Section V.

10. Such theories are suitably externalist when, in characterizing the notions of *reliability* or *warrant-conferring causal process*, they employ an account of truth that does not resolve truth into that which we have reason to believe—for example, a nontrivial correspondence theory.

11. Or if moral facts were supposed to be things of a kind to provide categorical reasons for action. However, this supposition is simply Hume's thesis of practicality in ontological garb.

12. J. L. Mackie, in *Ethics: Inventing Right and Wrong* (Harmondsworth, Middlesex: Penguin, 1977), and Gilbert Harman, in *The Nature of Morality: An Introduction to Ethics* (New York: Oxford University Press, 1977), both challenge moral realism in part by questioning its capacity to explain. Nicholas L. Sturgeon, in "Moral Explanations," David Copp and David Zimmerman, eds., *Morality, Reason and Truth: New Essays in the Foundations of Ethics* (Totowa, N.J.: Rowman and Allanheld, 1984), takes the opposite side, using arguments different from those offered below.

13. A full-scale theory of value would, I think, show the concept of someone's good to be slightly different from the concept of what is desirable for him. However, this difference will not affect the argument made here.

14. It was some work by Richard C. Jeffrey on epistemic probability that originally suggested to me the idea of objectifying subjective interests. See note 17. I have since benefited from Richard B. Brandt's work on "rational desire," although I fear that what I will say contains much that he would regard as wrong-headed. See *A Theory of the Good and the Right* (Oxford: Clarendon, 1979), pt. I.

15. We ask this question of $A+$, rather than what $A+$ wants for himself, because we are seeking the objectified subjective interests of A, and the interests of $A+$ might be quite different owing to the changes involved in the idealization of A. For example, $A+$ presumably does not want any more information for himself—there is no more to be had and he knows this. Yet it might still be true that $A+$ would want to want more knowledge were he to be put in the place of his less well-informed self, A. It may as a psychological matter be impossible for $A+$ to set aside entirely his desires *in his present circumstances* with regard to himself or to A in considering what he would want to want were he to be put *in the place of* his less-than-ideal self. This reveals a measurement problem for objective interests: giving an individual the information and capacities necessary to "objectify" his interests may perturb his psychology in ways that alter the phenomenon we wish to observe. Such difficulties attend even the measurement of subjective interests, since instruments for sampling preferences (indeed, mere acts of reflection upon one's preferences) tend to affect the preferences expressed. For obvious reasons, interference effects come with the territory. Though not in themselves sufficient ground for skepticism about subjective or objective interests, these measurement problems show the need for a "perturbation theory," and for caution about attributions of interests that are inattentive to interference effects.

16. 'Interest' is not quite the word wanted here, for in ordinary language we may speak of a want where we would not speak of a corresponding interest. See Brian Barry, *Political Argument* (London: Routledge & Kegan Paul, 1965), esp. chap. X, for discussion. A more accurate, but overly cumbersome, expression would be 'positive-valence-making characteristic'.

17. Suppose for a moment, contrary to what was urged above, that there is a workable notion of epistemic probability that determines rational degrees of belief independent of the contingent goals of the epistemic agent. Perhaps then the following analogy will be helpful. Consider a physically random process, such as alpha-decay. We can ask an individual what subjective probability he would assign to an event consisting in a certain rate of decay for a given sample of uranium; we can also ask what rational degree of belief the individual would assign to this event were he to become ideally informed about the laws of physics and the relevant initial conditions. Call the latter rational degree of belief the *objectified subjective probability* of the event, and suppose it to be equal to one fifth. (Compare Richard C. Jeffrey, *The Logic of Decision* (New York: McGraw-Hill, 1964), pp. 190–96.) But now consider the physical facts that, in conjunction with the laws of quantum mechanics, ground the idealized individual's judgment. Call these the *reduction basis* of that judgment. This reduction basis is a complex set of primary qualities that can be said to bring it about that the event in question has an *objective probability* of one fifth. (It should be said that it is not part of Jeffrey's approach to posit such objective probabilities.) The existence of this objective probability can explain why an ideally informed individual would select an objectified subjective probability equal to one fifth, but the probability judgment of an ideally informed individual cannot explain why the objective probability is one fifth—that is a matter of the laws of physics. Similarly, the existence of an individual's objective interest can explain why his ideally informed self would pick out for his less-informed self a given objectified subjective interest, but not *vice versa*.

18. More precisely, we may say that X is non-morally good for A at time t if and only if X would satisfy an objective interest of A the reduction basis of which exists at t. Considerations about the evolution of interests over time raise a number of issues that cannot be entered into here.

19. $A+$, putting himself in A's place, may find several different sets of wants equally appealing, so that several alternatives could be equal-best for A in this sense. This would not make the notion of 'the good for A' problematic, just pluralistic. However, a more serious question looms. Is there sufficient determinacy in the specification of $A+$'s condition, or in the psychology of desire, to make the notion of objective interest definite enough for my purposes? Without trying to say how definite *that* might be, let me suggest two ways in which an answer to the worry about definiteness might begin. (1) It seems that we do think that there are rather definite answers to questions about how an individual A's desires would change were his beliefs to change in certain limited ways. If Lonnie were to learn the consequences of drinking milk, he would no longer want his desire for milk to be effective. But a large change in belief can be accomplished piecemeal, by a sequence of limited changes in belief. Thus, if (admittedly, a big 'if') *order* of change is not in the end significant, then the facts and generalizations that support counterfactuals about limited changes might support an extrapolation all the way to $A+$. (2) Beliefs and desires appear to co-vary systematically. Typically, we find that individuals who differ markedly in their desires—for example, about career or style of life—differ markedly, and characteristically, in their beliefs; as individuals become more similar in their beliefs, they tend to become more similar in their desires. This suggests that if (another big 'if') the characterization given of $A+$ fixes the entire content of his beliefs in a definite way (at least, given a choice of language), then his desires may be quite comprehensively fixed as well. If we had in hand a general theory of the co-variation of beliefs and desires, then we could appeal directly to this theory—plus facts about A—to ground the counterfactuals needed to characterize A's objectified interests, eliminating any essential reference to the imaginary individual $A+$.

20. The account may, however, yield some counterintuitive results. Depending upon the nature and circumstances of given individuals, they might have objective interests in things we find wrong or repulsive, and that do not seem to us part of a good life. We can explain a good deal of our objection to certain desires—for example, those involving cruelty—by saying that they are not *morally* good; others—for example, those of a philisine nature—by saying that they are not *aesthetically* valuable; and so on. It seems to me preferable to express our distaste for certain ends in terms of specific categories of value, rather than resort to the device of saying that such ends could under no circumstances be part of anyone's non-moral good. People, or at least some people, might be put together in a way that makes some not-very-appetizing things essential to their flourishing, and we do not want to be guilty of wishful thinking on this score. (There will be wishful thinking enough before we are through.)

21. To put the matter in more strictly naturalistic terms, we can expect that evolution will have favored organisms so constituted that those behaviors requisite to their survival and flourishing are associated with positive internal states (such as pleasure) and those opposed to survival or flourishing with negative states (such as pain). 'Flourishing' here, even if understood as mere reproductive fitness, is not a narrow notion. In order for beings such as humans to be reproductively successful, they must as phenotypes have lives that are psychologically sustainable, internally motivating, and effectively social; lives, moreover, that normally would engage in a wide range of their peculiarly human capacities. Humankind could hardly have been a success story even at the reproductive level were not pursuit of the sorts of things that characteristically have moved humans to action associated with existences of this kind. However, it must be kept in mind that most human evolution occurred under circumstances different in important ways from the present. It therefore is quite possible that the interaction of evolved human motivational potentials with existing circumstances will produce incongruities between what we tend to aim at, or to be driven by, and what would produce the greatest pleasure for us. That is one reason for doubting hedonism as a theory of motivation.

22. 'Functional success' rather than 'representational accuracy' for the following reason. Selection favors organisms that have some-or-other feature that happens in their particular environment to contribute to getting their needs met. Whether that feature will be an accurate representational capacity cannot be settled by an argument of this kind. Of course, it would be a very great coincidence if beings who rely as heavily upon representations as we do were able to construct only grossly inaccurate representations while at the same time managing successfully in a range of environments over a long period of time. But such coincidences cannot be ruled out.

23. Although some elements of their reduction basis depend upon our past choices, our objective interests are not therefore subjective in a sense damaging to the present argument. After all, such unproblematically objective facts about us as our weight, income, and spatial location depend in the same way upon past choices. The point is not that our subjective interests have no role in shaping the reduction basis of our objective interests, but rather that they can affect our objective interests only in virtue of their actual (rather than merely desired) effects upon this reduction basis, just as they can affect our weight, income, or spatial location only in virtue of actual (rather than merely desired) effects upon our displacement, employment, or movement.

24. In a similar way, it would be incomplete and superficial to explain why, once large-scale production became possible, the world's consumption of refined sugar underwent such explosive development, by mentioning only the fact that people liked its taste. Why, despite wide differences in traditional diet and acquired tastes, has sugar made such inroads into human consumption? Why haven't the appearance and promotion of other equally cheap foodstuffs produced such remarkable shifts in consumption? Why, even in societies where sugar is recognized as a health hazard, does consumption of sugars, often in concealed forms, continue to climb? Facts about the way we are constituted, about the rather singular ways sugar therefore affects us, and about the ways forms of production and patterns of consumption co-evolved to generate both a growing demand and an expanding supply, must supplement a theory that stops at the level of subjective preferences. See Sidney W. Minz, *Sweetness and Power: The Place of Sugar in Modern History* (New York: Viking, 1985), for relevant discussion.

25. For a discussion of how informally expressed accounts may nonetheless convey explanatory information, see sec. II of my "Probability, Explanation, and Information," *Synthese* 48 (1981): 233–56.

26. Such explanation uses a naturalized criterion when rationality is defined in terms of relative efficiency given the agent's beliefs and desires. A (more or less) rational agent is thus someone disposed to act in (more or less) efficient ways. There is a deep difficulty about calling such explanation naturalistic, for the constraints placed upon attributions of beliefs and desires by a "principle of charity" may compromise the claim that rational-agent explanations are empirical. Although I believe this difficulty can be overcome, this is hardly the place to start *that* argument.

27. For a survey of the literature, see Richard Nisbett and Lee Ross, *Human Inference: Strategies and Shortcomings of Social Judgment* (Englewood Cliffs, N.J.: Prentice-Hall, 1980), where one unsurprisingly finds greater attention paid to drawbacks than advantages.

28. To recall a point from Section II: one may make assessments relative to particular evaluative criteria without thereby valuing that which satisfies them.

29. I realize that it is misleading to call a point of view that is "impartial, but equally concerned with all those potentially affected" a *social* point of view—some of those potentially affected may lie on the other side of an intersocial boundary. This complication will be set aside until Section V.

30. It also means that the relation of moral criteria to criteria of individual rationality has become problematic, since there can be no guarantee that what would be instrumentally rational from any given individual's point of view will coincide with what would be instrumentally rational from a social point of view.

31. A rather strong thesis of interpersonal comparison is needed here for purposes of social aggregation. I am not assuming the existence of some single good, such as happiness, underlying such comparisons. Thus the moral theory in question, although consequentialist, aggregative, and maximizing, is not equivalent to classical utilitarianism. I *am* assuming that when a choice is faced between satisfying interest X of A vs. satisfying interest Y of B, answers to the question "All else equal, would it matter more to me if I were A to have X satisfied than if I were B to have Y satisfied?" will be relatively determinate and stable across individuals under conditions of full and vivid information. A similar, though somewhat weaker, form of comparability-across-difference is presupposed when we make choices from among alternative courses of action that would lead us to have different desires in the future.

32. See, for example, Barrington Moore, Jr., *The Social Origins of Dictatorship and Democracy: Lord and Peasant in the Making of the Modern World* (Boston: Beacon, 1966) and *Injustice: The Social Bases of Obedience and Revolt* (White Plains, N.Y.: M. E. Sharpe, 1978); E. P. Thompson, *The Making of the English Working Class* (New York: Pantheon, 1963); William B. Taylor, *Drinking, Homicide, and Rebellion in Colonial Mexican Villages* (Stanford: Stanford University Press, 1979); Charles Tilly, *From Mobilization to Revolution* (Reading, Mass.: Addison-Wesley, 1978); and Charles Tilly et al., *The Rebellious Century, 1830–1930* (Cambridge, Mass.: Harvard University Press, 1975).

33. A common theme in the works cited in note 32 is that much social unrest is re-vindicative rather than revolutionary, since the discontent of long-suffering groups often is galvanized into action only when customary entitlements are threatened or denied. The overt ideologies of such groups thus frequently are particularistic and conservative, even as their unrest contributes to the emergence of new social forms that concede greater weight to previously discounted interests. In a similar way, individuals often fail to notice irrationalities in their customary behavior until they are led by it into uncustomary difficulties, which then arouse a sense that something has gone wrong. For familiar reasons, a typical initial individual response is to attempt to retrieve the *status quo ante*, although genuine change may result from these restorative efforts.

34. It should be emphasized that these mechanisms do not presuppose a background of democratic institutions. They have extracted concessions even within societies that remained very hierarchical. See, for example, Taylor, *Drinking, Homicide, and Rebellion*.

35. Indeed, the mechanism just described may push in several directions at once: toward the inclusion of some previously excluded interests, and toward the exclusion of some previously included

interests. To be sure, if interests come to be excluded even though their social and material basis remains more or less intact, a new potential for unrest is created. Some groups present a special problem, owing to their inherent inability to mobilize effectively, for example, children and future generations. To account for the pressures that have been exerted on behalf of these groups it is necessary to see how individuals come to include other individuals within their own interests. (Compare the way in which one's future selves, which can exert no pressure on their own behalf, come to be taken into account by one's present self in virtue of one's identification with them.) Unless one takes account of such processes of incorporation and identification, morality (or even prudence) will appear quite mysterious, but I will have little to say about them here. For some preliminary remarks, see sec. IX of my "Alienation, Consequentialism, and the Demands of Morality," *Philosophy and Public Affairs* 13 (1984): 134–71.

36. Here and elsewhere, I mean by 'contemporary moral theory' to refer to dominant views in the academies, and by 'contemporary moral discourse' to refer to widespread practices of public moral argumentation, in those societies that have achieved the highest levels of development of empirical science generally. Again, the moral realist, like the scientific realist, is not committed to worldwide consensus.

37. However, such prohibitions historically have shown limitations of scope that are no longer recognized as valid. The trend against such limitations is an instance of the first sort of pattern, toward increased generality.

38. Moreover, the accounts are highly general in character, operating at a level of description incapable of discriminating between hypotheses based upon the particular account of moral rightness proposed here and others rather close to it. (Roughly, those characterizing moral rightness in terms of instrumental rationality relative to the non-moral good of those affected, but differing on details regarding instrumental rationality—for example, is it straightforwardly maximizing or partly distributive?—or regarding non-moral goodness—for example, is it reducible to pleasure? For a discussion of not-very-close competitors, see Section VI.) If the method I have employed is to be used to make choices from among close competitors, the empirical analysis must be much more fine-grained. Similar remarks apply to the weak and extended theories of individual rationality appealed to above.

39. It is of no importance whether we say that he has *no* reason to do this or simply a vanishingly small one. I suppose we could say that a person has a vanishingly small reason to do anything—even to expend enormous effort to purge minor contradictions from his beliefs or to purge alligators from distant swamps—that might *conceivably* turn out to be to his benefit. But then we would have no trouble guaranteeing the existence of vanishingly small reasons for moral conduct. This would allow naturalized moral rightness to satisfy a Humean thesis of practicality after all, but in a way that would rob the thesis of its interest.

40. François (duc de) la Rochefoucauld, *Reflexions, ou sentences et maximes morales suivi de reflexions diverses*, ed. Jean Lafond (Paris: Gallimard, 1976), p. 79. La Rochefoucauld apparently borrowed the phrase from the cleric Du Moulin. I am grateful to a remark of Barrington Moore, Jr., for reminding me of it. See his *Injustice*, p. 508.

41. Contrast Harman's relativism about 'ought' in *The Nature of Morality*. Harman adopts the first of the two courses just mentioned, preserving the connection between an individual's moral obligations and what he has (instrumental) reason to do. He defends his approach in part by arguing that, if we suppose that Hitler was engaged in rational pursuit of his ends, an "internal" judgment like 'Hitler (morally) ought not to have killed six million Jews' would be "weak" and "odd" compared to an "external" judgment like 'Hitler was evil' (see pp. 107 ff). I would have thought the opposite, namely, that it is too "weak" and "odd" to give an account of morality such that Hitler can be judged to be consummately evil (which Harman claims, without explanation, his brand of relativism *can* do) but in which 'Hitler (morally) ought not to have acted as he did' is false.

42. This felt need is also reflected in the codification of laws, and in the development of legal theories. However contrived the law may at times seem, surely the general social conditions and needs that have driven its development are real enough. Indeed, the elaborate artifice of law and its language is in part an indication of how pressing the need to go beyond pretheoretic common sense has been.

43. I am indebted to a great many people, including Peter Achinstein, Robert Audi, Annette Baier, Michael Bratman, Stephen Darwall, Allan Gibbard, Thomas Nagel, Samuel Scheffler, Rebecca Scott, Nicholas Sturgeon, Nicholas White, and the editors at *The Philosophical Review*, who have kindly provided comments on previous drafts or presentations of this paper.

B

ANTIREALISM

9

How To Be an Ethical Antirealist

SIMON BLACKBURN

Some philosophers like to call themselves realists, and some like to call themselves antirealists. An increasing number, I suspect, wish to turn their backs on the whole issue.[1] Their strengths include those of naturalism, here counseling us that there is none except a natural science of human beings. From this it follows that there is no "first philosophy" lying behind (for instance) physics, or anthropology, enabling the philosopher to know how much of the world is "our construction" (antirealism) or, on the contrary, "independent of us" (realism).

This naturalism bestows small bouquets and small admonishments to each of the previous parties. The antirealists were right to deny that there exists a proper philosophical (a priori) explanation of things like the success of physics, which some people were acute enough to discern, from their armchairs, while others did not. A scientist can say that there was a certain result because a neutrino or electron did this and that, but a philosopher has nothing to *add* to this. If she tries to say "Not only did the result occur because of the neutrino, but also because neutrino theory depicts (corresponds with, matches, carves at the joints) the world," she adds nothing but only voices a vain, and vainglorious, attempt to underwrite the science. This attempt may have made sense in a Cartesian tradition, when the mind's contact with the world seemed so problematical, but its time has passed. On the other hand, antirealists, sensing the futility of this road, stress instead the dependence of the ordinary world on us, our minds and categories, and again the additions they offer are unacceptable.[2] Characteristically, if realism fails because it is vacuous, antirealism fails because it strays into mistakes—making things dependent on us when they obviously are not, for example.[3] Again, and perhaps even more clearly, it is plausible to see antirealism as attempting to theorize where no theory should be—in this case, making the unnatural. Cartesian mind into a source of worlds. These theories are naturally described as "transcendental," and the word reminds us that for all his hostility to rational psychology, Kant himself failed to escape this trap.

The transcendental aspect can be seen if we put the matter in terms of what I call "correspondence conditionals." We like to believe that if we exercise our sensory and cognitive faculties properly and end up believing that p, then p. What kind of theory might explain our right to any such confidence? If p is a thesis from basic physical theory, only the theory itself. To understand why, when we believe that neutrinos exist, having used such-and-such information in such-and-such a way, then they probably do, is just to understand whatever credentials neutrino theory has. That is physics. Any attempt at a background, an underwriting of the conditional from outside the theory, is certain to be bogus.

When considering such global matters as the success of our science, the nature of our world, it seems that naturalism ought to win. But in local areas, it seems instead that battle can be joined. In this paper I would like to say in a little more detail why I think this is so. The main problem to which I turn is that of seepage, or the way in which antirealism, once comfortably in command of some particular area of our thought, is apt to cast imperialistic eyes on neighboring territory. The local antirealist faces the problem of drawing a line, which may prove difficult, or that of reneging on naturalism, and allowing that global antirealism must after all make sense. The second part of my paper is thus an exploration of this specific problem.

Why can battle be joined in local areas? What I said about physics might be retorted upon any area. To understand how, when we believe that twice two is four, we are probably right requires arithmetical understanding. To understand why, when we believe that wanton cruelty is wrong, we are also right requires ethical understanding. Where is the asymmetry?

Let us stay with the example of ethics. Here a "projective" theory can be developed to give a perfectly satisfying way of placing our propensities for values. According to me the surface phenomena of moral thought do not offer any obstacle to it. They can be explained as being just what we should expect, if the projective metaphysics is correct. (I call the doctrine that this is so "quasi-realism"—a topic I return to later.) I have also argued that this package contains various explanatory advantages over other rivals and alleged rivals. The projectivism is not, of course, new—the package is intended indeed to be a modern version of Hume's theory of the nature of ethics, but without any commitment to particular operations of passions such as sympathy. Emotivism and Hare's prescriptivism are also immediate ancestors. Anything new comes in the quasi-realism, whose point is to show that, since projectivism is consistent with, and indeed explains, the important surface phenomena of ethics, many of the arguments standardly used against it miss their mark. These arguments allege that projectivism is inadequate to one or another feature of the way we think ethically; the quasi-realism retorts that it is not, and goes on to explain the existence of the features. Such features include the propositional as opposed to emotive or prescriptive form, the interaction of ethical commitments with ordinary propositional attitude verbs, talk of truth, proof, knowledge, and so forth. I must urge the reader to look elsewhere for the details of the program; here, it is its relationship with naturalism that is to be determined.

I

The first link is this. I think that naturalism demands this view of ethics, but in any case it motivates it. It does so because in this package the fundamental state of mind of one who has an ethical commitment makes natural sense. This state of mind is not located as a belief (the belief in a duty, right, value). We may *end up* calling it a belief, but that is after the work has been done. In fact, we may end up saying that there really are values (such as the value of honesty) and facts (such as the fact that you have a duty to your children). For in this branch of philosophy, it is not what you finish by saying, but how you manage to say it that matters. How many people think they can just *announce* themselves to be realists or antirealists, as if all you have to do is put your hand on your heart and say, "I really believe it!" (or, "I really don't")? The way I treat the issue of realism denies that this kind of avowal helps the matter at all. The question is one of the best theory of this state of commitment, and reiterating it, even with a panoply of dignities—truth, fact, perception, and the rest—is not to the point.

The point is that the state of mind starts theoretical life as something else—a stance, or conative state or pressure on choice and action. Such pressures need to exist if human beings are to meet their competing needs in a social, cooperative setting. The stance may be called an attitude, although it would not matter if the word fitted only inexactly: its function is to mediate the move from features of a situation to a reaction, which in the appropriate circumstances will mean choice. Someone with a standing stance is set to react in some way when an occasion arises, just as someone with a standing belief is set to react to new information cognitively in one way or another. It matters to us that people have some attitudes and not others, and we educate them and put pressure on them in the hope that they will.

So far, two elements in this story are worth keeping in mind, for it will be important to see whether a projective plus quasi-realist story can do without them. These are: (1) the fundamental identification of the commitment in question as something other than a belief; (2) the existence of a neat natural account of why the state that it is should exist.

Obviously, the emergence of cooperative and altruistic stances is not a mere armchair speculation. It can be supplemented by both theoretical and empirical studies.[4] It is noteworthy that the account will insist upon the nonrepresentative, conative function for the

stance. The evolutionary success that attends some stances and not others is a matter of the behavior to which they lead. In other words, it is the direct consequences of the pressure on action that matter. Evolutionary success may attend the animal that helps those that have helped it, but it would not attend an allegedly possible animal that thinks it ought to help but does not. In the competition for survival, it is what the animal *does* that matters. This is important, for it shows that only if values are intrinsically motivating, is a natural story of their emergence possible. Notice, too, the way the evolutionary success arises. Animals with standing dispositions to cooperate (say) do better in terms of other needs like freedom from fleas or ability to survive failed hunting expeditions by begging meals from others. No right, duty, or value plays any explanatory role in this history. It is not as if the creature with a standing disposition to help those who have helped it does well *because* that is a virtue. Its being a virtue is irrelevant to evolutionary biology. There is no such naturalistically respectable explanation.

The commitment may have psychological accretions consistently with this being its core or essence. The precise "feel" of an ethical stance may be a function of local culture, in its scope, or some of its interactions with other pressures and other beliefs. A pressure toward action can be associated variously with pride, shame, self-respect, and there is no reason to expect a simple phenomenology to emerge. The essence lies in the practical import, but the feelings that surround that can vary considerably. There is no reason for a stance to feel much like a desire, for example. Consider as a parallel the way in which a biological or evolutionary story would place attraction between the sexes, and the culturally specific and surprising ways in which that attraction can emerge—the varieties of lust and love (whose imperatives often do not feel much like desire either, and may equally be expressed by thinking that there are things one simply *must* do. I say more about this later.) So, if a theorist is attracted to the rich textures of ethical life, he need not, therefore, oppose projectivism. No "reduction" of an ethical stance to one of any other type is needed.

Now contrast the kind of evolution already sketched with any that might be offered for, say, our capacity to perceive spatial distance. Again, what matters here is action. But what we must be good at is acting according to the very feature perceived. A visual-motor mechanism enabling the frog's tongue to hit the fly needs to adapt the trajectory of the tongue to the place of the fly relative to the frog, and an animal using perceived distance to guide behavior will be successful only if it perceives distances as they are. It is because our visual mechanisms show us far-off things as far off and near things as near that we work well using them. That is what they are *for*. We can sum up this contrast by saying that although the teleology of spatial perception is spatial, the teleology of ethical commitment is not ethical. The good of spatial perception is to be representative, but the good of ethical stances is not.

The possibility of this kind of theory, then, provides the needed contrast between the general case of science, where an attempt to provide a further background "theory" is transcendental, and the local particular case of ethics, where there are natural materials for such a story ready at hand. It also means that philosophers wanting a general realism versus antirealism issue cannot take comfort from the local case: the materials to generate theory there exist, as it were, by contrast with anything that can be provided in the general case.

These simple naturalistic points are not always respected. Consider, for example, the position associated with John McDowell and David Wiggins. This goes some way in the same direction as projectivism, at least in admitting that a person's ethical outlook is dependent on affective or conative aspects of his make-up. But it takes those aspects as things that enable the subject to do something

else—to perceive value properties. It is only if one is moved or prone to be moved in a certain way that one sees the value of things, just as it is only if one is prone to be moved in some way that one perceives the sadness in a face.[5] This is supposed to do justice to the obvious point that sentiments have something to do with our capacity to make ethical judgment, yet to retain a "perceptual" and cognitive place for moral opinion.

Let us suppose that this is a substantial theory and different from projectivism (in the light of what is to come, neither supposition is beyond doubt). The view is substantial if it holds that changes in one's sensibilities enable one to do something else: *literally* to perceive ethical properties in things. Or if the "something else" is not literal perception, then at least its kinship with perception must be very close—so close that it cannot be explained as projection of a stance. For the view is no different from projectivism if this "something else" is nothing else at all, but merely a different label for reaching an ethical verdict because of one's sentiments. In other words, it is only different from projectivism if this literal talk of perceiving plays a theoretical role, and not just a relabeling of the phenomena. This is not at all obvious. Theoretically low-grade talk of perception is always available. Everyone can say that one can "see" what one must do or what needs to be done, just as one can see that 17 is prime. When I said that it is not what one finishes by saying, but the theory that gets one there, this is one of the crucial examples I had in mind.

Literal talk of perception runs into many problems. One is that the ethical very commonly, and given its function in guiding choice, even typically, concerns imagined or described situations, not perceived ones.[6] We reach ethical verdicts about the behavior of described agents or actions in the light of general standards. And it is stretching things to see these general standards as perceptually formed or maintained. Do I see that ingratitude is base only on occasions when I see an example of ingratitude? How can I be sure of the generalization to examples that I did not see (I could not do that for color, for instance. Absent pillar-boxes may be a different color from present ones; only an inductive step allows us to guess at whether they are). Or, do I see the timeless connection—but how? Do I have an antenna for detecting timeless property-to-value connections? Is such a thing that much like color vision? Perhaps these questions can be brushed aside. But in connection with naturalism, the question to ask of the view is why nature should have bothered. Having, as it were, forced us into good conative shape, why not sit back? Why should this be merely the curtain raiser for a perceptual system? It seems only to engender dangerous possibilities. It ought to make us slower to act, for we must process the new information perceived. Worse, it might be that someone moved, say, by gratitude comes to see the goodness of gratitude and then has, quite generally, some other (negative) reaction to what is seen. Perhaps typically, the conative pressure opens our eyes to these properties, about which we then have a different, conflicting feeling. Or is it somehow given that what comes back is what went in— that the property perceived impinges on us with the same emotional impact required for perceiving it? How convenient! But how clumsy of nature to go in for such a loop! And why did we not evolve to short-circuit it, as projectivism claims? In other words, we have here the typical symptoms of realism, which not only has to take us *to* the new properties but also has to take us back *from* them, showing how perception of them contrives to have exactly the effects it does.

This extravagance came from taking literally the talk of perception made possible by changes of sensibility. But the theory seems to be meant literally. Wiggins, for example, thinks that although projectivism can be dismissed (values "put into [or onto like varnish] the factual world"), the right view is that there are value properties and sensibilities for perceiving them "made for each other" as "equal and reciprocal partners."[7]

Can this be understood? Projectivism, from which the theory is supposed to be so different, can easily embrace one half of the doctrine—that the properties are made for the sensibility. The embrace ought to be a bit tepid, because we shall see better ways of putting the view that value predicates figure in thought and talk as reflections or projections of the attitudes that matter. But it is the other half, that the sensibilities are "made for" the properties, that really startles. Who or what makes them like that? (God? As we have seen, no natural story explains how the ethical sensibilities of human beings were made for the ethical properties of things, so perhaps it is a supernatural story.)

Wiggins, I think, would reply that nothing extraordinary or unfamiliar is called for here. Refinement or civilization makes both sensibility and property. It is the process of education or moral refinement that makes sensibilities end up in good harmony with values. "When this point is reached, a system of anthropocentric properties and human responses has surely taken on a life of its own. Civilization has begun." The implicit plea that we get our responses to life into civilized shape is admirable, but is it enough to locate a view of the nature of ethics, or is there a danger of confusing uplift with theory? Certainly, it is true that when we have gone through some process of ethical improvement, we can turn back and say that now we have got something *right*—now we appreciate the value of things as they are, whereas before we did not. This Whiggish judgment is often in place, but it is, of course, a moral judgment. It is not pertinent to explaining *how* sensibilities are "made for" values. Is it a good theoretical description or explanation of the fact that we value friendship that, first, it is good and, second, civilization has "made" our sensibilities "for" the property of goodness? It seems overripe, since it goes with no apparent theory of error (what if our sensibilities are unluckily not made for the properties?), no teleology, and no evolutionary background. Its loss of control becomes clear if we think how easy it is to generate parallels. Perhaps something similar made our arithmetical powers for the numbers, or our tastes for the niceness of things. Or, perhaps, on the contrary, the talk of our sensibilities being made for the properties is theoretically useless and the more economical remainder is all that is really wanted.

Might there still be room for a view that the properties are "made for" the sensibility, which avoids projectivism? The analogy with colors, for all its many defects, might be held to open such a possibility. But color at this point is a dangerous example. If we ask seriously what color vision is made for, an answer can be found—but it will not cite colors. Color vision is probably made for enhancing our capacities for quickly identifying and keeping track of objects and surfaces, and this asymmetry with, for instance, spatial perception remains the most important point of the primary-secondary property distinction.

Any analogy with color vision is bound to run into the problem of dependency. If we had a theory whereby ethical properties are literally made by or for sensibilities, ethical truth would be constituted by and dependent on the way we think. This might not repel Wiggins. It agrees with the analogy with colors, and in the course of discussing Russell's worry ("I find myself incapable of believing that all that is wrong with wanton cruelty is that I don't like it"), Wiggins freely asserts that "what is wrong with cruelty is not, even for Bertrand Russell, just that Bertrand Russell does not like it, but that it is not such as to call forth liking given our *actual* responses."[8] But is it? I should have said not. It is because of our responses that we *say* that cruelty is wrong, but it is not because of them that it is so. It is true that insertion of the "actual" into the sentence makes it wrong to test the alleged dependence by the usual device of imagining our responses otherwise and asking if that makes cruelty any better.[9] But our actual responses are inappropriate for the wrongness of cruelty to depend upon. What

makes cruelty abhorrent is not that it offends us, but all those hideous things that make it do so.

The projectivist can say this vital thing: that it is not because of our responses, scrutinized and collective or otherwise, that cruelty is wrong. The explanation flows from the way in which quasi-realism has us deal with oblique contexts. It issues an "internal" reading of the statement of dependence, according to which it amounts to an offensive ethical view, about (of course) what it is that makes cruelty wrong. Critics of this explanation allow the internal reading, but complain that the quasi-realist is being willfully deaf to an intended "external" reading, according to which the dependency is a philosophical thesis, and one to which the projectivist, it is said, must assent.[10] The crucial question. therefore, is whether the projectivist willfully refuses to hear the external reading. According to me, there is only one proper way to take the question "On what does the wrongness of wanton cruelty depend?": as a moral question, with an answer in which no mention of our actual responses properly figures. There *would* be an external reading if realism were true. For in that case there would be a fact, a state of affairs (the wrongness of cruelty) whose rise and fall and dependency on others could be charted. But antirealism acknowledges no such state of affairs, and no such issue of dependency. Its freedom from any such ontological headache is not the least of its pleasures. A realist might take this opportunity for dissent. He might say, "I can just *see* that the wrongness of cruelty is a fact (perhaps an eternal one) that needs an ontological theory to support it—no theory that avoids providing such support is credible." In that case I gladly part company, and he is welcome to his quest—for what kind of ontology is going to help? The Euthyphro dilemma bars all roads there.[11]

It is tempting to think: on this metaphysics the world contains nothing but us and our responses, so that fact that cruelty is bad *must* be created by our responses. What else is there for it to be dependent upon? The prejudice is to treat the moral fact as a natural one, capable of being constituted, made or unmade, by sensibilities. The wrongness of wanton cruelty does indeed depend on things—features of it which remind us how awful it is. But locating these is giving moral verdicts. Talk of dependency is moral talk or nothing. This is not, of course, to deny that "external" questions make sense—the projectivist plus quasi-realist package is an external philosophical theory about the nature of morality. But external questions must be conducted in a different key once this package is brought in. We may notice, too, how this undermines a common way of drawing up the realist versus antirealist issue, according to which antirealism asserts that truth in some or all areas is "mind dependent" and realism denies this. For here is the projection, as antirealist a theory of morality as could be wished, denying that moral truth is mind dependent in the only sense possible.

The point can be made as follows. As soon as one *uses* a sentence whose simple assertion expresses an attitude, one is in the business of discussing or voicing ethical opinion. Such sentences include "The fact that *cruelty is wrong* depends on . . ." or "Our refined consensus makes it true that *cruelty is wrong*," and so on. If one generalizes and says things like "moral facts depend on us," the generalization will be true only if instances are true or, in other words, if one can find examples of truths like those. Since these ethical opinions are unattractive, they must be judged incorrect, as must generalizations of them. If one attempts to discuss external questions, one must use a different approach—in my case, a naturalism that places the activities of ethics in the realm of adjusting, improving, weighing, and rejecting different sentiments or attitudes. The projectivist, then, has a perfect right to confine external questions of dependency to domains where real estates of affairs, with their causal relations, are in questions. The only things in this world are the attitudes of people, and

those, of course, are trivially and harmlessly mind dependent. But the projectivist can hear no literal sense in saying that moral properties are made for or by sensibilities. They are not in a world where things are made or unmade—not in this world at all. and it is only because of this that naturalism remains true.

The charge that projectivism refuses to hear an explanatory demand as it is intended can be returned with, I suggest, much more effect. I was severe earlier with Wiggins's theoretical description of us as indulging in a kind of coordination of responses and properties as we become civilized. But it is telling that the Whiggish appeal to a value ("civilization") is introduced at that point. For the introduction of values into explanatory investigations is echoed in other writings in this tradition, notably in those of John McDowell.[12] The strategy is that in a context purportedly comparing explanations of a practice—the practice of ethical judgment—we allow ourselves to invoke the very commitments of that practice. Why are we afraid of the dark? Because it is fearful. Why do we value friendship? Because it is good and we are civilized. Why do I dislike sentimentality? Because it merits it. And so on.

The refusal to stand outside ethics in order to place it is supposed to tie in with one strand in Wittgenstein. This is the thought that there is characteristically neither a reduction nor an explanation of the members of any major family of concepts in terms of those of another. Ethical notions require ethical sensibilities to comprehend them. Similarly, why should it not require an ethical sensibility to comprehend an explanation of the views we hold? Only those who perceive friendship as good will understand why we do so, and to them it can be explained why we do so by reminding them that it is good, or making them feel that it is so. The rest—aliens, outsiders, Martians—cannot be given the explanation, but this is as it must be. What I said about the explanation of our spatial capacities will make it apparent that the circularity exists there in exactly the same way. Only those who appreciate distance can understand the distance-centered explanation of visual perception.

This returns us to a theme that has been touched at many points in this essay. The insistence on hearing explanatory demands only in a way in which one can invoke values in answering them had a respectable origin. We agreed earlier that the parallel would be true of thinking about the correspondence conditionals in the case of physics. But I hope I have said enough to show that nature and our theory of nature surround our ethical commitments in a way that gives us a *place* from which to theorize about them. Nothing and no theory surround our physics. In other words, the difference in the ethical case comes in the theses I labeled (1) and (2)— the brute fact that an external explanatory story is possible. We already know that in even more local cases, where what is at question is not "the ethical" in a lump, but particular attitudes and their etiologies. Social anthropology is not confined to explaining the rise of puritanism to puritans or the evolution of polygamy to polygamists. Similarly, nothing in Wittgenstein offers any principled obstacle to explaining the general shape and nature of ethical attitudes and their expressions in projective terms.

Indeed much in Wittgenstein is sympathetic to doing so. Not only is Wittgenstein himself an antirealist about ethics. He is in general quite free in admitting propositions or quasi-propositions whose function is not to describe anything—the rules of logic and arithmetic, for instance. It is clear that what he wants to do is to place mathematical practice, not as a representation of the mathematical realm, but as "a different kind of instrument," commitment to which is not like central cases of belief, but much more like other kinds of stance. It is also interesting that some of the apparently irritating or evasive answers he gives when faced with the charge of anthropocentricity are exactly those which a projectivist can give if quasi-realism has done its work, and that according to me, no

other philosophy of these matters can give. For example, when Wittgenstein approaches the question whether on his anthropocentric view of mathematical activity, mathematical truth is yet independent of human beings, he says exactly what I would have him say:

> "But mathematical truth is independent of whether human beings know it or not!"— Certainly, the propositions 'Human beings believe that twice two is four' and 'twice two is four' do not mean the same. The latter is a mathematical proposition; the other, if it makes sense at all, may perhaps mean: human beings have *arrived* at the mathematical proposition. The two propositions have entirely different *uses*.[13]

The proposition expresses a norm that arises in the course of human activities, but it does not describe those activities, and it has no use in which the correctness of the norm (the truth of the proposition) depends upon the existence or form of those activities. *That* question simply cannot be posed; it treats what is not a dependent state of affairs belonging to the natural world at all, as if it were.

I have tried to show that naturalism, which turns away from realism and antirealism alike in the global case turns toward projective theories in the ethical case. This theory is visibly antirealist, for the explanations offered make no irreducible or essential appeal to the existence of moral "properties" or "facts"; they demand no "ontology of morals. They explain the activity from the inside out— from the naturally explicable attitudes to the forms of speech that communicate them, challenge them, refine them, and abandon them, and which so mislead the unwary.

So far I have talked of the issue of mind dependency in fairly abstract terms, and relied upon a relatively subtle move in the philosophy of language to defend my view. I now want to discuss these points in practical terms. It is evident that a more fundamental mistake underlies some discomfort with projectivism. The mistake is visible in Wiggins's critique of "non-cognitive theories" in his

British Academy Lecture.[14] It results in the charge that projectivism cannot be true to the "inside of lived experience." Other writers (I would cite Nagel, Williams, and Foot) seem to illustrate similar unease. The thought is something like this: it is important that there should be some kind of accord in our thinking about ethical stances from the perspective of the theorist, and from that of the participant. Our story about ethical commitment is to explain it, not to explain it away. But projectivism threatens to do the latter (many people who should know better think of Hume as a skeptic about ethics, and, of course. John Mackie saw himself as one). It threatens to do so because it shows us that our commitments are not external demands, claiming us regardless of our wills or in direct opposition to our passions. It makes our commitments facets of our own sentimental natures; this softens them, destroying the hardness of the moral must.

From the inside, the objects of our passions are their *immediate* objects: it is the death, the loved one, the sunset, that matters to us. It is not our own state of satisfaction or pleasure. Must projectivism struggle with this fact, or disown it? Is it that we projectivists, at the crucial moment when we are about to save the child, throw ourselves on the grenade, walk out into the snow, will think, "Oh, it's only me and my desires or other conative pressures—forget it"?

It ought to be sufficient refutation of this doubt to mention other cases. Does the lover escape his passion by thinking, "Oh it's only my passion, forget it"? When the world affords occasion for grief, does it brighten when we realize that it is we who grieve? (The worst thing to think is that if we are "rational," it should, as if rationality had anything to tell us about it.)

There is an important mistake in the philosophy of action that, I think, must explain the temptation to share Wiggins's doubt. The mistake is that of supposing that when we deliberate in the light of various features of a situation we are *at the same time* or "really"

deliberating—or that our reasoning can be "modeled" by representing us as deliberating—about our own conative functioning. Representing practical reasoning as if it consisted of contemplating a syllogism, one of whose premises describes what we want, encourages this mistake. But just as the eye is not part of the visual scene it presents, the sensibility responsible for the emotional impact of things is not part of the scene it takes for material. Nor is our sense of humor the main thing we find funny. This does not mean that our sensibility is hidden from us, and when we reflect on ourselves we can recognize aspects of it, just as we can know when we are in love or grieving. But it does mean that its own shape is no part of the input, when we react to the perceived features of things. Furthermore, even when we reflect on our sensibility, we will be using it if we issue a verdict: when we find our own sense of humor funny, we are not escaping use of it as we do so.

This misconstruction leads people to suppose that on a projective theory all obligations must be "hypothetical," because properly represented as dependent upon the existence of desires. But the lover who hears that she is there and feels he has to go, or the person who receiving bad news feels he must grieve, has no thoughts of the form "if I desire her / feel sad then I must go / grieve." Nothing corresponds to this. The news comes in and the emotion comes out; nothing in human life could be or feel more categorical. In ordinary emotional cases, of course, a third party may judge that it is only *if* he desires her that he must go; this is not so in ethical cases. One ought to look after one's young children, whether one wants to or not. But that is because we insist on some responses from others, and it is sometimes part of good moralizing to do so.

Once these mistakes are averted, is there any substance left to the worry about failure of harmony of the theoretical and deliberative points of view? I think not. Sometimes theory can help to change attitudes. One might become less attached to some virtue, or less eager in pursuing some vice, after thinking about its etiology or its functioning. One might qualify it a little (we see an example in what follows). But sometimes one might become more attached to the virtue, and sometimes everything stays the same. Does the story threaten to undermine the promise that the stances cited in this theory of ethics make good natural sense (does it take something divine to make the claims of obligation so pregnant with authority)? Not at all—I have already mentioned the "musts" of love and grief, and those of habit and obsession are just as common.

There is one last charge of the would-be realist. This claims that projectivism must lead to relativism. "Truth" must be relative to whatever set of attitudes is grounding our ethical stances; since these may vary from place to place and time to time, truth must be relative. The very analogies with other conative states press this result: what to one person is an occasion for love or grief or humor is not to another. Consider a young person gripped by the imperatives of fashion. The judgment that people must wear some style, that another is impossible, has its (naturally explicable and perfectly intelligible) function: it appears quite categorical, for the subject will think that it is not just for him or her that the style is mandatory or impossible (it was so in the parents' time as well, only they did not realize it). Yet, surely this is a mistake. The verdict is "relative," having no truth outside the local system of preferences that causes it. The image is plain: a projectivist may inhabit a particular ethical boat, but he must know of the actual or potential existence of others; where, then, is the absolute truth?

The answer is that it is not anywhere that can be visible from this sideways, theoretical perspective. It is not that this perspective is illegitimate, but that it is not the one adapted for finding ethical truth. It would be if such truth were natural truth, or consisted

of the existence of states of affairs in the real world. That is the world seen from the viewpoint that sees different and conflicting moral systems—but inevitably sees no truth in just one of them. To "see" the truth that wanton cruelty is wrong demands moralizing, stepping back into the boat, or putting back the lens of a sensibility. But once that is done, there is nothing relativistic left to say. The existence of the verdict, of course, depends on the existence of those capable of making it; the existence of the truth depends on nothing (externally), and on those features that make it wrong (internally). For the same reasons that operated when I discussed mind dependency, there is no doctrine to express relating the truth of the verdict to the existence of us, of our sentiments, or of rival sentiments.

What, then, of the parallel with the other emotions, or with the fashion example? The emotions of grief and love are naturally personal; if the subject feels they make a claim on others, so that those unstricken somehow *ought* to be, then, she is nonrelativistically, absolutely wrong. Similarly with fashion: the underlying story includes the need to a self-presentation that is admirable to the peer group, and if what is admirable changes rapidly as generations need to distance themselves from their immediate predecessors, then the teenager who thinks that her parents were wrong to like whatever clothes they did is mistaken in the same way as the subject of an emotion who imputes a mistake to those who cannot feel the same. But the strongest ethical judgments do not issue from stances that are properly variable. They may sometimes be absent, from natural causes, as if a hard life destroys a capacity for pity. But this is a cause for regret; it would be better if it were not so. In the variations of emotion, and still more of fashion, there is no cause for regret. In saying these things I am, of course, voicing some elements of my own ethical stances, but as I promised, it is only by doing this that ethical truth is found.

II

If projective theories have everything going for them in ethics, how much can they jettison and still have *something* going for them? The two ingredients I highlighted are: the possibility of identifying the commitment in a way that contrasts it usefully with belief, and a "neat, natural account" of why the state that it is should exist. In the case of ethics we have conative stances, and a visible place for them in our functioning. But what in other cases?

Color commitments might attract attention, because not everybody will be happy that the agreed story about what color vision is and why we have it leaves realism as a natural doctrine about colors. Here the second ingredient is present. There is a neat, natural story of our capacity for color discrimination, and in its explanatory side, both physically and evolutionarily, it makes no explanatory use of the *existence* of colors. But there is no way that I can see usefully to contrast color commitments with *beliefs*. Their functional roles do not differ. So, there will be no theory of a parallel kind to develop, explaining why we have propositional attitudes of various kinds toward color talk, or why we speak of knowledge, doubt, proof, and so forth in connection with them. If anything can be drawn from a realism versus antirealism debate over color (which I rather doubt), it would have to be found by different means.

Modal commitments are much more promising. Our penchant for necessities and possibilities, either in concepts or in nature, is not easy to square with a view that we are representing anything, be it a distribution of possible worlds, or (in the case of natural necessity) a timeless nomic connection between universals.[15]

First, consider the case of logical necessity. A theory insisting on a nonrepresentative function for modal commitment is clearly attractive. Here, however, although I think the first desideratum is met—we can do

something to place the stance as something other than belief in the first instance—the second is not so easy. The kind of stance involved in insistence upon a norm, an embargo on a trespass. Saying that $2 + 2$ is anything other than 4 offends against the embargo, and the embargo in turn makes shared practices, shared communication possible. So far so good, but what of a "neat, natural theory" of the emergence of the embargo? That shared practices should exist is good—but do they so clearly depend upon such policing? If they do, it appears to be because of something else: because we can make no sense of a way of thinking that flouts the embargo. It introduces apparent possibilities of which we can make nothing. This imaginative limitation is, in turn, something of which no natural theory appears possible, even in outline. For when we *can* make sense of the imaginative limitation, we do find it apt to explain away or undermine the original commitment to a necessity. If it seems only because of (say) confinement to a world in which relative velocities are always slow compared to that of light, that we find a relativistic view of simultaneity hard to comprehend, then that already shows how we would be wrong to deem the theory impossible. If it is only because of the range of our color vision that we cannot imagine a new primary color, then we would be unwise to rule out the possibility that some natural operation might result in our admitting one. Natural explanation is here the enemy of the hard logical must.

It is not obviously so in the case of natural necessity. Once more the paradigm is Hume—not the Hume of commentators, but the real Hume, who knew that talk of necessity was irreducible, but gave a projective theory of it. The explanation here has us responsive to natural regularity, and forming dispositions of expectation (we might add, of observing boundaries in our counterfactual reasoning), which in turn stand us in good stead as the regularities prove reliable. Here, once we accept the Humean metaphysics, the naturalism seems quite in place. The upshot—talk of causation—is not undermined but is explained by this interpretation. This accords exactly with the case of ethics. There is a difference, however, I do not think metaphysical obstacles stand in the way of the conception of nature that does the explanatory work in the example of ethics. But many writers have difficulty with the conception of nature that is supposed to do it in Hume's metaphysics of causation. Regularities—but between what? Events—but how are these to be conceived, stripped of the causal "bit" (to use the computer metaphor)? Events thought of as changes in ordinary objects will scarcely do, for as many writers have insisted, ordinary objects are permeated with causal powers. Nothing corresponds to the easy, sideways, naturalistic perspective that strips the world of values.

What is the option? All sides carry on talk of causation in whichever mode they find best. The new realists like to produce apparent ontologies—universals, timeless connections, and the rest. The Humean does not mind, so long as the explanatory pretensions of these retranslations are kept firmly in their place (outside understanding). Is there scope for a debate here? It is a place where the ghosts are hard to lay, and I for one do not like being there alone in the gloom.

NOTES

1. For example. see Arthur Fine, "Unnatural Attitudes: Realist and Instrumentalist Attachments to Science," *Mind* 95 (1986): 149–79.

2. On Putnam in this connection, see Ruth Garrett Millikan, "Metaphysical Anti-Realism?" *Mind* 95 (1986): 417–31.

3. My favorite example is Putnam, *Reason, Truth and History* (Cambridge: Cambridge University Press, 1981), p. 52.

4. R. Axelrod, *The Evolution of Cooperation* (New York: Basic Books, 1984).

5. John McDowell, "Non-Cognitivism and Rule Following," in *Wittgenstein: To Follow a Rule*, ed. S. Holtzman and C. Leich (London: Routledge & Kegan Paul, 1981). Also, Sabina Lovibond, *Realism and Imagination in Ethics* (Oxford: Blackwell, 1983). Other writers influenced by the analogy include Mark Platts, *The Ways of Meaning*, (London: Routledge & Kegan Paul, 1979); and Anthony Price, "Doubts about Projectivism," *Philosophy*, 61 (1986): 215–28.

6. John Locke, *An Essay concerning Human Understanding,* IV, chap. IV, 6–7.

7. D. Wiggins, *Truth, Invention and the Meaning of Life*, British Academy lecture *Proceedings of the British Academy* 62 (1976): 348.

8. "A Sensible Subjectivism," in *Needs, Values, Truth* (Oxford: Blackwell, 1987), 210; [see also this volume, chap. 13].

9. The use of "actual" to make rigid the reference to our present attitudes, and thereby fend off some natural objections to dispositional subjective analyses, is exploited in this connection by Michael Smith.

10. Quassim Cassam, "Necessity and Externality," *Mind*, 95: (1986) 446–64.

11. I enlarge upon this in "Morals and Modals," in *Fact, Science, and Morality*, ed. Graham MacDonald and Crispin Wright (Oxford: Blackwell, 1987).

12. For instance in his "Values and Secondary Properties," in *Morality and Objectivity: A Tribute to J. L. Mackie*, ed. T. Honderich (London: Routledge & Kegan Paul, 1985).

13. Ludwig Wittgenstein, *Philosophical Investigations* (Oxford: Blackwell, 1953) p. 226.

14. Ibid, (6) sec. 4.

15. David Armstrong, *What Is a Law of Nature* (Cambridge: Cambridge University Press, 1983), chap. 6.

10

Wise Choices, Apt Feelings

ALLAN GIBBARD

1. THE PUZZLE

Why ponder our lives? At one extreme, the question is not a live one. We are a pondering species—and not each by himself; we are conversants. Silence is a discipline; too much is torment, as children learn in school. Sometimes we discuss earnestly, and in any case we banter and tease; we quarrel and sulk. We gossip and tell stories, with verve if we can. These things engage us; is that because they have point? Are they ways of working matters through with each other, or playing them through? Even when we are not pondering outright, we are caught up in equivalents.

With human beings it was always so. The !Kung of the Kalihari are hunter-gatherers, and perhaps in them we can see what our hunting-gathering forebears were like. "Conversation in a !Kung encampment is a constant sound like the sound of a brook, and as low and lapping, except for shrieks of laughter. People cluster together in little groups

during the day, talking, perhaps making artifacts at the same time. At night, families talk late by their fires, or visit at other family fires with their children between their knees or in their arms if the wind is cold."[2] The !Kung criticize each other, they gossip, they make oblique hints; they tell about events, about comings and goings, and about past hunts. They plan their hunts, and the successful hunter may consult on the proper distribution of his kill. Occasionally they quarrel, and frequently they talk about gifts and their suitability.

Conversation, then, is far more than a carrier of bald information. In talk we work out not only what to believe about things and events and people, but how to live. We work out how to feel about things in our lives, and in the lives of others. Not that we strive always to get to the root of things: We think not so much how to live and to feel on the whole, but about one thing or another, as it catches our attention.

To ponder how to live, to reason about how

to live, is in effect to ask what kind of life it is *rational* to live. I offer no special answer to this question; my first worry is what the question is. What does it mean to call an alternative rational, or another irrational? That is puzzle of this study, and my hope is that from working on it, we can learn things worth learning about ourselves and about our questions.

In part the question how to live is moral—perhaps in whole. Once broad questions grip us, we shall want to know where morality fits in. What kind of morality, if any, would be worth heeding? Or does the rational life do without morality? Here again my puzzle will be what the questions are. Again I want to know what 'rational' means, and in addition I want to understand this talk of morality. What are moral questions; what do they mean? What, if anything, do they have to do with rationality?

My puzzle is about philosophers, but it is also about the !Kung. I ask about moral philosophy, but also about everyday, non-philosophic life and thought and talk. The two kinds of talk are not the same, but one grows out of the other. As part of a human way of living, we think and discuss what it makes sense to do, and how it makes sense to feel about things. This thought and talk contains its own nudges toward refinement, and responding to them makes for stronger nudges still. Wise choices and apt feelings figure in talk at both extremes: in refined, self-conscious philosophizing and in everyday banter and quarrel. I want to know what is at stake in normative talk of both kinds.

2. RATIONALITY AND MORALITY

To call a thing "rational" is to endorse it in some way. That suggests a scheme for getting at the meaning of the term. Instead of trying to define a property "rationality" by giving conditions under which a thing would have that property or lack it, start with the use of the term. Fix on the dictum, "To call a thing rational is to endorse it," and search for a sense of 'endorse' for which the dictum holds true.

We appraise a wide variety of human attributes as rational or irrational. Not only can a person act rationally or irrationally, but he can believe rationally or irrationally, and he can be angry or grateful or envious rationally or irrationally. It is irrational, say, to be angry at the messenger who brings bad tidings, but rational to be angry at the miscreant who deliberately wrongs one. Or at least this, I take it, is what we tend to think in the normal course of life. If the word "rational" seems overly learned here, substitutes come with a more homely flavor: "It doesn't make sense" to be angry at the person who brings bad news he had no part in making. The anger "isn't warranted." You "shouldn't be grateful" to someone who benefited you only inadvertently in seeking his own gain.

None of this is to say that when we call something "rational"—an act, belief, or emotion—we are saying anything intelligible. That remains to be seen. I am saying that we *talk* and *think* as if such appraisals are intelligible. It may be worth while, then, to see if we can interpret them as intelligible.

First, though, let me turn to morality and its tie to rationality. Suppose naively, for now, that we know what 'rational' means. Later I attempt an analysis of the term.

In the history of moral philosophy, there seem to be at least two sharply different conceptions of what morality is. On the broadest of conceptions, morality is simply practical rationality in the fullest sense: to say that an act is morally right is to say that it is rational. Sidgwick is a prime exponent of this broad conception, and perhaps Kant is; it is shared by many current writers. On this conception, it makes no sense to ask, "Is it always rational to do what is morally right?" for 'the morally right' simply means "the rational." On a narrow conception of morality, in contrast, moral considerations are just some of the considerations that bear on what it makes sense to do. Non-moral considerations matter too. On the narrow conception it is normally wrong, say, to injure others, to steal, or break one's word. It would normally not be morally wrong, though, to fritter away a day for which one had planned an enjoyable hike—however irrational that might be. On the broad conception of morality, morally right action simply is action that is truly rational, whereas on the narrow conception, an act may be truly irrational without being morally wrong. (Perhaps too an action can be morally wrong without being truly irrational.)

In Chapter 5 of *Utilitarianism*, John Stuart Mill uses the term 'morality' in this narrow sense, and offers an account of what is distinctive about morality so taken. "Morality," he says, "pertains to what is wrong or not wrong, and to say that an act is wrong is to say that there ought to be a sanction against it, a sanction of law, of public opinion, or of conscience." The 'ought' here, Mill proposes, should be judged by the standards of the greatest happiness principle—but that is part of the normative theory Mill is giving, not a part of his analysis of the term 'morally wrong'. What I propose to do is to take over Mill's analysis of what morality is in the narrow sense, with various interpretations and modifications.

When Mill says there ought to be a sanction, let us read him as saying that a sanction is rational—or, perhaps, rationally required. Let us also drop talk of legal sanctions. Suppose, say, we think that people who overpark at parking meters ought to be fined, but that they ought not to feel guilty, and ought not to be resented by others for overparking. In that case, it seems to me, we do not think overparking morally wrong; we merely think that a price should be charged. That leaves sanctions of conscience and of public opinion: sanctions of guilt and remorse, on the one hand, and of blame, resentment, and moral outrage on the other. Thus as the proposal now stands, what a person does is *morally wrong* if and only if it is rational for him to feel guilty for doing it, and for others to resent him for doing it.

'Resent' here is in some ways the wrong term. It suggests a sense of personal injury, injury to oneself, whereas blame may well be impartial. Resentment, outrage, condemnation, indignation, blame—all these get roughly at the sentiment I want. Now all these terms suggest anger, perhaps along with a sense of justification. The sense of justification goes with my talk of rationality, and so what is left is anger of various kinds. Try this formulation, then: What a person does is *morally wrong* if and only if it is rational for him to feel guilty for having done it, and for others to be angry at him for having done it.

As the formulation stands, it is more plausible for 'blameworthy' than for 'morally wrong'. What, then, might it mean to call an act wrong? Roughly, we might say, the standards of right and wrong are the standards we demand an agent use to rule out certain alternatives. In assessing blame, we apply two kinds of tests. First, we ask whether the agent's level of morally desirable motivation was satisfactory. If not, we ask whether there are extenuating circumstances that render the agent not fully responsible. Standards of right and wrong pertain to the first part: an agent's motives are morally acceptable if he is sufficiently motivated to avoid wrong acts. Standards for wrongness, then, are the standards such that an agent is prima facie blameworthy if he does not use them to rule out acts that violate them. The reason the blameworthiness is only prima facie is that facts about the person's motivational state may be extenuating. Blame thus depends both on standards for wrongness and on standards for responsibility. Formally put, then, the definitions I propose are these: An act is wrong if and only if it violates standards for ruling out actions, such that if an agent in a normal frame of mind violated those standards because he was not substantially motivated to conform to them, he would be to blame. To say that he would *be to blame*, here, is to say that it would be rational for him to feel guilty and for others to resent him.

3. THE NORM-EXPRESSIVISTIC ANALYSIS

What does it mean to call something "rational"? One way of tackling such a question is to psychologize it. What, we may ask, is the psychological state of *regarding* something as rational, of *taking* it to be rational, of *believing* it rational? Put roughly and cryptically, my hypothesis is that to *think something rational* is to accept norms that, on balance, permit it.

By a *norm* here, I mean a possible norm: a possible rule or prescription, expressible by an imperative. The prescription need not actually be made by anyone, or accepted by anyone, to count as a "norm" as I am using the term. The main thing to be explained is not what a "norm" is, but what "accepting a norm" is—or more precisely, what it is for something to be permitted or required by "the norms" a person "accepts." I mean these latter notions to be psychological: They are meant to figure in an explanatory theory of human experience and action.

I might have tried an analysis of quite a different form: that an act, belief, or attitude of a person *is* rational if someone—be it I, or he, or a commentator—accepts norms that prescribe it for that person's circumstances. My own analysis, though, is not directly a hypothesis about what it *is* for something to be rational at all. It is a hypothesis about what it is to *think* or *believe* something rational, to *regard* it as rational, to consider rational. An observer *believes* an action, belief, or attitude *A* of mine to be rational, the hypothesis is, if and only if he accepts norms that permit *A* for my circumstances. It follows that if we want to decide what really *is* rational, we shall have to settle what norms to accept ourselves—for that is what it is to form an opinion as to the rationality of something.

Return now to norms of morality. In analyzing the narrowly moral notions "blameworthy" and "wrong," I took the term 'rational' as understood. If we now combine these analyses with our rough analysis of 'rational',

we can derive an account of the distinction between moral norms and norms of rationality. All norms, in a sense, are norms of rationality, but moral norms in particular are norms for the rationality of guilt and resentment. Consider first what it is for an action to be "blameworthy." The analyses given so far tell us this: (1) An observer thinks an act *blameworthy*, or *morally reprehensible*, if and only if he thinks it rational for the agent to feel guilty over the act, and for others to resent the agent for it. (2) To think something 'rational' is to accept norms that prescribe it. Therefore, we may conclude, to think an act *morally reprehensible* is to accept norms that prescribe, for such a situation, guilt on the part of the agent and resentment on the part of others.

Next consider the term 'morally wrong'. The standards for whether an act is wrong, we have said, are the standards such that guilt and resentment are prima facie rational if the agent is not disposed to rule out alternatives that violate them. Thus to *think* an act *wrong* is to accept norms for guilt and resentment that, prima facie, would sanction guilt and resentment if the act were performed. 'Prima facie' here means before questions of the psychological peculiarities of the agent are raised—the psychological peculiarities, that is, that bear on whether the agent is to be considered fully responsible. Norms for wrongness are thus explained in terms of norms for guilt and resentment.

This proposal as it stands requires an independent account of responsibility. Now the psychic makeup of the agent has some bearing not only on whether the agent is responsible, but on what acts open to him are wrong. How do we separate the two? Suppose, for instance, that an act is the only one that is eligible, in the sense that all alternatives to it would leave the agent desperately unhappy. That fact may, in our opinion, tend to justify the act morally: It might be that even though the act would otherwise be wrong, this consideration turns it right. That, in any case, is what we might well think, and an analysis should allow for the possibility. In what ways, then, might psychological peculiarities of an agent bear on his degree of moral responsibility by itself, without bearing on the rightness and wrongness of the acts open to him?

So far I have offered no clear answer. Standards for responsibility, I might have said, are standards for when an agent is to blame for acting on prima facie blameworthy motivations, and prima facie blameworthy motivations are motives for which an agent is to blame if he is fully responsible. Then although 'blameworthy' itself would have been defined independently, the terms 'prima facie blameworthy' and 'responsible' would be defined only in terms of each other.

This circularity, I think, can be eliminated as follows: Consider an agent who has various psychological peculiarities, and an act for which I would consider the agent to blame if I thought him normal. Our problem, recall, is to untangle whether, because of his psychological peculiarities, I regard the act as right, or whether, rather, I consider the act to be wrong but the agent not to blame. The test I propose is this: Take an agent with psychological peculiarities, and imagine him for the moment rendered normal, but expecting to reacquire his psychological peculiarities once he had decided how to act on this occasion. He thus must take these psychological peculiarities into account in deciding what to do, though he is rid of them for the moment, apart from his belief that he has them. Whether I consider the act to be wrong, then, is a matter of whether I accept norms that would sanction guilt and anger if the agent, while temporarily rendered normal, were to perform that act.

4. NORMATIVE PSYCHOLOGY: COMPETING SYSTEMS OF CONTROL

How can the "acceptance of norms" be explained? The straightest course would be further analysis: we might look for a straight-forward definition of what it means to say that a person accepts such-and-such a norm. I doubt, though, that such an analysis is possible. Philosophers are familiar with crucial terms that stymie analysis. At times large numbers of philosophers have tried to analyze a concept, and all have failed. I shall sketch a picture that suggests that were all philosophers to turn to analyzing the "acceptance of norms," all would fail here too.

How, then, if not by analysis, might I hope to explain the acceptance of norms? What I shall do, in effect, is to engage in incipient psychological theorizing. "Accepting a norm," I want to suggest, is a significant kind of psychological state that we are far from entirely understanding. We can hope not to define this state precisely, but to point to it. There is a centrally important psychological state, I suggest, that roughly fits the ordinary notion of a person's "accepting a norm." I shall say what I can about this putative state, adducing various shreds of evidence and lines of reasoning that I think lend plausibility to the claim that there is such a state. The shreds of evidence consist in part of commonsense belief and vocabulary, and in part of observation, both systematic and casual. I shall then announce that I am interested in whatever theoretically significant psychological state, if any, roughly fits what I have said.

My goal, then, will be not just to elucidate ordinary concepts and beliefs, but to use them as a guide. They can guide us in speculating about what an adequate scientific psychology might be like. The vague hypothesis I shall be developing is that in a scientifically adequate psychology, there would figure a state that roughly fits the commonsense notion of "accepting a norm." This state would figure centrally in the story of human thinking and motivation.

Start by considering cases of "weakness of will" and the struggle for "self-control." Suppose I can't get myself to stop eating nuts at a party. What is happening? One commonsense description is this: I think it makes sense to stop eating the nuts—indeed that it doesn't make sense to go on eating them—but I nevertheless go on eating them. In this case, it seems, I accept a norm that prescribes eating no more nuts, but go on eating them even so.

In this commonsense account, it is assumed that the acceptance of a norm is motivating, at least to a degree: believing I ought to stop tends to make me stop. On this occasion, though, the motivation that stems from my accepting a norm is "overpowered" by motivation of another kind: my craving or appetite for nuts. The craving is not itself a matter of my accepting norms; indeed such cravings are sometimes referred to as "animal": we think that they are motivations of a kind we share with beasts.

This is a picture of two motivational systems in conflict. One system is of a kind we think peculiar to human beings; it works through a person's accepting norms. We might call this kind of motivation *normative* motivation, and the putative psychological faculty involved the *normative control system*. The other putative system we might call the *animal control system*, since it, we think, is the part of our motivational system that we share with the beasts. Let us treat this picture as a vague psychological hypothesis—a hypothesis about what is going on in typical cases of "weakness of will."

How plausible is this hypothesis? It draws some support, of course, simply from the fact that it fits the commonsense picture, and so has some claim to fit the motley array of observations that have shaped our ordinary views of the world. This plausibility alone, though, is weak: Common sense, after all, may stick to a picture that fits only a part of everyday observation. In any case, it is untouched by the further observations that can be made in the course of a systematic psychological investigation. Common sense may be a good starting point for psychological theorizing, but it is no place to stop.

Some plausibility is added to the hypothesis by considerations of human evolution.

Why did language evolve in the genus *Homo*? Why might linguistic ability have been fitness-enhancing in proto-humans? A significant part of the story must of course be that language allows the straightforward communication of beliefs. The story must also involve, though, the kinds of planned, coordinated activities that language makes possible. Humans plan together; they make agreements; they exhort. Their language facilitates both complex coordination among individuals and complex individual plans—and if words lacked all power to move us, none of these things would be possible. Words, then, must motivate. What does this have to do with norms? In many cases, at least, a norm is stated in language, or thought in words. A norm, we might say, is a linguistically encoded precept. Perhaps, then, we should think of the motivation I have been calling "normative" as motivation of a particular, linguistically infused kind—a kind of motivation that evolved because of the advantages of coordination and planning through language.

If language figures centrally in human motivation, then we should expect conflicts between motivation of different kinds: the peculiarly human, linguistically infused kind of motivation on the one hand, and evolutionarily prior kinds of motivation on the other. Biology, after all, offers numerous examples of duplicate systems sharing the same function, with one system evolutionarily more recent than the other. The normative control system and the animal control system might be a case in point.

To understand norms, we need to ask how language motivates. A special, linguistically infused motivational system might well have evolved as part of the evolution of human linguistic abilities, and if it did, we could introduce talk of "accepting a norm" by pointing to that system, and saying that *accepting a norm* is whatever that system does.

We cannot, I think, rest content with this proposal, but it makes a good start.

5. CONFLICTS WITH SOCIAL MOTIVATIONS

"Weakness of will" involves conflict, and so far in my discussion, the conflict has been between the norms a person accepts and an appetite. Many apparent cases of "weakness of will" are not of this kind. Often what we experience is not a conflict between the norms we accept and a bodily appetite, but a conflict between our "better judgment" and powerful social motivations. We are paralyzed by embarrassment, or a desire to ingratiate, or some other motivation that is peculiarly social. Examples abound: I may be unable to get myself to walk out of a lecture, even though it is important for me to be somewhere else. I may find myself unable to say something I know will be painful to my listener, even though I think it needs to be said. My discussion of "normative control" seems not to have addressed cases like these.

An especially powerful demonstration of this kind of conflict lies in Stanley Milgram's series of experiments on obedience.[3] Subjects of his experiments were told to administer electric shocks—shocks that were increasingly painful, and eventually lethal—to another subject (who in fact was not being shocked, but was acting as a confederate of the experimenter). Roughly two-thirds of the subjects eventually did all they were ordered to do, although they were upset and protested vigorously. Even when subjects balked, once the experimenter said such things as "The experiment requires that you continue," a majority complied.

Now when we read about these experiments, we are shocked by what the subjects did. Their actions violate norms that we accept. The near uniformity with which the subjects substantially acquiesced, however, should suggest to each of us, "Had I been a subject in one of these experiments before I first read or heard of them, I too would have cooperated with the experimenter—perhaps fully, and almost certainly more than I would like to acknowledge. I would have felt immensely disturbed about the situation in which I found myself, and I would have protested vigorously and regarded the experimenter as a madman. Nevertheless, I probably would have complied."

A typical subject in one of these experiments clearly experiences conflict of some sort; that is shown by his protests and his extreme agitation. The conflict, though, is not between a norm he accepts and a bodily appetite. It seems rather to be a conflict between one norm and another. The subject accepts the norm against intentional harm—the norm in terms of which we ourselves condemn his behavior. That is shown by the vigor of his protests. Nevertheless, he obeys an experimenter who tells him to violate that norm. He does so, it would appear, from a complex of motivations: he is set to be polite and cooperative, to do his job in the experiment, to follow the directions of the man in charge. The conflict, we might therefore say, is between opposing norms: a norm of non-harm on the one hand, and norms of following directions, cooperating, doing one's job on the other.

What are we to make of this conflict? Much of what I have been saying about the subject applies as well to us, as we read about the experiment. We, like the subject, accept norms of politeness, cooperativeness, and doing one's job—the norms that determine the subject's behavior. Like him, we accept norms against inflicting pain and endangering others. What, then, distinguishes us from the subject? The difference seems to be that we, the readers, take these norms of politeness and cooperation to be decisively overridden by the norms against inflicting pain and endangering people, whereas the subject is moved, in the end, by norms of politeness and cooperativeness despite his acceptance of these other norms. The difference is not one of character, but one of circumstance—of the context in which we think, judge, and act. The subject, had he been a reader instead, would have reacted very much as we do. Had we been subjects, the evidence is, we too might well have done as they did.

What is the role of norms in all this? The conflict is between one set of norms and another, true enough, but that suggests a symmetry that is specious. For Milgram's setup, the two sets of norms play different psychological roles. The norm of non-infliction of harm prevails in the judgments of detached observers, whereas the norms of cooperativeness, taking directions, doing one's job control the agent in the heat of social encounter. From our detached perspective, norms against the infliction of pain and danger are, in their application to this situation, plainly overriding. For the subject, the norms of cooperativeness prevail.

Ordinary language has devices that come close to labelling this contrast. We, as judges, *accept* a norm against infliction of harm, and *accept* that this norm, in the situation of Milgram's subjects, overrides norms of cooperativeness and doing one's job—norms that we also accept. The subjects, on the other hand, do not genuinely *accept* that in their situation, norms of cooperativeness and the like override all other norms. Rather, we might say, they are *in the grip* of these norms. In common language, then, the contrast is between *accepting* a norm (or more precisely, *accepting* that one set of norms outweighs another in a given situation) with *being in the grip of* a norm.

If there is a distinction of this kind to be drawn, how is it tied to ascriptions of rationality? To call something rational, I have proposed, is to express one's acceptance of norms that, on balance, permit it. Once "accepting" a norm has been distinguished from "being in its grip," we need to ask which of the two belongs in the norm-expressivistic analysis of 'rational'. In the examples I used to display the distinction, the answer seems clear: It is "accepting" norms that matters here, not "being in their grip." What, after all, does a subject in one of Milgram's obedience experiments think it rational to do? If his plight is genuinely one of "weakness of will," that is presumably because he thinks that it makes no sense to cooperate, but finds himself cooperating nevertheless. In other words, he does what he thinks irrational. Now what he actually does, in this case, is a matter of the norms that have him "in their grip"—norms of politeness and cooperativeness. What he thinks it "rational" to do, on the other hand, is what is required by norms against inflicting pain and danger—and these are the norms he "accepts" as having most weight in his situation. In this case, then, his thinking it irrational to cooperate apparently consists of his *accepting*, as having most weight in his circumstances, norms that turn out to prohibit cooperation. Thinking something rational or irrational thus seems to be a matter not of being in the grip of norms, but of accepting them.

6. THE BIOLOGY OF COORDINATION

So far I have illustrated the distinction between "accepting" a norm and "being in its grip," but I have offered no theory of the difference. What I can suggest will have to be quite speculative, but the speculation may be worth attempting. Speculation may prompt more solid investigation, and it may lend some plausibility to the central claim I am making: that something like the ordinary notion of "accepting a norm" must figure in an adequate human psychology

I want to understand acceptance of norms as a natural, biological phenomenon. I do not mean by this that we should fit the acceptance of norms to a crude preconception of what could be biological; human life demands a biology adequate to its subject. I do mean that I shall be drawing on biological theory for devices to help us understand the phenomena I have been displaying.

If there is such a thing as governance by norms, there must be psychic mechanisms that accomplish it, and we can ask about their biological function. That function, I want to suggest, is to *coordinate*. Accepting a norm and being in its grip manifest two different systems of coordination. Of these, the capacity to accept norms is peculiarly human and depends on language.

Human beings are adapted to live in societies of many kinds, to respond flexibly to a vast diversity of cues their cultures might offer—and who because of culture and its ramified effects, live throughout the world in evolutionarily novel circumstances. In applying Darwinian theory to the human psyche, we should look not for rigid patterns of behavior, but for capacities to respond differently to different environments. We should look, in effect, for nature's contingency plans for human thought, emotion, and motivation. Tendencies to respond differently to different kinds of situations may in some cases constitute adaptations. Whether they do is roughly a matter of whether, in early human environments, these patterns would have tended on balance to promote individuals' reproduction.

Systems of normative control in human beings, I am suggesting, are adapted to achieve interpersonal coordination. What might this mean? To answer this, I sketch work of Thomas Schelling on rational coordination in pursuit of human goals, and John Maynard Smith's evolutionary analog of Schelling's theory.[4]

Turn first, then, to coordination in the pursuit of human goals. Meeting a person provides one of Schelling's paradigms. Suppose it will further the purposes of both of us if we meet successfully in Chicago, and it matters relatively little to each of us where or when. If you are in front of the Art Institute at 12:30, I do best myself to be in front of the Art Institute at 12:30. If instead, you are behind the Picasso statue at City Hall at noon, I do best to be behind the statue at noon. The same goes for you with respect to me. We coordinate if we succeed in being at the same place at the same time. If we are, then each of us has done best for himself, given what the other does.

Here coordinated expectations could coordinate behavior. If I expect you to be in front of the Art Institute at 12:30, then I will find it advantageous to be there too. If we each expect the other, then each will find it advantageous to do what in fact fulfills the other's expectations.

In this case, there is a near-coincidence of interests, but coordinated expectations matter even when interests are substantially opposed. Take price haggling, for instance. The buyer wants to buy cheap; the seller to sell dear, but there may be a range of prices for which each prefers a sale at that price to no sale at all. Within this range, the buyer holds out for the lowest price he thinks he can get; the seller for the highest. There will be a sale if expectations are suitably coordinated—if the lowest price the buyer thinks he can get is no lower than the highest price the seller thinks he can get. Here again, coordinated expectations make for mutual benefit.

Indeed coordinated expectations matter even in systems of threats: In many circumstances, a threat will be carried out only if it has not been believed—only if the person threatened did not expect the threat to be carried out if he did what he did. Even with hostility, coordinated expectations can make for mutual restraint.

Cooperation requires coordinated expectations in at least two ways. There must, of course, be coordinated expectations of how each shall contribute to the project, or the project fails. In addition, though, there must be coordinated expectations of how the fruits of cooperation shall be shared. Hunting, for example, often requires cooperation, and there are various ways the kill can be divided. Hunters in effect trade benefits, and they must coordinate their expectations of the terms of trade. A system of cooperation may be mutually advantageous in the sense that everyone does better with the system than he would with no cooperation at all, and yet it may well be that for each person, there is an alternative mutually advantageous system of cooperation that would benefit him more.

Game theorists call situations of the kinds I have been discussing "bargaining problems." More specifically, a *bargaining prob-*

lem has these features: There are alternative systems of cooperation or mutual restraint, each of which is mutually beneficial in the sense that its implementation would make everyone involved better off than he would be with no cooperation or restraint. There is a conflict of interest, though, over which of these alternative mutually beneficial systems to implement: For each such system, there is another which makes someone better off.

Return now to natural selection. In discussing coordination and bargaining, I have spoken of "interests," "benefit," and "advantage," and this talk was to be understood in terms of human goals and preferences—in terms of "preference-satisfaction," let me say. We could, though, substitute "biological fitness" or "reproductive success" for "preference satisfaction," and consider situations that have the same formal structure as human bargaining problems. An *evolutionary bargaining situation* is a recurrent kind of interaction among organisms in which the following conditions hold. First, there are mutual benefits to be gained, with benefits now to be glossed in terms of fitness. That is to say, as compared to some combination of behaviors of the organisms involved, called their *threatened combination*, some other combinations result in greater fitness for all. Call any such combination a *mutual fitness enhancing combination*. Second, there is a conflict of interest over how these benefits are to be divided. That is, for any mutual fitness-enhancing combination, there is an individual whose fitness is more enhanced by some other mutual fitness-enhancing combination.

Evolutionary bargaining situations are recurrent in the annals of natural selection. From the point of view of fitness, having exclusive access to a territory without a fight beats ceding all access without a fight, but that in turn beats getting into a deadly fight. Various combinations of behavior, then, are mutually fitness-enhancing compared with the threatened combination, fighting—namely that A enjoys the territory and B keeps

out, that A and B share the territory, and that B enjoys the territory and A keeps out. Between any two of these combinations, though, the one that is more fitness-enhancing for A is less so for B.

What can we expect to happen in an evolutionary bargaining situation? Let P be a mutual fitness-enhancing combination of behaviors, and suppose each animal is genetically disposed to the following behavioral strategy: play its part in P if the others do, and otherwise carry out its threatened behavior. Then each animal's strategy will be what Maynard Smith calls an *evolutionarily stable strategy*: roughly, a strategy such that if all adopt it, then for each individual, that strategy is at least as fitness-enhancing as would be any other strategy easily accessible by mutation.

Consider now human beings evolving in hunting-gathering societies. We could expect them to face an abundance of human bargaining situations, involving mutual aid, personal property, mates, territory, use of housing, and the like. Now human bargaining situations tend to be evolutionary bargaining situations. Human goals tend toward biological fitness, toward reproduction. The point is not, of course, that a person's sole goal is to maximize his reproduction; few if any people have that as a goal at all. Rather, the point concerns propensities to develop goals. Those propensities that conferred greatest fitness were selected: hence in a hunting-gathering society, people tended to want the various things it was fitness-enhancing for them to want. Conditions of primitive human life must have required intricate coordination—both of the simple cooperative kinds involved, say, in meeting a person, and of the kind required for bargaining problems to yield mutually beneficial outcomes. Propensities well coordinated with the propensities of others would have been fitness-enhancing, and so we may view a vast array of human propensities as coordinating devices. Our emotional propensities, I suggest, are largely the results of these selection pressures, and so are our normative capacities.

Take guilt and resentment. If one person resents an action of another and the other does not feel a corresponding guilt, we may expect trouble. Guilt makes possible the acknowledgment of wrong, and such modes of reconciliation as restitution, compensation, apology, and forgiveness. One's chances of damaging conflict are reduced, then, if one feels guilty when a show of guilt and its normal accompaniments is demanded by others, and if one demands guilt and its normal accompaniments only when others are prepared to feel guilty. Hence it tends to be advantageous for an individual to coordinate his guilt with the resentment of others and his resentment with the guilt of others. That, of course, will not be the only tendency governing these emotions, but it is a tendency that may well explain many aspects of the significant and complex coordinating mechanisms of a complex social animal.

Now human beings, as we know them, have a capacity to be guided by words, in their actions and emotions. This capacity is central to our psychic makeup, and it must have much to do with the selection pressures that led to the evolution of linguistic ability in human beings. Being guided by language could enhance a proto-human's biological fitness, both by enabling him to develop complex plans for action, and by leading him to coordinate his emotions and actions with those of his fellows. It is in the role of language in coordinating behavior and expectations, I shall be suggesting, that we can discern what is special about accepting norms.

7. INTERNALIZING NORMS

What is it to be in the grip of a norm as opposed to accepting it? Presumably, whatever happens when I am in the grip of a norm that I do not accept happens also, much of the time, when I do accept a norm. Take again our ordinary norms of politeness and cooperativeness. In my usual dealings with people, I not only accept these norms as having some weight; I accept them as having enough weight to override any conflicting norms that apply to my situation. I normally give people directions when asked, even if I am in a slight hurry, and this I do not out of weakness of will, but because I accept that it makes sense to help people who need it when the cost is small. In these cases, we would not say that I am "in the grip" of the norms of politeness and cooperativeness that guide my conduct, since I accept them as reasonably controlling in the situation. It may well be, though, that these norms would control my behavior even if I did not accept them, or did not accept them as having greatest weight in my situation. In this respect, my psychological state is like the state of being in the grip of a norm.

We need, then, some term for what is common to situations in which I am in the grip of a norm and situations of the more usual kind: situations in which I accept no opposing norm, but would still tend to be in the grip of this norm even if on balance I did accept opposing norms. I propose the colorless, somewhat technical term *internalizing* a norm.

How are we to understand internalizing a norm? The capacity to do so is one we share with other mammals, especially those who live in groups. Consider dogs: A dog will mark off its territory and bark at other dogs who encroach; two dogs meeting on neutral ground will engage in elaborate rituals. My anthropomorphic language suggests that something akin to our own internalizing norms may be in play. As in the human case, these animal interactions follow certain regular patterns, and the patterns seem, in a way, to have a rationale. They constitute adaptations, we may presume; they are, that is to say, the result of natural selection favoring these patterns. The selection pressures are in large part a matter of coordinating the behavior of the animals as they interact, and so the patterns of behavior constitute evolutionarily stable strategies. It is as if these patterns of behavior were designed into the lives of social beasts, and in this special sense, the beasts "follow rules" for social interaction.

They have not, of course, decided to conduct themselves by these rules, and they do not criticize each other for deviations. In these respects, their behavior differs from some of the human behavior we call norm-governed. Human life as well, though, has its share of such behaviors. Many patterns of human behavior are not explicitly formulated and demanded, but serve nonetheless to coordinate our lives in various ways. Think of conversational distance: most people have no opinions about proper conversational distance, and yet conversational distance in a sense "signals" varying degrees of familiarity and intimacy. There is a strong cultural element to conversational distance: Though in any given culture, closer means more intimate, cultures differ on the distance that is appropriate for a given kind of relationship. That will sometimes become obvious when people from two cultures stand and talk, and one keeps advancing as the other retreats. A culture has norms of conversational distance, then, in some sense of the term 'norm', even though members of the culture are not explicitly aware of them and do not explicitly avow them. The "signals" by which people avoid bumping into each other on a crowded sidewalk make for another case in point. These cases seem in many respects like cases in which we may speak of "norms" and "rituals" in the lives of beasts, and the behaviors involved may well rest on like psychic mechanisms. As with animal ritual, we have here behavioral patterns without explicit rules. To the extent that the behaviors result from inborn mechanisms, it is as if their designer had hit on a useful rule. To the extent that they result as well from social training, the story is more complex, but still, even though there is no explicit awareness of a rule, what goes on is much like following a rule. Children are not normally given explicit instructions concerning conversational distance, but they

may be primed genetically to take closeness as a sign of intimacy, and to pick up the practices with which they grow up. The end result is the following of complex rules without explicit awareness of them.

In the same limited sense, then, in which various beasts have norms, we do too. In one respect the rules are in the eye of the beholder: Neither the beast nor the human can state them, but they can be formulated—with considerable ingenuity and effort—by a sophisticated observer. In another respect, the rules are really in the actor: if they were not somehow represented internally, it would be mysterious how these patterns of behavior could be maintained.

A norm prescribes a pattern of behavior, and to internalize a norm, I want to say, is to have a motivational tendency of a particular kind to act on that pattern. The particular kind of motivational tendency is the one I have tried to pick out—partly by example, and partly by giving a theory of what unites the examples. The examples, I have said, are united by a purpose of coordination. Tendencies to act on the pattern (or propensities to acquire these tendencies when growing up exposed to the pattern) constitute biological adaptations for coordination. I hope that in saying this, I have picked out a natural kind—a natural kind of motivational tendency. If I have, then I can say that where norm N prescribes a certain behavioral pattern B, an organism *internalizes N* if and only if it has a motivational tendency, of the kind I have picked out, to act on pattern B. We share the capacity to internalize norms with other animals, although the greater complexity of human social life may well mean that our capacities to internalize norms are more refined than those of any other animal.

8. ACCEPTING NORMS

Earlier I contrasted *internalizing* a norm with *accepting* one, but so far I have speculated only about internalization. Acceptance is what chiefly interests me. In the Milgram experiment, recall, the subject accepts norms against inflicting pain and danger, and accepts them as outweighing all other norms in the circumstance. These norms prevail in what he would say and think away from the scene. The norms he most strongly internalizes, though, say to do one's job, and so those are the ones that prevail in the heat of social encounter.

What is it, then, to "accept" a norm? To understand acceptance we should look to language. Think of what language has to do with motivation, apart from simply making us aware of the states of affairs we confront. Although the most obvious function of language is to convey information, much of language is more than merely informative. Language is used to exhort, to criticize, and to summon up emotions. Narrative has a fascination that does not disappear if the tale narrative is thought to be fiction. Language influences actions and emotions not only by conveying information, but in many other ways as well.

One way is by letting people think together on absent situations, and voice reactions. With language, people share not only their immediate situation, but past, future, and hypothetical situations as well. Various kinds of reactions can then be expressed, in various ways: Emotional responses can be shared simply by evincing them. Special language can be used to express hypothetical decisions—decisions on what to do in the place of someone in the situation under discussion. Emotionally laden words can be used to label actions and characters. Explicit precepts can be formulated. In a rich number of ways, then, language allows for shared evaluation of absent situations.

That opens great new scope for coordination, and so a capacity for shared evaluation would be fitness-enhancing in a species with a complex social life. Those who can work out together reactions to an absent situation—what to do and what to feel—are ready for like situations. They are better prepared

than they would otherwise be to do what is advantageous in a new situation, and they can rely on complex schemes of interpersonal coordination. On general evolutionary grounds, then, we might expect shared evaluation to figure centrally in a complex social life—and in human life it does. Much of our speech fosters shared reactions to absent circumstances. Think of the familiar human fascination with stories. Think of how much of overheard conversation on sidewalks, busses, and the like consists in recounting problematic events such as personal confrontations, apparently to elicit reactions. Think of gossip. Shared evaluation is central to human life, I suggest, because it serves biological functions of rehearsal and coordination.

Working out, in community, what to do, what to think, and how to feel in absent situations, if it has these biological functions, must presumably influence what we do, think, and feel when faced with like situations. I shall be calling this influence *normative governance*. It is in this governance of action, belief, and emotion that we might find a place for phenomena that constitute acceptance of norms, as opposed merely to internalizing them. When we work out at a distance, in community, what to do or think or feel in a situation we are discussing, we come to accept norms for the situation. This is the tentative hypothesis I want to develop, and I shall be calling the discussion involved *normative discussion*.

Here, then, in brief, is the proposal: Normative discussion might coordinate acts and feelings if two things hold. First, normative discussion tends toward consensus. The mechanisms here, I shall propose, are two: mutual influence, and a responsiveness to demands for consistency. Second, the consensus must move people to do or feel accordingly. That is where normative governance comes in.

We evaluate in community, but part of what goes on is individual. Groups often reach consensus, but sometimes they do not. Even when they do, the consensus may emerge from individuals' taking their separate positions and then, to some degree, persuading each other. Acceptance of norms is tied not only to a consensus that emerges from normative discussion, but to individuals' taking positions.

This taking of normative positions I shall call *normative avowal*. By "avowal" here, I mean to include a wide range of expressions we might count as taking a position in normative discussion—in the discussion of absent states of affairs. The simplest kind might just be evincing an emotion toward the absent situation. Other kinds of avowal are more explicit: we may express a hypothetical decision in words, or label an action in words that are emotively charged. To understand acceptance of norms, we need to look to such avowal—the kind of avowal from which consensus emerges when it does, and which may persist even when there is no approach to consensus.

Can we explain acceptance by tying it to avowal? Perhaps so, if we distinguish two kinds of sincerity. One kind is deliberately holding oneself to standards of honest avowal; the other is a childlike openness or spontaneity—speaking without the psychic complications of self-censorship. Perhaps we should begin with this sincerity as spontaneity, and explain acceptance as a disposition to avow spontaneously.

Acceptance, though, involves more than spontaneous avowal, or being disposed to avow in unconstrained contexts. It involves a response to demands for consistency. Normative discussion consists of taking positions; even a conversational groan stakes out a position. Consensus may then be reached partly by a mechanism that is incipiently Socratic. Discussants hold each other to consistency in their positions, and thus force each other to shift positions by exposing inconsistency. A person, then, must take positions in order to engage in normative discussion responsibly, and in doing so, he exposes himself to pressures toward consistency. To accept a norm, we might say, is in

part to be disposed to avow it in unconstrained normative discussion, as a result of the workings of demands for consistency in the positions one takes in normative discussion.

To prepare oneself to meet demands for consistency may require a strong imaginative life. A person will engage in imaginative rehearsal for actual normative discussion; he practices by holding himself to consistency. The pressure for consistency need not be so strong as it is in good philosophical discussion, but it will be there, and it may be significant. From this imaginative rehearsal, then, a kind of imaginative persona may emerge, an "I" who develops a consistent position to take in normative discussion. It is then that we can speak most clearly of what the person accepts; he then has a worked out normative position to take in unconstrained contexts.

Why expose oneself to these demands for consistency? We do so naturally, but what selection pressures might have shaped us to do so? The answer should be clear from what I have said. The demands for consistency are reciprocal, and the system of mutual demands is part of a coordinating device. It is partly because of these mutual demands that there is any hope of reaching consensus in normative discussion. A person who refuses these demands must therefore be a poor candidate for cooperation of any kind—and in human life, cooperation is vital. It is fitness-enhancing, then, to stand ready to engage in normative discussion, and so to accept the demands for consistency that are part of the package.

What, now, of the distinction between "accepting" a norm and "internalizing" it? The picture I have sketched is this. "Accepting" a norm is something that we do primarily in the context of normative discussion, actual and imaginary. We take positions, and thereby expose ourselves to demands for consistency. Normative discussion of a situation influences action and emotion in like situations. It is then that we can speak of norms as governing action and emotion, and it is through this governance that normative discussion serves to coordinate. The state of accepting a norm, then, is a syndrome of tendencies toward action and avowal—a syndrome produced by the language-infused system of coordination peculiar to human beings. The system works through discussion of absent situations, and it allows for the delicate adjustments of coordination that human social life requires. Internalizing a norm is likewise a matter of coordinating propensities, but the propensities are of a different kind: they work independently of normative discussion.

9. ACCEPTANCE, ACTION, PERSUASION

The chief biological function of normative discussion is to coordinate. Normative discussion allows for common enterprises and adjusts terms of reciprocity—both the friendly give and take of cooperative schemes and hostile standoffs with their threats and mutual restraint. So I have been hypothesizing. Now for such a mechanism to work as I am picturing, two things are needed: tendencies toward consensus, and normative governance. Normative discussion must tend toward all accepting the same norms, and acceptance of norms must tend to guide action. Selection pressures could develop and maintain these tendencies only if, in the context of others' having them, having these tendencies oneself enhanced one's fitness. The tendencies, in other words, would have to constitute an evolutionarily stable strategy. In this section I discuss why they might.

Turn first to normative governance. The ties that link avowal to action will be complex: Anthropologists warn us against uncritically taking the norms people avow to describe their behavior, and common sense supports this caution. Still, there must be some tie of avowal to action, or the entire co-

ordinative story I have been telling would have no basis. I need, then, to sketch a picture that will allow for the variety to be found in human life, with both its genuine normative motivation and its hypocrisy and self-serving argument.

Selection pressures shaped our propensities both to abide by norms and to violate them, and these pressures must have been diverse. On the one hand, as I have stressed, there are great gains to be had from coordinating one's actions and expectations with those of others. This coordination is fostered if one accepts the norms accepted by others, and acts on those norms. Opposing pressures, though, would stem from the gains to be had from avowing one thing and doing another. In an animal whose reproduction depends on a complex social life, these opposing pressures might well have shaped subtle and intricate psychic mechanisms—mechanisms as subtle and intricate as the ones we observe. We could expect, then, some tendency for the norms a person accepts to control his actions, but a mitigated tendency.

Normative governance, then, is like literal governance. Governments do not always prevail: What a government commands, people do not invariably do. On the other hand, what a government commands has some influence on what people do, or it is no government. Likewise normative governance will not always prevail, but it has some influence on what people do and feel.

So far I have assumed consensus, and discussed normative governance, the tendency of action to match avowal. Now I do the reverse: Given normative governance, I want to ask, what could give rise to consensus? My broad question, then, is whether the tendencies I am hypothesizing could exist in evolutionary equilibrium: Would each of these tendencies be maintained in the presence of the others? Suppose then, action tends to match avowal. Would some set of dispositions tending toward consensus be evolutionarily stable? Are there consensus-producing dispositions that would enhance an individual's fitness, if those he deals with have those same dispositions?

To reap gains from normative discussion takes both a certain firmness and a certain persuadability. Without persuadability, there can be no consensus. A person who is wholly unpersuadable would get few benefits from normative discussion—unless he were surrounded by people who were themselves completely persuadable. He would be a poor candidate for cooperative social life; he would risk ostracism. It would be costly too, though, to be a pushover in discussion. To evince compliance to any demands whatsoever, so long as they were made in the name of putative norms, would open a person to manipulation. What might be advantageous, then, is some tendency to gravitate toward the norms of those around one, together with some firmness in sticking to the norms one has hitherto accepted.

This balance of firmness and persuadability must not be the only force shaping norms. If it were, after all, there would be nothing to make the norms that emerged from discussion at all responsive to anyone's needs. The gains of sociability might then be outweighed by the price of accepting debilitating norms. We should expect a person, then, not only to respond to the advantages of having his norms well coordinated with norms around him, but to respond as well to other ways some norms pay and others cost.

The rewards and costs of avowal are many, and complex propensities toward normative discussion might evolve in response to these pressures. Avowal influences what the audience accepts, and it influences what others expect one to do and their attitudes toward one. These effects can work in all kinds of ways. Because one's avowals influence what others accept, self-serving arguments will sometimes pay, at least when they have a chance of being convincing. On the other hand, arguments that are too blatantly self-serving may discredit one as a partner in co-operative life—though not so thoroughly as would a proclaimed indifference to all norms. A person may often do best, then, from the standpoints that shape human nature, to profess his devotion to norms that can attract others, while bending the norms a little in his own favor. Still, self-serving arguments would be in vain if no one ever tended to accept normative conclusions that went against some of his interests. The importance of coordination explains why we often do genuinely accept norms.

To say all this is of course to caricature important aspects of human life, but the caricature is familiar, and even in the caricature we can see how central normative talk is to human life. The forms of life the caricature depicts would be impossible without an involved interplay of action, feeling, and avowal in normative discussion.

I have been hypothesizing psychic mechanisms that were shaped, in the course of human evolution, by pressures of reproductive advantage. The mechanisms themselves, though, are by no means fully egoistic. We care intrinsically about norms and their validity, and about whether we and others accept these norms and conform to them. Self-interested calculation, to be sure, could in principle serve the various functions I have pictured. It would not be as cheap and reliable, though, as our simpler general tendencies and intrinsic concerns. What I am suggesting, then, is not that a person's motives for action or avowal must lie chiefly in the kinds of gains and losses I have been listing. In many cases a simple integrity, say, may better foster reproduction than a finely calculated honesty as best policy. The gains and losses I cite, my point is, might be sources of pressures that shaped the human psyche in the course of evolution—and led to simple integrity in some cases and self-deception or unprincipled cunning in others. In these selection pressures, we may find clues to psychic mechanisms that yield the diversity of characters we see.

10. EXPRESSION AND SYSTEMS OF NORMS

What is it to express one's acceptance of a system of norms? It is not, I have stressed, to *say that* one accepts the system. The contrast is the same here as it is with the expression of straightforwardly factual beliefs. Let Cleopatra say

Antony's fleet outnumbers the enemy's.

She thereby expresses her belief that Antony's fleet outnumbers the enemy's, but she does not *say that* she has this belief. She is talking about the opposing fleets, not about her beliefs. Likewise, suppose she says

It makes sense for Antony to give battle.

Here again, she is expressing a state of mind, but she is not *saying that* she is in it. Specifically, she is expressing her acceptance of a system of norms, but not saying that she accepts it. When one says one is in a certain state of mind, then actually being in that state of mind constitutes speaking truly. When one expresses a state of mind, on the other hand, being in that state of mind constitutes not speaking truly but being sincere.

An expressivistic analysis of 'rational' takes this special form: What 'rational' means is explained by saying what it is to call something "rational," and to call something "rational," the analysis says, is to express a state of mind. We might call this state of mind the "judgment" that the thing is rational. The analysis, then, consists of two parts: (1) an account of what it is to *judge* that such-and-such is rational, and (2) an account of what it is in general to *express* a state of mind. Just as a straightforwardly factual assertion expresses a straightforwardly factual belief, so an assertion that such-and-such is rational expresses a normative judgment. To judge something rational is to accept a system of norms that on balance permits it.

That words express judgments will, of course, be accepted by almost anyone. The controversial elements of the Norm-Expressivistic Analysis are these: first, its account of what it is to make a normative judgment, and second, its claim that the meaning of normative terms is to be given by saying what judgments normative statements express—what states of mind they express.

Turn now to norms. The norm-expressivistic analysis should speak of a "system of norms," and not simply of norms. A person's normative judgments all told on a given matter will typically depend on his acceptance of more than one norm, and the norms he accepts may weigh in opposing directions. In the Milgram obedience experiments, we as observers accept the norms of cooperativeness and good faith on which the subjects act, but we think the subjects irrational. For although we accept these norms, we think them outweighed or overridden by norms against the infliction of suffering. Our normative judgments thus depend not on a single norm, but on a plurality of norms that we accept as having some force, and on the ways we take some of these norms to outweigh or override others.

The system of norms we accept is a matter both of the norms we accept as having some force and of the ways we cope with normative conflicts. How can all this be represented? What is it for one norm to "override" another, or for one set of norms to "outweigh" another in a given circumstance? We might respond by trying to develop careful definitions of such terms as 'norm', 'weight', 'priority', and the like, or by developing a system of axioms that defines these terms implicitly. My purposes, though, will be served by a simpler course: Describe the end result of all these weights and priorities of individual norms, and so consider a system of norms as a system of permissions and requirements, applicable to a wide range of actual and hypothetical circumstances.

What matters about a system of norms is what it requires and what it permits in various conceivable circumstances. We can characterize any system N of norms by a family of basic predicates 'N-forbidden', 'N-optional', and 'N-required'. Here 'N-forbidden' simply means "forbidden by system of norms N," and likewise for its siblings. Other predicates can be constructed from these basic ones; in particular 'N-permitted' will mean "either N-optional or N-required."

These predicates are descriptive rather than normative: Whether a thing, say, is N-permitted will be a matter of fact. It might be N-permitted without being rational, for the system N might have little to recommend it. People who agree on the facts will agree on what is N-permitted and what is not, even if they disagree normatively—even if, for instance, one accepts N and the other does not.

A system of norms will apply to alternatives of some kind: A system of norms for action, for instance, will apply to alternative courses of action, and a system of norms for anger, say, will apply to alternative degrees of anger one might have at someone for doing something. Now when a system N of norms applies in a definite way to an alternative, that results in the alternative's having exactly one of the three basic properties being N-forbidden, N-optional, or N-required. We can call a system *complete* if these predicates trichotomize the possibilities: if on every occasion, actual or hypothetical, each alternative is either N-forbidden, N-optional, or N-required. (So long as N is consistent, nothing will be more than one of these things.)

Ordinarily, a person will accept only a system of norms that is *incomplete*. He may be undecided whether to accept or reject certain norms, or he may be unsettled on the relative weights of the various norms he accepts—so that when those norms conflict, he is unsettled as to which one prevails. These kinds of normative uncertainty are different from factual uncertainty: even an observer who knew all the facts of a case might still be ambivalent in his normative judgments. Ordinarily, to be sure, normative uncertainty is combined with some degree of factual uncertainty, but factual certainty, even if achieved, might not resolve all normative uncertainty.

A person who accepts only an incomplete system of norms is, in effect, undecided among complete systems of norms that are compatible with it. He is undecided on how to extend or sharpen his incomplete system of norms to make it complete.

11. NORMATIVE CONTENT

The analysis so far applies to simple contexts, in which it is simply asserted or denied that such-and-such is rational. It says nothing about more complex normative assertions.

Normative statements are of many kinds. In the first place there are the general normative principles that combine to form systems of norms—such principles as "Whenever the chance arises, give battle" or "Never give battle unless cornered." In the second place, there are normative conclusions for particular situations. "It makes sense for Antony to give battle." This could follow from a set of general normative principles combined with a description of the circumstances. Finally, there are the various complex constructions that include normative terms. "Unless Antony finds his fleet outnumbered, it will make sense for him to give battle." Our problem is to give a uniform account of the content of normative statements of all these different kinds.

As a first way of saying what a normative statement means, we can try this: its meaning is what it rules out. That goes for simple normative statements, and also for complex statements with normative components—statements like "Unless Octavian has done something irrational, it makes no sense for Antony to attack." A normative statement rules out various combinations of factual possibilities with normative principles, and its meaning, we now say, lies in the set of combinations it rules out. The norm-expressivistic analysis as revised now runs as follows:

As before, when a speaker makes a normative statement, he expresses a state of mind. Now, though, the state of mind he expresses consists in his ruling out various combinations of normative systems with factual possibilities.

Still, what is all this supposed to mean? Does it give what the person has in mind when he thinks some normative thought? He could not have in mind consciously everything he rules out. Indeed the set of things he rules out is infinite, and so how could they all be in his finite mind at all? His logical powers are limited, and so with many things, even if he thought about whether he was ruling them out, he could not say. These are versions of wider questions of what logic has to do with meaning, and what meaning has to do with things that go on in the mind. With meaning in general it is puzzling what to say and controversial. Here I venture a few words on normative meaning in particular, and what it has to do with psychic reality.

To display the objects of belief as a system, we need to show two main things: the inferential relations among them and their connection to the world. Inferential relations are a matter of logic. As for a connection to the world, for straightforwardly factual propositions, it runs through sense-experience. We need some parallel for normative statements.

Normative content too connects to the world through sense experience, but not only through sense experience. It connects as well by normative governance. That is the theory I propose. Normative governance is the special kind of motivation that stems from making a normative judgment that applies to oneself right now. Cleopatra may have thought it made sense for Antony to give battle, but that judgment could govern no action of hers.

If Antony, though, thought it made sense to give battle at that very moment, his opinion could very well govern his actions. Whereas purely descriptive propositions are tied to the world through sense experience alone, pieces of normative content are tied to the world not only through sense experience but through normative governance of actions. And just as few descriptive propositions describe present sense experience, so few pieces of normative content directly govern present action. Propositions and normative content are tied to the world through a web of inference.

The problem of attributing normative content is thus one of radical interpretation of a person's thoughts. We match normative content to his thoughts under at least two constraints. First, the inferences he makes with confidence are to be explained by relations of entailment among the pieces of normative content we attribute to him. Second, his propensities toward normative governance are to match the content we attribute his normative judgments. When the normative judgments we interpret a person as making at a time apply to that person himself at that very time, he must be normatively motivated. Conversely when he is normatively motivated, we must attribute to him a normative judgment that applies to himself at that time.

What, then, is a person doing when he voices a complicated normative thought? He is doing nothing that could be put in a better mouthful. But I could say: he expresses his ruling out certain combinations of factual possibilities with norms. Better, I can say this: he expresses a thought that gets its meaning from its logical ties to other statements, and through them not only to sense experience, but also to normative governance.

NOTES

1. Excerpted and adapted from *Wise Choices, Apt Feelings: A Theory of Normative Judgment* (Cambridge, Mass.: Harvard University Press, and Oxford: Oxford University Press, 1990), pp. 3–102.

2. Lorna Marshall, "Sharing, Talking, and Giving: Relief of Social Tensions among the !Kung," Richard B. Lee and Irven DeVore, eds., *Kalihari Hunter-Gatherers* (Cambridge, Mass.: Harvard University Press, 1976), pp. 351–52.

3. Stanley Milgram, *Obedience to Authority* (New York: Harper & Row, 1974).

4. See Thomas Schelling, *The Strategy of Conflict* (Cambridge, Mass.: Harvard University Press, 1960), chap. 2; John Maynard Smith, "The Evolution of Behavior," *Scientific American* 239 (1978): 176–92.

C

SENSIBILITY THEORIES

11

Values and Secondary Qualities

JOHN McDOWELL

1. J. L. Mackie insists that ordinary evalua-tive thought presents itself as a matter of sen-sitivity to aspects of the world.[1] And this phe-nomenological thesis seems correct. When one or another variety of philosophical non-cognitivism claims to capture the truth about what the experience of value is like, or (in a familiar surrogate for phenomenology[2]) about what we mean by our evaluative lan-guage, the claim is never based on careful at-tention to the lived character of evaluative thought or discourse. The idea is, rather, that the very concept of the cognitive or factual rules out the possibility of an undiluted rep-resentation of how things are, enjoying, nev-ertheless, the internal relation to "attitudes" or the will that would be needed for it to count as evaluative.[3] On this view the phenome-nology of value would involve a mere inco-herence, if it were as Mackie says—a possi-bility that then tends (naturally enough) not to be so much as entertained. But, as Mackie sees, there is no satisfactory justification for supposing that the factual is, by definition,

attitudinatively and motivationally neutral. This clears away the only obstacle to ac-cepting his phenomenological claim; and the upshot is that non-cognitivism must offer to correct the phenomenology of value, rather than to give an account of it.[4]

In Mackie's view the correction is called for. In this paper I want to suggest that he at-tributes an unmerited plausibility to this the-sis, by giving a false picture of what one is committed to if one resists it.

2. Given that Mackie is right about the phe-nomenology of value, an attempt to accept the appearances makes it virtually irresistible to appeal to a perceptual model. Now Mackie holds that the model must be perceptual awareness of *primary* qualities (see *HMT*, pp. 32, 60–61, 73–74). And this makes it com-paratively easy to argue that the appearances are misleading. For it seems impossible—at least on reflection—to take seriously the idea of something that is like a primary quality in being simply *there*, independently of human sensibility, but is nevertheless intrinsically (not conditionally on contingencies about human sensibility) such as to elicit some "attitude" or state of will from someone who becomes aware of it. Moreover, the primary-quality model turns the epistemology of value into mere mystification. The perceptual model is no more than a model: perception, strictly so called, does not mirror the role of reason in evaluative thinking, which seems to require us to regard the apprehension of value as an intellectual rather than a merely sensory matter. But if we are to take account of this, while preserving the model's picture of values as brutely and absolutely *there*, it seems that we need to postulate a faculty— "intuition"—about which all that can be said is that it makes us aware of objective rational connections: the model itself ensures that there is nothing helpful to say about how such a faculty might work, or why its deliverances might deserve to count as knowledge.

But why is it supposed that the model must be awareness of primary qualities rather than secondary qualities? The answer is that Mackie, following Locke, takes secondary-quality perception, as conceived by a pre-philosophical consciousness, to involve a projective error: one analogous to the error he finds in ordinary evaluative thought. He holds that we are prone to conceive secondary-quality experience in a way that would be appropriate for experience of primary qualities. So a pre-philosophical secondary-quality model for awareness of value would in effect be, after all, a primary-quality model. And to accept a philosophically corrected secondary-quality model for the awareness of value would be simply to give up trying to go along with the appearances.

I believe, however, that this conception of secondary-quality experience is seriously mistaken.

3. A secondary quality is a property the ascriptiori of which to an object is not adequately understood except as true, if it is true, in virtue of the object's disposition to present a certain sort of perceptual appearance: specifically, an appearance characterizable by using a word for the property itself to say how the object perceptually appears. Thus an object's being red is understood as obtaining in virtue of the object's being such as (in certain circumstances) to look, precisely, red.

This account of secondary qualities is faithful to one key Lockean doctrine, namely the identification of secondary qualities with "powers to produce various sensations in us."[5] (The phrase "perceptual appearance," with its gloss, goes beyond Locke's unspecific "sensations," but harmlessly; it serves simply to restrict our attention, as Locke's word may not, to properties that are in a certain obvious sense perceptible.[6])

I have written of what property-ascriptions are understood to be true in virtue of, rather than of what they are true in virtue of. No doubt it is true that a given thing is red in virtue of some microscopic textural property of its surface; but a predication understood only in such terms—not in terms of how the object would look—would not be an ascription of the secondary quality of redness.[7]

Secondary-quality experience presents itself as perceptual awareness of properties genuinely possessed by the objects that confront one. And there is no general obstacle to taking that appearance at face value.[8] An object's being such as to look red is independent of its actually looking red to anyone on any particular occasion; so, notwithstanding the conceptual connection between being red and being experienced as red, an experience of something as red can count as a case of being presented with a property that is there anyway—there independently of the experience itself.[9] And there is no evident ground for accusing the appearance of being misleading. What would one expect it to be like to experience something's being such as to look red, if not to experience the thing in question (in the right circumstances) as looking, precisely, red?

On Mackie's account, by contrast, to take experiencing something as red at face value, as a non-misleading awareness of a property that really confronts one, is to attribute to the object a property which is "thoroughly objective" (*PFL*, p. 18), in the sense that it does not need to be understood in terms of experiences that the object is disposed to give rise to; but which nevertheless resembles redness as it figures in our experience—this to ensure that the phenomenal character of the experience need not stand accused of misleadingness, as it would if the "thoroughly objective" property of which it constituted an awareness were conceived as a microscopic textural basis for the object's disposition to look red. This use of the notion of resemblance corresponds to one key element in Locke's exposition of the concept of a primary quality.[10] In these Lockean terms Mackie's view amounts to accusing a naive perceptual consciousness of taking secondary qualities for primary qualities (see *PFL*, p. 16).

According to Mackie, this conception of primary qualities that resemble colours as we see them is coherent; that nothing is characterized by such qualities is established by merely empirical argument (see *PFL*, pp. 17–20). But is the idea coherent? This would require two things: first, that colours figure in perceptual experience neutrally, so to speak, rather than as essentially phenomenal qualities of objects, qualities that could not be adequately conceived except in terms of how their possessors would look; and, second, that we command a concept of resemblance that would enable us to construct notions of possible primary qualities out of the idea of resemblance to such neutral elements of experience. The first of these requirements is quite dubious. (I shall return to this.) But even if we try to let it pass, the second requirement seems impossible. Starting with, say, redness as it (putatively neutrally) figures in our experience, we are asked to form the notion of a feature of objects which resembles that, but which is adequately conceivable otherwise than in terms of how its possessors would look (since if it were adequately conceivable only in those terms it would simply be secondary). But the second part of these instructions leaves it wholly mysterious what to make of the first: it precludes the required resemblance being in phenomenal respects, but it is quite unclear what other sense we could make of the notion of resemblance to redness as it figures in our experience. (If we find no other, we have failed to let the first requirement pass; redness as it figures in our experience proves stubbornly phenomenal.)[11] I have indicated how we can make error-free sense of the thought that colours are authentic objects of perceptual awareness; in face of that, it seems a gratuitous slur on perceptual "common sense" to accuse it of this wildly problematic understanding of itself.

Why is Mackie resolved, nevertheless, to convict "common sense" of error? Secondary qualities are qualities not adequately conceivable except in terms of certain subjective states, and thus subjective themselves in a sense that that characterization defines. In the natural contrast, a primary quality would be objective in the sense that what it is for something to have it can be adequately understood otherwise than in terms of dispositions to give rise to subjective states. Now this contrast between objective and subjective is not a contrast between veridical and illusory experience. But it is easily confused with a different contrast, in which to call a putative object of awareness "objective" is to say that it is there to be experienced, as opposed to being a mere figment of the subjective state that purports to be an experience of it. If secondary qualities were subjective in the sense that naturally contrasts with this, naive consciousness would indeed be wrong about them, and we would need something like Mackie's Lockean picture of the error it commits. What is acceptable, though, is only that secondary qualities are subjective in the first sense, and it would be simply wrong to suppose that this gives any support to the idea that they are subjective in the second.[12]

More specifically, Mackie seems insufficiently whole-hearted in an insight of his about perceptual experiences. In the case of "realistic" depiction, it makes sense to think of veridicality as a matter of resemblance between aspects of a picture and aspects of what it depicts.[13] Mackie's insight is that the best hope of a philosophically hygienic interpretation for Locke's talk of "ideas," in a perceptual context, is in terms of "intentional objects": that is, aspects of representational content—aspects of how things seem to one in the enjoyment of a perceptual experience. (See *PFL*, pp. 47–50.) Now it is an illusion to suppose, as Mackie does, that this warrants thinking of the relation between a quality and an "idea" of it on the model of the relation between a property of a picture's subject and an aspect of the picture. Explaining "ideas" as "intentional objects" should direct our attention to the relation between how things are and how an experience represents them as being—in fact identity, not resemblance, if the representation is veridical.[14] Mackie's Lockean appeal to resemblance fits something quite different: a relation borne to aspects of how things are by intrinsic aspects of a bearer of representational content—not how things are represented to be, but features of an item that does the representing, with particular aspects of its content carried by particular aspects of what it is intrinsically (non-representationally) like.[15] Perceptual experiences have representational content; but nothing in Mackie's defense of the "intentional objects" gloss on "ideas" would force us to suppose that they have it in that sort of way.[16]

The temptation to which Mackie succumbs, to suppose that intrinsic features of experience function as vehicles for particular aspects of representational content, is indifferent to any distinction between primary and secondary qualities in the representational significance that these features supposedly carry. What it is for a colour to figure in experience and what it is for a shape to figure in experience would be alike, on this view, in so far as both are a matter of an experience's having a certain intrinsic feature. If one wants, within this framework, to preserve Locke's intuition that primary-quality experience is distinctive in potentially disclosing the objective properties of things, one will be naturally led to Locke's use of the notion of resemblance. But no notion of resemblance could get us from an essentially experiential state of affairs to the concept of a feature of objects intelligible otherwise than in terms of how its possessors would strike us. (A version of this point told against Mackie's idea of possible primary qualities answering to "colours as we see them"; it tells equally against the Lockean conception of shapes.)

If one gives up the Lockean use of resemblance, but retains the idea that primary and secondary qualities are experientially on a par, one will be led to suppose that the properties attributed to objects in the "manifest image" are all equally phenomenal—intelligible, that is, only in terms of how their possessors are disposed to appear. Properties that are objective, in the contrasting sense, can then figure only in the "scientific image."[17] On these lines one altogether loses hold of Locke's intuition that primary qualities are distinctive in being both objective and perceptible.[18]

If we want to preserve the intuition, as I believe we should, then we need to exorcize the idea that what it is for a quality to figure in experience is for an experience to have a certain intrinsic feature: in fact I believe that we need to reject these supposed vehicles of content altogether. Then we can say that colours and shapes figure in experience, not as the representational significance carried by features that are—being intrinsic features of experience—indifferently subjective (which makes it hard to see how a difference in respect of objectivity could show up in their representational significance); but simply as properties that objects are represented as having, distinctively phenomenal in the one case and not so in the other. (Without the supposed intrinsic features, we should be immune to the illusion that experiences cannot represent objects as having properties that are not phenomenal—properties that are adequately conceivable otherwise than in terms of dispositions to produce suitable experiences.[19]) What Locke unfelicitously tried to yoke together, with his picture of real resemblances of our "ideas," can now divide into two notions that we must insist on keeping separate: first, the possible veridicality of experience (the objectivity of its object, in the second of the two senses I distinguished), in respect of which primary and secondary qualities are on all fours; and, second, the not essentially phenomenal character of some properties that experience represents objects as having (their objectivity in the first sense), which marks off the primary perceptible qualities from the secondary ones.

In order to deny that a quality's figuring in experience consists in an experience's having a certain intrinsic feature, we do not need to reject the intrinsic features altogether; it would suffice to insist that a quality's figuring in experience consists in an experience's having a certain intrinsic feature *together with* the quality's being the representational significance carried by that feature. But I do not believe that this yields a position in which acceptance of the supposed vehicles of content coheres with a satisfactory account of perception. This position would have it that the fact that an experience represents things as being one way rather than another is strictly additional to the experience's intrinsic nature, and so extrinsic to the experience itself (it seems natural to say "read into it"). There is a phenomenological falsification here. (This brings out a third role for Locke's resemblance, namely to obviate the threat of such a falsification by constituting a sort of intrinsic representationality: Locke's "ideas" carry the representational significance they do by virtue of what they are like, and this can be glossed both as "how they are intrinsically" and as "what they resemble.") In any case, given that we cannot project ourselves from features of experience to nonphenome-

nal properties of objects by means of an appeal to resemblance, it is doubtful that the metaphor of representational significance being "read into" intrinsic features can be spelled out in such a way as to avoid the second horn of our dilemma. How could representational significance be "read into" intrinsic features of experience in such a way that what was signified did not need to be understood in terms of them? How could a not intrinsically representational feature of experience become imbued with objective significance in such a way that an experience could count, by virtue of having that feature, as a direct awareness of a not essentially phenomenal property of objects?[20]

How things strike someone as being is, in a clear sense, a subjective matter: there is no conceiving it in abstraction from the subject of the experience. Now a motive for insisting on the supposed vehicles of aspects of content might lie in an aspiration, familiar in philosophy, to bring subjectivity within the compass of a fundamentally objective conception of reality.[21] If aspects of content are not carried by elements in an intrinsic structure, their subjectivity is irreducible. By contrast, one might hope to objectivize any "essential subjectivity" that needs to be attributed to not intrinsically representational features of experience, by exploiting a picture involving special access on a subject's part to something conceived in a broadly objective way—its presence in the world not conceived as constituted by the subject's special access to it.[22] Given this move, it becomes natural to suppose that the phenomenal character of the "manifest image" can be explained in terms of a certain familiar picture: one in which a confronted "external" reality, conceived as having only an objective nature, is processed through a structured "subjectivity," conceived in this objectivistic manner. This picture seems to capture the essence of Mackie's approach to the secondary qualities.[23] What I have tried to suggest is that the picture is suspect in threatening to cut us off from the *primary* (not essentially phenomenal) qualities of the objects that we perceive: either (with the appeal to resemblance) making it impossible, after all, to keep an essentially phenomenal character out of our conception of the qualities in question, or else making them merely hypothetical, not accessible to perception. If we are to achieve a satisfactory understanding of experience's openness to objective reality, we must put a more radical construction on experience's essential subjectivity. And this removes an insidious obstacle—one whose foundation is summarily captured in Mackie's idea that it is not simply wrong to count "colours as we see them" as items in our minds (see the diagram at *PFL*, p. 17)—that stands in the way of understanding how secondary-quality experience can be awareness, with nothing misleading about its phenomenal character, of properties genuinely possessed by elements in a not exclusively phenomenal reality.

4. The empirical ground that Mackie thinks we have for not postulating "thoroughly objective features which resemble our ideas of secondary qualities" (*PFL*, pp. 18–19) is that attributing such features to objects is surplus to the requirements of explaining our experience of secondary qualities (see *PFL*, pp. 17–18). If it would be incoherent to attribute such features to objects, as I believe, this empirical argument falls away as unnecessary. But it is worth considering how an argument from explanatory superfluity might fare against the less extravagant construal I have suggested for the thought that secondary qualities genuinely characterize objects: not because the question is difficult or contentious, but because of the light it casts on how an explanatory test for reality—which is commonly thought to undermine the claims of values—should be applied.

A *"virtus dormitiva"* objection would tell against the idea that one might mount a satisfying explanation of an object's looking red on its being such as to look red. The weight of the explanation would fall through the dis-

position to its structural ground.[24] Still, however optimistic we are about the prospects for explaining colour experience on the basis of surface textures,[25] it would be obviously wrong to suppose that someone who gave such an explanation could in consistency deny that the object was such as to look red. The right explanatory test is not whether something pulls its own weight in the favoured explanation (it may fail to do so without thereby being explained away), but whether the explainer can consistently deny its reality.[26]

Given Mackie's view about secondary qualities, the thought that values fail an explanatory test for reality is implicit in a parallel that he commonly draws between them (see, for instance, *HMT*, pp. 51–52; *E*, pp. 19–20). It is nearer the surface in his "argument from queerness" (*E*, pp. 95–98 in this volume), and explicit in his citing "patterns of objectification" to explain the distinctive phenomenology of value experience (*E*, pp. 98–100 in this volume).[27] Now it is, if anything, even more obvious with values than with essentially phenomenal qualities that they cannot be credited with causal efficacy: values would not pull their weight in any explanation of value experience even remotely analogous to the standard explanations of primary-quality experience. But reflection on the case of secondary qualities has already opened a gap between that admission and any concession that values are not genuine aspects of reality. And the point is reinforced by a crucial disanalogy between values and secondary qualities. To press the analogy is to stress that evaluative "attitudes," or states of will, are like (say) colour experience in being unintelligible except as modifications of a sensibility like ours. The idea of value experience involves taking admiration, say, to represent its object as having a property which (although there in the object) is essentially subjective in much the same way as the property that an object is represented as having by an experience of redness—that is, understood adequately only in terms of the appropriate modification of human (or similar) sensibility. The disanalogy, now, is that a virtue (say) is conceived to be not merely such as to elicit the appropriate "attitude" (as a colour is merely such as to cause the appropriate experiences), but rather such as to *merit* it. And this makes it doubtful whether merely causal explanations of value experience are relevant to the explanatory test, even to the extent that the question to ask is whether someone could consistently give such explanations while denying that the values involved are real. It looks as if we should be raising that question about explanations of a different kind.

For simplicity's sake, I shall elaborate this point in connection with something that is not a value, though it shares the crucial feature: namely danger or the fearful. On the face of it, this might seem a promising subject for a projectivist treatment (a treatment that appeals to what Hume called the mind's "propensity to spread itself on external objects").[28] At any rate the response that, according to such a treatment, is projected into the world can be characterized, without phenomenological falsification, otherwise than in terms of seeming to find the supposed product of projection already there.[29] And it would be obviously grotesque to fancy that a case of fear might be explained as the upshot of a mechanical (or perhaps para-mechanical) process initiated by an instance of "objective fearfulness." But if what we are engaged in is an "attempt to understand ourselves,"[30] then merely causal explanations of responses like fear will not be satisfying anyway.[31] What we want here is a style of explanation that makes sense of what is explained (in so far as sense can be made of it). This means that a technique for giving satisfying explanations of cases of fear—which would perhaps amount to a satisfactory explanatory theory of danger, though the label is possibly too grand—must allow for the possibility of criticism; we make sense of fear by seeing it as a response to objects that *merit* such a response, or as the intelligibly

defective product of a propensity towards responses that would be intelligible in that way.[32] For an object to merit fear just is for it to be fearful. So explanations of fear that manifest our capacity to understand ourselves in this region of our lives will simply not cohere with the claim that reality contains nothing in the way of fearfulness.[33] Any such claim would undermine the intelligibility that the explanations confer on our responses.

The shared crucial feature suggests that this disarming of a supposed explanatory argument for unreality should carry over to the case of values. There is, of course, a striking disanalogy in the contentiousness that is typical of values; but I think it would be a mistake to suppose that this spoils the point. In so far as we succeed in achieving the sort of understanding of our responses that is in question, we do so on the basis of preparedness to attribute, to at least some possible objects of the responses, properties that would validate the responses. What the disanalogy makes especially clear is that the explanations that preclude our denying the reality of the special properties that are putatively discernible from some (broadly) evaluative point of view are themselves constructed from that point of view. (We already had this in the case of the fearful, but the point is brought home when the validation of the responses is controversial.) However, the critical dimension of the explanations that we want means that there is no question of just any actual response pulling itself up by its own bootstraps into counting as an undistorted perception of the relevant special aspect of reality.[34] Indeed, awareness that values are contentious tells against an unreflective contentment with the current state of one's critical outlook, and in favour of a readiness to suppose that there may be something to be learned from people with whom one's first inclination is to disagree. The aspiration to understand oneself is an aspiration to change one's responses, if that is necessary for them to become intelligible otherwise than as defective. But although a sensible person will never be confident that his evaluative outlook is incapable of improvement, that need not stop him supposing, of some of his evaluative responses, that their objects really do merit them. He will be able to back up this supposition with explanations that show how the responses are well-placed; the explanations will share the contentiousness of the values whose reality they certify, but that should not stop him accepting the explanations any more than (what nobody thinks) it should stop him endorsing the values.[35] There is perhaps an air of bootstrapping about this. But if we restrict ourselves to explanations from a more external standpoint, at which values are not in our field of view, we deprive ourselves of a kind of intelligibility that we aspire to; and projectivists have given no reason whatever to suppose that there would be anything better about whatever different kind of self-understanding the restriction would permit.

5. It will be obvious how these considerations undermine the damaging effect of the primary-quality model. Shifting to a secondary-quality analogy renders irrelevant any worry about how something that is brutely *there* could nevertheless stand in an internal relation to some exercise of human sensibility. Values are not brutely there—not there independently of our sensibility—any more than colours are: though, as with colours, this does not stop us supposing that they are there independently of any particular apparent experience of them. As for the epistemology of value, the epistemology of danger is a good model. (Fearfulness is not a secondary quality, although the model is available only after the primary-quality model has been dislodged. A secondary-quality analogy for value experience gives out at certain points, no less than the primary-quality analogy that Mackie attacks.) To drop the primary-quality model in this case is to give up the idea that fearfulness itself, were it real, would need to be intelligible from a standpoint independent of the propensity to fear; the

same must go for the relations of rational consequentiality in which fearfulness stands to more straightforward properties of things.[36] Explanations of fear of the sort I envisaged would not only establish, from a different standpoint, that some of its objects are really fearful, but also make plain, case by case, what it is about them that makes them so; this should leave it quite unmysterious how a fear response rationally grounded in awareness (unproblematic, at least for present purposes) of these "fearful-making characteristics" can be counted as being, or yielding, knowledge that one is confronted by an instance of real fearfulness.[37]

Simon Blackburn has written, on behalf of a projectivist sentimentalism in ethics, that "we profit . . . by realizing that a training of the feelings rather than a cultivation of a mysterious ability to spot the immutable fitnesses of things is the foundation of how to live."[38] This picture of what an opponent of projectivism must hold is of a piece with Mackie's primary-quality model; it simply fails to fit the position I have described.[39] Perhaps with Aristotle's notion of practical wisdom in mind, one might ask why a training of the feelings (as long as the notion of feeling is comprehensive enough) cannot *be* the cultivation of an ability—utterly unmysterious just because of its connections with feelings—to spot (if you like) the fitnesses of things; even "immutable" may be all right, so long as it is not understood (as I take it Blackburn intends) to suggest a "platonistic" conception of the fitnesses of things, which would reimport the characteristic ideas of the primary quality model.[40]

Mackie's response to this suggestion used to be, in effect, that it simply conceded his point.[41] Can a projectivist claim that the position I have outlined is at best a notational variant, perhaps an inferior notational variant, of his own position?

It would be inferior if, in eschewing the projectivist metaphysical framework, it obscured some important truth. But what truth would this be? It will not do at this point to answer "The truth of projectivism." I have disarmed the explanatory argument for the projectivist's thin conception of genuine reality. What remains is rhetoric expressing what amounts to a now unargued primary-quality model for genuine reality.[42] The picture that this suggests for value experience—objective (value-free) reality processed through a moulded subjectivity—is no less questionable than the picture of secondary-quality experience on which, in Mackie at any rate, it is explicitly modelled. In fact I should be inclined to argue that it is projectivism that is inferior. Deprived of the specious explanatory argument, projectivism has nothing to sustain its thin conception of reality (that on to which the projections are effected) but a contentiously substantial version of the correspondence theory of truth, with the associated picture of genuinely true judgment as something to which the judger makes no contribution at all.[43]

I do not want to argue this now. The point I want to make is that even if projectivism were not actually worse, metaphysically speaking, than the alternative I have described, it would be wrong to regard the issue between them as nothing but a question of metaphysical preference.[44] In the projectivist picture, having one's ethical or aesthetic responses rationally suited to their objects would be a matter of having the relevant processing mechanism functioning acceptably. Now projectivism can of course perfectly well accommodate the idea of assessing one's processing mechanism. But it pictures the mechanism as something that one can contemplate as an object in itself. It would be appropriate to say "something one can step back from," were it not for the fact that one needs to use the mechanism itself in assessing it; at any rate one is supposed to be able to step back from any naively realistic acceptance of the values that the first-level employment of the mechanism has one attribute to items in the world. How, then, are

we to understand this pictured availability of the processing mechanism as an object for contemplation, separated off from the world of value? Is there any alternative to thinking of it as capable of being captured, at least in theory, by a set of principles for superimposing values on to a value-free reality? The upshot is that the search for an evaluative outlook that one can endorse as rational becomes, virtually irresistibly, a search for such a set of principles: a search for a *theory* of beauty or goodness. One comes to count "intuitions" respectable only in so far as they can be validated by an approximation to that ideal.[45] (This is the shape that the attempt to objectivize subjectivity takes here.) I have a hunch that such efforts are misguided; not that we should rest content with an "anything goes" irrationalism, but that we need a conception of rationality in evaluation that will cohere with the possibility that particular cases may stubbornly resist capture in any general net. Such a conception is straightforwardly available within the alternative to projectivism that I have described. I allowed that being able to explain cases of fear in the right way might amount to having a theory of danger, but there is no need to generalize that feature of the case; the explanatory capacity that certifies the special objects of an evaluative outlook as real, and certifies its responses to them as rational, would need to be exactly as creative and case-specific as the capacity to discern those objects itself. (It would be the same capacity: the picture of "stepping back" does not fit here.)[46] I take it that my hunch poses a question of moral and aesthetic taste, which—like other questions of taste —should be capable of being argued about. The trouble with projectivism is that it threatens to bypass that argument, on the basis of a metaphysical picture whose purported justification falls well short of making it compulsory. We should not let the question seem to be settled by what stands revealed, in the absence of compelling argument, as a prejudice claiming the honour due to metaphysical good taste.

NOTES

This paper grew out of my contributions to a seminar on J. L. Mackie's *Ethics: Inventing Right and Wrong* (Harmondsworth, Middlesex, Penguin: 1977: I refer to this as *E*) which I had the privilege of sharing with Mackie and R. M. Hare in 1978. I do not believe that John Mackie would have found it strange that I should pay tribute to a sadly missed colleague by continuing a strenuous disagreement with him.

1. See *E*, pp. 31–35. I shall also abbreviate references to the following other books by Mackie: *Problems from Locke* (Clarendon Press, Oxford, 1976: hereafter *PFL*); and *Hume's Moral Theory* (London: Routledge & Kegan Paul, 1980; hereafter *HMT*).

2. An inferior surrogate: it leads us to exaggerate the extent to which expressions of our sensitivity to values are signalled by the use of a special vocabulary. See my "Aesthetic Value, Objectivity, and the Fabric of the World," in Eva Schaper, ed., *Pleasure, Preference, and Value* (Cambridge: Cambridge University Press, 1983), pp. 1–16, at pp. 1–2.

3. I am trying here to soften a sharpness of focus that Mackie introduces by stressing the notion of prescriptivity. Mackie's singleness of vision here has the perhaps unfortunate effect of discouraging a distinction such as David Wiggins has drawn between "valuations" and "directives or deliberative (or practical) judgments" (see "Truth, Invention, and the Meaning of Life," *Proceedings of the British Academy* 62 (1976): 331–78, at pp. 338–39). My topic here is really the former of these. (It may be that the distinction does not matter in the way that Wiggins suggests: see note 35 below.)

4. I do not believe that the "quasi-realism" that Simon Blackburn has elaborated is a real alternative to this. (See p. 358 of his "Truth, Realism, and the Regulation of Theory," in Peter A. French, Theodore E. Uehling, Jr., and Howard Wettstein, eds., *Midwest Studies in Philosophy V: Studies in Epistemology* [Minneapolis: University of Minnesota Press, 1980), pp. 353–71.] In so far as the quasi-realist holds that the values, in his thought and speech about which he imitates the practices supposedly characteristic of realism, are *really* products of projecting "attitudes" into the world, he must have a conception of genuine reality—that which the values lack and the things on to which they are projected have. And the phenomenological claim ought to be that *that* is what the appearances entice us to attribute to values.

5. *An Essay concerning Human Understanding*, II.viii.10.

6. Being stung by a nettle is an actualization of a power in the nettle that conforms to Locke's description, but it seems wrong to regard it as a perception of that power; the experience lacks an intrinsically representational character which that would require. (It is implausible that looking red is intelligible independently of being red; combined with the account of secondary qualities that I am giving, this sets up a circle. But it is quite unclear that we ought to have the sort of analytic or definitional aspirations that would make the circle problematic. See Colin McGinn, *The Subjective View* ([Oxford: Clarendon Press, 1983], pp. 6–8.)

7. See McGinn, op. cit., pp. 12–14.

8. Of course there is room for the concept of illusion, not only because the senses can malfunction but also because of the need for a modifier like my "(in certain circumstances)," in an account of what it is for something to have a secondary quality. (The latter has no counterpart with primary qualities.)

9. See the discussion of (one interpretation of the notion of) objectivity at pp. 77–78 of Gareth Evans, "Things Without the Mind," in Zak van Straaten, ed., *Philosophical Subjects: Essays Presented to P. F. Strawson* (Oxford: Clarendon Press, 1980), pp. 76–116. Throughout the present section I am heavily indebted to this most important paper.

10. See *Essay*, II.viii. 15.

11. Cf. pp. 56–7 of P. F Strawson, "Perception and Its Objects," in G. F. Macdonald, ed., *Perception and Identity: Essays Presented to A. J. Ayer* (London: Macmillan, 1979), pp. 41–60.

12. This is a different way of formulating a point made by McGinn, op. cit. p. 121. Mackie's phrase "the fabric of the world" belongs with the second sense of "objective," but I think his arguments really address only the first. *Pace* p. 103 of A. W. Price, "Varieties of Objectivity and Values," *Proceedings of the Aristotelian Society* 82 (1982–83): 103–19, I do not think the phrase can be passed over as unhelpful, in favour of what the arguments do succeed in establishing, without missing something that Mackie wanted to say. (A gloss on "objective" as "there to be experienced" does not figure in Price's inventory, p. 104. It seems to be the obvious response to his challenge at pp. 118–19.)

13. I do not say it is correct: skepticism about this is very much in point. (See Nelson Goodman, *Languages of Art* (London: Oxford University Press, 1969), chap. I.)

14. When resemblance is in play, it functions as a palliative to lack of veridicality, not as what veridicality consists in.

15. Intrinsic features of experience, functioning as vehicles for aspects of content, seem to be taken for granted in Mackie's discussion of Molyneux's problem (*PFL*, pp. 28–32). The slide from talk of content to talk that fits only bearers of content seems to happen also in Mackie's discussion of truth, in *Truth, Probability, and Paradox* (Oxford: Clarendon Press, 1973), with the idea that a formulation like "A true statement is one such that the way things are is the way it represents things as being" makes truth consist in a relation of correspondence (rather than identity) between how things are and how things are represented as being; pp. 56–57 come too late to undo the damage done by the earlier talk of "comparison," e.g., at pp. 50, 51. (A subject matter for the talk that fits bearers is unproblematically available in this case; but Mackie does not mean to be discussing truth as a property of sentences or utterances.)

16. Indeed, this goes against the spirit of a passage about the word "content" at *PFL*, p. 48. Mackie's failure to profit by his insight emerges particularly strikingly in his remarkable claim (*PFL*, p. 50) that the "intentional object" conception of the content of experience yields an account of perception that is within the target area of "the stock objections against an argument from an effect to a supposed cause of a type which is never directly observed." (Part of the trouble here is a misconception of direct realism as a surely forlorn attempt to make perceptual knowledge unproblematic: *PFL*, p. 43.)

17. The phrases "manifest image" and "scientific image" are due to Wilfrid Sellars; see "Philosophy and the Scientific Image of Man," in *Science, Perception and Reality* (London: Routledge & Kegan Paul, 1963).

18. This is the position of Strawson, op. cit. (and see also his "Reply to Evans" in van Straaten, ed., op. cit., pp. 273–82). I am suggesting a diagnosis, to back up McGinn's complaint, op. cit., p. 124n.

19. Notice Strawson's sleight of hand with phrases like "shapes-as-seen," at p. 280 of "Reply to Evans." Strawson's understanding of what Evans is trying to say fails altogether to accommodate Evans's remark ("Things Without the Mind," p. 96) that "to deny that . . . primary properties are *sensory* is not at all to deny that they are *sensible* or *observable*." Shapes as seen are *shapes*—that is, non-sensory properties; it is one thing to deny, as Evans does, that experience can furnish us with the concepts of such properties, but quite another to deny that experience can disclose instantiations of them to us.

20. Features of physiologically specified states are not to the point here. Such features are not apparent in experience; whereas the supposed features that I am concerned with would have to be aspects of what experience is like for us, in order to function intelligibly as carriers for aspects of the content that experience presents to us. There may be an inclination to ask why it should be any harder for a feature of experience to acquire an objective significance than it is for a word to do so. But the case of language affords no counterpart to the fact that the objective significance in the case we are concerned with is a matter of how things (e.g.) *look* to be; the special problem is how to stop that "look" having the effect that a supposed intrinsic feature of experience get taken up into its own representational significance, thus ensuring that the significance is phenomenal and not primary.

21. See Thomas Nagel, "Subjective and Objective," in *Mortal Questions* (Cambridge: Cambridge University Press, 1979), pp. 196–213.

22. Cf. Bernard Williams, *Descartes: The Project of Pure Enquiry* (Harmondsworth: Penguin, 1978), p. 295.

23. Although McGinn, op. cit., is not taken in by the idea that "external" reality has only objective characteristics, I am not sure that he sufficiently avoids the picture that underlies that idea: see pp. 106–9. (This connects with a suspicion that at pp. 9–10 he partly succumbs to a temptation to objectivize the subjective properties of objects that he countenances: it is not as clear as he seems to suppose that, say, redness can be, so to speak, abstracted from the way things strike *us* by an appeal to relativity. His worry at pp. 132–36, that secondary quality experience may after all be phenomenologically misleading, seems to betray the influence of the idea of content-bearing intrinsic features of experience.)

24. See McGinn, op. cit., p. 14.

25. There are difficulties over how complete such explanations could aspire to be: see Price, op. cit., pp. 114–15, and my "Aesthetic value, Objectivity, and the Fabric of the World," op. cit., pp. l0–12.

26. Cf. pp. 206–8, especially p. 208, of David Wiggins, "What Would Be a Substantial Theory of Truth?" in van Straaten, ed., op . cit., pp. 189–221. The test of whether the explanations in question are consistent with rejecting the item in contention is something that Wiggins once mooted, in the course of a continuing attempt to improve that formulation: I am indebted to discussion with him.

27. See also Simon Blackburn, "Rule-Following and Moral Realism," in Steven Holtzman and Christopher Leich, eds., *Wittgenstein: To Follow a Rule* (London: Routledge & Kegan Paul, 1981), pp. 163–87; and the first chapter of Gilbert Harman, *The Nature of Morality* (New York: Oxford University Press, 1977).

28. *A Treatise of Human Nature*, I.iii.14. "Projectivist" is Blackburn's useful label: see "Rule-Following and Moral Realism," op. cit., and "Opinions and Chances," in D. H. Mellor, ed., *Prospects for Pragmatism* (Cambridge: Cambridge University Press, 1980), pp. 175–96.

29. At pp. 180–81 of "Opinions and Chances," Blackburn suggests that a projectivist need not mind whether or not this is so; but I think he trades on a slide between "can . . . only be understood in terms of" and "our best vocabulary for identifying" (which allows that there may be an admittedly inferior alternative).

30. The phrase is from p. 165 of Blackburn, "Rule-Following and Moral Realism."

31. I do not mean that satisfying explanations will not be causal. But they will not be *merely* causal.

32. I am assuming that we are not in the presence of a theory according to which no responses of the kind in question *could* be well-placed. That would have a quite unintended effect. (See E, p. l6.) Notice that it will not meet my point to suggest that calling a response "well-placed" is to be understood only quasi-realistically. Explanatory indispensability is supposed to be the test for the *genuine* reality supposedly lacked by what warrants only quasi-realistic treatment.

33. Cf. Blackburn, "Rule-Following and Moral Realism," op. cit., p. 164.

34. This will be so even in a case in which there are no materials for constructing standards of criticism except actual responses: something that is not so with fearfulness, although given a not implausible holism it will be so with values.

35. I can see no reason why we should not regard the contentiousness as ineliminable. The effect of this would be to detach the explanatory test of reality from a requirement of convergence (cf. the passage by Wiggins cited in note 26 above). As far as I can see, this separation would be a good thing. It would enable resistance to projectivism to free itself, with a good conscience, of some unnecessary worries about relativism. It might also discourage a misconception of the appeal to Wittgenstein that comes naturally to such a position. (Blackburn, "Rule-Following and Moral Realism," pp. 170–74, reads into my "Non-cognitivism and Rule-Following," in Holtzman and Leich, eds., op. cit., pp. 141–62, an interpretation of Wittgenstein as, in effect, making truth a matter of consensus, and has no difficulty in arguing that this will not make room for hard cases: but the interpretation is not mine.) With the requirement of convergence dropped, or at least radically relativized to a point of view, the question of the claim to truth of directives may come closer to the question of the truth status of evaluations than Wiggins suggests, at least in "Truth, Invention, and the Meaning of Life," op. cit.

36. Mackie's question (E, p. 41) "Just what *in the world* is signified by this 'because'?" involves a tendentious notion of "the world."

37. See Price, op. cit., pp. 106–7, 115.

38. "Rule-Following and Moral Realism," p. 186.

39. Blackburn's realist evades the explanatory burdens that sentimentalism discharges, by making the world rich (cf. p. 181) and then picturing it as simply setting its print on us. Cf. E, p. 22: "If there were something in the fabric of the world that validated certain kinds of concern, then it would be possible to acquire these merely by finding something out, by letting one's thinking be controlled by how things were." This saddles an opponent of projectivism with a picture of awareness of value as an exercise of pure receptivity, preventing him from deriving any profit from an analogy with secondary-quality perception.

40. On "platonism," see my "Non-Cognitivism and Rule-Following," op. cit., at pp. 156–57. On Aristotle, see M. F. Burnyeat, "Aristotle on Learning To Be Good," in Amelie O. Rorty, ed., *Essays on Aristotle's Ethics* (Berkeley: University of California Press, Los Angeles, London, 1980), pp. 69–92.

41. Price, op. cit. p. 107, cites Mackie's response to one of my contributions to the 1978 seminar (see Acknowledgment above).

42. We must not let the confusion between the two notions of objectivity distinguished in Sec. 3 above seem to support this conception of reality.

43. Blackburn uses the correspondence theorist's pictures for rhetorical effect, but he is properly skeptical about whether this sort of realism makes sense (see "Truth, Realism, and the Regulation of Theory," op. cit.). His idea is that the explanatory argument makes a counterpart to its metaphysical favouritism safely available to a projectivist about values in particular. Deprived of the explanatory argument, this projectivism should simply wither away. (See "Rule-Following and Moral Realism," p. 165. Of course I am not saying that the thin conception of reality that Blackburn's projectivism needs is unattainable, in the sense of being unformulable. What we lack is reasons of a respectable kind to recognize it as a complete conception of *reality*.)

44. Something like this seems to be suggested by Price, op. cit., pp. 107–8.

45. It is hard to see how a rational *inventing* of values could take a more piecemeal form.

46. Why do I suggest that a particularistic conception of evaluative rationality is unavailable to a projectivist? (See Blackburn, "Rule-Following and Moral Realism," pp. 167–70.) In the terms of that discussion, the point is that (with no good explanatory argument for his metaphysical favouritism) a projectivist has no alternative to being "a *real* realist" about the world on which he thinks values are superimposed. He cannot stop this from generating a quite un-Wittgensteinian picture of what *really* going on in the same way would be; which means that *he* cannot appeal to Wittgenstein in order to avert, as Blackburn puts it, "the threat which shapelessness poses to a respectable notion of consistency" (p. 169). So, at any rate, I meant to argue in my "Non-Cognitivism and Rule-Following," to which Blackburn's paper is a reply. Blackburn thinks his projectivism is untouched by the argument, because he thinks he can sustain its metaphysical favouritism without appealing to "*real* realism," on the basis of the explanatory argument. But I have argued that this is an illusion. (At p. 181, Blackburn writes: "Of course, it is true that our reactions are 'simply felt' and, in a sense, not rationally explicable." He thinks he can comfortably say this because our conception of reason will go along with the quasi-realist truth that his projectivism confers on some evaluations. But how can one restrain the metaphysical favouritism that a projectivist must show from generating some such thought as "This is not *real* reason"? If that is allowed to happen, a remark like the one I have quoted will merely threaten—like an ordinary nihilism—to dislodge us from our ethical and aesthetic convictions.)

12

Projection and Truth in Ethics

JOHN McDOWELL

1. Projection is what the mind engages in when, as Hume puts the idea, it "spreads itself" on to the external world.[1] This image certainly seems to fit some ways of thinking and talking that we can be tempted into: consider for instance the confused notion that disgustingness is a property that some things have intrinsically or absolutely, independently of their relations to us—a property of which our feelings of disgust constitute a kind of perception. That this notion is confused is of course no reason to suppose it cannot be true that something is disgusting. But the image of projection, figuring as it does in an explanation of how the confused notion comes about, might be useful in correcting a possible misconception of what such truth would amount to. My question in this lecture is whether the image is well suited to a similar employment in the field of ethics.

In connection with the prospects for crediting ethical statements or judgments with truth, David Wiggins has pressed a distinction between what he calls "valuations," on

the one hand, and "directives or deliberative (or practical) judgements," on the other.[2] It is in relation to the former category that the attribution of truth is most immediately attractive: valuations are not easily assimilated to, for instance, decisions what to do, but naturally strike us as correct or incorrect according to whether or not they accurately delineate the values that are to be found in their subject matter. This feature of valuations makes them also the most immediately tempting field for an application of the idea of projection: the phenomenology that makes the attribution of truth attractive can seem well explained as the upshot of a projection of what Hume would call "sentiments" on to their objects. Without prejudice to the possibility of extending the discussion to Wiggins's other category, for the purposes of this lecture I shall generally have valuations in mind.

In the case of the supposedly absolute or intrinsic property of disgustingness, what projection leads to is error: one takes what one in fact spreads on to the external world to be something one finds in the world on to which one spreads it, something that is there anyway—that is, there independently of human or sentient responses to things. It may seem that any projective thinking must be metaphysically erroneous in this way: the associated "error theory" in ethics was embraced, as is well known, by J. L. Mackie.[3] But we have to take note of a different use of the image of projection, which has been elaborated in a number of writings by Simon Blackburn. The position Blackburn describes and recommends for ethics in particular, is what he calls "quasi-realism." This aims to demonstrate that, starting from the claim that a mode of thinking (valuation in our particular case) is projective, we can see how it can, without confusion, exemplify nevertheless all the twists of thought and speech that might seem to signal a fully realist metaphysic, although—since they are now provided for within a projectivist framework— it must be a mistake to suppose they signal any such thing.[4] According to Hume, when our "taste" is projected on to the world, it "raises in a manner a new creation."[5] Blackburn's proposal, in effect, is that this "new creation" can be sufficiently robust to underwrite the presence of the trappings of realism, so to speak, in thought and speech which is correctly understood as projective; and that participants in such thought and speech need not be led by those elements of it into missing its projective nature. We can be clear, even as we suppose that our judgments accurately delineate the contours of reality, that it is only the "new creation," a product of projection, that is in question.

2. A tension arises in Blackburn's separation of projectivism from an error theory. (I mention this not to make it a problem for him, but to bring out a point that will be important in what follows.) To begin with at least, it is natural to put the projectivist thought, and Blackburn characteristically does put it, by saying that ethical commitments should not be understood as having truth-conditions. That would represent ethical remarks as statements about how things are, and according to projectivism they should be taken rather to express attitudes or sentiments.[6] But quasi-realism is supposed to make room for *all* the trappings of realism, including the idea that the notion of truth applies after all to ethical remarks. In that case, the original sharp contrast between putting forward a candidate for being true and expressing an attitude or sentiment cannot be right: a remark that expresses an attitude can also affirm a truth. Does this mean that projectivist quasi-realism is self-defeating?[7]

Not if we can distinguish what the projectivist starting-point rejects from what the quasi-realist conclusion establishes as acceptable. It may be tempting to suppose that this can be done only if we discern two different *notions* of truth, one to figure in the projectivist denial that ethical statements can be true, and the other to figure in the quasi-realist reinstatement of ethical truth.[8] However, this is not how Blackburn resolves the tension.[9] What Blackburn does—and this is centrally important to the point I want to make—is to contrast an *unearned* appeal to the notion of truth, which is what the projectivist rejects, with an *earned* right to the use of the notion, which is what the quasi-realist reinstates. The point about the application of the notion of truth that quasi-realism is supposed to make available is that we do not merely help ourselves to it, but work for it.

The contrast—the unearned employment of the notion of truth that projectivism rejects—is a position that expands reality by mere postulation, beyond what the projectivist is comfortable with, to include an extra population of distinctively value-involving states of affairs or facts. Corresponding to this, it purports to equip us with special cognitive faculties by whose exercise we become aware of this special field of knowable fact. These special cognitive faculties are vaguely assimilated to the senses, but no detailed account can be given of how they operate, such as might make it clear to us—as clear as it is in the case of the senses—how their exercise affords us access to the relevant range of circumstances. The assimilation to the senses gives this intuitionistic position the superficial appearance of offering an epistemology of our access to valuational truth. but there is no substance behind this appearance.

How does projectivism improve on this rather clearly disreputable position?

The basic projectivist idea is that ethical remarks express not mysterious "cognizings" of valuational facts, but attitudes. Now if that were the whole story, there would not be much prospect of a substantial notion of truth; think of the practice of expressing one's attitudes to various flavors of ice cream. But there is an extra ingredient to the story, which quasi-realism exploits. The attitudes are the upshot of sensibilities: that is, propensities to form various attitudes in response to various features of situations. Ethical sensibilities are themselves subject to attitudes of approbation or disapprobation; and—that is the crucial thing—these attitudes to sensibilities are a matter for argument and criticism.[10] We are not content simply to go along with the flow of our sensibilities as they stand, regardless of how they fare under critical scrutiny; and we are not at liberty to rank sensibilities at random and still be taken seriously as participants in ethical discussion. Truth, in a remark that has to be understood in the first instance as expressive of an attitude can now be explained in terms of the fact that the sensibility from which the attitude issues stands up to the appropriate kind of criticism.

To complete the picture, we should need an account of the nature of the criticism to which ethical sensibilities are subject. In part the critical assessment in question is formal, involving requirements like consistency. But there are also substantive constraints on whether a sensibility is acceptable: these derive—so Blackburn seems to suggest—from the function of ethical thought and speech in helping to secure such goods as social order and co-operation.[11] This sketch will serve for the present: as we shall see. a crucial issue opens up when one sets out to be less schematic.

3. It is hard to imagine that anyone would explicitly deny that if truth in ethics is available, it needs to be earned. It seems clear. moreover, that one would be deceiving oneself if one thought that those vague analogies with perception amounted to earning it. If the idea that truth must be earned is located as, precisely, a corrective to the unhelpful intuitionistic realism that Blackburn is primarily concerned to reject, it can seem to establish a conclusion about a metaphysical basis on which ethical truth must be worked for: realism shirks the obligation and the clear alternative is projectivism. But it is questionable whether that is the right setting in which to place the idea that truth must be earned.

Consider a view of the current predicament of ethics on the lines of Alasdair MacIntyre's in *After Virtue*.[12] According to MacIntyre, the description of ethical language given by C. L. Stevenson—although it is not, as Stevenson claimed, a correct description of ethical language as such—has come to be true of the ethical language that is actually at our disposal. One crucial ingredient of Stevenson's picture is the implication that no substantial distinction can be drawn among methods of inducing people to change their minds on ethical matters, between making reasons available to them on the one hand and manipulating them in ways that have nothing in particular to do with rationality on the other. I do not want to go into the question whether MacIntyre is right in contending that we now lack the means to draw such distinctions; the point is that if he is right, then clearly there is no prospect of achieving, in ethical thought with its present conceptual resources. anything that we could count as truth in any serious sense. No doubt it is always possible for anyone to use "It is true that . . ." as an indication of willingness on his own part to affirm whatever follows "that." But if MacIntyre's Stevensonian picture is correct, we lack what a more substantial notion of truth seems plainly to require, a conception of better and worse ways to think about ethical questions which connects with the idea that there are reasons for being of a certain mind on a question, in contrast with the idea that there is nothing to ethical thinking but rationally arbitrary subjective stances and whatever power relations might be exploited to shift people's ethical allegiances.[13]

Earning the notion of truth, in the face of this sort of suggestion, would thus be a matter of arguing that we do after all have at our disposal a conception of reasons for ethical thinking which is sufficiently rich and substantial to mark off rationally induced improvements in ethical stances from alterations induced by merely manipulative persuasion.

Positions like MacIntyre's suggest a quite different context for the thought that the availability of truth in ethics is something that it would take work to establish. The problem about truth in ethics, viewed in this context, is not that it fails to be as the intuitionist realist supposes, so that establishing its availability requires a different metaphysical basis. The problem is that a question is raised whether our equipment for thinking ethically is suited only for mere attitudinizing— whether our ethical concepts are too sparse and crude for ethical thought to seem an exercise of reason, as it must if there is to be room in it for a substantial notion of truth.[14] It is really not clear why addressing a problem of this sort should seem to require a metaphysical move at all.

4. It may still seem that, even if earning truth in the face of this sort of challenge to its availability requires something other than an explicitly metaphysical move, namely vindicating the richness and robustness of the conception of reasons for ethical judgments that our conceptual resources equip us with, nevertheless, as soon as we concede that attaining truth is not simply a matter of "cognizing" valuational facts, we must have implicitly adopted a projectivist metaphysic. This appearance reflects an assumption that, at the metaphysical level, there are just two options: projectivism and the unattractive intuitionistic realism that populates reality with mysterious extra features and merely goes through the motions of supplying an epistemology for our supposed access to them. But the assumption is questionable.

The point of the image of projection is to explain certain seeming features of reality as reflections of our subjective responses to a world that really contains no such features. Now this explanatory direction seems to require a corresponding priority, in the order of understanding, between the projected response and the apparent feature: we ought to be able to focus our thought on the response without needing to exploit the concept of the apparent feature that is supposed to result from projecting the response. In the sort of case I cited at the beginning, it is plausible that this requirement is met: disgust, or nausea, we can plausibly suppose, are self-contained psychological items, conceptualizable without any need to appeal to any projected properties of disgustingness or nauseatingness. (No doubt a full explanation of the psychological phenomena would group things together in terms of their tendency to produce those responses, but those tendencies are not properties that need to be explained as projections of the responses.) The question, now, is this: if, in connection with some range of concepts whose application engages distinctive aspects of our subjective make-up in the sort of way that seems characteristic of evaluative concepts, we reject the kind of realism that construes subjective responses as perceptions of associated features of reality and does no work towards earning truth, are we entitled to assume that the responses enjoy this kind of explanatory priority, as projectivism seems to require?

It may help to consider a non-ethical case in which an intuitionistic realism is obviously unattractive, and in which Blackburn proceeds as if projectivism is obviously correct: the case of the comic or funny. To begin with at least, this looks like a good field for a projective account. But what exactly is it that we are to conceive as projected on to the world so as to give rise to our idea that things are funny? "An inclination to laugh" is not a satisfactory answer[15]: projecting an inclination to laugh would not necessarily yield an apparent instance of the comic. since laughter can signal, for instance. embarrassment just as well as amusement. Perhaps the right response cannot be identified except as amusement; and perhaps amusement cannot be understood except as finding something comic. I need not take a view on whether this is correct. But if it is correct, there is a serious question whether we can really *explain* the idea of something's being comic as a *projection* of that response. The suggestion is that there is no self-contained prior fact of our subjective lives that could enter into a projective account of the relevant way of thinking: in the only relevant response, the conceptual apparatus that figures in the relevant way of thinking is already in play. No doubt the propensity to laugh is in some sense a self-contained prior psychological fact. But differentiating some exercises of that unspecific propensity as cases of *amusement* is something we have to learn, and if the suggestion is correct, this learning is indistinguishable from coming to find some things comic. Surely it undermines a projective account of a concept if we cannot home in on the subjective state whose projection is supposed to result in the seeming feature of reality in question without the aid of the concept of that feature, the concept that was to be projectively explained. And surely this scepticism cannot tend in the direction of a relapse into the intuitionistic sort of realism.

Blackburn himself is remarkably casual about this. I know only one place where he discusses the question whether this kind of consideration poses a problem for projectivism; and in that place he simply asserts that there is no problem for projectivism if the only way to describe a supposedly projected subjective response is in terms of seeming to find the supposed upshot of projecting it in something one confronts.[16] I think this reflects the assumption I mentioned earlier, that if we are not realists of the unsatisfactorily intuitionistic sort then we cannot but be projectivists.

Blackburn's view of the available options is well summed up in these words of his (they apply to morality in particular, but the structure is quite general):

> The projectivist holds that our nature as moralists is well explained by regarding us as reacting to a reality which contains nothing in the way of values, duties, rights and so forth; a realist thinks it is well explained only by seeing us as able to perceive, cognize, intuit, an independent moral reality. He holds that the moral features of things are the parents of our sentiments, whereas the Humean holds that they are their children.[17]

Realism here is the unsatisfactory position that helps itself to an unearned notion of truth. So if the choice is the one Blackburn offers in this passage, it seems compulsory to opt for regarding the "features of things" that are in question as children of our sentiments rather than their parents. There is no room to raise a problem about whether the sentiments have the requisite explanatory independence. But why do we have to limit ourselves to those two options? What about a position which says that the extra features are neither parents nor children of our sentiments, but—if we must find an apt metaphor from the field of kinship relations—siblings?[18] Such a view would be appropriate for amusement and the comic, if that case is as I have suggested it might be. Denying that the extra features are prior to the relevant sentiments, such a view distances itself from the idea that they belong, mysteriously, in a reality that is wholly independent of our subjectivity and set over against it. It does not follow that the sentiments have a priority. If there is no comprehending the right sentiments independently of the concepts of the relevant extra features, a no-priority view is surely indicated. There are two possible ways of not being an intuitionistic realist, and the image of projection really fits only one of them.

In the case of the comic, the threat in face of which it would be necessary to earn truth—if one wanted to—would not be that any persuasion seems indistinguishable from manipulation; argument is not an important ingredient in that part of our lives. (The attempt to persuade someone that something is funny is typically self-defeating.) But there is a sameness underlying this difference. In both cases, the threat to a substantial notion of truth lies in the idea that there is nothing really to choose between different sensibilities, and that any convergence is best thought of as a mere coincidence of subjectivities rather than agreement on a range of truths—the sort of view that would be natural if everyone came to prefer one flavour of ice cream to any other. And in both cases, the threatening thought can be put like this: different sensibilities cannot be ranked according to whether there are better *reasons* for one sensibility's response than another's. Whether or not the sensibilities are conceived as typically altered by argument, so that the issue can be whether persuading someone counts as giving him reasons to change his mind, the challenge can be put as a query whether a mode of thought that engages subjective responses allows for a sufficiently substantial conception of reasons for exercises of it to be capable of truth.

The interest of the no-priority view, now, is that it opens up the possibility that it might be respectable to use the apparently world-describing conceptual resources with which we articulate our responses, in earning truth in one of the relevant areas. Blackburn's simpler structure of options suggests that we must deny ourselves those resources, on pain

of lapsing back into a bald intuitionism. A serious projective quasi-realism about the comic would construct a conception of what it is for things to be really funny on the basis of principles for ranking senses of humour which would have to be established from outside the propensity to find things funny. The contrasting idea would be that we might regard our conception of greater and less refinement and discrimination in senses of humour as derivative from an understanding of what it is for things to be really funny: something we can acceptably aim to elaborate from within the propensity to find things funny. The concept of the comic is not a device for a rationally isolated grouping of items, things whose satisfaction of it we take to be simply a matter of their eliciting the appropriate reaction from us; having the concept involves at least inklings of a place it occupies in a rationally interconnected scheme of concepts, and we should aim to exploit such inklings in working out an aesthetic, so to speak, of humour. A ranking of sensibilities would flow from that, rather than being independently constructed (from what materials?"[19]) and used to deliver verdicts on when things are really comic. Of course we might not be able to squeeze much in the way of rankings of senses of humour out of our understanding of the funny. And anything on these lines that we did come up with would be liable, as such constructions always are, to accusations of fraud, on behalf of people whose senses of humour we represented as blunter than they might be. We would need to take great care to be sure that we were not merely projectively conferring a bogus objectivity on the deliverances of a sensibility that was in fact rationally on a par with any other. But, although we must of course acknowledge the risks and do our best to guard against them, we would not be guaranteed to fall into self-deception of this sort, simply by virtue of working from within.

The no-priority view allows, then, that it might be possible to do something recognizable as earning truth by focusing on the funny itself. The idea of what is really funny need not be explained in terms of an independently established conception of what makes a sense of humour more discriminating. This contrasts with a constraint that seems to be implicit in a serious projectivism, according to which the idea of a superior discernment has to be made clear without exploiting exercises of the way of thinking which is to be explained as projective, so that it is available for use in certifying some such exercises as (quasi-realistically) true.

Analogously in the ethical case; here again, the possibility of the no-priority view brings out that we do not need to choose between, on the one hand, lapsing into intuitionism—simply helping ourselves to truth—and, on the other, disallowing ourselves, in earning truth, the conceptual equipment that projectivism sees as the product of projection. Earning truth is a matter of supplying something that does satisfactorily what is merely pretended by the bogus epistemology of intuitionism. Instead of a vague attempt to borrow the epistemological credentials of the idea of perception, the position I am describing aims, quite differently, at an epistemology that centres on the notion of susceptibility to reasons. The threat to truth is from the thought that there is not enough substance to our conception of reasons for ethical stances. When we try to meet this threat, there is no reason not to appeal to all the resources at our disposal, including all the ethical concepts that we can lay our hands on, so long as they survive critical scrutiny; and there need be no basis for critical scrutiny of one ethical concept except others, so the necessary scrutiny does not involve stepping outside the point of view constituted by an ethical sensibility.

Notice that this does not make it a foregone conclusion that the threat will be satisfactorily met: MacIntyre's picture of our present predicament, for instance, cannot be ruled out without actually looking into the resources we still have. Aiming to meet the threat from within is not helping ourselves to ethical truth in the manner of an intuitionistic realism; and it would be quite wrong to suppose that it is helping ourselves to ethical truth in the different sense that the issue is prejudged in favour of truth being attainable.

5. Blackburn has purported to respond to the suggestion that truth in ethics might be earned from within ethical thinking, and similarly in other areas where an issue about projection arises. His claim is that such a suggestion merely shirks a plainly necessary explanatory task: one in which

> we try to place the activity of moralizing, or the reaction of finding things funny ... In particular we try to fit our commitments in these areas into a metaphysical understanding of the kinds of fact the world contains: a metaphysical view which can properly be hostile to an unanalysed and *sui generis* area of moral or humorous ... facts. And relative to this interest, answers which merely cite the truth of various such verdicts are quite beside the point. This ... is because there is no theory connecting these truths to devices whereby we know about them—in other words no way of protecting our right to [conditionals of the form "If it hadn't been the case that p I would not be committed to p"].[20]

This passage raises several questions. I shall end this lecture by making three points about it.

First, note how the passage still strikes the note of theft as against honest toil, as if the target were still the kind of intuitionism that merely helps itself to a novel range of facts. This looks quite unwarranted once it is clear that there are three positions and not just two. The suggestion is not that we "merely cite the truth"—presumably alleged to be detected by some mysterious quasi-sensory capacities—of specific ethical verdicts, or judgments to the effect that something is funny. The aim is to give an account of how such verdicts and judgments are located in the appropriate region of the space of reasons. No particular verdict or judgment would be a sacrosanct starting-point, supposedly immune to critical scrutiny, in our earning the right to claim that some such verdicts or judgments stand a chance of being true. That is not at all to say that we must earn that right from an initial position in which *all* such verdicts or judgments are suspended at once, as in the projectivist picture of a range of responses to a world that does not contain values or instances of the comic.

The second point relates to the "metaphysical understanding" that Blackburn mentions. This fixes an inventory of "the kinds of fact the world contains." It fixes also, in parallel, a conception of the kinds of cognitive occurrence that can constitute access to facts: nothing will serve except what can be conceived in terms of the impact on us of the world as the "metaphysical understanding" understands it. That is why one is not allowed to count as protecting one's right to a conditional of the form "If it had not been the case that *p*, I would not have become committed to the belief that *p*" if one establishes that one would not have arrived at the belief that *p* had it not been for good reasons for it, with the excellence of the reasons vindicated from within the relevant way of thinking.

But how good are the credentials of a "metaphysical understanding" that blankly excludes values and instances of the comic from the world in advance of any philosophical enquiry into truth?[21] Surely if the history of philosophical reflection on the correspondence theory of truth has taught us anything, it is that there is ground for suspicion of the idea that we have some way of telling what can count as a fact, prior to and independent of asking what forms of words might count as expressing truths, so that a conception of facts could exert some leverage in the investigation of truth. We have no point of vantage on the question what can be the case, that is, what can be a fact, external to the modes of thought and speech we know our way around in, with whatever understanding of what counts as better and worse execution of them our mastery of them can give us. If

there is enough substance to that understanding to enable us to rule out positions like MacIntyre's with a clear conscience, that is what it is for truth to be attainable in such thought and speech, and so much the worse for any prior "metaphysical understanding" which holds that there cannot be facts of that kind.[22] It is a matter for diagnosis and exorcism, not something that can be allowed without further ado to be a good starting-point for a philosophy of ethics or humour. To reiterate the first point, we need not be frightened out of this line by the bogey of "an unanalysed and *sui generis* area of moral or humorous . . . facts." That is what one gets if one accepts a familiar "metaphysical understanding"—one which is in fact quite dubious even in the areas where it is most tempting—with its picture of facts and our access to them, and then tries to accommodate exercises of ethical sensibilities or senses of humour within its framework; but that was never the proposal.

The third point is about "placing" ethics or humour. I have been suggesting that an undefended "metaphysical understanding" cannot impose binding intellectual obligations on anyone. But that is not to say there are no good questions in this general vicinity. Consider the world as natural science describes it. It is plausible (although not beyond dispute) that that "world" would not contain moral values or instances of the comic. (This is no concession to the "metaphysical understanding": what is missing is a reason to suppose that natural science has a foundational status in philosophical reflection about truth—that there can be no facts other than those that would figure in a scientific understanding of the world.) Now there is no reason not to raise the question how ethics or humour relate to the scientifically useful truth about the world and our dealings with it. There is no reason to dispute that a good answer to such questions can contribute to our making ourselves intelligible to ourselves in a way that we ought to find desirable. Finding things funny, for instance, can seem, from a certain fully intelligible perspective, a peculiar and even mysterious aspect of our lives, quite unlike, say, being able to tell what shapes things have, or even what colours things have. Anything that alleviated this sense of mystery would be welcome, and it would be anti-intellectual or obscurantist to deny that. What is unclear, however, is why it seems so obvious to Blackburn that this kind of consideration supports projectivism. No doubt reflections about the benefits of co-operation and social order go some distance towards " placing" ethics—making it intelligible that we inculcate ethical sensibilities in our young, trying to give ethics the importance to them that we believe is proper. (It is not at all obvious what might play an analogous role with senses of humour.) But we do not need to suppose that such "placing" functions by allowing us to make sense of a range of subjective responses to a world that contains nothing valuable, or funny-responses that we can then see as projected on to that world

so as to generate the familiar appearances. What we "place" need not be the sort of sentiments that can be regarded as parents of apparent features: it may be pairs of sentiments and features reciprocally related—siblings rather than parents and children.

There is surely something right about the Humean idea of a "new creation"—the idea of a range of seeming states of affairs which would not be as they are if it were not for the distinctive affective colouration of our subjectivity. What does not follow is that the seeming states of affairs can be understood as creatures of independently intelligible operations of our affective nature. These seeming objectivities need not be a shadow or reflection of a self-contained subjectivity: understanding the genesis of the "new creation" may be understanding an interlocking complex of subjective and objective, of response and feature responded to. And in that case it is a mistake to think we can illuminate the metaphysics of these matters by appealing to the image of projection.

NOTES

1. See *A Treatise of Human Nature* I, iii. 14.

2. See his "Truth, Invention, and the Meaning of Life." *Proceedings of the British Academy* 62 (1976): 332–78, at pp. 338–39.

3. See chap. 1 of his *Ethics: Inventing Right and Wrong* (Harmondsworth: Penguin Books, 1977).

4. Among many other writings, see chap. 5 and 6 of Blackburn's *Spreading the Word* (Oxford: Clarendon Press, 1984).

5. *An Enquiry Concerning the Principles of Morals*, App. I.

6. See, e.g., *Spreading the Word*, pp. 167–71.

7. Blackburn raises the question whether "a projective approach is too good to be true" at p. 219.

8. See Crispin Wright, "Realism, Anti-Realism, Irrealism, Quasirealism," *Midwest Studies in Philosophy*.

9. See p. 257: "Does this make moral commitments true in the same sense as others, or only in a different sense? I do not greatly commend the question."

10. See *Spreading the Word*, p. 194.

11. See, e.g., pp. 192, 197. I think Blackburn would regard Hume's treatment of the artificial virtues as a model of the kind of thing that would be required in a full version of the quasi-realist project, constructing truth out of an account of how projective thinking can allow for a substantial notion of better and worse ways of doing it.

12. London: Duckworth, 1981.

13. I am not suggesting that any ethical thought and language of which an account which is in some sense emotivist is true must dissolve such distinctions: compare *Spreading the Word*, p. 197. (I have not questioned that ethical thought and speech engages our affective nature, and I suppose that is an emotivist insight.) But Stevenson's account does dissolve such distinctions: so it affords a good picture of a

kind of threat in face of which earning truth should seem a good thing to attempt. (If MacIntyre is right, earning truth would involve a conceptual reform.)

14. This requires me to take issue with Blackburn when he says things like the following (p. 181 of "Reply: Rule-Following and Moral Realism"): "Of course, it is true that our reactions are 'simply felt' and, in a sense, not rationally explicable. But we should not be too worried about reason here. In general. reason follows where truth leads." By my lights this is the wrong way round. If we could not convince ourselves that our rankings of sensibilities were capable of being grounded in reason (as Blackburn's appeals, when it suits, to argument and criticism suggest they are), there would not be any reason to suppose that we had regained an application for the notion of truth.

15. Compare Blackburn's "Errors and the Phenomenology of Value," in Ted Honderich, ed., *Morality and Objectivity* (London: Routledge & Kegan Paul, 1985), pp. 1–22, at p. 9

16. This is at pp. 180–81 of "Opinions and Chances," in D. H. Mellor. ed., *Prospects for Pragmatism* (Cambridge: Cambridge University Press, 1980), pp. 175–96. Blackburn makes the point that it would not be surprising, given a projectivist view, that "our best vocabulary for identifying the reaction should be the familiar one using the predicates we apply to the world we have spread." This seems right: once we have done the spreading, the resulting way of talking will no doubt seem more natural to us than any other. But that is not the same as saying that there is no alternative way of identifying the response; if there is *no* alternative way, then there is no way of saying what has happened, in detail, in terms of the image of projection, and it is obscure why we should allow *that* to be consistent with projectivism.

17. "Reply: Rule-Following and Moral Realism," in Steven Holtzman and Christopher Leich, eds., *Wittgenstein To Follow a Rule* (London: Routledge & Kegan Paul, 1981). pp. 163–87, at pp. 164–65. It may be worth mentioning in passing that the idea of rights as children of our sentiments seems an over-simplification of Hume's view.

18. See David Wiggins, "Truth, Invention, and the Meaning of Life," at p. 348; and for an elaboration of the thought there expressed that "an adequate account of these matters will have to treat psychological states and their objects as equal and reciprocal partners," see now "A Sensible Subjectivism?" in his *Needs, Values, Deliberation and Truth* (Oxford: Blackwell, 1987).

19. This is a serious question for anyone who is sympathetic to a quasi-realist projectivism about the comic. Much of what is ordinarily appealed to in ranking objects for amusement is suitably external but just for that reason not obviously relevant to *this* issue: for instance much humour that one may deplore as being "in bad taste" (usually on moralistic grounds) is not thereby shown not to be extremely *funny*. It seems highly implausible that we could extract out of the function of the sense of humour (if we knew it) something that would even seem to do the sort of work in a quasi-realist ranking of sensibilities that Blackburn seems to suggest is done in the ethical case by the function of ethical thinking.

20. "Errors and the Phenomenology of Value," pp. 17–8: the material in square brackets is supplied from p. 16.

21. Blackburn is extraordinarily unconcerned with this question. See *Spreading the Word*, p. 39, where "the best philosophical problems" are said to arise when "we get a sense of what the world is like, what it must be like," and cannot find room in it for this or that which we are loath to give up: for instance, "consciousness, agency, causation, or value." The question where we get this sense. and what its credentials might be, is not raised. Similarly at p. 146: "Once such doubts are felt—motivated in whatever way—a number of attitudes are possible." Again there is the striking lack of concern with the origin of the doubts, and this leaves no room for addressing the question of their merits. It is as if any bit of philosophy that comes naturally to us must be all right, ahead of any inquiry into why it comes naturally to us. (In my "Values and Secondary Qualities," in Honderich. ed., op. cit., pp. 110–29. I consider and reject the suggestion that the favouritism of the "metaphysical understanding" might be defended on the basis of a conception of the real as what is explanatorily indispensable. Blackburn's purported response, in "Errors and the Phenomenology of Value," pp. 17–18. still takes the "metaphysical understanding" not to need defending: the response does not make contact with its purported target.)

22. Blackburn considers (see *Spreading the Word*, p. 236) the thesis that "there is no way in which any mind can step back from its own system of belief, survey without its benefit a reality the system aims to depict, and discover whether it is doing well or badly." I am not sure I understand his attitude to this thesis. In the chapter from which I have quoted those words, he considers (as in the passage under discussion in my text) only "correspondence conditionals" with directly causal underpinnings—cases where we can take quite literally the idea of reality making an impact on us. It would surely be a mistake to suppose that when we cite such causal underpinnings for the idea that we are capable of attaining the truth in some area, we are somehow managing after all to step outside reliance on the best we can do, from within our "system of belief," to afford reasons for bits of it. And one might think this thought ought to neutralize "correspondence conditionals" in particular: that is just one shape that rationally underwritten "correspondence conditionals" can take. Blackburn, however, writes (pp. 247–8) as if such a thought involves a "gestalt-switch" akin to Idealism, and in competition with ascribing to objects and facts "their independence of us and our believings." It seems to me quite clear that there is no competition here. I am accordingly led to wonder if Blackburn is, in some submerged way, conceiving the causal impact on us of some facts as a way in which after all the World itself—what we would like to get a glimpse of head on, if we could only "step back"—penetrates the veil of our "system of belief" and gets through to us.

13

A Sensible Subjectivism

DAVID WIGGINS

I cannot see how to refute the arguments for the subjectivity of ethical values, but I find myself incapable of believing that all that is wrong with wanton cruelty is that I don't like it.

BERTRAND RUSSELL

1. Usually—if only for the purpose of having the position summarily dismissed as soon as possible—the doctrine of subjectivism is reported as claiming that "x is good" or "x is right" or "x is beautiful," as uttered by speaker S, says that S approves of x, or that x induces in S a certain sentiment of approbation.

The first and perhaps most obvious objection, that "good," "right," and "beautiful" do not themselves mean the same, might be countered by distinguishing different species of approbative sentiment. But there is a more familiar and more considerable second objection: at least when it is given in this form, subjectivism makes a difficulty for itself about disagreement. If, where John says x is good, Philip denies that x is good, Philip is not on this account necessarily disagreeing with John. Certainly, if they are disagreeing, the purported subjectivist analysis of "x is good" does not really bring out what they are disagreeing about.

To attend to this fault, the doctrine might be modified, by a shift from *me* to *us*, so as to claim that "x is good," as uttered by John, says that x is approved of by those whom John calls "us." If Philip is one of these persons, there can then be disagreement between John and Philip. But now the risk is that the disagreement in question will appear as merely sociological, whereas the disagreement that always needed to be accounted for and made room for was not disagreement about what we value, but disagreement *in valuation*. Rival attempts to speak for us as a community (if that is how the subjectivist ought to see disagreement) cannot be plausibly reduced to rival accounts of what, if anything, the community does already say.

2. Emotivists may be expected to butt in at this point to suggest that disagreement in valuation can be seen as disagreement in attitude *expressed* (Stevenson). But this suggestion, and the whole idea of an emotive meaning reckoned separately from cognitive content, does insufficient justice to our feel-

227

ing that divergence of attitude must itself be founded in something, and reflect a prior or coeval disagreement in something not itself reducible without residue to emotive attitude (i.e., in something the sentence is *about*, which is not so far accounted for). Even if it were plainer what emotive meaning was and clearer how it could work in concert with ordinary meaning (and more evident that in the end one will have to settle for it), there would still be something deeply unsatisfying about the suggestion.[1]

3. At this point I think we ought to feel the need to look again at the subjectivists who wrote before G. E. Moore's celebrated and influential critique of subjectivism—and especially at Hume, an author whom Moore cautiously refrains from mentioning by name in this connexion.[2]

In so far as Hume ever came anywhere near to suggesting a semantical account of "*x* is good/right/beautiful" (which is not, one may think, very near even at the points where he speaks of "defining" this or that), it may seem that the best proposal implicit in his theory of valuation is that this sentence says that *x* is the kind of thing to arouse a certain sentiment of approbation. This is not my approbation, or your approbation, or Hume's or society's approbation. If we want a form of words that can be the focus of real valuational disagreement as it was open to Hume to conceive this, then we do best *not to specify* whose approbation. *x* is simply such as to arouse that sentiment. (Note that it can still count against "*x* is good" that *x* in fact arouses a sentiment of approbation in nobody. Just as the claim that *x* is desirable falls into difficulty if nobody at all desires *x*. This is a point that one may register without making the error John Stuart Mill is often accused of making about "desired" and "desirable."

Not only is such subjectivism free from Moore's well-worn criticism about disagreement. It comes close to escaping Moore's earlier "open question" argument. If *x* is such as

to merit a certain feeling of approbation [when taken as one among the *f*s], the question is not wide open whether or not *x* is [a] good [*f*]. For if *x* is such as to arouse that sentiment, this surely need not be without influence upon the will.

Hume might have been easier to satisfy on this point than Moore would have been. But since the escape is still a rather narrow one, perhaps we should consider another suggestion that Hume could have made. If he had considered a question he does not consider and if he had disclaimed any intention to provide analyses of the ordinary terms of approbation, then Hume could have said that *x* is good/right/beautiful if and only if *x* is such as to make a certain sentiment of approbation *appropriate*.[3]

4. It may appear that this second account of Hume's theory makes it viciously circular in a way that it previously was not. But I reply that, on a proper understanding of the point of subjectivism and its having no need to supplant valuational by non-valuational language, the circularity is benign (see below and Sec. 9); and that in any case no *new* circularity has been introduced. There was already a kind of circle before this adjustment was made. What after all is a sentiment of approbation? (Or if the point of the word "certain," sometimes inserted by Hume, is that there are different, phenomenologically distinguishable kinds of approbation, numerous enough to differentiate the good, right, and beautiful, then what *are* sentiments of approbation?) Surely a sentiment of approbation cannot be identified except by its association with the thought or feeling that *x* is good (or right or beautiful) and with the various considerations in which that thought can be grounded, given some particular item and context, *in situ*.

Whether such circularities constitute a difficulty for subjectivism depends entirely on what the subjectivist takes himself to be attempting. If we treat it as already known and given that "*x* is good" (or "right" or "beautiful") is *fully analysable*, and if "*x* is such as to arouse the sentiment of approbation" (or "*x* is such as to make that sentiment appropriate") is the subjectivist's best effort in the analytical direction, and if this equivalent fails to deliver any proper analysis, then subjectivism is some sort of failure.[4] Certainly. But, even if classical subjectivists have given this impression to those who want to conceive of all philosophy as analysis, analysis as such never needed to be their real concern. What traditional subjectivists have really wanted to convey is not so much definition as commentary. Chiefly they have wanted to persuade us that, when we consider whether or not *x* is good or right or beautiful, there is no appeal to anything that is more fundamental than actually possible human sentiments—a declaration that seems both contentious and plausible (but more plausible when we take into account the intentionality of the sentiments, cp. Sec. 14–15). Circularity as such is no objection to it, provided that the offending formulation is also *true*. But what use (I shall be asked) is such a circular formulation? My answer is that, by tracing out such a circle, the subjectivist hopes to elucidate the concept of value by displaying it in its actual involvement with the sentiments. One would not, according to him, have sufficiently elucidated what value is *without* that detour.

5. In all these matters, an analogy with colour is suggestive. "*x* is red if and only if *x* is such as to give, under certain conditions specifiable as normal, a certain visual impression" naturally raises the question "which visual impression?" And that question attracts the answer "an impression as of seeing something red," which reintroduces *red*. But this finding of circularity scarcely amounts to proof that we can after all appeal to something beyond visual impressions to determine colour authoritatively. It only shows that "red" stands for something not in this sort of way *analysable*. Surely it is simply obvious

that colour is something subjective; and just as obvious that the unanalysability of colour words represents no difficulty in that claim.[5] The mere unanalysability or indefinability of colour terms does not release us from the task of finding means to elucidate these terms in a way that will bring out their subjectivity. Until one has done this much, one has not even reminded anyone of what he or she already knows about what colours are.

How then, without traducing it or treating it unfairly as a definition or an analysis, are we to develop and amplify the subjectivist claim that *x* is good if and only if *x* is such as to arouse/such as to make appropriate the sentiment of approbation? There are two main ways.

6. The first way is to follow Hume's lead and say that, just as in the colour case "the appearance of objects in daylight to the eye of a man in health is denominated their real and true colour, even while colour is . . . merely a phantasm of the senses,"[6] so value is merely a phantasm of the feelings or a "gilding or staining" of "natural objects with the colours borrowed from internal sentiment,"[7] (or in terms alien to Hume but in one way illuminating, value is the intentional object of *une certaine folie à presque tous*); and that to the extent that there is a standard of correctness in morals, this is determined by the verdicts of whoever judges "most coolly,"[8] "with the least prejudice," and on the basis of the fullest information—all of which, "if we consider the matter aright," is "a question of fact, not of sentiment."[9] When men argue and dispute in valuation, and when they succeed in instructing one another, what they are really seeking to do is to approximate to the verdicts of that judge.

What is remarkable here, among many other merits in Hume's explicit defence of this position as it applies in the case of aesthetic taste, is his anxiety to describe and make room for something that an ordinary or vulgar sceptic would simply deny or explain away. This is the remarkable degree of consensus that is sometimes achieved in the view that is reached about works of art and literature that survive the test of time:

> The same Homer, who pleased at Athens and Rome two thousand years ago, is still admired at Paris and at London. All the changes of climate, government, religion, and language have not been able to obscure his glory. Authority or prejudice may give a temporary vogue to a bad poet or orator; but his reputation will never be durable or general. When his compositions are examined by posterity or foreigners, the enchantment is dissipated and his faults appear in their true colours. On the contrary, a real genius, the longer his works endure, and the more wide they are spread, the more sincere is the admiration which they meet with.[10]

Hume contends that for a subjectivist simply to declare that "all sentiment is right because sentiment has reference to nothing beyond itself"—which might seem a little close to the position he had himself taken up in the Treatise—is for him to invite charges of advancing an "extravagant paradox, or rather a palpable absurdity."

It is one of the strengths of Hume's subjectivism that he distances himself from this paradox and works so hard to show how a standard of correctness is possible in taste and morals and to explain our many and frequent lapses from it. No plausible or life-like subjectivism can do less. It is however a difficulty in his execution of the task—and a further difficulty in extending Hume's account of the aesthetic case to the general case and the moral case in particular—that he has to place so much weight at certain points on an analogy between aesthetic taste and ordinary sensory (gustatory, etc.) taste:

> Some particular forms or qualities, from the original structure of the internal fabric, are calculated to please, and others to displease, and if they fail of their effect in any particular instance, it is from some apparent defect or imperfection in the organ. A man in a fever would not insist on his palate as able to decide concerning flavours; nor would one affected with

the jaundice pretend to give a verdict with regard to colours. In each creature there is a sound and a defective state; and the former alone can be supposed to afford us a true standard of taste and sentiment. If, in the sound state of the organ, there be an entire or a considerable uniformity of sentiment among men, we may thence derive an idea of the perfect beauty.

For the pleasures of the table such claims might just pass. But our chances of making the requisite analogy with an organ of perception, or of something a bit like an organ of perception (a sound judge, or organism or whatever) first weaken and then disappear altogether as we pass with Hume from the gustatory to the aesthetic-perceptual and thence to the aesthetic in general and the moral. And it is not enough, so long as we take the problem on Hume's official terms, to respond to this problem as Hume does (in effect) when he answers the question where the true judges and critics are to be found "whose joint verdict is the true standard of taste and beauty," by saying that:

> Where doubts occur men can do no more than in other disputable questions which are submitted to their understanding: they must produce the best arguments that their invention suggests to them; they must acknowledge a true and decisive standard to exist somewhere, to wit real existence and matter of fact; and they must have indulgence to such as differ from them in their appeals to this standard. It is sufficient for our present purposes if we have proved that the taste of all individuals is not upon an equal footing, and that some men in general however difficult to be pitched upon will be acknowledged by universal sentiment to have a preference above others.[11]

For one happy to speak the language of objects and their properties (as well as of their judges) such a stance may be sustainable. (See below Sec. 8.) But for Hume's own purposes the answer is not good enough—not so much because of the epistemological difficulty (which here, as always, one must learn to live with), but because, in the absence of any possible story about something comparable to sound organs of perception, it leaves us with insufficient grasp, and an insufficient account of our actual grasp (which I take to have regard for the properties attributed to objects within the critic's or judge's sentiment of approbation) of what constitutes a good critic or judge.

7. If Hume holds true to his doctrine that values are merely phantasms of the feelings, or gildings or stainings with colours borrowed from internal sentiment, then strictly speaking, he must never look to objects and properties themselves in characterizing the difference between good and bad judgments in taste and morals. (If he could do this then we should not need the independent standard, or the "sound organ" story.) So Hume looks instead to the *condition of the judge* (his "strong sense, united to delicate sentiment, improved by practice, perfected by comparison, cleared of all prejudice"), and this he then takes himself to need to see as (in his terms) a real existence or matter of fact. So that it suddenly appears that, if we pass over the properties of the object itself, then a life-like philosophical subjectivism requires a *non*-subjective foundation as well as the support of a substantial conception of a nearly homogeneous human nature.

This paradox deserves to be conjoined with another kind of puzzle. Our subjective reactions to objects or events will often impose groupings upon them that have no purely naturalistic rationale. (That, in a way, is the point of subjectivism—cp. Sec. 8 below.) But, at least for subjectivists who are serious in the fashion of Hume, there are good and bad ways of effecting such groupings. We are not simply to fire off *at random* in our responses to things. A feeble jest or infantile practical joke does not deserve to be grouped with the class of things that a true judge would find genuinely funny. How then in the case of a responsible judge are we to envisage Hume's process of gilding and staining? When the mind of such a man spreads itself upon objects, does it first de-

termine that x really belongs in the non-natural[12] class of genuine specimens of the funny—first determine the similarity-link of x with items a true judge would find funny—and then, when all is over bar the shouting, "gild and stain" x, or "project" or "discharge itself" upon x?[13] That seems a ludicrous suggestion. Is it not rather that there is something in the object that is *made for* the sentiment it would occasion in a qualified judge, and it brings down the sentiment upon the object as so qualified? Surely this feature of x, whatever it is, impinges on perception and sentiment simultaneously; and the time has come to enrich our ideas about what can fall under *each* of perception and sentiment in their engagement with the object.[14]

8. Does the subjectivism that we found reason in Section 4 above to search after admit of some alternative formulation? Let us seize for this purpose upon a Humean suggestion that has no clear place in his official theory: "It must be allowed that there are certain qualities in objects which are fitted by nature to produce particular ... feelings."[15] In Hume's official theory, this is not meant to count against the Humean denial that virtue, viciousness, merit, etc., are in the object itself. But let us now abandon Hume's aspiration to secure the standard of correctness in valuation from outside the domain of values, or by sole reference to the qualified judge. And let us restore to its proper place the ordinary idea in its ordinary construal that the criterion for a good judge is that he is apt to get things right. (If questions of value were not questions of real existence or matters of fact, then how could the criterion for being a good judge have that status?)

Suppose that objects that regularly please or help or amuse us ... or harm or annoy or vex us ... in various ways come to be grouped together by us under various categories or classifications to which we give various avowedly anthropocentric names; and suppose they come to be grouped together as they are precisely *because* they are such as to please, help, amuse us, . . . or harm, annoy, vex us . . . in their various ways. There will be then no saying, very often, what properties these names stand for independently of the reactions they provoke. (The point of calling this position subjectivism is that the properties in question are explained by reference to the reactions of human subjects.) But equally—at least when the system of properties and reactions diversifies, complicates, and enriches itself—there will often be no saying exactly *what* reaction a thing with the associated property will provoke without direct or indirect allusion to the property itself. Amusement for instance is a reaction we have to characterize by reference to its proper object, via something perceived as funny (or incongruous or comical or whatever). There is no object-independent and property-independent, "purely phenomenological" or "purely introspective" account of amusement. And equally there is no saying what exactly the funny is without reference to laughter or amusement or kindred reactions. Why should we expect there to be such an independent account?[16]

Of course, when we dispute whether x is really funny, there is a whole wealth of considerations and explanations we can adduce, and by no means all of them have to be given in terms simply synonymous or interdefinable with "funny." We can do a little better than say that the funny is that which makes people laugh. (Since laughter can come about in quite other ways, no doubt that is just as well.) What is improbable in the extreme is that, either singly or even in concert, further explanations will ever add up to a *reduction* of the funny or serve to characterize it in purely natural terms (terms that pull their weight in our theoretical cum explanatory account of the mechanisms of the natural world). If so, the predicate "funny" is an irreducibly subjective predicate. These diverse supporting considerations will however serve another purpose. By means of them, one person can improve another's grasp of the concept of the funny; and one person can improve another's focus or discrimination of what *is* funny. Furthermore, the process can be a collaborative one, without either of the participants to a dialogue counting as the absolutely better judge. The test of improvement in this process of mutual instruction and improvement can be at least partially internal to the perceptions of its participants. For, as Protagoras might (almost) have said, after the process has begun, those who participate in it may report not only that they discriminate more keenly, make more decisions, and are better satisfied with the classifications and subclassifications they now effect, but also that they get more and more cognitive cum affective satisfaction in their own responses.[17] Finer perceptions can both intensify and refine responses. Intenser responses can further heighten and refine perceptions. And more and more refined responses can lead to the further and finer and more variegated or more intense responses *and* perceptions.

9. When this point is reached, a system of anthropocentric properties and human responses has surely taken on a life of its own. Civilization has begun. One may surmise that at any stage in the process some ⟨property, response⟩ pairs will and some will not prove susceptible of refinement, amplification, and extension. One may imagine that some candidate pairs do and some do not relate in a reinforceable, satisfying way to the subjectivity of human life at a given time. Some pairs are such that refinement of response leads to refinement of perception and *vice versa*. Others are not. Some are and some are not capable of serving in the process of interpersonal education, instruction, and mutual enlightenment. Those pairs that do have this sort of advantage, we may expect to catch on and survive, and then to evolve further, generate further ⟨property, response⟩ pairs, and make room for the discovery of yet further properties that lie at a progressively greater distance from specific kinds of affect. Those pairs that do not have this sort of viability will no doubt fall by the wayside.

If we see matters in this sort of way, we

are surely not committed to suppose that the properties that figure within these ⟨property, response⟩ pairs will bear to natural properties any relation of supervenience that could be characterized in terms that were both general and illuminating of the particular properties in question. Rather they will be primitive, *sui generis*, incurably anthropocentric, and as unmysterious as any properties will ever be to us.[18]

Now, however, in order to embrace the great majority of the valuational predicates in common use, there is need to make room in the story for at least one further complication. Suppose that a point has been reached where a ⟨property, response⟩ pair is well established, the response is corrigible by reference to the question whether whatever is required for the presence of the property is present, and various supplementary considerations have become available that make possible the criticism, explanation, and vindication of attitudes and responses to a given thing. Suppose therefore that we are past the stage at which the critics of classical subjectivism like to see the position as stuck, where the non-accidental occurrence of some simple response is seen as simply sufficient for the presence of the property. (That is the stage where it can be said that any actual nausea caused by *x* suffices to prove that *x* is nauseating, and the claim may be preserved against doubt or difficulty by simple restriction— "*x* is nauseating *for John* even if not *for Philip*," or as in Heraclitus's example "Sea water is good *for fishes* and most poisonous *for men*.") Suppose then that the language of evaluation is past the point at which some semi-valuational predicates (such as the predicates like "nauseating" that we can qualify by explicit relativization) have stuck. Then something else also becomes possible. Instead of fixing on an object or class of objects and arguing about what response or responses they are such as to evoke, we can fix on a response—one that we value or disvalue for itself or value or disvalue for what it is a response to—and then argue about what the

marks are of the property that the response itself is made for. And without serious detriment to the univocity of the predicate, it can now become essentially contestable what a thing has to be like for there to be any reason to accord that particular appellation to it and correspondingly contestable what the extension is of the predicate.[19] (This was part of the point of the end of Sec. 3.)

Once we have the possibility of an attitude's being held relatively fixed, the attitude's being paired with some reciprocally appropriate property that is made for it, and its being essentially contestable what the marks are of the property, we shall have a sketch for an explanation of something that cognitivists have said too little about. We can explain the phenomenon that Stevenson (who was not the first to notice it—cp. Plato *Euthyphro* 8d, Aristotle *Nicomachean Ethics* 1107a, though Stevenson was first to see it so speech-functionally) called the "magnetism" of value terms. This is the same phenomenon as Hume notices in the second and third paragraphs of "Of the Standard of Taste"

> There are certain terms in every language which import blame, and others praise, and all men who use the same tongue must agree in their application of them. Every voice is united in applauding elegance, propriety, simplicity, spirit in writing, and in blaming fustian, affectation, coldness, and false brilliancy. But when critics come to particulars, this seeming unanimity vanishes; and it is found that they had affixed a very different meaning to their expressions. In all matters of opinion and science it is different. . . . The word *virtue*, with its equivalent in every tongue, implies praise: as that of *vice* does blame; and no man without the most obvious and grossest impropriety could affix reproach to a term which in general acceptation is understood in a good sense or bestow applause where the idiom requires disapprobation. . . .

No philosophy of value can ignore this phenomenon. Stevenson tries to account for it by his doctrine of emotive meanings. Richard

Hare would approach the phenomenon by characterizing the meaning of value words in terms of their commendatory function. If what I have just been saying is anywhere near right, however, perhaps we need not go to these lengths or involve ourselves in the difficulties they involve. If a property and an attitude are made for one another, it will be strange for one to use the term for the property if he is in no way party to the attitude and there is simply no chance of his finding that the item in question has the property. But if he is no stranger to the attitude and the attitude is favourable, it will be the most natural thing in the world if he regards it as a matter of keen argument what it takes for a thing to count as having the property that the attitude is paired with.

10. If we imagine that what the moralist or aesthetician always confronts is the end-product of a long and complicated evolutionary process of the sort I have described, we shall certainly find ethical naturalism an unattractive position (at least if we mean by naturalism what Moore started out meaning, cp. note 12), and we may well find subjectivism an overwhelmingly attractive one. If so, then I think we ought to prefer the second of our two formulations, that is the one described in Sections 8 through 9 above. There is still place for the sentient subject in our subjectivism—this is a subjectivism of subjects and properties *mutually* adjusted. But if we despair of letting the whole matter of correctness depend on the analogy between a sound, healthy sense-organ and a sound judge or organism, then we shall need to give up the idea of achieving any simple or single statement of the standard of correctness along the lines envisaged by Hume (or the lines sometimes envisaged by Aristotle, cp. *NE* 107a2). In which case we must keep faith in another way with Hume's desire to maintain the sovereignty of subjects simultaneously with the distinction between

sound and mistaken judgment. We shall do this by insisting that *genuinely* [funny/appalling/shocking/consoling/reassuring/disgusting/pleasant/delightful/ . . .] things are things that not only [amuse/appal/shock/console/reassure/disgust/please/delight/ . . .] but have these effects precisely because they *are* [funny/appalling/shocking/ consoling/reassuring/disgusting/pleasant/delightful/ . . .][20]—at the same time insisting that this "because" introduces an explanation that both explains and justifies. (In *something like* the way in which "there is a marked tendency for us all to think that $7 + 5 = 12$, and this tendency exists because there is really nothing else to think about what $7 + 5$ is" explains a tendency *by* justifying it. On request, the justificatory aspect can be made yet more evident by filling out the explanation with a calculation, or a proof. A similar complement for the valuational case could consist in an argued vindication of the claim that x is indeed funny, shocking . . .).

If this is how we work out the second approach, then the subjectivist who is committed to prefer the more Humean formulation of the subjectivist position will ask by what right I characterize the funny/appalling/shocking/consoling/reassuring/disgusting/pleasant/delightful . . . in these terms, and how I can propose to extend this method of elucidation to the good, the right and the beautiful. If he accepts Hume's own criterion of plausibility, however, then there is now a prospect of replying to him as follows: Hume has given the only imaginable external standard of correctness, but it appears more and more implausible the further we move from the gustatory and olfactory cases. If the only other standard we can imagine is an internal one, that is a subject-involving *and* property-involving, piecemeal standard, then we must conclude that what makes possible those discriminations that Hume insists upon our being properly impressed by is just what we think it is, namely the properties of objects as they impinge on us. Such a standard must be essentially contestable and internal to the thoughts and practices it relates to—indeed all of a piece with the practice of criticism, and vulnerable to anything that that can establish. But then (as Hume says, and we have the better right to say this) when critical doubts occur, "men can do no more than in other disputable questions which are submitted to the understanding; they must produce the best arguments that their invention suggests to them." The practices and the standards stand or fall (or, having fallen, are shored up again) together. Perhaps it is a shame that nothing vindicates the standard once and for all. But, conceiving the standard in these humble terms, at least we can prefer the obvious to the devious in stating it, and in doing so speak boldly of objects and their subjective properties. Either we hold our ground in making the discriminations that Hume insists that we contrive to make or (cp. Sec. 17 below) we don't. If we do, the standard itself—for that sort of evaluation—is surviving another day, and we can continue to employ it in distinguishing between what is really ϕ and what is not really ϕ. It is not inevitable that the standard will withstand criticism. But it does not need to be inevitable that it will. So the response to the objection I envisaged at the beginning of this paragraph is that if there is a problem about this "really," or if its natural link with the ideas of truth and objectivity ought to be severed, then the onus is on him who prefers the first, more Humean formulation of subjectivism to say what the problem is, to make out the case against these natural appearances, and also to show how, even if talk of objects were only *a façon de parler*, Hume's criteria of adequacy could be satisfied. For the following possibility has now become visible: that we should characterize the *subjective* (and then perhaps the valuational) positively, in terms of a subjective judgment's being one that is however indirectly answerable for its correctness to the responses of conscious subjects; that we should characterize the *objective* positively, in terms of an objective judgment's being one that is a candidate for

plain truth: and that, having characterized each of these categories of judgment positively and independently, we need to be ready for the possibility that a judgment may fall into both, may both rest upon sentiment *and* relate to a matter of fact.

I should not for my positive preference call such a position *realism*, as if to contrast it with *mentalism* or whatever. Nor should I claim that this preliminary elaboration and defence. can go anywhere near to showing the final tenability of the position itself. What is much more urgent than any final assessment of the position is some fuller appreciation of its motivation and commitments. In this essay I attempt little more than this.

11. (a) Whether we prefer the first or the second of the two ways of expounding subjectivism, it will be appropriate and natural to declare with Protagoras the sophist, the first systematic subjectivist,

Man is the measure of all things,

restricting the Protagorean doctrine to valuational things, and taking "man" to mean not "this man" or "that man" or "any man"[21] but "men in so far as we can reach them or they can reach us and are not alien to us."

(b) Given our development of the position at Sections 8 and 9 it will be equally natural to say that, where the ascription of value is concerned, *finding x* to be ϕ is prior to (or at least coeval with) *thinking x* to be ϕ.

(c) It will also be natural to say that what is ϕ (simply, not "ϕ for us" or "ϕ here") is *relative*, in a special sense to be explained. An object's or person's or event's being ϕ— or ϕ in our sense, if you will (but that of course is what the predicate will mean in this sentence, the sentence being our sentence)— consists in its being such as to evoke in the right way or such as to make appropriate some response, call it A,—still no relativity so far, but now it comes—where A is *our* response, or the response that *we* owe to it if it really is ϕ. The relativity to us that is here in question consists in the fact that it is we who owe x the response A and owe it that even though one who is not party to the set of associations of paired ⟨property, response⟩ associations to which the ⟨ϕ, A⟩ association belongs may fail to respond in that way. What this relativity imports is the possibility that there may be simply no point in urging that a stranger to our associations owes the object this response.[22] Even if a stranger can, by an imaginative effort, get himself some idea of what the property ϕ is and what the associated reaction A is, this may not suffice to effect the connexion between his discerning ϕ in a thing and his participating fully in A. It may not result in his identifying or associating himself with that sort of response. Even when the response A becomes possible for him, then, this may not trigger any readiness on his part to participate in all the collateral aesthetic or practical responses normally associated with A. (It is for investigation whether that means that he has an imperfect grasp of what ϕ is.)

A relativity of this kind was always to have been expected if it is by the process speculatively reconstructed in Sections 8 through 9 above that we get our value terms. For this process was a historical and particular one, and it comprised some contribution by the mind unlike that which is postulated in Kantian epistemology. What imports the relativity is a contribution that need not be everywhere the same or similar in its content.[23] There is the possibility (at least) of distinct and different moral and aesthetic worlds whose inhabitants need to struggle long and hard to appreciate the differences. They must understand not only the nature and extent of these differences, but also something of the way in which these differences are shaped substantively by the conditions of human life, before it is even an option for them to come properly to disagree with one another in their valuations.[24] (And when they disagree they are not thereby committed to dwell on the Humean question whether the differences are "blameless" or "not blameless." The various

circumstances that make up the differences may condition the sense and proper understanding of judgments.)

12. At this point I should expect the intuitionist objectivist and the champion of Hume's version of subjectivism (and several other parties perhaps, e.g., the emotivist) to combine forces in a joint protest: "In something like the way we each expected, you have now talked yourself into a really impossible position: you are trying to ground a distinction that you like to describe as the distinction between what is really ϕ and not really ϕ upon what are by your own account mere responses—upon a convergence in the inclinations various people feel or do not feel to say that x is ϕ or that x is not ϕ. Surely this distinction between the really ϕ and not really ϕ, like everything else that is distinctive of your subjectivism, is either plain bluff or a mere *façon de parler*. (No wonder you disclaimed the title "realist.") In a phrase Williams uses in criticism of intuitionism, you are confusing resonance with reference. Surely the relativity you have now deduced from your subjectivism and described in terms that are both object-involving and blatantly metaphorical ("owing an object a response" and the rest) precisely demonstrates the necessity to treat all such talk as a *façon de parler*. It is no less a *façon de parler* for sounding like the natural continuation of the ordinary language of evaluation."

It would be a defeat if this were so. We were trying to formulate a variant upon classical subjectivism both positively and literally. Pending a more challenging statement of the objection, however, I believe that I can defend the subjectivist position as we now have it by pointing out that these responses we have been speaking of are not "mere" responses. They are responses that are correct when and only when they are occasioned by what has the corresponding property ϕ and are occasioned by it because it *is* ϕ. If the objector persists: "How can human agreement in these responses decide what *really* is

ϕ or not ϕ?" I reply that the sort of agreement that is in question here is only agreement in *susceptibility* to respond thus and so to ϕ things. It is agreement at most (as one might say, evoking a very familiar passage of Wittgenstein)[25] in what property/response associations we are able to catch onto and work up into a shared way of talking, acting, and reacting. Since this agreement is not in itself agreement in *opinions* about what is ϕ or not ϕ (even though the existence of the shared language presupposes the possibility of such agreement), there is no question of the agreement in the belief that x is ϕ being the *criterion* for x's really being ϕ. x is only really ϕ if it is such as to evoke and make appropriate the response A among those who are sensitive to ϕ-ness. That is a far cry from agreement about the ϕ-ness of x simply *constituting* the actual ϕ-ness of x.[26]

13. The response is likely to excite another sort of objection: "You have spoken of morality's depending, at least in part, upon agreement in susceptibility to respond thus and so to certain things. But what if these susceptibilities changed? Could that make what is now right wrong, what is now good bad. . . ? Again, you suggested at the very outset that Hume could be read as proposing that x is good if and only if x is such as to arouse or make appropriate a certain sentiment of approbation. But whether x is such depends not only on the condition of x but on the nature and range of susceptibilities of the subjects of the sentiments. What sentiment is appropriate to a thing of a given character will depend at least in part upon what the range is of the sentiments themselves. But how can goodness, goodness itself, depend on anything of this sort?"

The objection is instructive and demonstrates the importance of detaching any development of Humean or Protagorean subjectivism from the Moorean conception of philosophy. I believe it also casts further light upon relativity.

The objection would be dead right if the subjectivist were saying that "x is good" may be paraphrased as "x is such as to arouse or make appropriate [a certain] sentiment of approbation," and if he were saying that this paraphrase could then be intersubstituted with "good" *salvo sensu* (or more or less *salvo sensu*). But the subjectivist need not be saying that. His distinctive claim is rather that x is good if and only if x is the sort of thing that calls forth or makes appropriate a certain sentiment of approbation *given the range of propensities that we actually have to respond in this or that way;*[27] or generalizing a little, and still disclaiming the attempt to provide an equivalent, his claim is that, for each value predicate ϕ (or for a very large range of such), there is an attitude or response of subjects *belonging to a range of propensities that we actually have* such that an object has the property ϕ stands for if and only if the object is fitted by its characteristics to bring down that extant attitude or response upon it and bring it down *precisely because* it has those characteristics.

To take the matter any further would involve an articulation of the response or attitude and of the associated marks that are annexed to particular value predicates. This articulation would have to be given in a way that threw into relief the organizing point of applying the predicate to anything or withholding it. The existence of a substantial body of attempts at what used to be called the theory of laughter (see the instructive review of these in D. H. Munro's *Argument of Laughter*[28]), all devoted to the understanding of just two or three such predicates, is evidence of the potential difficulty and of the interest of this sort of work. But such a theory need not promise to carry us even one inch nearer to an intersubstitutable equivalent for the predicates that stand for the properties that it studies. It may or may not succeed in this.

14. But does the subjectivist want to remain perfectly satisfied with the actual condition of our actual response to the objects of moral and aesthetic attention? What of criticism and progress?

It was for this reason that I tried to secure the irrelevance of a change in human nature and susceptibilities, by stressing not the relativity of value to the *totality of our actual responses* but its relativity to our *actual propensities*, these being propensities that are answerable to criticism, etc., to respond in this or that way to this or that feature of things. But to fill out this answer, I must hark back to the claims in Section 9 about the essential contestability of valuational language, and also to the claim that the standard of correctness for each predicate is all of a piece with the day to day practice of using it and criticizing or vindicating the uses that are made of it. In prosecuting that practice (in adjusting the mind's spread upon objects, you can say if you insist—but remember then that the account offered here will construe this process in terms of the discovery of properties or the lighting up of properties that are there, and not in terms of projecting properties onto the black, white, and grey of the pre-subjective world) in prosecuting that practice, we shall reach wherever we reach, for such reasons as seem good and appropriate. Subjectivism itself prescribes no limit to the distance that reflection can carry us from the starting point in the sentiments. (No more than cognitivism does, cp. Sabina Lovibond in *Reason and Imagination in Ethics*.) It does not imprison us in the system of evaluations we begin with; nor does it insulate from criticism the attitudes and responses that sustain glib, lazy, or otherwise suspect predications.

15. But someone will now ask: what if, by a sequence of minute shifts in our responses, an evil demon were to work us round to a point where we took what is actually evil to be good? Perhaps the demon might do this without our even noticing it. Yes, I reply, he might. But this is not an objection to sensible subjectivism. It would not follow from our not noticing the magnitude of the shift and everything that went with it that the very

same thing that once told the presence of good was now fastened constitutively upon evil. For the subjectivism we have envisaged does not treat the response as a criterion, or even as an indicator. In the full theory of the last stage of the processes we have been describing, it counts as nothing less than an act of judging a content; it is a judgment indispensably sustained by the perceptions and feelings and thoughts that are open to criticism that is based on norms that are open to criticism. It is not that *by which we tell*. It is part of the telling itself.

What the objection does do, however, is to point clearly at the thing that has given subjectivism a bad name. This is all the associations that are commonly imputed to subjectivism with the thought that evaluative judgments may be assimilated to "mere responses" and with the idea that the responses the subjectivist interests himself in are autonomously inner states—or states such that, if you are in one of them, you can tell and tell infallibly, without looking outward, whether you are in it or not. (These really would be states that "have no reference to anything beyond themselves.") These associations are made explicit by the objection. But they were already under acute pressure in Hume's more mature statement of ethical subjectivism, and none of them is maintained in the position as we have defended it.

16. What needs to be emphasized again at this point is that subjectivism ought not to be represented as offering any guarantee that for most (or for any) of the predicates and properties we put our trust in, the very best judgments that we can make involving them *will* gather a consensus such that the best explanation of the consensus is that those who take x to be ϕ do so precisely because x is ϕ. Of course our shared linguistic practice commits us strongly to that belief. But our practice can operate without any special or philosophical guarantee that truth and correctness *will* stay around in this way. Our practice can even continue to operate in full awareness of the flimsiness and contingency of the natural facts that it reposes upon, in the awareness that so often impinges upon valuation as we know it of our proneness to error and self-deception, even in awareness of the theoretical possibility that our minds and nervous systems may have been poisoned or perverted. What we can do about that danger is only to take ordinary precautions, and to have ordinary regard (regard not insulated from thoughts about the subject matter itself) for the credentials with which and conditions from out of which people's judgments are made. Better, we can take ordinary precautions, and then, in deference to the inherent difficulty of the subject matter, a few more. And it is well worth remembering that, by preferring over Hume's subjectivism a subjectivism that was object- and property-involving, we did not disqualify ourselves from insisting upon its also being *conscious subject*-involving. If there is something fishy in either the agreements or the disagreements that we encounter, then we must investigate their etiology case by case, and as best we can, having proper regard for everything, not excluding the characters and sensibilities of those participating in the agreements and disagreements.

17. If nothing can exclude in advance the possibility that the very best judgments we can arrive at involving this or that predicate will fail to gather any consensus, let alone underwrite a consensus such that the best explanation of the consensus is that those who take x to be ϕ do so because x is ϕ, then what is to be said about such failure? Well. Where we seem to encounter such a thing, it may be that what we call ϕ-ness is different things to different people. That is one possibility. If so, there is less strict *disagreement* than may appear. But it may be that there is no escape by that route. It may not be possible to establish any sufficient difference in the "value-focus" of those who appear to be in disagreement.

In that case there are two other possibili-

ties. We may simply give up on the predicate; or we may remain undeterred. Sometimes, of course, where the latter seems to be the right attitude Hume's formulation of subjectivism may seem superior to the cognitivist formulation of subjectivism that I have advocated (especially if the Humean version can be freed of the difficulties I have claimed there are in it). It is strange, however, that the pull towards Hume's formulation should be at its strongest precisely where the sense of the predicate gives the appearance of being in danger of the kind of collapse from which Hume himself believed that he needed our shared human nature and our shared proclivity towards certain sentiments to protect it. So long as it is Hume's struggle to make the sovereignty of moral subjects consist with the distinction he wanted between sound and unsound judgments that remains at the centre of Hume's theoretical concern, I think there is no clear advantage for him in the shift back to the first formulation.

In truth, whatever difficulties there are in the possibility of irresoluble substantive disagreement, no position in moral philosophy can render itself simply immune from them. We should not tumble over ourselves to assert that there is irresoluble substantive disagreement. We should simply respect the possibility of such disagreement, I think, and in respecting it register the case for a measure of cognitive underdetermination. Some have wished to find a philosophical position that ruled out this possibility in advance, by espousing some anti-subjectivist theory—a Kantian or intuitionist or utilitarian or dogmatically realist theory. But how can such a possibility be simply ruled out? And why on the other hand should the subjectivist be deemed to have *ruled it in*? In this matter the subjectivist really has to do the same as everyone else: he can only urge that, in spite of the possibility of irresoluble substantive disagreement, but in a manner partially conditioned by that possibility, we should persevere as best we can in the familiar processes of reasoning, conversion, and criticism—without guarantees of success, which are almost as needless as they are unobtainable.

18. In 1960, Bertrand Russell wrote "I cannot see how to refute the arguments for the subjectivity of ethical values, but I find myself incapable of believing that all that is wrong with wanton cruelty is that I don't like it."[29] How close have our prosubjectivist efforts carried us to the answer to this difficulty? First, reverting to Hume we can drop the first person. What is wrong with cruelty is not, even for Bertrand Russell, just that Bertrand Russell doesn't like it, but that it is not such as to call forth liking given our *actual* collectively scrutinized responses. Those responses are directed at cruelty, and at what cruelty itself consists in on the level of motive, intention, outcome. . . . To be sure, we should not care about these things, these things would not impinge as they do upon us, if our responses were not there to be called upon. In the presence of a good reason to call them in question, we should not be able to trust them or take too much for granted about the well-foundedness of the properties they are keyed to. But, in the total absence of such a reason, it will not be at all question-begging for Russell simply to remind himself as thoroughly and vividly as he can of just what it is that he dislikes, abhors, detests . . . about cruelty and its antique and hideous marks.

NOTES

I am indebted to Anthony Price for detailed comments on the penultimate version. In notes 17, 21, and 27, acknowledgement is made to unpublished writing of Hidé Ishiguro, Michael Smith, and Edward Hussey. The essay was originally conceived as a justification and expansion of the claims made in "Truth, Invention, and the Meaning of Life" at section V. In the time that has elapsed since that essay was written I have benefited especially (if insufficiently) from reading Warren S. Quinn's essay "Moral and Other Realisms: Some Initial Difficulites," in Goldman and Kim, eds., *Values and Morals* (Dordrecht, Netherlands: Reidel, 1978). The *strictly* valuational predicates singled out in section 4 of Essay III [not in the anthology; see "A Sensible Subjectivism?" in *Needs, Values, Truth: Essays in the Philosophy of Value*] will be the most conspicuous verifiers, if there are any, of the subjectivist doctrine to be developed here.

1. The dissatisfaction was of course anticipated by C. L. Stevenson, but not, one may feel, answered by him. Cf. "The Emotive Meaning of Ethical Terms," *Mind* (1937): esp. p. 30.

2. See *Philosophical Studies* (Boston: Routledge & Kegan Paul, 1922): 329–39; *Ethics* (London: Home University Library, Thornton Butterworth, 1912), chaps. III, IV. For the apparently paralysing effect of this critique, see Russell's "Notes on *Philosophy* January 1960," *Philosophy* 35 (1960): 146–47, and his difficulty, surely consequential upon Moore's discussion, in seeing his way past the dilemma I have quoted at the head of this essay and shall discuss in sec. 18 below.

3. Compare John McDowell's discussion of the phrase "such as to merit" in "Values and Secondary Qualities" in *Morality and Objectivity*, ed. Ted Honderich (London: Routledge & Kegan Paul, 1985), pp. 117–20.

4. Observe that by this failure. if it were a failure, nothing would have been established against the *truth* of the biconditional "x is good just if x is such as to arouse a certain sentiment of approbation." Consider the statement "If x is the same as y then, if y is the same as z, then x is the same as z." As a contribution to an analysis of the meaning of "same" (or "identical") this is circular because it employs the word or a mere synonym. But, in pointing this out as a defect in the sentence when it is put forward within an analysis, we do nothing to show the falsity of the sentence. Indeed it might well serve in a partial elucidation of sameness. For elucidation, as contrasted with analysis, see secs. 2–4 of "Truth as Predicated of Moral Judgments," in *Needs, Values, Truth.*

5. The analogy can be taken one point further. When asked what red is like, we can say how dark a pure unsaturated shade of red is compared with how light a pure shade of yellow is. This doesn't say what red is. But, while presupposing our colour categories, it does say something more about what red

is like. Similarly, given a particular x and the question of its title to have some particular determination of good ascribed to it, we can say some more about what it is about things like x that makes them such as to arouse a particular species of sentiment of approbation when taken as among the fs. Explanations as such do not give out altogether; but those we find will tend to *presuppose* some relevant standard for thinking about the merits and demerits of x and things like x as among fs.

For the non-significance of unanalysability, see further "Truth, Invention, and the Meaning of Life," sec. 8, para. 3.

6. "Of the Standard of Taste," para. 12.

7. *Inquiry concerning Principles of Morals*, app. I.

8. See, e.g., Hume's essay "Of the Delicacy of Taste and of Passion."

9. Cp. "Standard" op. cit. para. 24–25.

10. Para. 11. Compare the following passage from Longinus, *On the Sublime*, chap. VIII, "when men of different pursuits, lives, ambitions, ages, languages, hold identical views on one and the same subject, then that verdict which results so to speak from a concert of discordant elements makes our faith in the object of admiration strong and unassailable."

11. Para. 25.

12. For "non-natural" cp. the explanation given by G. E. Moore in *Principia Ethica*, (Cambridge, Cambridge University Press, 1903), pp. 40–41 ("By nature then I do mean . . . that which is the subject matter of the natural sciences, and also of psychology"); also my *Sameness & Substance* (Oxford: Blackwell, 1981), p. 183 with n. 40.

13. Cp. *Inquiry* (app. I)". . . *after* every circumstance, every relation is known, the understanding has no further room to operate, nor any object on which it could employ itself. The approbation or blame which *then* ensues cannot be the work of the judgment, but of the heart . . ." (italics mine).

14. Something similar is conceded—indeed insisted upon—in Richard Wollheim's psycho-analytically motivated enrichment of subjectivism in *The Sheep and the Ceremony* (Cambridge University Press, 1981), and in Essay VI ("Art & Evaluation") in the second, expanded edition of *Art and its Objects* (Cambridge University Press, 1980). If anything at all puzzles me in this treatment, it is only how it can see itself (if it does) as able to resist the attractions of the alternative version of subjectivism that is sketched in Section 8 and further refined in Section 12 below. See also in this connexion Thomas Reid, Essay VIII, *Essays on the Intellectual Powers of Man* (Edinburgh, 1785).

15. Hume, op. cit., para. 16. Compare and contrast Thomas Reid's insistence upon the point, in opposition to the view he complained had become "a fashion among modern philosophers," ("even those who hold it, find themselves obliged to use language that contradicts it"): "This excellence [in an air in music] is not in me; it is in the music. But the pleasure it gives is not in the music; it is in me. Perhaps I cannot say what it is in the tune that pleases my ear, as I cannot say what it is in a sapid body that pleases my palate; but there is a quality in the sapid body which pleases my palate, and I call it a delicious taste; and there is a quality in the tune that pleases my taste, and I call it a fine or excellent air." (op. cit., chap. 1, sec. 1.)

16. Indeed how could there be? By hypothesis, the linked properties and responses we are speaking of are arrived at by a historical process. How then could these things be *defined*? (Cp. Nietzsche, *Genealogy of Morals* II. xiii, cited at pp. 67–68.)

It is along the lines of the speculations in the text that I should explicate the metaphor of properties and sentiments being "made for one another."

17. Cp. Plato *Theaetetus* 166–67. A similar point is urged by Hidé Ishiguro in an unpublished manuscript, and made out in intriguing detail for the application of the Japanese predicate "*monono awaré*."

18. This is not to deny of course that, in a given context with a given object, evaluative properties will rub shoulders with, and have relations of compossibility and non-compossibility with, other properties. That is the normal condition of properties from different ranges converging upon a single object. But this familiar circumstance will shed no particular light upon value-properties either in particular or in general.

In deference to established philosophical usage, I use the word "property" here and throughout to denominate what predicates stand for, instead of using the Fregean word "concept" (which I should have greatly preferred). On this point, and the reality of properties (concepts), see the defence-cum-amendment of Frege's doctrine given in my article "The Sense and Reference of Predicate Expressions," *Philosophical Quarterly* (July 1984).

19. See Longer Note 19.

20. For various further defences of this sort of formulation, see "Truth, Invention, and the Meaning of Life," sec. 5; "Truth as Predicated of Moral Judgments," sec. 5, mark (2) and sec. 10 following; Ishiguro, op. cit.; John McDowell, "Aesthetic Value, Objectivity, and the Fabric of the World," in E. Schaper, ed., *Pleasure. Preference. and Value* (Cambridge: Cambridge University Press, 1983), esp. his sec. IV. The "because" is meant literally, with the full sense that is conferred on it by the English language in this context. "Because" introduces explanations. So questions of causality come into consideration, but only by virtue of the way in which statements of causation can figure within explanations. (Cp. Donald Davidson "Causal Relations," in *Journal of Philosophy* (1967); also, on a connected point, McDowell, loc. cit., note 3 above.) Certainly what the predicate "funny" stands for (cp. note 18) enters into the truth-conditions of "John laughed because what Philip said was funny"; for certainly the backing for that particular explanatory "because" comprises something causal. Philip's remark's being funny was causally responsible for John's amusement, let us suppose. Is it necessary to go on to claim that the value-property *funny* itself causes the response of amusement?

21. Note that the reading we give to Protagoras's famous formula (Plato, *Theaetetus*, 151e6–152c7) is not the undoubtedly authentic individualistic interpretation but the possibly equally authentic inter-subjective social interpretation which I for one believe he was aware of and *also* intended. I am fortified in this belief by an unpublished essay "Protagoras and the Theory of the Natural Consensus" by Edward Hussey. Hussey translates Protagoras's doctrine as follows: "A man is a measure of all things: of those which are that and how they are, and of those that are not and how they are not."

22. Compare the formulation Williams gives of a connected point in his "The Truth in Relativism," *Moral Luck* (New York: Cambridge University Press, 1981), pp. 141–42.

23. For an account of the way in which Kant's epistemology suggested to Herder and others the possibility of this different sort of contribution, see P. L. Gardiner in *The Monist* (1981). For another aspect of this matter, see also Kenneth Burke, *Grammar of Motives* (University of California Press, 1969), p. 59: "[We] seek for vocabularies that will be faithful *reflections* of reality. To this end, we must develop vocabularies that are *selections* of reality. And any selection of reality must, in certain circumstances, function as a *deflection* of reality. Insofar as the vocabulary meets the needs of reflection, we can say that it has the necessary scope. In its selectivity, it is a reduction. Its scope and reduction become a deflection when the given terminology, or calculus, is not suited to the subject matter."

24. See longer note 24.

25. L. Wittgenstein, *Philosophical Investigations*, sec. 241.

26. See longer note 26.

27. Cp. M. K. Davies and I. L. Humberstone, "Two Notions of Necessity," *Philosophical Studies* 38 (1980): esp. 22–25; also Michael Smith, "An Argument for Moral Realism," unpublished; and for the general point, see Saul Kripke, *Naming and Necessity* (Oxford: Blackwell, 1980), p. 140, n. 71.

28. *The Argument of Laughter* (London and Melbourne, 1951).

29. Op. cit. at note 4 above.

LONGER NOTES

Longer Note 19: *Essential contestability.* By showing (if it will show) how essential contestability can come to attach to a predicate and how questions of appropriateness get in (cp. sec. 4 and note 3 above), the argument of Section 9 will complete the subjectivist's vindication of his right to give the "such as to make approbation appropriate" elucidation proposed in Section 3 above. But of course it is at this point that I shall be asked how can I claim it is possible for the process described in the text to occur without serious detriment to the univocity of the predicate. If people disagree about the extension and disagree about the marks of the property that serve to collect its extension (i.e., the property the predicate stands for), surely they can only focus their disagreement (can only disagree, instead of simply talking past one another) if they agree in what the attitude of response itself is. But the trouble is that there is no saying—or so I have insisted—what that attitude *is* except by reference to the property that is its proper object.

The right response to this objection is not to seek to explode it, but simply to suggest that it depends for its whole force on a certain quantum of exaggeration. To get an attitude that can be held sufficiently fixed to focus disagreement about the marks of the property it is made for, we do indeed need to effect some delimitation or further determination of the attitude. Only in this way can a subjectivist distinguish different senses for "good." "right," "beautiful." Approving of some x had better not be a barely determinable state, approving *tout court*. It had better be approving of x as a good g, as a good f, or as a good $fg, \ldots$. Certainly if even this cannot be supplied, the parties may be talking past one another when they dispute about the marks of the property. But then the case we have to be interested in is the case where this much *can* be made clear, and there is *still* room for disagreement about what it takes to be good, a good f a good $fg \ldots$ or whatever. So my answer to the question about univocity is simply that you do not need complete agreement about the marks of the property, or total coincidence in your conceptions of it, in order to mean the same by the predicate that stands for the property, or to be concerned with the same attitude directed towards it. (Do you need complete agreement about magnetic compasses—do we all have to have identical conceptions of a magnetic compass—in order to mean the same by "magnetic compass"? Surely not.) This is a complicated terrain I am trying to make a short cut through. But I cannot help thinking that what my critic is finding hard to accept is really the mutual inextricability I continually insist upon of the anthropocentric properties of an object and the attitudes towards it that are made for these properties. But why should not the ball be rolled as tightly as this: so tightly that nothing will count as unrolling it. (Contrast with unrolling a curled up hedgehog trying to untwist the volutes of a snail's shell.) Remember that we are not inventing these predicates. We have found them already in occupation.

Longer Note 24: *Relativity*. Let us distinguish the relativity that subjectivism appears to import from others that are in the offing here and frequently compresent with it.

In the first place, any particular item x's goodness (say) will almost always consist in its being, for some $f, g \ldots$ a good f, or a good g or. . . . And this "attributivity" may either come down to x's being good *relative to a comparison-class*, as among whose members it is assessed (the more straightforward sort of attributivity), or, as in the case of "good man," "good thing to do," it may consist in x's being good *relative to a certain specifiable point of view*, the moral point of view or whatever (as well perhaps as relative to a comparison class).

In the second place, such goodness-as-among-the-fs and goodness-relative-to-such-and-a-point-of-view may themselves be relative to the circumstances, the actors, the patients, the cultural context. (Indeed, if we didn't have regard for these things we sometimes might not be assessing that very item.)

These two kinds of relativity can of course interact with one another, but neither singly nor in concert could they ever be rationally conflated with the relativity introduced in Section 11. I announced this as relativity to us. But the kind of relativity I intended there does not (I emphasize) introduce *us* as the value of an extra parameter. Nor does it search out some potentially explicit extra argument-place, as in "x is [a] good relative to us $[f]$" or "x is [a] for-our-purposes good $[f]$" or whatever. . . . Once the point is passed that we described at paragraph 3 of Section 9, and once the option disappears of vindicating judgements of ϕ-ness by simply restricting them as ϕ-ness for such and such person, nothing like this can be what is at issue. (There is less wrong with "x is [a] good $[f]$ *on our view*," precisely because this version makes *oratio obliqua* manifest. What it means is "According to us, x is [a] good $[f]$" or "In our scheme of things, x is [a] good $[f]$". In this form "us" or "our scheme of things" precisely does not fill an extra *argument*-place belonging to "good $[f]$" and made available by the mode of combination "x is [a] good $[f]$.")

If it is not obvious why the hidden argument place would be a wrong approach, then consider the following dilemma. Suppose two cultures or subcultures S_1 and S_2 differ with respect to the question whether x is a good f, and suppose that their names are to be written into the new slot, subscript "S," supposedly discovered for the insertion of one or the other—as in "x is a good $_s f$." Now ask: do S_1, and S_2 really disagree? Either they do or they don't. Suppose they don't and their difference is not a disagreement about the answer to a common question with a common sense. Then there is no point in using the subscripted predicate because there is then the *prior* problem that one of S_1 and S_2 (or both) is such that its opinion cannot strictly be given *at all* by a content-sentence that either ascribes or denies the property of being [a] good $[f]$ to x. (For being [a] good $[f]$ is the property that "[a] good $[f]$" stands for when used in *our* sense, and this either S_1 or S_2 does not have available to it.) On the other hand, if S_1 and S_2 are giving incompatible answers to a common question and they do disagree, then there is some common judgment they disagree about, and *ex hypothesi* there is a common text and the predicate therein comprises neither of these fillings. To make different insertions into the subscript slot would effectively lose us our whole grasp on their disagreement.

It was for this sort of reason that our preferred way of stating the relativity imported by the subjectivity of value was to say that, where we owe x the response A in virtue of x's being ϕ, there will not necessarily be a point in insisting that others not party to the system of associations that comprises the $<\phi, A>$ linkage owe x that response.

Longer Note 26: *Responses*. Anthony Price has pointed out to me that there are *two* sorts of worry that someone may feel in this area, of which only the first is directly addressed in the text. There is the worry the objector actually expresses about "mere" responses and the attempt to make these validate the reality of that to which they purport to be keyed. And there is another worry. No doubt, *if* the responses in question are ever appropriate, then sensitivity to ϕ-ness is sometimes certifiable independently of a sensitivity to x's ϕ-ness. But is the response *ever* appropriate? "It would seem like lifting oneself up by one's own bootstraps to appeal to ϕ-ness to justify the shared sensibility and appeal to the shared sensibility to confirm the reality of ϕ-ness."

My reply to this would be first that the sensibility and the supposition that there is something it is keyed to are indeed in *joint* danger from the kind of upset that is discussed in Sections 16–17 below. But they may or may not suffer that mishap. They would also be in joint danger from the notion of rationality envisaged in Section 10 of Essay III [of "A Sensible Subjectivism?"] if there were any future in that. But that was an illusory notion.

Given that something could count against the sensibility and the property considered jointly, and given that they are not arbitrary constructs but things that have survived the evolutionary process described in Section 9, and continue to survive criticism (albeit criticism internal to a whole whirl of going practices, cp. Essay III, sec. 5), there need be no question of having to justify the claim that what seems to be a sensibility really is a sensibility (i.e., a sensibility *to something*)—not at least *ab initio* or from a standing start. What is required is the readiness to take criticism seriously, and to recognize a case where we do have the situation described in Sections 16–17.

D

CONSTRUCTIVISM

14

Kantian Constructivism in Moral Theory

JOHN RAWLS

LECTURE I

RATIONAL AND FULL AUTONOMY

In these lectures I examine the notion of a constructivist moral conception, or, more exactly, since there are different kinds of constructivism, one Kantian variant of this notion. The variant I discuss is that of justice as fairness, which is presented in my book *A Theory of Justice*.[1] I have two reasons for doing this: one is that it offers me the opportunity to consider certain aspects of the conception of justice as fairness which I have not previously emphasized and to set out more clearly the Kantian roots of that conception. The other reason is that the Kantian form of constructivism is much less well understood than other familiar traditional moral conceptions, such as utilitarianism, perfectionism, and intuitionism. I believe that this situation impedes the advance of moral theory. Therefore, it may prove useful simply to explain the distinctive features of Kantian constructivism, to say what it is, as illustrated by justice as fairness, without being concerned to defend it. To a degree that it is hard for me to estimate, my discussion assumes some acquaintance with A *Theory of Justice,* but I hope that, for the most part, a bare familiarity with its main intuitive ideas will suffice; and what these are I note as we proceed. . . .

I

What distinguishes the Kantian form of constructivism is essentially this: it specifies a particular conception of the person as an element in a reasonable procedure of construction, the outcome of which determines the content of the first principles of justice. Expressed another way: this kind of view sets up a certain procedure of construction which answers to certain reasonable requirements, and within this procedure persons characterized as rational agents of construction specify, through their agreements, the first principles of justice. (I use 'reasonable' and 'rational' to express different notions throughout, notions which will be explained below, in Sec. V.) The leading idea is to establish a suitable connection between a particular conception of the person and first principles of justice, by means of a procedure of construction. In a Kantian view the conception of the person, the procedure, and the first principles must be related in a certain manner—which, of course, admits of a number of variations. Justice as fairness is not, plainly, Kant's view, strictly speaking; it departs from his text at many points. But the adjective 'Kantian' expresses analogy and not identity; it means roughly that a doctrine sufficiently resembles Kant's in enough fundamental respects so that it is far closer to his view than to the other traditional moral conceptions that are appropriate for use as benchmarks of comparison.

On the Kantian view that I shall present, conditions for justifying a conception of justice hold only when a basis is established for political reasoning and understanding within a public culture. The social role of a conception of justice is to enable all members of society to make mutually acceptable to one another their shared institutions and basic arrangements, by citing what are publicly recognized as sufficient reasons, as identified by that conception. To succeed in doing this, a conception must specify admissible social institutions and their possible arrangements into one system, so that they can be justified to all citizens, whatever their social position or more particular interests. Thus, whenever a sufficient basis for agreement among citizens is not presently known, or recognized, the task of justifying a conception of justice becomes: how can people settle on a conception of justice, to serve this social role, that is (most) reasonable for them in virtue of how they conceive of their persons and construe the general features of social cooperation among persons so regarded?

. . . [A] Kantian doctrine joins the content of justice with a certain conception of the person; and this conception regards persons as both free and equal, as capable of acting both reasonably and rationally, and therefore as capable of taking part in social cooperation among persons so conceived. In addressing the public culture of a democratic society, Kantian constructivism hopes to invoke a conception of the person implicitly affirmed in that culture, or else one that would prove acceptable to citizens once it was properly presented and explained.

I should emphasize that what I have called the "real task" of justifying a conception of justice is not primarily an epistemological problem. The search for reasonable grounds for reaching agreement rooted in our conception of ourselves and in our relation to society replaces the search for moral truth interpreted as fixed by a prior and independent order of objects and relations, whether natural or divine, an order apart and distinct from how we conceive of ourselves. The task is to articulate a public conception of justice that all can live with who regard their person and their relation to society in a certain way. And though doing this may involve settling theoretical difficulties, the practical social task is primary. What justifies a conception of justice is not its being true to an order antecedent to and given to us, but its congruence with our deeper understanding of ourselves and our aspirations, and our realization that, given our history and the traditions embedded in our public life, it is the most reasonable doctrine for us. We can find no better basic charter for our social world. Kantian constructivism holds that moral objectivity is to be understood in terms of a suitably constructed social point of view that all can accept. Apart from the procedure of constructing the principles of justice, there are no moral facts. Whether certain facts are to be recognized as reasons of right and justice, or how much they are to count, can be ascertained only from within the constructive procedure, that is, from the undertakings of rational agents of construction when suitably represented as free and equal moral persons.

II

... Justice as fairness tries to uncover the fundamental ideas (latent in common sense) of freedom and equality, of ideal social co-operation and of the person, by formulating what I shall call "model-conceptions." We then reason within the framework of these conceptions, which need be defined only sharply enough to yield an acceptable public understanding of freedom and equality. Whether the doctrine that eventually results fulfills its purpose is then decided by how it works out: once stated, it must articulate a suitable conception of ourselves and of our relation to society, and connect this conception with workable first principles of justice, so that, after due consideration, we can acknowledge the doctrine proposed.

Now the two basic model-conceptions of justice as fairness are those of a *well-ordered society* and of a *moral person*. Their general purpose is to single out the essential aspects of our conception of ourselves as moral persons and of our relation to society as free and equal citizens. They depict certain general features of what a society would look like if its members publicly viewed themselves and their social ties with one another in a certain way. The *original position* is a third and mediating model-conception: its role is to establish the connection between the model-conception of a moral person and the principles of justice that characterize the relations of citizens in the model-conception of a well-ordered society. It serves this role by modeling the way in which the citizens in a well-ordered society, viewed as moral persons, would ideally select first principles of justice for their society. The constraints imposed on the parties in the original position, and the manner in which the parties are described, are to represent the freedom and equality of moral persons as understood in such a society. If certain principles of justice would indeed be agreed to (or if they would belong to a certain restricted family of principles), then the aim of Kantian constructivism to connect definite principles with a particular conception of the person is achieved.

For the present, however, I am concerned with the parties in the original position only as rationally autonomous agents of construction who (as such agents) represent the aspect of rationality, which is part of the conception of a moral person affirmed by citizens in a well-ordered society. The rational autonomy of the parties in the original position contrasts with the full autonomy of citizens in society. Thus *rational* autonomy is that of the parties as agents of construction: it is a relatively narrow notion, and roughly parallels Kant's notion of hypothetical imperatives (or the notion of rationality found in neo-classical economics); *full* autonomy is that of citizens in everyday life who think of themselves in a certain way and affirm and act from the first principles of justice that would be agreed to. In Section V, I shall discuss the constraints imposed on the parties which enable the original position to represent the essential elements of full autonomy.

Let us briefly recall the features of a well-ordered society most relevant here.[3] First, such a society is effectively regulated by a public conception of justice; that is, it is a society in which every one accepts, and knows that others likewise accept, the same first principles of right and justice. It is also the case that the basic structure of society, the arrangement of its main institutions into one social scheme, actually satisfies, and is believed by all on good grounds to satisfy, these principles. Finally, the public principles of justice are themselves founded on reasonable beliefs as established by the society's generally accepted methods of inquiry; and the same is true of the application of these principles to judge social institutions.

Second, the members of a well-ordered society are, and view themselves and one another in their political and social relations (so far as these are relevant to questions of justice) as, free and equal moral persons. Here there are three distinct notions, specified independently freedom, equality, and moral (as applied to) person. The members of a well-ordered society are moral persons in that, once they have reached the age of reason, each has, and views the others as having, an effective sense of justice, as well as an understanding of a conception of their good. Citizens are equal in that they regard one another as having an equal right to determine, and to assess upon due reflection, the first principles of justice by which the basic structure of their society is to be governed. Finally, the members of a well-ordered society are free in that they think they are entitled to make claims on the design of their common institutions in the name of their own fundamental aims and highest-order interests. At the same time, as free persons, they think of themselves not as inevitably tied to the pursuit of the particular final ends they have at any given time, but rather as capable of revising and changing these ends on reasonable and rational grounds. . . .

III

Let us descend from these abstractions, at least a bit, and turn to a summary account of the original position. As I have said, justice as fairness begins from the idea that the most appropriate conception of justice for the basic structure of a democratic society is one that its citizens would adopt in a situation that is fair between them and in which they are represented solely as free and equal moral persons. This situation is the original position: we conjecture that the fairness of the circumstances under which agreement is reached transfers to the principles of justice agreed to; since the original position situates free and equal moral persons fairly with respect to one another, any conception of justice they adopt is likewise fair. Thus the name: 'justice as fairness'.

In order to ensure that the original position is fair between individuals regarded solely as free and equal moral persons, we require that, when adopting principles for the basic structure, the parties be deprived of certain information; that is, they are behind what I shall call a "veil of ignorance." For example, they do not know their place in society, their class position, or social status, nor do they know their fortune in the distribution of natural talents and abilities. It is assumed also that they do not know their conception of the good, that is, their particular final ends; nor finally, their own distinctive psychological dispositions and propensities, and the like. Excluding this information is required if no one is to be advantaged or disadvantaged by natural contingencies or social chance in the adoption of principles. Otherwise the parties would have disparate bargaining advantages that would affect the agreement reached. The original position would represent the parties not solely as free and equal moral persons, but instead as persons also affected by social fortune and natural accident. Thus, these and other limitations on information are necessary to establish fairness between the parties as free and equal moral persons and, therefore, to guarantee that it is as such persons that they agree to society's basic principles of justice. . . .

One reason for describing the original position as incorporating pure procedural justice is that it enables us to explain how the parties, as the rational agents of construction, are also autonomous (as such agents). For the use of pure procedural justice implies that the principles of justice themselves are to be constructed by a process of deliberation, a process visualized as being carried out by the parties in the original position. The appropriate weight of considerations for and against various principles is given by the force of these considerations for the parties, and the force of all reasons on balance is expressed by the agreement made. Pure procedural justice in the original position allows that in their deliberations the parties are not required to apply, nor are they bound by, any antecedently given principles of right and justice. Or, put another way, there exists no standpoint external to the parties' own perspective from which they are constrained by prior and independent principles in questions of justice that arise among them as members of one society. . . .

V

. . . I now turn to the notion of full autonomy; although this notion is realized only by the citizens of a well-ordered society in the course of their daily lives, the essential features of it must nevertheless be represented in a suitable manner in the original position. For it is by affirming the first principles that would be adopted in this situation and by publicly recognizing the way in which they would be agreed to, as well as by acting from these principles as their sense of justice dictates, that citizens' full autonomy is achieved. We must ask, then, how the original position incorporates the requisite elements of full autonomy.

Now these elements are not expressed by how the parties' deliberations and motivation are described. The parties are merely artificial agents, and are presented not as fully but only as rationally autonomous. To explain full autonomy, let us note two elements of any notion of social cooperation. The first is a conception of the *fair terms of cooperation*, that is, terms each participant may reasonably be expected to accept, provided that everyone else likewise accepts them. Fair terms of cooperation articulate an idea of reciprocity and mutuality: all who cooperate must benefit, or share in common burdens, in some appropriate fashion as judged by a suitable benchmark of comparison. This element in social cooperation I call the *Reasonable*. The other element corresponds to the *Rational*: it expresses a conception of each participant's rational advantage, what, as individuals, they are trying to advance. As we have seen, the rational is interpreted by the original position in reference to the desire of persons to real-

ize and to exercise their moral powers and to secure the advancement of their conception of the good. Given a specification of the parties' highest-order interests, they are rational in their deliberations to the extent that sensible principles of rational choice guide their decisions. Familiar examples of such principles are: the adoption of effective means to ends; the balancing of final ends by their significance for our plan of life as a whole and by the extent to which these ends cohere with and support each other; and finally, the assigning of a greater weight to the more likely consequences; and so on. Although there seems to be no one best interpretation of rationality, the difficulties in explaining Kantian constructivism do not lie here. Thus I ignore these matters, and focus on the more obscure notion of the Reasonable and how it is represented in the original position.

This representing is done essentially by the nature of the constraints within which the parties' deliberations take place and which define their circumstances with respect to one another. The Reasonable is incorporated into the background setup of the original position which frames the discussions of the parties and situates them symmetrically More specifically, in addition to various familiar formal conditions on first principles, such as generality and universality, ordering and finality, the parties are required to adopt a public conception of justice and must assess its first principles with this condition in mind.

Again, the veil of ignorance implies that persons are represented solely as moral persons and not as persons advantaged or disadvantaged by the contingencies of their social position, the distribution of natural abilities, or by luck and historical accident over the course of their lives. As a result they are situated equally as moral persons, and in this sense fairly. Here I appeal to the idea that, in establishing the truly basic terms of social cooperation, the possession of the minimum adequate powers of moral personality (the powers that equip us to be normally cooperating members of society over a complete life) is the sole relevant characteristic. This presumption, plus the precept that equals in all relevant respects are to be represented equally, ensures that the original position is fair.

The last constraint I shall mention here is this: the stipulation that the first subject of justice is the basic structure of society, that is, the main social institutions and how they cohere together into one system, supports situating the parties equally and restricting their information by the veil of ignorance. For this stipulation requires the parties to assess alternative conceptions as providing first principles of what we may call *background justice*: it is only if the basic structure satisfies the requirements of background justice that a society treats its members as equal moral persons. Otherwise, its fundamental regulative arrangements do not answer to principles its citizens would adopt when fairly represented solely as such persons.

Let us pull together these remarks as follows: the Reasonable presupposes and subordinates the Rational. It defines the fair terms of cooperation acceptable to all within some group of separately identifiable persons, each of whom possesses and can exercise the two moral powers. All have a conception of their good which defines their rational advantage, and everyone has a normally effective sense of justice: a capacity to honor the fair terms of cooperation. The Reasonable presupposes the Rational, because, without conceptions of the good that move members of the group, there is no point to social cooperation nor to notions of right and justice, even though such cooperation realizes values that go beyond what conceptions of the good specify taken alone. The Reasonable subordinates the Rational because its principles limit, and in a Kantian doctrine limit absolutely, the final ends that can be pursued.

Thus, in the original position we view the Reasonable as expressed by the framework of constraints within which the deliberations of the parties (as rationally au-

tonomous agents of construction) take place. Representative of these constraints are the condition of publicity, the veil of ignorance and the symmetry of the parties' situation with respect to one another, and the stipulation that the basic structure is the first subject of justice. Familiar principles of justice are examples of reasonable principles, and familiar principles of rational choice are examples of rational principles. The way the Reasonable is represented in the original position leads to the two principles of justice. These principles are constructed by justice as fairness as the content of the Reasonable for the basic structure of a well-ordered society. . . .

VI

[T]he way in which the Reasonable frames the Rational in the original position represents a feature of the unity of practical reason. In Kant's terms, empirical practical reason is represented by the rational deliberations of the parties; pure practical reason is represented by the constraints within which these deliberations take place. The unity of practical reason is expressed by defining the Reasonable to frame the Rational and to subordinate it absolutely; that is, the principles of justice that are agreed to are lexically prior in their application in a well-ordered society to claims of the good. This means, among other things, that the principles of justice and the rights and liberties they define cannot, in such a society, be overridden by considerations of efficiency and a greater net balance of social well-being. This illustrates one feature of the unity of reason: the Reasonable and the Rational are unified within one scheme of practical reasoning which establishes the strict priority of the Reasonable with respect to the Rational. This priority of the right over the good is characteristic of Kantian constructivism.

Now in a well-ordered society we stipulate that the justification of the principles of justice as the outcome of the original position is publicly understood. So not only do citizens have a highest-order desire, their sense of justice, to act from the principles of justice, but they understand these principles as issuing from a construction in which their conception of themselves as free and equal moral persons who are both reasonable and rational is adequately represented. By acting from these principles, and affirming them in public life, as so derived, they express their full autonomy. The rational autonomy of the parties is merely that of artificial agents who inhabit a construction designed to model this more inclusive conception. It is the inclusive conception which expresses the ideal to be realized in our social world. . . .

LECTURE III

CONSTRUCTION AND OBJECTIVITY

In the preceding lectures I sketched the main idea of Kantian constructivism, which is to establish a connection between the first principles of justice and the conception of moral persons as free and equal. These first principles are used to settle the appropriate understanding of freedom and equality for a modern democratic society. The requisite connection is provided by a procedure of construction in which rationally autonomous agents subject to reasonable conditions agree to public principles of justice. With the sketch of these ideas behind us, I consider in this final lecture how a Kantian doctrine interprets the notion of objectivity in terms of a suitably constructed social point of view that is authoritative with respect to all individual and associational points of view. This rendering of objectivity implies that, rather than think of the principles of justice as true, it is better to say that they are the principles most reasonable for us, given our conception of persons as free and equal, and fully cooperating members of a democratic society. [Here 'reasonable' is used, as explained later, in contrast with 'true' as understood in ra-

tional intuitionism, and not, as previously, with 'rational', as in the notion of rational autonomy.]

I

To fix ideas. let's look back roughly a hundred years to Henry Sidgwick. *The Methods of Ethics* (first edition 1874) is, I believe, the outstanding achievement in modern moral theory.[4] By "moral theory" I mean the systematic and comparative study of moral conceptions, starting with those which historically and by current estimation seem to be the most important. Moral philosophy includes moral theory, but takes as its main question justification and how it is to be conceived and resolved; for example, whether it is to be conceived as an epistemological problem (as in rational intuitionism) or as a practical problem (as in Kantian constructivism). Sidgwick's *Methods* is the first truly academic work in moral theory, modern in both method and spirit. Treating ethics as a discipline to be studied like any other branch of knowledge, it defines and carries out in exemplary fashion, if not for the first time, some of the comprehensive comparisons that constitute moral theory. By pulling together the work of previous writers, and through its influence on G. E. Moore and others, this work defined much of the framework of subsequent moral philosophy. Sidgwick's originality lies in his conception and mode of presentation of the subject and in his recognition of the significance of moral theory for moral philosophy.

It is natural, then, that the limitations of *Methods* have been as important as its merits. Of these limitations I wish to mention two. First, Sidgwick gives relatively little attention to the conception of the person and the social role of morality as main parts of a moral doctrine. He starts with the idea of a method of ethics as a method specified by certain first principles, principles by which we are to arrive at a judgment about what we ought to do. He takes for granted that these methods aim at reaching true judgments that hold for all rational minds. Of course, he thinks it is best to approach the problem of justification only when a broad understanding of moral theory has been achieved. In the preface of the first edition of *Methods* he explains that he wants to resist the natural urgency to discover the true method of ascertaining what it is right to do. He wishes instead to expound, from a neutral position and as impartially as possible, the different methods found in the moral consciousness of humankind and worked into familiar historical systems.[5] But these detailed expositions—necessary as they are—are merely preparation for comparing the various methods and evaluating them by criteria that any rational method that aims at truth must satisfy.

But a consequence of starting with methods of ethics defined as methods that seek truth is not only that it interprets justification as an epistemological problem, but also that it is likely to restrict attention to the first principles of moral conceptions and how they can be known. First principles are however only one element of a moral conception; of equal importance are its conception of the person and its view of the social role of morality. Until these other elements are clearly recognized, the ingredients of a constructivist doctrine are not at hand. It is characteristic of Sidgwick's *Methods* that the social role of morality and the conception of the person receive little notice. And so the possibility of constructivism was closed to him.

Sidgwick overlooked this possibility because of a second limitation: he failed to recognize that Kant's doctrine (and perfectionism also for that matter) is a distinctive method of ethics. He regarded the categorical imperative as a purely formal principle, or what he called "the principle of equity": whatever is right for one person is right for all similar persons in relevantly similar circumstances. This principle Sidgwick accepts, but, since it is plainly not a sufficient basis for a moral view, Kant's doctrine could

not be counted a substantive method (pp. 209–10). This formal reading of Kant, together with the dismissal of perfectionism, led Sidgwick to reduce the traditional moral conceptions essentially to three main methods: rational egoism, (pluralistic) intuitionism, and classical utilitarianism. Surely he was right to restrict himself to a few conceptions so that each could be explored in considerable detail. Only in this way can depth of understanding be achieved. But rational egoism, which he accepted as a method of ethics, is really not a moral conception at all, but rather a challenge to all such conceptions, although no less interesting for that. Left with only (pluralistic) intuitionism and classical utilitarianism as methods of ethics in the usual sense, it is no surprise that utilitarianism seemed superior to Sidgwick, given his desire for unity and system in a moral doctrine.

Since Kant's view is the leading historical example of a constructivist doctrine, the result once again is that constructivism finds no place in *Methods*. Nor is the situation altered if we include another leading representative work, F. H. Bradley's *Ethical Studies* (first edition 1876); following Hegel, Bradley likewise regarded Kant's ethics as purely formal and lacking in content and, therefore, to be assigned to an early stage of the dialectic as an inadequate view.[6] The result of these formal interpretations of Kant is that constructivism was not recognized as a moral conception to be studied and assimilated into moral theory. Nor was this lack made good in the first half of this century; for in this period beginning with Moore's *Principia Ethica* (1903), interest centered mainly on philosophical analysis and its bearing on justification regarded as an epistemological problem and on the question whether its conclusions support or deny the notion of moral truth. During this time, however, utilitarianism and intuitionism made important advances. A proper understanding of Kantian constructivism, on a par with our grasp of these views, is still to be achieved.

II

Let us now try to deepen our understanding of Kantian constructivism by contrasting it with what I shall call *rational intuitionism*. This doctrine has, of course, been expressed in various ways; but in one form or another it dominated moral philosophy from Plato and Aristotle onwards until it was challenged by Hobbes and Hume, and, I believe, in a very different way by Kant. To simplify matters, I take rational intuitionism to be the view exemplified in the English tradition by Clarke and Price, Sidgwick and Moore, and formulated in its minimum essentials by W. D. Ross.[7] With qualifications, it was accepted by Leibniz and Wolff in the guise of perfectionism, and Kant knows of it in this form.

For our purposes here, rational intuitionism may be summed up by two theses: first, the basic moral concepts of the right and the good. and the moral worth of persons, are not analyzable in terms of nonmoral concepts (although possibly analyzable in terms of one another); and, second, first principles of morals (whether one or many), when correctly stated, are self-evident propositions about what kinds of considerations are good grounds for applying one of the three basic moral concepts, that is, for asserting that something is (intrinsically) good, or that a certain action is the right thing to do, or that a certain trait of character has moral worth. These two theses imply that the agreement in judgment which is so essential for an effective public conception of justice is founded on the recognition of self-evident truths about good reasons. And what these reasons are is fixed by a moral order that is prior to and independent of our conception of the person and the social role of morality. This order is given by the nature of things and is known, not by sense, but by rational intuition. It is with this idea of moral truth that the idea of first principles as reasonable will be contrasted.

It should be observed that rational intuitionism is compatible with a variety of contents for the first principles of a moral conception Even classical utilitarianism, which Sidgwick was strongly inclined to favor (although he could not see how to eliminate rational egoism as a rival) was sometimes viewed by him as following from three principles each self-evident in its own right.[8] In brief, these three propositions were: the principle of equity so-called: that it cannot be right to treat two different persons differently merely on the ground of their being numerically different individuals; a principle of rational prudence: that mere difference of position in time is not by itself a reasonable ground for giving more regard to well-being at one moment than to well-being at another; and a principle of rational benevolence: the good of one person is of no more importance from the point of view of the universe than the good of any other person. These three principles, when combined with the principle that, as reasonable beings. we are bound to aim at good generally and not at any particular part of it, Sidgwick thought yielded the principle of utility: namely, to maximize the net balance of happiness. And this principle, like those from which it followed, he was tempted to hold as self-evident.

Of all recent versions of rational intuitionism, the appeal to self-evidence is perhaps most striking in Moore's so-called "ideal utilitarianism" in *Principia Ethica* (1903). A consequence of Moore's principle of organic unity is that his view is extremely pluralistic; there are few if any useful first principles, and distinct kinds of cases are to be decided by intuition as they arise. Moore held a kind of Platonic atomism:[9] moral concepts (along with other concepts) are subsisting and independent entities grasped by the mind. That pleasure and beauty are good, and that different combinations of them alone or together with other good things are also good, and to what degree, are truths known by intuition: by seeing with the mind's eye how these separate and distinct objects (universals) are (timelessly) related. This picture is even more vivid in the early philosophy of mathematics of Bertrand Russell, who talks of searching for the indefinable concepts of mathematics with a mental telescope (as one might look for a planet).[10]

Now my aim in recalling these matters is to point out that rational intuitionism, as illustrated by Sidgwick, Moore, and Ross, is sharply opposed to a constructivist conception along Kantian lines. That Kant would have rejected Hume's psychological naturalism as heteronomous is clear.[11] I believe that the contrast with rational intuitionism, no matter what the content of the view (whether utilitarian, perfectionist, or pluralist) is even more instructive. It is less obvious that for Kant rational intuitionism is also heteronomous. The reason is that from the first thesis of rational intuitionism, the basic moral concepts are conceptually independent of natural concepts, and first principles are independent of the natural world and, as grasped by rational intuition, are regarded as synthetic a priori. This may seem to make these principles not heteronomous. Yet it suffices for heteronomy that these principles obtain in virtue of relations among objects the nature of which is not affected or determined by the conception of the person. Kant's idea of autonomy requires that there exist no such order of given objects determining the first principles of right and justice among free and equal moral persons. Heteronomy obtains not only when first principles are fixed by the special psychological constitution of human nature, as in Hume, but also when they are fixed by an order of universals or concepts grasped by rational intuition, as in Plato's realm of forms or in Leibniz's hierarchy of perfections.[12] Perhaps I should add, to prevent misunderstanding, that a Kantian doctrine of autonomy need not deny that the procedures by which first principles are selected are synthetic a priori. This thesis, however, must be properly interpreted. The essential idea is that such procedures must be suitably founded on practical reason, or, more exactly, on notions which characterize persons as reasonable and rational and which are incorpo-rated into the way in which, as such persons, they represent to themselves their free and equal moral personality. Put another way, first principles of justice must issue from a conception of the person through a suitable representation of that conception as illustrated by the procedure of construction in justice as fairness.

Thus in a Kantian doctrine a relatively complex conception of the person plays a central role. By contrast, rational intuitionism requires but a sparse notion of the person, founded on the self as knower. This is because the content of first principles is already fixed, and the only requirements on the self are to be able to know what these principles are and to be moved by this knowledge. A basic assumption is that the recognition of first principles as true and self-evident gives rise, in a being capable of rationally intuiting these principles, to a desire to act from them for their own sake. Moral motivation is defined by reference to desires that have a special kind of cause, namely, the intuitive grasp of first principles.[13] This sparse conception of the person joined with its moral psychology characterizes the rational intuitionism of Sidgwick, Moore, and Ross, although there is nothing that forces rational intuitionism to so thin a notion. The point is rather that. in rational intuitionism in contrast to a Kantian view, since the content of first principles is already given, a more complex conception of the person, of a kind adequate to determine the content of these principles, together with a suitable moral psychology, is simply unnecessary.

III

Having contrasted Kantian constructivism to rational intuitionism with respect to the idea of a moral order that is prior to and independent from our conception of the person, I now consider a second contrast, namely, how each regards the inevitable limitations that constrain our moral deliberations. The constructionist view accepts from the start that a moral conception can establish but a loose framework for deliberation which must rely very considerably on our powers of reflection and judgment. These powers are not fixed once and for all, but are developed by a shared public culture and hence shaped by that culture. In justice as fairness this means that the principles adopted by the parties in the original position are designed by them to achieve a public and workable agreement on matters of social justice which suffices for effective and fair social cooperation. From the standpoint of the parties as agents of construction, the first principles of justice are not thought to represent, or to be true of, an already given moral order, as rational intuitionism supposes. The essential point is that a conception of justice fulfills its social role provided that citizens equally conscientious and sharing roughly the same beliefs find that, by affirming the framework of deliberation set up by it, they are normally led to a sufficient convergence of opinion. Thus a conception of justice is framed to meet the practical requirements of social life and to yield a public basis in the light of which citizens can justify to one another their common institutions. Such a conception need be only precise enough to achieve this result.

On the constructivist view, the limitations that constrain our moral deliberations affect the requirements of publicity and support the use of priority rules. These limitations also lead us to take the basic structure of a well-ordered society as the first subject of justice and to adopt the primary goods as the basis of interpersonal comparisons. To begin with publicity: at the end of the preceding lecture I mentioned why in a constructivist view first principles are to satisfy the requirements of publicity. The moral conception is to have a wide social role as a part of public culture and is to enable citizens to appreciate and accept the conception of the person as free and equal. Now if it is to play this wide role, a conception's first principles cannot be so complex that they cannot be generally un-

derstood and followed in the more important cases. Thus, it is desirable that knowing whether these principles are satisfied, at least with reference to fundamental liberties and basic institutions. should not depend on information difficult to obtain or hard to evaluate. To incorporate these desiderata in a constructivist view, the parties are assumed to take these considerations into account and to prefer (other things equal) principles that are easy to understand and simple to apply. The gain in compliance and willing acceptance by citizens more than makes up for the rough and ready nature of the guiding framework that results and its neglect of certain distinctions and differences. In effect, the parties agree to rule out certain facts as irrelevant in questions of justice concerning the basic structure, even though they recognize that in regard to other cases it may be appropriate to appeal to them. From the standpoint of the original position, eliminating these facts as reasons of social justice sufficiently increases the capacity of the conception to fulfill its social role. Of course, we should keep in mind that the exclusion of such facts as reasons of social justice does not alone entail that they are not reasons in other kinds of situation where different moral notions apply. Indeed, it is not even ruled out that the account of some notions should be constructivist, whereas the account of others is not.

It is evident, then, why a constructivist view such as justice as fairness incorporates into the framework of moral deliberation a number of schematic and practical distinctions as ways that enable us to deal with the inevitable limitations of our moral capacities and the complexity of our social circumstances. The need for such distinctions supports and helps to account for the use of certain priority rules to settle the relative weight of particular kinds of grounds in extremely important cases. Two such rules in justice as fairness are: first, the priority of justice over efficiency (in the sense of Pareto) and the net balance of advantages (summed over all individuals in society), and second, the priority of the principle of equal liberty (understood in terms of certain enumerated basic liberties) over the second principle of justice.[14] These rules are introduced to handle the complexity of the many prima facie reasons we are ready to cite in everyday life; and their plausibility depends in large part on the first principles to which they are adjoined. But although these rules are intended to narrow the scope of judgment in certain fundamental questions of justice, this scope can never be entirely eliminated, and for many other questions sharp and definite conclusions cannot usually be derived. Sharp and definite conclusions are not needed, however, if sufficient agreement is still forthcoming (*TJ*, p. 44–45).

Similar considerations apply in beginning with the basic structure of a well-ordered society as the first subject of justice and trying to develop a conception of justice for this case alone. The idea is that this structure plays a very special role in society by establishing what we may call *background justice*; and if we can find suitable first principles of background justice, we may be able to exclude enough other considerations as irrelevant for this case, so as to develop a reasonably simple and workable conception of justice for the basic structure. The further complexities of everyday cases that cannot be ignored in a more complete moral conception may be dealt with later in the less general situations that occur within the various associations regulated by the basic structure, and in that sense subordinate to it.[15]

Finally, parallel observations hold in finding a feasible basis for interpersonal comparisons of well-being relevant for questions of justice that arise in regard to the basic structure. These comparisons are to be made in terms of primary goods (as defined in the first lecture), Which are, so far as possible, certain public features of social institutions and of people's situations with respect to them, such as their rights, liberties, and opportunities, and their income and wealth, broadly understood. This has the consequence that the comparison of citizens' shares in the benefits of social cooperation is greatly simplified and put on a footing less open to dispute.

Thus the reason why a constructivist view uses the schematic or practical distinctions we have just noted is that such distinctions are necessary if a workable conception of justice is to be achieved. These distinctions are incorporated into justice as fairness through the description of the parties as agents of construction and the account of how they are to deliberate. Charged with the task of agreeing to a workable conception of justice designed to achieve a sufficient convergence of opinion, the parties can find no better way in which to carry out this task. They accept the limitations of human life and recognize that at best a conception of justice can establish but a guiding framework for deliberation.

A comparison with classical utilitarianism will highlight what is involved here. On that view, whether stated as a form of rational intuitionism (Sidgwick) or as a form of naturalism (Bentham), every question of right and justice has an answer: whether an institution or action is right depends upon whether it will produce the greatest net balance of satisfaction. We may never be in a position to know the answer, or even to come very near to it, but, granting that a suitable measure of satisfaction exists, there is an answer: a fact of the matter. Of course, utilitarianism recognizes the needs of practice: working precepts and secondary rules are necessary to guide deliberation and coordinate our actions. These norms may be thought of as devised to bring our actions as close as possible to those which would maximize utility, so far as this is feasible. But of course, such rules and precepts are not first principles; they are at best directives that when followed make the results of our conduct approximate to what the principle of utility enjoins. In this sense, our working norms are approximations to something given.

By contrast, justice as fairness, as a constructivist view, holds that not all the moral questions we are prompted to ask in everyday life have answers. Indeed, perhaps only a few of them can be settled by any moral conception that we can understand and apply. Practical limitations impose a more modest aim upon a reasonable conception of justice, namely, to identify the most fundamental questions of justice that can be dealt with, in the hope that, once this is done and just basic institutions established, the remaining conflicts of opinion will not be so deep or widespread that they cannot be compromised. To accept the basic structure as the first subject of justice together with the account of primary goods is a step toward achieving this more modest goal. But in addition, the idea of approximating to moral truth has no place in a constructivist doctrine: the parties in the original position do not recognize any principles of justice as true or correct and so as antecedently given; their aim is simply to select the conception most rational for them, given their circumstances. This conception is not regarded as a workable approximation to the moral facts: there are no such moral facts to which the principles adopted could approximate.

As we have just seen, the differences between constructivism and classical utilitarianism are especially sharp in view of the content of the principle of utility: it always yields an answer that we can at least verbally describe. With the rational (pluralistic) intuitionism of Ross, however, the contrast is less obvious, since Ross's list of self-evident prima facie principles that identify good reasons also specifies but a loose guiding framework of moral deliberation which shares a number of the features of the framework provided by constructivism. But though these resemblances are real, the underlying idea of Ross's view is still essentially different from constructivism. His pluralistic intuitionism rejects utilitarianism (even an ideal utilitarianism) as oversimplifying the given moral facts, especially those concerning the correct weight of special duties and obligations. The complexity of the moral facts in particular

kinds of cases is said to force us to recognize that no family of first principles that we can formulate characterizes these facts sufficiently accurately to lead to a definite conclusion. Decision and judgment are almost always to some degree uncertain and must rest with "perception,"[16] that is, with our intuitive estimate of where the greatest balance of prima facie reasons lies in each kind of case. And this perception is that of a balance of reasons each of which is given by an independent moral order known by intuition. The essential contrast with constructivism remains.

IV

Having examined several contrasts between Kantian constructivism and rational intuitionism, we are now in a position to take up a fundamental point suggested by the discussion so far. an essential feature of a constructivist view, as illustrated by justice as fairness, is that its first principles single out what facts citizens in a well-ordered society are to count as reasons of justice. Apart from the procedure of constructing these principles, there are no reasons of justice. Put in another way, whether certain facts are to count as reasons of justice and what their relative force is to be can be ascertained only on the basis of the principles that result from the construction. This connects with the use of pure procedural justice at the highest level. It is, therefore, up to the parties in the original position to decide how simple or complex the moral facts are to be, that is, to decide on the number and complexity of the principles that identify which facts are to be accepted as reasons of justice by citizens in society (see *TJ*, p. 45). There is nothing parallel to this in rational intuitionism.

This essential feature of constructivism may be obscured by the fact that in justice as fairness the first principles of justice depend upon those general beliefs about human nature and how society works which are allowed to the parties in the original position. First principles are not, in a constructivist view, independent of such beliefs, nor, as some forms of rational intuitionism hold, true in all possible worlds. In particular, they depend on the rather specific features and limitations of human life that give rise to the circumstances of justice. Now, given the way the original position is set up, we can allow, in theory, that, as the relevant general beliefs change, the beliefs we attribute to the parties likewise change, and conceivably also the first principles that would be agreed to. We can say, if we like that *the* (most reasonable) principles of justice are those which would be adopted if the parties possessed all relevant general information and if they were properly to take account of all the practical desiderata required for a workable public conception of justice. Though these principles have a certain preeminence, they are still the outcome of construction. Furthermore. it is important to notice here that no assumptions have been made about a theory of truth. A constructivist view does not require an idealist or a verificationist, as opposed to a realist, account of truth. Whatever the nature of truth in the case of general beliefs about human nature and how society works, a constructivist moral doctrine requires a distinct procedure of construction to identify the first principles of justice. To the extent that Kant's moral doctrine depends upon what to some may appear to be a constructivist account of truth in the *First Critique* (I don't mean to imply that such an interpretation is correct), justice as fairness departs from that aspect of Kant's view and seeks to preserve the overall structure of his moral conception apart from that background.

In the preceding paragraph I said that the way justice as fairness is set up allows the possibility that, as the general beliefs ascribed to the parties in the original position change, the first principles of justice may also change. But I regard this as a mere possibility noted in order to explain the nature of a constructivist view. To elaborate: at the end of the first lecture I distinguished between the roles of a conception of the person and of a theory of human nature, and I remarked that in justice as fairness these are distinct elements and enter at different places. I said that a conception of the person is a companion moral ideal paired with the ideal of a well-ordered society. A theory of human nature and a view of the requirements of social life tell us whether these ideals are feasible, whether it is possible to realize them under normally favorable conditions of human life. Changes in the theory of human nature or in social theory generally which do not affect the feasibility of the ideals of the person and of a well-ordered society do not affect the agreement of the parties in the original position. It is hard to imagine realistically any new knowledge that should convince us that these ideals are not feasible, given what we know about the general nature of the world, as opposed to our particular social and historical circumstances. In fact, the relevant information on these matters must go back a long time and is available to the common sense of any thoughtful and reflective person. Thus such advances in our knowledge of human nature and society as may take place do not affect our moral conception, but rather may be used to implement the application of its first principles of justice and suggest to us institutions and policies better designed to realize them in practice.[17]

In justice as fairness, then, the main ideals of the conception of justice are embedded in the two model-conceptions of the person and of a well-ordered society. And, granting that these ideals are allowed by the theory of human nature and so in that sense feasible, the first principles of justice to which they lead, via the constructivist procedure of the original position, determine the long-term aim of social change. These principles are not, as in rational intuitionism, given by a moral order prior to and independent from our conception of the person and the social role of morality; nor are they, as in some naturalist doctrines, to be derived from the truths of science and adjusted in accordance with advances in human psychology and social theory. (These remarks are admittedly too brief, but we must return to the main line of discussion.)

V

The rational intuitionist may object that an essential feature of constructivism—the view that the facts to count as reasons of justice are singled out by the parties in the original position as agents of construction and that, apart from such construction, there are no reasons of justice—is simply incoherent.[18] This view is incompatible not only with the notion of truth as given by a prior and independent moral order, but also with the notions of reasonableness and objectivity, neither of which refer to what can be settled simply by agreement, much less by choice. A constructivist view, the objection continues, depends on the idea of adopting or choosing first principles, and such principles are not the kind of thing concerning which it makes sense to say that their status depends on their being chosen or adopted. We cannot "choose" them; what we can do is choose whether to follow them in our actions or to be guided by them in our reasoning, just as we can choose whether to honor our duties, but not what our duties are.

In reply, one must distinguish the three points of view . . . : that of the parties in the original position, that of the citizens in a well-ordered society, and that of you and me who are examining justice as fairness to serve as a basis for a conception that may yield a suitable understanding of freedom and equality. It is, of course, the parties in the original position whose agreement singles out the facts to count as reasons. But their agreement is subject to all the conditions of the original position which represent the Reasonable and the Rational. And the facts singled out by the first principles count as reasons not for the parties, since they are moved by their highest order interests, but for the citizens of a

well-ordered society in matters of social justice. As citizens in society we are indeed bound by first principles and by what our duties are, and must act in the light of reasons of justice. Constructivism is certain to seem incoherent unless we carefully distinguish these points of view.

The parties in the original position do not agree on what the moral facts are, as if there already were such facts. It is not that, being situated impartially, they have a clear and undistorted view of a prior and independent moral order. Rather (for constructivism), there is no such order, and therefore no such facts apart from the procedure of construction as a whole; the facts are identified by the principles that result. Thus the rational intuitionists' objection, properly expressed, must be that no hypothetical agreement by rationally autonomous agents, no matter how circumscribed by reasonable conditions in a procedure of construction, can determine the reasons that settle what we as citizens should consider just and unjust; right and wrong are not, even in that way, constructed. But this is merely to deny what constructivism asserts. If, on the other hand, such a construction does yield the first principles of a conception of justice that matches more accurately than other views our considered convictions in general and wide reflective equilibrium, then constructivism would seem to provide a suitable basis for objectivity.

The agreement of the parties in the original position is not a so-called "radical" choice: that is, a choice not based on reasons, a choice that simply fixes, by sheer fiat, as it were, the scheme of reasons that we, as citizens, are to recognize, at least until another such choice is made. The notion of radical choice, commonly associated with Nietzsche and the existentialists, finds no place in justice as fairness. The parties in the original position are moved by their preference for primary goods, which preference in turn is rooted in their highest-order interests in developing and exercising their moral powers. Moreover, the agreement of the parties takes place subject to constraints that express reasonable conditions.

In the model-conception of a well-ordered society, citizens affirm their public conception of justice because it matches their considered convictions and coheres with the kind of persons they, on due reflection, want to be. Again, this affirmation is not radical choice. The ideals of the person and of social cooperation embedded in the two model-conceptions mediated by the original position are not ideals that, at some moment in life, citizens are said simply to choose. One is to imagine that, for the most part, they find on examination that they hold these ideals, that they have taken them in part from the culture of their society.

The preceding paragraph ties in with what I said at the beginning of the first lecture, except that there I was talking about us and not about a well-ordered society. Recall that a Kantian view, in addressing the public culture of a democratic society, hopes to bring to awareness a conception of the person and of social cooperation conjectured to be implicit in that culture, or at least congenial to its deepest tendencies when properly expressed and presented. Our society is not well-ordered: the public conception of justice and its understanding of freedom and equality are in dispute. Therefore, for us—you and me—a basis of public justification is still to be achieved. In considering the conception of justice as fairness we have to ask whether the ideals embedded in its model-conceptions are sufficiently congenial to our considered convictions to be affirmed as a practicable basis of public justification. Such an affirmation would not be radical choice (if choice at all); nor should it be confused with the adoption of principles of justice by the parties in the original position. To the contrary, it would be rooted in the fact that this Kantian doctrine as a whole, more fully than other views available to us, organized our considered convictions.

Given the various contrasts between Kantian constructivism and rational intu-

itionism, it seems better to say that in constructivism first principles are reasonable (or unreasonable) than that they are true (or false)—better still, that they are most reasonable for those who conceive of their person as it is represented in the procedure of construction. And here 'reasonable' is used instead of 'true' not because of some alternative theory of truth, but simply in order to keep to terms that indicate the constructivist standpoint as opposed to rational intuitionism. This usage, however, does not imply that there are no natural uses for the notion of truth in moral reasoning. To the contrary, for example, particular judgments and secondary norms may be considered true when they follow from, or are sound applications of, reasonable first principles. These first principles may be said to be true in the sense that they would be agreed to if the parties in the original position were provided with all the relevant true general beliefs.

Nor does justice as fairness exclude the possibility of there being a fact of the matter as to whether there is a single most reasonable conception. For it seems quite likely that there are only a few viable conceptions of the person both sufficiently general to be part of a moral doctrine and congruent with the ways in which people are to regard themselves in a democratic society. And only one of these conceptions may have a representation in a procedure of construction that issues in acceptable and workable principles, given the relevant general beliefs.[19] Of course, this is conjecture, intended only to indicate that constructivism is compatible with there being, in fact, only one most reasonable conception of justice, and therefore that constructivism is compatible with objectivism in this sense. However, constructivism does not presuppose that this is the case, and it may turn out that, for us, there exists no reasonable and workable conception of justice at all. This would mean that the practical task of political philosophy is doomed to failure.

VI

My account of Kantian constructivism in moral theory (as illustrated by justice as fairness) is now concluded. I should stress, however, that for all I have said it is still open to the rational intuitionist to reply that I have not shown that rational intuitionism is false or that it is not a possible basis for the necessary agreement in our judgments of justice. It has been my intention to describe constructivism by contrast and not to defend it, much less to argue that rational intuitionism is mistaken. In any case, Kantian constructivism, as I would state it, aims to establish only that the rational intuitionist notion of objectivity is unnecessary for objectivity. Of course, it is always possible to say, if we ever do reach general and wide reflective equilibrium, that now at last we intuit the moral truths fixed by a given moral order; but the constructivist will say instead that our conception of justice, by all the criteria we can think of to apply, is now the most reasonable for us.

We have arrived at the idea that objectivity is not given by "the point of view of the universe," to use Sidgwick's phrase. Objectivity is to be understood by reference to a suitably constructed social point of view, an example of which is the framework provided by the procedure of the original position. This point of view is social in several respects. It is the publicly shared point of view of citizens in a well-ordered society, and the principles that issue from it are accepted by them as authoritative with regard to the claims of individuals and associations. Moreover, these principles regulate the basic structure of society within which the activities of individuals and associations take place. Finally, by representing the person as a free and equal citizen of a well-ordered society, the constructivist procedure yields principles that further everyone's highest-order interests and define the fair terms of social cooperation among persons so understood. When citizens invoke these principles they speak as members of a political community and appeal to its shared point of view either in their own behalf or in that of others. Thus, the essential agreement in judgments of justice arises not from the recognition of a prior and independent moral order, but from everyone's affirmation of the same authoritative social perspective.

The central place of the conception of the person in these lectures prompts me to conclude with a note of warning, addressed as much to me as to anyone else: ever since the notion of the person assumed a central place in moral philosophy in the latter part of the eighteenth century, as seen in Rousseau and Kant and the philosophy of idealism, its use has suffered from excessive vagueness and ambiguity. And so it is essential to devise an approach that disciplines our thought and suitably limits these defects. I view the three model-conceptions that underlie justice as fairness as having this purpose.

To elucidate: suppose we define the concept of a person as that of a human being capable of taking full part in social cooperation, honoring its ties and relationships over a complete life. There are plainly many specifications of this capacity, depending, for example, on how social cooperation or a complete life is understood; and each such specification yields another conception of the person falling under the concept. Moreover, such conceptions must be distinguished from specifications of the concept of the self as knower, used in epistemology and metaphysics, or the concept of the self as the continuant carrier of psychological states: the self as substance, or soul. These are prima facie distinct notions, and questions of identity, say, may well be different for each; for these notions arise in connection with different problems. This much is perhaps obvious. The consequence is that there are numerous conceptions of the person as the basic unit of agency and responsibility in social life, and of its requisite intellectual, moral, and active powers. The specification of these conceptions by philosophical analysis alone, apart from any background theoretical structure or general requirements, is likely to prove fruitless. In isolation these notions play no role that fixes or limits their use, and so their features remain vague and indeterminate.

One purpose of a model-conception like that of the original position is that, by setting up a definite framework within which a binding agreement on principles must be made, it serves to fix ideas. We are faced with a specific problem that must be solved, and we are forced to describe the parties and their mutual relations in the process of construction so that appropriate principles of justice result. The context of the problem guides us in removing vagueness and ambiguity in the conception of the person, and tells us how precise we need to be. There is no such thing as absolute clarity or exactness; we have to be only clear or exact enough for the task at hand. Thus the structure defined by the original position may enable us to crystallize our otherwise amorphous notion of the person and to identify with sufficient sharpness the appropriate characterization of free and equal moral personality.

The constructivist view also enables us to exploit the flexibility and power of the idea of rational choice subject to appropriate constraints. The rational deliberations of the parties in the original position serve as a way to select among traditional or other promising conceptions of justice. So understood, the original position is not an axiomatic (or deductive) basis from which principles are derived but a procedure for singling out principles most fitting to the conception of the person most likely to be held, at least implicitly, in a modern democratic society. To exaggerate, we compute via the deliberations of the parties and in this way hope to achieve sufficient rigor and clarity in moral theory. Indeed, it is hard to see how there could be any more direct connection between the conception of free and equal moral persons and first principles of justice than this construction allows. For here persons so conceived and moved by their highest-order interests are themselves, in their rationally autonomous deliberations, the agents who select the principles that are to govern the basic structure of their social life. What connection could be more intimate than this?

Finally, if we ask, what is clarity and exactness enough? the answer is: enough to find an understanding of freedom and equality that achieves workable public agreement on the weight of their respective claims. With this we return to the current impasse in the understanding of freedom and equality which troubles our democratic tradition and from which we started. Finding a way out of this impasse defines the immediate practical task of political philosophy. Having come full circle, I bring these lectures to a close.

NOTES

Presented as three lectures, on Kantian Constructivism in Moral Theory, given at Columbia University in April 1980; the first, "Rational and Full Autonomy," on April 14; the second, "Representation of Freedom and Equality," on April 15; the third, "Construction and Objectivity," on April 16. These lectures constitute the fourth series of John Dewey Lectures, which were established in 1967 to honor the late John Dewey, who had been from 1905 to 1930 a professor of philosophy at Columbia.

In revising these lectures for publication I should like to thank Burton Dreben for helpful discussion which has led to numerous improvements and clarifications, and also Joshua Cohen and Samuel Scheffler for valuable criticisms of an earlier version of material included in Lectures I and III, originally prepared for the Howison Lecture at Berkeley in May 1979. As always, I am indebted, at many points, to Joshua Rabinowitz.

1. Cambridge, Mass.: Harvard University Press, 1971. Hereafter referred to as *TJ*.

2. See, e.g., Dewey's *Outlines of a Critical Theory of Ethics* (1891) and *The Study of Ethics: A Syllabus* (1894), reprinted in *John Dewey: The Early Works. 1882–1898* (Carbondale: Southern Illinois University Press, 1971), in vols. 3 and 4, respectively. From Dewey's critique of Kant in *Outlines*, pp. 290–300, and his statement of his own form of the self-realization doctrine, pp. 300–327, Dewey's debt to idealism is plain enough.

3. These features were not conveniently stated at any one place in *TJ*. In this and the next lecture I try to give a clearer and more systematic account of this notion and to indicate its basic role as a model-conception.

4. On Sidgwick now, see the comprehensive work by J. B. Schneewind, *Sidgwick's Ethics and Modern Victorian Moral Philosophy* (New York: Oxford, 1977).

5. *The Methods of Ethics*, 7th ed. (London: Macmillan 1907), pp. v–vi; parenthetical page references to Sidgwick are to this book, this edition.

6. See Essay IV: "Duty for Duty's Sake," 2d ed. (New York: Oxford University Press, 1927).

7. See *The Right and the Good* (Oxford: Clarendon Press, 1930), esp. chaps. 1–2. I shall adopt Ross's characterization of rational intuitionism, adjusted to allow for any number of first principles and, thus, as fitting either single-principle or pluralistic intuitionism. I should add that, for my purposes here, I interpret Aristotle's view as combining teleological and metaphysical perfectionism. Although this may not be a sound interpretation in the light of contemporary scholarship, it suits well enough how Aristotle was interpreted up to Kant's time.

8. *Methods*, Bk. III, chap. 13, pp. 379–89. See Schneewind's discussion, chap. 10, pp. 286–309.

9. I borrow this expression from Peter Hylton's discussion, *The Origins of Analytic Philosophy*, chap. 3 (diss., Harvard University, 1978).

10. See *The Principles of Mathematics* 2d ed. (London: Allen & Unwin, 1937; 1st ed. 1903), pp. xv–xvi. The analogy of the mental telescope is Russell's.

11. Because it formulates definitions of the basic moral concepts in terms of nonmoral concepts, this being the mode of identifying those facts which are to count as good reasons in applying the basic moral concepts, naturalism is a form of heteronomy from the Kantian standpoint. The various definitions, presumably arrived at by the analysis of concepts, convert moral judgments into statements about the world on all fours with those of science and common sense. Therefore, these definitions, combined with the natural order itself, now come to constitute the moral order, which is prior to and independent from our conception of ourselves as free and equal moral persons. If time permitted, this could be substantiated by setting out, for example, the details of Hume's view (as often interpreted) and of Bentham's hedonistic utilitarianism, at least once these views are expressed in the requisite naturalistic format. (Rational intuitionism tries to secure a kind of independence of the moral order from the order of nature.)

12. This fundamental contention is unfortunately obscured by the fact that although in the *Grundlegung* Kant classifies the view of Leibniz and Wolff as a form of heteronomy, his criticism of it is that it is circular and therefore empty. See Academy Edition, p. 443. Much the same happens in the *Second Critique*, Academy Edition, p. 41, where Kant argues that the notion of perfection in practical reasoning means fitness for any given ends and therefore is again empty until these ends are specified independently. These arguments give the erroneous impression that, if perfectionism had sufficient content, it would be compatible with autonomy.

13. See, for example, *Methods*, pp. 23–28, 34–37, 39 f, read together with the discussion of the self-evident basis of the principle of utility, cited in note 8 above.

14. For a statement of these principles and priority rules, see *TJ*, pp. 60–62, 250, 302–3.

15. See "The Basic Structure as Subject," in A. I. Goldman and Jaegwon Kim, eds., *Values and Morals* (Boston: Reidel, 1978), esp. secs. IV–V, pp. 52–57.

16. See *The Right and the Good*, pp. 41–42. Ross refers to Aristotle's remark: "The decision rests with perception" (*Nicomachean Ethics* 1109b23, 1126b4).

17. Therefore these advances in our knowledge of human psychology and social theory might be relevant at the constitutional, legislative, and judicial stages in the application of the principles of justice, as opposed to the adoption of principles in the original position. For a brief account of these stages, see *TJ*, sec. 31.

18. For this and other objections to what I call "constructivism" in this lecture, see the review of *TJ* by Marcus Singer, *Philosophy of Science* 64, no. 4 (December 1977): 594–618, 612–15. I am grateful to him for raising this objection, which I here try to meet. Singer's criticism starts from the passage on p. 45 of *TJ* (also referred to above). It should not be assumed that Singer's own position is that of rational intuitionism. I simply suppose that a rational intuitionist would make this objection.

19. I am indebted to Samuel Scheffler for valuable discussion on this point.

15

Contractualism and Utilitarianism

T. M. SCANLON

Utilitarianism occupies a central place in the moral philosophy of our time. It is not the view which most people hold; certainly there are very few who would claim to be act utilitarians. But for a much wider range of people it is the view towards which they find themselves pressed when they try to give a theoretical account of their moral beliefs. Within moral philosophy it represents a position one must struggle against if one wishes to avoid it. This is so in spite of the fact that the implications of act utilitarianism are wildly at variance with firmly held moral convictions, while rule utilitarianism, the most common alternative formulation, strikes most people as an unstable compromise.

The wide appeal of utilitarianism is due, I think, to philosophical considerations of a more or less sophisticated kind which pull us in a quite different direction than our first order moral beliefs. In particular, utilitarianism derives much of its appeal from alleged difficulties about the foundations of rival views. What a successful alternative to utilitarian-

ism must do, first and foremost, is to sap this source of strength by providing a clear account of the foundations of non-utilitarian moral reasoning. In what follows I will first describe the problem in more detail by setting out the questions which a philosophical account of the foundations of morality must answer. I will then put forward a version of contractualism which, I will argue, offers a better set of responses to these questions than that supplied by straightforward versions of utilitarianism. Finally I will explain why contractualism, as I understand it, does not lead back to some utilitarian formula as its normative outcome.

Contractualism has been proposed as the alternative to utilitarianism before, notably by John Rawls in *A Theory of Justice* (Rawls 1971). Despite the wide discussion which this book has received, however, I think that the appeal of contractualism as a foundational view has been underrated. In particular, it has not been sufficiently appreciated that contractualism offers a particularly plausible account of moral motivation. The version of contractualism that I shall present differs from Rawls's in a number of respects. In particular, it makes no use, or only a different and more limited kind of use, of his notion of choice from behind a veil of ignorance. One result of this difference is to make the contrast between contractualism and utilitarianism stand out more clearly.

I

There is such a subject as moral philosophy for much the same reason that there is such a subject as the philosophy of mathematics. In moral judgements, as in mathematical ones, we have a set of putatively objective beliefs in which we are inclined to invest a certain degree of confidence and importance. Yet on reflection it is not at all obvious what, if anything, these judgements can be about, in virtue of which some can be said to be correct or defensible and others not. This question of subject matter, or the grounds of truth, is the first philosophical question about both morality and mathematics. Second, in both morality and mathematics it seems to be possible to discover the truth simply by thinking or reasoning about it. Experience and observation may be helpful, but observation in the normal sense is not the standard means of discovery in either subject. So, given any positive answer to the first question—any specification of the subject matter or ground of truth in mathematics or morality—we need some compatible epistemology explaining how it is possible to discover the facts about this subject matter through something like the means we seem to use.

Given this similarity in the questions giving rise to moral philosophy and to the philosophy of mathematics, it is not surprising that the answers commonly given fall into similar general types. If we were to interview students in a freshman mathematics course many of them would, I think, declare themselves for some kind of conventionalism.

They would hold that mathematics proceeds from definitions and principles that are either arbitrary or instrumentally justified, and that mathematical reasoning consists in perceiving what follows from these definitions and principles. A few others, perhaps, would be realists or platonists according to whom mathematical truths are a special kind of nonempirical fact that we can perceive through some form of intuition. Others might be naturalists who hold that mathematics, properly understood, is just the most abstract empirical science. Finally there are, though perhaps not in an average freshman course, those who hold that there are no mathematical facts in the world "outside of us," but that the truths of mathematics are objective truths about the mental constructions of which we are capable. Kant held that pure mathematics was a realm of objective mind-dependent truths, and Brouwer's mathematical Intuitionism is another theory of this type (with the important difference that it offers grounds for the warranted assertability of mathematical judgements rather than for their truth in the classical sense). All of these positions have natural correlates in moral philosophy. Intuitionism of the sort espoused by W. D. Ross is perhaps the closest analogue to mathematical platonism, and Kant's theory is the most familiar version of the thesis that morality is a sphere of objective, mind-dependent truths.

All of the views I have mentioned (with some qualification in the case of conventionalism) give positive (i.e., non-sceptical) answers to the first philosophical question about mathematics. Each identifies some objective, or at least intersubjective, ground of truth for mathematical judgements. Outright scepticism and subjective versions of mind-dependence (analogues of emotivism or prescriptivism) are less appealing as philosophies of mathematics than as moral philosophies. This is so in part simply because of the greater degree of intersubjective agreement in mathematical judgement. But it is also due to the difference in the further questions that philosophical accounts of the two fields must answer.

Neither mathematics nor morality can be taken to describe a realm of facts existing in isolation from the rest of reality. Each is supposed to be connected with other things. Mathematical judgements give rise to predictions about those realms to which mathematics is applied. This connection is something that a philosophical account of mathematical truth must explain, but the fact that we can observe and learn from the correctness of such predictions also gives support to our belief in objective mathematical truth. In the case of morality the main connection is, or is generally supposed to be, with the will. Given any candidate for the role of subject matter of morality we must explain why anyone should care about it, and the need to answer this question of motivation has given strong support to subjectivist views.

But what must an adequate philosophical theory of morality say about moral motivation? It need not, I think, show that the moral truth gives anyone who knows it a reason to act which appeals to that person's present desires or to the advancement of his or her interests. I find it entirely intelligible that moral requirement might correctly apply to a person even though that person had no reason of either of these kinds for complying with it. Whether moral requirements give those to whom they apply reasons for compliance of some third kind is a disputed question which I shall set aside. But what an adequate moral philosophy must do, I think, is to make clearer to us the nature of the reasons that morality does provide, at least to those who are concerned with it. A philosophical theory of morality must offer an account of these reasons that is, on the one hand, compatible with its account of moral truth and moral reasoning and, on the other, supported by a plausible analysis of moral experience. A satisfactory moral philosophy will not leave concern with morality as a simple special preference, like a fetish or a special taste,

which some people just happen to have. It must make it understandable why moral reasons are ones that people can take seriously, and why they strike those who are moved by them as reasons of a special stringency and inescapability.

There is also a further question whether susceptibility to such reasons is compatible with a person's good or whether it is, as Nietzsche argued, a psychological disaster for the person who has it. If one is to defend morality one must show that it is not disastrous in this way, but I will not pursue this second motivational question here. I mention it only to distinguish it from the first question, which is my present concern.

The task of giving a philosophical explanation of the subject matter of morality differs both from the task of analysing the meaning of moral terms and from that of finding the most coherent formulation of our first order moral beliefs. A maximally coherent ordering of our first order moral beliefs could provide us with a valuable kind of explanation: it would make clear how various, apparently disparate moral notions, precepts, and judgements are related to one another, thus indicating to what degree conflicts between them are fundamental and to what degree, on the other hand, they can be resolved or explained away. But philosophical inquiry into the subject matter of morality takes a more external view. It seeks to explain what kind of truths moral truths are by describing them in relation to other things in the world and in relation to our particular concerns. An explanation of how we can come to know the truth about morality must be based on such an external explanation of the kind of things moral truths are rather than on a list of particular moral truths, even a maximally coherent list. This seems to be true as well about explanations of how moral beliefs can give one a reason to act.[1]

Coherence among our first order moral beliefs—what Rawls has called narrow reflective equilibrium[2]—seems unsatisfying[3] as an account of moral truth or as an account of the basis of justification in ethics just because, taken by itself, a maximally coherent account of our moral beliefs need not provide us with what I have called a philosophical explanation of the subject matter of morality. However internally coherent our moral beliefs may be rendered, the nagging doubt may remain that there is nothing to them at all. They may be merely a set of socially inculcated reactions, mutually consistent perhaps but not judgements of a kind which can properly be said to be correct or incorrect. A philosophical theory of the nature of morality can contribute to our confidence in our first order moral beliefs chiefly by allaying these natural doubts about the subject. Insofar as it includes an account of moral epistemology, such a theory may guide us towards new forms of moral argument, but it need not do this. Moral argument of more or less the kind we have been familiar with may remain as the only form of justification in ethics. But whether or not it leads to revision in our modes of justification, what a good philosophical theory should do is to give us a clearer understanding of what the best forms of moral argument amount to and what kind of truth it is that they can be a way of arriving at. (Much the same can be said, I believe, about the contribution which philosophy of mathematics makes to our confidence in particular mathematical judgements and particular forms of mathematical reasoning.)

Like any thesis about morality, a philosophical account of the subject matter of morality must have some connection with the meaning of moral terms: it must be plausible to claim that the subject matter described is in fact what these terms refer to at least in much of their normal use. But the current meaning of moral terms is the product of many different moral beliefs held by past and present speakers of the language, and this meaning is surely compatible with a variety of moral views and with a variety of views about the nature of morality. After all, moral terms are used to express many different views of these kinds, and people who express

these views are not using moral terms incorrectly, even though what some of them say must be mistaken. Like a first order moral judgement, a philosophical characterisation of the subject matter of morality is a substantive claim about morality, albeit a claim of a different kind.

While a philosophical characterisation of morality makes a kind of claim that differs from a first order moral judgement, this does not mean that a philosophical theory of morality will be neutral between competing normative doctrines. The adoption of a philosophical thesis about the nature of morality will almost always have some effect on the plausibility of particular moral claims, but philosophical theories of morality vary widely in the extent and directness of their normative implications. At one extreme is intuitionism, understood as the philosophical thesis that morality is concerned with certain non-natural properties. Rightness, for example, is held by Ross[4] to be the property of "fittingness" or "moral suitability." Intuitionism holds that we can identify occurrences of these properties, and that we can recognise as self-evident certain general truths about them, but that they cannot be further analysed or explained in terms of other notions. So understood, intuitionism is in principle compatible with a wide variety of normative positions. One could, for example, be an intuitionistic utilitarian or an intuitionistic believer in moral rights, depending on the general truths about the property of moral rightness which one took to be self-evident.

The other extreme is represented by philosophical utilitarianism. The term "utilitarianism" is generally used to refer to a family of specific normative doctrines—doctrines which might be held on the basis of a number of different philosophical theses about the nature of morality. In this sense of the term one might, for example, be a utilitarian on intuitionist or on contractualist grounds. But what I will call "philosophical utilitarianism" is a particular philosophical thesis about the subject matter of morality, namely the thesis that the only fundamental moral facts are facts about individual well-being.[5] I believe that this thesis has a great deal of plausibility for many people, and that, while some people are utilitarians for other reasons, it is the attractiveness of philosophical utilitarianism which accounts for the widespread influence of utilitarian principles.

It seems evident to people that there is such a thing as individuals' being made better or worse off. Such facts have an obvious motivational force; it is quite understandable that people should be moved by them in much the way that they are supposed to be moved by moral considerations. Further, these facts are clearly relevant to morality as we now understand it. Claims about individual well-being are one class of valid starting points for moral argument. But many people find it much harder to see how there could be any other, independent starting points. Substantive moral requirements independent of individual well-being strike people as intuitionist in an objectionable sense. They would represent "moral facts" of a kind it would be difficult to explain. There is no problem about recognising it as a fact that a certain act is, say, an instance of lying or of promise breaking. And a utilitarian can acknowledge that such facts as these often have (derivative) moral significance: they are morally significant because of their consequences for individual well-being. The problems, and the charge of "intuitionism," arise when it is claimed that such acts are wrong in a sense that is not reducible to the fact that they decrease individual well-being. How could this independent property of moral wrongness be understood in a way that would give it the kind of importance and motivational force which moral considerations have been taken to have? If one accepts the idea that there are no moral properties having this kind of intrinsic significance, then philosophical utilitarianism may seem to be the only tenable account of morality. And once philosophical utilitarianism is accepted, some form of normative utilitarianism seems to be forced on

us as the correct first order moral theory. Utilitarianism thus has, for many people, something like the status which Hilbert's Formalism and Brouwer's Intuitionism have for their believers. It is a view which seems to be forced on us by the need to give a philosophically defensible account of the subject. But it leaves us with a hard choice: we can either abandon many of our previous first order beliefs or try to salvage them by showing that they can be obtained as derived truths or explained away as useful and harmless fictions.

It may seem that the appeal of philosophical utilitarianism as I have described it is spurious, since this theory must amount either to a form of intuitionism (differing from others only in that it involves just one appeal to intuition) or else to definitional naturalism of a kind refuted by Moore and others long ago. But I do not think that the doctrine can be disposed of so easily. Philosophical utilitarianism is a philosophical thesis about the nature of morality. As such, it is on a par with intuitionism or with the form of contractualism which I will defend later in this paper. None of these theses need claim to be true as a matter of definition; if one of them is true it does not follow that a person who denies it is misusing the words "right," "wrong," and "ought." Nor are all these theses forms of intuitionism, if intuitionism is understood as the view that moral facts concern special nonnatural properties, which we can apprehend by intuitive insight but which do not need or admit of any further analysis. Both contractualism and philosophical utilitarianism are specifically incompatible with this claim. Like other philosophical theses about the nature of morality (including, I would say, intuitionism itself), contractualism and philosophical utilitarianism are to be appraised on the basis of their success in giving an account of moral belief, moral argument and moral motivation that is compatible with our general beliefs about the world: our beliefs about what kinds of things there are in the world, what kinds of observation and reasoning we are capable of, and what kinds of reasons we have for action. A judgement as to which account of the nature of morality (or of mathematics) is most plausible in this general sense is just that: a judgement of overall plausibility. It is not usefully described as an insight into concepts or as a special intuitive insight of some other kind.

If philosophical utilitarianism is accepted then some form of utilitarianism appears to be forced upon us as a normative doctrine, but further argument is required to determine which form we should accept. If all that counts morally is the well-being of individuals, no one of whom is singled out as counting for more than the others, and if all that matters in the case of each individual is the degree to which his or her well-being is affected, then it would seem to follow that the basis of moral appraisal is the goal of maximising the sum^6 of individual well-being. Whether this standard is to be applied to the criticism of individual actions, or to the selection of rules or policies, or to the inculcation of habits and dispositions to act is a further question, as is the question of how "well-being" itself is to be understood. Thus the hypothesis that much of the appeal of utilitarianism as a normative doctrine derives from the attractiveness of philosophical utilitarianism explains how people can be convinced that some form of utilitarianism must be correct while yet being quite uncertain as to which form it is, whether it is "direct" or "act" utilitarianism or some form of indirect "rule" or "motive" utilitarianism. What these views have in common, despite their differing normative consequences, is the identification of the same class of fundamental moral facts.

II

If what I have said about the appeal of utilitarianism is correct, then what a rival theory must do is to provide an alternative to philosophical utilitarianism as a conception of the subject matter of morality. This is what the theory which I shall call contractualism seeks to do. Even if it succeeds in this, however, and is judged superior to philosophical utilitarianism as an account of the nature of morality, normative utilitarianism will not have been refuted. The possibility will remain that normative utilitarianism can be established on other grounds, for example as the normative outcome of contractualism itself. But one direct and, I think, influential argument for normative utilitarianism will have been set aside.

To give an example of what I mean by contractualism, a contractualist account of the nature of moral wrongness might be stated as follows. "An act is wrong if its performance under the circumstances would be disallowed by any system of rules for the general regulation of behaviour which no one could reasonably reject as a basis for informed, unforced general agreement." This is intended as a characterisation of the kind of property which moral wrongness is. Like philosophical utilitarianism, it will have normative consequences, but it is not my present purpose to explore these in detail. As a contractualist account of one moral notion, what I have set out here is only an approximation, which may need to be modified considerably. Here I can offer a few remarks by way of clarification.

The idea of "informed agreement" is meant to exclude agreement based on superstition or false belief about the consequences of actions, even if these beliefs are ones which it would be reasonable for the person in question to have. The intended force of the qualification "reasonably," on the other hand, is to exclude rejections that would be unreasonable *given* the aim of finding principles which could be the basis of informed, unforced general agreement. Given this aim, it would be unreasonable, for example, to reject a principle because it imposed a burden on you when every alternative principle would impose much greater burdens on others. I will have more to say about grounds for rejection later in the paper.

The requirement that the hypothetical agreement which is the subject of moral argument be unforced is meant not only to rule out coercion, but also to exclude being forced to accept an agreement by being in a weak bargaining position, for example because others are able to hold out longer and hence to insist on better terms. Moral argument abstracts from such considerations. The only relevant pressure for agreement comes from the desire to find and agree on principles which no one who had this desire could reasonably reject. According to contractualism, moral argument concerns the possibility of agreement among persons who are all moved by this desire, and moved by it to the same degree. But this counter-factual assumption characterises only the agreement with which morality is concerned, not the world to which moral principles are to apply. Those who are concerned with morality look for principles for application to their imperfect world which they could not reasonably reject, and which others in this world, who are not now moved by the desire for agreement, could not reasonably reject should they come to be so moved.[7]

The contractualist account of moral wrongness refers to principles "which no one could reasonably reject" rather than to principles "which everyone could reasonably accept" for the following reason.[8] Consider a principle under which some people will suffer severe hardships, and suppose that these hardships are avoidable. That is, there are alternative principles under which no one would have to bear comparable burdens. It might happen, however, that the people on whom these hardships fall are particularly self-sacrificing, and are willing to accept these burdens for the sake of what they see as the greater good of all. We would not say, I think, that it would be unreasonable of them to do this. On the other hand, it might not be unreasonable for them to refuse these burdens, and, hence, not unreasonable for someone to reject a principle requiring him to bear them. If this rejection would be reasonable, then the principle imposing these burdens is put in doubt, despite the fact that some particularly self-sacrificing people could (reasonably) accept it. Thus it is the reasonableness of rejecting a principle, rather than the reasonableness of accepting it, on which moral argument turns.

It seems likely that many non-equivalent sets of principles will pass the test of non-rejectability. This is suggested, for example, by the fact that there are many different ways of defining important duties, no one of which is more or less "rejectable" than the others. There are, for example, many different systems of agreement-making and many different ways of assigning responsibility to care for others. It does not follow, however, that any action allowed by at least one of these sets of principles cannot be morally wrong according to contractualism. If it is important for us to have *some* duty of a given kind (some duty of fidelity to agreements, or some duty of mutual aid) of which there are many morally acceptable forms, then one of these forms needs to be established by convention. In a setting in which one of these forms *is* conventionally established, acts disallowed by it will be wrong in the sense of the definition given. For, given the need for such conventions, one thing that could not be generally agreed to would be a set of principles allowing one to disregard conventionally established (and morally acceptable) definitions of important duties. This dependence on convention introduces a degree of cultural relativity into contractualist morality. In addition, what a person can reasonably reject will depend on the aims and conditions that are important in his life, and these will also depend on the society in which he lives. The definition given above allows for variation of both of these kinds by making the wrongness of an action depend on the circumstances in which it is performed.

The partial statement of contractualism which I have given has the abstract character appropriate in an account of the subject matter of morality. On its face, it involves no specific claim as to which principles could be agreed to or even whether there is a unique set of principles which could be the basis of agreement. One way, though not the only way, for a contractualist to arrive at substantive moral claims would be to give a technical definition of the relevant notion of agreement, for example, by specifying the conditions under which agreement is to be reached, the parties to this agreement and the criteria of reasonableness to be employed. Different contractualists have done this in different ways. What must be claimed for such a definition is that (under the circumstances in which it is to apply) what it describes is indeed the kind of unforced, reasonable agreement at which moral argument aims. But contractualism can also be understood as an informal description of the subject matter of morality on the basis of which ordinary forms of moral reasoning can be understood and appraised without proceeding via a technical notion of agreement.

Who is to be included in the general agreement to which contractualism refers? The scope of morality is a difficult question of substantive morality, but a philosophical theory of the nature of morality should provide some basis for answering it. What an adequate theory should do is to provide a framework within which what seem to be relevant arguments for and against particular interpretations of the moral boundary can be carried out. It is often thought that contractualism can provide no plausible basis for an answer to this question. Critics charge either that contractualism provides no answer at all, because it must begin with some set of contracting parties taken as given, or that contractualism suggests an answer which is obviously too restrictive, since a contract requires parties who are able to make and keep agreements and who are each able to offer the others some benefit in return for their cooperation. Neither of these objections applies to the version of contractualism that I am defending. The general specification of the scope of morality which it implies seems

to me to be this: morality applies to a being if the notion of justification to a being of that kind makes sense. What is required in order for this to be the case? Here I can only suggest some necessary conditions. The first is that the being have a good, that is, that there be a clear sense in which things can be said to go better or worse for that being. This gives partial sense to the idea of what it would be reasonable for a trustee to accept on the being's behalf. It would be reasonable for a trustee to accept at least those things that are good, or not bad, for the being in question. Using this idea of trusteeship we can extend the notion of acceptance to apply to beings that are incapable of literally agreeing to anything. But this minimal notion of trusteeship is too weak to provide a basis for morality, according to contractualism. Contractualist morality relies on notions of what it would be reasonable to accept, or reasonable to reject, which are essentially comparative. Whether it would be unreasonable for me to reject a certain principle, given the aim of finding principles which no one with this aim could reasonably reject, depends not only on how much actions allowed by that principle might hurt me in absolute terms but also on how that potential loss compares with other potential losses to others under this principle and alternatives to it. Thus, in order for a being to stand in moral relations with us it is not enough that it have a good, it is also necessary that its good be sufficiently similar to our own to provide a basis for some system of comparability. Only on the basis of such a system can we give the proper kind of sense to the notion of what a trustee could reasonably reject on a being's behalf.

But the range of possible trusteeship is broader than that of morality. One could act as a trustee for a tomato plant, a forest, or an ant colony, and such entities are not included in morality. Perhaps this can be explained by appeal to the requirement of comparability: while these entities have a good, it is not comparable to our own in a way that provides a basis for moral argument. Beyond this, however, there is in these cases insufficient foothold for the notion of justification *to* a being. One further minimum requirement for this notion is that the being constitute a point of view; that is, that there be such a thing as what it is like to be that being, such a thing as what the world seems like to it. Without this, we do not stand in a relation to the being that makes even hypothetical justification *to it* appropriate.

On the basis of what I have said so far contractualism can explain why the capacity to feel pain should have seemed to many to count in favour of moral status: a being which has this capacity seems also to satisfy the three conditions I have just mentioned as necessary for the idea of justification to it to make sense. If a being can feel pain, then it constitutes a centre of consciousness to which justification can be addressed. Feeling pain is a clear way in which the being can be worse off; having its pain alleviated a way in which it can be benefited; and these are forms of weal and woe which seem directly comparable to our own.

It is not clear that the three conditions I have listed as necessary are also sufficient for the idea of justification to a being to make sense. Whether they are, and, if they are not, what more may be required, are difficult and disputed questions. Some would restrict the moral sphere to those to whom justifications could in principle be communicated, or to those who can actually agree to something, or to those who have the capacity to understand moral argument. Contractualism as I have stated it does not settle these issues at once. All I claim is that it provides a basis for argument about them which is at least as plausible as that offered by rival accounts of the nature of morality. These proposed restrictions on the scope of morality are naturally understood as debatable claims about the conditions under which the relevant notion of justification makes sense, and the arguments commonly offered for and against them can also be plausibly understood on this basis.

Some other possible restrictions on the scope of morality are more evidently rejectable. Morality might be restricted to those who have the capacity to observe its constraints, or to those who are able to confer some reciprocal benefit on other participants. But it is extremely implausible to suppose that the beings excluded by these requirements fall entirely outside the protection of morality. Contractualism as I have formulated it[9] can explain why this is so: the absence of these capacities alone does nothing to undermine the possibility of justification to a being. What it may do in some cases, however, is to alter the justifications which are relevant. I suggest that whatever importance the capacities for deliberative control and reciprocal benefit may have is as factors altering the duties which beings have and the duties others have towards them, not as conditions whose absence suspends the moral framework altogether.

III

I have so far said little about the normative content of contractualism. For all I have said, the act utilitarian formula might turn out to be a theorem of contractualism. I do not think that this is the case, but my main thesis is that whatever the normative implications of contractualism may be it still has distinctive content as a philosophical thesis about the nature of morality. This content—the difference, for example, between being a utilitarian because the utilitarian formula is the basis of general agreement and being a utilitarian on other grounds—is shown most clearly in the answer that a contractualist gives to the first motivational question.

Philosophical utilitarianism is a plausible view partly because the facts which it identifies as fundamental to morality—facts about individual well-being—have obvious motivational force. Moral facts can motivate us, on this view, because of our sympathetic identification with the good of others. But as we move from philosophical utilitarianism to a specific utilitarian formula as the standard of right action, the form of motivation that utilitarianism appeals to becomes more abstract. If classical utilitarianism is the correct normative doctrine then the natural source of moral motivation will be a tendency to be moved by changes in aggregate well-being, however these may be composed. We must be moved in the same way by an aggregate gain of the same magnitude whether it is obtained by relieving the acute suffering of a few people or by bringing tiny benefits to a vast number, perhaps at the expense of moderate discomfort for a few. This is very different from sympathy of the familiar kind toward particular individuals, but a utilitarian may argue that this more abstract desire is what natural sympathy becomes when it is corrected by rational reflection. This desire has the same content as sympathy—it is a concern for the good of others—but it is not partial or selective in its choice of objects.

Leaving aside the psychological plausibility of this even-handed sympathy, how good a candidate is it for the role of moral motivation? Certainly sympathy of the usual kind is one of the many motives that can sometimes impel one to do the right thing. It may be the dominant motive, for example, when I run to the aid of a suffering child. But when I feel convinced by Peter Singer's article[10] on famine, and find myself crushed by the recognition of what seems a clear moral requirement, there is something else at work. In addition to the thought of how much good I could do for people in drought-stricken lands, I am overwhelmed by the further, seemingly distinct thought that it would be wrong for me to fail to aid them when I could do so at so little cost to myself. A utilitarian may respond that his account of moral motivation cannot be faulted for not capturing this aspect of moral experience, since it is just a reflection of our non-utilitarian moral upbringing. Moreover, it must be groundless. For what kind of fact could this supposed further fact of moral wrongness be, and how

could it give us a further, special reason for acting? The question for contractualism, then, is whether it can provide a satisfactory answer to this challenge.

According to contractualism, the source of motivation that is directly triggered by the belief that an action is wrong is the desire to be able to justify one's actions to others on grounds they could not reasonably[11] reject. I find this an extremely plausible account of moral motivation—a better account of at least my moral experience than the natural utilitarian alternative—and it seems to me to constitute a strong point for the contractualist view. We all might like to be in actual agreement with the people around us, but the desire which contractualism identifies as basic to morality does not lead us simply to conform to the standards accepted by others whatever these may be. The desire to be able to justify one's actions to others on grounds they could not reasonably reject will be satisfied when we know that there is adequate justification for our action even though others in fact refuse to accept it (perhaps because they have no interest in finding principles which we and others could not reasonably reject). Similarly, a person moved by this desire will not be satisfied by the fact that others accept a justification for his action if he regards this justification as spurious.

One rough test of whether you regard a justification as sufficient is whether you would accept that justification if you were in another person's position. This connection between the idea of "changing places" and the motivation which underlies morality explains the frequent occurrence of "Golden Rule" arguments within different systems of morality and in the teachings of various religions. But the thought experiment of changing places is only a rough guide; the fundamental question is what would it be unreasonable to reject as a basis for informed, unforced, general agreement. As Kant observed,[12] our different individual points of view, taken as they are, may in general by simply irreconcilable. "Judgemental harmony" requires the construction of a genuinely interpersonal form of justification which is nonetheless something that each individual could agree to. From this interpersonal standpoint, a certain amount of how things look from another person's point of view, like a certain amount of how they look from my own, will be counted as bias.

I am not claiming that the desire to be able to justify one's actions to others on grounds they could not reasonably reject is universal or "natural." "Moral education" seems to me plausibly understood as a process of cultivating this desire and shaping it, largely by learning what justifications others are in fact willing to accept, by finding which ones you yourself find acceptable as you confront them from a variety of perspectives, and by appraising your own and others' acceptance or rejection of these justifications in the light of greater experience.

In fact it seems to me that the desire to be able to justify one's actions (and institutions) on grounds one takes to be acceptable is quite strong in most people. People are willing to go to considerable lengths, involving quite heavy sacrifices, in order to avoid admitting the unjustifiability of their actions and institutions. The notorious insufficiency of moral motivation as a way of getting people to do the right thing is not due to simple weakness of the underlying motive, but rather to the fact that it is easily deflected by self-interest and self-deception.

It could reasonably be objected here that the source of motivation I have described is not tied exclusively to the contractualist notion of moral truth. The account of moral motivation which I have offered refers to the idea of a justification which it would be unreasonable to reject, and this idea is potentially broader than the contractualist notion of agreement. For let M be some non-contractualist account of moral truth. According to M, we may suppose, the wrongness of an action is simply a moral characteristic of that action in virtue of which it ought not to be done. An act which has this characteristic, according to M, has it quite independently of any tendency of informed persons to come to agreement about it. However, since informed persons are presumably in a position to recognise the wrongness of a type of action, it would seem to follow that if an action is wrong then such persons would agree that it is not to be performed. Similarly, if an act is not morally wrong, and there is adequate moral justification to perform it, then there will presumably be a moral justification for it which an informed person would be unreasonable to reject. Thus, even if M, and not contractualism, is the correct account of moral truth, the desire to be able to justify my actions to others on grounds they could not reasonably reject could still serve as a basis for moral motivation.

What this shows is that the appeal of contractualism, like that of utilitarianism, rests in part on a qualified scepticism. A non-contractualist theory of morality can make use of the source of motivation to which contractualism appeals. But a moral argument will trigger this source of motivation only in virtue of being a good justification for acting in a certain way, a justification which others would be unreasonable not to accept. So a non-contractualist theory must claim that there are moral properties which have justificatory force quite independent of their recognition in any ideal agreement. These would represent what John Mackie has called instances of intrinsic "to-be-doneness" and "not-to-be-doneness."[13] Part of contractualism's appeal rests on the view that, as Mackie puts it, it is puzzling how there could be such properties "in the world." By contrast, contractualism seeks to explain the justificatory status of moral properties, as well as their motivational force, in terms of the notion of reasonable agreement. In some cases the moral properties are themselves to be understood in terms of this notion. This is so, for example, in the case of the property of moral wrongness, considered above. But there are also right- and wrong-making properties which are themselves independent of the contractualist notion of agreement. I take the property of being an act of killing for the pleasure of doing so to be a wrong-making property of this kind. Such properties are wrong-making because it would be reasonable to reject any set of principles which permitted the acts they characterise. Thus, while there are morally relevant properties "in the world" which are independent of the contractualist notion of agreement, these do not constitute instances of intrinsic "to-be-doneness" and "not-to-be-doneness": their moral relevance—their force in justifications as well as their link with motivation—is to be explained on contractualist grounds.

In particular, contractualism can account for the apparent moral significance of facts about individual well-being, which utilitarianism takes to be fundamental. Individual well-being will be morally significant, according to contractualism, not because it is intrinsically valuable or because promoting it is self-evidently a right-making characteristic, but simply because an individual could reasonably reject a form of argument that gave his well-being no weight. This claim of moral significance is, however, only approximate, since it is a further difficult question exactly how "well-being" is to be understood and in what ways we are required to take account of the well-being of others in deciding what to do. It does not follow from this claim, for example, that a given desire will always and everywhere have the same weight in determining the rightness of an action that would promote its satisfaction, a weight proportional to its strength or "intensity." The right-making force of a person's desires is specified by what might be called a conception of morally legitimate interests. Such a conception is a product of moral argument; it is not given, as the notion of individual well-being may be, simply by the idea of what it is rational for an individual to desire. Not everything for which I have a rational desire will be something in which others need concede me to have a legitimate interest which they undertake to weigh in deciding

what to do. The range of things which may be objects of my rational desires is very wide indeed, and the range of claims which others could not reasonably refuse to recognise will almost certainly be narrower than this. There will be a tendency for interests to conform to rational desire—for those conditions making it rational to desire something also to establish a legitimate interest in it—but the two will not always coincide.

One effect of contractualism, then, is to break down the sharp distinction, which arguments for utilitarianism appeal to, between the status of individual well-being and that of other moral notions. A framework of moral argument is required to define our legitimate interests and to account for their moral force. This same contractualist framework can also account for the force of other moral notions such as rights, individual responsibility, and procedural fairness.

IV

It seems unlikely that act utilitarianism will be a theorem of the version of contractualism which I have described. The positive moral significance of individual interests is a direct reflection of the contractualist requirement that actions be defensible to each person on grounds he could not reasonably reject. But it is a long step from here to the conclusion that each individual must agree to deliberate always from the point of view of maximum aggregate benefit and to accept justifications appealing to this consideration alone. It is quite possible that, according to contractualism, *some* moral questions may be properly settled by appeal to maximum aggregate well-being, even though this is not the sole or ultimate standard of justification.

What seems less improbable is that contractualism should turn out to coincide with some form of "two level" utilitarianism. I cannot fully assess this possibility here. Contractualism does share with these theories the important features that the defense of individual actions must proceed via a defense of principles that would allow those acts. But contractualism differs from *some* forms of two level utilitarianism in an important way. The role of principles in contractualism is fundamental; they do not enter merely as devices for the promotion of acts that are right according to some other standard. Since it does not establish two potentially conflicting forms of moral reasoning, contractualism avoids the instability which often plagues rule utilitarianism.

The fundamental question here, however, is whether the principles to which contractualism leads must be ones whose general adoption (either ideally or under some more realistic conditions) would promote maximum aggregate well-being. It has seemed to many that this must be the case. To indicate why I do not agree I will consider one of the best known arguments for this conclusion and explain why I do not think it is successful. This will also provide an opportunity to examine the relation between the version of contractualism I have advocated here and the version set forth by Rawls.

The argument I will consider, which is familiar from the writings of Harsanyi[14] and others, proceeds via an interpretation of the contractualist notion of acceptance and leads to the principle of maximum average utility. To think of a principle as a candidate for unanimous agreement I must think of it not merely as acceptable to *me* (perhaps in virtue of my particular position, my tastes, etc.) but as acceptable[15] to others as well. To be relevant, my judgement that the principle is acceptable must be impartial. What does this mean? To judge impartially that a principle is acceptable is, one might say, to judge that it is one which you would have reason to accept no matter who you were. That is, and here is the interpretation, to judge that it is a principle which it would be rational to accept if you did not know which person's position you occupied and believed that you had an equal chance of being in any of these positions. ("Being in a person's position" is here

understood to mean being in his objective circumstances and evaluating these from the perspective of his tastes and preferences.) But, it is claimed, the principle which it would be rational to prefer under these circumstances—the one which would offer the chooser greatest expected utility—would be that principle under which the average utility of the affected parties would be highest.

This argument might be questioned at a number of points, but what concerns me at present is the interpretation of impartiality. The argument can be broken down into three stages. The first of these is the idea that moral principles must be impartially acceptable. The second is the idea of choosing principles in ignorance of one's position (including one's tastes, preferences, etc.). The third is the idea of rational choice under the assumption that one has an equal chance of occupying anyone's position. Let me leave aside for the moment the move from stage two to stage three, and concentrate on the first step, from stage one to stage two. There is a way of making something like this step which is, I think, quite valid, but it does not yield the conclusion needed by the argument. If I believe that a certain principle, *P*, could not reasonably be rejected as a basis for informed, unforced general agreement, then I must believe not only that it is something which it would be reasonable for me to accept but something which it would be reasonable for others to accept as well, insofar as we are all seeking a ground for general agreement. Accordingly, I must believe that I would have reason to accept *P* no matter which social position I were to occupy (though, for reasons mentioned above, I may not believe that I *would* agree to *P* if I were in some of these positions). Now it may be thought that no sense can be attached to the notion of choosing or agreeing to a principle in ignorance of one's social position, especially when this includes ignorance of one's tastes, preferences, etc. But there is at least a minimal sense that might be attached to this notion. If it would be reasonable for everyone to choose or agree to *P*, then my knowledge that I have reason to do so need not depend on my knowledge of my particular position, tastes, preferences, etc. So, insofar as it makes any sense at all to speak of choosing or agreeing to something in the absence of this knowledge, it could be said that I have reason to choose or agree to those things which everyone has reason to choose or agree to (assuming, again, the aim of finding principles on which all could agree). And indeed, this same reasoning can carry us through to a version of stage three. For if I judge *P* to be a principle which everyone has reason to agree to, then it could be said that I would have reason to agree to it if I thought that I had an equal chance of being anybody, or indeed, if I assign any other set of probabilities to being one or another of the people in question.

But it is clear that this is not the conclusion at which the original argument aimed. That conclusion concerned what it would be rational for a self-interested person to choose or agree to under the assumption of ignorance or equal probability of being anyone. The conclusion we have reached appeals to a different notion: the idea of what it would be unreasonable for people to reject given that they are seeking a basis for general agreement. The direction of explanation in the two arguments is quite different. The original argument sought to explain the notion of impartial acceptability of an ethical principle by appealing to the notion of rational self-interested choice under special conditions, a notion which appears to be a clearer one. My revised argument explains how *a* sense might be attached to the idea of choice or agreement in ignorance of one's position given some idea of what it would be unreasonable for someone to reject as a basis for general agreement. This indicates a problem for my version of contractualism: it may be charged with failure to explain the central notion on which it relies. Here I would reply that my version of contractualism does not seek to explain this notion. It only tries to describe it

clearly and to show how other features of morality can be understood in terms of it. In particular, it does not try to explain this notion by reducing it to the idea of what would maximise a person's self-interested expectations if he were choosing from a position of ignorance or under the assumption of equal probability of being anyone.

The initial plausibility of the move from stage one to stage two of the original argument rests on a subtle transition from one of these notions to the other. To believe that a principle is morally correct one must believe that it is one which all could reasonably agree to and none could reasonably reject. But my belief that this is the case may often be distorted by a tendency to take its advantage to me more seriously than its possible costs to others. For this reason, the idea of "putting myself in another's place" is a useful corrective device. The same can be said for the thought experiment of asking what I could agree to in ignorance of my true position. But both of these thought experiments are devices for considering more accurately the question of what *everyone* could reasonably agree to or what no one could reasonably reject. That is, they involve the pattern of reasoning exhibited in my revised form of the three-stage argument, not that of the argument as originally given. The question, what would maximise the expectations of a single self-interested person choosing in ignorance of his true position, is a quite different question. This can be seen by considering the possibility that the distribution with the highest average utility, call it *A*, might involve extremely low utility levels for some people, levels much lower than the minimum anyone would enjoy under a more equal distribution.

Suppose that *A* is a principle which it would be rational for a self-interested chooser with an equal chance of being in anyone's position to select. Does it follow that no one could reasonably reject *A*? It seems evident that this does not follow.[16] Suppose that the situation of those who would fare worst under *A*, call them the Losers, is extremely bad, and that there is an alternative to A, call it E, under which no one's situation would be nearly as bad as this. Prima facie, the losers would seem to have a reasonable ground for complaint against A. Their objection may be rebutted, by appeal to the sacrifices that would be imposed on some other individual by the selection of E rather than A. But the mere fact that A yields higher average utility, which might be due to the fact that many people do very slightly better under A than under E while a very few do much worse, does not settle the matter.

Under contractualism, when we consider a principle our attention is naturally directed first to those who would do worst under it. This is because if anyone has reasonable grounds for objecting to the principle it is *likely* to be them. It does not follow, however, that contractualism always requires us to select the principle under which the expectations of the worse off are highest. The reasonableness of the Losers' objection to A is not established simply by the fact that they are worse off under A and no one would be this badly off under E. The force of their complaint depends also on the fact that their position under A is, in absolute terms, very bad, and would be significantly better under E. This complaint must be weighed against those of individuals who would do worse under E. The question to be asked is, is it unreasonable for someone to refuse to put up with the Losers' situation under A in order that someone else should be able to enjoy the benefits which he would have to give up under E? As the supposed situation of the Loser under A becomes better, or his gain under E smaller in relation to the sacrifices required to produce it, his case is weakened.

One noteworthy feature of contractualist argument as I have presented it so far is that it is non-aggregative: what are compared are individual gains, losses, and levels of welfare. How aggregative considerations can enter into contractualist argument is a further question too large to be entered into here.

I have been criticising an argument for Average Utilitarianism that is generally associated with Harsanyi, and my objections to this argument (leaving aside the last remarks about maximin) have an obvious similarity to objections raised by Rawls.[17] But the objections I have raised apply as well against some features of Rawls's own argument. Rawls accepts the first step of the argument I have described. That is, he believes that the correct principles of justice are those which "rational persons concerned to advance their interests" would accept under the conditions defined by his Original Position, where they would be ignorant of their own particular talents, their conception of the good, and the social position (or generation) into which they were born. It is the second step of the argument which Rawls rejects, that is, the claim that it would be rational for persons so situated to choose those principles which would offer them greatest expected utility under the assumption that they have an equal chance of being anyone in the society in question. I believe, however, that a mistake has already been made once the first step is taken.

This can be brought out by considering an ambiguity in the idea of acceptance by persons "concerned to advance their interests." On one reading, this is an essential ingredient in contractual argument; on another it is avoidable and, I think, mistaken. On the first reading, the interests in question are simply those of the members of society to whom the principles of justice are to apply (and by whom those principles must ultimately be accepted). The fact that they have interests which may conflict, and which they are concerned to advance, is what gives substance to questions of justice. On the second reading, the concern "to advance their interests" that is in question is a concern of the parties to Rawls's Original Position, and it is this concern which determines, in the first instance,[18] what principles of justice they will adopt. Unanimous agreement among these parties, each motivated to do as well for himself as he can, is to be achieved by depriving them of any information that could give them reason to choose differently from one another. From behind the veil of ignorance, what offers the best prospects for one will offer the best prospects for all, since no one can tell what would benefit him in particular. Thus the choice of principles can be made, Rawls says, from the point of view of a single rational individual behind the veil of ignorance.

Whatever rules of rational choice this single individual, concerned to advance his own interests as best he can, is said to employ, this reduction of the problem to the case of a single person's self-interested choice should arouse our suspicion. As I indicated in criticising Harsanyi, it is important to ask whether this single individual is held to accept a principle because he judges that it is one he could not reasonably reject whatever position he turns out to occupy, or whether, on the contrary, it is supposed to be acceptable to a person in any social position because it would be the rational choice for a single self-interested person behind the veil of ignorance. I have argued above that the argument for average utilitarianism involves a covert transition from the first pattern of reasoning to the second. Rawls's argument also appears to be of this second form; his defence of his two principles of justice relies, at least initially, on claims about what it would be rational for a person, concerned to advance his own interests, to choose behind a veil of ignorance. I would claim, however, that the plausibility of Rawls's arguments favouring his two principles over the principle of average utility is preserved, and in some cases enhanced, when they are interpreted as instances of the first form of contractualist argument.

Some of these arguments are of an informal moral character. I have already mentioned his remark about the unacceptability of imposing lower expectations on some for the sake of the higher expectations of others. More specifically, he says of the parties to the Original Position that they are concerned "to choose principles the consequences of which they are prepared to live with whatever generation they turn out to belong to"[19] or, presumably, whatever their social position turns out to be. This is a clear statement of the first form of contractualist argument. Somewhat later he remarks, in favour of the two principles, that they "are those a person would choose for the design of a society in which his enemy is to assign him a place."[20] Rawls goes on to dismiss this remark, saying that the parties "should not reason from false premises,"[21] but it is worth asking why it seemed a plausible thing to say in the first place. The reason, I take it, is this. In a contractualist argument of the first form, the object of which is to find principles acceptable to each person, assignment by a malevolent opponent is a thought experiment which has a heuristic role like that of a veil of ignorance: it is a way of testing whether one really does judge a principle to be acceptable from all points of view or whether, on the contrary, one is failing to take seriously its effect on people in social positions other than one's own.

But these are all informal remarks, and it is fair to suppose that Rawls's argument, like the argument for average utility, is intended to move from the informal contractualist idea of principles "acceptable to all" to the idea of rational choice behind a veil of ignorance, an idea which is, he hopes, more precise and more capable of yielding definite results. Let me turn then to his more formal arguments for the choice of the Difference Principle by the parties to the Original Position. Rawls cites three features of the decision faced by parties to the Original Position which, he claims, make it rational for them to use the maximin rule and, therefore, to select his Difference Principle as a principle of justice. These are (1) the absence of any objective basis for estimating probabilities, (2) the fact that some principles could have consequences for them which "they could hardly accept" while (3) it is possible for them (by following maximin) to ensure themselves of a minimum prospect, advances above which, in comparison, matter very little.[22] The first of these features is slightly puzzling, and I leave it aside. It seems clear, however, that the other considerations mentioned have at least as much force in an informal contractualist argument about what all could reasonably agree to as they do in determining the rational choice of a single person concerned to advance his interests. They express the strength of the objection that the "losers" might have to a scheme that maximised average utility at their expense, as compared with the counter-objections that others might have to a more egalitarian arrangement.

In addition to this argument about rational choice, Rawls invokes among "the main grounds for the two principles" other considerations which, as he says, use the concept of contract to a greater extent.[23] The parties to the Original Position, Rawls says, can agree to principles of justice only if they think that this agreement is one that they will actually be able to live up to. It is, he claims, more plausible to believe this of his two principles than of the principle of average utility, under which the sacrifices demanded ("the strains of commitment") could be much higher. A second, related claim is that the two principles of justice have greater psychological stability than the principle of average utility. It is more plausible to believe, Rawls claims, that in a society in which they were fulfilled people would continue to accept them and to be motivated to act in accordance with them. Continuing acceptance of the principle of average utility, on the other hand, would require an exceptional degree of identification with the good of the whole on the part of those from who sacrifices were demanded.

These remarks can be understood as claims about the "stability" (in a quite practical sense) of a society founded on Rawls's two principles of justice. But they can also be seen as an attempt to show that a principle arrived at via the second form of contractualist reasoning will also satisfy the requirements of the first form, that is, that it is something no one could reasonably reject. The question "Is the acceptance of this principle an agreement you could actually live up to?" is, like the idea of assignment by one's worst enemy, a thought experiment through which we can use our own reactions to test our judgement that certain principles are ones that no one could reasonably reject. General principles of human psychology can also be invoked to this same end.

Rawls's final argument is that the adoption of his two principles gives public support to the self-respect of individual members of society, and "give a stronger and more characteristic interpretation of Kant's idea"[24] that people must be treated as ends, not merely as means to the greater collective good. But, whatever difference there may be here between Rawls's two principles of justice and the principle of average utility, there is at least as sharp a contrast between the two patterns of contractualist reasoning distinguished above. The connection with self-respect, and with the Kantian formula, is preserved by the requirement that principles of justice be ones which no member of the society could reasonably reject. This connection is weakened when we shift to the idea of a choice which advances the interests of a single rational individual for whom the various individual lives in a society are just so many different possibilities. This is so whatever decision rule this rational chooser is said to employ. The argument from maximin seems to preserve this connection because it reproduces as a claim about rational choice what is, in slightly different terms, an appealing moral argument.

The "choice situation" that is fundamental to contractualism as I have described it is obtained by beginning with "mutually disinterested" individuals with full knowledge of their situations and adding to this (not, as is sometimes suggested, benevolence but) a desire on each of their parts to find principles which none could reasonably reject insofar as they too have this desire. Rawls several times considers such an idea in passing.[25] He rejects it in favour of his own idea of mutually disinterested choice from behind a veil of ignorance on the ground that only the latter enables us to reach definite results: "if in choosing principles we required unanimity even where there is full information, only a few rather obvious cases could be decided."[26] I believe that this supposed advantage is questionable. Perhaps this is because my expectations for moral argument are more modest than Rawls's. However, as I have argued, almost all of Rawls's own arguments have at least as much force when they are interpreted as arguments within the form of contractualism which I have been proposing. One possible exception is the argument from maximin. If the Difference Principle were taken to be generally applicable to decisions of public policy, then the second form of contractualist reasoning through which it is derived would have more far reaching implications than the looser form of argument by comparison of losses, which I have employed. But these wider applications of the principle are not always plausible, and I do not think that Rawls intends it to be applied so widely. His intention is that the Difference Principle should be applied only to major inequalities generated by the basic institutions of a society, and this limitation is a reflection of the special conditions under which he holds maximin to be the appropriate basis for rational choice: some choices have outcomes one could hardly accept, while gains above the minimum one can assure one's self matter very little, and so on. It follows, then, that in applying the Difference Principle—in identifying the limits of its applicability— we must fall back on the informal comparison of losses which is central to the form of contractualism I have described.

V

I have described this version of contractualism only in outline. Much more needs to be said to clarify its central notions and to work out its normative implications. I hope that I have said enough to indicate its appeal as a philosophical theory of morality and as an account of moral motivation. I have put forward contractualism as an alternative to utilitarianism, but the characteristic feature of the doctrine can be brought out by contrasting it with a somewhat different view.

It is sometimes said[27] that morality is a device for our mutual protection. According to contractualism, this view is partly true but in an important way incomplete. Our concern to protect our central interests will have an important effect on what we could reasonably agree to. It will thus have an important effect on the content of morality if contractualism is correct. To the degree that this morality is observed, these interests will gain from it. If we had no desire to be able to justify our actions to others on grounds they could reasonably accept, the hope of gaining this protection would give us reason to try to instil this desire in others, perhaps through mass hypnosis or conditioning, even if this also meant acquiring it ourselves. But given that we have this desire already, our concern with morality is less instrumental.

The contrast might be put as follows. On one view, concern with protection is fundamental, and general agreement becomes relevant as a means or a necessary condition for securing this protection. On the other, contractualist view, the desire for protection is an important factor determining the content of morality because it determines what can reasonably be agreed to. But the idea of general agreement does not arise as a means of securing protection. It is, in a more fundamental sense, what morality is about.

I am greatly indebted to Derek Parfit for patient criticism and enormously helpful discussion of many earlier versions of this paper. Thanks are due also to the many audiences who have heard parts of those versions delivered as lectures and kindly responded with helpful comments. In particular, I am indebted to Marshall Cohen, Ronald Dworkin, Owen Fiss, and Thomas Nagel for valuable criticism.

NOTES

1. Though here the ties between the nature of morality and its content are more important. It is not clear that an account of the nature of morality which left its content *entirely* open could be the basis for a plausible account of moral motivation.

2. See John Rawls, "The Independence of Moral Theory," *Proceedings and Addresses of the American Philosophical Association* 47 (1974–75): 8; and Norman Daniels, "Wide Reflective Equilibrium and Theory Acceptance in Ethics," *Journal of Philosophy* 76 (1979): 257–58. How closely the process of what I am calling philosophical explanation will coincide with the search for "wide reflective equilibrium" as this is understood by Rawls and by Daniels is a further question which I cannot take up here.

3. For expression of this dissatisfaction see Peter Singer, "Sidgwick and Reflective Equilibrium," *Monist* 58 (1974): 490–517, and Richard Brandt, A *Theory of the Good and the Right* (Oxford: Oxford University Press, 1979), pp. 16–21.

4. W. D. Ross, *The Right and the Good* (Oxford: Oxford University Press, 1939), pp. 52–54, 315.

5. For purposes of this discussion I leave open the important questions of which individuals are to count and how "well-being" is to be understood. Philosophical utilitarianism will retain the appeal I am concerned with under many different answers to these questions.

6. "Average Utilitarianism" is most plausibly arrived at through quite a different form of argument, one more akin to contractualism. I discuss one such argument in section IV below.

7. Here I am indebted to Gilbert Harman for comments which have helped me to clarify my statement of contractualism.

8. A point I owe to Derek Parfit

9. On this view (as contrasted with some others in which the notion of a contract is employed) what is fundamental to morality is the desire for reasonable agreement, not the pursuit of mutual advantage. See Section V below. It should be clear that this version of contractualism can account for the moral standing of future persons who will be better or worse off as a result of what we do now. It is less clear how it can deal with the problem presented by future people who would not have been born but for actions of ours which also made the conditions in which they live worse. Do such people have reason to reject principles allowing these actions to be performed? This difficult problem, which I cannot explore here, is raised by Derek Parfit in "On Doing the Best for Our Children," in *Ethics and Population*, ed. Michael Bayles (Cambridge: Schenkman Publishing, 1976).

10. Peter Singer, "Famine, Affluence, and Morality," *Philosophy and Public Affairs* 1 (1972): 229–43.

11. Reasonably, that is, given the desire to find principles which others similarly motivated could not reasonably reject.

12. Immanuel Kant, *Groundwork of the Metaphysics of Morals*, sec. 2, n. 14.

13. J. L. Mackie, *Ethics: Inventing Right and Wrong* (Harmondsworth, Middlesex: Pelican, 1977), p. 42.

14. See J. C. Harsanyi, "Cardinal Utility, Individualistic Ethics, and Interpersonal Comparisons of Utility," *Journal of Political Economy* 63 (1955): 309–21, sec. IV. He is there discussing an argument which he presented earlier in "Cardinal Utility in Welfare Economics and in the Theory of Risk-Taking," *Journal of Political Economy* 61 (1953): 434–35.

15. In discussing Harsanyi and Rawls I will generally follow them in speaking of the acceptability of principles rather than their unrejectability. The difference between these, pointed out above, is important only within the version of contractualism I am presenting; accordingly, I will speak of rejectability only when I am contrasting my own version with theirs.

16. The discussion which follows has much in common with the contrast between majority principles and unanimity principles drawn by Thomas Nagel in "Equality," chap. 8 of *Mortal Questions* (Cambridge: Cambridge University Press, 1979). I am indebted to Nagel's discussion of this idea.

17. For example, the intuitive argument against utilitarianism on page 14 of Rawls's *A Theory of Justice* and his repeated remark that we cannot expect some people to accept lower standards of life for the sake of the higher expectations of others.

18. Though they must then check to see that the principles they have chosen will be stable, not produce intolerable strains of commitment, and so on. As I argue below, these further considerations can be interpreted in a way that brings Rawls's theory closer to the version of contractualism presented here.

19. A *Theory of Justice*, p. 137.

20. Ibid., p. 152.

21. Ibid., p. 153.

22. Ibid., p. 154.

23. Ibid., sec. 29, pp. 175ff.

24. Ibid., p. 183.

25. E.g., ibid., pp. 141, 148, although these passages may not clearly distinguish between this alternative and an assumption of benevolence.

26. Ibid., p. 141.

27. In different ways by G. J. Warnock in *The Object of Morality* (London: Methuen & Co., 1971), and by J. L. Mackie in *Ethics: Inventing Right and Wrong*. See also Richard Brandt's remarks on justification in chap. X of *A Theory of the Good and the Right*.

16

Discourse Ethics: Notes on a Program of Philosophical Justification

JÜRGEN HABERMAS

... I call interactions *communicative* when the participants coordinate their plans of action consensually, with the agreement reached at any point being evaluated in terms of the intersubjective recognition of validity claims. In cases where agreement is reached through explicit linguistic processes, the actors make three different claims to validity in their speech acts as they come to an agreement with one another about something. Those claims are claims to truth, claims to rightness, and claims to truthfulness, according to whether the speaker refers to something in the objective world (as the totality of existing states of affairs), to something in the shared social world (as the totality of the legitimately regulated interpersonal relationships of a social group) or to something in his own subjective world (as the totality of experiences to which one has privileged access). Further, I distinguish between communicative and strategic action. Whereas in strategic action one actor seeks to *influence* the behavior of another by means of the threat of sanctions or the prospect of gratification in order to *cause* the interaction to continue as the first actor desires, in communicative action one actor seeks *rationally* to *motivate* another by relying on the illocutionary binding/bonding effect (*Bindungseffekt*) of the offer contained in his speech act.

The fact that a speaker can rationally motivate a hearer to accept such an offer is due not to the validity of what he says but to the speaker's guarantee that he will, if necessary, make efforts to redeem the claim that the hearer has accepted. It is this guarantee that effects the coordination between speaker and hearer. In the case of claims to truth or rightness, the speaker can redeem his guarantee discursively, that is, by adducing reasons; in the case of claims to truthfulness he does so through consistent behavior. (A person can convince someone that he means what he says only through his actions, not by giving reasons.) As soon as the hearer accepts the guarantee offered by the speaker, obligations are assumed that have consequences for the interaction, obligations that are contained in the meaning of what was said. In the case of orders and directives, for instance, the obligations to act hold primarily for the hearer, in the case of promises and announcements, they hold for the speaker, in the case of agreements and contracts, they are symmetrical, holding for both parties, and in the case of substantive normative recommendations and warnings, they hold asymmetrically for both parties.

Unlike these regulative speech acts, the meaning of a constative speech act gives rise to obligations only insofar as the speaker and the hearer agree to base their actions on situational definitions that do not contradict the propositions they accept as true at any given point. Obligations to act flow directly from the meaning of an expressive speech act in that the speaker specifies what it is that his behavior does not contradict and will not contradict in the future. Owing to the fact that communication oriented to reaching understanding has a validity basis, a speaker can persuade a hearer to accept a speech-act offer by guaranteeing that he will redeem a criticizable validity claim. In so doing, he creates a binding/bonding effect between speaker and hearer that makes the continuation of their interaction possible.

The two *discursively redeemable* claims to validity that are of particular interest to us, claims to propositional truth and claims to normative rightness, play their roles as coordinators of action in different ways. A number of asymmetries between them suggest that they occupy different "positions" in the communicative practice of everyday life.

On the face of it, *assertoric statements* used in *constative speech acts* appear to be related to *facts* as *normative statements* used in *regulative speech acts* are related to *legitimately ordered interpersonal relations*. The *truth* of propositions seems to signify the *existence* of states of affairs in much the same way as the *rightness* of actions signifies the *observance* of norms. If we look at the matter more closely, however, we notice some

interesting differences. The relation of speech acts to norms is not the same as the relation of speech acts to facts. Let us look at the case of moral norms that can be formulated in terms of universal "ought" sentences or commandments:

(a) One ought not to kill anybody.
(a′) It is commanded not to kill anybody.

We make reference to norms of action of the above kind in regulative speech acts, and we do so in a variety of ways: by giving orders, making contracts, opening meetings, issuing warnings, granting exceptions, giving advice, etc. A moral norm, however, lays claim to meaning and validity regardless of whether it is promulgated or made use of in a specific way. A norm may be formulated in a statement like (a), but this act of formulating it, that is, of writing a sentence, *need not* itself be conceived of as a speech act, that is, as something other than the impersonal expression of the norm. Statements such as (a) are commands that we can address *secondarily* in one way or another through speech acts. This has no equivalent in the domain of facts. There are no assertoric propositions that have an existence independent of speech acts, as norms do. If such assertoric statements are to have pragmatic meaning at all, they *must* be used in a speech act. Unlike sentences (a) and (a′), descriptive statements such as "Iron is magnetic" or "It is the case that iron is magnetic" cannot be expressed or used independently of the illocutionary role of a certain type of speech act if they are to retain their assertoric power.

We can account for this asymmetry by saying that claims to truth reside *only* in speech acts, whereas the locus of normative claims to validity is primarily in norms and only derivatively in speech acts.[1] To use an ontological mode of expression, we might say that this asymmetry is due to the fact that the orders of society, which we either conform to or deviate from, are not constituted *independently of validity*, as are the orders of nature, toward which we can assume an objectivating attitude. The social reality that we address in our regulative speech acts has by its very nature an *intrinsic* link to normative validity claims. Claims to truth, on the other hand, have no such intrinsic link to entities; they are inherently related only to the constative speech acts by which we refer to entities when we use fact-stating locutions to represent states of affairs.

Owing to the fact that normative validity claims are built into the universe of norms, the latter reveals a peculiar kind of objectivity vis-à-vis regulative speech acts, an objectivity that the universe of facts does not possess vis-à-vis constative speech acts. To be sure, "objectivity" in this connection refers only to the independence of "objective spirit," for entities and facts are, of course, independent in a completely different sense than is everything we consider part of the social world when we take a norm-conformative attitude. For example, norms are dependent upon the continual reestablishment of legitimately ordered interpersonal relationships. They would assume a utopian character in the negative sense and lose their very meaning if we did not *complement* them, at least in our minds, with actors who might follow them and actions that might fulfill them. States of affairs, for their part, must be assumed to exist independently of whether we formulate them by means of true propositions or not.

Normative claims to validity, then, *mediate a mutual dependence* of language and the social world that does not exist for the relation of language to the objective world. This interlocking of claims to validity that reside in norms and claims to validity raised in regulative speech acts is also connected with the *ambiguous nature of normative validity*. While there is an unequivocal relation between existing states of affairs and true propositions about them, the "existence" or social currency of norms says nothing about whether the norms are valid. We must distinguish between the social fact that a norm

is intersubjectively recognized and its worthiness to be recognized. There may be good reasons to consider the validity claim raised in a socially accepted norm to be unjustified. Conversely, a norm whose claim to validity is in fact redeemable does not necessarily meet with actual recognition or approval. Gaining acceptance on the part of a norm is encoded in a twofold fashion because our motives for recognizing normative claims to validity are rooted both in convictions and in sanctions, that is, they derive from a complex mixture of rational insight and force. Typically, rationally motivated assent will be combined with empirical *acquiescence*, effected by weapons or goods, to form a belief in legitimacy whose component parts are difficult to isolate. Such alloys are interesting in that they indicate that a positivistic enactment of norms is not sufficient to secure their *lasting* social acceptance. Enduring acceptance of a norm *also* depends on whether, in a given context of tradition, reasons for obedience can be mobilized, reasons that suffice to make the corresponding validity claim at least appear justified in the eyes of those concerned. Applied to modern societies, this means that there is no mass loyalty without legitimacy.[2]

But if in the long run the social currency of a norm depends on its being accepted as valid in the group to which it is addressed and if this recognition is based in turn on the expectation that the corresponding claim to validity can be redeemed with reasons, it follows that there is a connection between the "existence" of norms and the anticipated justifiability of the corresponding "ought" statements, a connection for which there is no parallel in the ontic sphere. While there is an internal connection between the existence of states of affairs and the truth of assertoric statements, there is no inner connection between the existence of states of affairs and the *expectation*, held by a certain group of people, that such statements can be justified. This difference may also explain why, when we ask what makes valid moral judgments possible, we are compelled to proceed *directly* to a logic of practical discourse, whereas determining the conditions for the validity of empirical judgments requires analysis in terms of epistemology and the philosophy of science, an analysis that is, at least initially, independent of a logic of theoretical discourse.

4. The Moral Principle, or the Criterion for Generalizing Maxims of Action

. . . In what follows, I presuppose that a theory of argumentation must take the form of an "informal logic," because it is impossible to *force* agreement on theoretical and moral-practical issues either by means of deduction or on the basis of empirical evidence. To the degree to which arguments are deductively valid, that is, compelling in terms of logical inference, they reveal nothing substantively new. To the degree to which arguments do have substantive content, they are based on experiences and needs/wants that are open to various interpretations in the light of changing theories using changing systems of description. Such experiences and needs/wants thus fail to offer an *ultimate* basis for argumentation.

In theoretical discourse the gap between particular observations and general hypotheses is bridged by some canon or other of induction. An analogous bridging principle is needed for practical discourse.[3] Accordingly, all studies of the logic of moral argumentation end up having to introduce a moral principle as a rule of argumentation that has a function equivalent to the principle of induction in the discourse of the empirical sciences.

Interestingly enough, in trying to identify such a moral principle, philosophers of diverse backgrounds always come up with principles whose basic idea is the same. *All* variants of cognitivist ethics take their bearings from the basic intuition contained in Kant's categorical imperative. What I am concerned with here is not the diversity of Kantian formulation but their underlying idea, which is designed to take into account the impersonal or general character of valid universal commands.[4] The moral principle is so conceived as to exclude as invalid any norm that could not meet with the qualified assent of all who are or might be affected by it. This bridging principle, which makes consensus possible, ensures that only those norms accepted as valid that express a *general will*. As Kant noted time and again, moral norms must be suitable for expression as "universal laws." The categorical imperative can be understood as a principle that requires the universalizability of *modes of action* and *maxims*, or of the *interests* furthered by them (that is, those embodied in the norms of action). Kant wants to eliminate as invalid all those norms that "contradict" this requirement. He focuses on "that inner contradiction which promptly arises for an agent's maxim when his behavior can lead to its desired goal only upon the condition that it is not universally followed".[5] Admittedly, this and similar versions of the bridging principle imply a requirement of consistency which has led to *formalistic misunderstandings* and *selective interpretations.*

The principle of universalization is by no means exhausted by the requirement that moral norms must take the *form* of unconditionally universal "ought" statements. The *grammatical form* of normative statements alone, which does not permit such sentences to refer to or be addressed to particular groups or individuals, is not a sufficient condition for valid moral commands, for we could give such universal form to commands that are plainly immoral. What is more, in some respects the requirement of formal universality may well be too restrictive; it may make sense to submit nonmoral norms of action (whose range of jurisdiction is socially and spatiotemporally limited) to a practical discourse (restricted in this case to those affected and hence relative), and to test them for generalizability.

. . . True impartiality pertains only to that standpoint from which one can generalize precisely those norms that can count on universal assent because they perceptibly embody an interest common to all affected. It is these norms that deserve intersubjective recognition. Thus the impartiality of judgment is expressed in a principle that constrains *all* affected to adopt the perspectives of *all others* in the balancing of interests. The principle of universalization is intended to compel the *universal exchange of roles* that G. H. Mead called "ideal role taking" or "universal discourse."[6] Thus every valid norm has to fulfill the following condition:

(U) *All* affected can accept the consequences and the side effects its *general* observance can be anticipated to have for the satisfaction of *everyone's* interests (and these consequences are preferred to those of known alternative possibilities for regulation).[7]

We should not mistake this principle of universalization (U) for the following principle, which already contains the distinctive idea of an ethics of discourse.

(D) Only those norms can claim to be valid that meet (or could meet) with the approval of all affected in their capacity *as participants in a practical discourse.*

This principle of discourse ethics (D), to which I will return after offering my justification for (U), already *presupposes* that we *can* justify our choice of a norm. At this point in my argument, that presupposition is what is at issue. I have introduced (U) as a rule of argumentation that makes agreement in practical discourses possible whenever matters of concern to all are open to regulation in the equal interest of everyone. Once this bridging principle has been justified, we will be able to make the transition to discourse ethics. I have formulated (U) in a way that precludes a monological application of the

principle. First, (U) regulates only argumentation among a plurality of participants; second, it suggests the perspective of real-life argumentation, in which all affected are admitted as participants. In this respect my universalization principle differs from the one John Rawls proposes.

Rawls wants to ensure impartial consideration of all affected interests by putting the moral judge into a fictitious "original position," where differences of power are eliminated, equal freedoms for all are guaranteed, and the individual is left in a condition of ignorance with regard to the position he might occupy in a future social order. Like Kant, Rawls operationalizes the standpoint of impartiality in such a way that every individual can undertake to justify basic norms on his own. The same holds for the moral philosopher himself. It is only logical, therefore, that Rawls views the substantive parts of his study (e.g., the principle of average utility), not as the *contribution* of a participant in argumentation to a process of discursive will formation regarding the basic institutions of late capitalist society, but as the outcome of a "theory of justice," which he as an expert is qualified to construct.

If we keep in mind the action-coordinating function that normative validity claims play in the communicative practice of everyday life, we see why the problems to be resolved in moral argumentation cannot be handled monologically but require a cooperative effort. By entering into a process of moral argumentation, the participants continue their communicative action in a reflexive attitude with the aim of restoring a consensus that has been disrupted. Moral argumentation thus serves to settle conflicts of action by consensual means. Conflicts in the domain of norm-guided interactions can be traced directly to some disruption of a normative consensus. Repairing a disrupted consensus can mean one of two things: restoring intersubjective recognition of a validity claim after it has become controversial or assuring intersubjective recognition for a new validity claim that is a substitute for the old one. Agreement of this kind expresses a *common will*. If moral argumentation is to produce this kind of agreement, however, it is not enough for the individual to reflect on whether he can assent to a norm. It is not even enough for each individual to reflect in this way and then to register his vote. What is needed is a "real" process of argumentation in which the individuals concerned cooperate. Only an intersubjective process of reaching understanding can produce an agreement that is reflexive in nature; only it can give the participants the knowledge that they have collectively become convinced of something.

From this viewpoint, the categorical imperative needs to be reformulated as follows: "Rather than ascribing as valid to all others any maxim that I can will to be a universal law, I must submit my maxim to all others for purposes of discursively testing its claim to universality. The emphasis shifts from what each can will without contradiction to be a general law, to what all can will in agreement to be a general law, to what all can will in agreement to be a universal norm."[8] This version of the universality principle does in fact entail the idea of a cooperative process of argumentation. For one thing, nothing better prevents others from perspectively distorting one's own interests than actual participation. It is in this pragmatic sense that the individual is the last court of appeal for judging what is in his best interest. On the other hand, the descriptive terms in which each individual perceives his interests must be open to criticism by others. Needs and wants are interpreted in the light of cultural values. Since cultural values are always components of intersubjectively shared traditions, the revision of the values used to interpret needs and wants cannot be a matter for individuals to handle monologically.[9] . . .

Discourse ethics, then, stands or falls with two assumptions: (a) that normative claims to validity have cognitive meaning and can be treated *like* claims to truth and (b) that the justification of norms and commands requires that a real discourse be carried out and thus cannot occur in a strictly monological form, that is, in the form of a hypothetical process of argumentation occurring in the individual mind. . . .

III. DISCOURSE ETHICS AND ITS BASES IN ACTION THEORY

With the introduction of the principle of universalization, the first step in the justification of a discourse ethics has been accomplished. We can review the systematic content of the argument in the form of an imaginary debate between an advocate of ethical cognitivism and an advocate of moral skepticism.

The opening round was a matter of opening the die-hard skeptic's eyes to the domain of *moral phenomena*. In the second round the issue was whether practical questions *admit of truth*. We saw that as an ethical subjectivist the skeptic could score some points against the ethical objectivist. The cognitivist could salvage his position by asserting that for normative statements a claim to validity is only *analogous to a truth claim*. The third round opened with the skeptic's realistic observation that it is often impossible to reach a consensus on questions of moral principle, despite the best intentions of all concerned. Faced with a *pluralism of ultimate value orientations*, which seems to support the skeptic's position, the cognitivist has to try to demonstrate the existence of a bridging principle that makes consensus possible. A moral principle having been proposed, the question of cultural relativism occupies the next round of the argumentation. The skeptic voices the objection that (U) represents a hasty generalization of moral intuitions peculiar to our own Western culture, a challenge to which the cognitivist will respond with a *transcendental justification* of his moral principle. In round 5 the skeptic brings in further objections to the strategy of transcendental justification, and the cognitivist meets them with a more cautious version of Apel's argument. In the sixth round, in the face of this promising justification of a discourse ethics, the skeptic can take refuge in a *refusal to enter into discourse*. But as we will see, by doing so he has maneuvered himself into a hopeless position. The theme of the seventh and last round of the debate is the skeptic's revival of the objections to ethical formalism that Hegel brought up in his criticism of Kant. On this issue the astute cognitivist will not hesitate to meet the well-considered reservations of his opponent halfway. . . .

This is where the debate stands now. Next the skeptic will demand a justification for this bridging principle. In Section 6 I will meet the charge of having committed the ethnocentric fallacy with Apel's proposal for a transcendental-pragmatic justification of ethics. I will modify Apel's argument (in Section 7) so as to give up any claim to "ultimate justification," without damage to the argument. In Section 8 I will defend the principle of discourse ethics against the skeptic's renewed objections by showing that moral arguments are embedded in contexts of communicative action. This internal connection between morality and ethical life does not impose limits on the universality of moral claims of validity, but it does subject practical discourses to constraints to which theoretical discourses are not subject in the same way.

6. Is a Justification of the Moral Principle Necessary and Possible?

. . . Where he does not simply appeal to a "fact of reason," Kant bases his justification of the categorical imperative on the substantive normative concepts of autonomy and free will; by doing so he makes himself vulnerable to the objection that he has committed a *petitio principii*. In any case, the justification of the categorical imperative is so closely intertwined with the overall design of Kant's system that it would not be easy to defend it if the premises were changed.

Contemporary moral theorists do not even offer a justification of the moral principle but content themselves with reconstructing pretheoretical knowledge. A case in point is John Rawls's concept of reflective equilibrium.[10] Another example is the constructivist proposal to erect a language of moral argumentation on a systematic basis; the introduction of a moral principle that regulates language is convincing only because it conceptually explicates *extant* intuitions.[11]

I am not dramatizing the situation when I say that faced with the demand for a justification of the universal validity of the principle of universalization, cognitivists are in trouble.[12]

The skeptic feels emboldened to recast his *doubts* about the possibility of justifying a universalist morality as an *assertion* that it is impossible to justify such a morality. . . .

[T]he necessary justification of the proposed moral principle could take the following form: every argumentation, regardless of the context in which it occurs, rests on pragmatic presuppositions from whose propositional content the principle of universalism (U) can be derived.

7. The Structure and Status of the Transcendental-Pragmatic Argument

. . . I will begin in section 1 by enumerating certain conditions that all transcendental-pragmatic arguments must satisfy. I will then use these criteria to assess two of the best known proposals of this kind, namely those of R. S. Peters and K. O. Apel. In section 2 I will present a version of the transcendental-pragmatic argument that can stand up to the familiar objections against it. Finally, in section 3 I will show that this justification of discourse ethics cannot have the status of an ultimate justification and why there is no need to claim this status for it.

1. Following Collingwood, a type of philosophical analysis has gained credence in

England that corresponds quite closely to the procedure Apel terms "transcendental pragmatics." A. J. Watt calls it "analysis of the presuppositions of a mode of discourse." Watt characterizes the structure of this approach as follows:

> The strategy of this form of argument is to accept the skeptical conclusion that these principles are not open to any proof, being presuppositions of reasoning rather than conclusions from it, but to go on to argue that commitment to them is rationally inescapable because they must, logically, be assumed if one is to engage in a mode of thought essential to any rational human life. The claim is not exactly that the principles are *true*, but that their adoption is not a result of mere social convention or free personal decision: that a mistake is involved in repudiating them while continuing to use the form of thought and discourse in question.[13]

Collingwood's influence shows up in the application of presuppositional analysis to the way specific *questions* are posed and dealt with: "A presuppositional justification would show that one was committed to certain principles by raising and considering a certain range of *questions*."[14] The purpose of such arguments is to prove that certain discourses entail inescapable presuppositions; moral principles have to be derivable from the propositional content of such presuppositions. The significance of these arguments is proportional to the degree of generality of the discourses that entail substantive normative presuppositions. Strictly speaking, arguments cannot be called transcendental unless they deal with discourses, or the corresponding competences, so general that it is impossible to replace them by functional equivalents; they must be constituted in such a way that they can be replaced only with discourses or competences of the same kind. Accordingly, it is of the utmost importance to specify the precise object domain to which presuppositional analysis is to be applied. . . .

2. We must return to the justification of the principle of universalization. We are now in a position to specify the role that the transcendental-pragmatic argument can play in this process. Its function is to help to show that the principle of universalization, which acts as a rule of argumentation, is implied by the presuppositions of argumentation in general. This requirement is met if the following can be shown:

> Every person who accepts the universal and necessary communicative presuppositions of argumentative speech and who knows what it means to justify a norm of action implicitly presupposes as valid the principle of universalization, whether in the form I gave it above or in an equivalent form.

It makes sense to distinguish three levels of presuppositions of argumentation along the lines suggested by Aristotle: those at the logical level of products, those at the dialectical level of procedures, and those at the rhetorical level of processes.[15] First, reasoning or argumentation is designed to *produce* intrinsically cogent arguments with which we can redeem or repudiate claims to validity. This is the level at which I would situate the rules of a minimal logic currently being discussed by Popperians, for example, and the consistency requirements proposed by Hare and others. For simplicity I will follow the catalog of presuppositions of argumentation drawn up by R. Alexy.[16] For the logical-semantic level, the following rules[17] can serve as *examples*:

(1.1) No speaker may contradict himself.
(1.2) Every speaker who applies predicate F to object A must be prepared to apply F to all other objects resembling A in all relevant aspects.
(1.3) Different speakers may not use the same expression with different meanings.

The presuppositions of argumentation at this level are logical and semantic rules that have no ethical content. They are not a suitable point of departure for a transcendental-pragmatic argument.

In *procedural* terms, arguments are processes of reaching understanding that are ordered in such a way that proponents and opponents, having assumed a hypothetical attitude and being relieved of the pressures of action and experience, can test validity claims that have become problematic. At this level are located the pragmatic presuppositions of a special form of interaction, namely everything necessary for a search for truth organized in the form of a competition. Examples include recognition of the accountability and truthfulness of all participants in the search. At this level I also situate general rules of jurisdiction and relevance that regulate themes for discussion, contributions to the argument, etc.[18] Again I cite a few examples from Alexy's catalog of rules:

(2.1) Every speaker may assert only what he really believes.

(2.2) A person who disputes a proposition or norm not under discussion must provide a reason for wanting to do so.

Some of these rules obviously have an ethical import. At this level what comes to the fore are presuppositions common both to discourses and to action oriented to reaching understanding as such, for example, presuppositions about relations of mutual recognition.

But to fall back here directly on the basis of argumentation in action theory would be to put the cart before the horse. Yet the presuppositions of an unrestrained competition for better arguments are relevant to our purpose in that they are irreconcilable with traditional ethical philosophies that have to protect a dogmatic core of fundamental convictions from all criticism.

Finally, in *process* terms, argumentative speech is a process of communication that, in light of its goal of reaching a rationally motivated agreement, must satisfy improbable conditions. In argumentative speech we see the structures of a speech situation immune to repression and inequality in a particular way: it presents itself as a form of communication that adequately approximates ideal conditions. This is why I tried at one time to describe the presuppositions of argumentation as the defining characteristics of an ideal speech situation.[19] I cannot here undertake the elaboration, revision, and clarification that my earlier analysis requires, and accordingly, the present essay is rightly characterized as a sketch or a proposal. The intention of my earlier analysis still seems correct to me, namely the reconstruction of the general symmetry conditions that every competent speaker who believes he is engaging in an argumentation must presuppose as adequately fulfilled. The presupposition of something like an "unrestricted communication community," an idea that Apel developed following Peirce and Mead, can be demonstrated through systematic analysis of performative contradictions. Participants in argumentation cannot avoid the presupposition that, owing to certain characteristics that require formal description, the structure of their communication rules out all external or internal coercion other than the force of the better argument and thereby also neutralizes all motives other than that of the cooperative search for truth.

Following my analysis, R. Alexy has suggested the following rules of discourse for this level:[20]

(3.1) Every subject with the competence to speak and act is allowed to take part in a discourse.

(3.2) a. Everyone is allowed to question any assertion whatever.
b. Everyone is allowed to introduce any assertion whatever into the discourse.
c. Everyone is allowed to express his attitudes, desires, and needs.[21]

(3.3) No speaker may be prevented, by internal or external coercion, from exercising his rights as laid down in (3.1) and (3.2).

A few explanations are in order here. Rule (3.1) defines the set of potential participants. It includes all subjects without exception who have the capacity to take part in argumentation. Rule (3.2) guarantees all participants equal opportunity to contribute to the argumentation and to put forth their own arguments. Rule (3.3) sets down conditions under which the rights to universal access and to equal participation can be enjoyed equally by all, that is, without the possibility of repression, be it ever so subtle or covert.

If these considerations are to amount to more than a definition favoring an ideal form of communication and thus prejudging everything else, we must show that these rules of discourse are not mere *conventions*; rather, they are inescapable presuppositions.

The presuppositions themselves are identified by convincing a person who contests the hypothetical reconstructions offered that he is caught up in performative contradictions.[22] In this process I must appeal to the intuitive preunderstanding that every subject competent in speech and action brings to a process of argumentation. Here I will content myself with discussing a few examples, indicating what such an analysis might actually look like.

The statement

(1) Using good reasons, I finally convinced H that p

can be read as someone's report on the outcome of a discourse. In this discourse the speaker, by using reasons, motivated the hearer to accept the truth claim connected with the assertion that p, that is, to consider p true. Central to the meaning of the word "convince" is the idea that a subject other than the speaker adopts a view on the basis of good reasons. This is why the statement

(2) *Using lies, I finally convinced H that p is nonsensical. It can be revised to

(3) Using lies, I finally talked H into believing that p.

I can refer someone to a dictionary to look up the meaning of the verb "to convince." But that will not explain *why* statement (2) is a semantic paradox that can be reso!ved by statement (3). To explain that, I can start with the internal connection between the expressions "to convince someone of something" and "to come to a reasoned agreement about something." In the *final* analysis, convictions rest on a consensus that has been attained discursively. Now statement (2) implies that H has formed his conviction under conditions that simply do not permit the formation of convictions. Such conditions contradict the pragmatic presuppositions of argumentation as such (in this case rule [2.1]). This presupposition holds not only for particular instances but inevitably for every process of argumentation. I can prove this by making a proponent who defends the truth of statement (2) aware that he thereby gets himself into a performative contradiction. For as soon as he cites a reason for the truth of (2), he enters a process of argumentation and has thereby accepted the presupposition, among others, that he can never *convince* an opponent of something by resorting to lies; at most, he can talk him into believing something to be true. But then the content of the assertion to be justified contradicts one of the presuppositions the proponent must operate with if his statement is to be regarded as a justification.

Similarly, performative contradictions can be demonstrated in the statements of a proponent who tries to justify the following sentence:

(4) *Having excluded persons A, B, C, . . . from the discussion by silencing them or by foisting our interpretation on them, we were able to convince ourselves that N is justified.

Here A, B, C . . . are assumed to be among the persons who would be affected by putting norm *N* into effect and to be indistinguishable in their capacity as *participants in argumentation* in all relevant respects from the other participants. In any attempt to justify statement (4), a proponent necessarily contradicts the presuppositions set out in rules (3.1) to (3.3).

In giving these presuppositions the form of rules, Alexy may well be promoting the misconception that all actual discourses must conform to these rules. In many cases this is clearly not so, and in all cases we have to be content with approximations. This misconception may have something to do with the ambiguity of the word "rule." Rules of discourse in Alexy's sense are not *constitutive* of discourses in the sense in which chess rules are constitutive of real chess games. Whereas chess rules *determine* the playing of actual chess games, discourse rules are merely the *form* in which we present the implicity adopted and intuitively known pragmatic presuppositions of a special type of speech, presuppositions that are adopted implicitly and known intuitively. If one wanted to make a serious comparison between argumentation and chess playing, one would find that the closest equivalents to the rules of chess are the rules to the construction and exchange of arguments. These rules must be followed in *actual fact* if error-free argumentation is to take place in real life. By contrast, discourse rules (3.1) to (3.3) state only that participants in argumentation must assume these conditions to be approximately realized, or realized in an approximation adequate enough for the purpose of argumentation, regardless of whether and to what extent these assumptions are counterfactual in a given case or not.

Discourses take place in particular social contexts and are subject to the limitations of time and space. Their participants are not Kant's intelligible characters but real human beings driven by other motives in addition to the one permitted motive of the search for truth. Topics and contributions have to be organized. The opening, adjournment, and resumption of discussions must be arranged.

Because of all these factors, institutional measures are needed to sufficiently neutralize empirical limitations and avoidable internal and external interference so that the idealized conditions always already presupposed by participants in argumentation can at least be adequately approximated. The need to institutionalize discourses, trivial though it may be, does not contradict the partly counterfactual content of the presuppositions of discourse. On the contrary, attempts at institutionalization are subject in turn to normative conceptions and their goal, which spring *spontaneously* from our intuitive grasp of what argumentation is. This assertion can be verified empirically by studying the authorizations, exemptions, and procedural rules that have been used to institutionalize theoretical discourse in science or practical discourse in parliamentary activity.[23] To avoid the fallacy of misplaced concreteness, one must carefully differentiate between rules of discourse and conventions serving the institutionalization of discourses, conventions that help to actualize the ideal content of the presuppositions of argumentation under empirical conditions.

If after these cursory remarks we accept the rules tentatively set down by Alexy (pending a more detailed analysis), we have at our disposal, in conjunction with a weak idea of normative justification (i.e., one that does not prejudge the matter), premises that are strong enough for the derivation of the universalization principle (U).

If every person entering a process of argumentation must, among other things, make presuppositions whose content can be expressed in rules (3.1) to (3.3) and if we understand what it means to discuss hypothetically whether norms of action ought to be adopted, then everyone who seriously tries to *discursively* redeem normative claims to validity intuitively accepts procedural conditions that amount to implicitly acknowledging (U). It follows from the aforementioned rules of discourse that a contested norm cannot meet with the consent of the participants in a practical discourse unless (U) holds, that is,

> Unless all affected can *freely* accept the consequences and the side effects that the *general* observance of a controversial norm can be expected to have for the satisfaction of the interests of *each individual.*

But once it has been shown that (U) can be grounded upon the presuppositions of argumentation through a transcendental-pragmatic derivation, discourse ethics itself can be formulated in terms of the principle of discourse ethics (D), which stipulates,

> Only those norms can claim to be valid that meet (or could meet) with the approval of all affected in their capacity as participants in a practical discourse.[24]

The justification of discourse ethics outlined here avoids confusions in the use of the term "moral principle." The only moral principle here is the universalization principle (U), which is conceived as a rule of argumentation and is part of the logic of practical discourses. (U) must be carefully distinguished from the following:

- Substantive principles or basic norms, which can only be the *subject matter* of moral argumentation
- The normative content of the presuppositions of argumentation, which can be expressed in terms of rules, as in (3.1) to (3.3)
- The principle of discourse ethics (D), which stipulates the basic idea of a moral theory but does not form part of a logic of argumentation

Previous attempts to ground discourse ethics were flawed because they tended to collapse *rules, contents, presuppositions* of argumentation and in addition confused all of these with moral principles in the sense of principles of philosophical ethics. (D) is the

assertion that the philosopher as moral theorist ultimately seeks to justify. The program of justification I have outlined in this essay describes what I regard as the most promising *road* to that goal. This road is the transcendental-pragmatic justification of a rule of argumentation with normative content. This rule is selective, to be sure, but it is also formal. It is not compatible with all substantive legal and moral principles, but it does not prejudge substantive regulations, as it is a rule of argumentation only. All contents, no matter how fundamental the action norm involved may be, must be made to depend on real discourses (or advocatory discourses conducted as substitutes for them). The moral theorist may take part in them as one of those concerned, perhaps even as an expert, but he cannot conduct such discourses by *himself alone.* To the extent to which a moral theory touches on substantive areas—as Rawls's theory of justice does, for example—it must be understood as a contribution to a discourse among citizens. . . .

3. . . . My programmatic justification of discourse ethics requires all of the following:

1. A definition of a universalization principle that functions as a rule of argumentation

2. The identification of pragmatic presuppositions of argumentation that are inescapable and have a normative content

3. The explicit statement of that normative content (e.g., in the form of discourse rules)

4. Proof that a relation of material implication holds between steps (3) and (1) in connection with the idea of the justification of norms

Step (2) in the analysis, for which the search for performative contradictions provides a guide, relies upon a maieutic method that serves

2a. to make the skeptic who presents an objection aware of presuppositions he knows intuitively,

2b. to cast this pretheoretical knowledge in an explicit form that will enable the skeptic to recognize his intuitions in this description,

2c. to corroborate, through counterexamples, the proponent's assertion that there are no alternatives to the presuppositions he has made explicit.

Substeps (2b) and (2c) contain unmistakable hypothetical elements. The description we employ to pass from knowing how to knowing that is a hypothetical reconstruction that can provide only a more or less correct rendering of intuitions. It needs maieutic confirmation. Similarly, the assertion that there is no alternative to a given presuppositon, that it is one of the inescapable (i.e., necessary and general) presuppositions, has the status of an assumption. Like a lawlike hypothesis (*Gesetzeshypothese*), it must be checked against individual cases. To be sure, the intuitive knowledge of rules that subjects capable of speech and action must use if they are to be able to participate in argumentation is in a certain sense not fallible. But this is not true of *our reconstruction* of this pretheoretical knowledge and the claim to universality that we connect with it. The *certainty* with which we put our knowledge of rules into practice does not extend to the *truth* of proposed reconstructions of presuppositions hypothesized to be general, for we have to put our reconstructions up for discussion in the same way in which the logician or the linguist, for example, presents his theoretical descriptions.

No harm is done, however, if we deny that the transcendental-pragmatic justification constitutes an ultimate justification. Rather, discourse ethics then takes its place among the reconstructive sciences concerned with the rational bases of knowing, speaking, and acting. If we cease striving for the foundationalism of traditional transcendental philosophy, we acquire new corroborative pos-

sibilities for discourse ethics. In competition with other ethical approaches, it can be used to describe empirically existing moral and legal ideas. It can be built into theories of the development of moral and legal consciousness at both the sociocultural and the ontogenetic levels and in this way can be made susceptible to indirect corroboration.

Nor need moral philosophy maintain the claim to ultimate justification because of its presumed relevance for the lifeworld. The *moral* intuitions of everyday life are not in need of clarification by the philosopher. In this case the therapeutic self-understanding of philosophy initiated by Wittgenstein is for once, I think, appropriate. Moral philosophy does have an enlightening or clarificatory role to play vis-à-vis the confusions that it has created in the minds of the educated, that is, to the extent to which value skepticism and legal positivism have established themselves as professional ideologies and have infiltrated everyday consciousness by way of the educational system. Together skepticism and positivism have misinterpreted and thus neutralized the intuitions people acquire in a quasi-natural manner through socialization. Under extreme conditions they can contribute to the moral disarmament of academics already in the grip of a cultivated skepticism.[25]

8. Morality and Ethical Life (*Sittlichkeit*)

1. The principle of discourse ethics (D) makes reference to a *procedure*, namely the discursive redemption of normative claims to validity. To that extent discourse ethics can properly be characterized as *formal*, for it provides no substantive guidelines but only a procedure: practical discourse. Practical discourse is not a procedure for generating justified norms but a procedure for testing the validity of norms that are being proposed and hypothetically considered for adoption. That means that practical discourses depend on content brought to them from outside. It would be utterly pointless to engage in a practical discourse without a horizon provided by the lifeworld of a specific social group and without real conflicts in a concrete situation in which the actors consider it incumbent upon them to reach a consensual means of regulating some controversial social matter. Practical discourses are always related to the concrete point of departure of a disturbed normative agreement. These antecedent disruptions determine the topics that are up for discussion. This procedure, then, is not formal in the sense that it abstracts from content. Quite the contrary, in its openness, practical discourse is dependent upon contingent content being fed into it from outside. In discourse this content is subjected to a process in which particular values are ultimately discarded as being not susceptible to consensus. The question now arises as to whether this very selectivity might not make the procedure unsuitable for resolving practical questions.

2. If we define practical issues as issues of the good life, which invariably deal with the totality of a particular form of life or the totality of an individual life history, then ethical formalism is incisive in the literal sense: the universalization principle acts like a knife that makes razor-sharp cuts between evaluative statements and strictly normative ones, between the good and the just. While cultural values may imply a claim to intersubjective acceptance, they are so inextricably intertwined with the totality of a particular form of life that they cannot be said to claim normative validity in the strict sense. By their very nature, cultural values are at best *candidates* for embodiment in norms that are designed to express a general interest.

Participants can distance themselves from norms and normative systems that have been set off from the totality of social life only to the extent necessary to assume a hypothetical attitude toward them. Individuals who have been socialized cannot take a hypothetical attitude toward the form of life and the personal life history that have shaped their own identity. We are now in a position to define the scope of application of a deontological ethics: it covers only practical questions that can be debated rationally, that is, those that hold out the prospect of consensus. It deals not with value preferences but with the normative validity of norms of action.

3. . . . [I]deas of the good life are not something we hold before us as an abstract "ought." Rather, they shape the identities of groups and individuals in such a way that they form an intrinsic part of culture or personality. Thus the development of the moral point of view goes hand in hand with a differentiation within the practical into *moral questions* and *evaluative questions*. Moral questions can in principle be decided rationally, that is, in terms of *justice* or the generalizability of interests. Evaluative questions present themselves at the most general level as issues of the *good life* (or of self-realization); they are accessible to rational discussion only *within* the unproblematic horizon of a concrete historical form of life or the conduct of an individual life.

If we consider the abstraction achieved by morality, two things become clear: (1) the increase in rationality achieved when we isolate issues of justice and (2) the problems of mediating morality and ethical life that arise therefrom. Within the horizon of the lifeworld, practical judgments derive both their concreteness and their power to motivate action from their inner connection to unquestioningly accepted ideas of the good life, in short, from their connection to ethical life and its institutions. Under these conditions, problematization can never be so profound as to risk all the assets of the existing ethical substance. But the abstractive achievements required by the moral point of view do precisely that. This is why Kohlberg speaks of a transition to the *postconventional* stage of moral consciousness. At this stage, moral judgment becomes dissociated from the local conventions and historical coloration of a particular form of life. It can no longer appeal to the naive validity of the context of the lifeworld. Moral answers retain only the rationally motivating force of insights. Along with the naive self-certainty of their lifeworld background they lose the thrust and efficacy of empirical motives for action. To become effective in practice, every universalist morality has to make up for this loss of concrete ethical substance, which is initially accepted because of the cognitive advantages attending it. Universalist moralities are dependent on forms of life that are rationalized in that they make possible the prudent application of universal moral insights and support motivations for translating insights into moral action. Only those forms of life that meet universalist moralities halfway in this sense fulfill the conditions necessary to reverse the abstractive achievements of decontextualization and demotivation.

NOTES

1. At most we can compare theories, as higher-level systems of propositions, with norms. But it is debatable whether theories can be said to be true or false in the same sense as the descriptions, predictions, and explanations that we derive from them, whereas norms, for their part are right or wrong in the same sense as the actions that satisfy or violate them.

2. J. Habermas, "Legitimation Problems in the Modern State," in Habermas, *Communication and the Evolution of Society* (Boston, 1979), pp. 178ff. On the relation between the justification of norms, their being put into effect, and their being accepted, see also W. Kuhlmann, "1st eine philosophische Letztbegründung von Normen möglich?" in *Funkkolleg Ethik*, Studienbegleitbrief 8 (Weinheim, 1981) p.32.

3. On the logic of practical discourse, see T. McCarthy, *The Critical Theory of Jürgen Habermas* (Cambridge, Mass., 1978), pp. 310ff

4. R. Wimmer, *Universalisierung in der Ethik* (Frankfurt am Main, 1980), pp. 174 ff.

5. G. Patzig, *Tatsachen, Normen, Sätze* (Stuttgart, 1980), p. 162

6. G. H. Mead, "Fragments on Ethics," in *Mind, Self, and Society* (Chicago, 1934), pp. 379 ff. See also H. Joas, *G. H. Mead: A Contemporary Reexamination of His Thought* (Cambridge, Mass., 1985), and J. Habermas, *The Theory of Communicative Action*, vol. 2 (Boston, 1987), pp. 92 ff.

7. With reference to B. Gert's *Moral Rules*, p. 72, G. Nunner-Winkler has raised the objection that (U) is unable to single out from among the norms that fulfill the stated conditions those that are moral in the narrow sense and to exclude others (e.g., "You ought to smile when you say hello to people"). This objection is met when one proposes to call moral only those norms that are strictly universalizable, that is, those that are invariable over historical time and across social groups. This usage of the moral theorist does not, of course, coincide with that of the sociologist and the historian, who tend to describe epoch-specific and culture-specific rules as moral rules if they accepted as such by members of the group under study.

8. T. McCarthy (1978), p. 326.

9. S. Benhabib, "The Methodological Illusions of Modern Political Theory: The Case of Rawls and Habermas," in *Neue Hefte für Philosophie* 21 (1982) 47 ff.

10. J. Rawls, *A Theory of Justice* (Cambridge, Mass., 1971), pp. 20 ff and 48 ff.

11. P. Lorenzen and O. Schwemmer, *Konstuktive Logik, Ethik und Wissenschaftstheorie* (Mannheim, 1973), pp. 107 ff.

12. Wimmer (1980), pp. 358f.

13. A. J. Watt, "Transcendental Arguments and Moral Principles," *Philosophical Quarterly* 25 (1975): 40.

14. Watt (1975), p. 41.

15. B. R. Burleson, "On the Foundation of Rationality," *Journal of The American Forensic Association* 1979: 112 ff.

16. R. Alexy, "Eine Theorie des praktischen Diskurses," in W. Oelmüller, ed., *Normenbegründung, Normendurchsetzung* (Paderborn, 1978).

17. Alexy (1978), p. 37. The numbering has been changed.

18. To the degree to which these are of a special kind and cannot be distilled from the general meaning of a competition for better arguments, they are *institutional* mechanisms that belong to a *different* level of analysis (see below).

19. Habermas, "Wahrheitstheorien" (1973), pp. 211 ff.

20. Alexy (1978), p. 40.

21. This presupposition is obviously irrelevant for theoretical discourses, since they only test assertoric validity claims. All the same, it is one of the pragmatic presuppositions of argumentation as such.

22. In what follows, Habermas contrasts *überzeugen* and *überreden*, here translated as "convince" and "talk into." The contrast is more emphatic in German than in English; *überzeugen* implies the use of argument, while "to cause to believe by argument" is one but not the only meaning of "convince." (Translator's note.)

23. See J. Habermas, "Die Utopie des guten Herrschers," in Habermas, *Kleine Politische Schriften*, vols. 1–4 (Frankfurt, 1981), pp. 318 ff.

24. A somewhat different formulation of the same principle can be found in F. Kambartel, "Moralisches Argumentieren," in Kambartel, ed., *Praktische Philosophie und kunstruktive Wissenschaftstheorie* (Frankfurt, 1974), pp. 54 ff. According to Kambartel, those norms for which the consent of all concerned can be obtained through "rational dialogue" are justified. Justification is based on "a rational dialogue (or the outline of such a dialogue) leading to an agreement by all participants that the orientation which is being questioned can be agreed to by all concerned in an imaginary situation of undistorted communication" (p. 68).

25. When we talk about the political relevance of an ethics of discourse, things are different to the degree to which the ethics of discourse affects the moral-practical basis of the legal system or any political aspect transcending the private sphere of morality. In this regard, that is, in regard to providing guidance for an emancipatory practice, discourse ethics can acquire a significance for orienting action. It does so, however not as an ethics, that is, not prescriptively in the direct sense, but indirectly, by becoming part of a critical social theory that can be used to interpret situations, as for example when it is used to differentiate between particular and universalizable interests.

IV

Reasons, Motives, and the Demands of Morality

17

Reasons, Motives, and the Demands of Morality: An Introduction

STEPHEN DARWALL

MORALITY AND AUTHORITY I

Moral demands present themselves as *categorical imperatives*, as Kant put it. It's a fine day, and you'd like nothing better than to go for a walk, but you promised your students to return their papers. You could put them off, but you think that would be wrong. And that, you think, is reason enough to stay in and finish them. But is it really? An observer might take your staying in as evidence that discharging your obligation is what, under the circumstances, you want most to do. After all, no one is forcing you to stay inside. Perhaps, if there is reason for you to finish the papers, it derives from this. But this is unlikely to be the way it will seem to you, from the inside. In taking your moral obligation seriously, you are unlikely to think that the reason you have for finishing your students' papers is that this will satisfy your desires. Of course, if you do stay in and finish them, you will be acting voluntarily, and so, doing what you want. But as Thomas Nagel points out, *this* desire of yours is not a source of reasons since it is itself motivated by them.[1] It is because you think you should not break your promise that you want most not to do so, not vice versa. And, you are apt to think, if, counterfactually, you didn't want to do what was right—if your moral obligation didn't happen to weigh with you—this would not mean it *should* not. It would not lessen the weight of reasons you think there are for you to finish the papers. Viewed from the inside, moral demands appear to present us with reasons for acting that are unconditional on our desires and, it seems, that override any considerations based in these.

Whether this appearance is correct is the question of whether morality has the *authority* or, as philosophers also say, the *normativity* it appears to claim. There are actually two questions here. First, if it is morally obligatory that S do A, will there necessarily exist some *reason* for S to do A consisting in the fact that S morally ought to do A or in considerations that make this a fact? In the above example, you think that not giving back the papers would be wrong because of your promise. But does this guarantee that either the fact that you promised or the fact that not returning the papers would be wrong is a *reason* to give them back? In a fairly trivial sense, the answer is yes. Any moral "ought" is grounded in reasons—moral reasons—so there are guaranteed always to be such reasons for doing what one morally ought to do. But any scheme of "oughts" we might cook up can be grounded *internally* in what *that scheme* recognizes as reasons, so this answer is unhelpful. It cannot show that the scheme has any genuine claim on us or that we really ought or must do what it says we should.

Philippa Foot makes this point forcefully with the example of etiquette.[2] By etiquette's lights, one ought always to use forks from left to right as they are placed before one. We could say, equivalently, that there are reasons of etiquette for using forks in this order. It does not follow, however, that this is something one really ought to do, or that there is a reason with genuine deliberative weight for so acting. Etiquette-reasons are not guaranteed to be reasons unqualifiedly, or with the qualifier removed. And without further argument, the same might be true of moral reasons.

Nevertheless, moral obligations and the reasons that ground them do seem to present themselves as necessarily bearing on what a person genuinely ought or has reason to do. And so we can ask, "Is this appearance correct?" "Does the moral 'ought' guarantee reasons for acting as it directs?"

If the first question, "Is there a reason to do what you are morally obligated to do?" can be answered affirmatively, a second arises. Considering your moral obligation to return your students' papers, it may seem to you not just that this is, or is grounded in, *a* reason to act, but that the relevant moral reasons *override* all others, for example, those connected to your desire to enjoy a walk. The idea is not that the reason not to break your promise must outweigh any other reason that

could have existed in the situation. If other reasons were to trump, however, it may seem that this must be because these also change the moral situation. For example, if putting off the papers were the only way to prevent some disaster, then not only would that be a trumping reason, it would also change what you morally should do. Or if it were the only way of averting some significant harm to yourself, then either this would become your moral duty or, at least, it would no longer be morally wrong. Here again, we can ask whether this appearance is correct. Do moral demands necessarily provide overriding reasons for acting, either in themselves or in what grounds them?

INTERNALISM AND EXTERNALISM I: MORALITY/REASONS

The thesis that moral "ought"s do guarantee rational "ought"s is one of the things philosophers refer to by the term *internalism*.[3] *Morality/reasons internalism*, as we may call it, holds that reasons for acting are internal to moral demands in the following sense: If *S* morally ought to do *A*, then necessarily there is reason for *S* to do *A* consisting either in the fact that *S* morally ought so to act, or in considerations that ground that fact. *Morality/reasons externalism* denies this. It holds that we may not have reason to do what we morally ought; moral reasons are not necessarily, in themselves, reasons for acting, or, at least, not overriding reasons. Even if moral demands present themselves as intrinsically authoritative or categorically binding, this appearance may be in error.

Of course, someone might simply define moral demands as whatever is categorically binding or dictated by the best reasons for acting. This would make morality/reasons internalism true by definition, but it would not settle whether, for example, you necessarily have reason to keep your promise to your students. It would simply turn that question into the issue of whether it would really be wrong for you to break your promise. If we adopt a more familiar, narrower conception, one on which it is relatively uncontroversial that persons morally ought to keep their promises, other things being equal, then whether morality/reasons internalism holds becomes a significant issue. And if, as our example suggests, taking morality seriously involves regarding its demands as authoritative, then it may seem that Kant must have been right in thinking that establishing morality/reasons internalism will be central to a philosophical vindication of morality.

Whether it can be established, however, depends on what a reason for acting is and on what reasons there are. Morality/reasons externalists, such as Philippa Foot, begin with the widely held idea, represented as much in modern social science as in modern society, that rational conduct is that which advances the satisfaction of an agent's desires and interests.[4] Since the latter are at best contingently related to moral demands, an agent's moral obligations may not coincide with what she has reason to do. Much less are moral demands and the considerations that ground them guaranteed to be reasons for her in themselves. Externalists do not view this with alarm, however. Whatever the appearances, it may be, as Foot argues, that morality requires no more than contingent connections to agents' practical reasoning to be a fully respectable concern.

INTERNALISM AND EXTERNALISM II: REASONS/MOTIVES

To make headway on the issue that divides morality/reasons externalists and internalists, it is necessary to ask, "What makes conduct rational or a consideration a reason for acting?" Or, as we might also put it, "What does rational authority or normativity itself consist in?" One very attractive thought to many morality/reasons externalists *and* internalists is a different form of internalism, this one concerning the relation between practical reasons and what can *motivate the will*. *Reasons/motives internalism* holds that a necessary condition of *p*'s being a reason for *S* to do *A* is that *S* can have, and under suitable conditions would have, some motivation to do *A* by virtue of a suitable awareness of *p*. This thesis is hardly uncontroversial. There is a conceptual distinction, after all, between normative or justifying reasons, on the one hand, and motivating or explaining reasons, on the other. Something can be a (normative) reason for someone to do something without that person actually acting on it or even being moved by it—without, that is, its being a motivating reason for that person. Still, reasons/motives internalism has significant philosophical appeal, and since it attracts philosophers who differ so sharply concerning the relation between morality and reasons, it offers the hope of shedding light on whether moral demands have intrinsic authority.

Here is one source of its appeal: "What is there reason for me to do?" and "What should I do?" are *practical questions*. This is not just because they are *about* action. "When will I give my students' papers back?" also concerns action in this sense. Rather, they are practical in the further sense that they are the questions that confront an agent deliberating about what *to* do. They are, we might say, the defining questions of an agent's deliberative perspective. It is distinctive of agency that agents act for reasons. Deliberation just *is* the search for and weighing of reasons for acting in order to resolve what to do. It can seem, therefore, that there must be some connection between an agent's deliberative judgment and being moved so to act.

This thought is confirmed when we take up the perspective of a deliberating agent. You are deciding whether or not to finish your students' papers or to go for a walk. If you take this question seriously, and if you see your promise as a reason to stay in and finish the papers, will you not assume that you *can act for that reason*, that is, that it can motivate you? And similarly for taking the pleasures of the walk as reasons to do that. An intrinsic connection of some sort between practical judgment and motivation seems to be a presupposition of serious deliberation.

It's a sign of the deep connection between normative and motivating reasons that we use the language of force with both. To say that reasons are forceful, weighty, or compelling is, strictly speaking, to make a remark in "normative space." But it can be hard to see how there could be merely a contingent connection between judging reasons weighty, forceful, or compelling and being moved by them.

Judgment Internalism

Even if it is agreed that there is some necessary connection in this area, however, there may still be disagreement concerning exactly what this connection is. We can distinguish three broadly different forms of reasons/motives internalism (henceforth: internalism). *Judgment internalism* holds that if S judges (or believes, or sincerely asserts) that she ought to do A (or that she has reason to do A), then, necessarily, she has some motivation to do A.[5] This is a view about the nature of normative thought and language. It says that nothing counts as a genuinely normative thought or as a sincere normative assertion unless it is related in this way to motivation. Some form of judgment internalism frequently figures in arguments for noncognitivist metaethics. Allan Gibbard argues, for example, that fundamental disagreements concerning what a person has reason to do—in his terms, what it "makes sense" to do—are best understood as expressing the acceptance of different norms, where norm-acceptance is a motivational rather than a cognitive state.[6] And similar theses are at work in the arguments of prescriptivists like Hare or emotivists such as Stevenson.[7]

Existence Internalism

Because the two other forms of internalism put forward necessary conditions of the truth of a normative proposition or the holding of a normative fact, I call them both *existence internalisms*.

Perceptual Internalism. One kind, an *epistemic* or *perceptual* (*existence*) *internalism*, is typified by Platonism, rational intuitionism, and in a different form by contemporary sensibility theories such as those of Wiggins and McDowell. Perceptual internalism holds that it is impossible for a person to know directly or perceive the truth of a normative proposition without being moved. This was Plato's view about direct knowledge of the Good, and early modern rational intuitionists such as Samuel Clarke and Richard Price held the same about rational perception of what they believed to be the fundamental normative facts concerning, respectively, the fitting and the right. Sensibility theorists reject intuitionist metaphysics, but they, too, speak of the perception of reasons as seeing an action in an intrinsically motivating "favorable light."[8]

Metaphysical Internalism. For both intuitionists and sensibility theorists, motivation necessarily attends direct epistemic contact with normative facts; it is no part of normative facts themselves. As Price put it, motivation is "an *effect* of obligation perceived, rather than *obligation itself*."[9] Sensibility theorists do speak of matched sets of normative property and affective/motivational sense or sentiment, but much like the intuitionists, they reject any reductive account of normative properties or facts. *Metaphysical (existence) internalism*, on the other hand, asserts that an agent's being moved (under appropriate conditions) is either part of what it is for a normative proposition to be true of him, or a necessary condition for the holding of that normative fact.

Perceptual internalism is a form of existence rather than of judgment internalism since it sees motivation as an aspect or consequence of direct knowledge of normative *facts*, rather than of normative belief or sincere normative assertion. But metaphysical versions are the purest case of existence internalism since they assert the agent's being moved under appropriate conditions to be necessary for the holding of the fact of there being some reason for her to act, quite independently of any knowledge of this fact.

According to *metaphysical internalism, p* is a reason for *S* to do *A* only if *S* would have some motivation to do *A* were she aware that *p* under the appropriate conditions. As Bernard Williams puts the idea, it is a condition of something's being a reason for someone that it be something that person *could have*, or *act on*, as *her reason* for acting. In order, that is, for something, *p*, to be a (normative or justifying) reason for *S* to do *A*, it must be case that *p* could function as *S*'s (motivating) reason for doing *A*.[10] Specifically, there must be some deliberative path, including some appropriate awareness of *p*, that would take *S* from her current "motivational set" to one that contains some motivation to do *A*. Williams calls considerations that meet this condition "internal reasons." Those that do not, but which someone puts forward as a reason for acting nonetheless, he calls "external reasons." The problem with external reasons claims is that they assert the practical relevance of a consideration even though the agent herself might remain utterly unmoved by engaging that consideration in rational deliberation. With no purchase on the agent's practical reasoning, however, it is hard for external reasons claims to avoid the suspicion of being "mere bluff."

But how are we to understand "rational deliberation" here? And what is to count as part of what Williams calls an agent's "motivational set"? Williams mentions means/end reasoning, and the informed mutual adjustment of ends as examples of the former, but he takes no definite stand on the precise contours of rational deliberation, much less does he offer any principled rationale for a specific position. Without clarity on these issues, however, it is impossible to determine

how accepting metaphysical internalism and the thesis that all reasons are "internal reasons" affects the issue of morality's authority. Some morality/reasons externalists tend to view their position as the inevitable consequence of metaphysical (reasons/motives) internalism, but this is almost certainly too quick. Frequently, this line of thought involves a purely instrumentalist picture of practical reasoning, or some version of the view that all reasons for acting must be based in the agent's desires. It goes something like this: All reasons must be capable of motivating, but since any source of motivation must be some form of desire, any reason for acting must be desire-based. Non-desire-based reasons would be a possibility only if practical reason can itself be a source of motivation. But that is impossible.

Christine Korsgaard argues that this amounts to a kind of skepticism about practical reason. Even the instrumentalist about practical reason is bound to hold that someone who deliberates rationally will be moved to take the means to his ends, despite the fact that this motivation is not guaranteed by his desire for the end. Of course, in a *rational* person, motivation from the desire for an end will be transmitted to a desire for the means. But the latter is only *rationally* necessary. It is not guaranteed simply by the fact that someone desires some goal that he will come to have motivation for an acknowledged means to it, even if he sees that to be the only means. Consequently, Korsgaard concludes, even instrumentalists are obliged to accept that practical reason can motivate.

The proper way to understand (metaphysical) internalism, she argues, is as holding that *p* is a reason for *S* to do *A* only if *rational* awareness of *p* would give *S* motivation to do *A*. If they accept metaphysical internalism, consequently, morality/reasons internalists will then be committed to holding that the recognition of moral demands can be intrinsically motivating in rational deliberation, without reliance on further desires. But this thesis is no different *in kind* from that to which any nonskeptic about practical reason is committed. All must believe that reason can be inherently practical.

The real issue must then be what rational awareness or deliberation consists in. If, however, we must be careful not to oversimplify the relations between reason, desire, and motivation so as to prejudice the issue against morality/reasons internalism, so also should we take care not to beg important questions against morality/reasons externalism. One line of defense of morality/reasons internalism is simply to insist that moral demands have authority and to argue that anyone who fails to be moved by them is thereby shown to be irrational since he fails to be moved by what should move him. If metaphysical internalism is interpreted as the constraint that something can be a reason for someone only if he would be motivated by it were he *rational*, or were he to deliberate in a *rational* way, then such a position will in fact satisfy this constraint. But surely what this shows is that the theses of reasons/motives internalism and internal reasons can do no substantive philosophical work when they are interpreted in this way. Any considerations put forward as reasons can be held to satisfy internalism, so construed, since a person would be motivated by them if rational (that is, if he were adequately responsive to reasons).

A way around this impasse is to require that "rational deliberation or consideration" be treated as an independent variable, and "reasons for acting" as a dependent variable. Unlike rational intuitionism, which holds there to be a metaphysically independent order of normative fact, direct knowledge of which is intrinsically motivating, the lines of thought that underlie metaphysical internalism are Humean and Kantian doctrines, according to which there can be no such independent order of normative fact. For the Humean (Williams can serve as an example), such a metaphysical supposition violates naturalist scruples and also makes it mysterious how epistemic contact with such an order would necessarily motivate the will.[11] For a

Kantian such as Korsgaard, the idea of an independent order of normative fact is inconsistent with *the autonomy of the will*.[12] Practical reasoning is not a matter of orienting oneself properly in relation to some external source of value. Rather it is a *self-government or autonomy*—the agent determining herself in accord with principles she can prescribe for herself as one rational person among others.

It seems more faithful to the lines of thought underlying metaphysical internalism, therefore, to treat rational deliberation as a formal ideal, defined independently of any specific view about which facts are reasons for acting. *Reason for acting* is then a status a consideration *earns* by virtue of the fact that it would be a motivating reason for someone were she to deliberate rationally.

MORALITY AND AUTHORITY II

We can view several of the arguments concerning morality's authority given in the essays that follow in this broad context. First, a morality/reasons externalism built on a reasons/motives internalist foundation might take the form that Williams suggests but does not explicitly defend, namely, that rational deliberation includes no more than informed means/end instrumental thinking and mutual adjustment of ends, and so there is no a priori reason to expect any connection between what morality demands and what reason recommends.

Gauthier, Nagel, and Korsgaard can all be read as defending versions of morality/reasons internalism on reasons/motives internalist grounds. Gauthier may seem to begin with the same familiar desire- and self-interest-based theory of reasons on which Foot grounds her morality/reasons externalism. But actually, Gauthier's argument depends on no premise about the relation between an agent's interests and desires and rational *conduct*, and hence on no premise that all reasons must be desire- or interest-based. True to what we have identified as the line of thought underlying metaphysical internalism, Gauthier holds that reasons for acting earn that status by virtue of their being motivating reasons in rational deliberation, where it is the *latter*, he thinks, that must be properly related to an agent's desires and interests. Roughly, rational deliberation is whatever form of deliberative thinking most advances the agent's interests, and considerations are normative reasons if they would function as motivating reasons in that form. This enables Gauthier then to argue that agents do better if they regard certain interest-constraining demands, such as those requiring them to keep mutually advantageous agreements, as authoritative since, under normal circumstances, they would not be able to make such agreements unless they were disposed so to regard demands to keep them.[13]

Nagel and Korsgaard both sound more Kantian themes. Unlike Gauthier, neither assumes a material standard even for evaluating deliberation as a process. For both Nagel and Korsgaard, the standards of practical reasoning are entirely formal. Nagel argues that avoiding a practical analogue of solipsism requires being able to make practical judgments with the same content from first-personal and third-personal standpoints and that, because of the motivational content intrinsic to practical judgments, this is possible only if all reasons for acting are agent-neutral. That this would satisfy *my* desire or interest can be a reason for me, consequently, only if that this would satisfy *someone's* interest can be a reason for me—first-personal pronouns drop out of the proper expression of genuine reasons. This doesn't amount to a direct defense of morality's authority. Rather it seeks to undermine the major, desire-based form of morality/reasons externalism.[14]

Korsgaard elaborates and defends Kant's doctrine that action is possible only under the concepts of freedom and practical law. Certain ways of regarding our conduct are inescapable for us as agents. We cannot but see what we do as chosen by us for reasons. And in so choosing, we commit ourselves to normative judgments and, consequently, to universal normative principles or practical laws. So far there is nothing with which someone holding a desire- or interest-based theory of reasons, for example, a rational egoist, need disagree. The egoist might concede that he is committed by his choices to the principle that everyone should do what is in his own best interest or what would most satisfy his desires. But what about the egoist's commitment to universal egoism itself? What underlies that? If no metaphysically independent order of normative facts exists, no universal principle can simply be *given*. In particular, therefore, the principle of universal egoism cannot be taken as given. As autonomous agents, we can always step back from any principle and ask, "Is this a principle on which we should act?" And this, Korsgaard argues, gives Kant a way to ground what he regards as the fundamental principle of morality—the Categorical Imperative—*within* the deliberative standpoint of a free rational agent. If we cannot act but on a universal principle to which we commit ourselves, and if no universal principles are given, then we should act only on what we are prepared to "legislate" as universal law by willing that all agents be guided by it in their practical reasoning.

NOTES

1. Thomas Nagel, *The Possibility of Altruism*. See Chapter 19 below.

2. In "Morality as a System of Hypothetical Imperatives." See Chapter 18 below.

3. The term "internalism" derives from W. D. Falk's " 'Ought' and Motivation," *Proceedings of the Aristotelian Society* 48 (1947–48): 111–38, reprinted in *Ought, Reasons, and Morality: The Collected Papers of W. D. Falk* (Ithaca, N.Y.: Cornell University Press, 1986). Other important discussions include William Frankena, "Obligation and Motivation in Recent Moral Philosophy," in A. I. Melden, ed.,

Essays in Moral Philosophy (Seattle: University of Washington Press, 1958); Thomas Nagel, *The Possibility of Altruism* (Chapter 19 below); Bernard Williams, "Internal and External Reasons," Chapter 21 below; Stephen Darwall, *Impartial Reason* (Ithaca, N.Y.: Cornell University Press, 1983), pp. 51–61; Christine Korsgaard, "Skepticism About Practical Reason," Chapter 22 below; and Stephen Darwall, "Internalism and Agency," *Philosophical Perspectives* 6 (1992): 155–74.

4. In "Morality as a System of Hypothetical Imperatives" and "Reasons for Action and Desires," *Proceedings of the Aristotelian Society*, supp. vol. 46 (1972): 203–10. See also, however, her Recantation in Chapter 18 below, in which Foot makes clear that this is no longer her position.

5. For the distinction between judgment and existence internalism, see *Impartial Reason* (Ithaca, N.Y.: Cornell University Press, 1983), pp. 54–55.

6. Allan Gibbard, *Wise Choices, Apt Feelings* (Cambridge, Mass.: Harvard University Press, 1990), pp. 3–82. See Chapter 10 above.

7. R. M. Hare, *The Language of Morals* (Oxford: Oxford University Press, 1952); Charles Stevenson, "The Emotive Meaning of Ethical Terms," Chapter 4 above.

8. John McDowell, "Are Moral Requirements Hypothetical Imperatives?" *Proceedings of the Aristotelian Society*, supp. vol. 52 (1978): 13–29; David Wiggins, "Truth, Invention, and the Meaning of Life," in his *Needs, Values, Truth: Essays in the Philosophy of Value* (Oxford: Basil Blackwell, 1987), see esp. p. 137.

9. Richard Price, *A Review of the Principal Questions in Morals*, ed. D. D. Raphael (Oxford: Clarendon Press, 1974), p. 114.

10. Bernard Williams, "Internal and External Reasons," see Chapter 21 below.

11. On the latter, cf. Mackie's argument from queerness, Chapter 6 above.

12. I discuss early modern formulations of these different internalist rationales—empirical naturalist and autonomist, respectively—in *The British Moralists and the Internal "Ought": 1640–1740* (Cambridge: Cambridge University Press, 1995).

13. These circumstances are contingent, but they may be the same contingent circumstances that give rise to the existence of moral demands.

14. Nagel no longer holds that all reasons must be agent-neutral. Nor, as he has been especially prominent in pointing out, are all moral demands agent-neutral. Our example above—that one ought to keep *one's* promise—is an agent-relative demand. See Thomas Nagel, *The View from Nowhere* (New York: Oxford University Press, 1986).

18

Morality as a System of Hypothetical Imperatives

PHILIPPA FOOT

There are many difficulties and obscurities in Kant's moral philosophy, and few contemporary moralists will try to defend it all. Many, for instance, agree in rejecting Kant's derivation of duties from the mere form of the law expressed in terms of a universally legislative will. Nevertheless, it is generally supposed, even by those who would not dream of calling themselves his followers, that Kant established one thing beyond doubt—namely, the necessity of distinguishing moral judgements from hypothetical imperatives. That moral judgements cannot be hypothetical imperatives has come to seem an unquestionable truth. It will be argued here that it is not.

In discussing so thoroughly Kantian a notion as that of the hypothetical imperative, one naturally begins by asking what Kant himself meant by a hypothetical imperative, and it may be useful to say a little about the idea of an imperative as this appears in Kant's works. In writing about imperatives Kant seems to be thinking at least as much of state-ments about what ought to be or should be done, as of injunctions expressed in the imperative mood. He even describes as an imperative the assertion that it would be "good to do or refrain from doing something"[1] and explains that for a will that "does not always do something simply because it is presented to it as a good thing to do" this has the force of a command of reason. We may therefore think of Kant's imperatives as statements to the effect that something ought to be done or that it would be good to do it.

The distinction between hypothetical imperatives and categorical imperatives, which plays so important a part in Kant's ethics, appears in characteristic form in the following passages from the *Foundations of the Metaphysics of Morals*:

> All imperatives command either hypothetically or categorically. The former present the practical necessity of a possible action as a means to achieving something else which one desires (or which one may possibly desire). The cate-

gorical imperative would be one which presented an action as of itself objectively necessary, without regard to any other end.[2]

If the action is good only as a means to something else, the imperative is hypothetical; but if it is thought of as good in itself, and hence as necessary in a will which of itself conforms to reason as the principle of this will, the imperative is categorical.[3]

The hypothetical imperative, as Kant defines it, "says only that the action is good to some purpose" and the purpose, he explains, may be possible or actual. Among imperatives related to actual purposes Kant mentions rules of prudence, since he believes that all men necessarily desire their own happiness. Without committing ourselves to this view it will be useful to follow Kant in classing together as "hypothetical imperatives" those telling a man what he ought to do because (or if) he wants something and those telling him what he ought to do on grounds of self-interest. Common opinion agrees with Kant in insisting that a moral man must accept a rule of duty whatever his interests or desires.[4]

Having given a rough description of the class of Kantian hypothetical imperatives it may be useful to point to the heterogeneity within it. Sometimes what a man should do depends on his passing inclination, as when he wants his coffee hot and should warm the jug. Sometimes it depends on some long-term project, when the feelings and inclinations of the moment are irrelevant. If one wants to be a respectable philosopher one should get up in the mornings and do some work, though just at that moment when one should do it the thought of being a respectable philosopher leaves one cold. It is true nevertheless to say of one, at that moment, that one wants to be a respectable philosopher,[5] and this can be the foundation of a desire-dependent hypothetical imperative. The term "desire" as used in the original account of the hypothetical imperative was meant as a grammatically convenient substitute for "want," and was not meant to carry any implication of inclination rather than long-term aim or project. Even the

word "project," taken strictly, introduces undesirable restrictions. If someone is devoted to his family or his country or to any cause, there are certain things he wants, which may then be the basis of hypothetical imperatives, without either inclinations or projects being quite what is in question. Hypothetical imperatives should already be appearing as extremely diverse; a further important distinction is between those that concern an individual and those that concern a group. The desires on which a hypothetical imperative is dependent may be those of one man, or may be taken for granted as belonging to a number of people engaged in some common project or sharing common aims.

Is Kant right to say that moral judgements are categorical, not hypothetical, imperatives? It may seem that he is, for we find in our language two different uses of words such as "should" and "ought," apparently corresponding to Kant's hypothetical and categorical imperatives, and we find moral judgements on the "categorical" side. Suppose, for instance, we have advised a traveller that he should take a certain train, believing him to be journeying to his home. If we find that he has decided to go elsewhere, we will most likely have to take back what we said: the "should" will now be unsupported and in need of support. Similarly, we must be prepared to withdraw our statement about what he should do if we find that the right relation does not hold between the action and the end—that it is either no way of getting what he wants (or doing what he wants to do) or not the most eligible among possible means. The use of "should" and "ought" in moral contexts is, however, quite different. When we say that a man should do something and intend a moral judgement we do not have to back up what we say by considerations about his interests or his desires; if no such connexion can be found the "should" need not be withdrawn. It follows that the agent cannot rebut an assertion about what, morally speaking, he should do by showing that the action is not ancillary to his interests or desires. Without such a connexion the "should" does not stand unsupported and in need of support;[6] the support that *it* requires is of another kind.[7]

There is, then, one clear difference between moral judgements and the class of "hypothetical imperatives" so far discussed. In the latter "should" is "used hypothetically," in the sense defined, and if Kant were merely drawing attention to this piece of linguistic usage his point would easily be proved. But obviously Kant meant more than this; in describing moral Judgements as non-hypothetical—that is, categorical imperatives—he is ascribing to them a special dignity and necessity which this usage cannot give. Modern philosophers follow Kant in talking, for example, about the "unconditional requirement" expressed in moral judgements. These, they say, tell us what we have to do whatever our interests or desires, and by their inescapability they are distinguished from hypothetical imperatives.

The problem is to find proof for this further feature of moral judgements. If anyone fails to see the gap that has to be filled it will be useful to point out to him that we find "should" used non-hypothetically in some non-moral statements to which no one attributes the special dignity and necessity conveyed by the description "categorical imperative." For instance, we find this non-hypothetical use of "should" in sentences enunciating rules of etiquette, as, for example, that an invitation in the third person should be answered in the third person, where the rule does not *fail to apply* to someone who has his own good reasons for ignoring this piece of nonsense, or who simply does not care about what, from the point of view of etiquette, he should do. Similarly, there is a non-hypothetical use of "should" in contexts where something like a club rule is in question. The club secretary who has told a member that he should not bring ladies into the smoking-room does not say, "Sorry, I was mistaken" when informed that this member is resigning tomorrow and cares nothing about his reputation in the club. Lacking a connexion with the agent's desires or interests, this "should" does not stand "unsupported and in need of support"; it requires only the backing of the rule. The use of "should" is therefore "non-hypothetical" in the sense defined.

It follows that if a hypothetical use of "should" gave a hypothetical imperative, and a non-hypothetical use of "should" a categorical imperative, then "should" statements based on rules of etiquette, or rules of a club would be categorical imperatives. Since this would not be accepted by defenders of the categorical imperative in ethics, who would insist that these other "should" statements give hypothetical imperatives, they must be using this expression in some other sense. We must therefore ask what they mean when they say that "You should answer . . . in the third person" is a hypothetical imperative. Very roughly the idea seems to be that one may reasonably ask why anyone should bother about what should (from the point of view of etiquette) be done, and that such considerations deserve no notice unless reason is shown. So although people give as their reason for doing something the fact that it is required by etiquette, we do not take this consideration as *in itself giving us reason to act.* Considerations of etiquette do not have any automatic reason-giving force, and a man might be right if he denied that he had reason to do "what's done."

This seems to take us to the heart of the matter, for, by contrast, it is supposed that moral considerations necessarily give reasons for acting to any man. The difficulty is, of course, to defend this proposition which is more often repeated than explained. Unless it is said, implausibly, that all "should" or "ought" statements give reasons for acting, which leaves the old problem of assigning a special categorical status to moral judgement, we must be told what it is that makes the moral "should" relevantly different from the "shoulds" appearing in normative statements of other kinds.[8] Attempts have sometimes been made to show that some kind of irrationality is involved in ignoring the "should" of morality: in saying "Immoral—so what?" as one says "Not *comme il faut*—so what?" But as far as I can see these have all rested on some illegitimate assumption, as, for instance, of thinking that the amoral man, who agrees that some piece of conduct is immoral but takes no notice of that, is inconsistently disregarding a rule of conduct that he has accepted; or again of thinking it inconsistent to desire that others will not do to one what one proposes to do to them. The fact is that the man who rejects morality because he sees no reason to obey its rules can be convicted of villainy but not of inconsistency. Nor will his action necessarily be irrational. Irrational actions are those in which a man in some way defeats his own purposes, doing what is calculated to be disadvantageous or to frustrate his ends. Immorality does not *necessarily* involve any such thing.

It is obvious that the normative character of moral judgement does not guarantee its reason-giving force. Moral judgements are normative, but so are judgements of manners, statements of club rules, and many others. Why should the first provide reasons for acting as the others do not? In every case it is because there is a background of teaching that the non-hypothetical "should" can be used. The behaviour is required, not simply recommended, but the question remains as to why we should do what we are required to do. It is true that moral rules are often enforced much more strictly than the rules of etiquette, and our reluctance to press the non-hypothetical "should" of etiquette may be one reason why we think of the rules of etiquette as hypothetical imperatives. But are we then to say that there is nothing behind the idea that moral judgements are categorical imperatives but the relative stringency of our moral teaching? I believe that this may have more to do with the matter than the defenders of the categorical imperative would like to admit. For if we look at the kind of thing that is said in its defence we may find

ourselves puzzled about what the words can even mean unless we connect them with the feelings that this stringent teaching implants. People talk, for instance, about the "binding force" of morality, but it is not clear what this means if not that we *feel* ourselves unable to escape. Indeed the "inescapability" of moral requirements is often cited when they are being contrasted with hypothetical imperatives. No one, it is said, escapes the requirements of ethics by having or not having particular interests or desires. Taken in one way this only reiterates the contrast between the "should" of morality and the hypothetical "should," and once more places morality alongside of etiquette. Both are inescapable in that behaviour does not cease to offend against either morality or etiquette because the agent is indifferent to their purposes and to the disapproval he will incur by flouting them. But morality is supposed to be inescapable in some special way and this may turn out to be merely the reflection of the way morality is taught. Of course, we must try other ways of expressing the fugitive thought. It may be said, for instance, that moral judgements have a kind of necessity since they tell us what we "must do" or "have to do" whatever our interests and desires. The sense of this is, again, obscure. Sometimes when we use such expressions we are referring to physical or mental compulsion. (A man has to go along if he is pulled by strong men and he has to give in if tortured beyond endurance.) But it is only in the absence of such conditions that moral judgements apply. Another and more common sense of the words is found in sentences such as "I caught a bad cold and had to stay in bed" where a penalty for acting otherwise is in the offing. The necessity of acting morally is not, however, supposed to depend on such penalties. Another range of examples, not necessarily having to do with penalties, is found where there is an unquestioned acceptance of some project or rôle, as when a nurse tells us that she has to make her rounds at a certain time, or we say that we have to run for a certain train.[9] But these too are irrelevant in the present context, since the acceptance condition can always be revoked.

No doubt it will be suggested that it is in some other sense of the words "have to" or "must" that one has to or must do what morality demands. But why should one insist that there must be such a sense when it proves so difficult to say what it is? Suppose that what we take for a puzzling thought were really no thought at all but only the reflection of our *feelings* about morality? Perhaps it makes no sense to say that we "have to" submit to the moral law, or that morality is "inescapable" in some special way. For just as one may feel as if one is falling without believing that one is moving downward, so one may feel as if one has to do what is morally required without believing oneself to be under physical or psychological compulsion, or about to incur a penalty if one does not comply. No one thinks that if the word "falling" is used in a statement reporting one's sensations it must be used in a special sense. But this kind of mistake may be involved in looking for the special sense in which one "has to" do what morality demands. There is no difficulty about the idea that we feel we *have to* behave morally, and given the psychological conditions of the learning of moral behaviour it is natural that we should have such feelings. What we cannot do is quote them in support of the doctrine of the categorical imperative. It seems, then, that in so far as it is backed up by statements to the effect that the moral law *is* inescapable, or that we *do* have to do what is morally required of us, it is uncertain whether the doctrine of the categorical imperative even makes sense.

The conclusion we should draw is that moral judgements have no better claim to be categorical imperatives than do statements about matters of etiquette. People may indeed follow either morality or etiquette without asking why they should do so, but equally well they may not. They may ask for reasons and may reasonably refuse to follow either if reasons are not to be found.

It will be said that this way of viewing moral considerations must be totally destructive of morality, because no one could ever act morally unless he accepted such considerations as in themselves sufficient reason for action. Actions that are truly moral must be done "for their own sake," "because they are right," and not for some ulterior purpose. This argument we must examine with care, for the doctrine of the categorical imperative has owed much to its persuasion.

Is there anything to be said for the thesis that a truly moral man acts "out of respect for the moral law" or that he does what is morally right because it is morally right? That such propositions are not *prima facie* absurd depends on the fact that moral judgement concerns itself with a man's reasons for acting as well as with what he does. Law and etiquette require only that certain things are done or left undone, but no one is counted as charitable if he gives alms "for the praise of men," and one who is honest only because it pays him to be honest does not have the virtue of honesty. This kind of consideration was crucial in shaping Kant's moral philosophy. He many times contrasts acting out of respect for the moral law with acting from an ulterior motive, and what is more from one that is self-interested. In the early *Lectures on Ethics* he gave the principle of truth-telling under a system of hypothetical imperatives as that of not lying *if it harms one* to lie. In the *Metaphysics of Morals* he says that ethics cannot start from the ends which a man may propose to himself, since these are all "selfish."[10] In the *Critique of Practical Reason* he argues explicitly that when acting not out of respect for moral law but "on a material maxim" men do what they do for the sake of pleasure or happiness. "All material practical principles are, as such, of one and the same kind and belong under the general principle of self love or one's own happiness."[11] Kant, in fact, was a psychological hedonist in respect of all actions except those done for the sake of the moral law, and this faulty theory of human nature was one of the things preventing him from seeing that moral virtue might be compatible with the rejection of the categorical imperative.

If we put this theory of human action aside, and allow as ends the things that seem to be ends, the picture changes. It will surely be allowed that quite apart from thoughts of duty a man may care about the suffering of others, having a sense of identification with them, and wanting to help if he can. Of course he must want not the reputation of charity, nor even a gratifying rôle helping others, but, quite simply, their good. If this is what he does care about, then he will be attached to the end proper to the virtue of charity and a comparison with someone acting from an ulterior motive (even a respectable ulterior motive) is out of place. Nor will the conformity of his action to the rule of charity be merely contingent. Honest action may happen to further a man's career; charitable actions do not *happen* to further the good of others.[12]

Can a man accepting only hypothetical imperatives possess other virtues besides that of charity? Could he be just or honest? This problem is more complex because there is no end related to such virtues as the good of others is related to charity. But what reason could there be for refusing to call a man a just man if he acted justly because he loved truth and liberty, and wanted every man to be treated with a certain respect? And why should the truly honest man not follow honesty for the sake of the good that honest dealing brings to men? Of course, the usual difficulties can be raised about the rare case in which no good is foreseen from an individual act of honesty. But it is not evident that a man's desires could not give him reason to act honestly even here. He wants to live openly and in good faith with his neighbours; it is not all the same to him to lie and conceal.

If one wants to know whether there could be a truly moral man who accepted moral principles as hypothetical rules of conduct, as many people accept rules of etiquette as hypothetical rules of conduct, one must consider the right kind of example. A man who

demanded that morality should be brought under the heading of self-interest would not be a good candidate, nor would anyone who was ready to be charitable or honest only so long as he felt inclined. A cause such as justice makes strenuous demands, but this is not peculiar to morality, and men are prepared to toil to achieve many ends not endorsed by morality. That they are prepared to fight so hard for moral ends—for example, for liberty and justice—depends on the fact that these are the kinds of ends that arouse devotion. To sacrifice a great deal for the sake of etiquette one would need to be under the spell of the emphatic "ought." One could hardly be devoted to behaving *comme il faut*.

In spite of all that has been urged in favour of the hypothetical imperative in ethics, I am sure that many people will be unconvinced and will argue that one element essential to moral virtue is still missing. This missing feature is the recognition of a *duty* to adopt those ends which we have attributed to the moral man. We have said that he *does* care about others, and about causes such as liberty and justice; that it is on this account that he will accept a system of morality. But what if he never cared about such things, or what if he ceased to care? Is it not the case that he *ought* to care? This is exactly what Kant would say, for though at times he sounds as if he thought that morality is not concerned with ends, at others he insists that the adoption of ends such as the happiness of others is itself dictated by morality.[13] How is this proposition to be regarded by one who rejects all talk about the binding force of the moral law? He will agree that a moral man has moral ends and cannot be indifferent to matters such as suffering and injustice. Further, he will recognise in the statement that one ought to care about these things a correct application of the non-hypothetical moral "ought" by which society is apt to voice its demands. He will not, however, take the fact that he ought to have certain ends as in itself reason to adopt them. If he himself is a moral man then he cares about such things, but not "because he ought." If he is an amoral man he may deny that he has any reason to trouble his head over this or any other moral demand. Of course he may be mistaken, and his life as well as others' lives may be most sadly spoiled by his selfishness. But this is not what is urged by those who think they can close the matter by an emphatic use of "ought." My argument is that they are relying on an illusion, as if trying to give the moral "ought" a magic force.[14]

This conclusion may, as I said, appear dangerous and subversive of morality. We are apt to panic at the thought that we ourselves, or other people, might stop caring about the things we do care about, and we feel that the categorical imperative gives us some control over the situation. But it is in-teresting that the people of Leningrad were not struck by the thought that only the *contingent* fact that other citizens shared their loyalty and devotion to the city stood between them and the Germans during the terrible years of the siege. Perhaps we should be less troubled than we are by fear of defection from the moral cause; perhaps we should even have less reason to fear it if people thought of themselves as volunteers banded together to fight for liberty and justice and against inhumanity and oppression. It is often felt, even if obscurely, that there is an element of deception in the official line about morality. And while some have been persuaded by talk about the authority of the moral law, others have turned away with a sense of distrust.[15]

NOTES

"Morality as a System of Hypothetical Imperatives" originally appeared in *Philosophical Review* 81, 3 (July 1972).

1. *Foundations of the Metaphysics of Morals*, sec. II, trans. by L. W. Beck.
2. Ibid.
3. Ibid.
4. According to the position sketched here we have three forms of hypothetical imperative: "If you want x you should do y." "Because you want x you should do y." And "Because x is in your interest you should do y." For Kant the third would automatically be covered by the second.
5. To say that at that moment one wants to be a respectable philosopher would be another matter. Such a statement requires a special connexion between the desire and the moment.
6. I am here going back on something I said in an earlier article ("Moral Beliefs," reprinted in [Foot, *Virtues and Vices and Other Essays in Moral Philosophy* (Berkeley, CA: University of California Press, 1978)]) where I thought it necessary to show that virtue must benefit the agent. I believe the rest of the article can stand.
7. Op. cit., p. 119. See also Foot, "Moral Arguments," p. 105.
8. To say that moral considerations are *called* reasons is blatantly to ignore the problem.
In the case of etiquette or club rules it is obvious that the non-hypothetical use of "should" has resulted in the loss of the usual connexion between what one should do and what one has reason to do. Someone who objects that in the moral case a man cannot be justified in restricting his practical reasoning in this way, since every moral "should" gives reasons for acting, must face the following dilemma. Either it is possible to create reasons for acting simply by putting together any silly rules and introducing a non-hypothetical "should," or else the non-hypothetical "should" does not necessarily imply reasons for acting. If it does not necessarily imply reasons for acting we may ask why it is supposed to do so in the case of morality. Why cannot the indifferent amoral man say that for him "should$_m$" gives no reason for acting, treating "should$_m$" as most of us treat "should$_e$?" Those who insist that "should$_m$" is categorical in this second "reason-giving" sense do not seem to realise that they never prove this to be so. They sometimes say that moral considerations "just do" give reasons for acting, without explaining why some devotee of etiquette could not say the same about the rules of etiquette.

9. I am grateful to Rogers Albritton for drawing my attention to this interesting use of expressions such as "have to" or "must."

10. Pt. II, Introduction, sec. II.

11. Immanuel Kant, *Critique of Practical Reason*, trans. L. W. Beck, p. 133.

12. It is not, of course, necessary that charitable actions should *succeed* in helping others; but when they do so they do not *happen* to do so, since that is necessarily their aim. (Note added, 1977.)

13. See, e.g., *Metaphysics of Morals*, pt. II, sec. 30.

14. See G. E. M. Anscombe, "Modern Moral Philosophy," *Philosophy* (1958). My view is different from Miss Anscombe"s, but I have learned from her.

15. So many people have made useful comments on drafts of this article that I despair of thanking them all. Derek Parfit's help has been sustained and invaluable, and special thanks are also due to Barry Stroud.

An earlier version of this paper was read at the Center for Philosophical Exchange, Brockport, N. Y., and published in *Philosophical Exchange* (Summer 1971). Note 8 is mostly from this paper, and I add here some other paragraphs that may throw light on the present paper.

My own view is that while there are ends within ethics which one should adopt (as, e.g., that one's children get a good education) there are difficulties about saying that one "ought" to take account of the general good. For either the "ought" means "morally ought" or "ought from a moral point of view" or else it does not. If it does we have a tautological principle. If it does not the problem is to know what is being said. By hypothesis a prudential "ought" is not intended here, or one related to others of the agent's contingent ends. Nor do we have the "ought" and "ought not" operating within the system of etiquette, or some system of institutional rules. This "ought"—the one in the sentence "One ought to be moral"—is supposed to be free floating and unsubscripted, and I have never found anyone who could explain the use of the word in such a context. (They are apt to talk about the expressing of resolves, or of decisions, but it is then not clear why we need the "ought" terminology when "I resolve" and "I've decided" are already in use.) My own conclusion is that "One ought to be moral" makes no sense at all unless the "ought" has the moral subscript, giving a tautology, or else relates morality to some other system such as prudence or etiquette. I am, therefore putting forward quite seriously a theory that disallows the possibility of saying that a man ought (free unsubscripted "ought") to have ends other than those he does have: for instance, that the uncaring, amoral man ought to care about the relief of suffering or the protection of the weak. In my view we must start from the fact that some people do care about such things, and even devote their lives to them; they may therefore talk about what should be done presupposing such common aims. These things are necessary, but only subjectively and conditionally necessary, as Kant would put it.

Kant would of course object that I am treating men as if, in the army of duty, they were volunteers, and this is exactly my thought. Why does Kant so object to the idea that those who are concerned about morality are joining together with like-minded people to fight against injustice and oppression, or to try to relieve suffering, and that they do so because, caring about such things, they are ready to volunteer in the cause? Kant says that there is a kind of conceit involved in such a conception. Why does he think this? He supposes that in so viewing the matter (In seeing ourselves as volunteers) we are forgetting our nature as human beings, members of the phenomenal as well as the noumenal world, whose will may be determined by the moral law but also by desire, so that we do not automatically act as a being with a holy will would act, and are beings for whom the dictates of reason take the form of a command. Let us agree that a human being doesn't necessarily have moral ends, and that even when he does his inclination may be stronger than his moral resolves. Both of these things being true a man could be mistaken either in supposing that his concern for others could not fail, or in supposing that by merely following his inclinations he could serve moral causes with no need for resolution or self-discipline. We have already pointed out that a morality of hypothetical imperatives is not a morality of inclination; resolution and self-discipline being at least as necessary to achieve moral ends as to achieve anything else. So let us consider the other suggestion, that the supporter of the hypothetical imperative is failing to recognise that the desires of even the most moral of men could always change. This charge should be denied. One who supports the hypothetical imperative does not forget that desires might change; he has simply given up trying to deal, in advance, with such a contingency by saying to himself that he would still be under command. That this seems hard to accept is the fact that lies, I think, at the heart of Kantianism in ethics, and to the neo-Kantianism of those who accept his strictures on the hypothetical imperative though rejecting the rest of his theory. It will seem to many impossible that one should have nothing to say about the case where moral concerns have vanished, except, of course, to note the character of the man concerned, and in the case of other people, to take what measures one can to stop them from doing harm. Perhaps the greatest fear is of a change in oneself; one wants as it were to make sure one is stuck with the idea of acting morally whatever one's concerns have become. The move betrays a lack of confidence which oddly does not often trouble people when their devotion is to causes other than those of morality.

These suggestions are, of course, directly relevant to Kant's arguments against the hypothetical imperative, for the same problems arise about the meaning of the things that he says. What, for instance, does it mean to say that moral rules are categorical commands? In the first place they are not commands at all, neither commands of men nor commands of God; or rather if they are commands of God it is not as commanded by God that they are in Kant's sense categorical commands. (This he says explicitly.) What we actually have are rules of conduct adopted by certain societies, and individuals within these societies; and Kant is saying that these rules are universally valid. But when we put it this way, in terms of rules, the difficulty of understanding the notion of universal validity is apparent. (It can no longer mean that everyone is commanded, which shows that there is some point in denying Kant the picturesque language of commands.) Kant's thought seems to be that moral rules are universally valid in that they are inescapable, that no one can contract out of morality, and above all that no one can say that as he does not happen to care about the ends of morality, morality does not apply to him. This thought about inescapability is very important, and we should pause to consider it. It is perhaps Kant's most compelling argument against the hypothetical imperative, and the one that may make Kantians of us all.

There is, of course, a sense in which morality is inescapable. Consider, for instance, moral epithets such as "dishonest," "unjust," "uncharitable"; these do not cease to apply to a man because he is indifferent to the ends of morality: they may indeed apply to him because of his indifference. He is judged by the criteria of morality when moral character is in question, and Kant is indeed right in saying that these criteria are independent of his desires. (*Contrast* a word such as "rash"). No one can escape the application of the moral terms by pleading his indifference. Nor can he escape them by turning to ways of life in which he can be counted as being neither morally good or morally bad, as he can escape being a good or a bad husband by simply not marrying, or a good or bad carpenter by refusing to take up the tools. In this sense, then, morality is inescapable, but this can be accepted, and insisted on, by Kant's opponent, the defender of the hypothetical imperative. The latter may also agree that the application of such epithets will often be the vehicle for the expression of opposition, disgust, or hatred. It has already been agreed that with our present "non-hypothetical" use of "should" in moral contexts the application of the moral "should" is also inescapable. But someone who thinks that significant concessions have now been made to Kant must answer the following question. Has anything been said about the inescapability of morality which could not also be said about the inescapability of etiquette? For just as a man is immoral if he does certain things, despite his indifference to the nature and result of his actions, so he is rude or unmannerly, or one who does what is "not done," whatever his views about etiquette. Since no one says that the rules of etiquette are categorical imperatives the task must be to explain the additional inescapability belonging to morality.

We must return, therefore, to the difficulty of discovering what Kant can have meant by saying that moral rules have objective necessity, are categorical commands, are universally valid, or are binding upon the will of every free agent. Nothing that we have yet considered has given Kant what he wants, and one cannot, I think, avoid the following conclusion. Kant's argument that moral rules have a peculiar and dignified status depends wholly upon his attempt to link moral action with rationality through the mere concept of the form of law and the principle of universalisability. as interpreted by him. In acting morally Kant thinks that we do as reason dictates. In acting immorally we are acting irrationally, and if this is not how Kant puts it, it is what he must show in order to make his point; if it could be proved, then any man, whatever his desires, could be shown to have reason to act morally, since one has reason to do what it is rational to do. The difficulty, as everyone knows, is to accept Kant's arguments purporting to show that morally bad actions are those whose maxim could not belong to a universally legislative will, and moreover that action according to such maxims is irrational action. These difficulties have been argued *ad nauseam*, and I shall not repeat the arguments here. All I would claim to have shown is that no one who rejects Kant's attempts to derive morality from reason has been given any reason to reject the hypothetical imperative in morals. It is commonly believed that even if Kant has not shown the connexion between reason and morality he has at least destroyed the hypothetical imperative. I have urged that, on the contrary, there is no valid argument against the hypothetical imperative to be found in Kant should the argument from reason fail. (Note added in 1977.)

RECANTATION 1994

The idea that morality is a system of hypothetical imperatives is so alien to my present views that I no longer want to reprint this paper without explaining that I have long thought the positive part of it misconceived. It is true that the challenge that the paper started with was good, and that it has not, perhaps, to this day been satisfactorily answered. I pointed out that if we say that it is rational to follow moral injunctions but not rational to follow just any old rule, as, for example, a rule of etiquette or of the proper procedure for fighting a duel, it will not do to invoke usage to show that moral imperatives are categorical and the rest hypothetical. If we have reason, quite apart from our desires, to keep promises or tell the truth but not to bother about etiquette or dueling rules, then it must be shown that and why this is so.

At the time that I was writing the article I was unable to see how this could be done, because I was still under the influence of Humean theories of reasons for action. To be sure I had elsewhere (rather inconsistently) allowed self-interest an independent reason giving force; but I nevertheless insisted, for example, that only one who could be described as a lover of justice would have reason to be just. What I was doing, in my own mind, was to contrast rational action with the unthinking, perhaps habitual, following of rules one had been trained to follow; and I simply assumed that I had to find the difference within the mentality of the agent. I therefore dismissed as irrelevant the obvious difference between, say, morality and etiquette which would be the first to strike anyone innocent of philosophy: I mean the fact that much good for human beings hangs on such things as promise-keeping and truth-telling, whereas rules of etiquette may have to do with unimportant matters, and often seem designed to produce anxiety rather than to safeguard the good things of human life.

In my present view, facts about human life are the ones we should call on to develop an account of practical rationality: that is an account of goodness in respect of the recognising and following of reasons for action as it is for creatures situated as human being are. Moral virtues are needed for this practical rationality, as is a modicum of self-love, and the rightful pursuit of more desire-dependent ends. Someone acts well in all these respects only if he recognises what he has reason to do in each area, and allows this to influence his conduct. Wherever exactly we want to use the word "irrationality," we must admit that someone is *deficient in practical rationality* if he fails to recognize moral considerations as reasons for acting; as also if he thinks he has no reason to look after himself, or to take trouble to attain his more particular ends. But of course he can also be defective if, in spite of knowing what he should do, he does not do it. "Hypothetical imperatives" having to do with the pursuit of ends that are not mandatory belongs only to part of this story, and definitely not to the part that concerns morality.

For an exposition of the later view of the practical rationality I must refer readers to a lecture of mine called "Does Moral Subjectivism Rest on a Mistake?" printed in the *Oxford Journal of Legal Studies*, 15, no. 1 (January 1995). The present note will not stand on its own, except as a statement of my firm opposition to the theses of the earlier piece.

For an excellent criticism of "Morality as a System of Hypothetical Imperatives" see Gavin Lawrence "The Rationality of Morality," in R. Hursthouse et al., eds., *Virtues and Reasons* (Oxford: Oxford University Press, 1995).

19

From *The Possibility of Altruism*

THOMAS NAGEL

I. THE FOUNDATION OF MORALS

1. Just as there are rational requirements on thought, there are rational requirements on action, and altruism is one of them. This book defends a conception of ethics, and a related conception of human nature, according to which certain important moral principles state rational conditions on desire and action which derive from a basic requirement of altruism. Altruism itself depends on a recognition of the reality of other persons, and on the equivalent capacity to regard oneself as merely one individual among many.

I conceive ethics as a branch of psychology. My claims concern its foundation, or ultimate motivational basis. If the requirements of ethics are rational requirements, it follows that the motive for submitting to them must be one which it would be contrary to reason to ignore. So it must be shown that susceptibility to certain motivational influences, including altruism, is a condition of rationality, just as the capacity to accept certain theoret-

ical arguments is thought to be a condition of rationality. The view presented here is opposed not only to ethical relativism but to any demand that the claims of ethics appeal to our interests: either self-interest or the interest we may happen to take in other things and other persons. The altruism which in my view underlies ethics is not to be confused with generalized affection for the human race. It is not a feeling.

2. Philosophers interested in the motivational problems of ethics commonly seek a *justification* for being moral: a consideration which can persuade everyone or nearly everyone to adhere to certain moral principles, by connecting those principles with a motivational influence to which everyone is susceptible. The question arises, however, whether any grounding of this sort can meet the conditions of inescapability which should attach to ethics. Any justification, it would seem, must rest on empirical assumptions about the influences to which people are susceptible. The justification will have neither validity nor persuasive force if those assumptions are not true of the individual to whom it is addressed.

One can escape a rational requirement if one fails to meet its conditions in some way. One is then allowed to beg off, and the permissible grounds depend on the general principle from which the particular application of the requirement follows. That principle may in turn apply in virtue of a still more general principle plus further conditions, and if those conditions are not met, escape is again possible. But at some point the retreat must come to an end: one must reach a requirement (it need not be conditional, for it may have been the original one) from which it is not possible to escape by begging off. It is natural to suppose that principles of this sort must underlie ethics, if it exists.

It is also natural to assume that the enterprise of justification should focus on these basic requirements, thus yielding an ethical system with cast iron motivational backing. But such a programme appears doomed from the start. For if we justify a requirement, it is in terms of a principle from which that requirement follows, perhaps with the aid of further conditions. But that principle must itself represent a requirement, or else what it is adduced to justify will not be one. Therefore any requirement which we set out to justify will not be ultimate. Something beyond justification is required.

3. I assume that a normative requirement on action must have correspondingly strict motivational backing. If ethics is to contain practical requirements, motivation theory, specifically the theory of rational motivation, must contain results that are similarly inescapable. It may be thought that this excludes from an essential role in the foundation of ethics the factor of desire (although it is a mystery how one could account for the motivational source of ethical action without referring to desires). The problem about appealing ultimately to human desires is that this appears to exclude rational criticism of ethical motivations at the most fundamental level. As ordinarily conceived, any desire, even if it is in fact universal, is nevertheless merely an affection (not susceptible to rational assessment) to which one is either subject or not. If that is so, then moral considerations whose persuasiveness depends on desires depend ultimately on attitudes which we are not required to accept. On the other hand, the picture of human motivational structure as a system of given desires connected in certain ways with action is a very appealing one, and it can seem that any persuasive justification of ethical conduct must find its foothold in such a system.

There are two possible paths out of this dilemma, which are not in the end completely distinct. (a) One may dispute the standard views of motivation and of the role which desires play in it; or (b) one may hold that though all motivation involves desire, some desires are open to rational assessment and need not be regarded simply as given inclinations. I shall propose that the basis of ethics in human motivation is something other than desire; but this factor will itself enable us to criticize certain desires as contrary to practical reason.

4. Denial that justification is the appropriate final defence of ethics suggests the familiar view that the question "Why should I be moral?" is senseless or in principle unanswerable. Strictly the suggestion is correct, but not in a sense which supports intuitionism. I believe that an *explanation* can be discovered for the basic principles of ethics, even though it is not a justification. A satisfactory explanation must account for the motivational force appropriate to requirements on action. Psychology, specifically motivation theory, may therefore be the appropriate field in which to make progress in ethical theory. But this appears to involve radical changes in what is thought possible for psychology. Psychological investigation leading to ethical conclusions may require the reintroduction of metaphysics. One does not ordinarily expect to find in motivation theory any principles which lend themselves to interpretation as normative requirements on action. Motivation theory is automatically regarded as an empirical science; it is assumed that at best we may hope to discover the influences to which men are subject and the patterns into which their behaviour falls—perhaps even certain patterns and influences which are universal. But the suggestion that there must be motivational requirements on which to base ethical requirements (or perhaps that the two are identical) seems to demand a priori reasoning in motivation theory—something rather unexpected.

This is the possibility which I propose to explore. Human motivation possesses features which are susceptible to metaphysical investigation and which carry some kind of necessity (though this last requires elaborate qualification). The need to find sufficiently firm psychological ground for ethics has prompted the search for such features, but fortunately there is independent support for their existence.

It will in any case not do to rest the motivational influence of ethical considerations on fortuitous or escapable inclinations. Their hold on us must be deep, and it must be essentially tied to the ethical principles themselves, and to the conditions of their truth. The alternative is to abandon the objectivity of ethics. That is a course which cannot be excluded in advance, but it should not be taken before serious attempts to rescue the subject have failed.

II. THE TRADITIONAL CONTROVERSY

1. The names "internalism" and "externalism" have been used to designate two views of the relation between ethics and motivation.[1] Internalism is the view that the presence of a motivation for acting morally is guaranteed by the truth of ethical propositions themselves. On this view the motivation must be so tied to the truth, or meaning, of ethical statements that when in a particular case someone is (or perhaps merely believes that he is) morally required to do something, it follows that he has a motivation for doing it. Externalism holds, on the other hand, that the necessary motivation is not supplied by ethical principles and judgments themselves, and that an additional psychological sanction is required to motivate our compliance. Externalism is compatible with a variety of views about the motivation for being moral. It is even compatible with the view that such a motivation is always present—so long as its presence is not guaranteed by moral judgments themselves, but by something external to ethics. The present discussion attempts to construct the basis of an internalist position.

Internalists appeal to various types of motivation: self-interest, sympathy, benevolence, even the amorphously general "approval" or "pro-attitude." Even emotivism can be counted as an internalist position of sorts, so the conditions which internalism places on the organization of the motivational factor need not be very rigorous. Internalism's appeal derives from the conviction that one cannot accept or assert sincerely any ethical proposition without accepting at least a prima facie motivation for action in accordance with it. Philosophers who believe that there is no room for rational assessment of the basic springs of motivation will tend to be internalists, but at the cost of abandoning claims to moral objectivity. One way to do this is to build motivational content into the meaning of ethical assertions by turning them into expressions of a special sort of inclination, appropriate only when that inclination is present, and rooted only in the motivations of the speaker. The result is a basically anti-rational ethical theory, having as its foundation a commitment, inclination, feeling, or desire that is simply given (though the superstructure may be characterized by a high degree of rational articulation). Motivational content is thereby tied to the meaning of ethical *utterances*—

what the speaker means or expresses—rather than to the truth conditions of those utterances, which are left vague or non-existent.

A stronger position, one which ties the motivation to the cognitive content of ethical claims, requires the postulation of motivational influences which one cannot reject once one becomes aware of them. If such influences can be shown to belong to the content of ethics, then someone who recognizes the truth of an ethical claim will have to accept the corresponding motivation.

2. Mill and Moore appear to be externalists. In Moore's case, the attribution is by elimination, for at least in *Principia Ethica*, he does not consider the motivation for being moral at all. Mill devotes a separate chapter of *Utilitarianism* to what he calls the sanctions for the principle of utility. He regards the question as separate from that of the principle's truth, and the answers he provides are unrelated to his arguments for the principle.

On Moore's stated view it can only be regarded as a mysterious fact that people care whether what they do is right or wrong. I suspect, however, that it is really an unrecognized assumption of internalism that underlies Moore's "refutation" of naturalism. The evaluative factor which is always left out by any naturalistic description of the object of ethical assessment is in fact the relevant inclination or attitude.[2] But Moore did not realize this, and consequently did not produce an internalist position but an externalist one in which a peculiar non-natural quality served to flesh out the content of ethical claims.

Such views are, it seems to me, unacceptable on their surface, for they permit someone who has acknowledged that he should do something and has seen *why* it is the case that he should do it to ask whether he has any reason for doing it. Of course one line of retreat from this unacceptable conclusion is to deny that the evaluative portion or aspect of an ethical assertion has any truth value, and to attach the evaluation instead to the individual's expression of the ethical claim.

But if one wishes to tie the requirement of motivational influence to the truth-conditions of moral claims, with the consequence that if someone recognizes their grounds, he cannot but be affected accordingly, then a stricter motivational connection will be required.

3. One example of such a view is provided by Hobbes, whose ethical system is solidly grounded in motivational energies derived from a universal desire for self-preservation. The ethical system is simply a development of certain consequences of that motive in the conduct of a rational and fully informed individual. Human nature is according to Hobbes subject to other, irrational influences as well, so one will not necessarily do what one ought even when one knows what it is; but given the universality and fundamental nature of the desire to live, a recognition of the grounds for one of Hobbes's ethical imperatives cannot fail to move us to some extent.

Hobbes derives the system of moral requirements from the operation of a motivational factor which can be independently understood, together with certain highly general assumptions about the human condition. The basic motive is taken as given, and only its consequences qualify as ethical conclusions. It is not an ethical principle that all men should want to preserve their own lives; so in that sense motivation theory is at the most fundamental level prior to ethics, which constitutes a development of one branch of it. Claims about what we should do simply *are* on this view claims about what we have a certain sort of motivation for doing; ethical arguments are persuasive because, if someone with the assumed desire understands the argument for an ethical conclusion, he must be aware of those circumstances and interconnections which, according to the argument, would motivate him if he were aware of them.

4. The most influential anti-rational internalist is of course Hume. The motivational basis of his ethical system is weaker and less clearly defined than that of Hobbes, since sympathy (later general benevolence), the specifically moral motivation, requires buttressing by self-interest if it is to be sufficiently powerful to resist contrary claims stemming from self-interest directly. But he does make explicit an extremely attractive theory of the justification of action which has had enormous effect on ethical theory. The view is that any justification must appeal to an inclination in the individual to whom it is offered, and that the justification proceeds by drawing connections between that inclination and other things (notably actions) which are means to its satisfaction. The inclination then becomes transferred to these by association, which is what makes persuasive justification possible. If we cast this view in terms of reasons, it will state that among the conditions for the presence of a reason for action there must always be a desire or inclination capable of motivating one to act accordingly.

Hobbes's system satisfies these conditions on justification. In fact he and Hume approach the task in similar ways: both assume that ethics must represent the domain of the objective, the common, in practical matters—that is, that which all men equally have reason to promote—and both seek a motivational basis for the possibility of such agreement. Hobbes finds it in men's common interest in certain security conditions, social structures, and conventions necessary for the fulfilment of their desire to survive; Hume finds it in the capacity for sympathetic participation in the happiness and unhappiness of others, or even in the mere thought of the likelihood of their happiness or unhappiness. Both regard ethics as a codification of only part of the motivational apparatus; there remains ample room for practical disagreement among men, and, for Hume at least, given the weakness of sympathy in contrast to self-interest, moral considerations alone are by no means decisive.

On Hume's view one begins with psychology, and ethics is an elaboration of it.

The basic psychological factors are not themselves brought to light by ethical investigation (though the need for a foundation for ethics may have led to the search for them). And given Hume's famous restrictions on rational assessment of the passions and of preferences, the possibility of justifying morality is strictly limited. Any justification ends finally with the rationally gratuitous presence of the emotion of sympathy; if that condition were not met, one would simply have no reason to be moral. Now it may in fact follow from Hume's theory of imagination that susceptibility to sympathy is a necessary trait of all beings who can think about the feelings of others.[3] But he does not appear to recognize that his psychological factor has this status; so far as he is concerned the edifice of ethics rests on a psychological contingency. In the case of Hobbes, the love of life may be thought somewhat closer to being a necessary motive for human beings. But still the motivational basis is prior to and independent of the ethical system which derives from it. A quite different sort of theory would be necessary to alter that relation of priority.

5. Plato and Aristotle, each in his own way, constitute examples of such a rebellion against the priority of psychology. Both felt, I think, that the motivation for being moral does not come from elsewhere, that is, from any independently comprehensible desire or feeling. The ethical motivation, even at its most basic level, can on this view be understood only through ethics. But since the issue is not clearly posed by either of these writers, a discussion of their views would require heavier exegetical work than I wish to undertake here.

Fortunately we have a far better example in the person of Kant, who is explicitly and consciously driven by the demand for an ethical system whose motivational grip is not dependent on desires which must simply be taken for granted. His insistence that the imperatives of morality be categorical is essentially an insistence that their application not depend on the presence of a motivational factor prior to ethics, from which they are extracted as consequences. From Kant's efforts one sees what a struggle is required to undercut the priority of ethically neutral motivations, and to put ethical principles themselves at the absolute source of our moral conduct. It seems possible that Kant's postulation of moral interest as the motivating impulse for phenomenal moral behaviour compromised the effort. But that need not be settled here. We must try to understand Kant's enterprise.

A hypothetical imperative is the only kind which Hume regards as possible. It states what a given desire provides one with a motivation to do, and it applies only if one is subject to that desire. The desire itself is not commanded by the imperative. Consequently no hypothetical imperative can state an unconditional requirement on action.

Kant's effort to produce a categorical imperative is an attempt to discover requirements on action which apply to a man on no conditions about what he wants, how he feels, and so forth. They must nevertheless be requirements whose validity involves the capacity to be motivated in accordance with them. Since that motivational factor cannot come from a presupposed motivation which is made a condition of the requirements, it must, if it is to exist at all, come from the requirements themselves. That is, what makes the requirements valid for us must itself determine the capacity of our motivational structure to yield corresponding action. Thus, according to Kant, ethics, rather than appropriating an antecedently comprehensible motivational foundation on which to build its requirements, actually uncovers a motivational structure which is specifically ethical and which is explained by precisely what explains those requirements. It is the conception of ourselves as free which he alleges to be the source of our acceptance of the imperatives of morality, and it is the acceptance of the imperatives thus grounded by which he explains moral motivation. This is more-

over not a motivational explanation, since instead of making use of the motivational system, it explains one of its fundamental features.

III. THE SOLUTION

1. The issue of priority between ethics and motivation theory is for an internalist of crucial importance. The position which I shall defend resembles that of Kant in two respects: First, it provides an account of ethical motivation which does not rely on the assumption that a motivational factor is already present among the *conditions* of any moral requirement. On this view the possibility of appropriate motivation must be guaranteed by the truth of the moral claim itself—but *not* because the existence of such motivation is included in advance among the independently comprehensible truth conditions of every moral claim. There are reasons for action which are specifically moral; it is because they represent moral requirements that they can motivate, and not vice versa.

If this is correct, ethics must yield discoveries about human motivation. But of what kind? Not just information about what people want. If ethics is not to presuppose any motivations, but must instead reveal their possibility, the discoveries must be at a more fundamental level than that.

Admittedly other internalist theories, of the Humian sort, offer to explain how the motivation of ethical conduct is possible. Hobbes's theory begins with a desire for self-preservation, and requirements of contractual fidelity and political allegiance are deduced therefrom by a complicated argument which shows how the postulated interest can motivate one to adhere to those requirements. Such a derivation does not start from scratch, however; the basic motivation is presupposed even though ethics reveals the possibility of its extended influence (thereby extending its *actual* influence). Ethical theory does not, in the system of Hobbes, explain how the fear of death is possible. So there is a component in human motivation, which can be understood independently of ethics, on which the force of ethics ultimately depends. That is the sort of dependence that I contend must be eliminated from ethical theory.

Certain ethical principles are themselves propositions of motivation theory so fundamental that they cannot be derived from or defined in terms of previously understood motivations. These principles specify how reasons for action follow from certain given conditions. Thus they *define* motivational possibilities, rather than presupposing them. Consequently the final understanding of action motivated by those reasons will be ethical. To understand the motivation we must understand how the ethical principle governs us.

The second way in which my position resembles Kant's is that it assigns a central role in the operation of ethical motives to a certain feature of the agent's metaphysical conception of himself. On Kant's view the conception is that of freedom, whereas on my view it is the conception of oneself as merely a person among others equally real. However, different as they are, both are thought to be conceptions which we cannot escape, and are thought to provide that basis for ethical motivation which in other internalist theories is provided by various motives and desires. Because of the alleged inescapability of these conceptions, a view of the Kantian type entails that we are not fully free to be amoral, or insusceptible to moral claims. That is what makes us men.

2. I shall argue that the motivational counterpart of an ethical requirement is not any particular desire or sentiment, but rather a matter of structure. Any theory of motivation must contain some structural features. They may be very simple. In the limiting case, they may amount simply to the conditions on causal explanation in general, without special features facilitating its application to human conduct. Even the simplest drive theory assumes some additional structure; a theory which explains all rational action by the combination of desires and beliefs assumes somewhat more. I suggest that the contribution of structural factors to the generation of reasons, and of actions done for those reasons, is very important. That is where the foundation of ethics must be sought (though by no means all of the important structural contributions will be ethical).

We are therefore in search of principles which belong both to ethics and to motivation theory, and which state structural conditions on the forms and interrelations of reasons for action. This solution may appear to involve an illegitimate conflation of explanatory and normative inquiries. But a close connection between the two is already embodied in the ordinary concept of a reason, for we can adduce reasons either to explain or to justify action. We may explain what a man does by referring to his reasons. On the other hand we may assert that circumstances *provide* someone with a reason to act in certain ways, without implying that he will be accordingly motivated (if only because of the possibility of his ignorance). But though the explanatory and normative claims can diverge, this does not mean that we are faced with two disparate concepts finding refuge in a single word. When action is explained by reasons, it is brought under the control of normative principles. A consideration can operate as a motivating reason only if it has, or is thought to have, the status of a reason in the system of normative principles by which individuals govern their conduct. Such normative principles therefore specify significant features of the motivational structure. This structure is neither arbitrary nor accidental. Its form is determined in certain ways by the fact that conscious beings must apply the system of normative principles to themselves when forming their intentions.

3. The eventual goal of our investigation is an analysis of altruism along the above lines.

However, such an analysis can emerge only as the result of a broader examination of reasons, which will include detailed attention to the motive of prudence as well. Actually, the notions of prudence and altruism indicate a range of motives narrower than that to be discussed; the conclusions which I shall defend are quite general. My aim is to discover for prudence and altruism, and other motivations related to them, a basis which depends not on desires, but rather on formal aspects of practical reason. One of the steps in the argument will be to show that the most natural alternative, namely explanation by means of desires, cannot adequately account for the facts, so that another account is necessary. The detailed support for this general thesis will be presented in connection with prudence: a less controversial motive, which provides the model for a subsequent analysis of altruism.

The general thesis to be defended concerning altruism is that one has a *direct* reason to promote the interests of others—a reason which does not depend on intermediate factors such as one's own interests or one's antecedent sentiments of sympathy and benevolence. This is both a claim of ethics, and a claim about what happens when someone is altruistically motivated. . . .

IV. DESIRES

1. Beginning with relatively uncontroversial cases, we must try to arrive at general conclusions about the sources of reasons and their mode of operation. Eventually we shall deal with prudence as a model for the treatment of altruism: the difficulties which arise in the two cases depend on similar arguments and fallacies. Most important, the interpretation of that feature of reasons on which prudence depends provides a model for the parallel enterprise in the case of altruism.

I shall argue that the superficially plausible method of accounting for all motivations in terms of the agent's desires will not work, and that the truth is considerably less obvious and more significant. It is therefore necessary to begin with an investigation of the role of desires in rational motivation generally, in order to demonstrate that what they can explain is limited, and that even in simple cases they produce action by a mechanism which is not itself explicable in terms of desires.

The attempt to derive all reasons from desires stems from the acknowledgment that reasons must be capable of motivating, together with an assumption which I shall attack—that all motivation has desire at its source. The natural position to be opposed is this: since all motivated action must result from the operation of some motivating factor within the agent, and since belief cannot by itself produce action, it follows that a desire of the agent must always be operative if the action is to be genuinely his. Anything else, any external factor or belief adduced in explanation of the action, must on this view be connected with it through some desire which the agent has at the time, a desire which can take the action or its goal as object. So any apparently prudential or altruistic act must be explained by the connection between its goal—the agent's future interest or the interest of another—and a desire which activates him now. Essentially this view denies the possibility of motivational action at a distance, whether over time or between persons. It bridges any apparent gaps with desires of the agent, which are thought to supply the necessary links to the future and to external situations.

Prudence cannot on this view be explained merely by the perception that something is in one's future interest; there must be a desire to further one's future interests if the perception is to have an effect. What follows about altruism is similar: I cannot be motivated simply by the knowledge that an act of mine will have certain consequences for the interests of others; I must care what happens to them if this knowledge is to be effective. There seems little doubt that most people have the desire that makes prudence possible, though it is sometimes overcome by other, more immediate impulses. Altruistic or benevolent desires on the other hand seem less common. In neither case are we in any sense required to possess the desires in question: consequently we are not required to act on the specified considerations. If one lacks the relevant desire, there is nothing more to be said.

The consequence of this view, for a system of normative reasons, is that the interests of others, or his own future interests, cannot themselves provide a person with reasons for action unless we are prepared to admit also that reasons by themselves, or conditions sufficient for their presence, may provide us with no motivation for action whatever. The separation of normative from motivational discourse has of course been attempted. But if one finds that move implausible, and wishes some guarantee that reasons will provide a motive, then one is left with no alternative, on the motivational premises already laid out, but to include a present desire of the agent, one with appropriate scope, among the conditions for the presence of any reason for action whatever. Therefore another's interest, or my own future interest, can provide me with a reason—a reason capable of motivating—only if a desire for that object is present in me at the time.

The consequences for any other-regarding morality are extreme, for if one wishes to guarantee its universal application, one must make the presence of reasons for altruistic behaviour depend on a desire present in all men. (No wonder self-interest has so often been preferred to altruism as the foundation for justice and the other social virtues.) This view eliminates the possibility of construing ethical principles so based as requirements on action, unless one can somehow show that the appropriate underlying *desires* are required of us.

2. The assumption that a motivating desire underlies every intentional act depends, I believe, on a confusion between two sorts of

desires, motivated and unmotivated. It has been pointed out before[4] that many desires, like many beliefs, are *arrived at* by decision and after deliberation. They need not simply assail us, though there are certain desires that do, like the appetites and in certain cases the emotions. The same is true of beliefs, for often, as when we simply perceive something, we acquire a belief without arriving at it by decision. The desires which simply come to us are unmotivated though they can be explained. Hunger is produced by lack of food, but is not motivated thereby. A desire to shop for groceries, after discovering nothing appetizing in the refrigerator, is on the other hand motivated by hunger. Rational or motivational explanation is just as much in order for that desire as for the action itself.

The claim that a desire underlies every act is true only if desires are taken to include motivated as well as unmotivated desires, and it is true only in the sense that *whatever* may be the motivation for someone's intentional pursuit of a goal, it becomes in virtue of his pursuit *ipso facto* appropriate to ascribe to him a desire for that goal. But if the desire is a motivated one, the explanation of it will be the same as the explanation of his pursuit, and it is by no means obvious that a desire must enter into this further explanation. Although it will no doubt be generally admitted that some desires are motivated, the issue is whether another desire always lies behind the motivated one, or whether sometimes the motivation of the initial desire involves no reference to another, unmotivated desire.

Therefore it may be admitted as trivial that, for example, considerations about my future welfare or about the interests of others cannot motivate me to act without a desire being present at the time of action. That I have the appropriate desire simply *follows* from the fact that these considerations motivate me; if the likelihood that an act will promote my future happiness motivates me to perform it now, then it is appropriate to ascribe to me a desire for my own future happiness. But nothing follows about the role of the desire as a condition contributing to the motivational efficacy of those considerations. It is a necessary condition of their efficacy to be sure, but only a logically necessary condition. It is not necessary either as a contributing influence, or as a causal condition.

In fact, if the desire is itself motivated, it and the corresponding motivation will presumably be possible for the same reasons. Thus it remains an open question whether an additional, unmotivated desire must always be found among the conditions of motivation by any other factor whatever. If considerations of future happiness can motivate by themselves, then they can explain and render intelligible the desire for future happiness which is ascribable to anyone whom they do motivate. Alternatively, there may be another factor operating in such cases, one which explains both the motivational influence of considerations about the future and the motivated desire which embodies that influence. But if a further, unmotivated desire is always among those further conditions, it has yet to be proved.

If we bring these observations to bear on the question whether desires are always among the necessary conditions of *reasons* for action, it becomes obvious that there is no reason to believe that they are. Often the desires which an agent necessarily experiences in acting will be motivated exactly as the action is. If the act is motivated by reasons stemming from certain external factors, and the desire to perform it is motivated by those same reasons, the desire obviously cannot be among the conditions for the presence of those reasons. This will be true of any motivated desire which is ascribable to someone simply in virtue of his intentional pursuit of a goal. The fact that the presence of a desire is a logically necessary condition (because it is a logical consequence) of a reason's motivating, does not entail that it is a necessary condition of the *presence* of the reason; and if it is motivated by that reason it *cannot* be among the reason's conditions.

3. As I have said earlier, the temptation to postulate a desire at the root of every motivation is similar to the temptation to postulate a belief behind every inference. Now we can see that the reply in both cases is the same: that this is true in the trivial sense that a desire or belief is always present when reasons motivate or convince—but not that the desire or belief explains the motivation or conclusion, or provides a reason for it. If someone draws conclusions in accordance with a principle of logic such as *modus ponens*, it is appropriate to ascribe to him the belief that the principle is true; but that belief is explained by the *same* thing which explains his inferences in accordance with the principle. The belief that this principle is true is certainly not among the *conditions* for having reasons to draw conclusions in accordance with it. Rather it is the perception of those reasons which explains both the belief and the particular conclusions drawn.

Beliefs provide the material for theoretical reasoning, but finally there is something besides belief, namely reason, which underlies our inferences from one set of beliefs to another, and explains both the conclusions and those logical beliefs which embody our inferential principles in general propositional form. Correspondingly, desires are among the materials for practical reasoning, but ultimately something besides desire explains how reasons function. This element accounts for many of the connections between reasons (including the reasons which stem from desires) and action. It also explains those general desires which embody our acceptance of the principles of practical reason.

The omnipresence of desires in action is misleading, for it suggests that a desire must form the basis of every motivation. But in fact, when we examine the logical reason why desire must always be present, we see that it may often be motivated by precisely what motivates the action. An alternative basis for that motivation must therefore be discovered. The alternative which I shall defend does not require one to abandon the assumption that reasons must be capable of motivating. It merely points out that they may have this capacity precisely because they are reasons, and not because a motivationally influential factor is among their conditions of application.

An account in terms of the structure of reasons and their relations to their conditions and to each other has the advantage of rendering the motivation of action by those conditions significantly more intelligible than does the mere postulation of intervening desires. It explains the peculiar intelligibility of prudential motivation, and also, I hope to show, the possibility of altruistic motivation—both without the assistance of intervening desires for future happiness or the welfare of others.

4. To summarize the argument briefly:

Though all motivation implies the presence of desire, the sense in which this is true does not warrant us in concluding that all motivation requires that desire be operative as a motivational *influence*. To that extent it remains open that there can be motivation without any motivating desire.

Some desires are themselves motivated by reasons. Those desires at any rate cannot be among the conditions of the reasons which motivate them. And since there may in principle be motivation without motivating desires, those reasons may be motivationally efficacious even without the presence of any *further* desires among their conditions.

There are two ways in which this might be so; either some other motivating factor besides desire may be present among the conditions for the existence of those reasons; or else their motivational efficacy may derive not from the conditions themselves, but rather from the principle which governs the derivation of reasons from those conditions.

In the latter event, the motivational efficacy of reasons for action would be due only to the system by which they are derived from their conditions. This would be explained by a connection between the structure of a system of reasons and the structure of human motivation. In that sense it would still be true that a reason is necessarily capable of motivating. That is the possibility which I shall pursue. . . .

V. ALTRUISM: THE INTUITIVE ISSUE

1. The problem of how, if at all, altruism is possible has much in common with the corresponding problem about prudence. By altruism I mean not abject self-sacrifice, but merely a willingness to act in consideration of the interests of other persons, without the need of ulterior motives.[5] How is it possible that such considerations should motivate us at all? What sort of system, and what further intervening factors, are necessary in order to justify and to explain behaviour which has as its object the benefit of others? (As in the case of prudence, the problem can be treated without attempting to provide too fine an analysis of benefit and harm, happiness, unhappiness, pleasure, pain, or whatever the principal determinants, positive and negative, are to be. The question is not why these particular factors motivate, but how, given that they motivate in one way, they can also motivate in another—over time or across the gap between persons.)

The problem at this stage is not how the interests of others can motivate us to some specific policy of altruistic conduct, but how they can motivate us at all. Obviously *some* account of such behaviour is needed by most ethical theories, since there are few which do not include some requirements of other-regarding action. Even if the required social behaviour does not include serious self-sacrifice, it will almost certainly include cases in which no obviously self-interested motive is present, and in which some inconvenience or at least no benefit to the agent is likely to result. A defence of altruism in terms of self-interest is therefore unlikely to be successful. But there are other interests to which appeal may be made, including the indiscriminate general sentiments of sympathy or benevolence.

It is possible to argue against such hypotheses on the ground that the psychological and societal principles to which they appeal are neither universal nor obvious enough to account for the extent of altruistic motivation, and that they are evidently false to the phenomena.[6] However, I prefer to concentrate instead on trying to provide a better account, thereby showing that an appeal to our interests or sentiments, to account for altruism, is superfluous. My general reply to such suggestions is that without question people may be motivated by benevolence, sympathy, love, redirected self-interest, and various other influences, on some of the occasions on which they pursue the interests of others, but that there is also something else, a motivation available when none of those are, and also operative when they are present, which has genuinely the status of a rational requirement on human conduct. There is in other words such a thing as pure altruism (though it may never occur in isolation from all other motives). It is the direct influence of one person's interest on the actions of another, simply because in itself the interest of the former provides the latter with a reason to act. If any further internal factor can be said to interact with the external circumstances in such a case, it will be not a desire or an inclination but the structure represented by such a system of reasons.

A suggestion of this sort will have to deal with opposition similar to that evoked by the corresponding thesis about prudential motives. With regard to prudence, we had to contend with the intuition that since even when preparing for the future I am acting in the present, it must be a present reason which motivates me, something which I want *now*. With regard to altruism, the corresponding intuition is that since it is I who am acting, even when I act in the interests of another, it must be an interest of mine which provides the impulse. If so, any convincing justification of apparently altruistic behaviour must appeal to what *I* want.

The same prejudices are in operation here which have been observed to influence discussions of prudence: the conviction that every motivation must conform to the model of an inner force; the view that behind every motivated action lies a desire which provides the active energy for it; the assumption that to provide a justification capable also of *explaining* action, an appropriate motivation, usually a desire, must be among the conditions of the justification. If, as seems unavoidable, we are to explain the influence on a person of factors external to him in terms of their interaction with something internal to him, it is natural to assume that a desire, which can take the good of others directly or indirectly as its object, must provide the motivational force behind altruistic conduct. Bluntly: the belief that an act of mine will benefit someone else can motivate me only because I want his good, or else want something which involves it.[7]

The general assumptions behind such a view have been criticized at length in Chapter V, and I do not propose to repeat those criticisms here, for they apply without significant variation and with equal validity to the present employment of these assumptions. Briefly: in so far as a desire must be present if I am motivated to act in the interest of another, it need not be a desire of the sort which can form the *basis* for a motivation. It may, instead, be a desire which is itself motivated by reasons which the other person's interests provide. And if that is so, it cannot be among the conditions for the presence of such reasons. Desire is not the only possible source of motivation. Therefore we may look for other internal factors which connect belief and action in the altruistic case. Instead of ending the explanation with an altruistic desire which is simply postulated, we can do better by inquiring how such desires are possible, and what in our nature makes us capable of wanting other people's happiness or well-being.

The account I offer will depend on a formal feature of practical reasoning which has a metaphysical explanation.

Alternative hypotheses fail as plausible candidates for a complete account of altruistic action because none of them provides the type of simple, absolute generality which is required. There is a considerateness for others which is beyond the reach of complicated reflections about social advantage, and which does not require the operation of any specific sentiment. The task is to discover an account of this general, passionless motivation which will make its existence plausible. Introspective and empirical investigation are not very useful in this area since the motivation is often partly or completely blocked in its operation by the interference of corrupting factors: repression, rationalization, blindness, weakness. Arguments and theoretical considerations can, however, reveal the form of an altruistic *component* in practical reason, which will be one contribution among others to the genesis of action.

2. The rational altruism which I shall defend can be intuitively represented by the familiar argument, "How would you like it if someone did that to you?" It is an argument to which we are all in some degree susceptible; but how it works, how it can be persuasive, is a matter of controversy. We may assume that the situation in which it is offered is one in which you would not like it if another person did to you what you are doing to someone now (the formula can be changed depending on the type of case; it can probably be used, if it works at all, to persuade people to help others as well as to avoid hurting them). But what follows from this? If no one *is* doing it to you, how can your conduct be influenced by the hypothetical admission that if someone were, you would not like it?

Various hypotheses suggest themselves. It could be that you are afraid that your present behaviour will have the result that someone *will* do the same to you; your behaviour might bring this about either directly or through the encouragement of a general practice of some kind. It could be that the thought of yourself in a position similar to that of your victim is so vivid and unpleasant that you find it distasteful to go on persecuting the wretch. But what if you have neither this belief nor this degree of affective response? Or alternatively, why cannot such considerations motivate you to increase your security against retaliation, or take a tranquilizer to quell your pity, rather than to desist from your persecutions?

There is something else to the argument; it does not appeal solely to the passions, but is a genuine argument whose conclusion is a judgment. The essential fact is that you would not only *dislike* it if someone else treated you in that way; you would resent it. That is, you would think that your plight gave the other person a reason to terminate or modify his contribution to it, and that in failing to do so he was acting contrary to reasons which were plainly available to him. In other words, the argument appeals to a *judgment* that you would make in the hypothetical case, a judgment applying a general principle which is relevant to the present case as well. It is a question not of compassion but of simply connecting, in order to see what one's attitudes commit one to.

Recognition of the other person's reality, and the possibility of putting yourself in his place, is essential. You see the present situation as a specimen of a more general scheme, in which the characters can be exchanged. The crucial factor injected into this scheme is an attitude which you have towards your own case, or rather an aspect of the view which you take of your own needs, actions, and desires. You attribute to them, in fact, a certain objective interest, and the recognition of others as persons like yourself permits extension of this objective interest to the needs and desires of persons in general, or to those of any particular individual whose situation is being considered. That is accomplished by the schematic argument. But the initial intuition in your own case is what must be investigated.

It is important that the reasons which you believe others have to consider your interests, should not refer to them specifically as *yours*. That is, you must be prepared to grant that if you were in the position in question, other people would have as their reason to help you simply that *someone* was in need of help. Otherwise there would be no way of concluding from the presence of such reasons in the event that you needed help to the presence of similar reasons in the present case, when someone else is in the unfortunate situation and you are in a position to help him. So to explain how the argument works, we must discover an aspect of your attitude towards your own needs, desires, and interests which permits you to regard them as worthy of consideration simply as *someone's* needs, desires, and interests, rather than as yours.

If there actually is such an attitude, then the form of the intuitive argument we have been considering is not really essential—since it will be possible to bring that attitude to bear on the needs, desires, and interests of another person directly. His interests are *someone's* interests as much as yours are. However, the argument at least reveals the connection between attitudes towards your own and towards other cases, and allows us to focus our analysis on attitudes of the former type, which are more vivid and require less imaginative effort. If one's sense of the reality of other persons is already sufficiently vivid, the argument may be superfluous; but since most of us are in varying degrees blind to other people, it is useful to be asked to imagine ourselves in their place, thus appealing to an objective element in the concern we feel for ourselves, and generalizing from that.

I shall therefore concentrate on each person's practical and evaluative judgments about his own needs, and so forth; especially the relation between the reasons they give him to act because they are *his* needs, and the reasons he thinks they provide for others to act, simply because they are *someone's*

needs. Our primary task will be to discover a foundation for the latter belief.

3. The primary opposition to my view comes from egoism, a general position which corresponds in this controversy to the preference of dated to timeless reasons in the controversy over prudence. Egoism holds that each individual's reasons for acting and possible motivations for acting, must arise from his own interests and desires, however those interests may be defined. The interests of one person can on this view motivate another or provide him with a reason only if they are connected with his interests or are objects of some sentiment of his, like sympathy, pity, or benevolence.

Those who occupy this philosophical position may believe that they are, as a matter of psychological fact, egoists, but I doubt that there are any genuine specimens of the type. It should be noticed how peculiar egoism would be in practice; it would have to show itself not only in the lack of a direct concern for others but also in an inability to regard one's own concerns as being of interest to anyone else, except instrumentally or contingently upon the operation of some sentiment. An egoist who needs help, before concluding that anyone else has reason to assist him, must be able to answer the question "What's it to him?" He is precluded from feeling resentment, which embodies the judgment that another is failing to act on reasons with which one's own needs provide him. No matter how extreme his own concern the egoist will not feel that this in itself need be of interest to anyone else. The pain which gives him a reason to remove his gouty toes from under another person's heel does not in itself give the other any reason to remove the heel, since it is not his pain.

Anyone who thinks he is an egoist should imagine himself in either role in such a situation. Can he truly affirm that the owner of the heel has no reason whatever to remove it from the gouty toes? Particularly if one owns the toes, it shows a rare detachment not to regard the pain as simply in itself a bad thing, which there is reason for anyone to avert. It is difficult, in other words, to resist the tendency to objectify the negative value which one assigns to pain, or would assign to it if one experienced it, regarding the identity of its owner as irrelevant.

The procedure may be different for different kinds of reasons, but the idea is the same: that in accepting goals or reasons myself I attach objective value to certain circumstances, not just value for myself; similarly when I acknowledge that others have reason to act in their own interests, these must finally be reasons not just for them, but objective reasons for the goals which they pursue or the acts which they perform.

Arguments against the coherency of ethical egoism have been offered in the past, and it may be in order to distinguish them from the one I propose to offer. The arguments with which I am familiar all focus on egoism as a universal position, and find incoherencies in the judgments which it requires a man to make about other people, and in what it requires him in general to urge or support. I wish to suggest, on the other hand, that ethical egoism is already objectionable in its application by each person to his *own* case, and to his own reasons for action. Let me mention briefly some earlier arguments.

There is the position of G. E. Moore, who claimed that egoism involves a straightforward contradiction, for it asserts "that *each* man's happiness is the sole good—that a number of different things are *each* of them the only good thing there is—an absolute contradiction!" An egoist may be inclined to object that his view is only that each man's happiness or interest is the sole good *for him* but Moore has already disallowed this move.

> When I talk of a thing as "my own good," all that I can mean is that something which will be exclusively mine (whatever be the various senses of this relation denoted by "possession"), is also *good absolutely*; or rather that my possession of it is *good absolutely*. The

good of it can in no possible sense be "private" or belong to me; any more than a thing can *exist* privately, or *for* one person only. The only reason I can have for aiming at "my own good," is that it is *good absolutely* that what I so call should belong to me—*good absolutely* that I should *have* something, which, if I have it, others cannot have. But it is *good absolutely* that I should have it, then everyone else has as much reason for aiming at *my* having it, as I have myself.[8]

He goes on to say more to the same effect, but nothing resembling an argument is offered for these claims.[9] What I wish to explain is exactly what he assumes: that in order to accept something as a goal for oneself, one must be able to regard its achievement by oneself as an *objective* good.

Other arguments, such as those of Medlin[10] and Baier,[11] point out that egoism leads to inconsistent attitudes and behaviour if as an ethical doctrine, it is to govern not only one's own actions but also what one wants and encourages others to do, or what one is obliged to permit them to do. But if these objections are correct, they leave a more fundamental question unanswered: Why should the acceptance of a universal principle of conduct commit one to any desires at all about the conformity of others to that principle? Why should the judgment that another person has reason to act in certain ways provide you with *any* reason for wanting him to do so?

There is a further question: Why need one adopt *general* principles of action at all—that is, principles applying to others besides oneself? Why can one not restrict oneself to the acceptance of personal principles of action—which may be construed as intentions, some longer-term or more general than others but all nevertheless applicable only to one's own behaviour? About this question something will be said later on.

It is a requirement of universality on practical principles, in a specific form which excludes most types of egoism, that will be defended here. And it will be supported by reflections about what happens when one acts in one's own interest. That case by itself contains the basis for a challenge to egoism.

It should be emphasized that by "egoism" I mean the relatively narrow and specific view that the only *source* of reasons for action lies in the interests of the agent. The term might also be applied to a variety of other views, and I do not propose to argue against all of them. Some fall prey to the general argument which will be offered; others do not. And of the latter, some (e.g., egoism as an instrumental policy likely to lead to everyone's happiness if generally practised) can be refuted on empirical grounds,[12] whereas others perhaps cannot (e.g., the view that life is like a competitive game, which it is objectively good that everyone should play to win). More will be said on this subject in the course of the argument.

4. I shall attempt to explain altruism, like prudence, as a rational requirement on action. Just as it became clear in the earlier discussion that prudence is not fundamental, but derives from the requirement that reasons be timelessly formulable, so it will turn out that altruism is not fundamental, but derives from something more general: a formal principle which can be specified without mentioning the interests of others at all. That principle will, moreover, be closely analogous to the formal principle of timelessness, in that it will deny the possibility of restricting to one *person* the derivative influence of a reason for action, just as the formal principle which underlies prudence denies the possibility of restricting such derivative influence to one *time*. The principle underlying altruism will require, in other words, that all reasons be construable as expressing objective rather than subjective values. In both cases the relevant condition on reasons is a purely formal one, compatible with considerable variety in the content of those reasons which satisfy it. Therefore the acceptance of prudence, or of altruism, is no substitute for a general theory of value and human interests. Both prudence

and altruism impose conditions on the derivative influence of primary reasons whose sources lie elsewhere.

The attempt to discover such a general requirement on conduct as I have described, and to provide a plausible interpretation of it, is indebted to the earlier efforts to defend prudence. Not only the general enterprise, but also the form of the present principle and the method of interpretation will parallel those of the earlier case. Specifically, it will be argued that the condition of *objectivity* (as I shall call it) is the practical expression of a conception possessed by any rational, acting subject, though not in this case the conception of himself as temporally extended. As has been indicated in Chapter IV, Section I, the conception underlying altruism is that of oneself as merely one person among others, and of others as persons in just as full a sense. This is parallel to the central element in a conception of oneself as temporally extended: that the present is just a time among others, and that other times are equally real. As we shall see, the two views have similar analyses and parallel consequences.

My argument is intended to demonstrate that altruism (or its parent principle) depends on a full recognition of the reality of other persons. Nevertheless the central conception in my proposed interpretation will be a conception of *oneself*, and the argument will rest on an analysis of how this conception bears on self-interested action. This method is allowable, because recognition of the reality of others depends on a conception of oneself, just as recognition of the reality of the future depends a conception of the present.[13]

The precise form of altruism which derives from this argument will depend on a further factor, namely the nature of the primary reasons for action which individuals possess. If these are tied to the pursuit of their interests, in some ordinary sense of that term, then a normal requirement of altruism will be the result. But if the general reasons with which we begin are not tied to individual goals, the resulting objective system may require the common pursuit of certain goals without involving altruism in the usual sense at all, that is, concern for the needs and interests of other individuals.

It is not at all obvious what our interests are, let alone what part they play in determining reasons for our conduct. I doubt, for one thing, that the satisfaction of basic desires comes anywhere near to exhausting the notion of interest. Moreover, there may be values which have nothing to do with interests at all. I do not in fact possess a general theory of the values to be embodied in a catalogue of primary reasons, but I am fairly certain that they are complicated enough to ensure that even if the formal result defended here is correct, what will emerge from it is neither utilitarianism, nor any other moral system which is simply altruistic. . . .

NOTES

1. See W. K. Frankena, "Obligation and Motivation in Recent Moral Philosophy," in *Essays in Moral Philosophy*, ed. A. I. Melden (Seattle: University of Washington Press, 1958). Frankena derives the terms from W. D. Falk; see " 'Ought' and Motivation," *Proceedings of the Aristotelian Society* (1947–48).

2. This has been observed by R. M. Hare. Cf. pp. 83–84 of *The Language of Morals* (Oxford: Oxford University Press, 1952).

3. Because he holds that to imagine the feeling or sensation of another is to have a faint copy of that feeling oneself; hence the imagination of the pain of others will itself be painful.

4. For example by Aristotle: *Nicomachean Ethics*, Bk. III, chap. 3.

5. I shall put aside for the time being all questions about the relative weight to be assigned to the interests of oneself and others, in a system of reasons which can qualify as altruistic.

6. There is one common account which can perhaps be disposed of here; the view that other-regarding behaviour is motivated by a desire to avoid the guilt feelings which would result from selfish behaviour. Guilt cannot provide the basic reason, because guilt is precisely the pained recognition that one is acting or has acted contrary to a reason which the claims, rights, or interests of others provide— a reason which must therefore be antecedently acknowledged.

Let me add that a similar argument can be given against appeals to a generalized sympathy as the basis of moral motivations. Sympathy is not, in general, just a feeling of discomfort produced by the recognition of distress in others, which in turn motivates one to relieve their distress. Rather, it is the pained awareness of their distress *as something to be relieved.*

7. The bluntness of this position may be modified, however, by the observation that it permits a distinction between selfish and unselfish behaviour. If what I want is genuinely another's happiness, the object of my actions may simply *be* his happiness, rather than the satisfaction of my own desire for it. This point was made by Joseph Butler long ago, in opposition to the claim that all action is motivated by self-love; *Fifteen Sermons Preached at the Rolls Chapel* (London, 1726), esp. Sermon XI, "Upon the Love of Our Neighbor."

8. *Principia Ethica* (Cambridge, 1903), p. 99. Although Moore treats egoism as a theory about the good, while I treat it as a theory about reasons, the two are clearly related, since Moore believes that the good is that at which one has reason to aim. I myself do not wish to make any claims about good and bad, or about their relation to reasons for action.

9. They seem to him self-evident because he regards it as already established that "good" is a one-place predicate denoting a simple, non-natural property. But that would not be granted by an egoist, whose fundamental evaluative concept would be a *relation*: "X is good for Y." A similar criticism is made by C. D. Broad, "Certain Features in Moore's Ethical Doctrines," in *The Philosophy of G. E. Moore*, ed. P. A. Schlipp (Evanston and Chicago, 1942).

10. Brian Medlin, "Ultimate Principles and Ethical Egoism," *Australasian Journal of Philosophy* (1957).

11. Kurt Baier, *The Moral Point of View* (Ithaca, N.Y.: Cornell University Press, 1958), abridged ed. (New York: Random House, 1965), p. 95.

12. On the other hand, if an instrumental egoism should be supported by *true* empirical premises, it need not conflict with altruism. If in fact egoistic conduct is the best means to the general happiness, then altruism probably requires it. But that is not the egoism that I am talking about.

13. In fact, since altruism is in a sense a hypothetical principle, stating what one has reason to do *if* what one does will affect the interests of others, it could be accepted even by someone who believed that there were no other people. Without believing in their actual existence, he could still believe in the reality of other persons in the sense that he might regard himself as a type of individual of which there could be other specimens, as real as he was. The source of this hypothetical altruism towards these possible other beings would lie in the connection between the conception of himself which allowed him to believe in their possibility, and his own self-interested concerns.

20

From *Morals by Agreement*

DAVID GAUTHIER

VI. COMPLIANCE: MAXIMIZATION CONSTRAINED

1.1 . . . The just person is fit for society because he has internalized the idea of mutual benefit, so that in choosing his course of action he gives primary consideration to the prospect of realizing the co-operative outcome. If he is able to bring about, or may reasonably expect to bring about, an outcome that is both (nearly) fair and (nearly) optimal, then he chooses to do so; only if he may not reasonably expect this does he choose to maximize his own utility.

In order to relate our account of the co-operative person to the conditions on rational interaction stated in Chapter III, let us define a fair optimizing strategy (or choice, or response) as one that, given the expected strategies of the others, may be expected to yield an outcome that is nearly fair and optimal—an outcome with utility pay-offs close to those of the co-operative outcome. . . . We speak of the response as nearly fair and op-

timal because in many situations a person will not expect others to do precisely what would be required by minimax relative concession, so that he may not be able to choose a strategy with an expected outcome that is completely fair or fully optimal. But we suppose that he will still be disposed to co-operative rather than to non-co-operative interaction.

A just person then accepts this reading of condition A [Each person's choice must be a rational response to the choices she expects the others to make]: A′: Each person's choice must be a fair optimizing response to the choice he expects the others to make, provided such a response is available to him; otherwise, his choice must be a utility-maximizing response. A just person is disposed to interact with others on the basis of condition A′.

A just person must however be aware that not all (otherwise) rational persons accept this reading of the original condition A. In forming expectations about the choices of others, he need not suppose that their choices will satisfy A'. Thus as conditions of strategic interaction, we cannot dispense with the original conditions A, B, and C; "rational response" remains (at least until our theory has gained universal acceptance) open to several interpretations. . . .

In defending condition A', we uphold the external rationality of co-operation against the objections of the egoist. Whatever else he may do, the egoist always seeks to maximize his expected utility. Recognizing that co-operation offers the prospect of mutual benefit, he nevertheless denies that it is rational to behave co-operatively, where this would constrain maximization. This egoist makes his philosophical debut as the Foole in Thomas Hobbes's *Leviathan*, where we shall now observe him.

1.2. Hobbes begins his moral theory with a purely permissive conception of the right of nature, stating what one may do, not what one must be let do, or what must be done for one. The permission is rational, for as Hobbes says, "Neither by the word *right* is anything else signified, than that liberty which every man hath to make use of his natural faculties according to right reason."[1] And Hobbes claims that in the natural condition of humankind this liberty is unlimited, so that "every man has a Right to every thing; even to one anothers body."[2] In so treating the right of nature, Hobbes expresses a straightforwardly maximizing view of rational action, subject to the material condition, central to his psychology, that each seeks above all his own preservation. For Hobbes each person has the initial right to do whatever he can to preserve himself, but there is no obligation on others, either to let him do or to do for him what is necessary to his preservation.

The condition in which this unlimited right is exercised by all persons is, Hobbes claims, one in which "there can be no security to any man, (how strong or wise soever he be,) of living out the time, which Nature ordinarily alloweth men to live."[3] Persons who seek their own preservation find themselves locked in mortal combat. But if reason brings human beings to this condition of war, it can also lead them out of it. Hobbes says, "Reason suggesteth convenient Articles of Peace, upon which men may be drawn to agreement. These Articles . . . are called the Lawes of Nature."[4] Laws of nature are precepts, "found out by Reason, by which a man is forbidden to do, that, which is destructive of his life, or taketh away the means of preserving the same; and to omit, that, by which he thinketh it may be best preserved."[5]

Since war is inimical to preservation, the fundamental or first law of nature is, "That every man, ought to endeavour Peace, as farre as he has hope of obtaining it," to which Hobbes adds, "and when he cannot obtain it, that he may seek, and use, all helps, and advantages of Warre."[6] From this Hobbes immediately derives a second law, setting out, as the fundamental means to peace, "That a man be willing, when others are so too, as farre-forth, as for Peace, and defence of himselfe he shall think it necessary, to lay down this right to all things; and be contented with so much liberty against other men, as he would allow other men against himselfe."[7] Since the unlimited right of nature gives rise to war, renouncing some part of this right is necessary for peace. The renunciation must of course be mutual; each person expects to benefit, not from his own act of renunciation, but from that of his fellows, and so no one has reason to renounce his rights unilaterally. What Hobbes envisages is a rational bargain in which each accepts certain constraints on his freedom of action so that all may avoid the costs of the natural condition of war.

The defence of this second law is perfectly straightforward. Hobbes needs to say only that "as long as every man holdeth this Right, of doing any thing he liketh; so long are all men in the condition of Warre."[8] And the mutuality required by the law is defended in an equally simple way: "if other men will not lay down their Right, as well as he; then there is no Reason for any one, to devest himselfe of his: For that were to expose himselfe to Prey, (which no man is bound to) rather than to dispose himselfe to Peace."[9] It is directly advantageous for each to agree with his fellows to a mutual renunciation or laying down of right, and so a mutual acceptance of constraint. Hobbes conceives such constraint as obligation, arising only through agreement, for there is "no Obligation on any man, which ariseth not from some Act of his own; for all men equally, are by Nature Free."[10] Hobbes's theory, as our own, introduces morals by agreement.

Hobbes recognizes that it is one thing to make an agreement or covenant, quite another to keep it. He does not suppose that the second law of nature, enjoining us to agree, also enjoins us to compliance. Thus he introduces a third law of nature, "That men performe their Covenants made," which he considers to be the "Originall of JUSTICE."[11] A just person is one who keeps the agreements he has rationally made.

Hobbes's defence of this third law lacks the straightforwardness of his defence of the second. As he recognizes, without it "Covenants are in vain, and but Empty words; and the Right of all men to all things remaining, wee are still in the condition of Warre."[12] But this does not show that conformity to it yields any direct benefit. Each person maximizes his expected utility in making a covenant, since each gains from the mutual renunciation it involves. But each does not maximize his expected utility in keeping a covenant, in so far as it requires him to refrain from exercising some part of his previous liberty. And this opens the door to the objection of the Foole.

We shall let him speak for himself.

The Foole hath sayd in his heart, there is no such thing as Justice; and sometimes also with his tongue; seriously alleaging, that every mans conservation, and contentment, being committed to his own care, there could be no reason, why every man might not do what he thought conduced thereunto: and therefore also to make, or not make; keep, or not keep

Covenants, was not against Reason, when it conduced to ones benefit. He does not therein deny, that there be Covenants; and that they are sometimes broken, sometimes kept; and that such breach of them may be called Injustice, and the observance of them Justice: but he questioneth, whether Injustice . . . may not sometimes stand with that Reason, which dictateth to every man his own good. . . .[13]

The Foole does not seriously challenge the second law of nature, for Hobbes assumes that each person will make only those covenants that he expects to be advantageous, and such behaviour the Foole does not question. What the Foole challenges is the third law, the law requiring compliance, or adherence to one's covenants, for let it be ever so advantageous to make an agreement, may it not then be even more advantageous to violate the agreement made? And if advantageous, then is it not rational? The Foole challenges the heart of the connection between reason and morals that both Hobbes and we seek to establish—the rationality of accepting a moral constraint on the direct pursuit of one's greatest utility.

1.3. In replying to the Foole, Hobbes claims that the question is, given sufficient security of performance by one party, "whether it be against reason, that is, against the benefit of the other to performe, or not."[14] On the most natural interpretation, Hobbes is asking whether keeping one's covenant is a rational, that is, utility-maximizing, response to covenant-keeping by one's fellows. If this is indeed Hobbes's view, then he is endeavouring to refute the Foole by appealing, in effect, to condition *A* for strategically rational choice, taking a rational response to be simply a utility-maximizing response. We may not be very hopeful about Hobbes's prospect of success.

Hobbes's first argument reminds the Foole that the rationality of choice depends on expectations, not actual results. It need not detain us. His second argument joins issue with the Foole at a deeper level.

> He . . . that breaketh his Covenant, and consequently declareth that he thinks he may with reason do so, cannot be received into any Society, that unite themselves for Peace and Defence, but by the errour of them that receive him; nor when he is received, be retayned in it, without seeing the danger of their errour; which errours a man cannot reasonably reckon upon as the means of his security.[15]

A person disposed to violate his covenants cannot be admitted as a party to co-operative arrangements by those who are both rational and aware of his disposition, and so such a person cannot rationally expect to reap the benefits available to co-operators. Even if his particular breaches of covenant would benefit him, yet the disposition that leads him to such breaches does not.

In effect Hobbes moves the question from whether it be against reason, understood as utility-maximization, to keep one's agreement (given sufficient security of others keeping their agreements), to whether it be against reason to be disposed to keep one's agreement. The disposition to decide whether or not to adhere to one's covenants or agreements by appealing to directly utility-maximizing considerations, is itself disadvantageous, if known, or sufficiently suspected, because it excludes one from participating, with those who suspect one's disposition, in those co-operative arrangements in which the benefits to be realized require each to forgo utility-maximization—or in Hobbes's terminology, require each to lay down some portion of his original, unlimited right of nature. The disposition to keep one's agreement, given sufficient security, without appealing to directly utility-maximizing considerations, makes one an eligible partner in beneficial co-operation, and so is itself beneficial. This will prove to be the key to our demonstration that a fully rational utility-maximizer disposes himself to compliance with his rationally undertaken covenants or agreements.

But for Hobbes to take full advantage of this response to the Foole, he must revise his conception of rationality, breaking the direct connection between reason and benefit with which he began his reply. Hobbes needs to say that it is rational to perform one's covenant even when performance is not directly to one's benefit, provided that it is to one's benefit to be disposed to perform. But this he never says. And as long as the Foole is allowed to relate reason directly to benefit in performance, rather than to benefit in the disposition to perform, he can escape refutation.

Hobbes does suggest a revision in his conception of rationality in his discussion with Bishop Bramhall. Agreeing with Bramhall that "moral goodness is the conformity of an action with right reason," he does not claim that what is morally good is conducive to one's benefit, but instead holds that

> All the real good . . . is that which is not repugnant to the law . . . for the law is all the right reason we have, and . . . is the infallible rule of moral goodness. The reason whereof is this, that because neither mine nor the Bishop's reason is . . . fit to be a rule of our moral actions, we have therefore set up over ourselves a sovereign governor, and agreed that his laws shall . . . dictate to us what is really good.[16]

To the Foole's contention that injustice may "sometimes stand with that Reason, which dictateth to every man his own good,"[17] Hobbes can reply that injustice may not stand with that reason that is constituted by the law of the sovereign. Just as it is unprofitable for each man to retain his entire natural right, so it is unprofitable for each man to retain his natural reason as guide to his actions. But Hobbes does not suppose that each man internalizes the right reason of the sovereign. His egoistic psychology allows the internalization of no standard other than that of direct concern with individual preservation and contentment. And so it is only in so far as the sovereign is able to enforce the law that compliance with it is rationally binding on the individual. But this is to propose a political, not a moral, solution to the problem posed by the Foole.

If the market acts as an invisible hand, directing the efforts of each person intending only his own benefit to a social optimum, the sovereign acts as a very visible foot, directing, by well-placed kicks, the efforts of each to the same social end. Each device performs the same task, ensuring the coincidence of an equilibrium in which each person maximizes his expected utility given the actions of his fellows, with an optimum in which each person gains the maximum utility compatible with the utilities of his fellows. Each device affects the conditions under which interaction occurs, leaving every individual free to maximize his utility given those conditions. Of course, the sovereign appears as a constraint on each person's freedom whereas the market does not, but this is the difference between visibility and invisibility; the sovereign visibly shapes the conditions that reconcile each person's interest with those of his fellows, whereas the market so shapes these conditions simply in virtue of its structure.

The sovereign makes morality, understood as a constraint on each person's endeavour to maximize his own utility, as unnecessary as does the market. Our moral enquiry has been motivated by the problems created for utility-maximizers by externalities. Adam Smith reminds us of the conditions in which externalities are absent, so that the market ensures that each person's free, maximizing behaviour results in an optimal outcome. Thomas Hobbes introduces the sovereign, who constrains each person's options so that maximizing behaviour results in a seemingly optimal outcome even when externalities are present. We may retain the idea of justice as expressing the requirement of impartiality for principles that regulate social interaction, but it no longer expresses a constraint on individual maximization. It would seem that between them, economics and politics resolve our problem with no need for morality.

But Hobbes's sovereign lacks the appeal of the market, and for good reason. The invisible hand is a costless solution to the problems of natural interaction, but the visible foot is a very costly solution. Those subject to the Hobbesian sovereign do not, in fact, attain an optimal outcome; each pays a portion of the costs needed to enforce adherence to agreements, and these costs render the outcome sub-optimal. Even if we suppose that power does not corrupt, so that the sovereign is the perfect instrument of his subjects, acting only in their interests, yet each would expect to do better if all would adhere voluntarily to their agreements, so that enforcement and its costs would be unnecessary. We pay a heavy price, if we are indeed creatures who rationally accept no internal constraint on the pursuit of our own utility, and who consequently are able to escape from the state of nature, in those circumstances in which externalities are unavoidably present, only by political, and not by moral, devices. Could we but voluntarily comply with our rationally undertaken agreements, we should save ourselves this price.

We do not suppose that voluntary compliance would eliminate the need for social institutions and practices, and their costs. But it would eliminate the need for some of those institutions whose concern is with enforcement. Authoritative decision-making cannot be eliminated, but our ideal would be a society in which the coercive enforcement of such decisions would be unnecessary. More realistically, we suppose that such enforcement is needed to create and maintain those conditions under which individuals may rationally expect the degree of compliance from their fellows needed to elicit their own voluntary compliance. Internal, moral constraints operate to ensure compliance under conditions of security established by external, political constraints. But before we can expect this view to be accepted we must show, what the Foole denies, that it is rational to dispose oneself to co-operate, and so to accept internal, moral constraints.

Hobbes's argument that those not so disposed may not rationally be received into society, is the foundation on which we shall build.

2.1. The Foole, and those who share his conception of practical reason, must suppose that there are potentialities for co-operation to which each person would rationally agree, were he to expect the agreement to be carried out, but that remain unactualized. since each rationally expects that someone, perhaps himself, perhaps another, would not adhere to the agreement. In Chapter V we argued that co-operation is rational if each co-operator may expect a utility nearly equal to what he would be assigned by the principle of minimax relative concession. The Foole does not dispute the necessity of this condition, but denies its sufficiency. He insists that for it to be rational to comply with an agreement to co-operate, the utility an individual may expect from co-operation must also be no less than what he would expect were he to violate his agreement. And he then argues that for it to be rational to agree to co-operate, then, although one need not consider it rational to comply oneself, one must believe it rational for the others to comply. Given that everyone is rational, fully informed, and correct in his expectations, the Foole supposes that co-operation is actualized only if each person expects a utility from co-operation no less than his noncompliance utility. The benefits that could be realized through co-operative arrangements that do not afford each person at least his non-compliance utility remain forever beyond the reach of rational human beings—forever denied us because our very rationality would lead us to violate the agreements necessary to realize these benefits. Such agreements will not be made.

The Foole rejects what would seem to be the ordinary view that, given neither unforeseen circumstances nor misrepresentation of terms, it is rational to comply with an agreement if it is rational to make it. He insists that holders of this view have failed to think out the full implications of the maximizing conception of practical rationality. In choosing one takes one's stand in the present, and looks to the expected utility that will result from each possible action. What has happened may affect this utility; that one has agreed may affect the utility one expects from doing, or not doing, what would keep the agreement. But what has happened provides in itself no reason for choice. That one had reason for making an agreement can give one reason for keeping it only by affecting the utility of compliance. To think otherwise is to reject utility-maximization.

Let us begin our answer to the Foole by recalling the distinction introduced in V.1.3 between an individual strategy and a joint strategy.[18] An individual strategy is a lottery over the possible actions of a single actor. A joint strategy is a lottery over possible outcomes. Co-operators have joint strategies available to them.

We may think of participation in a co-operative activity, such as a hunt, in which each huntsman has his particular role co-ordinated with that of the others, as the implementation of a single joint strategy. We may also extend the notion to include participation in a practice, such as the making and keeping of promises, where each person's behaviour is predicated on the conformity of others to the practice.

An individual is not able to ensure that he acts on a joint strategy, since whether he does depends, not only on what he intends, but on what those with whom he interacts intend. But we may say that an individual bases his action on a joint strategy in so far as he intentionally chooses what the strategy requires of him. Normally, of course, one bases one's action on a joint strategy only if one expects those with whom one interacts to do so as well, so that one expects actually to act on that strategy. But we need not import such an expectation into the conception of basing one's action on a joint strategy.

A person co-operates with his fellows only if he bases his actions on a joint strategy; to agree to co-operate is to agree to employ a joint rather than an individual strategy. The Foole insists that it is rational to co-operate only if the utility one expects from acting on the co-operative joint strategy is at least equal to the utility one would expect were one to act instead on one's best individual strategy. This defeats the end of co-operation, which is in effect to substitute a joint strategy for individual strategies in situations in which this substitution is to everyone's benefit.

A joint strategy is fully rational only if it yields an optimal outcome, or in other words, only if it affords each person who acts on it the maximum utility compatible in the situation with the utility afforded each other person who acts on the strategy. Thus we may say that a person acting on a rational joint strategy maximizes his utility, subject to the constraint set by the utilities it affords to every other person. An individual strategy is rational if and only if it maximizes one's utility given the *strategies* adopted by the other persons; a joint strategy is rational only if (but not if and only if) it maximizes one's utility given the *utilities* afforded to the other persons.

Let us say that a *straightforward* maximizer is a person who seeks to maximize his utility given the strategies of those with whom he interacts. A *constrained* maximizer, on the other hand, is a person who seeks in some situations to maximize her utility, given not the strategies but the utilities of those with whom she interacts. The Foole accepts the rationality of straightforward maximization. We, in defending condition A' for strategic rationality (stated in 1.1), accept the rationality of constrained maximization.

A constrained maximizer has a conditional disposition to base her actions on a joint strategy, without considering whether some individual strategy would yield her greater expected utility. But not all constraint could be rational; we must specify the characteristics of the conditional disposition. We shall therefore identify a constrained maximizer thus: (i) someone who is conditionally disposed to base her actions on a joint strategy or practice should the utility she expects were everyone so to base his action be no less than what she would expect were everyone to employ individual strategies, and approach what she would expect from the co-operative outcome determined by minimax relative concession; (ii) someone who actually acts on this conditional disposition should her expected utility be greater than what she would expect were everyone to employ individual strategies. Or in other words, a constrained maximizer is ready to co-operate in ways that, if followed by all, would yield outcomes that she would find beneficial and not unfair, and she does co-operate should she expect an actual practice or activity to be beneficial. In determining the latter she must take into account the possibility that some persons will fail, or refuse, to act co-operatively. Henceforth, unless we specifically state otherwise, we shall understand by a constrained maximizer one with this particular disposition.

There are three points in our characterization of constrained maximization that should be noted. The first is that a constrained maximizer is conditionally disposed to act, not only on the unique joint strategy that would be prescribed by a rational bargain, but on any joint strategy that affords her a utility approaching what she would expect from fully rational co-operation. The range of acceptable joint strategies is, and must be left, unspecified. The idea is that in real interaction it is reasonable to accept co-operative arrangements that fall short of the ideal of full rationality and fairness, provided they do not fall too far short. At some point, of course, one decides to ignore a joint strategy, even if acting on it would afford one an expected utility greater than one would expect were everyone to employ an individual strategy, because one hopes thereby to obtain agreement on, or acquiescence in, another joint strategy which in being fairer is also more favourable to oneself. At precisely what point one decides this we make no attempt to say. We simply defend a conception of constrained maximization that does not require that all acceptable joint strategies be ideal.

Constrained maximization thus links the idea of morals by agreement to actual moral practice. We suppose that some moral principles may be understood as representing joint strategies prescribed to each person as part of the ongoing co-operative arrangements that constitute society. These principles require each person to refrain from the direct pursuit of her maximum utility, in order to achieve mutually advantageous and reasonably fair outcomes. Actual moral principles are not in general those to which we should have agreed in a fully rational bargain. but it is reasonable to adhere to them in so far as they offer a reasonable approximation to ideal principles. We may defend actual moral principles by reference to ideal co-operative arrangements, and the closer the principles fit, the stronger the defence. We do not of course suppose that our actual moral principles derive historically from a bargain, but in so far as the constraints they impose are acceptable to a rational constrained maximizer, we may fit them into the framework of a morality rationalized by the idea of agreement.

The second point is that a constrained maximizer does not base her actions on a joint strategy whenever a nearly fair and optimal outcome would result were everyone to do likewise. Her disposition to co-operate is conditional on her expectation that she will benefit in comparison with the utility she could expect were no one to cooperate. Thus she must estimate the likelihood that others involved in the prospective practice or interaction will act co-operatively, and calculate, not the utility she would expect were all to co-operate, but the utility she would expect if she co-operates, given her estimate of the degree to which others will co-operate. Only if this exceeds what she would expect from universal non-co-operation, does her conditional disposition to constraint actually manifest itself in a decision to base her actions on the co-operative joint strategy.

Thus, faced with persons whom she believes to be straightforward maximizers, a constrained maximizer does not play into their hands by basing her actions on the joint strategy she would like everyone to accept, but rather, to avoid being exploited, she behaves as a straightforward maximizer, acting on the individual strategy that maximizes her utility given the strategies she expects the others to employ. A constrained maximizer makes reasonably certain that she is among like-disposed persons before she actually constrains her direct pursuit of maximum utility.

But note that a constrained maximizer may find herself required to act in such a way that she would have been better off had she not entered into co-operation. She may be engaged in a co-operative activity that, given the willingness of her fellows to do their part, she expects to be fair and beneficial, but that, should chance so befall, requires her to act so that she incurs some loss greater than had she never engaged herself in the endeavour. Here she would still be disposed to comply, acting in a way that results in real disadvantage to herself, because given her *ex ante* beliefs about the dispositions of her fellows and the prospects of benefit, participation in the activity affords her greater expected utility than non-participation.

And this brings us to the third point, that constrained maximization is not straightforward maximization in its most effective disguise. The constrained maximizer is not merely the person who, taking a larger view than her fellows. serves her overall interest by sacrificing the immediate benefits of ignoring joint strategies and violating co-operative arrangements in order to obtain the long-run benefits of being trusted by others.[19] Such a person exhibits no real constraint. The constrained maximizer does not reason more effectively about how to maximize her utility, but reasons in a different way. We may see this most clearly by considering how each faces the decision whether to base her action on a joint strategy. The constrained maximizer considers (i) whether the outcome, should everyone do so, be nearly fair and optimal, and (ii) whether the outcome she realistically expects should she do so affords her greater utility than universal non-co-operation. If both of these conditions are satisfied she bases her action on the joint strategy. The straightforward maximizer considers simply whether the outcome he realistically expects should he base his action on the joint strategy affords him greater utility than the outcome he would expect were he to act on any alternative strategy—taking into account, of course, long-term as well as short-term effects. Only if this condition is satisfied does he base his action on the joint strategy.

Consider a purely isolated interaction, in which both parties know that how each chooses will have no bearing on how each fares in other interactions. Suppose that the situation has the familiar Prisoner's Dilemma structure; each benefits from mutual cooperation in relation to mutual non-co-operation, but each benefits from non-co-operation whatever the other does. In such a situation, a straightforward maximizer chooses not to co-operate. A constrained maximizer chooses to co-operate if, given her estimate of whether or not her partner will choose to co-operate, her own expected utility is greater than the utility she would expect from the non-co-operative outcome.

Constrained maximizers can thus obtain co-operative benefits that are unavailable to straightforward maximizers, however far-sighted the latter may be. But straightforward maximizers can, on occasion, exploit unwary constrained maximizers. Each supposes her disposition to be rational. But who is right?

2.2. To demonstrate the rationality of suitably constrained maximization we solve a problem of rational choice. We consider what a rational individual would choose, given the alternatives of adopting straightforward maximization, and of adopting constrained maximization, as his disposition for strategic behaviour. Although this choice is about interaction, to make it is not to engage in interaction. Taking others' dispositions as fixed, the individual reasons parametrically to his own best disposition. Thus he compares the expected utility of disposing himself to maximize utility given others' expected strategy choices, with the utility of disposing himself to co-operate with others in bringing about nearly fair and optimal outcomes.

To choose between these dispositions, a person needs to consider only those situations in which they would yield different behaviour. If both would be expressed in a maximizing individual strategy, or if both would lead one to base action on the joint strategy one expects from others, then their utility expectations are identical. But if the disposition to constraint would be expressed in basing action on a joint strategy, whereas the disposition to maximize straightforwardly would be expressed in defecting from the joint strategy, then their utility expectations differ. Only situations giving rise to such differences need be considered. These situations must satisfy two conditions. First, they must afford the prospect of mutually beneficial and fair co-operation, since otherwise constraint would be pointless. And second, they must afford some prospect for individually beneficial defection, since otherwise no constraint would be needed to realize the mutual benefits.

We suppose, then, an individual, considering what disposition to adopt, for situations in which his expected utility is u should each person act on an individual strategy, u' should all act on a cooperative joint strategy, and u'' should he act on an individual strategy and the others base their actions on a co-operative joint strategy, and u is less than u' (so that he benefits from co-operation as required by the first condition) and u' in turn is less than u'' (so that he benefits from defection as required by the second condition).

Consider these two arguments which this person might put to himself:

Argument (1): Suppose I adopt straightforward maximization. Then if I expect the others to base their actions on a joint strategy, I defect to my best individual strategy, and expect a utility, u''. If I expect the others to act on individual strategies, then so do I, and expect a utility, u. If the probability that others will base their actions on a joint strategy is p, then my overall expected utility is $[pu'' + (1 - p)u]$.

Suppose I adopt constrained maximization. Then if I expect the others to base their actions on a joint strategy, so do I, and expect a utility u'. If I expect the others to act on individual strategies, then so do I, and expect a utility, u. Thus my overall expected utility is $[pu' + (1 - p)u]$.

Since u'' is greater than u', $[pu'' + (1 - p)u]$ is greater than $[pu' + (1 - p)u]$, for any value of p other than 0 (and for $p = 0$, the two are equal). Therefore, to maximize my overall expectation of utility, I should adopt straightforward maximization.

Argument (2): Suppose I adopt straightforward maximization. Then I must expect the others to employ maximizing individual strategies in interacting with me; so do I, and expect a utility, u.

Suppose I adopt constrained maximization. Then if the others are conditionally disposed to constrained maximization, I may expect them to base their actions on a co-operative joint strategy in interacting with me; so do I, and expect a utility u'. If they are not so disposed, I employ a maximizing strategy and expect u as before. If the probability that others are disposed to constrained maximization is p, then my overall expected utility is $[pu' + (1 - p)u]$.

Since u' is greater than u, $[pu' + (1 - p)u]$ is greater than u for any value of p other than 0 (and for $p = 0$, the two are equal). Therefore, to maximize my overall expectation of utility, I should adopt constrained maximization.

Since these arguments yield opposed conclusions, they cannot both be sound. The first has the form of a dominance argument. In any situation in which others act non-co-operatively, one may expect the same utility whether one is disposed to straightforward or to constrained maximization. In any situation

in which others act co-operatively, one may expect a greater utility if one is disposed to straightforward maximization. Therefore one should adopt straightforward maximization. But this argument would be valid only if the probability of others acting co-operatively were, as the argument assumes, independent of one's own disposition. And this is not the case. Since persons disposed to co-operation only act co-operatively with those whom they suppose to be similarly disposed, a straightforward maximizer does not have the opportunities to benefit which present themselves to the constrained maximizer. Thus argument (1) fails.

Argument (2) takes into account what argument (1) ignores—the difference between the way in which constrained maximizers interact with those similarly disposed, and the way in which they interact with straightforward maximizers. Only those disposed to keep their agreements are rationally acceptable as parties to agreements. Constrained maximizers are able to make beneficial agreements with their fellows that the straightforward cannot, not because the latter would be unwilling to agree, but because they would not be admitted as parties to agreement given their disposition to violation. Straightforward maximizers are disposed to take advantage of their fellows should the opportunity arise; knowing this, their fellows would prevent such opportunity arising. With the same opportunities, straightforward maximizers would necessarily obtain greater benefits. A dominance argument establishes this. But because they differ in their dispositions, straightforward and constrained maximizers differ also in their opportunities, to the benefit of the latter.

But argument (2) unfortunately contains an undefended assumption. A person's expectations about how others will interact with him depend strictly on his own choice of disposition only if that choice is known by the others. What we have shown is that, if the straightforward maximizer and the constrained maximizer appear in their true colours, then the constrained maximizer must do better. But need each so appear? The Foole may agree, under the pressure of our argument and its parallel in the second argument we ascribed to Hobbes, that the question to be asked is not whether it is or is not rational to keep (particular) covenants, but whether it is or is not rational to be (generally) disposed to the keeping of covenants, and he may recognize that he cannot win by pleading the cause of straightforward maximization in a direct way. But may he not win by linking straightforward maximization to the appearance of constraint? Is not the Foole's ultimate argument that the truly prudent person, the fully rational utility-maximizer, must seek to appear trustworthy, an upholder of his agreements? For then he will not be excluded from the co-operative arrangements of his fellows, but will be welcomed as a partner, while he awaits opportunities to benefit at their expense—and, preferably, without their knowledge, so that he may retain the guise of constraint and trustworthiness.

There is a short way to defeat this maneuvre. Since our argument is to be applied to ideally rational persons, we may simply add another idealizing assumption, and take our persons to be *transparent*.[20] Each is directly aware of the disposition of his fellows, and so aware whether he is interacting with straightforward or constrained maximizers. Deception is impossible; the Foole must appear as he is.

But to assume transparency may seem to rob our argument of much of its interest. We want to relate our idealizing assumptions to the real world. If constrained maximization defeats straightforward maximization only if all persons are transparent, then we shall have failed to show that under actual, or realistically possible, conditions, moral constraints are rational. We shall have refuted the Foole but at the price of robbing our refutation of all practical import.

However, transparency proves to be a stronger assumption than our argument requires. We may appeal instead to a more realistic *translucency*, supposing that persons are neither transparent nor opaque, so that their disposition to co-operate or not may be ascertained by others, not with certainty, but as more than mere guesswork. Opaque beings would be condemned to seek political solutions for those problems of natural interaction that could not be met by the market. But we shall show that for beings as translucent as we may reasonably consider ourselves to be, moral solutions are rationally available.

2.3. If persons are translucent, then constrained maximizers (CMs) will sometimes fail to recognize each other, and will then interact non-co-operatively even if co-operation would have been mutually beneficial. CMs will sometimes fail to identify straightforward maximizers (SMs) and will then act co-operatively; if the SMs correctly identify the CMs they will be able to take advantage of them. Translucent CMs must expect to do less well in interaction than would transparent CMs; translucent SMs must expect to do better than would transparent SMs. Although it would be rational to choose to be a CM were one transparent, it need not be rational if one is only translucent. Let us examine the conditions under which the decision to dispose oneself to constrained maximization is rational for translucent persons, and ask if these are (or may be) the conditions in which we find ourselves.

As in the preceding subsection, we need consider only situations in which CMs and SMs may fare differently. These are situations that afford both the prospect of mutually beneficial co-operation (in relation to non-co-operation) and individually beneficial defection (in relation to co-operation). Let us simplify by supposing that the non-co-operative outcome results unless (i) those interacting are CMs who achieve mutual recognition, in which case the co-operative outcome results, or (ii) those interacting include CMs who fail to recognize SMs but are themselves recognized, in which case the outcome affords the SMs the benefits of individual defection and the CMs the costs of having advantage taken of mistakenly basing their actions on a co-operative strategy. We ignore the inadvertent taking of advantage when CMs mistake their fellows for SMs.

There are then four possible pay-offs—non-co-operation, co-operation, defection, and exploitation (as we may call the outcome for the person whose supposed partner defects from the joint strategy on which he bases his action). For the typical situation, we assign defection the value 1, co-operation u'' (less than 1), non-co-operation u' (less than u''), and exploitation 0 (less than u'). We now introduce three probabilities. The first, p, is the probability that CMs will achieve mutual recognition and so successfully co-operate. The second, q, is the probability that CMs will fail to recognize SMs but will themselves be recognized, so that defection and exploitation will result. The third, r, is the probability that a randomly selected member of the population is a CM. (We assume that everyone is a CM or an SM, so the probability that a randomly selected person is an SM is $(1 - r)$.) The values of p, q, and r must of course fall between 0 and 1.

Let us now calculate expected utilities for CMs and SMs in situations affording both the prospect of mutually beneficial cooperation and individually beneficial defection. A CM expects the utility u' unless (i) she succeeds in co-operating with other CMs or (ii) she is exploited by an SM. The probability of (i) is the combined probability that she interacts with a CM, r, and that they achieve mutual recognition, p, or rp. In this case she gains $(u'' - u')$ over her non-co-operative expectation u'. Thus the effect of (i) is to increase her utility expectation by a value $[rp(u'' - u')]$. The probability of (ii) is the combined probability that she interacts with an SM, $1 - r$, and that she fails to recognize him but is recognized, q, or $(1 - r)q$. In this case she receives 0, so she loses her non-co-operative expectation u'. Thus the effect of (ii) is to re-

duce her utility expectation by a value $[(1 - r)qu'']$ Taking both (i) and (ii) into account, a CM expects the utility $\{u' + [rp(u'' - u')] - (1 - r)qu'\}$.

An SM expects the utility u' unless he exploits a CM. The probability of this is the combined probability that he interacts with a CM, r, and that he recognizes her but is not recognized by her, q, or rq. In this case he gains $(1 - u')$ over his non-co-operative expectation u'. Thus the effect is to increase his utility expectation by a value $[rq(1 - u')]$. An SM thus expects the utility $\{u' + [rq(1 - u')]\}$.

It is rational to dispose oneself to constrained maximization if and only if the utility expected by a CM is greater than the utility expected by an SM, which obtains if and only if p/q is *greater* than $\{(1 - u')/(u'' - u') + [(1 - r)u']/[r(u'' - u')]\}$.

The first term of this expression, $[(1 - u')/(u'' - u')]$, relates the gain from defection to the gain through co-operation. The value of defection is of course greater than that of co-operation, so this term is greater than 1. The second term, $\{[(1 - r)u']/[r(u'' - u')]\}$, depends for its value on r. If $r = 0$ (i.e., if there are no CMs in the population), then its value is infinite. As r increases, the value of the expression decreases, until if $r = 1$ (i.e., if there are only CMs in the population) its value is 0.

We may now draw two important conclusions. First, it is rational to dispose oneself to constrained maximization only if the ratio of p to q, that is, the ratio between the probability that an interaction involving CMs will result in co-operation and the probability that an interaction involving CMs and SMs will involve exploitation and defection, is greater than the ratio between the gain from defection and the gain through co-operation. If everyone in the population is a CM, then we may replace "only if" by "if and only if" in this statement, but in general it is only a necessary condition of the rationality of the disposition to constrained maximization.

Second, as the proportion of CMs in the

population increases (so that the value of r increases), the value of the ratio of p to q that is required for it to be rational to dispose oneself to constrained maximization decreases. The more constrained maximizers there are, the greater the risks a constrained maximizer may rationally accept of failed co-operation and exploitation. However, these risks, and particularly the latter, must remain relatively small.

We may illustrate these conclusions by introducing typical numerical values for co-operation and non-co-operation, and then considering different values for r. One may suppose that on the whole, there is no reason that the typical gain from defection over co-operation would be either greater or smaller than the typical gain from co-operation over non-co-operation, and in turn no reason that the latter gain would be greater or smaller than the typical loss from non-co-operation to exploitation. And so, since defection has the value 1 and exploitation 0, let us assign co-operation the value 2/3 and non-co-operation 1/3.

The gain from defection, $(1 - u')$, thus is 2/3; the gain through cooperation, $(u'' - u')$, is 1/3. Since p/q must exceed $\{(1 - u')/(u'' - u') + [(1 - r)u']/[r(u'' - u')]\}$ for constrained maximization to be rational, in our typical case the probability p that CMs successfully co-operate must be more than twice the probability q that CMs are exploited by SMs, however great the probability r that a randomly selected person is a CM. If three persons out of four are CMs, so that $r = 3/4$, then p/q must be greater than 7/3; if one person out of two is a CM, then p/q must be greater than 3; if one person in four is a CM, then p/q must be greater than 5. In general, p/q must be greater than $2 + (1 - r)/r$, or $(r + 1)/r$.

Suppose a population evenly divided between constrained and straightforward maximizers. If the constrained maximizers are able to co-operate successfully in two-thirds of their encounters, and to avoid being exploited by straightforward maximizers in four-fifths of their encounters, then constrained maximizers may expect to do better than their fellows. Of course. the even distribution will not be stable; it will be rational for the straightforward maximizers to change their disposition. These persons are sufficiently translucent for them to find morality rational.

2.4. A constrained maximizer is conditionally disposed to cooperate in ways that, followed by all, would yield nearly optimal and fair outcomes, and does co-operate in such ways when she may actually expect to benefit. In the two preceding subsections, we have argued that one is rationally so disposed if persons are transparent, or if persons are sufficiently translucent and enough are like-minded. But our argument has not appealed explicitly to the particular requirement that co-operative practices and activities be nearly optimal and fair. We have insisted that the co-operative outcome afford one a utility greater than non-co-operation, but this is much weaker than the insistence that it approach the outcome required by minimax relative concession.

But note that the larger the gain from co-operation, $(u'' - u')$, the smaller the minimum value of p/q that makes the disposition to constrained maximization rational. We may take p/q to be a measure of translucency; the more translucent constrained maximizers are, the better they are at achieving co-operation among themselves (increasing p) and avoiding exploitation by straightforward maximizers (decreasing q). Thus as practices and activities fall short of optimality, the expected value of co-operation, u'', decreases, and so the degree of translucency required to make cooperation rational increases. And as practices and activities fall short of fairness, the expected value of co-operation for those with less than fair shares decreases, and so the degree of translucency to make co-operation rational for them increases. Thus our argument does appeal implicitly to the requirement that co-operation yield nearly fair and optimal outcomes.

But there is a further argument in support of our insistence that the conditional disposition to co-operate be restricted to practices and activities yielding nearly optimal and fair outcomes. And this argument turns, as does our general argument for constraint, on how one's dispositions affect the characteristics of the situations in which one may reasonably expect to find oneself. Let us call a person who is disposed to co-operate in ways that, followed by all, yield nearly optimal and fair outcomes, *narrowly compliant*. And let us call a person who is disposed to co-operate in ways that, followed by all, merely yield her some benefit in relation to universal non-cooperation, *broadly compliant*. We need not deny that a broadly compliant person would expect to benefit in some situations in which a narrowly compliant person could not. But in many other situations a broadly compliant person must expect to lose by her disposition. For in so far as she is known to be broadly compliant, others will have every reason to maximize their utilities at her expense, by offering "co-operation" on terms that offer her but little more than she could expect from non-co-operation. Since a broadly compliant person is disposed to seize whatever benefit a joint strategy may afford her, she finds herself with opportunities for but little benefit.

Since the narrowly compliant person is always prepared to accept co-operative arrangements based on the principle of minimax relative concession, she is prepared to be co-operative whenever cooperation can be mutually beneficial on terms equally rational and fair to all. In refusing other terms she does not diminish her prospects for co-operation with other rational persons, and she ensures that those not disposed to fair co-operation do not enjoy the benefits of any co-operation, thus making their unfairness costly to themselves, and so irrational.

In the next chapter we shall extend the conception of narrow compliance, so that it includes taking into account not only satisfaction of minimax relative concession, but also satisfaction of a standard of fairness for the initial bargaining position. [F]or some circumstances, narrow compliance sets too high a standard. If the institutions of society fail to be both rational and impartial, then the narrowly compliant person may be unable to effect any significant reform of them, while depriving herself of what benefits an imperfect society nevertheless affords. Then—we must admit—rationality and impartiality can fail to coincide in individual choice.

But we suppose that among fully rational persons, institutions, practices, and agreements that do not satisfy the requirements of minimax relative concession must prove unstable. There would, of course, be some persons with an interest in maintaining the unfairness inherent in such structures. But among the members of a society each of whom is, and knows her fellows to be, rational and adequately informed, those who find themselves with less than they could expect from fair and optimal co-operation can, by disposing themselves to narrow compliance, effect the reform of their society so that it satisfies the requirements of justice. Reflection on how partiality sustains itself shows that, however important coercive measures may be, their effectiveness depends finally on an uncoerced support for norms that directly or indirectly sustain this partiality, a support which would be insufficiently forthcoming from clearheaded constrained maximizers of individual utility.

2.5. To conclude this long section, let us supplement our argument for the rationality of disposing ourselves to constrained maximization with three reflections on its implications—for conventional morality, for the treatment of straightforward maximizers, and for the cultivation of translucency.

First, we should not suppose that the argument upholds all of conventional morality, or all of those institutions and practices that purport to realize fair and optimal outcomes. If society is, in Rawls's words "a cooperative venture for mutual advantage," then it is rational to pay one's share of social costs—

one's taxes. But it need not be rational to pay one's taxes, at least unless one is effectively coerced into payment, if one sees one's tax dollars used (as one may believe) to increase the chances of nuclear warfare and to encourage both corporate and individual parasitism. If tax evasion seems to many a rational practice, this does not show that it is irrational to comply with fair and optimal arrangements, but only, perhaps, that it is irrational to acquiesce willingly in being exploited.

Second, we should not suppose it is rational to dispose oneself to constrained maximization, if one does not also dispose oneself to exclude straightforward maximizers from the benefits realizable by co-operation. Hobbes notes that those who think they may with reason violate their covenants, may not be received into society except by the error of their fellows. If their fellows fall into that error, then they will soon find that it pays no one to keep covenants. Failing to exclude straightforward maximizers from the benefits of co-operative arrangements does not, and cannot, enable them to share in the long-run benefits of co-operation; instead, it ensures that the arrangements will prove ineffective, so that there are no benefits to share. And then there is nothing to be gained by constrained maximization; one might as well join the straightforward maximizers in their descent to the natural condition of humankind.

A third consideration relates more closely to the conceptions introduced in 2.3. Consider once again the probabilities p and q, the probability that CMs will achieve mutual recognition and cooperate, and the probability that CMs will fail to recognize SMs but will be recognized by them and so be exploited. It is obvious that CMs benefit from increasing p and decreasing q. And this is reflected in our calculation of expected utility for CMs; the value of $\{u' + [rp(u'' - u')] - (1 - r)qu'\}$ increases as p increases and as q decreases.

What determines the values of p and q? p depends on the ability of CMs to detect the sincerity of other CMs and to reveal their own sincerity to them. q depends on the ability of CMs to detect the insincerity of SMs and conceal their own sincerity from them, and the ability of SMs to detect the sincerity of CMs and conceal their own insincerity from them. Since any increase in the ability to reveal one's sincerity to other CMs is apt to be offset by a decrease in the ability to conceal one's sincerity from SMs, a CM is likely to rely primarily on her ability to detect the dispositions of others, rather than on her ability to reveal or conceal her own.

The ability to detect the dispositions of others must be well developed in a rational CM. Failure to develop this ability, or neglect of its exercise, will preclude one from benefiting from constrained maximization. And it can then appear that constraint is irrational. But what is actually irrational is the failure to cultivate or exercise the ability to detect others' sincerity or insincerity.

Both CMs and SMs must expect to benefit from increasing their ability to detect the dispositions of others. But if both endeavour to maximize their abilities (or the expected utility, net of costs, of so doing), then CMs may expect to improve their position in relation to SMs. For the benefits gained by SMs, by being better able to detect their potential victims, must be on the whole offset by the losses they suffer as the CMs become better able to detect them as potential exploiters. On the other hand, although the CMs may not enjoy any net gain in their interactions with SMs, the benefits they gain by being better able to detect other CMs as potential co-operators are not offset by corresponding losses, but rather increased as other CMs become better able to detect them in return.

Thus as persons rationally improve their ability to detect the dispositions of those with whom they interact, the value of p may be expected to increase, while the value of q remains relatively constant. But then p/q increases, and the greater it is, the less favourable need be other circumstances for it to be rational to dispose oneself to constrained maximization. Those who believe rationality and morality to be at loggerheads may have failed to recognize the importance of cultivating their ability to distinguish sincere co-operators from insincere ones.

David Hume points out that if "it should be a virtuous man's fate to fall into the society of ruffians," then "his particular regard to justice being no longer of use to his own safety or that of others, he must consult the dictates of self-preservation alone."[21] If we fall into a society—or rather into a state of nature—of straightforward maximizers, then constrained maximization, which disposes us to justice, will indeed be of no use to us, and we must then consult only the direct dictates of our own utilities. In a world of Fooles, it would not pay to be a constrained maximizer, and to comply with one's agreements. In such circumstances it would not be rational to be moral.

But if we find ourselves in the company of reasonably just persons, then we too have reason to dispose ourselves to justice. A community in which most individuals are disposed to comply with fair and optimal agreements and practices, and so to base their actions on joint co-operative strategies, will be self-sustaining. And such a world offers benefits to all which the Fooles can never enjoy.

Hume finds himself opposed by "a sensible knave" who claimed that "*honesty is the best policy*, may be a good general rule, but is liable to many exceptions; and he . . . conducts himself with most wisdom, who observes the general rule, and takes advantage of all the exceptions."[22] Hume confesses candidly that "if a man think that this reasoning much requires an answer, it would be a little difficult to find any which will to him appear satisfactory and convincing."[23] A little difficult, but not, if we are right, impossible. For the answer is found in treating honesty, not as a policy, but as a disposition. Only the person truly disposed to honesty and justice may expect fully to realize their benefits, for only such a person may rationally be admitted to

those mutually beneficial arrangements—whether actual agreements or implicitly agreed practices—that rest on honesty and justice, on voluntary compliance. But such a person is not able, given her disposition, to take advantage of the "exceptions"; she rightly judges such conduct irrational. The Foole and the sensible knave, seeing the benefits to be gained from the exceptions, from the advantageous breaches in honesty and compliance, but not seeing beyond these benefits, do not acquire the disposition. Among knaves they are indeed held for sensible, but among us, if we be not corrupted by their smooth words, they are only fools.

3.1. In defending constrained maximization we have implicitly reinterpreted the utility-maximizing conception of practical rationality. The received interpretation, commonly accepted by economists and elaborated in Bayesian decision theory and the Von Neumann–Morgenstern theory of games, identifies rationality with utility-maximization at the level of particular choices. A choice is rational if and only if it maximizes the actor's expected utility. We identify rationality with utility-maximization at the level of dispositions to choose. A disposition is rational if and only if an actor holding it can expect his choices to yield no less utility than the choices he would make were he to hold any alternative disposition. We shall consider whether particular choices are rational if and only if they express a rational disposition to choose.

It might seem that a maximizing disposition to choose would express itself in maximizing choices. But we have shown that this is not so. The essential point in our argument is that one's disposition to choose affects the situations in which one may expect to find oneself. A straightforward maximizer, who is disposed to make maximizing choices, must expect to be excluded from co-operative arrangements which he would find advantageous. A constrained maximizer may expect to be included in such arrangements. She benefits from her disposition, not in the choices she makes, but in her opportunities to choose.

We have defended the rationality of constrained maximization as a disposition to choose by showing that it would be rationally chosen. Now this argument is not circular; constrained maximization is a disposition for strategic choice that would be parametrically chosen. But the idea of a choice among dispositions to choose is a heuristic device to express the underlying requirement, that a rational disposition to choose be utility-maximizing. In parametric contexts, the disposition to make straightforwardly maximizing choices is uncontroversially utility-maximizing. We may therefore employ the device of a parametric choice among dispositions to choose to show that in strategic contexts, the disposition to make constrained choices, rather than straightforwardly maximizing choices, is utility-maximizing. We must however emphasize that it is not the choice itself, but the maximizing character of the disposition in virtue of which it is choiceworthy, that is the key to our argument.

But there is a further significance in our appeal to a choice among dispositions to choose. For we suppose that the capacity to make such choices is itself an essential part of human rationality. We could imagine beings so wired that only straightforward maximization would be a psychologically possible mode of choice in strategic contexts. Hobbes may have thought that human beings were so wired, that we were straightforwardly-maximizing machines. But if he thought this, then he was surely mistaken. At the core of our rational capacity is the ability to engage in self-critical reflection. The fully rational being is able to reflect on his standard of deliberation, and to change that standard in the light of reflection. Thus we suppose it possible for persons, who may initially assume that it is rational to extend straightforward maximization from parametric to strategic contexts, to reflect on the implications of this extension, and to reject it in favour of constrained maximization. Such

persons would be making the very choice, of a disposition to choose, that we have been discussing in this chapter.

And in making that choice, they would be expressing their nature not only as rational beings, but also as moral beings. If the disposition to make straightforwardly maximizing choices were wired in to us, we could not constrain our actions in the way required for morality. Moral philosophers have rightly been unwilling to accept the received interpretation of the relation between practical rationality and utility-maximization because they have recognized that it left no place for a rational constraint on directly utility-maximizing behaviour, and so no place for morality as ordinarily understood. But they have then turned to a neo-Kantian account of rationality which has led them to dismiss the idea that those considerations that constitute a person's reasons for acting must bear some particular relationship to the person.[24] They have failed to relate our nature as moral beings to our everyday concern with the fulfilment of our individual preferences. But we have shown how morality issues from that concern. When we correctly understand how utility-maximization is identified with practical rationality, we see that morality is an essential part of maximization.

3.2. An objector might grant that it may be rational to dispose oneself to constrained maximization, but deny that the choices one is then disposed to make are rational.[25] The objector claims that we have merely exhibited another instance of the rationality of not behaving rationally. And before we can accuse the objector of paradox, he brings further instances before us.

Consider, he says, the costs of decision-making. Maximizing may be the most reliable procedure, but it need not be the most cost-effective. In many circumstances, the rational person will not maximize but satisfice—set a threshold level of fulfilment and choose the first course of action of those coming to mind that one expects to meet this level. Indeed, our objector may suggest, human beings, like other higher animals, are natural satisficers. What distinguishes us is that we are not hard-wired, so that we can choose differently, but the costs are such that it is not generally advantageous to exercise our option, even though we know that most of our choices are not maximizing.

Consider also, he says, the tendency to wishful thinking. If we set ourselves to calculate the best or maximizing course of action, we are likely to confuse true expectations with hopes. Knowing this, we protect ourselves by choosing on the basis of fixed principles, and we adhere to these principles even when it appears to us that we could do better to ignore them, for we know that in such matters appearances often deceive. Indeed, our objector may suggest, much of morality may be understood, not as constraints on maximization to ensure fair mutual benefit, but as constraints on wish-fulfilling behaviour to ensure closer approximation to maximization.

Consider again, he says, the benefits of threat behaviour. I may induce you to perform an action advantageous to me if I can convince you that, should you not do so, I shall then perform an action very costly to you, even though it would not be my utility-maximizing choice. Hijackers seize aircraft, and threaten the destruction of everyone aboard, themselves included, if they are not transported to Havana. Nations threaten nuclear retaliation should their enemies attack them. Although carrying out a threat would be costly, if it works the cost need not be borne, and the benefit, not otherwise obtainable, is forthcoming.

But, our objector continues, a threat can be effective only if credible. It may be that to maximize one's credibility, and one's prospect of advantage, one must dispose oneself to carry out one's threats if one's demands are not met. And so it may be rational to dispose oneself to threat enforcement. But then, by parity of reasoning with our claims about constrained maximization, we

must suppose it to be rational actually to carry out one's threats. Surely we should suppose instead that, although it is clearly irrational to carry out a failed threat, yet it may be rational to dispose oneself to just this sort of irrationality. And so similarly we should suppose that although it is clearly irrational to constrain one's maximizing behaviour, yet it may be rational to dispose oneself to this irrationality.

We are unmoved. We agree that an actor who is subject to certain weaknesses or imperfections may find it rational to dispose himself to make choices that are not themselves rational. Such dispositions may be the most effective way of compensating for the weakness or imperfection. They constitute a second-best rationality, as it were. But although it may be rational for us to satisfice, it would not be rational for us to perform the action so chosen if, cost free, the maximizing action were to be revealed to us. And although it may be rational for us to adhere to principles as a guard against wish-fulfilment, it would not be rational for us to do so if, beyond all doubt, the maximizing action were to be revealed to us.

Contrast these with constrained maximization. The rationale for disposing oneself to constraint does not appeal to any weakness or imperfection in the reasoning of the actor; indeed, the rationale is most evident for perfect reasoners who cannot be deceived. The disposition to constrained maximization overcomes externalities; it is directed to the core problem arising from the structure of interaction. And the entire point of disposing oneself to constraint is to adhere to it in the face of one's knowledge that one is not choosing the maximizing action.

Imperfect actors find it rational to dispose themselves to make less than rational choices. No lesson can be drawn from this about the dispositions and choices of the perfect actor. If her dispositions to choose are rational, then surely her choices are also rational.

But what of the threat enforcer? Here we

disagree with our objector; it may be rational for a perfect actor to dispose herself to threat enforcement, and if it is, then it is rational for her to carry out a failed threat. Equally, it may be rational for a perfect actor to dispose herself to threat resistance, and if it is, then it is rational for her to resist despite the cost to herself. Deterrence, we have argued elsewhere, may be a rational policy, and non-maximizing deterrent choices are then rational.[26]

In a community of rational persons, however, threat behaviour will be proscribed. Unlike co-operation, threat behaviour does not promote mutual advantage. A successful threat simply redistributes benefits in favour of the threatener; successful threat resistance maintains the status quo. Unsuccessful threat behaviour, resulting in costly acts of enforcement or resistance, is necessarily nonoptimal; its very *raison d'être* is to make everyone worse off. Any person who is not exceptionally placed must then have the *ex ante* expectation that threat behaviour will be overall disadvantageous. Its proscription must be part of a fair and optimal agreement among rational persons; one of the constraints imposed by minimax relative concession is abstinence from the making of threats. Our argument thus shows threat behaviour to be both irrational and immoral.

Constrained maximizers will not dispose themselves to enforce or to resist threats among themselves. But there are circumstances, beyond the moral pale, in which a constrained maximizer might find it rational to dispose herself to threat enforcement. If she found herself fallen among straightforward maximizers, and especially if they were too stupid to become threat resisters, disposing herself to threat enforcement might be the best thing she could do. And for her, carrying out failed threats would be rational, though not utility-maximizing.

Our objector has not made good his case. The dispositions of a fully rational actor issue in rational choices. Our argument identifies practical rationality with utility-maxi-mization at the level of dispositions to choose, and carries through the implications of that identification in assessing the rationality of particular choices.

3.3. To conclude this chapter, let us note an interesting parallel to our theory of constrained maximization—Robert Trivers's evolutionary theory of reciprocal altruism.[27] We have claimed that a population of constrained maximizers would be rationally stable; no one would have reason to dispose herself to straightforward maximization. Similarly, if we think of constrained and straightforward maximization as parallel to genetic tendencies to reciprocal altruism and egoism, a population of reciprocal altruists would be genetically stable; a mutant egoist would be at an evolutionary disadvantage. Since she would not reciprocate, she would find herself excluded from co-operative relationships.

Trivers argues that natural selection will favour the development of the capacity to detect merely simulated altruism. This of course corresponds to our claim that constrained maximizers, to be successful, must be able to detect straightforward maximizers whose offers to co-operation are insincere. Exploitative interactions between CMs and SMs must be avoided.

Trivers also argues that natural selection will favour the development of guilt, as a device motivating those who fail to reciprocate to change their ways in future.[28] In our argument, we have not appealed to any affective disposition; we do not want to weaken the position we must defeat, straightforward maximization, by supposing that persons are emotionally indisposed to follow it. But we may expect that in the process of socialization, efforts will be made to develop and cultivate each person's feelings so that, should she behave as an SM, she will experience guilt. We may expect our affective capacities to be shaped by social practices in support of cooperative interaction.

If a population of reciprocal altruists is genetically stable, surely a population of egoists is also stable. As we have seen, the argument for the rationality of constrained maximization turns on the proportion of CMs in the population. A small proportion of CMs might well suffer more from exploitation by undetected SMs than by cooperation among themselves unless their capacities for detecting the dispositions of others were extraordinarily effective. Similarly, a mutant reciprocal altruist would be at a disadvantage among egoists; her attempts at co-operation would be rebuffed and she would lose by her efforts in making them.

Does it then follow that we should expect both groups of reciprocal altruists and groups of egoists to exist stably in the world? Not necessarily. The benefits of co-operation ensure that, in any given set of circumstances, each member of a group of reciprocal altruists should do better than a corresponding member of a group of egoists. Each reciprocal altruist should have a reproductive advantage. Groups of reciprocal altruists should therefore increase relative to groups of egoists in environments in which the two come into contact. The altruists must prevail—not in direct combat between the two (although the co-operation possible among reciprocal altruists may bring victory there), but in the indirect combat for evolutionary survival in a world of limited resources.

In his discussion of Trivers's argument, Jon Elster notes two points of great importance which we may relate to our own account of constrained maximization. The first is, "The altruism is the more efficient because it is *not* derived from calculated self-interest."[29] This is exactly our point at the end of 2.1—constrained maximization is not straightforward maximization in its most effective guise. The constrained maximizer genuinely ignores the call of utility-maximization in following the co-operative practices required by minimax relative concession. There is no simulation; if there were, the benefits of co-operation would not be fully realized.

The second is that Trivers's account "does not purport to explain specific instances of altruistic behaviour, such as, say, the tendency to save a drowning person. Rescue attempts are explained by a general tendency to perform acts of altruism, and this tendency is then made the object of the evolutionary explanation."[30] In precisely the same way, we do not purport to give a utility-maximizing justification for specific choices of adherence to a joint strategy. Rather we explain those choices by a general disposition to choose fair, optimizing actions whenever possible, and this tendency is then given a utility-maximizing justification.

We do not, of course, have the competence to discuss whether or not human beings are genetically disposed to utility-maximizing behaviour. But if human beings are so disposed, then we may conclude that the disposition to constrained maximization increases genetic fitness.

NOTES

1. Hobbes, *De Cive*, chap. I, para. 7; in *Man and Citizen*, p. 115.
2. Hobbes, *Leviathan*, chap. 14, p. 64.
3. Ibid.
4. Ibid., chap. 13, p. 63.
5. Ibid., chap. 14, p. 64.
6. Ibid.
7. Ibid., chap. 14, pp. 64–65.
8. Ibid., chap. 14, p. 65.
9. Ibid.
10. Ibid., chap. 21, p. 111.

11. Ibid., chap. 15, p. 71.

12. Ibid.

13. Ibid., chap. 15, p. 72.

14. Ibid., chap. 15, p. 73.

15. Ibid.

16. Hobbes, *The Questions Concerning Liberty. Necessity, and Chance* (1656), no. xiv; in Sir William Molesworth, ed., *The English Works of Thomas Hobbes*, 11 vols. (London, 1839–45), vol. 5, pp. 193–94.

17. Hobbes, *Leviathan*, chap. 15, p. 72.

18. Our answer to the Foole builds on, but supersedes, my discussion in "Reason and Maximization," *Canadian Journal of Philosophy* 4 (1975): 424–33.

19. Thus constrained maximization is not parallel to such strategies as "tit-for-tat" that have been advocated for so-called iterated Prisoner's Dilemmas. Constrained maximizers may co-operate even if neither expects her choice to affect future situations. Thus our treatment of co-operation does not make the appeal to reciprocity necessary to Robert Axelrod's account; see "The Emergence of Cooperation Among Egoists," *American Political Science Review* 75 (1981): 306–18.

20. That the discussion in "Reason and Maximization" assumes transparency was pointed out to me by Derek Parfit. See his discussion of "the self-interest theory" in *Reasons and Persons* (Oxford, 1984), esp. pp. 18–19. See also the discussion of "Reason and Maximization," in S. L. Darwall, *Impartial Reason* (Ithaca, N.Y., 1983), esp. pp. 197–98.

21. Hume, *Enquiry*, iii. i, p. 187.

22. Ibid., ix. ii, pp. 282–93.

23. Ibid., ix. ii, p. 283.

24. See, e.g., T. Nagel, *The Possibility of Altruism* (Oxford, 1970), pp. 90–124.

25. The objector might be Derek Parfit; see *Reasons and Persons*, pp. 19–23. His book appeared too recently to permit discussion of his arguments here.

26. See "Deterrence, Maximization, and Rationality," *Ethics* 94 (1984): 474–95; also in D. MacLean, ed., *The Security Gamble: Deterrence Dilemmas in the Nuclear Age* (Totowa, N.J., 1984), 101–22.

27. See R. L. Trivers, "The Evolution of Reciprocal Altruism," *Quarterly Review of Biology* 46 (1971): 35–57.

28. Ibid., p. 50,

29. J. Elster, *Ulysses and the Sirens: Studies in Rationality and Irrationality* (Cambridge, 1979), p. 145.

30. Ibid., pp. 145–46.

21

Internal and External Reasons

BERNARD WILLIAMS

Sentences of the forms "A has a reason to ϕ" or "There is a reason for A to ϕ" (where "ϕ" stands in for some verb of action) seem on the face of it to have two different sorts of interpretation. On the first, the truth of the sentence implies, very roughly, that A has some motive which will be served or furthered by his ϕ-ing, and if this turns out not to be so the sentence is false: there is a condition relating to the agent's aims, and if this is not satisfied it is not true to say, on this interpretation, that he has a reason to ϕ. On the second interpretation, there is no such condition, and the reason-sentence will not be falsified by the absence of an appropriate motive. I shall call the first the "internal," the second the "external," interpretation. (Given two such interpretations, and the two forms of sentence quoted, it is reasonable to suppose that the first sentence more naturally collects the internal interpretation, and the second the external, but it would be wrong to suggest that either form of words admits only one of the interpretations.)

I shall also for convenience refer sometimes to "internal reasons" and "external reasons," as I do in the title, but this is to be taken only as a convenience. It is a matter for investigation whether there are two sorts of reasons for action, as opposed to two sorts of statements about people's reasons for action. Indeed. as we shall eventually see, even the interpretation in one of the cases is problematical.

I shall consider first the internal interpretation, and how far it can be taken. I shall then consider, more sceptically, what might be involved in an external interpretation. I shall end with some very brief remarks connecting all this with the issue of public goods and free-riders.

The simplest model for the internal interpretation would be this: A has a reason to ϕ if A has some desire the satisfaction of which will be served by his ϕ-ing. Alternatively, we might say . . . some desire, the satisfaction of which A believes will be served by his ϕ-ing; this difference will concern us later. Such a model is sometimes ascribed to Hume, but since in fact Hume's own views are more complex than this, we might call it *the sub-Humean model*. The sub-Humean model is certainly too simple. My aim will be, by addition and revision, to work it up into something more adequate. In the course of trying to do this, I shall assemble four propositions which seem to me to be true of internal reason statements.

Basically, and by definition, any model for the internal interpretation must display a relativity of the reason statement to the agent's *subjective motivational set*, which I shall call the agent's *S*. The contents of *S* we shall come to, but we can say:

(i) An internal reason statement is falsified by the absence of some appropriate element from *S*.

The simplest sub-Humean model claims that any element in *S* gives rise to an internal reason. But there are grounds for denying this, not because of regrettable, imprudent, or deviant elements in *S*—they raise different sorts of issues—but because of elements in *S* based on false belief.

The agent believes that this stuff is gin, when it is in fact petrol. He wants a gin and tonic. Has he reason, or a reason, to mix this stuff with tonic and drink it? There are two ways here (as suggested already by the two alternatives for formulating the sub-Humean model). On the one hand, it is just very odd to say that he has a reason to drink this stuff, and natural to say that he has no reason to drink it, although he thinks that he has. On the other hand, if he does drink it, we not only have an explanation of his doing so (a reason why he did it), but we have such an explanation which is of the reason-for-action form. This explanatory dimension is very important, and we shall come back to it more than once. If there are reasons for action, it must be that people sometimes act for those reasons, and if they do, their reasons must figure in some correct explanation of their ac-

tion (it does not follow that they must figure in all correct explanations of their action). The difference between false and true beliefs on the agent's part cannot alter the *form* of the explanation which will be appropriate to his action. This consideration might move us to ignore the intuition which we noticed before, and lead us just to legislate that in the case of the agent who wants gin, he has a reason to drink this stuff which is petrol.

I do not think, however, that we should do this. It looks in the wrong direction, by implying in effect that the internal reason conception is only concerned with explanation, and not at all with the agent's rationality, and this may help to motivate a search for other sorts of reason which are connected with his rationality. But the internal reasons conception is concerned with the agent's rationality. What we can correctly ascribe to him in a third-personal internal reason statement is also what he can ascribe to himself as a result of deliberation, as we shall see. So I think that we should rather say:

(ii) A member of *S*, *D*, will not give *A* a reason for ϕ-ing if either the existence of *D* is dependent on false belief, or *A*'s belief in the relevance of ϕ-ing to the satisfaction of *D* is false.

(This double formulation can be illustrated from the gin/petrol case: *D* can be taken in the first way as the desire to drink what is in this bottle, and in the second way as the desire to drink gin.) It will, all the same, be true that if he does ϕ in these circumstances, there was not only a reason why he ϕ-ed, but also that that displays him as, relative to his false belief, acting rationally.

We can note the epistemic consequence:

(iii) (a) *A* may falsely believe an internal reason statement about himself, and (we can add)

(b) *A* may not know some true internal reason statement about himself.

(b) comes from two different sources. One is that A may be ignorant of some fact such that if he did know it he would, in virtue of some element in S, be disposed to ϕ: we can say that he has a reason to ϕ, though he does not know it. For it to be the case that he actually has such a reason, however, it seems that the relevance of the unknown fact to his actions has to be fairly close and immediate; otherwise one merely says that A would have a reason to ϕ if he knew the fact. I shall not pursue the question of the conditions for saying the one thing or the other, but it must be closely connected with the question of when the ignorance forms part of the explanation of what A actually does.

The second source of (iii) is that A may be ignorant of some element in S. But we should notice that an unknown element in S, D, will provide a reason for A to ϕ only if ϕ-ing is rationally related to D; that is to say, roughly, a project to ϕ could be the answer to a deliberative question formed in part by D. If D is unknown to A because it is in the unconscious, it may well not satisfy this condition, although of course it may provide the reason why he ϕ's, that is, may explain or help to explain his ϕ-ing. In such cases, the ϕ-ing may be related to D only symbolically.

I have already said that

(iv) internal reason statements can be discovered in deliberative reasoning.

It is worth remarking the point, already implicit, that an internal reason statement does not apply only to that action which is the uniquely preferred result of the deliberation. "A has reason to ϕ" does not mean "the action which A has overall, all-in, reason to do is ϕ-ing." He can have reason to do a lot of things which he has other and stronger reasons not to do.

The sub-Humean model supposes that ϕ-ing has to be related to some element in S as causal means to end (unless, perhaps, it is straightforwardly the carrying out of a desire which is itself that element in S). But this is only one case: indeed, the mere discovery that some course of action is the causal means to an end is not in itself a piece of practical reasoning.[1] A clear example of practical reasoning is that leading to the conclusion that one has reason to ϕ because ϕ-ing would be the most convenient, economical, pleasant, and so forth, way of satisfying some element in S, and this of course is controlled by other elements in S, if not necessarily in a very clear or determinate way. But there are much wider possibilities for deliberation, such as: thinking how the satisfaction of elements in S can be combined, for instance, by time-ordering; where there is some irresoluble conflict among the elements of S, considering which one attaches most weight to (which, importantly, does not imply that there is some one commodity of which they provide varying amounts); or, again, finding constitutive solutions, such as deciding what would make for an entertaining evening, granted that one wants entertainment.

As a result of such processes an agent can come to see that he has reason to do something which he did not see he had reason to do at all. In this way, the deliberative process can add new actions for which there are internal reasons, just as it can also add new internal reasons for given actions. The deliberative process can also subtract elements from S. Reflection may lead the agent to see that some belief is false, and hence to realise that he has in fact no reason to do something he thought he had reason to do. More subtly, he may think he has reason to promote some development because he has not exercised his imagination enough about what it would be like if it came about. In his unaided deliberative reason, or encouraged by the persuasions of others, he may come to have some more concrete sense of what would be involved, and lose his desire for it, just as, positively, the imagination can create new possibilities and new desires. (These are important possibilities for politics as well as for individual action.)

We should not, then, think of S as statically given. The processes of deliberation can have all sorts of effect on S, and this is a fact which a theory of internal reasons should be very happy to accommodate. So also it should be more liberal than some theorists have been about the possible elements in S. I have discussed S primarily in terms of desires, and this term can be used, formally, for all elements in S. But this terminology may make one forget that S can contain such things as dispositions of evaluation, patterns of emotional reaction, personal loyalties, and various projects, as they may be abstractly called, embodying commitments of the agent. Above all, there is of course no supposition that the desires or projects of an agent have to be egoistic; he will, one hopes, have non-egoistic projects of various kinds, and these equally can provide internal reasons for action.

There is a further question, however, about the contents of S: whether it should be taken, consistently with the general idea of internal reasons, as containing *needs*. It is certainly quite natural to say that A has a reason to pursue X, just on the ground that he needs X, but will this naturally follow in a theory of internal reasons? There is a special problem about this only if it is possible for the agent to be unmotivated to pursue what he needs. I shall not try to discuss here the nature of needs, but I take it that insofar as there are determinately recognisable needs, there can be an agent who lacks any interest in getting what he indeed needs. I take it, further, that that lack of interest can remain after deliberation, and, also that it would be wrong to say that such a lack of interest must always rest on false belief. (Insofar as it does rest on false belief, then we can accommodate it under [ii], in the way already discussed.)

If an agent really is uninterested in pursuing what he needs; and this is not the product of false belief; and he could not reach any such motive from motives he has by the kind of deliberative processes we have discussed; then I think we do have to say that in the in-ternal sense he indeed has no reason to pursue these things. In saying this, however, we have to bear in mind how strong these assumptions are, and how seldom we are likely to think that we know them to be true. When we say that a person has reason to take medicine which he needs, although he consistently and persuasively denies any interest in preserving his health, we may well still be speaking in the internal sense, with the thought that really at some level he *must* want to be well.

However, if we become clear that we have no such thought, and persist in saying that the person has this reason, then we must be speaking in another sense, and this is the external sense. People do say things that ask to be taken in the external interpretation. In James's story of Owen Wingrave, from which Britten made an opera, Owen's father urges on him the necessity and importance of his joining the army, since all his male ancestors were soldiers, and family pride requires him to do the same. Owen Wingrave has no motivation to join the army at all, and all his desires lead in another direction: he hates everything about military life and what it means. His father might have expressed himself by saying that *there was a reason for Owen to join the army.* Knowing that there was nothing in Owen's S which would lead, through deliberative reasoning, to his doing this would not make him withdraw the claim or admit that he made it under a misapprehension. He means it in an external sense. What is that sense?

A preliminary point is that this is not the same question as that of the status of a supposed categorical imperative, in the Kantian sense of an "ought" which applies to an agent independently of what the agent happens to want: or rather, it is not undoubtedly the same question. First, a categorical imperative has often been taken, as by Kant, to be necessarily an imperative of morality, but external reason statements do not necessarily relate to morality. Second, it remains an obscure issue what the relation is between "there is a reason for A to . . ." and "A ought to . . . ." Some philosophers take them to be equivalent, and under that view the question of external reasons of course comes much closer to the question of a categorical imperative. However, I shall not make any assumption about such an equivalence, and shall not further discuss "ought."[2]

In considering what an external reason statement might mean, we have to remember again the dimension of possible explanation, a consideration which applies to any reason for action. If something can be a reason for action, then it could be someone's reason for acting on a particular occasion, and it would then figure in an explanation of that action. Now no external reason statement could *by itself* offer an explanation of anyone's action. Even if it were true (whatever that might turn out to mean) that there was a reason for Owen to join the army, that fact by itself would never explain anything that Owen did, not even his joining the army. For if it was true at all, it was true when Owen was not motivated to join the army. The whole point of external reason statements is that they can be true independently of the agent's motivations. But nothing can explain an agent's (intentional) actions except something that motivates him so to act. So something else is needed besides the truth of the external reason statement to explain action, some psychological link; and that psychological link would seem to be belief. A's believing an external reason statement about himself may help to explain his action.

External reason statements have been introduced merely in the general form "there is a reason for A to . . . ," but we now need to go beyond that form, to specific statements of reasons. No doubt there are some cases of an agent's φ-ing because he believes that there is a reason for him to φ, while he does not have any belief about what that reason is. They would be cases of his relying on some authority whom he trusts, or, again, of his recalling that he did know of some reason for his φ-ing, but his not being able to remember what it was. In these respects, reasons for action are like reasons for belief. But, as with reasons for belief, they are evidently secondary cases. The basic case must be that in which A φ's, not because he believes only that there is some reason or other for him to φ, but because he believes of some determinate consideration that it constitutes a reason for him to φ. Thus Owen Wingrave might come to join the army because (now) he believes that it is a reason for him to do so that his family has a tradition of military honour.

Does believing that a particular consideration is a reason to act in a particular way provide, or indeed constitute, a motivation to act? If it does not, then we are no further on. Let us grant that it does—this claim indeed seems plausible, so long at least as the connexion between such beliefs and the disposition to act is not tightened to that unnecessary degree which excludes *akrasia*. The claim is in fact *so* plausible, that this agent, with this belief, appears to be one about whom, now, an *internal* reason statement could truly be made: he is one with an appropriate motivation in his S. A man who does believe that considerations of family honour constitute reasons for action is a man with a certain disposition to action, and also dispositions of approval, sentiment, emotional reaction, and so forth.

Now it does not follow from this that there is nothing in external reason statements. What does follow is that their content is not going to be revealed by considering merely the state of one who believes such a statement, nor how that state explains action, for that state is merely the state with regard to which an internal reason statement could truly be made. Rather, the content of the external type of statement will have to be revealed by considering what it is to *come to believe* such a statement—it is there, if at all, that their peculiarity will have to emerge.

We will take the case (we have implicitly been doing so already) in which an external reason statement is made about someone who, like Owen Wingrave, is not already motivated in the required way, and so is some-one about whom an internal statement could not also be truly made. (Since the difference between external and internal statements turns on the implications accepted by the speaker, external statements can of course be made about agents who are already moti-vated; but that is not the interesting case.) The agent does not presently believe the external statement. If he comes to believe it, he will be motivated to act; so coming to believe it must, essentially, involve acquiring a new motivation. How can that be?

This is closely related to an old question, of how "reason can give rise to a motivation," a question which has famously received from Hume a negative answer. But in that form, the question is itself unclear, and is unclearly related to the argument—for of course rea-son, that is to say, rational processes, can give rise to new motivations, as we have seen in the account of deliberation. Moreover, the traditional way of putting the issue also (I shall suggest) picks up an onus of proof about what is to count as a "purely rational process" which not only should it not pick up, but which properly belongs with the critic who wants to oppose Hume's general conclusion and to make a lot out of external reason state-ments—someone I shall call "the external reasons theorist."

The basic point lies in recognising that the external reasons theorist must conceive *in a special way* the connexion between acquir-ing a motivation and coming to believe the reason statement. For of course there are var-ious means by which the agent could come to have the motivation and also to believe the reason statement, but which are the wrong kind of means to interest the external reasons theorist. Owen might be so persuaded by his father's moving rhetoric that he acquired both the motivation and the belief. But this excludes an element which the external rea-sons theorist essentially wants, that the agent should acquire the motivation *because* he comes to believe the reason statement, and that he should do the latter, moreover, be-cause, in some way, he is considering the matter aright. If the theorist is to hold on to these conditions, he will, I think, have to make the condition under which the agent ap-propriately comes to have the motivation something like this, that he should deliberate correctly; and the external reasons statement itself will have to be taken as roughly equiv-alent to, or at least as entailing, the claim that if the agent rationally deliberated, then, what-ever motivations he originally had, he would come to be motivated to ϕ.

But if this is correct, there does indeed seem great force in Hume's basic point, and it is very plausible to suppose that all exter-nal reason statements are false. For, *ex hy-pothesi*, there is no motivation for the agent to deliberate *from*, to reach this new motiva-tion. Given the agent's earlier existing moti-vations, and this new motivation, what has to hold for external reason statements to be true, on this line of interpretation, is that the new motivation could be in some way rationally arrived at, granted the earlier motivations. Yet at the same time it must not bear to the earlier motivations the kind of rational rela-tion which we considered in the earlier dis-cussion of deliberation—for in that case an internal reason statement would have been true in the first place. I see no reason to sup-pose that these conditions could possibly be met.

It might be said that the force of an ex-ternal reason statement can be explained in the following way. Such a statement implies that a rational agent would be motivated to act appropriately, and it can carry this impli-cation, because a rational agent is precisely one who has a general disposition in his S to do what (he believes) there is reason for him to do. So when he comes to believe that there is reason for him to ϕ, he is motivated to ϕ, even though, before, he neither had a motive to ϕ, nor any motive related to ϕ-ing in one of the ways considered in the account of de-liberation.

But this reply merely puts off the prob-lem. It reapplies the desire and belief model (roughly speaking) of explanation to the actions in question, but using a desire and a belief the content of which are in question. *What* is it that one comes to believe when he comes to believe that there is reason for him to φ, if it is not the proposition, or something that entails the proposition, that if he deliberated rationally, he would be motivated to act appropriately? We were asking how any true proposition could have that content; it cannot help, in answering that, to appeal to a supposed desire which is activated by a belief which has that very content.

These arguments about what it is to accept an external reason statement involve some idea of what is possible under the account of deliberation already given, and what is excluded by that account. But here it may be objected that the account of deliberation is very vague, and has for instance allowed the use of the imagination to extend or restrict the contents of the agent's S. But if that is so, then it is unclear what the limits are to what an agent might arrive at by rational deliberation from his existing S.

It *is* unclear, and I regard it as a basically desirable feature of a theory of practical reasoning that it should preserve and account for that unclarity. There is an essential indeterminacy in what can be counted a rational deliberative process. Practical reasoning is a heuristic process, and an imaginative one, and there are no fixed boundaries on the continuum from rational thought to inspiration and conversion. To someone who thinks that reasons for action are basically to be understood in terms of the internal reasons model, this is not a difficulty. There is indeed a vagueness about "A has reason to φ," in the internal sense, insofar as the deliberative processes which could lead from A's present S to his being motivated to φ may be more or less ambitiously conceived. But this is no embarrassment to those who take as basic the internal conception of reasons for action. It merely shows that there is a wider range of states, and a less determinate one, than one

might have supposed, which can be counted as A's having a reason to φ.

It is the external reasons theorist who faces a problem at this point. There are of course many things that a speaker may say to one who is not disposed to φ when the speaker thinks that he should be, as that he is inconsiderate, or cruel, or selfish, or imprudent; or that things, and he, would be a lot nicer if he were so motivated. Any of these can be sensible things to say. But one who makes a great deal out of putting the criticism in the form of an external reason statement seems concerned to say that what is particularly wrong with the agent is that he is *irrational*. It is this theorist who particularly needs to make this charge precise: in particular, because he wants any rational agent, as such, to acknowledge the requirement to do the thing in question.

Owen Wingrave's father indeed expressed himself in terms other than "a reason," but, as we imagined, he could have used the external reasons formulation. This fact itself provides some difficulty for the external reasons theorist. This theorist, who sees the truth of an external reason statement as potentially grounding a charge of irrationality against the agent who ignores it, might well want to say that if Wingrave *père* put his complaints against Owen in this form, he would very probably be claiming something which, in this particular case, was false. What the theorist would have a harder time showing would be that the words *meant* something different as used by Wingrave from what they mean when they are, as he supposes, truly uttered. But what they mean when uttered by Wingrave is almost certainly *not* that rational deliberation would get Owen to be motivated to join the army—which is (very roughly) the meaning or implication we have found for them, if they are to bear the kind of weight such theorists wish to give them.

The sort of considerations offered here strongly suggest to me that external reason statements, when definitely isolated as such, are false, or incoherent, or really something else misleadingly expressed. It is in fact harder to isolate them in people's speech than the introduction of them at the beginning of this chapter suggested. Those who use these words often seem, rather, to be entertaining an optimistic internal reason claim, but sometimes the statement is indeed offered as standing definitely outside the agent's S and what he might derive from it in rational deliberation, and then there is, I suggest, a great unclarity about what is meant. Sometimes it is little more than that things would be better if the agent so acted. But the formulation in terms of reasons does have an effect, particularly in its suggestion that the agent is being irrational, and this suggestion, once the basis of an internal reason claim has been clearly laid aside, is bluff. If this is so, the only real claims about reasons for action will be internal claims.

A problem which has been thought to lie very close to the present subject is that of public goods and free riders, which concerns the situation (very roughly) in which each person has egoistic reason to want a certain good provided, but at the same time each has egoistic reason not to take part in providing it. I shall not attempt any discussion of this problem, but it may be helpful, simply in order to make clear my own view of reasons for action and to bring out contrasts with some other views, if I end by setting out a list of questions which bear on the problem, together with the answers that would be given to them by one who thinks (to put it cursorily) that the only rationality of action is the rationality of internal reasons.

1. Can we define notions of rationality which are not purely egoistic?

   Yes.

2. Can we define notions of rationality which are not purely means–end?

   Yes.

3. Can we define a notion of rationality where the action rational for A is in no way relative to A's existing motivations?

   No

4. Can we show that a person who only has egoistic motivations is irrational in not pursuing non-egoistic ends?

   Not necessarily, though we may be able to in special cases. (The trouble with the egoistic person is not characteristically irrationality.)

Let there be some good, G, and a set of persons, P, such that each member of P has egoistic reason to want G provided, but delivering G requires action C, which involves costs, by each of some proper sub-set of P; and let A be a member of P: then

5. Has A egoistic reason to do C if he is reasonably sure either that too few members of P will do C for G to be provided, or that enough other members of P will do C, so that G will be provided?

   No.

6. Are there any circumstances of this kind in which A can have egoistic reason to do C?

   Yes, in those cases in which reaching the critical number of those doing C is sensitive to his doing C, or he has reason to think this.

7. Are there any motivations which would make it rational for A to do C, even though not in the situation just referred to?

   Yes, if he is not purely egoistic: many. For instance, there are expressive motivations—appropriate, for instance, in the celebrated voting case.[3] There are also motivations which derive from the sense of fairness. This can precisely transcend the dilemma of "either useless or unnecessary," by the form of argument "somebody, but no reason to omit any particular body, so everybody."

8. It is irrational for an agent to have such motivations?

In any sense in which the question is intelligible, no.

9. Is it rational for society to bring people up with these sorts of motivations?

Insofar as the question is intelligible, yes. And certainly we have reason to encourage people to have these dispositions—for instance, in virtue of possessing them ourselves.

I confess that I cannot see any other major questions which, at this level of generality, bear on these issues. All these questions have clear answers which are entirely compatible with a conception of practical rationality in terms of internal reasons for action, and are also, it seems to me, entirely reasonable answers.

NOTES

1. A point made by Aurel Kolnai: see his "Deliberation Is of Ends," in *Ethics, Value and Reality* (London and Indianapolis: Hackett, 1978). See also David Wiggins, "Deliberation and Practical Reason," *Proceedings of the Aristotelian Society* 76 (1975–76); reprinted in part in *Practical Reasoning*, ed. J. Raz (Oxford: Oxford University Press, 1978).

2. It is discussed in " 'Ought' and Moral Obligation," in *Moral Luck* (Cambridge: Cambridge University Press, 1981).

3. A well-known treatment is by M. Olson, Jr., *The Logic of Collective Action* (Cambridge, Mass.: Harvard University Press, 1965). On expressive motivations in this connexion, see S. I. Benn, "Rationality and Political Behaviour," in S. I. Benn and G. W. Mortimore, eds., *Rationality and the Social Sciences* (London: Routledge & Kegan Paul, 1976). On the point about fairness, which follows in the text, there is of course a very great deal more to be said: for instance, about how members of a group can, compatibly with fairness, converge on strategies more efficient than everyone's doing *C* (such as people taking turns).

22

Skepticism about Practical Reason

CHRISTINE KORSGAARD

The Kantian approach to moral philosophy is to try to show that ethics is based on practical reason: that is, that our ethical judgments can be explained in terms of rational standards that apply directly to conduct or to deliberation. Part of the appeal of this approach lies in the way that it avoids certain sources of skepticism that some other approaches meet with inevitably. If ethically good action is simply rational action, we do not need to postulate special ethical properties in the world or faculties in the mind, in order to provide ethics with a foundation. But the Kantian approach gives rise to its own specific form of skepticism, skepticism about practical reason.

By *skepticism about practical reason*, I mean doubts about the extent to which human action is or could possibly be directed by reason. One form that such skepticism takes is doubt about the bearing of rational considerations on the activities of deliberation and choice; doubts, that is to say, about

whether "formal" principles have any content and can give substantive guidance to choice and action. An example of this would be the common doubt about whether the contradiction tests associated with the first formulation of the categorical imperative succeed in ruling out anything. I will refer to this as *content skepticism*. A second form taken by skepticism about practical reason is doubt about the scope of reason as a motive. I will call this *motivational skepticism*. In this paper my main concern is with motivational skepticism and with the question whether it is justified. Some people think that motivational considerations alone provide grounds for skepticism about the project of founding ethics on practical reason. I will argue, against this view, that motivational skepticism must always be based on content skepticism. I will not address the question of whether or not content skepticism is justified. I want only to establish the fact that motivational skepticism has no independent force.

Skepticism about practical reason gets its classical formulation in the well-known passages in the *Treatise of Human Nature* that lead Hume to the conclusion that "Reason is, and ought only to be the slave of the passions, and can never pretend to any other office than to serve and obey them."[1] According to these passages, as they are usually understood, the role of reason in action is limited to the discernment of the means to our ends. Reason can teach us how to satisfy our desires or passions, but it cannot tell us whether those desires or passions are themselves "rational", that is, there is no sense in which desires or passions are rational or irrational. Our ends are picked out, so to speak, by our desires, and these ultimately determine what we do. Normative standards applying to conduct may come from other sources (such as a moral sense), but the only standard that comes from reason is that of effectiveness in the choice of means.

The limitation of practical reason to an instrumental role does not only prevent reason from determining ends; it even prevents reason from ranking them, except with respect to their conduciveness to some other end. Even the view that those choices and actions which are conducive to our over-all self-interest are rationally to be preferred to self-destructive ones is undermined by the instrumental limitation. Self-interest itself has no rational *authority* over even the most whimsical desires. As Hume says:

> 'Tis not contrary to reason to prefer the destruction of the whole world to the scratching of my finger. 'Tis not contrary to reason for me to chuse my total ruin, to prevent the least uneasiness of an *Indian* or person wholly unknown to me. 'Tis as little contrary to reason to prefer even my own acknowledg'd lesser good to my greater, and have a more ardent affection for the former than the latter (*Treatise*, p. 416).

Under the influence of self-interest [or of "a general appetite to good, and aversion to evil, consider'd merely as such" (p. 417)] we may rank our ends, according to the amount of good that each represents for us, and determine which are, as Hume puts it, our "greatest and most valuable enjoyments" (p. 416). But the self-interest that would make us favor the greater good need not itself be a stronger desire, or a stronger reason, than the desire for the lesser good, or than any of our more particular desires. Reason by itself neither selects nor ranks our ends.

Hume poses his argument as an argument against "the greatest part of moral philosophy, ancient and modern" (p. 413). Moral philosophers, Hume says, have claimed that we ought to regulate our conduct by reason, and either suppress our passions or bring them into conformity with it; but he is going to show the fallacy of all this by showing, first, that reason alone can never provide a motive to any action, and, second, that reason can never oppose passion in the direction of the will. His argument for the first point goes this way: all reasoning is concerned either with abstract relations of ideas or with relations of objects, especially causal relations, which we learn about from experience. Abstract relations of ideas are the subject of logic and mathematics, and no one supposes that those by themselves give rise to any motives. They yield no conclusions about action. We are sometimes moved by the perception of causal relations, but only when there is a pre-existing motive in the case. As Hume puts it, if there is "the prospect of pleasure or pain from some object," we are concerned with its causes and effects. The argument that reason cannot oppose a passion in the direction of the will depends on, and in fact springs directly from, the argument that reason by itself cannot give rise to a motive. It is simply that reason *could* oppose a passion only if it could give rise to an *opposing motive*.

What is important to notice in this discussion is the relation between Hume's views about the possible content of principles of reason bearing on action and the scope of its motivational efficacy. The answer to the question what sorts of operation, procedure, or judgment of reason exist is presupposed in these passages. In the first part of the argument Hume goes through what by this point in the *Treatise* is a *settled* list of the types of rational judgment. The argument is a sort of process of elimination: there are rational judgments concerning logical and mathematical relations; there are empirical connections such as cause and effect: Hume looks at each of these in turn in order to see under what circumstances it might be thought to have a bearing on decision and action. In other words, Hume's arguments against a more extensive practical employment of reason depend upon Hume's own views about what reason is—that is, about what sorts of operation and judgment are "rational." His motivational skepticism (skepticism about the scope of reason as a motive) is entirely dependent upon his content skepticism (skepticism about what reason has to *say* about choice and action).

Yet Hume's arguments may give the impression of doing something much stronger: of placing independent constraints, based solely on motivational considerations, on what might count as a principle of practical reason. Hume seems to say simply that all reasoning that has a motivational influence must start from a passion, that being the only possible source of motivation. and must proceed to the means to satisfy that passion, that being the only operation of reason that transmits motivational force. Yet these are separate points: they can be doubted, and challenged, separately. One could disagree with Hume about his list of the types of rational judgment, operation, or possible deliberation, and yet still agree with the basic point about the source of motivation: that all rational motivation must ultimately spring from some nonrational source, such as passion. At least one contemporary philosopher, Bernard Williams, has taken something like Hume's argument to have this kind of independent force, and has so argued in his essay "Internal

and External Reason,"[2] which I will take up later in this paper.

The Kantian must go further, and disagree with Hume on both counts, since the Kantian supposes that there are operations of practical reason which yield conclusions about actions and which do not involve discerning relations between passions (or any pre-existing sources of motivation) and those actions. What gives rise to the difficulty about this further possibility is the question of how such operations could yield conclusions that can motivate us.

II

The problem can best be stated in some terms provided by certain recent discussions in moral philosophy. W. D. Falk, William Frankena, and Thomas Nagel, among others, have distinguished between two kinds of moral theories, which are called "internalist" and "externalist."[3] An *internalist* theory is a theory according to which the knowledge (or the truth or the acceptance) of a moral judgment implies the existence of a motive (not necessarily overriding) for acting on that judgment. If I judge that some action is right, it is implied that I have, and acknowledge, some motive or reason for performing that action. It is part of the sense of the judgment that a motive is present: if someone agrees that an action is right, but cannot see any motive or reason for doing it, we must suppose, according to these views, that she does not quite know what she means when she agrees that the action is right. On an *externalist* theory, by contrast, such a conjunction of moral comprehension and total unmotivatedness is perfectly possible: knowledge is one thing and motivation another.

Examples of unquestionably external theories are not easy to find. As Falk points out (pp. 125–26), the simplest example would be a view according to which the motives for moral action come from something wholly separate from a grasp of the correctness of the judgments—say, an interest in obeying divine commands. In philosophical ethics the best example is John Stuart Mill (see Nagel pp. 8–9), who firmly separates the question of the proof of the principle of utility from the question of its "sanctions." The reason why the principle of utility is true and the motive we might have for acting on it are not the same: the theoretical proof of its truth is contained in chapter IV of *Utilitarianism*, but the motives must be acquired in a utilitarian upbringing. It is Mill's view that *any* moral principle would have to be motivated by education and training and that "there is hardly anything so absurd or so mischievous" that it cannot be so motivated.[4] The "ultimate sanction" of the principle of utility is *not* that it can be proved, but that it is in accordance with our natural social feelings. Even to some who, like Mill himself, realize that the motives are acquired, "It does not present itself . . . as a superstition of education or a law despotically imposed by the power of society, but as an attribute which it would not be well for them to be without" (Mill p. 36). The modern intuitionists, such as W. D. Ross and H. A. Prichard, seem also to have been externalists, but of a rather minimal kind. They believed that there was a distinctively moral motive, a sense of right or desire to do one's duty. This motive is triggered by the news that something is your duty, and only by that news, but it is still separate from the rational intuition that constitutes the understanding of your duty. It would be possible to have that intuition and not be motivated by it.[5] The reason why the act is right and the motive you have for doing it are separate items, although it is nevertheless the case that the motive for doing it is "because it is right." This falls just short of the internalist position, which is that the reason why the act is right is the reason, and the motive, for doing it: it is a practical reason. Intuitionism is a form of rationalist ethics, but intuitionists do not believe in practical reason, properly speaking. They believe there is a branch of theoretical reason that is specifically concerned with morals, by which

human beings can be motivated because of a special psychological mechanism: a desire to do one's duty. One can see the oddity of this if one considers what the analogue would be in the case of theoretical reasoning. It is as if human beings could not be convinced by arguments acknowledged to be sound without the intervention of a special psychological mechanism: a belief that the conclusions of sound arguments are true.

By contrast, an internalist believes that the reasons why an action is right and the reasons why you do it are the same. The reason that the action is right is both the reason and the motive for doing it. Nagel gives as one example of this the theory of Hobbes: the reason for the action's rightness and your motive for doing it are both that it is in your interest. The literature on this subject splits, however, on the question of whether the Kantian position is internalist or not. Falk, for instance, characterizes the difference between internalism and externalism as one of whether the moral command arises from a source outside the agent (like God or society) or from within. If the difference is described this way, Kant's attempt to derive morality from autonomy makes him a paradigmatic internalist (see Falk, p. 125, 129). On the other hand, some have believed that Kant's view that the moral command is indifferent to our desires, needs, and interests—that it is categorical—makes him a paradigmatic externalist.[6] Since Kant himself took the categorical character of the imperative and autonomy of the moral motive to be necessarily connected, this is a surprising difference of opinion. I will come back to Kant in Section VII.

This kind of reflection about the motivational force of ethical judgments has been brought to bear by Bernard Williams on the motivational force of reason claims generally. In "Internal and External Reasons" Williams argues that there are two kinds of reason claims, or two ways of making reason claims. Suppose I say that some person *P* has a reason to do action *A*. If I intend this to imply that the person *P* has a motive to do the action *A*, the claim is of an internal reason, if not, the claim is of an external reason. Williams is concerned to argue that only internal reasons really exist. He points out (pp. 106–7) that, since an external-reason claim does not imply the existence of a motive, it cannot be used to explain anyone's action: that is, we cannot say that the person *P* did the action *A* because of reason *R*; for *R* does not provide *P* with a motive for doing *A*, and *that* is what we need to explain *P*'s doing *A*: a motive. Nagel points out that if acknowledgment of a reason claim did not include acknowledgment of a motive, someone presented with a reason for action could ask: Why do what I have a reason to do? (p. 9; see also Falk, pp. 121–22). Nagel's argument makes from the agent's perspective the same point that Williams makes from the explainer's perspective, namely, that unless reasons are motives, they cannot prompt or explain actions. And, unless reasons are motives, we cannot be said to be practically rational.

Thus, it seems to be a requirement on practical reasons, that they be capable of motivating us. This is where the difficulty arises about reasons that do not, like means/end reasons, draw on an obvious motivational source. So long as there is doubt about whether a given consideration is able to motivate a rational person, there is doubt about whether that consideration has the force of a practical *reason*. The consideration that such and such action is a means to getting what you want has a clear motivational source; so no one doubts that this is a reason. Practical-reason claims, if they are really to present us with reasons for action, must be capable of motivating rational persons. I will call this the *internalism requirement*.

III

In this section I want to talk about how the internalism requirement functions—or, more precisely, malfunctions—in skeptical arguments. Hume winds up his argument by putting the whole thing in a quite general form. Reason is the faculty that judges of truth and falsehood, and it can judge our ideas to be true or false because they represent other things. But a passion is an original existence or modification of existence, not a copy of anything: it cannot be true or false, and therefore it cannot in itself be reasonable or unreasonable. Passions can be unreasonable, then, only if they are accompanied by judgments, and there are two cases of this kind. One is when the passion is founded on the supposition of the existence of objects that do not exist. You are outraged at the mocking things you heard me say about you, but I was talking about somebody else. You are terrified by the burglars you hear whispering in the living room, but in fact you left the radio on. It is of course only in an extended sense that Hume can think of these as cases where a passion is irrational. Judgments of irrationality, whether of belief or action, are, strictly speaking, relative to the subject's beliefs. Conclusions drawn from mistaken premises are not *irrational*.[7] The case of passions based on false beliefs seems to be of this sort.

The second kind of case in which Hume says that the passion might be called unreasonable is ". . . when, in exerting any passion in action, we chuse means insufficient for the design'd end, and deceive ourselves in our judgment of causes and effects" (*Treatise*, p. 416). This is in itself an ambiguous remark. Hume might, and in fact does, mean simply that we base our action on a false belief about causal relations. So this is no more genuinely a case of irrationality than the other. Relative to the (false) causal belief, the action is not irrational. But it is important that there is something else one might mean in this case, which is that, knowing the truth about the relevant causal relations in the case, we might nevertheless choose means insufficient to our end or fail to choose obviously sufficient and readily available means to the end. This would be what I will call *true irrationality*, by which I mean a failure to respond appropriately to an available reason.

If the only possibility Hume means to be putting forward here is the possibility of action based on false belief about causes and effects, we get a curious result. Neither of the cases that Hume considers is a case of true irrationality: relative to their beliefs, people *never* act irrationally. Hume indeed says this: ". . . the moment we perceive the falsehood of any supposition, or the insufficiency of any means, our passions yield to our reason without any opposition" (*Treatise*, p. 416). But it looks as if a theory of means/end rationality ought to allow for at least one form of true irrationality, namely, failure to be motivated by the consideration that the action is the means to your end. Even the skeptic about practical reason admits that human beings can be motivated by the consideration that a given action is a means to a desired end. But it is not enough, to explain this fact, that human beings can engage in causal reasoning. It is perfectly possible to imagine a sort of being who could engage in causal reasoning and who could, therefore, engage in reasoning that would point out the means to her ends, but who was not motivated by it.

Kant, in a passage early in the *Foundations*, imagines a human being in just such a condition of being able to reason, so to speak, theoretically but not practically. He is talking about what the world would have been like if nature had had our happiness as her end. Our actions would have been controlled entirely by instincts designed to secure our happiness, and: ". . . if, over and above this, reason should have been granted to the favored creature, it would have served only to let it contemplate the happy constitution of its nature."[8] The favored creature is portrayed as able to see that his actions are rational in the sense that they promote the means to his end (happiness); but he is not motivated by their reasonableness; he acts from instinct. Reason allows him to admire the rational appropriateness of what he does,

but this is not what gets him to do it—he has the sort of attitude toward all his behavior that we in fact might have toward the involuntary well-functioning of our bodies.

Being motivated by the consideration that an action is a means to a desirable end is something beyond merely reflecting on that fact. The motive force attached to the end must be transmitted to the means in order for this to be a consideration that sets the human body in motion—and only if this is a consideration that sets the human body in motion can we say that reason has an influence on action. A practically rational person is not merely capable of performing certain rational mental operations, but capable also of transmitting motive force, so to speak, along the paths laid out by those operations. Otherwise even means/end reasoning will not meet the internalism requirement.

But the internalism requirement does not imply that nothing can interfere with this motivational transmission. And generally, this is something there seems to be no reason to believe: there seem to be plenty of things that could interfere with the motivational influence of a given rational consideration. Rage, passion, depression, distraction, grief, physical or mental illness: all these things could cause us to act irrationally, that is, to fail to be motivationally responsive to the rational considerations available to us.[9] The necessity, or the compellingness, of rational considerations lies in those considerations themselves, not in us: that is, we will not necessarily be motivated by them. Or rather, to put the point more properly and not to foreclose any metaphysical possibilities, their necessity may lie in the fact that, when they do move us—either in the realm of conviction or in that of motivation—they move us with the force of necessity. But it will still not be the case that they necessarily move us. So a person may be irrational, not merely by failing to observe rational connections—say, failing to see that the sufficient means are at hand—

but also by being "willfully" blind to them, or even by being indifferent to them when they are pointed out.[10]

In this respect practical reason is no different from theoretical reason. Many things might cause me to fail to be convinced by a good argument. For me to be a theoretically rational person is not merely for me to be capable of performing logical and inductive operations, but for me to be appropriately *convinced* by them: my conviction in the premises must carry through, so to speak, to a conviction in the conclusion. Thus, the internalism requirement for theoretical reasons is that they be capable of convincing us—insofar as we are rational. It is quite possible for me to be able to perform these operations without generating any conviction, as a sort of game, say, and then I would not be a rational person.

Aristotle describes the novice in scientific studies as being able to repeat the argument, but without the sort of conviction that it will have for him later, when he fully understands it. In order for a theoretical argument or a practical deliberation to have the status of reason, it must of course be capable of motivating or convincing a rational person, but it does not follow that it must at all times be capable of motivating or convincing any given individual. It may follow from the supposition that we are rational persons and the supposition that a given argument or deliberation is rational that, if we are not convinced or motivated, there must be some explanation of that failure. But there is no reason at all to believe that such an explanation will always show that we had mistaken reasons, which, if true, would have been good reasons. Many things can interfere with the functioning of the rational operations in a human body. Thus there is no reason to deny that human beings might be practically irrational in the sense that Hume considers impossible: that, even with the truth at our disposal, we might from one cause or another fail to be interested in the means to our ends.

IV

My speculation is that skepticism about practical reason is sometimes based on a false impression of what the internalism requirement requires. It does not require that rational considerations always succeed in motivating us. All it requires is that rational considerations succeed in motivating us insofar as we are rational. One can admit the possibility of true irrationality and yet still believe that all practical reasoning is instrumental. But once this kind of irrationality is allowed in the means/end case, some of the grounds for skepticism about more ambitious forms of practical reasoning will seem less compelling. The case of prudence or self-interest will show what I have in mind. I have already mentioned Hume's account of this matter: he thinks that there is "a general appetite to good, and aversion to evil" and that a person will act prudently insofar as this calm and general passion remains dominant over particular passions. It is under the influence of this end that we weigh one possible satisfaction against another, trying to determine which conduces to our greater good. But if this general desire for the good does not remain predominant, not only the motive, but the reason, for doing what will conduce to one's greater good, disappears. For Hume says it is not contrary to reason to prefer an acknowledged lesser good to a greater.

Suppose, then, that you are confronted with a choice and, though informed that one option will lead to your greater good, you take the other. If true irrationality is excluded, and you fail to take the means to some end, this is evidence either that you don't really have this end or that it is not the most important thing to you. Thus, in this imagined case, where you do not choose your greater good, this is evidence either that you do not care about your greater good or that you do not care about it as much as you do about this particular lesser good. On the other hand, if you do respond to the news that one option leads to your greater good, then we have evidence that you do care about your greater good. This makes it seem as if your greater good is an end you might care about or not, and rationality is relative to what you care about. But, once we admit that one might from some other cause fail to be responsive to a rational consideration, there is no special reason to accept this analysis of the case. I do not mean that there is a reason to reject it, either, of course; my point is that whether you accept it depends on whether you *already* accept the limitation to means/end rationality. If you do, you will say that the case where the lesser good was chosen was a case where there was a stronger desire for it, and so a stronger reason; if you do not, and you think it *is* reasonable to choose the greater good (because prudence has rational authority), you will say that this is a case of true irrationality. The point is that the motivational analysis of the case *depends* upon your views of the content of rational principles of action, not the reverse. The fact that one might or might not be motivated to choose a certain course of action by the consideration that it leads to the greater good does not by itself show that the greater good is just one end among others, without special rational authority, something that some people care about and some people do not. Take the parallel case. The fact that one might or might not be motivated to choose a certain course of action by the consideration that it is the best available means to one's end does not show that taking the means to one's ends is just one end among others, an end some people care about and some people do not. In both cases, what we have is the fact that people are sometimes motivated by considerations of this sort, and that we all think in the latter case and some think in the former case that it is rational to be so motivated.

The argument about whether prudence or the greater good has any special rational authority—about whether it is a rational consideration—will have to be carried out on another plane: it will have to be made in terms of a more metaphysical argument about just what reason does, what its scope is, and what sorts of operation, procedure, and judgment are rational. This argument will usually consist in an attempt to arrive at a general notion of reason by discovering features or characteristics that theoretical and practical reason share; such characteristic features as universality, sufficiency, timelessness, impersonality, or authority will be appealed to.[11] What the argument in favor of prudence would be will vary from theory to theory; here, the point is this: the fact that someone might fail to be motivated by the consideration that something will serve her greater good cannot by itself throw any doubt on the argument, whatever it is, that preferring the greater good is rational. If someone were not convinced by the logical operation of conjunction, and so could not reason with conviction from "*A*" and from "*B*" to "*A* and *B*," we would not be eager to conclude that conjunction was just a theory that some people believe and some people do not. Conjunction is not a theory to believe or disbelieve, but a principle of reasoning. Not everything that drives us to conclusions is a theory. Not everything that drives us to action need be a desired end (see Nagel, pp. 20–22).

V

An interesting result of admitting the possibility of true irrationality is that it follows that it will not always be possible to argue someone into rational behavior. If people are acting irrationally only because they do not know about the relevant means/end connection, they may respond properly to argument: point the connection out to them, and their behavior will be modified accordingly. In such a person the motivational path, so to speak, from end to means is open. A person in whom this path is, from some cause, blocked or nonfunctioning may not respond to argument, even if this person understands the argument in a theoretical way. Aristotle thinks of the incontinent person as being in a condition of this sort: this happens to people in fits of passion or rage, and the condition is actually physiological.[12] Now this is important; for it is sometimes thought, on the basis of the internalism requirement, that if there is a reason to do something it must be possible to argue someone into doing it: anyone who understands the argument will straightaway act. (The conclusion of a practical syllogism is an action.) Frankena, for example, argues against an internalist construal of the moral "ought" on the grounds that even after full reflection we do not always do what is right (p. 71). But if there is a gap between understanding a reason and being motivated by it, then internalism does not imply that people can always be argued into reasonable conduct. The reason motivates someone who is capable of being motivated by the perception of a rational connection. Rationality is a condition that human beings are capable of, but it is not a condition that we are always in.

It is for this reason that some ethical theories centered on the idea of practical reason are best thought of as establishing ideals of character. A person with a good character will be, on such a view, one who responds to the available reasons in an appropriate way, one whose motivational structure is organized for rational receptivity, so that reasons motivate in accord with their proper force and necessity. It is not an accident that the two major philosophers in our tradition who thought of ethics in terms of practical reason—Aristotle and Kant—were also the two most concerned with the methods of moral education. Human beings must be taught, or habituated, to listen to reason: we are, as Kant says, imperfectly rational.

In fact, the argument of the last section can be recast in terms of virtues. Suppose that it *is* irrational not to prefer the greater good: this need have nothing at all to do with having the greater good *among* your desired ends. It is of course true that some people are more steadily motivated by considerations of what conduces to their greater good than others: call such a person *the prudent person.* The fact that the prudent is more strongly motivated by reasons of greater good need not be taken to show that he has stronger reasons for attending to his greater good. (People have varying theoretical virtues too.[13]) We may, indeed say that the prudent person "cares more" about his greater good, but that is just another way of saying that he responds more strongly to these kinds of consideration, that he has the virtue of prudence. It need not be taken to imply that his greater good is a more heavily weighted end with him and that, therefore, it really does matter more to him that he achieve his greater good than it does to another person, an imprudent person, that he achieve his. It makes more sense to say that this other person ignores reasons that he has. Again, take the parallel: some people respond much more readily and definitely to the consideration that something is an effective means to their end. We might call such a person a *determined* or *resolute* person. Presumably no one feels like saying that the determined or resolute person has a stronger reason for taking the means to her ends than anyone else does. We all have just the same reason for taking the means to our ends. The fact that people are motivated differently by the reasons they have does not show that they have different reasons. It may show that some have virtues that others lack. On a practical-reason theory, the possibility of rationality sets a standard for character; but that standard will not always be met. But this is not by itself a reason for skepticism about the scope of the deliberative guidance that reason *can* provide. This is a reason for skepticism only about the extent to which that guidance will ever be taken advantage of.

VI

Nevertheless, the fact that a practical reason must be capable of motivating us might still seem to put a limitation on the scope of practical reason: it might be thought that it is a subjective matter which considerations can motivate a given individual and that, therefore, all judgments of practical reason must be conditional in form. In Hume's argument, this kind of limitation is captured in the claim that motivation must originate in a passion. In the means/end case, we are able to be motivated by the consideration that action A will promote purpose P because, and only if, we have a pre-existing motivational impulse (a passion) attached to purpose P. As Hume says, a relation between two things will not have any motivational impact on us unless one of the two things has such impact. This does not limit practical reason to the means/end variety, but it might seem to impose a limitation of this sort: practical-reason claims must be reached by something that is recognizably a rational deliberative process from interests and motives one already has. This position is advocated by Bernard Williams in "Internal and External Reasons." Williams, as I have mentioned, argues that only internal reasons exist; but he takes this to have a strong Humean implication. Williams takes it that internal reasons are by definition relative to something that he calls the agent's "subjective motivational set": this follows from the fact that they can motivate. The contents of this set are left open, but one kind of thing it will obviously contain is the agent's desires and passions. Internal reasons are reasons reached by deliberation from the subjective motivational set: they can motivate us because of their connection to that set. Means/end deliberation, where the end is in the set and the means are what we arrive at by the motivating deliberation, is the most characteristic, but not the only, source of reasons for action. Williams calls the means/end view the "sub-Humean model," and he says this:

> The sub-Humean model supposes that ϕ-ing [where ϕ-ing is some action we have a reason for doing] has to be related to some element in [the subjective motivational set] as causal means to end (unless perhaps it is straightfor-

wardly the carrying out of a desire which is itself that element in [the subjective motivational set].) But this is only one case . . . there are much wider possibilities for deliberation, such as: thinking how the satisfaction of elements in [the subjective motivational set] can be combined, e.g. by time-ordering; where there is some irresoluble conflict among the elements of [the subjective motivational set,] considering which one attaches most weight to . . . ; or again, finding constitutive solutions, such as deciding what would make for an entertaining evening, granted that one wants entertainment (pp. 104–5).[14]

Anything reached by a process of deliberation from the subjective motivational set may be something for which there is an internal reason, one that can motivate. External reasons, by contrast, exist regardless of what is in one's subjective motivational set. In this case, Williams points out, there must be some rational process, not springing from the subjective motivational set and therefore not relative to it, which could bring you to acknowledge something to be a reason and at the same time to be motivated by it. Reason must be able to produce an entirely new motive, the thing that Hume said could not be done.

Thus, Williams takes up one part of the skeptic's argument: that a piece of practical reasoning must start from something that is capable of motivating you; and drops the other, that the only kind of reasoning is means/end. One might suppose that this limits the operations or judgments of practical reason to those functions which are natural extensions or expansions of the means/end variety, and the things Williams mentions in this passage, such as making a plan to satisfy the various elements in the set, or constitutive reasoning, are generally thought to be of that sort. But in fact this is not Williams's view, nor is it necessitated by his argument, as he points out.

> The processes of deliberation can have all sorts of effect on [the subjective motivational set],

and this is a fact which a theory of internal reasons should very happy to accommodate. So also it should be more liberal than some theorists have been about the possible elements in the [subjective motivational set]. I have discussed [the subjective motivational set] primarily in terms of desires, and this term can be used, formally, for all elements in [the subjective motivational set]. But this terminology may make one forget that [the subjective motivational set] can contain such things as dispositions of evaluation, patterns of emotional reaction, personal loyalties, and various projects, as they may be abstractly called, embodying commitments of the agent (p. 105).

Williams can accommodate the case of someone's acting for reasons of principle, and in this case the form the deliberation will take is that of applying the principle or of seeing that the principle applies to the case at hand. The advocate of the view that all deliberation is strictly of the means/ends variety may claim to assimilate this case by the formal device of saying that the agent must have a desire to act on this principle, but this will not change the important fact, which is that the reasoning in this case will involve the application of the principle, which is not the same as means/end reasoning.[15]

In this kind of case, Williams's point will be that in order for the principle to provide reasons for a given agent, acceptance of the principle must constitute part of the agent's subjective motivational set. If the principle is not accepted by the agent, its dictates are not reasons for her. Reasons are relativized to the set. If this is true, it looks at first as if all practical reasons will be relative to the individual, because they are conditioned by what is in the subjective motivational set. Reasons that apply to you regardless of what is in your subjective motivational set will not exist.

This argument, however, having been cut loose from Hume's very definite ideas about what sort of rational operations and processes exist, has a very unclear bearing on claims about pure practical reason. If one accepts the internalism requirement, it follows that pure practical reason will exist if and only if we are capable of being motivated by the conclusions of the operations of pure practical reason as such. Something in us must make us capable of being motivated by them, and this something will be part of the subjective motivational set. Williams seems to think that this is a reason for doubting that pure practical reasons exist, whereas what seems to follow from the internalism requirement is this: if we can be motivated by considerations stemming from pure practical reason, then that capacity belongs to the subjective motivational set of every rational being. One cannot argue that the subjective motivational set contains only ends or desires; for that would be true only if all reasoning were of the means/end variety or its natural extensions. What sorts of items can be found in the set does not limit, but rather depends on, what kinds of reasoning are possible. Nor can one assume that the subjective motivational set consists only of individual or idiosyncratic elements; for that is to close off without argument the possibility that reason could yield conclusions that every rational being must acknowledge and be capable of being motivated by. As long as it is left open what kinds of rational operations yield conclusions about what to do and what to pursue, it must be left open whether we are capable of being motivated by them.

Consider the question of how an agent comes to accept a principle: to have it in her subjective motivational set. If we say that the agent comes to accept the principle through reasoning—through having been convinced that the principle admits of some ultimate justification—then there are grounds for saying that this principle is in the subjective motivational set of every rational person: for all rational persons could be brought to see that they have reason to act in the way required by the principle, and this is all that the internalism requirement requires. Now this is of course not Williams's view: he believes that the principles are acquired by education, training, and so forth, and that they do not admit of any ultimate justification.[16] There are two important points to make about this.

First, consider the case of the reflective agent who, after being raised to live by a certain principle, comes to question it. Some doubt, temptation, or argument has made her consider eliminating the principle from her subjective motivational set. Now what will she think? The principle does not, we are supposing, admit of an ultimate justification, so she will not find that. But this does not necessarily mean that she will reject the principle. She may, on reflection, find that she thinks it better (where this will be relative to what other things are in her motivational set) that people should have and act on such a principle, that it is in some rough way a good idea—perhaps not the only but an excellent basis for community living, and so forth— and so she may retain it and even proceed to educate those under her influence to adopt it. The odd thing to notice is that this is almost exactly the sort of description Mill gives of the reflective utilitarian who, on realizing that his capacity to be motivated by the principle of utility is an acquirement of education, is not sorry. But Mill's position, as I mentioned earlier, is often taken to be the best example of an *externalist* ethical position.

More immediately to the point, what this kind of case shows is that for Williams, as for Hume, the motivational skepticism depends on what I have called the "content skepticism." Williams's argument does not show that if there were unconditional principles of reason applying to action we could not be motivated by them. He only thinks that there are none. But Williams's argument, like Hume's, gives the appearance of going the other way around: it looks as if the motivational point—the internalism requirement— is supposed to have some force in limiting what might count as a principle of practical reason. Whereas in fact, the real source of the skepticism is a doubt about the existence of principles of action whose content shows them to be ultimately justified.

VII

The internalism requirement is correct, but there is probably no moral theory that it excludes. I do not think that it even excludes utilitarianism or intuitionism, although it calls for a reformulation of the associated views about the influence of ethical reasoning or motivation. The force of the internalism requirement is psychological: what it does is not to refute ethical theories, but to make a psychological demand on them.

This is in fact how philosophers advocating a connection between morality and practical reason have thought of the matter. From considerations concerning the necessity that reasons be internal and capable of motivating us which are almost identical to Williams's, Nagel, in the opening sections of *The Possibility of Altruism*, argues that investigations into practical reason will yield discoveries about our motivational capacities. Granting that reasons must be capable of motivating us, he thinks that if we then are able to show the existence of reasons, we will have shown something capable of motivating us. In Nagel's eyes, the internalism requirement leads not to a limitation on practical reason, but to a rather surprising increase in the power of moral philosophy: it can teach us about human motivational capacities; it can teach us psychology.[17]

As Nagel points out, this approach also characterizes the moral philosophy of Kant. By the end of the Second Section of the *Foundations*, there is in *one* sense no doubt that Kant has done what he set out to do: he has shown us what sort of demand pure reason would make on action. Working from the ideas that reasons in general (either theoretical or practical) must be universal, that reason seeks the unconditioned, and that its binding force must derive from autonomy, he has shown us what a law of pure reason applying to action would look like. But until it has been shown that we can be motivated to act according to the categorical imperative, it has not been completely shown that the categorical imperative really exists—that there really is a law of pure practical reason. And this is because of the internalism requirement. The question how the imperative is possible is equated to that of "how the constraint of the will, which the imperative expresses in the problem, can be conceived" (Beck, p. 34; Acad., p. 417). Thus, what remains for proof by a "deduction" is that we are capable of being motivated by this law of reason: that we have an autonomous will. In the Third Section of the *Foundations*, Kant does try to argue that we can be motivated by the categorical imperative, appealing to the pure spontaneity of reason as evidence for our intelligible nature and so for an autonomous will (Beck, pp. 70–71; Acad., p. 452). In the *Critique of Practical Reason*,[18] however, Kant turns his strategy around. He argues that we know that we are capable of being motivated by the categorical imperative and therefore that we know (in a practical sense) that we have an autonomous will. Again, explorations into practical reason reveal our nature. It is important, however, that although in the *Critique of Practical Reason* Kant does not try to argue *that* pure reason can be a motive, he has detailed things to say about *how* it can be a motive—about how it functions as an incentive in combatting other incentives.[19] Something is still owed to the internalism requirement: namely, to show what psychological conclusions the moral theory implies.

It may be that we are immune to motivation by pure practical reason. But, for that matter, it may be that we are immune to motivation by means/ends connections. Perhaps our awareness of these in cases where we seem to act on them is epiphenomenal. In fact we are quite sure that we are not immune to the reasons springing from means/ends connections; and Kant maintained that, if we thought about it, we would see that we are not immune to the laws of pure practical reason: that we know we can do what we ought. But there is no guarantee of this; for our knowledge of our motives is limited. The conclusion is that, if we are rational, we will

act as the categorical imperative directs. But we are not necessarily rational.

VIII

I have not attempted to show in this paper that there is such a thing as pure practical reason, or that reason has in any way a more extensive bearing on conduct than empiricism has standardly credited it with. What I have attempted to show is that this question is open in a particular way: that motivational considerations do not provide any reason, in advance of specific proposals, for skepticism about practical reason. If a philosopher can show us that something that is recognizably a law of reason has bearing on conduct, there is no special reason to doubt that human beings might be motivated by that consideration. The fact that the law might not govern conduct, even when someone understood it, is no reason for skepticism: the necessity is in the law, and not in us.

To the extent that skepticism about pure practical reason is based on the strange idea that an acknowledged reason can never fail to motivate, there is no reason to accept it. It is based on some sort of a misunderstanding, and I have suggested a misunderstanding of the internalism requirement as a possible account. To the extent that skepticism about pure practical reason is based on the idea that no process or operation of reason yielding unconditional conclusions about action can be found, it depends on—and is not a reason for believing—the thesis that no process or operation of reason yielding unconditional conclusions about action can be found. To the extent that skepticism about pure practical reason is based on the requirement that reasons be capable of motivating us, the correct response is that if someone discovers what are recognizably reasons bearing on conduct and those reasons fail to motivate us, that only shows the limits of our rationality. Motivational skepticism about practical reason depends on, and cannot be the basis for, skepticism about the possible content of rational requirements. The extent to which people are actually moved by rational considerations, either in their conduct or in their credence, is beyond the purview of philosophy. Philosophy can at most tell us what it would be like to be rational.

NOTES

I would like to thank Timothy Gould, Charlotte Brown, and audiences of an earlier version of this paper at Columbia and the University of Chicago, for comments on and discussions of the issues of this paper, from which I have learned a great deal.

1. David Hume, *Treatise of Human Nature*, L. A. Selby-Bigge, ed. (London: Oxford University Press, 1888), p. 415. Page references to the *Treatise* will be to this edition.

2. This paper was originally published in Ross Harrison, ed., *Rational Action* (New York: Cambridge University Press, 1980), and is reprinted in Williams, *Moral Luck* (New York: Cambridge University Press, 1981), pp. 101–13. Page references to Williams are to this article, as it appears in *Moral Luck*.

3. Actually, Falk and Frankena speak of internalist and externalist senses of 'ought.' See Falk, " 'Ought' and Motivation," *Proceedings of the Aristotelian Society* (1947–48). Frankena's discussion, "Obligation and Motivation in Recent Moral Philosophy," was originally published in A. I. Melden, ed., *Essays in Moral Philosophy* (Seattle: University of Washington Press, 1958), and is reprinted in *Perspectives on Morality: Essays of William K. Frankena*, Kenneth E. Goodpaster, ed. (Notre Dame, Ind.: University of Notre Dame Press, 1976), pp. 49–73 (page references are to this volume). Nagel's discussion is in *The Possibility of Altruism* (New York: Oxford University Press, 1970), Pt. I.

4. *Utilitarianism*, in Samuel Gorovitz, ed., *Utilitarianism with Critical Essays* (Indianapolis: Bobbs-Merrill, 1971), p. 34.

5. See Prichard, "Duty and Interest," in *Duty and Interest* (London: Oxford University Press, 1928). Falk's original use of the distinction between internal and external senses of ought in " 'Ought' and Motivation" is in an argument responding to Prichard's paper.

6. See Frankena, op. cit., p. 63 for a discussion of this surprising view.

7. I am ignoring here the more complicated case in which the passion in question is parent to the false beliefs. In my examples, for instance, there might be cases such as these: irritation at me predisposes you to think my insults are aimed at you; terror of being alone in the house makes you more likely to mistake the radio for a burglar. Hume does discuss this phenomenon (*Treatise* 120). Here, we might say that the judgment is irrational, not merely false, and that its irrationality infects the passions and actions based on the judgment. If Hume's theory allows him to say that the judgment is irrational, he will be able to say that some passions and actions are truly irrational, and not merely mistaken, although he does not do this.

8. Immanuel Kant, *Foundations of the Metaphysics of Morals*, Lewis White Beck, trans. (New York: Library of Liberal Arts, 1959), p. 11; Prussian Academy Edition [hereafter cited as "Acad."], p. 395.

9. "Available to us" is vague, for there is a range of cases in which one might be uncertain whether or not to say that a reason was available to us. For instance there are (1) cases in which we don't know about the reason, (2) cases in which we couldn't possibly know about the reason, (3) cases in which we deceive ourselves about the reason, (4) cases in which some physical or psychological condition makes us unable to see the reason, and (5) cases in which some physical or psychological condition makes us fail to respond to the reason, even though in some sense we look it right in the eye. Now no one will want to say that reason claims involving reasons people do not know about are therefore external, but as we move down the list there will be a progressive uneasiness about whether the claim is becoming external. For toward the end of the list we will come to claim that someone is psychologically incapable of responding to the reason, and yet that it is internal: capable of motivating a rational person. I do not think there is a problem about any of these cases; for all that is necessary for the reason claim to be internal is that we can say that, if a person did know and *if nothing were interfering with her rationality*, she would respond accordingly. This does not trivialize the limitation to internal reasons as long as the notion of a psychological condition that interferes with rationality is not trivially defined.

10. I have in mind such phenomena as self-deception, rationalization, and the various forms of weakness of will. Some of these apply to theoretical as well as practical reason, and for the former we can add the various forms of intellectual resistance or ideology (though "willful" is not a good way to characterize these). For some reason, people find the second thing that I mention—being indifferent to a reason that is pointed out to you—harder to imagine in a theoretical than in a practical case. To simply shrug in the face of the acknowledged reason seems to some to be possible in practice in a way that it is not in theory. I think part of the problem is that we can push what the practically paralyzed person accepts over into the realm of theory: he *believes* "that he ought to do such-and-such," although he is not moved to; whereas there seems to be nowhere further back (except maybe to a suspense of judgment) to push what the theoretically paralyzed person accepts. It may also be that the problem arises because we do not give enough weight to the difference between being convinced by an argument and being left without anything to say by it, or it may be just that what paralysis *is* is less visible in the case of belief than in the case of action.

11. Universality and sufficiency are appealed to by Kant; timelessness and impersonality by Nagel; and authority by Joseph Butler.

12. *Nicomachean Ethics,* V11.3, 1147b5–10.

13. The comparisons I have been drawing between theoretical and practical reason now suggest that there should also be something like an ideal of good theoretical character: a receptivity to theoretical reasons. The vision of someone free of all ideology and intellectual resistance might be such an ideal.

14. Williams uses the designation 'S' for 'subjective motivational set,' but I have put back the original phrase wherever it occurs; hence the brackets.

15. It is true that the application of a principle may be so simple or immediate that it will be a matter of judgment or perception rather than deliberation. In such a case there will be some who want to deny that practical reason has been used. On the other hand, the reasoning involved in applying a principle may be quite complicated (as in the case of the contradiction tests under the categorical imperative), and so be such that anyone should be willing to call it reasoning. If the fact that you hold the principle gives motivational force to either the insight or the deliberative argument to the effect that this case falls under the principle, then the result is a practical reason.

16. Williams himself remarks that the "onus of proof about what is to count as a 'purely rational process' . . . properly belongs with the critic who wants to oppose Hume's general conclusion and to make a lot out of external reason statements" (108). Although I think he is quite right in saying that the burden of proof about what is to count as a purely rational process—about *content*—belongs to Hume's opponents, I am arguing that there is no reason to suppose that if this burden is successfully picked up the reasons will be external.

17. Op. cit., p. 13. Nagel calls this a "rebellion against the priority of psychology" (p. 11) and accordingly distinguishes two kinds of internalism: one that takes the psychological facts as given and supposes that we must somehow derive ethics from them in order to achieve an internalist theory, and one that supposes that metaphysical investigations—investigations into what it is to be a rational person—will have psychological conclusions. Hobbes would be an example of the first kind and Kant of the second.

18. See esp. pp. 30 and 43–51 in the translation by Lewis White Beck (New York: Library of Liberal Arts, 1956) and pp. 30 and 41–50 in the Prussian Academy Edition.

19. In chapter III of the Analytic of the *Critique of Practical Reason*, where Kant's project is "not . . . to show a priori why the moral law supplies an incentive but rather what it effects (or better, must effect) in the mind, in so far as it is an incentive" (Beck, p. 17; Acad., p. 72).

23

The Sources of Normativity

CHRISTINE KORSGAARD

LECTURE III: THE AUTHORITY OF REFLECTION

INTRODUCTION

Over the course of the last two lectures I have sketched the way in which the normative question took shape in the debates of modern moral philosophy. Voluntarism tries to explain normativity in what is in some sense the most natural way: we are subject to laws, including the laws of morality, because we are subject to lawgivers. But when we ask why we should be subject to those lawgivers, an infinite regress threatens. Realism tries to block that regress by postulating the existence of entities—objective values, reasons, or obligations—whose intrinsic normativity forbids further questioning. But why should we believe in these entities? In the end, it seems we will be prepared to assert that such entities exist only because—and only if—we are already confident that the claims of morality are justified.

The reflective endorsement theorist tries a new tack. Morality is grounded in human nature. Obligations and values are projections of our own moral sentiments and dispositions. To say that these sentiments and dispositions are justified is not to say that they track the truth, but rather to say that they are good. We are the better for having them, for they perfect our social nature and promote our self-interest.

But the normative question is one that arises in the heat of action. So it is not just our dispositions, but rather the particular motives and impulses that spring from them, that must seem to us to be normative. It is this line of thought that presses us toward Kant. Kant, like the realist, thinks we must show that particular actions are right and particular ends are good. Each impulse as it offers itself to the will must pass a kind of test for normativity before we can adopt it as a reason for action. But the test that it must pass is not the test of knowledge or truth. For Kant, like Hume and Williams, thinks that morality is grounded in human nature and that moral properties are projections of human dispositions. So the test is one of reflective endorsement.

In what follows I will lay out the elements of a theory of normativity. This theory derives its main inspiration from Kant, but with some modifications that I have come to think are needed. What I say will necessarily be sketchy, and sketchily argued. My attention here will be focused on four points: first, that autonomy is the source of obligation, and in particular of our ability to obligate ourselves; second, that we have *moral* obligations, by which I mean obligations to humanity as such; third, that since we can obligate ourselves, we can also be obligated by other people; and fourth, that we have obligations to other living things. I will have little to say about the content of any of these obligations. And it will be no part of my argument to suggest either that all obligations are moral or that obligations can never conflict. My aim is to show you where obligation comes from. Exactly which obligations we have and how to negotiate among them is a topic for another day.

THE PROBLEM

The human mind is self-conscious. Some philosophers have supposed that this means that our minds are internally luminous, that their contents are completely accessible to us, that we always can be certain what we are thinking and feeling and wanting, and so that introspection yields certain knowledge of the self. Like Kant, and many philosophers nowadays, I do not think that this is true. Our knowledge of our own mental states and activities is no more certain than anything else.

But the human mind *is* self-conscious in the sense that it is essentially reflective. I'm not talking about being *thoughtful*, which of course is an individual property, but about the structure of our minds that makes thoughtfulness possible. A lower animal's attention is fixed on the world. Its perceptions are its beliefs and its desires are its will. It is engaged in conscious activities, but it is not conscious *of* them. That is, they are not the objects of its attention. But we human animals turn our attention on to our perceptions and desires themselves, and we are conscious *of* them. That is why we can think *about* them.

And this sets us a problem no other animal has. It is the problem of the normative. For our capacity to turn our attention onto our own mental activities is also a capacity to distance ourselves from them and to call them into question. I perceive, and I find myself with a powerful impulse to believe. But I back up and bring that impulse into view and then I have a certain distance. Now the impulse doesn't dominate me and now I have a problem. Shall I believe? Is this perception really a *reason* to believe? I desire and I find myself with a powerful impulse to act. But I back up and bring that impulse into view and then I have a certain distance. Now the impulse doesn't dominate me and now I have a problem. Shall I act? Is this desire really a *reason* to act? The reflective mind cannot settle for perception and desire, not just as such. It needs a *reason*. Otherwise, at least as long as it reflects, it cannot commit itself or go forward.

If the problem springs from reflection then the solution must do so as well. If the problem is that our perceptions and desires might not withstand reflective scrutiny, then the solution is that they might. We need reasons because our impulses must be able to withstand reflective scrutiny. We have reasons if they do. The normative word "reason" refers to a kind of reflective success. If "good" and "right" are also taken to be intrinsically normative words then they too must refer to reflective success. And they do. Think of what they mean when we use them as *exclamations*: "Good!" "Right!" There they mean: I'm satisfied, I'm happy, I'm committed, you've convinced me, let's go. They mean the work of reflection is done.

"Reason" then means reflective success. So if I decide that my desire is a reason to act, I must decide that on reflection I endorse that desire. And here we find the problem. For how do I decide that? Is the claim that I look at the desire and see that it is intrinsically normative or that its object is? Then all of the arguments against realism await us. Does the desire or its object inherit its normativity from something else? Then we must ask what makes that other thing normative, what makes it the source of a reason. And now of course the usual regress threatens. So what brings reflection to an end?

Kant described this same problem in terms of freedom. It is because of the reflective structure of the mind that we must act, as he puts it, under the idea of freedom. He says, "We cannot conceive of a reason which consciously responds to a bidding from the outside with respect to its judgments."[1] If the bidding from outside is desire, then his point is that the reflective mind must endorse the desire before it can act on it—it must say to itself that the desire is a reason. We must, as he puts it, *make it our maxim* to act on the desire. And this is something we must do of our own free will.

Kant defines a free will as a rational causality that is effective without being determined by any alien cause. Anything outside of the will counts as an alien cause, including the desires and inclinations of the person. The free will must be entirely self-determining. Yet, because the will is a causality, it must act according to some law or other. Kant says, "Since the concept of a causality entails that of laws . . . it follows that freedom is by no means lawless. . . ."[2] Alternatively, we may say that since the will is practical reason, it cannot be conceived as acting and choosing for no reason. Since reasons are derived from principles, the free will must have a principle. But because the will is free, no law or principle can be imposed on it from outside. Kant concludes that the will must be autonomous: that is, it must have its *own* law or principle. And here again we

arrive at the problem. For where is this law to come from? If it is imposed on the will from outside then the will is not free. So the will must adopt the law for itself. But until the will has a law or principle, there is nothing from which it can derive a reason. So how can it have any reason for adopting one law rather than another?

Well, here is Kant's answer. The categorical imperative tells us to act only on a maxim that we could will to be a law. And *this*, according to Kant, *is* the law of a free will. To see why, we need only compare the problem faced by the free will with the content of the categorical imperative. The problem faced by the free will is this: the will must have a law, but because the will is free, it must be its own law. And nothing determines what that law must be. *All that it has to be is a law*. Now consider the content of the categorical imperative. The categorical imperative simply tells us to choose a law. Its only constraint on our choice is that it have the form of a law. And nothing determines what that law must be. *All that it has to be is a law*.

Therefore the categorical imperative is the law of a free will. It does not impose any external constraint on the free will's activities, but simply arises from the nature of the will. It describes what a free will must do in order to be what it is. It must choose a maxim it can regard as a law.[3]

Now I'm going to make a distinction that Kant doesn't make. I am going to call the law of acting only on maxims you can will to be laws "the categorical imperative." And I am going to distinguish it from what I will call "the moral law." The moral law, in the Kantian system, is the law of what Kant calls the Kingdom of Ends, the republic of all rational beings. The moral law tells us to act only on maxims that all rational beings could agree to act on together in a workable cooperative system. Now the Kantian argument that I have just described establishes that *the categorical imperative* is the law of a free will. But it does not establish that *the moral law* is the law of a free will. Any law is universal, but the argument doesn't settle the question of the *domain* over which the law of the free will must range. And there are various possibilities here. If the law is the law of acting on the desire of the moment, then the agent will treat each desire as it arises as a reason, and her conduct will be that of a wanton.[4] If the law ranges over the interests of an agent's whole life, then the agent will be some sort of egoist. It is only if the law ranges over every rational being that the resulting law will be the moral law, the law of the Kingdom of Ends.

Because of this, it has sometimes been claimed that the categorical imperative is an empty formalism. And this in turn has been conflated with another claim, that the moral law is an empty formalism. Now that second claim is false.[5] But it is true that the argument that shows that we are bound by the categorical imperative does not show that we are bound by the moral law. For that we need another step. The agent must think of *herself* as a Citizen of the Kingdom of Ends.

THE SOLUTION

Those who think that the human mind is internally luminous and transparent to itself think that the term "self-consciousness" is appropriate because what we get in human consciousness is a direct encounter with the self. Those who think that the human mind has a reflective structure use the term too, but for a different reason. The reflective structure of the mind is a source of "self-consciousness" because it forces us to have a *conception* of ourselves. As Kant argues, this is a fact about what it is *like* to be reflectively conscious and it does not prove the existence of a metaphysical self. From a third person point of view, outside of the deliberative standpoint, it may look as if what happens when someone makes a choice is that the strongest of his conflicting desires wins. But that isn't the way it is *for you* when you deliberate. When you deliberate, it is as if there

were something over and above all of your desires, something that is *you*, and that *chooses* which desire to act on. This means that the principle or law by which you determine your actions is one that you regard as being expressive of *yourself*. To identify with such a principle or law is to be, in St. Paul's famous phrase, a law to yourself.[6]

An agent might think of herself as a Citizen in the Kingdom of Ends. Or she might think of herself as a member of a family or an ethnic group or a nation. She might think of herself as the steward of her own interests, and then she will be an egoist. Or she might think of herself as the slave of her passions, and then she will be a wanton. And how she thinks of herself will determine whether it is the law of the Kingdom of Ends, or the law of some smaller group, or the law of the egoist, or the law of the wanton that is the law that she is to herself.

The conception of one's identity in question here is not a theoretical one, a view about what as a matter of inescapable scientific fact you are. It is better understood as a description under which you value yourself, a description under which you find your life to be worth living and your actions to be worth undertaking. So I will call this a conception of your practical identity. Practical identity is a complex matter and for the average person there will be a jumble of such conceptions. You are a human being, a woman or a man, an adherent of a certain religion, a member of an ethnic group, someone's friend, and so on. And all of these identities give rise to reasons and obligations. Your reasons express your identity, your nature; your obligations spring from what that identity forbids.

Our ordinary ways of talking about obligation reflect this connection to identity. A century ago a European could admonish another to civilized behavior by telling him to act like a Christian. It is still true in many quarters that courage is urged on males by the injunction "Be a man!" Duties more obviously connected with social roles are of course enforced in this way. "A psychiatrist doesn't violate the confidence of her patients." No "ought" is needed here because the normativity is built right into the role. But it isn't only in the case of social roles that the idea of obligation invokes the conception of practical identity. Consider the astonishing but familiar "I couldn't live with myself if I did that." Clearly there are two selves here, me and the one I must live with and so must not fail. Or consider the protest against obligation ignored: "Just who do you think you are?"

The connection is also present in the concept of integrity. Etymologically, integrity is oneness, integration is what makes something one. To be a thing, one thing, a unity, an entity; to be anything at all: in the metaphysical sense, that is what it means to have integrity. But we use the term for someone who lives up to his own standards. And that is because we think that living up to them is what makes him one, and so what makes him a person at all.

It is the conceptions of ourselves that are most important to us that give rise to unconditional obligations. For to violate them is to lose your integrity and so your identity, and no longer to be who you are. That is, it is no longer to be able to think of yourself under the description under which you value yourself and find your life worth living and your actions worth undertaking. That is to be for all practical purposes dead or worse than dead. When an action cannot be performed without loss of some fundamental part of one's identity, and an agent would rather be dead, then the obligation not to do it is unconditional and complete. If reasons arise from reflective endorsement, then obligation arises from reflective *rejection*.

But the question how exactly an agent *should* conceive her practical identity, the question which law she should be to herself, is not settled by the arguments I have given. So moral obligation is not yet on the table. To that extent the argument is formal, and in one sense empty.

But in another sense it is not empty at all.

What we have established is this. The reflective structure of human consciousness requires that you identify yourself with some law or principle that will govern your choices. It requires you to be a law to yourself. And that is the source of normativity. So the argument shows just what Kant said that it did: that our autonomy is the source of obligation.

It will help to put the point in Joseph Butler's terms, in terms of the distinction between power and authority. We do not always do what upon reflection we would do or even what upon reflection we have already decided to do. Reflection does not have irresistible power over us. But when we do reflect we cannot but think that we ought to do what on reflection we conclude we have reason to do. And when we don't do that we punish ourselves, by guilt and regret and repentance and remorse. We might say that the acting self concedes to the thinking self its right to government. And the thinking self, in turn, tries to govern as well as it can. So the reflective structure of human consciousness establishes a relation here, a relation that we have to ourselves. And it is a relation not of mere power but rather of *authority*. And *that* is the authority that is the source of obligation.

Notice that this means that voluntarism is true after all. The source of obligation is a legislator, one whose authority is beyond question and does not need to be established. But there is only one such authority and it is the authority of your own mind and will.[7] So Pufendorf and Hobbes were right. It is not the bare fact that it would be a good idea to perform a certain action that obligates us to perform it. It is the fact that we *command ourselves* to do what we find it would be a good idea to do.

One more step is necessary. The acting self concedes to the thinking self its right to govern. But the thinking self in turn must try to govern well. It is its job to make what is in any case a good idea into law. How do we know what is a good idea or what should be a law? Kant proposes that we can tell whether our maxims should be laws by attending not to their matter but to their form.

To understand this idea, we need to return to its origins, which are in Aristotle. According to Aristotle, a thing is composed of a form and a matter. The matter is the material, the parts, from which it is made. The form of a thing is its functional arrangement. That is, it is the arrangement of the matter or of the parts that enables the thing to serve its purpose, to do whatever it does. For example, the purpose of a house is to be a shelter, so the form of a house is the way the arrangement of the parts—the walls and the roof— enables it to serve as a shelter. "Join the walls at the corner, put the roof on top, and that's how we keep the weather out." That is the form of a house.[8]

Next consider the maxim of an action. Since every human action is done for an end, a maxim has two parts, the act and the end. The form of the maxim is the arrangement of its parts. Take, for instance, Plato's famous example of the three maxims.[9]

1. I will keep my weapon, because I want it for myself.
2. I will refuse to return your weapon, because I want it for myself.
3. I will refuse to return your weapon, because you have gone mad and may hurt someone.

Maxims 1 and 3 are good; maxim 2 is bad. What makes them so? Not the actions, for maxims 2 and 3 have the same actions; not the purposes, for maxims 1 and 2 have the same purposes. The goodness does not rest in the parts; but rather in the way the parts are combined and related; so the goodness does not rest in the matter, but rather in the form of the maxim. But form is not merely the arrangement of the parts; it is the *functional* arrangement—the arrangement that enables the thing to do what it does. If the walls are joined and roof placed on top *so*

that the building can keep the weather out, then the building has the form of a house. So: if the action and the purpose are related to one another *so that* the maxim can be willed as a law, then the maxim is good.

Notice what this establishes. A good maxim is good in virtue of its internal structure. Its internal structure, its form, makes it fit to be willed as a law. A good maxim is therefore an *intrinsically normative entity*. So realism is true after all, and Nagel, in particular, was right. When an impulse presents itself to us, as a kind of candidate for being a reason, we look to see whether it really is a reason, whether its claim to normativity is true.

But this isn't an exercise of intuition or a discovery about what is out there in the world. The test for determining whether an impulse is a reason is whether *we* can will the maxim of acting on that impulse as law. So the test is a test of endorsement.

This completes the first part of my argument, so let me sum up what I've said. What I have shown so far is why there is such a thing as obligation. The reflective structure of human consciousness forces us to act for reasons. At the same time, and relatedly, it forces us to have a conception of our own identity, a conception that identifies us with the source of our reasons. In this way, it makes us laws to ourselves. When an impulse presents itself to us we ask whether it could be a reason. We answer that question by seeing whether the maxim of acting on it can be willed as a law by a being with the identity in question. If it can be willed as a law, it is a reason, for it has an intrinsically normative structure. If it cannot be willed as a law, we must reject it, and in that case we get obligation.

A moment ago I said that realism is true after all. But that could be misleading. That we obligate ourselves is simply a fact about human nature. But whether a maxim can serve as a law still depends upon the way that we think of our identities. So there is still an element of relativism in the system. In order to establish that there are *moral* obligations we will need another step.

MORAL OBLIGATION

There is another way to make the points I have been making, and in approaching the problem of relativism it will be helpful to employ it. We can take as our model the way Rawls employs the concept/conception distinction in *A Theory of Justice*. There, the *concept* of justice refers to a problem, the problem of how the benefits of social cooperation are to be distributed. A *conception* of justice is a principle that is proposed as a solution to that problem.[10]

In the same way, the most general normative concepts, the right and the good, are names for problems—for the normative problems that spring from our reflective nature. "Good" names the problem of what we are to strive for, aim for, and care about in our lives. "Right" names the more specific problem of what we are to do. The "thinness" of these terms, to use Bernard Williams's language, comes from the fact that they are only concepts, names for whatever it is that solves the problems in question.

How do we get from concepts to conceptions? What mediates is a conception of practical identity. In Rawls's argument, we move from concept to conception by taking up the standpoint of the pure citizen and asking what principles such a citizen would have reason to adopt. In Kant's argument, we move from concept to conception by taking up the standpoint of a Citizen in the Kingdom of Ends and asking what principles that citizen would have reason to adopt.

Because they are normative, thick ethical concepts stand to thin ones as conceptions to concepts. They represent solutions, or at least reasons that will be weighed in arriving at solutions, to the problems that are set by reflection. And that means that they embody a view about what is right or good. If this is right, then Williams is wrong to say that reflection is not inherent in, or already implied by, thick ethical concepts. As normative concepts, they are essentially reflective.

Furthermore, our thin ethical concepts, although not necessarily our thick ones, will be shared with those alien scientific investigators. For the fact that they are scientific investigators means that they have asked themselves what they ought to believe and that they have decided that the question is worth pursuing. And that in turn means that they are rational and social beings, who face normative problems like our own and sometimes solve them. The exact shape of their problems may be different from ours, and so they may have different conceptions. But if we can see their conceptions as solutions to the normative problems that *they* face, there will even be a kind of convergence.

But this does not eliminate the element of relativism that Williams has sought to preserve. The mediation between concepts and conceptions comes by way of practical identity. And human identity has been differently constituted in different social worlds. Sin, dishonor, and moral wrongness all represent conceptions of what one cannot do without being diminished or disfigured, without loss of identity, and therefore conceptions of what one must not do. But they belong to different worlds in which human beings thought of themselves and of what made them themselves in very different ways. Where sin is the conception, my identity is my soul and it exists in the eyes of my God. Where dishonor is the conception, my identity is my reputation, my position in some small and knowable social world. The conception of *moral* wrongness as we now understand it belongs to the world *we* live in, the one brought about by the Enlightenment, where one's identity is one's relation to humanity itself. Hume said at the height of the Enlightenment that to be virtuous is to think of yourself as a member of the "party of humankind, against vice or disorder, its common enemy."[11] And that is now true. But we coherently can grant that it was not always so.

But this is not to say that there is nothing to be said in favor of the Enlightenment conception. This sort of relativism has its limits, and they come from two different but related lines of thought.

We have already seen one of them set forward by Bernard Williams. We could, with the resources of a knowledge of human nature, rank different sets of values according to their tendency to promote human flourishing. If values are associated with ways of thinking of what we most fundamentally are, then the point will be that some ways of conceiving one's identity are healthier and better for us than others.

But it is also important to remember that no argument can preserve any form of relativism without on another level eradicating it. This is one of the main faults with one well-known criticism of liberalism, that the conception of the person that is employed in its arguments is an "empty self."[12] It is urged by communitarians that people need to conceive themselves as members of smaller communities, essentially tied to particular others and traditions. This is an argument about how human beings need to constitute our practical identities, and if it is successful what it establishes is a *universal* fact, namely that our practical identities must be constituted in part by particular ties and commitments. And the communitarian who has reflected and reached this conclusion now has a conception of his own identity that is universal: he is an animal that needs to live in community.

And there is a further implication of this that is important. Once the communitarian sees himself this way, his particular ties and commitments will remain normative for him only if this more fundamental conception of his identity is one that he can see as normative as well. A further stretch of reflection requires a further stretch of endorsement. So he must endorse this new view of his identity. He is an animal that needs to live in community, and he now takes *this* to be a normative identity. He treats it as a source of

reasons, for he argues that it matters that he gets what he needs. And this further stretch of endorsement is exactly what occurs. Someone who is moved to urge the value of *having* particular ties and commitments has discovered that part of their normativity comes from the fact that human beings need to have them. He urges that our lives are meaningless without them. That is not a reason that *springs from* one of his own particular ties and commitments. It is a plea on behalf of all human beings. And that means that he is no longer immersed in a normative world of particular ties and commitments. Philosophical reflection does not leave everything just where it was.

This is just a fancy new model of an argument that first appeared in a much simpler form, Kant's argument for his Formula of Humanity. The form of relativism with which Kant began was the most elementary one we encounter—the relativity of value to human desires and interests. He started from the fact that when we make a choice we must regard its object as good. His point is the one I have been making—that being human we must endorse our impulses before we can act on them. Kant asked what it is that makes these objects good, and, rejecting one form of realism, he decided that the goodness was not in the objects themselves. Were it not for our desires and inclinations, we would not find their objects good. Kant saw that we take things to be important because they are important to us—and he concluded that we must therefore take ourselves to be important. In this way, the value of humanity itself is implicit in every human choice.[13] If normative skepticism is to be avoided—if there is any such thing as a reason for action—then humanity as the source of all reasons and values must be valued for its own sake.[14]

The point I want to make now is the same. In this lecture I have offered an account of the source of normativity. I have argued that a human being is an animal who needs a practical conception of her own identity, a conception of who she is that is normative for her. Otherwise she could have no reasons to act, and since she is reflective she needs reasons to act. But you are a human being and so if you believe my argument you can now see that *this* is your identity. You are an animal of the sort I have just described. And that is not merely a contingent conception of your identity, which you have constructed or chosen for yourself or could conceivably reject. It is simply the truth. Now that you see that your need to have a normative conception of yourself comes from the sort of animal you are, you can ask whether it really matters whether animals of this kind conform to their normative practical identities. Does it really matter what human beings do? And here you have no option but to say yes. Since you are human you *must* take something to be normative, that is, some conception of practical identity must be normative for you. If you had no normative conception of your identity, you could have no reasons for action, and because your consciousness is reflective, you could then not act at all. Since you cannot act without reasons and your humanity is the source of your reasons, you must endorse your own humanity if you are to act at all.

It follows from this argument that human beings are valuable. Enlightenment morality is true.

OBLIGATING ONE ANOTHER

So far I have argued that the reflective structure of human consciousness gives us legislative authority over ourselves. That is why we are able to obligate ourselves. And just now I argued that once we understand how all of this works, we must concede that our humanity is an end in itself, that human nature as the source of our values is itself a value. This, I should add, is what gives rise to *moral* obligation.

You might suppose that I am claiming that this settles the question of our obligations to others. Since I regard my humanity as a source of value, I must in the name of consistency regard your humanity that way as well. So I must value the things that you value. Or, to put it another way, since I think my humanity is what makes my desires into normative reasons, I must suppose that the humanity of others makes their desires into normative reasons as well.

This is a familiar form of argument. Versions of it appear in Thomas Nagel's book *The Possibility of Altruism*, and in Alan Gewirth's book *Reason and Morality*. And the criticism of this form of argument is always the same. Consistency can force me to grant that your humanity is normative for you just as mine is normative for me. It can force me to acknowledge that your desires have the status of reasons for you, in exactly the same way that mine do for me. But it does not force me to share in your reasons or make *your* humanity normative for me.[15] It could still be true that I have my reasons and you have yours, and indeed that they leave us eternally at odds.[16] Human beings might be egoistic, not in the sense of being concerned only about themselves, but in the sense defined by Nagel in *The Possibility of Altruism*. The egoist thinks that reasons are a kind of private property. We each act on our own private reasons, and we need some special reason, like friendship or contract, for taking the reasons of others into account.

In one sense this objection is correct. Consistency is not what forces us to share our reasons. And even if these arguments did work, they would work in the wrong way. They would show that I have an obligation *to myself* to treat you in ways that respect the value that I place on you. But they would not show that I have obligations *to you*. So we need something more.

As we have seen, I can obligate myself because I am conscious of myself. So if you are going to obligate me I must be conscious of you. You must be able to intrude on my reflections—you must be able to get under my skin. People suppose that practical reasons are private because they suppose that reflection is a private activity. And they suppose that, in turn, because they believe in the privacy of consciousness. So what we need at this point is some help from Wittgenstein.

Consider the private language argument. As Wittgenstein defines it, a private language would be a language that referred to something essentially private and incommunicable, say for instance a sensation that is yours alone, and cannot be described in any other way than by a name that you give to it. You can't even call it a tickle or an itch, for then it would be communicable. So you just call it 'S.' And whenever you experience it, you say to yourself, "That was S."[17]

Wittgenstein argues that there couldn't be any such language. One way to understand his argument goes like this: Meaning is relational because it is a *normative* notion: to say that X means Y is to say that one ought to take X for Y; and this requires two, a legislator to lay it down that one ought to take X for Y and a citizen to obey. And the relation between these two is not merely causal because the citizen can disobey: there must be a possibility of misunderstanding or mistake. Since it is a relation in which one gives a law to another, it takes two to make a meaning. So you cannot peer inwardly at an essentially private and incommunicable sensation and say, "That is what I mean by S" and so in that way mean something. For if that is what you mean by S, then when you call something S it must be *that*, and if you call something else S you must be wrong. But if what you call S is just that sensation that makes you feel like saying "S," and it cannot be identified in any other way, then you cannot be wrong.[18] The idea of a private language is inconsistent with the normativity of meaning.

If we read Wittgenstein that way, there is an obvious similarity between the kind of normativity that he thinks characterizes language and the kind of normativity that I have been attributing to practical reasons. We could make a parallel argument against private reasons: Reasons are relational because

reason is a normative notion: to say that R is a reason for A is to say that one should do A because of R; and this requires two, a legislator to lay it down and a citizen to obey. And the relation between them is not just causal because the citizen can disobey: there must be a possibility of irrationality—or wrongdoing. Since it is a relation in which one gives a law to another, it takes two to make a reason. And here the two are the two elements of reflective consciousness, the thinking self and the active self: what I have been talking about all along is how you can make laws and reasons for your self.[19]

There are two important points here. The first point is that the mistake involved in thinking that a meaning is a mental entity is exactly like that involved in thinking that a reason or a value is a mental entity. To talk about reasons and meanings is not to talk about entities, but to talk in a shorthand way about relations we have with ourselves and one another. The normative demands of meaning and reason are not demands that are made on us by objects, but are demands that we make on ourselves and each other.

The second point concerns privacy. The private language argument does not show that I could not have my own personal language. It shows that I could not have a language that is in principle incommunicable to anybody else. When I make a language, I make its meanings normative for me. As Wittgenstein puts it, I *undertake* to use words in certain ways.[20] And however I go about binding myself to those meanings, it must be possible for me to bind another in exactly the same way.

If I say to you, "Picture a yellow spot!" you will. What exactly is happening? Are you simply cooperating with me? No, because at least without a certain active resistance you will not be able to help it. Is it a causal connection then? No, or at least not merely that, for if you picture a *pink* spot you will be mistaken, wrong. Causal connections cannot be wrong. What kind of necessity is this, both normative and compulsive? It is *obligation*.

Philosophers have been concerned for a long time about how we understand the meanings of words, but we have not paid enough attention to the fact that it is so hard not to. It is nearly impossible to hear the words of a language you know as mere noise. And this has implications for the supposed privacy of human consciousness. For it means that I can always intrude myself into your consciousness. All I have to do is talk to you in the words of a language you know, and in this way I can force you to think. The space of linguistic consciousness is essentially public, like a town square. You might happen to be alone in yours, but I can get in anytime. Wittgenstein says, "Think in this connection how singular is the use of a person's name to *call* him."[21]

If I call out your name, I make you stop in your tracks. (If you love me, I make you come running.) Now you cannot proceed as you did before. Oh, you can proceed, all right, but not just as you did before. For now if you walk on, you will be ignoring me and slighting me. It will probably be difficult for you, and you will have to muster a certain active resistance, a sense of rebellion. But why should you have to rebel against me? It is because I am a law to you. By calling out your name, I have obligated you. I have given you a reason to stop.[22]

Of course you might not stop. You have reasons of your own, and you might decide, rightly or wrongly, that they outweigh the one I have given you. But that I have given you a reason is clear from the fact that, in ordinary circumstances, you will feel like giving me one back. "Sorry, I must run, I'm late for an appointment." We all know that reasons must be met with reasons, and that is why we are always exchanging them.

We do not seem to need a reason to take the reasons of others into account. We seem to need a reason not to. Certainly we do things because others want us to, ask us to, tell us to, all the time. We give each other the time and directions, open doors and step aside, warn each other of imminent perils

large and small. We respond with the alacrity of obedient soldiers to telephones and doorbells and cries for help. You could say that it is because we want to be cooperative, but that is like saying that you understand my words because you want to be cooperative. It ignores the same essential point, which is that it is so hard not to.

Now the egoist may reply that this does not establish that other people's reasons are reasons for me. He'll say that I am merely describing a deep psychological fact—that human beings are very susceptible to one another's pressure. We tend to cave in to the demands of others. But nothing I have said so far shows that we have to treat the demands of others as *reasons*. It is at this point that Thomas Nagel's argument, from *The Possibility of Altruism*, comes into its own.

Suppose that we are strangers and that you are tormenting me, and suppose that I call upon you to *stop*. I say, "How would you like it if someone did that to you?" Now you cannot proceed as you did before. Oh, you can proceed all right, but not just as you did before. For I have obligated you to stop.

How does the obligation come about? Just the way that Nagel says that it does. I invite you to consider how you would like it if someone did that to you. You realize that you would not merely dislike it, you would resent it. You would think that the other has a reason to stop—more, that he has an obligation to stop. And that obligation would spring from your own objection to what he does to you. You make yourself an end for others; you make yourself a law to them. But if you are a law to others insofar as you are just a person, just *someone*, then others are also laws to you.[23] By making you think these thoughts, I force you to acknowledge the value of *my* humanity, and I obligate you to act in a way that respects it.

As Nagel observes, the argument does not go through if you fail to see yourself, to identify yourself, as just someone, a person, one person among others who are equally real.[24] The argument invites you to change places with the other, and you cannot do this if you fail to see what you and the other have in common. Suppose you could say, "Someone doing that to *me*, why that would be terrible! But then I am *me*, after all." Then the argument would fail of its effect; it would not find a foothold in you. But the argument never really fails in *that* way.

For it to fail in that way, I would have to hear your words as mere noise, not as intelligible speech. And it is impossible to hear the words of a language you know as mere noise. In hearing your words as *words*, I acknowledge that you are *someone*. In acknowledging that I can hear them, I acknowledge that I am *someone*. If I listen to the argument at all, I have already admitted that each of us is *someone*.

Consider an exchange of reasons. A student comes to your office door and says, "I need to talk to you. Are you free now?" You say, "No, I've got to finish this letter right now and then I've got to go home. Could you possibly come around tomorrow, say about three?" And your student says, "Yes, that will be fine. I'll see you tomorrow at three then."

What is happening here? On my view, the two of you are reasoning together, to arrive at a decision, a single shared decision, about what to do. And I take that to be the natural view. But if egoism is true, and reasons cannot be shared, then that is not what is happening. Instead, each of you backs into the privacy of his practical consciousness, reviews his own reasons, comes up with a decision, and then reemerges to announce the result to the other. And the process stops when the results happen to coincide, and the agents know it, because of the announcements they have made to each other.

Now consider an exchange of ideas, rather than an exchange of practical reasons. Here we do not find these two possibilities. If meanings could not be shared, there would be no point in announcing the results of one's private thinking to anybody else. If they can be shared, then it is in principle possible to think the issues through together, and that is

what people do when they talk. But if we have to grant that meanings can be shared, why not grant that practical reasons can be shared too?

The egoist may reply that I am leaving out an option. The student/teacher relation is a personal one. People who enter into particular personal relationships have special reasons to take each other's reasons into account. So the exchange I've just described takes place against a background agreement that the parties involved will take each other's reasons into account. The egoist is someone who only acts on his own reasons, not someone who has no concern for others. So you and your student reason together because you have tacitly agreed to, but this does not show that this is what usually happens.

But the objection reemerges within this framework. How are we to understand this personal relationship? If reasons are still private then it goes like this: each of you has a private reason to take the reasons of the other into account. A personal relationship is an interest in one another's interests.[25] This doesn't change the shape of the deliberation—you still back into your private deliberative spaces and then reemerge to announce the results. This only shows why you think there's a point in the exercise at all, why you hope to reach a convergence. But if you are really reasoning together, if you have joined your wills to arrive at a single decision—well, then that can happen, can't it? And why shouldn't it be what usually happens? Why shouldn't language force us to reason practically together, in just the same way that it forces us to think together?

I believe that the myth of egoism will die with the myth of the privacy of consciousness. Now you may object that the way in which I have argued against the privacy of consciousness—by arguing that we can think and reason together—has nothing to do with what philosophers mean when they discuss that privacy. What they mean by privacy is that you don't always know what someone else is thinking or feeling. The way in which you have access to the contents of another person's mind—through words and expressions and other such forms of evidence—doesn't allow you to look around in it freely, and make sure that you know what's there and what's not.

But that's not an issue about privacy. If you accept the thesis that consciousness is reflective rather than internally luminous, then you must admit that you don't have access to your *own* mind in *that* way. So that doesn't mark a difference between the kind of relationship you have to yourself and the kind that you have to other people. All we've got here is a matter of degree. You know some people better than others; if you're honest and lucky, you know yourself pretty well.

Human beings are social animals in a deep way. It is not just that we go in for friendship or prefer to live in swarms or packs. The space of linguistic consciousness—the space in which meanings and reasons exist—is a space that we occupy together.

THE ORIGIN OF VALUE AND THE VALUE OF LIFE

Pain is an objection. Interestingly, it is an objection to several of the views that I have discussed here. First, for many, pain is the biggest stumbling block to accepting Wittgenstein's views about our mental lives. It seems to them that pain is a sensation and that it is in the mind and therefore that what it is to be in pain is to have a sensation in your mind. And it seems to them that there could be a pain that was private in just the sense that Wittgenstein denied. Second, for many, pain is the biggest temptation to some form of naturalistic realism about normativity. One can have doubts about pleasure, for there are pleasures we deplore, but pain seems obviously to be a normative fact. And, third, if that is so, pain is an objection to Kantian ethics, or to any ethics that makes the value of humanity the foundation of value. For the other animals suffer pain, and

if pain is intrinsically normative, then it matters that they do. Animals just as such should have moral standing.

The first two objections are related. Wittgenstein's argument against a private language deploys one of the standard objections against any form of normative naturalism—that you cannot be wrong. Hobbes said you could only be obligated by the law if the sovereign is able to punish you. But if you break the law and get away with it, then the sovereign was not after all able to punish you and so you were not wrong. Hume says that your reason is your strongest desire. But if you always act from your strongest desire, then you always do what you have reason to do, and you cannot be wrong. Wittgenstein says that if a word just refers to the very sensation that makes you feel like saying that word, then you cannot be wrong.

But both the opponent of Wittgenstein and the normative realist point to pain, and more generally to sensation, as a case where it seems to be no objection to say that we cannot be wrong. In fact it creates a foundation. The utilitarian claims that pleasure and pain are facts that are also values, a place where the natural and the normative are one, and so where ethics can find a foundation in the world. And this is exactly analogous to the epistemological claim that our sensations are the place where the natural and the normative are one, and so where knowledge can find a foundation in the world. Sensations are seen to be intrinsically normative entities, about which we cannot be wrong.

But can't we? "I cannot be wrong about whether I am seeing red." If you mean that the object before you is red, you can certainly be wrong "No, I mean that I am having a red sensation." And what is that? It is the sensation that makes you feel like saying that a thing is red. You are not describing a condition that explains what you are inclined to say. You are simply announcing what you are inclined to say. In the same way, someone who says he is in pain is not describing a condition that gives him a reason to change his condition. He is announcing that he has a *very* strong impulse to change his condition.

Now that way of putting it, inspired by Wittgenstein, has a problem. People have thought that Wittgenstein was making a point about *language*, to the effect that when people talk about their own inner states and sensations they must be using language expressively, as if "I am in pain" could only be a cry of pain, and you could not simply be reporting your condition. Of course you can report your condition; once you've mastered the language, you can do anything that you like. His point is rather about mental activities, and whether a way of talking leaves anything for them to *be*. If "I see something red" *means* "I am having a red sensation" then one can never perceive; one can only announce the results of a perception that has already taken place. For what is this "having"? Did the little person in your mind perceive the red sensation? Wittgenstein is attacking a certain picture of what it is like to be conscious, which reduces all mental activity to the contemplation of sensations and ideas. And the language of "having" supports this picture. Does "I am in pain" mean "I am having a horrible sensation"? What here is the form of the "having"? Are you contemplating it? What would be so horrible about that?

But surely, you will reply, a *physical* pain is not just an impulse to change your condition. It *is* a sensation of a certain character. Now I am not denying that when we are in pain part of what is going on is that we are having sensations of a certain character. I am however denying that the painfulness of pain consists entirely in the character of those sensations. The painfulness of pain consists in the fact that these are sensations that we are inclined to fight. You may want to ask: why are we inclined to fight them if they are not horrible in themselves? Well, in some cases we are biologically wired this way; pain could not do its biological job if we were not inclined to fight it. When nature equipped us with pain she was giving us a way of taking care of ourselves, not a *reason* to take care

of ourselves. Why do you thrash? Is it as if you were trying to hurl your body away from itself? Why do you say "as if"? Pain really is less horrible if you can curb your inclination to fight it. This is why it helps, in dealing with pain, to take a tranquilizer or to lie down. Ask yourself how, if the painfulness of pain rested just in the character of the sensations, it could help to lie down? The sensations do not change. Pain wouldn't hurt if you could just relax and enjoy it.

If the painfulness of pain rested in the character of the sensations rather than in our tendency to revolt against them, our belief that physical pain has something in common with grief, rage, and disappointment would be inexplicable. For that matter, what physical pains have in common with each other would be inexplicable, for the sensations are of many different kinds. What do nausea, migraine, menstrual cramps, pinpricks, and pinches have in common that makes us call them all pains? What emotional pains have in common with physical ones is that in these cases too we are in the grip of an overwhelming urge to do battle, not now against our sensations, but against the world. Stoics and Buddhists are right in thinking that we could put an end to pain if we could just stop fighting. The person who cared only for his own virtue, if there could *be* such a person, would be happy on the rack.[26] They are wrong if they conclude that we should therefore stop fighting. Many pains are worth having; one may even say that they are true. Pain is not the condition that is a reason to change your condition, the condition in which the natural and the normative are one. It is our *perception* that we have a reason to change our condition.[27] Pain itself is not a reason at all.

But pain is the perception of a reason. Since animals have pain, and until now I have seemed to suggest that only human beings have reasons, this will take a moment to explain.

The best account of what an animal is comes from Aristotle. We have already seen that Aristotle thought that the form of a thing is the organization or arrangement of its parts that allows it to be what it is, to do what it does, to do its job. Now Aristotle thought that a *living* thing is a thing with a special kind of form. A living thing is so designed as to maintain and reproduce itself. It has what we might call a self-maintaining form. So it is its own end; its job is just to keep on being what it is. Its business in life is to preserve its own *identity*. And its organs and activities are arranged to that end.[28]

If a living thing is an animal, if it is conscious, then part of the way it preserves its own identity is through its sensations. And this is where pain comes in. When something is a threat to its physical existence, or would be if it went on long enough, the animal perceives that fact and revolts against it. The animal is moved to take action to fix what is wrong. Suppose for instance that the animal needs nourishment. It perceives that by getting hungry. It finds this unpleasant and is moved to get something to eat. Don't be confused here: it is not that the pain is an unpleasant sensation that gives the animal a reason to eat. The animal has a reason to eat, which is that it will die if it does not. It does not know that it has that reason, but it does perceive it. The sensation in question is the sensation of hunger, not of pain. But an animal is designed to perceive and revolt against threats to the preservation of its identity, such as hunger. When it does that, it is in pain.

Now consider this comparison. A human being is an animal whose nature it is to construct a practical identity that is normative for her. She is a law to herself. When some way of acting is a threat to her practical identity and reflection reveals that fact, the person finds that she must reject that way of acting, and act in another way. In that case, she is obligated.

A living thing is an entity whose nature it is to preserve and maintain its physical identity. It is a law to itself. When something it is doing is a threat to that identity and perception reveals that fact, the animal finds that it must reject what it is doing and do something else instead. In that case, it is in pain.

Obligation is the reflective rejection of a threat to your identity. Pain is the *unreflective* rejection of a threat to your identity. So pain is the *perception* of a reason, and that is why it seems normative.

To say that life is a value is almost a tautology. Since a living thing is a thing for which the preservation of identity is imperative, life is a form of morality. Or to put the point less strangely and in a way that has been made more familiar to us by Aristotle, morality is just the form that *human life* takes.

From here the argument proceeds as it did in the case of other people. I won't spell out the details here. Roughly it will look like this: I first point out to you that your animal nature is a fundamental form of identity on which your human identity depends. A further stretch of reflection requires a further stretch of endorsement. If you don't value your animal nature, you can value nothing. So you must endorse its value. Perhaps that by itself doesn't show us that we have obligations to the other animals, since the value could still be private. To show us that we have obligations, animals must have a way of impressing their value upon us, the way we impress our value on each other when we ask, "How would you like it if someone did that to you?" They must be able to intrude into our consciousness and make us think.

But that isn't a problem, is it? The cries of an animal are no more mere noise than the words of a person. An animal's cries express pain, and they mean that there is a reason to change its condition. Another animal can obligate you in exactly the same way another person can. It is a way of being *someone* that you share. So of course we have obligations to animals.

CONCLUSION

I hope by now it is clear that all of the accounts of normativity that I have discussed in these lectures are true.

Voluntarists like Pufendorf and Hobbes held that normativity must spring from the commands of a legislator. A good legislator commands us to do only what it is in any case a good idea to do, but the bare fact that an action is a good idea cannot make it a requirement. For that, it must be made law by someone in a position to command us.

As we saw, that view is true. What it describes is the relation in which we stand to ourselves. The fact that we must act in the light of reflection gives us a double nature. The thinking self has the power to command the acting self, and it is only its command that can make action obligatory. A good thinking self commands the acting self only to do what is good, but the acting self must in any case do what it says.

Realists like Nagel think that reasons are intrinsically normative entities and that what we should do when a desire presents itself is to look at it more objectively, to see whether it is such an entity. This view is also true. What it describes is the activity of the thinking self as it assesses the impulses that present themselves to us, the legislative proposals of our nature.

Reflection has the power to compel obedience and to punish us for disobedience. It in turn is bound to govern us by laws that are good. Together these facts yield the conclusion that the relation of the thinking self to the acting self is the relation of legitimate authority. That is to say, the necessity of acting in the light of reflection makes us authorities over ourselves. And insofar as we have authority over ourselves, we can make laws for ourselves, and those laws will be normative. So Kant's view is also true. Autonomy is the source of obligation.

Once we see this, we can see that the reflective endorsement theory is true on another level as well. In the end, nothing can be normative unless we endorse our own nature, unless we place a value upon ourselves. Reflection reveals to us that the normativity of our values springs from the fact that we are animals of a certain kind, autonomous moral animals. That is, in the Aristotelian sense, our human form. If we do not place a value on being such animals, then nothing will be normative at all.

That means realism is true on another level too. To see this, recall once again John Mackie's famous "argument from queerness." According to Mackie, it is fantastic to think that the world contains objective values or intrinsically normative entities. For in order to do what values do, they would have to be entities of a very strange sort, utterly unlike anything else in the universe. The way that we know them would have to be different from the way that we know ordinary facts. Knowledge of them, Mackie says, would have to provide the knower with both a direction and a motive. For when you met an objective value, according to Mackie, it would have to be—and I'm nearly quoting now—able both to tell you what to do and to make you do it. And nothing is like that.

But Mackie is wrong and realism is right. Of course there are entities that meet these criteria. It's true that they are queer sorts of entities and that knowing them isn't like anything else. But that doesn't mean that they don't exist. John Mackie must have been alone in his room with the Scientific World View when he wrote those words. For it is the most familiar fact of human life that the world contains entities that can tell us what to do and make us do it. They are people, and the other animals.[29]

NOTES

1. Kant, *Foundations of the Metaphysics of Morals*, p. 448; in Lewis White Beck's translation (Indianapolis: Bobbs-Merrill, 1959), p. 66.
   2. Ibid., p. 446; in Beck's translation, p. 65.

3. This is a reading of the argument Kant gives in ibid., pp. 446–48; in Beck's translation, pp. 64–67; and in *The Critique of Practical Reason* under the heading "Problem II," p. 29; in Beck's translation (Indianapolis, Bobbs-Merrill, 1955), pp. 28–29. It is explained in greater detail in my "Morality as Freedom," in *Kant's Practical Philosophy Reconsidered*, ed. Y. Yovel (Dordrecht, Netherlands: Kluwer Academic Publishers, 1989).

4. I have a reason for saying that her behavior will be that of a wanton rather than simply saying that she will be a wanton. Harry Frankfurt, from whom I am borrowing the term, defines a wanton as someone who has no second-order volitions. An animal, whose desire is its will, is a wanton. I am arguing here that a person cannot be like that, because of the reflective structure of human consciousness. A person must act on a reason, and so the person who acts like a wanton must be treating the desire of the moment as a reason. That commits her to the principle that the desire of the moment is a reason, and her commitment to that principle counts as a second-order volition. See H. Frankfurt, "Freedom of the Will and the Concept of a Person," *Journal of Philosophy* 68 (1971): 5–20, esp. the discussion on pp. 16–19. The affinity of my account with Frankfurt's will be evident.

5. Bradley and others understood Hegel's famous objection this way, and if it is taken this way it is a mistake. I argue for this in my paper "Kant's Formula of Universal Law," *Pacific Philosophical Quarterly* 66 (1985): 24–47. In that paper, however, I do not distinguish the categorical imperative from the moral law, and my arguments there actually only show that the moral law has content.

6. Romans II:14.

7. This remark needs a qualification, which springs from the fact that we can unite our wills with the wills of others. In Kant's theory, this happens when we are citizens who together form a general will or when we make friends or get married. In those cases it is sometimes the united will that has authority over our conduct. For further discussion, see my "Creating the Kingdom of Ends: Reciprocity and Responsibility in Personal Relations," *Philosophical Perspectives* 6 (1992): 305–32.

8. These views are found throughout Aristotle's writings, but centrally discussed in books VII–IX of the *Metaphysics* and in *On the Soul*.

9. Plato, *Republic*, I, 331c., p. 580.

10. Rawls, *A Theory of Justice*, (Cambridge, Mass.: Harvard University Press, 1971), p. 5.

11. Hume, *Enquiry concerning the Principles of Morals*, in *Enquiries concerning Human Understanding and concerning the Principles of Morals*, ed. L. A. Selby-Bigge, 3d ed. (Oxford: Clarendon, 1975), p. 275.

12. See, e.g., Michael Sandel, *Liberalism and the Limits of Justice*.

13. Kant, *Foundations of the Metaphysics of Morals*, pp. 427–28; in Beck's translation, pp. 45–47. I am here summarizing the interpretation of this argument I give in "Kant's Formula of Humanity," *Kantstudien* 77 (1986): 183–202.

14. This implies that you must accept the laws that arise from this more fundamental view of your identity, the laws of morality. But it does not imply that the less fundamental laws no longer exist or that the more fundamental ones always trump them. The view I have as I have spelled it out so far leaves room for conflict. Some account of how such conflicts might be negotiated is desirable, but I do not mean to be giving or implying any such account here.

15. See, e.g., Williams's criticism of Gewirth in chap. 4 of *Ethics and the Limits of Philosophy* (Cambridge, Mass.: Harvard University Press, 1985).

16. In contemporary jargon, the objection is that the reasons the argument reveals are "agent-relative" rather than "agent-neutral."

17. See Wittgenstein, *Philosophical Investigations*, trans. G. E. M. Anscombe (London: Macmillan, 1953), secs. 243 ff., pp. 88 ff.

18. See especially ibid., sec. 258, p. 92: "But 'I impress it on myself' can only mean: this process brings it about that I remember the connection *right* in the future. But in the present case I have no criterion of correctness. One would like to say: whatever is going to seem right to me is right. And that only means that here we cannot talk about 'right.' "

19. It may look as if there is a disanalogy here. The private language argument shows that you cannot mean a certain sensation by '*S*' just now and never again, because then you could not be wrong. The remark I just made makes it look as if you could have a reason just now and never again—the thinking self could bind the acting self to act a certain way just now. Actually, however, I do not think that is a possibility, since the acting self cannot coherently be taken to exist just at a particular moment. See my

"Personal Identity and the Unity of Agency: A Kantian Response to Parfit," *Philosophy and Public Affairs* 18 (1989): 113–14.

20. Wittgenstein, *Philosophical Investigations*, sec. 262, p. 93.

21. Ibid., sec. 27, p. 13.

22. More strictly speaking, the needs and demands of others present us with what Kant calls "incentives," just as our own inclinations do. Incentives come up for automatic consideration as candidates for being reasons. I thank Ulrike Heuer for prompting me to be clearer on this point.

23. See Nagel, *The Possibility of Altruism* (Princeton: Princeton University Press, 1978), pp. 82–84.

24. Ibid., chap. 9.

25. And that's not what a personal relationship is. See note 7 above.

26. Of course there could not be such a person, or at least, he could not *have* the virtues that were the only things he cared about. To have the virtues is in part to care about certain external things.

27. When you feel pity for someone, why does it strike you as a reason to help him? Why don't you just take a tranquilizer? Hucheson says, "If our sole Intention, in Compassion or Pity, was the Removal of our Pain, we should run away, shut our Eyes, divert our Thoughts from the miserable Object, to avoid the Pain of Compassion, which we seldom do . . ." (this passage is not in Raphael; one may find it in L. A. Selby-Bigge, *British Moralists* (Indianapolis: Bobbs-Merrill, 1964), p. 93). The point is reiterated by Nagel: "Sympathy is not, in general, just a feeling of discomfort produced by the recognition of distress in others, which in turn motivates one to relieve their distress. Rather, it is the pained awareness of their distress as *something to be relieved*" (*The Possibility of Altruism*, p. 80n). Wittgenstein says, "How am I filled with pity *for this man*? How does it come out what the object of my pity is? (Pity, one may say, is a form of conviction that someone else is in pain)" (*Philosophical Investigations*, sec. 287, p.98). Pity is painful because it is the perception of *another's* pain, and so the perception that there is a reason to change *his* condition.

28. This account of the nature of an animal is based primarily on *On the Soul*, bk. II.

29. I would like to thank Charlotte Brown, Peter Hylton, Arthur Kuflik, Andrews Reath, Amélie Rorty, Thomas Scanlon, Jay Schleusener, and my commentators on the occasion of the lectures, Gerald Cohen, Raymond Geuss, Thomas Nagel, and Bernard Williams, for comments on earlier versions of these lectures. A longer version of the lectures, together with commentary by Cohen, Geuss, Nagel, and Williams, is forthcoming from Cambridge University Press.

BIBLIOGRAPHY

Adams, Robert Merrihew. "Motive Utilitarianism." *Journal of Philosophy* 73 (1976): 467–81.

Allison, Henry. "Morality and Freedom: Kant's Reciprocity Thesis." *Philosophical Review* 95 (1986): 393–425.

Alston, William. "Meta-Ethics and Meta-Epistemology. In Goldman and Kim, *Values and Morals*.

Altham, J. E. J. "The Legacy of Emotivism." In Macdonald and Wright, *Fact, Science, and Morality*.

———, and R. Harrison, eds. *World, Mind and Ethics: Essays on the Ethical Philosophy of Bernard Williams*. Cambridge: Cambridge University Press, 1995.

Anderson, Elizabeth. *Value in Ethics and Economics*. Cambridge, Mass.: Harvard University Press, 1993.

Anscombe, G. E. M. *Intention*. Oxford: Basil Blackwell, 1957.

———. "Modern Moral Philosophy." *Philosophy* 33 (1958): 1–19. Also in Dworkin and Thomson, *Ethics*.

———. "On Brute Facts." *Analysis* 18 (1958): 69–72.

Audi, Robert. "Ethical Naturalism and the Explanatory Power of Moral Concepts." In Steven J. Wagner, ed. *Naturalism: A Critical Appraisal*. Notre Dame, Ind.: University of Notre Dame Press, 1993.

———. "Ethical Reflectionism." *Monist* 76 (1993): 295–315.

———. "Internalism and Externalism in Moral Epistemology." *Logos* 10 (1989): 13–37.

———. "Moral Epistemology and the Supervenience of Ethical Concepts." *Southern Journal of Philosophy* (1990): 1–24.

Austin, J. L. *How To Do Things With Words*. Cambridge, Mass.: Harvard University Press, 1962.

Axelrod, Robert. *The Evolution of Cooperation*. New York: Basic Books, 1984.

Baier, Annette. "Doing Without Moral Theory?" In *Postures of the Mind*.

———. "Extending the Limits of Moral Theory." *Journal of Philosophy* 83 (1986): 538–44.

———. *Moral Prejudices*. Cambridge, Mass.: Harvard University Press, 1994.

———. "Moralism and Cruelty: Reflections on Hume and Kant." *Ethics* 103 (1993): 436–57.

———. *Postures of the Mind*. Minneapolis: University of Minnesota Press, 1985.

———. "Theory and Reflective Practices." In *Postures of the Mind*

———. Trust and Antitrust." *Ethics* 96 (1986): 231–60.

———. "What Do Women Want in Moral Theory?" *Nous* 19 (1985): 53–63.

Baier, Kurt. "The Conceptual Link Between Morality and Rationality." *Nous* 16 (1982): 78–88.

———. "Moral Obligation." *American Philosophical Quarterly* 3 (1966): 1–17.

———. *The Moral Point of View*. Ithaca, N.Y.: Cornell University Press, 1958.

———. "Moral Reasons." *Midwest Studies in Philosophy* 3 (1978): 62–74.

———. "Moral Reasons and Reasons To Be Moral." In Goldman and J. Kim, *Value and Morals*.

———. *The Rational and the Moral Order*. Chicago and La Salle, Ill.: Open Court, 1995.

———. "Rationality and Morality." *Erkenntnis* 11 (1977): 197–223.

———. "Rationality, Reason, and the Good." In Copp and Zimmerman, *Morality, Reason and Truth*.

———. "Reason and Experience." *Nous* 7 (1973): 56–67.

———. "The Social Source of Reason." *Proceedings and Addresses of the American Philosophical Association* 51 (1978): 707–33.

Baldwin, Thomas. "Ethical Non-Naturalism." In Hacking, *Exercises in Analysis*.

Bales, R. E. "Act-Utilitarianism: Account of Right-Making Characteristics or Decision-Making Procedure?" *American Philosophical Quarterly* 8 (1971): 257–65.

Bambrough, Renford, *Moral Skepticism and Moral Knowledge*. Atlantic Heights, N.J.: Humanities Press, 1979.

Baron, Marcia. "The Alleged Moral Repugnance of Acting from Duty." *Journal of Philosophy* 81 (1984): 197–219.

———. "Varieties of Ethics of Virtue." *American Philosophical Quarterly* 22 (1985): 47–54.

Barry, Brian. *Theories of Justice*. Berkeley: University of California Press, 1989.

Beardsmore, R. W. *Moral Reasoning*. London: Routledge, 1969.

Becker, Lawrence. *On Justifying Moral Judgments*. New York: Humanities Press, 1973.

Bittner, Rudiger. *What Reason Demands*. Cambridge: Cambridge University Press, 1989.

Blackburn, Simon. "Errors and the Phenomenology of Value." In Honderich, ed., *Morality and Objectivity*.

———. *Essays in Quasi-Realism*. New York: Oxford University Press, 1993.

———. "How To Be an Ethical Antirealist." *Midwest Studies in Philosophy* 12 (1988): 361–75.

———. "Moral Realism." In Casey, *Morality and Moral Reasoning*.

———. "Morality and Thick Concepts—II, Through Thick and Thin." *Proceedings of the Aristotelian Society*, supp. vol. 66 (1992): 285–99.

———. "Morals and Modals." In Macdonald and Wright, *Fact, Science, and Morality*.

———. "Rule-Following and Moral Realism." In Holtzman and Leich, *Wittgenstein: To Follow a Rule*.

———. *Spreading the Word*. Oxford: Oxford University Press, 1984.

Blum, Lawrence. *Friendship, Altruism, and Morality*. London: Routledge & Kegan Paul, 1980.

———. *Moral Perception and Particularity*. Cambridge: Cambridge University Press, 1994.

Boghossian, Paul, and Velleman, J. David. "Colour as a Secondary Quality." *Mind* 98 (1989): 81–103.

Boghossian, Paul. "The Rule-Following Considerations." *Mind* 98 (1989): 507–49.

Bond, E. J. *Reason and Value*. Cambridge: Cambridge University Press, 1983.

Boxill, Bernard. "How Injustice Pays." *Philosophy and Public Affairs* 9 (1980): 359–71.

Boyd, Richard. "How To Be a Moral Realist." In Sayre-McCord, *Essays on Moral Realism*.

Bradie, Michael. "Rationality and the Objectivity of Values." *Monist* 67 (1984): 467–82.

Brandt, R. B. "The Explanation of Moral Language." In Copp and Zimmerman, *Morality, Reason and Truth*.

———. *Ethical Theory*. Englewood Cliffs, N.J.: Prentice Hall, 1959.

———. *Morality, Utilitarianism, and Rights*. New York: Cambridge University Press, 1992.

———. "Rationality, Egoism, and Morality." *Journal of Philosophy* 69 (1972): 681–97.

———. "The Status of Empirical Assertion Theories in Ethics." *Mind* 61 (1952): 458–79.

———. *A Theory of the Good and the Right*. New York: Oxford University Press, 1979.

Brink, David O. "Externalist Moral Realism." *Southern Journal of Philosophy*, supp. vol. 24 (1986): 111–25.

———. "Internalism and Moral Realism." *Southern Journal of Philosophy*, supp. vol. 24 (1986): 23–42.

———. "Moral Conflict and Its Structure." *Philosophical Review* 103 (1994): 215–47.

———. *Moral Realism and the Foundations of Ethics*. Cambridge: Cambridge University Press, 1989.

———. "Moral Realism and the Skeptical Arguments from Disagreement and Queerness." *Australasian Journal of Philosophy* 62 (1984): 111–25.

———. "A Puzzle About the Rational Authority of Morality." *Philosophical Perspectives* 6 (1992): 1–26.

———. Rawlsian Constructivism in Moral Theory." *Canadian Journal of Philosophy* 17(1987): 71–90.

———. "A Reasonable Morality." *Ethics* 104 (1994): 593–619.

———. "Sidgwick and the Rationale for Rational Egoism" In Schultz, *Essays on Henry Sidgwick*.

———. "Sidgwick's Dualism of Practical Reason." *Australasian Journal of Philosophy* 66 (1988): 291–307.

Broad, C. D. "Certain Features in Moore's Ethical Doctrines." In Schilpp, *The Philosophy of G. E. Moore*.

———. "Is 'Goodness' a Name of a Simple Non-Natural Quality?" *Proceedings of the Aristotelian Society* 34 (1933–34): 249–68.

———. "Some Reflections on Moral-Sense Theories in Ethics." *Proceedings of the Aristotelian Society* 45 (1944–45): 131–66.

Brody, Baruch. "Intuitions and Objective Moral Knowledge." *Monist* 62 (1979): 446–56.

Broome, John. *Weighing Goods*. Oxford: Blackwell, 1991.

Brower, Bruce. "Dispositional Ethical Realism." *Ethics* 103 (1993): 221–49.

Brown, Erik. "Sympathy and Moral Objectivity." American *Philosophical Quarterly* 23 (1986): 179–88.

Brown, S. C., ed. *Objectivity and Cultural Divergence*. Cambridge: Cambridge University Press, 1984.

Buchanan, A. "Revisability and Rational Choice." *Canadian Journal of Philosophy* 5 (1975): 395–408.

Butchvarov, Panayot. "Realism in Ethics." *Midwest Studies in Philosophy* 12 (1987): 395–412.

———. *Skepticism in Ethics*. Bloomington: Indiana University Press, 1989.

Calhoun, Cheshire. "Justice, Care, Gender Bias." *Journal of Philosophy* 85 (1988): 451–463.

———. "Responsibility and Reproach." *Ethics* 99 (1989): 389–406.

Campbell, John. "A Simple View of Colour." In Haldane and Wright, *Reality, Representation and Projection*.

Campbell, Richmond. "Can Inconsistency Be Reasonable?" *Canadian Journal of Philosophy* 11 (1981): 245–270.

———. *Self-Love and Self-Respect: A Philosophical Study of Egoism*. Ottawa: Canadian Library of Philosophy, 1979.

———. "Sociobiology and the Possibility of Naturalism." In Copp and Zimmerman, *Morality, Reason and Truth*.

Casey, John, ed. *Morality and Moral Reasoning*. London: Methuen, 1971.

Castaneda, H., and G. Nakhnikian, eds. *Morality and the Language of Conduct*. Detroit: Wayne State University Press, 1963.

Charles, David, and Kathleen Lennon, eds. *Reduction, Explanation and Realism*. New York: Oxford University Press, 1992.

Clarke, Stanley G., and Evan Simpson, eds. *Anti-Theory in Ethics and Moral Conservatism*. Albany: State University of New York Press, 1989.

Coburn, Robert. "Morality, Truth and Relativism." *Ethics* 92 (1982): 661–69.

———. "Relativism and the Basis of Morality." *Philosophical Review* 85 (1976): 87–93.

Cohon, Rachel. "Are External Reasons Impossible?" *Ethics* 96 (1986): 545–56.

———. "Internalism about Reasons for Action." *Pacific Philosophical Quarterly* 74 (1993): 265–88.

Collins, John. "Belief, Desire and Revision." *Mind* (1988): 333–42.

Conly, Sarah. "The Objectivity of Morals and the Subjectivity of Agents." *American Philosophical Quarterly* 22 (1985): 275–86.

———. "Review: Samuel Scheffler, *The Rejection of Consequentialism*." *Philosophical Review* 93 (1984): 489–92.

Cooper, David E. "Moral Relativism." *Midwest Studies in Philosophy* 3 (1978): 97–108.

Copp, David."Considered Judgements and Moral Justification: Conservatism in Moral Theory." In Copp and Zimmerman, *Morality, Reason, and Truth*.

———. "Explanation and Justification in Ethics." *Ethics* 100 (1990): 237–58.

———. "Harman on Internalism, Relativism and Logical Form." *Ethics* 92 (1978): 227–42.

———. "Moral Realism: Facts and Norms." *Ethics* 101 (1991): 610–24.

———. "Moral Skepticism." *Philosophical Studies* 62 (1991): 203–33.

———. *Morality, Normativity, and Society*. New York: Oxford University Press 1995.

———. "Normativity and the Very Idea of Moral Epistemology." *Southern Journal of Philosophy*, supp. vol. 29 (1990): 189–210.

————. "The Possibility of a Categorical Imperative." *Philosophical Perspectives* 6 (1992): 261–84.

————, and David Zimmerman, eds. *Morality, Reason and Truth*. Totowa, N.J.: Rowman and Allanheld, 1985.

Cummiskey, David. "Kantian Consequentialism." *Ethics* 100 (1990): 586–615.

————. *Kantian Consequentialism*. Oxford: New York, 1995.

Dancy, Jonathan. "Agent-Relativity: The Very Idea." In Frey and Morris, *Value, Welfare, and Morality*.

————. "Contemplating One's Nagel." *Philosophical Books* 29 (1988): 1–16.

————. "An Ethic of Prima Facie Duties." In Peter Singer, *A Companion to Ethics*.

————. "Ethical Particularism and Morally Relevant Properties." *Mind* 92 (1983): 530–47.

————. *Moral Reasons*. Oxford: Basil Blackwell, 1993.

————. "On Moral Properties." *Mind* 90 (1981): 367–85.

————. "Supererogation and Moral Realism." In Dancy, Moravcsik, and Taylor, *Human Agency*.

————. "Two Conceptions of Moral Realism." *Proceedings of the Aristotelian Society*, supp. vol. 60 (1986): 167–87.

————, J. Moravcsik, and C. C. W. Taylor, eds. *Human Agency: Language, Duty, Value*. Stanford: Stanford University Press, 1988.

Daniels, Norman. "Can Cognitive Psychotherapy Reconcile Reason and Desire?" *Ethics* 93 (1983): 772–85.

————. "Reflective Equilibrium and Archimedian Points." *Canadian Journal of Philosophy* 10 (1980): 83–103.

————. "Some Methods of Ethics and Linguistics." *Philosophical Studies* 37 (1980): 21–36.

————. "Two Approaches to Theory Acceptance in Ethics." In Copp and Zimmerman, *Morality, Reason and Truth*.

————. "Wide Reflective Equilibrium and Theory Acceptance in Ethics." *Journal of Philosophy* 76 (1979): 256–82.

————, ed. *Reading Rawls*. Oxford: Blackwell, 1975.

D'Arms, Justin, and Daniel Jacobson. "Expressivism, Morality, and the Emotions." *Ethics* 104(1994): 739–763.

Darwall, Stephen. "Agent-Centered Restrictions from the Inside Out." *Philosophical Studies* 50(1986): 291–319.

————. "Autonomist Internalism and the Justification of Morals." *Nous* 24 (1990): 257–67.

————. "How Nowhere Can You Get (and Do Ethics)?" *Ethics* 98 (1987): 137–57.

————. *Impartial Reason*. Ithaca, N.Y.: Cornell University Press, 1983.

————. "Internalism and Agency." *Philosophical Perspectives* 6 (1992): 155–74.

————. "Rational Agent, Rational Act." *Philosophical Topics* 14 (1986): 33–57.

————, Allan Gibbard, and Peter Railton "Toward *Fin de siècle* Ethics: Some Trends." *Philosophical Review* (1992): 115–89.

Davidson, Donald. "Actions, Reasons and Causes." In *Essays on Actions and Events*.

————. *Essays on Actions and Events*. New York: Oxford University Press, 1980.

————. "How is Weakness of the Will Possible?" In *Essays on Actions and Events*.

Davies, Martin, and Lloyd Humberstone. "Two Notions of Necessity." *Philosophical Studies* 38 (1980): 1–30.

Deigh, John. "Sidgwick on Ethical Judgment." In Schultz, *Essays on Henry Sidgwick*.

Dennet, Daniel. *Brainstorms*. Cambridge, Mass.: MIT Press, 1978.

————. *Content and Consciousness*. London: Routledge & Kegan Paul, 1969.

Divers, Martin, and Alex Miller. "Why Expressivists about Value Should Not Love Minimalism about Truth." *Analysis* 54 (1994): 12–19.

Donagan, Alan. *The Theory of Morality*. Chicago: University of Chicago Press, 1977.

Dreier, James. "Internalism and Speaker Relativism." *Ethics* 100 (1990): 6–26.

Dummett, Michael. *Truth and Other Enigmas*. Cambridge, Mass.: Harvard University Press, 1978.

Dworkin, Gerald, and Judith Jarvis Thomson. *Ethics*. New York: Harper & Row, 1968.

Dworkin, Ronald. *A Matter of Principle*. Cambridge, Mass.: Harvard University Press, 1985.

————. "The Original Position." In Daniels, *Reading Rawls*.

————. *Taking Rights Seriously*. London: Duckworth, 1978.

Elster, J. *Ulysses and the Sirens: Studies in Rationality and Irrationality*. Cambridge: Cambridge University Press, 1979.

Evans, Gareth. "Things Without the Mind—A Commentary on Chapter Two of Strawson's *Individuals*." In Van Straaten, *Philosophical Subjects*.

Ewing, A. C. *The Definition of Good*. New York: Macmillan, 1947.

———. *Ethics*. London: English Universities Press, 1962.

Falk, W. D. "Action-Guiding Reasons." *Journal of Philosophy* 60 (1963): 702–18.

———. "Morality, Self and Others." In Castaneda and Nakhnikian, *Morality and the Language of Conduct*.

———. "'Ought' and Motivation." *Proceedings of the Aristotelian Society* (1947–48): 111–38.

———. *Ought, Reasons, and Morality*. Ithaca, N.Y.: Cornell University Press, 1986.

Field, G.C. *Moral Theory*. London: Methuen & Co., 1932.

Field, H. "Realism and Relativism." *Journal of Philosophy* 79 (1982): 653–67.

Finnis, John. *Fundamentals of Ethics*. Washington, D.C.: Georgetown University Press, 1983.

Firth, R. M. "Ethical Absolutism and the Ideal Observer." *Philosophy and Phenomenological Research* 12 (1952): 317–45.

Flanagan, Owen. *Varieties of Moral Personality: Ethics and Psychological Realism* . Cambridge, Mass.: Harvard University Press, 1991.

———, and Amelie Rorty, eds. *Identity, Character, and Morality: Essays in Moral Psychology*. Cambridge, Mass.: MIT Press, Bradford Books, 1990.

Fodor, Jerry. "Special Sciences (or: The Disunity of Science as a Working Hypothesis)." *Synthese* 28 (1974): 97–115.

Føllesdall, D. "The Status of Rationality Assumptions in Interpretation and in the Explanation of Action." *Dialectica* 36 (1982): 301–16.

Foot, Philippa. "Approval and Disapproval." In Foot, *Virtues and Vices*.

———. "Moral Arguments." *Proceedings of the Aristotelian Society* 59 (1958–59): 502–13. Also in *Virtues and Vices*.

———. "Moral Beliefs." In *Proceedings of the Aristotelian Society* 59 (1958–59): 83–104. Also in *Virtues and Vices*.

———. "Moral Realism and Moral Dilemma." *Journal of Philosophy* 80 (1983): 379–98.

———. *Moral Relativism*. Lawrence: University of Kansas Press, 1978.

———. "Morality, Action, and Outcome." In Honderich, *Morality and Objectivity*.

———. "Morality as a System of Hypothetical Imperatives." *Philosophical Review* 81 (1972): 305–16. Reprinted in *Virtues and Vices*.

———. "Reasons for Action and Desire." In *Virtues and Vices*.

———. "Utilitarianism and the Virtues." *Mind* 94 (1985): 196–209.

———. *Virtues and Vices*. Los Angeles: University of California Press, 1978.

———, ed. *Theories of Ethics*. London: Oxford University Press, 1967.

Forester, Mary Gore. *Moral Language*. Madison: University of Wisconsin Press, 1982.

Frankena, William K. "Ethical Naturalism Renovated." *Review of Metaphysics* 10 (1957): 459–73.

———. *Ethics*, 2d ed. Englewood Cliffs, N.J.: Prentice-Hall, 1973.

———. "MacIntyre and Modern Morality." *Ethics* 93 (1983): 579–87.

———. "The Naturalistic Fallacy." *Mind* 48 (1939): 464–77.

———. "Obligation and Motivation in Recent Moral Philosophy." In Melden, *Essays on Moral Philosophy*.

———. *Perspectives on Morality*. Edited by K. E. Goodpaster. Notre Dame, Ind.: University of Notre Dame Press, 1976.

Frankfurt, Harry. "Freedom of the Will and the Concept of a Person." *Journal of Philosophy* 68 (1971): 5–20.

Frey, Raymond, and Christopher Morris, eds. *Value, Welfare, and Morality*. Cambridge: Cambridge University Press, 1992.

Friedman, Marilyn. "Going Nowhere: Nagel on Normative Objectivity." *Philosophy* 65 (1990): 501–9.

———. "The Impracticality of Impartiality." *Journal of Philosophy* 86 (1989): 645–56.

Fumerton, Richard. *Reason and Morality: A Defense of the Egocentric Perspective*. Ithaca, N.Y.: Cornell University Press, 1990.

Gauthier, David "Justice as Social Choice." In Copp and Zimmerman, *Morality, Reason and Truth*.

———. *Moral Dealing: Contract, Ethics, and Reason*. Ithaca, N.Y.: Cornell University Press, 1990.

———. *Morals by Agreement*. Oxford: Oxford University Press, 1986.

———. "Morality and Advantage." *Philosophical Review* 76 (1967): 460–75.

———. "Rational Cooperation." *Nous* 8 (1974): 53–65.

———. "Reason and Maximization." *Canadian Journal of Philosophy* 4 (1975): 411–33.

———. "Why Contractarianism." In Vallentyne, *Contractarianism and Rational Choice.*

———, ed. *Morality and Rational Self-Interest.* Englewood Cliffs, N.J.: Prentice-Hall, 1970.

Gay, Robert "Ethical Pluralism: A Reply to Dancy." *Mind* 94 (1985): 250–62.

Geach, Peter T. "Ascriptivism." *Philosophical Review* 69 (1960): 221–5.

———. "Assertion." *Philosophical Review* 74 (1965): 449–65.

———. "Good and Evil." *Analysis* 17 (1956): 23–42.

Gert, Bernard. *The Moral Rules.* New York: Harper & Row, 1966.

Gewirth, Alan. "Positive 'Ethics' and Normative 'Science'." *Philosophical Review* 69 (1960): 311–30.

———. *Reason and Morality.* Chicago: University of Chicago Press, 1978.

Gibbard, Alan. "An Expressivistic Theory of Normative Discourse." *Ethics* 96 (1986): 472–85.

———. "Moral Concepts: Substance and Sentiment." *Philosophical Perspectives* 6 (1992): 267–83.

———. "Moral Judgment and the Acceptance of Norms." *Ethics* 96 (1985): 5–21.

———. "Morality and Thick Concepts—I, Thick Concepts and Warrant for Feelings." *Proceedings of the Aristotelian Society*, supp. vol. 66 (1992): 267–83.

———. "Normative Objectivity." *Nous 19* (1985): 41–51.

———. *Wise Choices, Apt Feelings.* Cambridge, Mass.: Harvard University Press, 1990.

Goldman, Alvin I. and Jaegwon Kim. *Values and Morals.* Dordrecht, Netherlands: D. Reidel, 1978.

Gowans, C. W., ed. *Moral Dilemmas.* Oxford: Oxford University Press, 1987.

Greenspan, Patricia. "Conditional Oughts and Hypothetical Imperatives." *Journal of Philosophy* 72 (1975): 259–76.

———. *Emotions and Reason: An Inquiry into Emotional Justification.* London: Routledge & Kegan Paul, 1988.

———. "Guilt and Virtue." *Journal of Philosophy* 91 (1994): 57–70.

———. "Moral Dilemmas and Guilt." *Philosophical Studies* 43 (1983): 117–25.

———. *Practical Guilt.* New York: Oxford University Press, 1995.

Grice, Geoffrey Russell. *The Grounds of Moral Judgement.* Cambridge: Cambridge University Press, 1967.

Griffin, James. *Well-Being.* Oxford: Oxford University Press, 1986.

Guttenplan, Samuel. "Hume and Contemporary Ethical Naturalism." *Midwest Studies in Philosophy* 8 (1983): 309–20.

———. "Moral Realism and Moral Dilemmas." *Proceedings of the Aristotelian Society* 80 (1979–80): 61–80.

———, ed. *Mind and Language.* New York: Oxford University Press, 1975.

Hacking, Ian, ed. *Exercises in Analysis.* New York: Cambridge University Press, 1985.

Haldane, John, and Crispin Wright. *Reality, Representation and Projection.* New York: Oxford University Press, 1993.

Hale, Bob. "The Compleat Projectivist." *Philosophical Quarterly* 36 (1986): 65–84.

———. "Can There Be a Logic of Attitudes?" In Haldane and Wright, *Reality, Representation and Projection.*

Hall, Everett. *What Is Value?* New York: Humanities Press, 1952.

Hampshire, Sir Stuart. "Ethics: A Defence of Aristotle." In *Freedom of Mind and Other Essays.* Princeton: Princeton University Press, 1971.

———. "Morality and Pessimism." In *Public and Private Morality.* New York: Cambridge University Press, 1978.

Hampton, Jean. "Hobbes and Ethical Naturalism." *Philosophical Perspectives* 6 (1992): 333–53.

———. "Rethinking Reason." *American Philosophical Quarterly* 29 (1992): 219–36.

———. "Two Faces of Contractarian Thought." In Vallentyne, *Contractarianism and Rational Choice.*

Hardin, Russell. *Collective Action.* Baltimore: Johns Hopkins University Press, 1982.

———. *Morality Within the Limits of Reason.* Chicago: University of Chicago Press, 1988.

Hare, R. M. *Applications of Moral Philosophy.* Los Angeles: University of California Press, 1972.

———. "Descriptivism." In Hudson, *The Is-Ought Question.*

———. *Essays in Ethical Theory.* Oxford: Oxford University Press, 1989.

———. "Ethical Theory and Utilitarianism." In Sen and Williams, *Utilitarianism and Beyond.*

———. *Freedom and Reason.* Oxford: Oxford University Press, 1963.

———. *The Language of Morals.* New York: Oxford University Press, 1952.

———. *Moral Thinking.* New York: Oxford University Press, 1981.

———. "Ontology in Ethics." In Honderich, *Morality and Objectivity.*

———. "Rawls' Theory of Justice." In Daniels, *Reading Rawls.*

———. "Some Questions about Subjectivity." In *Freedom and Morality.* Lawrence: University of Kansas Press, 1976.

———. "Supervenience." *Proceedings of the Aristotelian Society, supp. vol.* 58 (1984): 1–16.

———. "Wanting: Some Pitfalls." In Robert Binkley, Richard Bronaugh, and Ausonio Marras, eds., *Agent, Action, and Reason.* Toronto: University of Toronto Press, 1971.

Harman, Gilbert. "Human Flourishing, Ethics, and Liberty." *Philosophy and Public Affairs* 12 (1983): 307–22.

———. "Is There a Single True Morality?" In Copp and Zimmerman, *Morality, Reason, and Truth.*

———. "Metaphysical Realism and Moral Relativism." *Journal of Philosophy* 79 (1982): 568–75.

———. "Moral Explanations of Natural Facts—Can Moral Claims Be Tested Against Moral Reality?" *Southern Journal of Philosophy*, supp. vol. 24 (1986).

———. "Moral Relativism Defended." *Philosophical Review* 84 (1975): 3–22.

———. *The Nature of Morality: An Introduction to Ethics.* New York: Oxford University Press, 1977.

———. "Relativistic Ethics: Morality as Politics." *Midwest Studies in Philosophy* 3 (1978): 109–21.

———. "What Is Moral Relativism?" In Goldman and Kim, *Values and Morals.*

Harrison, Jonathan. "Mackie's Moral 'Scepticism'." *Philosophy* 57 (1982): 173–91.

———. *Our Knowledge of Right and Wrong.* New York: Humanities Press, 1971.

Harsanyi, John C. "Basic Moral Decisions and Alternative Concepts of Rationality." *Social Theory and Practice* 9 (1983): 231–44.

———. "Cardinal Welfare, Individualistic Ethics, and Interpersonal Comparisons of Utility." *Journal of Political Economy* 63 (1955): 309–21.

———. *Essays on Ethics, Social Behavior, and Scientific Explanation.* Dordrecht, Netherlands & Boston: Reidel, 1976.

———. "Morality and the Theory of Rational Behaviour." In Sen and Williams, *Utilitarianism and Beyond.*

———. *Rational Behaviour and Bargaining Equilibrium in Games and Social Situations.* Cambridge: Cambridge University Press, 1977.

Helm, Paul, ed. *Divine Commands and Morality.* Oxford: Oxford University Press, 1981.

Hellman, Geoffrey, and Frank Thompson. "Physicalism: Ontology, Determination, and Reduction." *Journal of Philosophy* 72 (1975): 551–64.

Hill, Thomas E., Jr. "Kantian Constructivism in Ethics." *Ethics* 99 (1989): 752–70.

———. "Kant's Argument for the Rationality of Moral Conduct." *Pacific Philosophical Quarterly* 66 (1985): 3–23.

———. "Kant's Theory of Practical Reason." *Monist* 72 (1989): 363–83.

Hoffman, Martin. "Developmental Synthesis of Affect and Cognition and Its Implications for Altruistic Motivation." *Developmental Psychology, Personality and Social Psychology* 40 (1981): 121–37.

———. "Moral Development." In *Carmichael's Manual of Child Psychology*, vol. 2. New York: John Wiley, 1970.

Holtzman, Steven, and Christopher Leich, eds. *Wittgenstein: To Follow a Rule.* Boston: Routledge & Kegan Paul, 1981.

Honderich, Ted, ed. *Morality and Objectivity.* London: Routledge & Kegan Paul, 1985.

Hooker, Brad, ed. *Rationality, Rules, Utility.* Boulder, Colo.: Westview Press, 1993.

Hookway, Christopher. "Two Conceptions of Moral Realism." *Proceedings of the Aristotelian Society,* supp. vol. 60 (l986): 188–205.

Horgan, Terence, and Mark Timmons. "Troubles for New Wave Moral Semantics. The Open Question Argument Revived." *Philosophical Papers* 21 (1992): 153–75.

———. "Troubles on Moral Twin Earth: Moral Queerness Revived." *Synthese* 92 (1992): 221–60.

Horwich, Paul. "The Essence of Expressivism." *Analysis* 54 (1994): 19–20.

———. "Gibbard's Theory of Norms." *Philosophy and Public Affairs* (1992): 67–78.

————. "Three Forms of Realism." *Synthese* 51: 181–201.

Hubin, Donald Clayton. "Prudential Reasons." *Canadian Journal of Philosophy* 10 (1980): 63–81.

Hudson, W. D. *Modern Moral Philosophy*. London: Macmillan, 1970.

————, ed. *The Is-Ought Question*. London: Macmillan, 1969.

————, ed. *New Studies in Ethics*. London: Macmillan, 1974.

Humberstone, I. L. "Direction of Fit." *Mind* (1992): 59–83.

Hurley, Susan. L. *Natural Reasons*. New York: Oxford University Press, 1992.

————. "Objectivity and Disagreement." In Honderich, *Morality and Objectivity*.

Jackson, Frank, Graham Oppy, and Michael Smith. "Minimalism and Truth-Aptness." *Mind* 103 (1994): 287–302.

Jacobson, Daniel, and Justin D'Arms. "Expressivism, Morality, and the Emotions." *Ethics* 104 (1994): 739–63.

Jeffrey, Richard C. *The Logic of Decision*. New York: McGraw-Hill, 1964.

Johnston, Mark "Dispositional Theories of Value." *Proceedings of the Aristotelian Society*, supp. vol. 63 (1989): 139–74.

————. "Objectivity Refigured." In Haldane and Wright, *Reality, Representation and Projection*.

Kagan, Shelly. "Does Consequentialism Demand Too Much?: Recent Work on the Limits of Obligation." *Philosophy and Public Affairs* 13 (1984): 239–54.

————. *The Limits of Morality*. Oxford: Oxford University Press, 1989.

————. "Present-Aim Theories of Rationality." *Ethics* 96 (1986): 746–59.

Kamm, Frances Myrna. *Creation and Abortion*. New York: Oxford University Press, 1989.

————. "Non-consequentialism, the Person as an End-in-Itself, and the Significance of Status." *Philosophy and Public Affairs* 21 (1992): 354–89.

————. "Supererogation and Obligation." *Journal of Philosophy* 82 (1985): 118–38.

Kavka, Gregory S. "The Reconciliation Project." In Copp and Zimmerman, *Morality, Reason and Truth*.

————. "The Toxin Puzzle." *Analysis* 43 (1983): 33–36.

Kim, Jaegwon. "Concepts of Supervenience." *Philosophy and Phenomenological Research* 45 (1984): 153–76.

————. "Epiphenomenal and Supervenient Causation." *Midwest Studies in Philosophy* 9 (1984): 257–70.

Klagge, James. "An Alleged Difficulty Concerning Moral Properties." *Mind* 93 (1984): 370–80.

Kohlberg, Lawrence. "The Claim to Moral Adequacy of a Highest Stage of Moral Judgment." *Journal of Philosophy* 70 (1973): 630–46.

Kolnai, Aurel. "Deliberation Is of Ends." In Kolnai, *Ethics, Value and Reality*.

————. *Ethics, Value and Reality*. Indianapolis: Hackett, 1978.

Korsgaard, Christine. "Creating the Kingdom of Ends: Reciprocity and Responsibility in Personal Relations." *Philosophical Perspectives* 6 (1992): 305–32.

————. "Kant's Analysis of Obligation: The Argument of Foundations I." *Monist* 72 (1989): 311–40.

————. "Morality as Freedom." In Yovel, *Kant's Practical Philosophy Reconsidered*.

————. "Personal Identity and the Unity of Agency: A Kantian Response to Parfit." *Philosophy and Public Affairs* 18 (1989): 101–32.

————. "Skepticism about Practical Reason." *Journal of Philosophy* 83 (1986): 5–25.

————. "The Reasons We Can Share." In Paul, *Altruism*.

————. "The Sources of Normativity." In Grethe Peterson, ed., *The Tanner Lectures on Human Values*, vol. 15. Salt Lake City: University of Utah Press, 1994.

————. "Two Distinctions in Goodness." *Philosophical Review* 92 (1983): 169–96.

Krausz, Michael, and Jack Meiland, eds. *Relativism: Cognitive and Moral*. Notre Dame, Ind.: University of Notre Dame Press, 1982.

Kripke, Saul. *Naming and Necessity*. Oxford: Blackwell, 1980.

————. *Wittgenstein on Rules and Private Language*. Cambridge, Mass.: Harvard University Press, 1982.

Kupperman, J. J. *Ethical Knowledge*. New York: Humanities Press, 1970.

————. "Moral Objectivity." In S. C. Brown, *Objectivity and Cultural Divergence*.

Lewis, C. I. *An Analysis of Knowledge and Valuation*. La Salle, Ill.: Open Court, 1947.

Lewis, David K. *Convention: A Philosophical Study*. Cambridge, Mass.: Harvard University Press, 1969.

————. "Desire as Belief." *Mind* 97 (1988): 323–32.

———. "Dispositional Theories of Value." *Proceedings of the Aristotelian Society*, supp. vol. 63 (1989): 113–37.

Lewis, H. D., ed. *Contemporary British Philosophy*. London: Allen & Unwin, 1976.

Lewy, Casimir. "G. E. Moore on the Naturalistic Fallacy." *Proceedings of the British Academy* 50 (1964): 251–62.

Little, I. M. D. *A Critique of Welfare Economics*. New York: Oxford University Press, 1957.

Lovibond, Sabina. *Realism and Imagination in Ethics*. Minneapolis: University of Minnesota Press, 1983.

Luce, R. D., and H. Raiffa. *Games and Decisions*. New York: Wiley, 1957.

Lyons, David. "Ethical Relativism and the Problem of Incoherence." *Ethics* 86 (1976): 107–21.

———. "Mill's Theory of Morality." *Nous* 10 (1976): 101–20.

———. "Nature and Soundness of the Contract and Coherence Arguments." In Daniels, *Reading Rawls*.

Machan, Tibor. "Epistemology and Moral Knowledge." *Review of Metaphysics* 36 (1982): 23–49.

Mackie, J. L. "A Refutation of Morals." *Australasian Journal of Philosophy* 24 (1946): 77–90.

———. *Ethics: Inventing Right and Wrong*. Harmondsworth, Middlesex: Penguin, 1977.

———. *Hume's Moral Theory*. London: Routledge & Kegan Paul. 1980.

———. *Persons and Values*. New York: Oxford University Press, 1985.

Marcus, Ruth Barcan. "Moral Dilemmas and Consistency." *Journal of Philosophy* 77 (1980): 121–36.

Marks, Joel, ed. *The Ways of Desire*. Chicago: Precedent, 1986.

McCloskey, H. J. *Meta-Ethics and Normative Ethics*. The Hague: Martinus Nijhoff, 1969.

McConnell, Terrance. "Metaethical Principles, Meta-Prescriptions, and Moral Theories. *American Philosophical Quarterly* 22 (1985): 299–309.

Macdonald, Graham, and Crispin Wright, eds. *Fact, Science, and Morality: Essays on A. J. Ayer's Language, Truth and Logic*. Oxford: Basil Blackwell, 1986.

McDowell, John. "Aesthetic Value, Objectivity, and the Fabric of the World." In Eva Schaper, *Pleasure, Preference, and Value* (Cambridge, Cambridge University Press, 1983).

———. "Are Moral Requirements Hypothetical Imperatives?" *Proceedings of the Aristotelian Society*, supp. vol. 52 (1978): 13–29.

———. "Are There External Reasons?" In Altham and Harrison, *World, Mind and Ethics*.

———. Critical notice of *Ethics and the Limits of Philosophy*. *Mind* 95 (1986): 377–86.

———. "Noncognitivism and Rule Following." In Holtzman and Leich, *Wittgenstein: To Follow a Rule*.

———. "Values and Secondary Qualities." In Honderich, *Morality and Objectivity*.

———. "Virtue and Reason." *Monist* 62 (1979): 331–50.

———. "Projection and Truth in Ethics." Lindley Lecture. University of Kansas, 1987.

———. "Values and Secondary Properties." In Honderich, *Morality and Objectivity*.

McGinn, Colin. *The Character of the Mind*. Oxford: Oxford University Press, 1982.

———. *The Subjective View*. Oxford: Oxford University Press, 1983.

MacIntyre, Alasdair. *After Virtue*. Notre Dame, Ind.: University of Notre Dame Press, 1981.

———. "What Morality Is Not." *Philosophy* 32 (1957): 325–55.

MacKenzie, J. C. "Moral Scepticism and Moral Conduct." *Philosophy* 59 (1984): 473–79.

McNaughton, David. *Moral Vision*. Oxford: Basil Blackwell, 1988.

———, and P. Rawling. "Agent-Relativity and the Doing/Happening Distinction." *Philosophical Studies* 63 (1991): 167–85.

Melden, A. I., ed. *Essays on Moral Philosophy*. Seattle: University of Washington Press, 1958.

———. "On the Method of Ethics." *Journal of Philosophy* 75 (1948): 169–81.

———. "Reasons for Action and Matters of Fact." *Proceedings of the American Philosophical Association* 35 (1962): 46–60.

Mendola, Joseph. "Normative Realism, or Bernard Williams at the Limit." *Australasian Journal of Philosophy* 67 (1989): 306–18.

———. "Objective Value and Subjective States." *Philosophical and Phenomenological Research* 50 (1990): 695–713.

Midgley, M. *Beast and Man: The Roots of Human Nature*. Ithaca, N.Y.: Cornell University Press, 1978.

Miller, Richard. *Fact and Method Explanation, Confirmation, and Reality in the Natural and Social Sciences*. Princeton: Princeton University Press, 1987.

———. "Reason and Commitment in the Social Sciences." *Philosophy and Public Affairs* 8 (1979): 241–66.

———. "Ways of Moral Learning." *Philosophical Review* 94 (1985): 507–56.

Mischel, Theodore, ed. *The Self.* Oxford: Basil Blackwell, 1977.

Monro, D. H. *Empiricism and Ethics.* Cambridge: Cambridge University Press, 1967.

Montague, Phillip. "On the Relation of Natural Properties to Normative and Evaluative Properties." *Philosophy and Phenomenological Research* 35 (1975): 341–51.

Montefiore, A., ed. *Philosophy and Personal Relations.* London: Routledge & Kegan Paul, 1973.

Moore, G. E. "The Conception of Intrinsic Value." In *Philosophical Studies.*

———. *Ethics.* Oxford: Oxford University Press, 1921.

———. "Is Goodness a Quality?" In *Philosphical Papers.*

———. *Philosophical Papers.* London: George Allen & Unwin, 1959.

———. *Philosophical Studies.* Boston: Routledge & Kegan Paul, 1922.

———. *Principia Ethica.* Cambridge: Cambridge University Press, 1903.

———. "Reply to My Critics." In Schilpp, *The Philosophy of G. E. Moore.*

Murdoch, Iris. *Metaphysics as a Guide to Morals.* London: Chatto, 1992.

———. *The Sovereignty of Good.* London: Cambridge University Press, 1970.

Nagel, E., "The Meaning of Reduction in the Natural Sciences." In Stauffer, *Science and Civilization.*

———. *The Structure of Science.* Boston: Routledge & Kegan Paul, 1961.

Nagel, Thomas. *Equality and Partiality.* New York: Oxford University Press, 1991.

———. "The Fragmentation of Value." In *Mortal Questions.*

———. *Mortal Questions.* New York: Cambridge University Press, 1979.

———. *The Possibility of Altruism.* Princeton: Princeton University Press, 1978.

———. "Review of *Moral Thinking* by R. M. Hare." *London Review of Books.* 15 January 1982.

———. "Subjective and Objective." In *Mortal Questions.*

———. *The View From Nowhere.* New York: Oxford University Press, 1987.

Narveson, Jan. "Reason in Ethics—Or Reason versus Ethics." In Copp and Zimmerman, *Morality, Reason and Truth.*

Nesbitt, W. "Categorical Imperatives: A Defense." *Philosophical Review* 86 (1977): 217–25.

Nielsen, Kai. "The 'Good Reasons' Approach and Ontological Justification of Morality." *Philosophical Quarterly* 9 (1959): 116–30.

———. "Must the Immoralist Act Contrary to Reason?" In Copp and Zimerman, *Morality, Reason and Truth.*

———. "On Deriving an Ought from an Is: A Retrospective Look." *Review of Metaphysics* 32 (1979): 487–514.

Norman, Richard. *Reasons for Actions.* Oxford: Blackwell, 1971.

Nowell-Smith, P. H. *Ethics.* London: Penguin, 1954.

Nozick, Robert. *Anarchy, State and Utopia.* New York: Basic Books, 1974.

———. "Moral Complications and Moral Structures." *Natural Law Forum* 13 (1968): 1–50.

———. *The Nature of Rationality.* Princeton, N.J.: Princeton University Press, 1993.

———. *Philosophical Explanations.* Cambridge, Mass.: Harvard University Press, 1981.

Nussbaum, Martha. " 'Finely Aware and Richly Responsible': Moral Attention and the Moral Task of Literature." *Journal of Philosophy* 82 (1985): 516–29.

O'Neill, Onora. *Constructions of Reason: Explorations of Kant's Practical Philosophy.* New York: Cambridge University Press, 1989.

Ogden, C. K. and I. A. Richards. *The Meaning of Meaning.* London: Routledge & Kegan Paul, 1949.

Olson, Mancur, Jr. *The Logic of Collective Action.* Cambridge, Mass.: Harvard University Press, 1965.

Parfit, Derek. "Later Selves and Moral Principles." In Montefiore, *Philosophy and Personal Relations.*

———. "Prudence, Morality and the Prisoner's Dilemma." *Proceedings of the British Academy* (1979): 539–64.

———. *Reasons and Persons.* Oxford: Oxford University Press, 1984.

Paul, Ellen Frankel, ed. *Altruism.* Cambridge: Cambridge University Press, 1993.

Pettit, Phillip. "Backgrounding Desire." *Philosophical Review* (1990): 565–92.

———. *The Common Mind.* New York: Oxford University Press, 1993.

———. "Evaluative 'Realism' and Interpretation." In Holtzman and Leich, *Wittgenstein: To Follow a Rule.*

————. "Humeans, Anti-Humeans and Motivation." *Mind* (1987): 53–79.

Pettit, Phillip, and Michael Smith. "Brandt on Self-Control." In Hooker, *Rationality, Rules, Utility*.

————. "Practical Unreason." *Mind* (1993): 53–79.

Perry, R. B. *General Theory of Value*. New York: Longmans, Green, 1926.

Perry, Thomas D. *Moral Reasoning and Truth*. Oxford: Oxford University Press, 1976.

Philips, M. "Weighing Moral Reasons." *Mind* 96 (1987): 367–75.

Phillips, D. Z. "Does it Pay to be Good?" In Dworkin and Thomson, *Ethics*.

————. "In Search of the Moral Must." *Philosophical Quarterly* 27 (1977): 140–57.

Phillips, D. Z., and H. O. Mounce. *Moral Practices*. London: Routledge & Kegan Paul, 1969.

————. "On Morality's Having a Point." *Philosophy* 40 (1965): 308–19.

Piper, Adrian M. S. "Instrumentalism, Objectivity, and Moral Justification." *American Philosophical Quarterly* 23 (1986): 373–81.

————. "Two Conceptions of the Self." *Philosophical Studies* 48 (1985): 173–98.

Platts, Mark. "Moral Realism and the End of Desire." in *Reference, Truth and Meaning*.

————. *Moral Realities*. London: Routledge, 1992.

————. *Ways of Meaning*. London: Routledge & Kegan Paul, 1979.

————, ed. *Reference, Truth and Meaning*. London: Routledge & Kegan Paul, 1981.

Postow, B. C. "Moral Relativism Avoided." *Personalist* 60 (1979): 95–100.

————. "Werner's Ethical Realism." *Ethics* 95 (1985): 285–91.

Price, A. W. "Varieties of Objectivity and Values." *Proceedings of the Aristotelian Society* 82 (1982–83): 103–19.

Price, Huw. "Defending Desire-as-Belief." *Mind* (1989): 119–27.

————. *Facts and the Function of Truth*. Oxford: Basil Blackwell, 1988.

Prichard, H. A. "Does Moral Philosophy Rest On A Mistake?" *Mind* 21 (1912): 21–37.

————. "Duty and Interest." In *Duty and Interest*. London: Oxford University Press, 1928.

————. *Moral Obligation*. New York: Oxford University Press, 1949.

Prior, A. N. *Logic and the Basis of Ethics*. New York: Oxford University Press, 1949.

————. *Papers in Logic and Ethics*. London: Duckworth, 1976.

————. "The Autonomy of Ethics." *Australasian Journal of Philosophy* 38 (1960): 199–206.

Putnam, Hilary. *How Not To Solve Ethical Problems*. Lindley Lectures. Lawrence: University of Kansas, 1983.

————. *The Many Faces of Realism*. LaSalle, Ill.: Open Court, 1987.

————. *Mathematics, Matter and Method: Philosophical Papers, Vol. I*. Cambridge: Cambridge University Press, 1977.

————. *Meaning and the Moral Sciences*. Boston: Routledge & Kegan Paul, 1978.

————. "The Meaning of 'Meaning'." In *Mind, Language and Reality*.

————. *Mind, Language, and Reality: Philosophical Papers*. Cambridge: Cambridge University Press, 1975.

————. *Realism and Reason: Philosophical Papers*. Cambridge: Cambridge University Press, 1983.

————. *Reason, Truth, and History*. New York: Cambridge University Press, 1981.

Quine, W. V. "Epistemology Naturalized." In *Ontological Relativity and Other Essays*.

————. *From a Logical Point of View*. New York: Harper & Row, 1961.

————. "Moral and Other Realisms: Some Initial Difficulties." In Goldman and Kim, *Values and Morals*.

————. *Ontological Relativity and Other Essays*. New York: Columbia University Press, 1969.

————. "The Nature of Natural Knowledge." In Guttenplan, *Mind and Language*.

————. "Two Dogmas of Empiricism." *Philosophical Review* 60 (1951): 20–43.

————. *Word and Object*. Cambridge, Mass.: MIT Press, 1960.

Quinn, Warren. "Egoism as an Ethical System." *Journal of Philosophy* 71 (1974): 456–72.

————. "Moral and Other Realisms." In Goldman and Kim, *Values and Morals*.

————. *Morality and Action*. New York: Cambridge University Press, 1993.

————. "Putting Rationality in Its Place." In Frey and Morris, *Value, Welfare, and Morality*.

————. "Rationality and the Human Good." *Social Philosophy and Policy* 9 (1992): 81–95.

————. "Reflection and the Loss of Moral Knowledge." *Philosophy and Public Affairs* 16 (1987): 195–209.

————. "Truth and Explanation in Ethics." *Ethics* 96 (1986): 524–44.

Railton, Peter. "Alienation, Consequentialism, and The Demands of Morality." *Philosophy and Public Affairs* 13 (1984): 134–71.

———. "Facts and Values." *Philosophical Topics* 24 (1986): 5–31.

———. "Moral Realism." *Philosophical Review* 95 (1986): 163–207.

———. "Naturalism and Prescriptivity." *Social Philosophy and Policy* 7 (1989): 151–74.

———. "Nonfactualism about Normative Discourse." *Philosophy and Phenomenological Research* 52 (1992): 961–68.

———. "Reply to David Wiggins." In Haldane and Wright, *Reality, Representation and Projection*.

———. "Some Questions About the Justification of Morality." *Philosophical Perspectives* 6 (1992): 27–54.

———. "Subject-ive and Objective," *Ratio* 8 new series (1995): 259–76.

———. "What the Noncognitivist Helps Us To See the Naturalist Must Help Us To Explain." In Haldane and Wright, *Reality, Representation and Projection*.

Ramsey, Frank P. "Theories." In *Foundations of Mathematics*. London: Routledge & Kegan Paul, 1931.

Rapoport, Anatol, ed. *Game Theory as a Theory of Conflict Resolution*. Dordrecht, Netherlands: Reidel, 1974.

Rawls, John. "The Independence of Moral Theory." *Proceedings of the American Philosophical Association* (1975): 5–22.

———. "Justice as Fairness." In Bedeau, *Justice and Equality*.

———. "Kantian Constructivism in Moral Theory." *Journal of Philosophy* 77 (1980): 515–72.

———. "Outline of a Decision Procedure for Ethics." *Philosophical Review* 60 (1951): 177–97.

———. *A Theory of Justice*. Cambridge, Mass.: Harvard University Press, 1971.

Raz, J. "Mixing Values." *Proceedings of the Aristotelian Society*, supp. vol. 65 (1991): 83–101.

———. *The Morality of Freedom*. Oxford: Oxford University Press, 1986.

———. *Practical Reason and Norms*. Princeton: Princeton University Press, 1990.

———. "Reasons for Action, Decisions and Norms." *Mind* 84 (1975): 481–99.

———. "Value Incommensurability." *Proceedings of the Aristotelian Society* 86 (1985–86): 117–34.

Regan, Donald H. "Against Evaluator Relativity: A Response to Sen." *Philosophy and Public Affairs* 12 (1983): 93–112.

———. *Utilitarianism and Cooperation*. Oxford: Oxford University Press, 1980.

Rescher, N. *Unselfishness*. Pittsburgh: University of Pittsburgh Press, 1975.

Richards, David A. J. *A Theory of Reasons for Action*. Oxford: Oxford University Press, 1971.

Robinson, H. M. "Is Hare a Naturalist?" *Philosophical Review* 91 (1982): 73–86.

Rorty, Richard. *Philosophy and the Mirror of Nature*. Princeton: Princeton University Press, 1979.

Rosati, Connie S. "Naturalism, Normativity, and the Open Question Argument." *Nous* 29 (1995): 46–70.

———. "Persons, Perspectives, and Full Information Accounts of the Good." *Ethics* 105 (1995): 296–325.

Ross, W. D. *Foundations of Ethics*. Oxford: Oxford University Press, 1939.

———. *The Right and the Good*. Oxford: Oxford University Press, 1930.

Russell, Bruce. "Moral Relativism and Moral Realism." *Monist* 67 (1984): 435–51.

Sartorius, R. *Individual Conduct and Social Norms*. Encino, Calif.: Dickenson, 1975.

Sayre-McCord, Geoffrey, "Coherence and Models for Moral Theorizing." *Pacific Philosophical Quarterly* 66 (1986): 170–90.

———. "The Many Moral Realisms." *Southern Journal of Philosophy*, supp. vol. 24 (1986): 1–22.

———. "Moral Theory and Explanatory Impotence." In *Essays on Moral Realism*.

———. "Normative Explanations." *Philosophical Perspectives* 6 (1992): 55–72.

———, ed. *Essays on Moral Realism*. Ithaca, N.Y.: Cornell University Press, 1988.

Scanlon, T. M. "Contractualism and Utilitarianism." In Sen and Williams, *Utilitarianism and Beyond*.

———. "Preference and Urgency." *Journal of Philosophy* 72 (1975): 655–69.

———. "Rawls' Theory of Justice." In Daniels, *Reading Rawls*.

———. "The Significance of Choice." In Sterling M. McMurrin, ed., *The Tanner Lectures on Human Values*, vol. 8. Salt Lake City: University of Utah Press, 1988.

Scheffler, Samuel. "Agent-Centered Restrictions, Rationality, and the Virtues." *Mind* 94 (1985): 409–19.

———. *Human Morality*. New York: Oxford University Press, 1992.

———. "Morality's Demands and Their Limits." *Journal of Philosophy* 83 (1986): 531–37.

————. "Prerogatives Without Restrictions." *Philosophical Perspectives* 6 (1992): 377–98.

————. *The Rejection of Consequentialism*. Oxford: Oxford University Press, 1982.

————, ed. *Consequentialism and Its Critics*. Oxford: Oxford University Press, 1988.

Schilpp, P. A., ed. *The Philosophy of G. E. Moore*. La Salle, Ill.: Open Court, 1968.

Schlick, Moritz. *Problems of Ethics*. New York: Dover, 1962.

Schmidtz, David. "Choosing Ends." *Ethics* 104 (1994): 226–51.

————. *Rational Choice and Moral Agency*. Princeton, N.J.: Princeton University Press, 1995.

————. "Rationality Within Reason." *Journal of Philosophy* 89 (1992): 445–66.

Schneewind, J. B. *Sidgwick's Ethics and Modern Victorian Moral Philosophy*. New York: Oxford, 1977.

Schueler, G. F. "Pro-Attitudes and Directions of Fit." *Mind* (1991): 277–81.

Schultz, Bart. *Essays on Henry Sidgwick*. Cambridge: Cambridge University Press, 1992.

Scott, Robert B., Jr. "Five Types of Ethical Naturalism." *American Philosophical Quarterly* 17 (1980): 261–70.

Searle, John. "How to Derive 'Ought' from 'Is.' " *Philosophical Review* 73 (1964): 43–58.

Sellars, W. "Empiricism and the Philosophy of Mind." Reprinted in *Science, Perception, and Reality*. Boston: Routledge & Kegan Paul, 1963.

Sen, Amartya. *Choice, Welfare, and Measurement*. Oxford: Blackwell, 1982.

————. *Collective Choice and Social Welfare*. San Francisco: Holden-Day, 1970.

————. "Rights and Agency." *Philosophy and Public Affairs* 11 (1982): 3–39.

————. "Utilitarianism and Welfarism." *Journal of Philosophy* 76 (1979): 463–89.

————, and Bernard Williams, eds. *Utilitarianism and Beyond*. Cambridge: Cambridge University Press, 1982.

Shope, R. "The Conditional Fallacy in Contemporary Philosophy." *Journal of Philosophy* 75 (1978): 397–413.

Sidgwick, Henry. "The Establishment of Ethical First Principles." *Mind* 4 (1879): 106–11.

————. *The Methods of Ethics*, 7th ed. New York: Macmillan, 1962.

Singer, Marcus. *Generalization in Ethics*. New York: Knopf, 1961.

Singer, Peter. *The Expanding Circle: Ethics and Sociobiology*. New York: Farrar, Straus & Giroux, 1981.

————. "Sidgwick and Reflective Equilibrium." *Monist* 57 (1974): 490–517.

————. *Practical Ethics*. Cambridge: Cambridge University Press, 1979.

————. "The Triviality of the Debate over 'Is-Ought' and the Definition of 'Moral'." *American Philosophical Quarterly* 10 (1973): 51–56.

————, ed. *A Companion to Ethics*. Oxford: Blackwell, 1991.

Sinnott-Armstrong, Walter. *Moral Dilemmas*. Oxford: Blackwell, 1988.

————. "Moral Realisms and Moral Dilemmas." *Journal of Philosophy* 84 (1987): 263–76.

Slote, Michael. *Beyond Optimizing: A Study of Rational Choice*. Cambridge, Mass.: Harvard University Press, 1989.

————. *Common-sense Morality and Consequentialism*. London: Routledge & Kegan Paul, 1985.

————. "Ethics Naturalized." *Philosophical Perspectives* 6 (1992): 355–76.

————. *From Morality to Virtue*. New York: Oxford University Press, 1992.

Smart, J. J. C. *Ethics, Persuasion and Truth*. London: Routledge & Kegan Paul, 1984.

Smart, J. J. C. "An Outline of a System of Utilitarian Ethics." In Smart and Williams, *Utilitarianism*.

————, and B. Williams. *Utilitarianism: For and Against*. Cambridge: Cambridge University Press, 1973.

Smith, Holly M. "Deriving Morality from Rationality." In Vallentyne, *Contractarianism and Rational Choice*.

————. "Moral Realism, Moral Conflict, and Compound Acts." *Journal of Philosophy* 83 (1986): 341–43.

Smith, Michael. "Dispositional Theories of Value." *Proceedings of the Aristotelian Society*, supp. vol. 63 (1989): 89–111.

————. "The Humean Theory of Motivation." *Mind* (1987): 36–61.

————. "Internal Reasons." *Philosophy and Phenomenological Research* 55 (1995): 109–31.

————. "Internalism's Wheel." *Ratio* 8 new series (1995): 277–302.

————. "Minimalism, Truth-Aptitude and Belief." *Analysis* (1994): 21–26.

————. *The Moral Problem*. Oxford: Blackwell, 1994.

————. "Objectivity and Moral Realism: On the Significance of the Phenomenology of Moral Experience." In Haldane and Wright, *Reality, Representation and Projection*.

————. "On Humeans, Anti-Humeans and Motivation: A Reply to Pettit." *Mind* 97 (1988): 589–95.

————. "Reason and Desire." *Proceedings of the Aristotelian Society* (1988): 243–56.

————. "Should We Believe in Emotivism?" In Macdonald and Wright, *Fact, Science, and Morality*.

————. "Why Expressivists about Value Should Love Minimalism about Truth." *Analysis* (1994): 1–12.

————, Frank Jackson, and Graham Oppy. "Minimalism and Truth Aptness." *Mind* 103 (1994): 287–302.

Snare, Frank. "The Argument from Motivation." *Mind* 84 (1975): 1–9.

————. "The Diversity of Morals." *Mind* 89 (1980): 353–69.

————. "The Empirical Bases of Moral Scepticism." *American Philosophical Quartery* 21 (1984): 215–25.

————. "Externalism in Ethics." *Philosophical Quarterly* 24 (1974): 362–65.

————. "Three Sceptical Theses in Ethics." *American Philosophical Quarterly* 14 (1977): 129–36.

Sobel, David. "Full Information Accounts of Well-Being. *Ethics* 104 (1994): 784–810.

Solomon, Wm. David. "Moral Realism and the Amoralist." *Midwest Studies in Philosophy* 12 (1987): 377–94.

Stauffer, Robert, ed. *Science and Civilization*. Madison: University of Wisconsin Press, 1949.

Sterba, James. "Justifying Morality." *Synthese* 72 (1987): 45–69.

Stevenson, C. L. "The Emotive Meaning of Ethical Terms." *Mind* 46 (1937): 14–31.

————. *Ethics and Language*. New Haven: Yale University Press, 1944.

————. *Facts and Values*. New Haven: Yale University Press, 1963.

Stocker, Michael. "Agent and Other: Against Ethical Universalism." *Australasian Journal of Philosophy* 54 (1976): 206–20.

————. "Akrasia and the Object of Desire." In Marks, *The Ways of Desire*.

————. "Desiring the Bad: An Essay in Moral Psychology." *Journal of Philosophy* 76 (1979): 738–53.

————. "Emotional Thoughts." *American Philosophical Quarterly* 24 (1987): 59–69.

————. *Plural and Conflicting Values*. New York: Oxford University Press, 1990.

————. "The Schizophrenia of Modern Ethical Theories." *Journal of Philosophy* 73 (1976): 453–66.

Sturgeon, Nicholas. "Altruism, Solipsism, and the Objectivity of Reasons." *Philosophical Review* 83 (1974): 374–402.

————. "Brandt's Moral Empiricism." *Philosophical Review* 91 (1982): 389–422.

————. "Gibbard on Moral Judgment and Norms." *Ethics* 96 (1985): 22–33.

————. "Harman on Moral Explanations of Natural Facts." *Southern Journal of Philosophy*, supp. vol. 24 (1986): 69–78.

————. "Moral Disagreement and Moral Relativism." *Social Philosophy and Policy* 11 (1994): 80–115.

————. "Moral Explanations." In Copp and Zimmerman, *Morality, Reason and Truth*.

————. "What Difference Does It Make Whether Moral Realism Is True?" *Southern Journal of Philosophy*, supp. vol. 24 (1986): 115–42.

Taylor, Charles. "The Diversity of Goods." In Sen and Williams, *Utilitarianism and Beyond*.

————. "What Is Human Agency." In Mischel, *The Self*.

Thomas, Laurence. *Living Morally: A Psychology of Moral Character*. Philadelphia: Temple University Press, 1989.

Thomson, Judith Jarvis. *The Realm of Rights*. Cambridge, Mass.: Harvard University Press, 1990.

————, and Gerald Dworkin, ed. *Ethics*. New York: Harper & Row, 1968.

Timmons, Mark. "Irrealism and Error in Ethics." *Philosophia* 22 (1993): 373–406.

————, and Terrence Horgan. "Troubles for New Wave Moral Semantics. The Open Question Argument Revived." *Philosophical Papers* 21 (1992): 153–75.

————. "Troubles on Moral Twin Earth: Moral Queerness Revived." *Synthese* 92 (1992): 221–60.

Toulmin, Stephen. *The Place of Reason in Ethics*. Cambridge: Cambridge University Press, 1961.

Trigg, Roger. *Reason and Commitment*. Cambridge: Cambridge University Press, 1973.

Trivers, R. L. "The Evolution of Reciprocal Altruism." *Quarterly Review of Biology* 46 (1971): 35–57.

Tversky, A., and D. Kahneman. "Rational Choice and the Framing of Decisions." *Journal of Business* 59 (1986): 251–78.

Urmson, J. O. "A Defence of Intuitionism." *Proceedings of the Aristotelian Society* 75 (1975): 144–52.

————. *The Emotive Theory of Ethics*. Oxford: Oxford University Press, 1968.

———. "On Grading." *Mind* 59 (1950): 145–69.

———. "Saints and Heroes." In Melden, *Essays on Moral Philosophy*.

Vallentyne, Peter, ed. *Contractarianism and Rational Choice*. Cambridge: Cambridge University Press, 1991.

Van Straaten, ed. *Philosophical Subjects: Essays Presented to P. F. Strawson*. Oxford: Oxford University Press, 1980.

Velleman, J. David. "The Guise of the Good." *Nous* 26 (1992): 3–26.

———. *Practical Reflection*. Princeton: Princeton University Press, 1989.

———. "Well-Being and Time." *Pacific Philosophical Quarterly* 72 (1991): 48–77.

———. "What Happens When Someone Acts?" *Mind* 101 (1992): 461–81.

Von Neumann, John, and Oskar Morgenstern. *Theory of Games and Economic Behavior*. Princeton: Princeton University Press, 1944.

Von Wright, G. H. *The Varieties of Goodness*. London: Routledge & Kegan Paul, 1963.

Wallace, James. *Moral Relevance and Moral Conflict*. Ithaca, N.Y.: Cornell University Press, 1988.

———. *Virtues and Vices*. Ithaca, N.Y.: Cornell University Press, 1978.

Wallace, Jay. "How To Argue about Practical Reason." *Mind* (1990): 267–97.

Walker, Maragaret Urban. "Feminism, Ethics, and the Question of Theory." *Hypatia* 7 (1992): 23–38.

Warnock, G. J. *Contemporary Moral Philosophy*. London: Macmillan, N.Y.: St. Martin's Press, 1967.

———. *The Object of Morality*. London: Methuen, 1971.

Watson, Gary. "Free Agency." In *Free Will*.

———, ed. *Free Will*. New York: Oxford University Press, 1982.

Wellman, Carl. "Emotivism and Ethical Objectivity." *American Philosophical Quarterly* 5 (1968): 90–99.

———. "Ethical Disagreement and Objective Truth." *American Philosophical Quarterly* 12 (1975): 211–21.

Werner, Richard. "Ethical Realism." *Ethics* 93 (1983): 653–79.

———. "Ethical Realism Defended." *Ethics* 95 (1983): 292–96.

Westermarck, Edvard Alexander. *Ethical Relativity*. New York: Humanities Press, 1932.

White, Morton. *What Is and What Ought To Be Done*. New York: Oxford University Press, 1981.

Whiting, J. "Friends and Future Selves." *Philosophical Review* 95 (1986): 547–80.

Wiggins, D. "Categorical Requirements: Hume and Kant on the Idea of Duty." Inaugural Lecture, Birbeck College, London, 1991.

———. "Cognitivism, Naturalism, and Normativity: A Reply to Peter Railton." In Haldane and Wright, *Reality, Representation and Projection*.

———. "Deliberation and Practical Reason." *Proceedings of the Aristotelian Society* 76 (1975–76): 29–51.

———. *Needs, Values, Truth: Essays in the Philosophy of Value*. Oxford: Blackwell, 1987.

———. "A Neglected Position?" In Haldane and Wright, *Reality, Representation and Projection*.

———. "Objective and Subjective in Ethics, with Two Postscripts on Truth." *Ratio* 8 new series (1995):227–42.

———. "A Sensible Subjectivism?" In *Needs, Values, Truth*.

———. "Truth, and Truth as Predicated of Moral Judgments." In *Needs, Values, Truth*.

———. "Truth, Invention, and the Meaning of Life." *Proceedings of the British Academy* 62 (1976): 331–78. Reprinted in *Needs, Values, Truth*.

———. "Weakness of Will, Commensurability, and the Objects of Desire." *Proceedings of the Aristotelian Society* 79 (1979): 251–77.

Williams, Bernard. "A Critique of Utilitarianism." In Smart and Williams, *Utilitarianism*.

———. "Ethical Consistency." In *Problems of the Self*.

———. "Ethics and the Fabric of the World." In Honderich, *Morality and Objectivity*.

———. *Ethics and the Limits of Philosophy*. Cambridge, Mass.: Harvard University Press, 1985.

———. "Internal and External Reasons." In *Moral Luck*.

———. "Internal Reasons and the Obscurity of Blame." *Logos* 10 (1989): 1–11.

———. *Making Sense of Humanity*. Cambridge: Cambridge University Press, 1995.

———. *Moral Luck*. New York: Cambridge University Press, 1981.

———. *Morality: An Introduction to Ethics*. New York: Harper & Row and Cambridge University Press, 1972.

————. "Persons, Character and Morality." In *Moral Luck*.

————. *Problems of the Self*. Cambridge: Cambridge University Press, 1973.

————. "The Scientific and the Ethical." In S. C. Brown, *Objectivity and Cultural Divergence*.

————. "Truth in Ethics." *Ratio* 8 new series (1995): 227–42.

————. "The Truth in Relativism." In *Moral Luck*.

————. "What Does Intuitionism Imply?" In Dancy, Moravcsik, and Taylor, *Human Agency*.

————, and J. J. C. Smart. *Utilitarianism: For and Against*. Cambridge: Cambridge University Press, 1973.

Winch, Peter. *Ethics and Action*. Oxford: Blackwell, 1972.

————. "The Universalizability of Moral Judgments." *Monist* 49 (1965): 196–214.

Wittgenstein, Ludwig. "Lecture on Ethics." *Philosophical Review* 74 (1965): 3–11.

————. *On Certainty*. Oxford: Basil Blackwell, 1969.

————. *Philosophical Grammar*. Berkeley: University of California Press, 1974.

————. *Philosophical Investigations*. Translated by G. E. M. Anscombe. London: Macmillan, 1953.

Wolf, Susan. "Above and Below the Line of Duty." *Philosophical Topics* 14 (1986): 131–48.

————. "Asymmetrical Freedom" *Journal of Philosophy* 77 (1980): 151–66.

————. "Moral Saints." *Journal of Philosophy* 79 (1982): 419–39.

Wong, David. *Moral Relativity*. Berkeley: University of California Press, 1984.

Woods, Michael. "Reasons for Action and Desire." *Proceedings of the Aristotelian Society*, supp. vol. 46 (1972): 189–201.

Wright, Crispin. "Moral Values, Projection, and Secondary Qualities." *Proceedings of the Aristotelian Society*, supp. vol. 62 (1988): 1–26.

————. "Realism, Antirealism, Irrealism, Quasi-Realism." *Midwest Studies in Philosophy* 12 (1987): 25–50.

————. "Realism: The Contemporary Debate—Whither Now?" In Haldane and Wright, *Reality, Representation and Projection*.

————. *Truth and Objectivity*. Cambridge, Mass.: Harvard University Press, 1992.

————. "Truth in Ethics." *Ratio* 8 new series (1995): 209–26.

Yovel, Y., ed. *Kant's Practical Philosophy Reconsidered*. Dordrecht, Netherlands: Kluwer Academic Publishers, 1989.

Zimmerman, David. "The Force of Hypothetical Commitment." *Ethics* 93 (1983): 467–83.

————. "Moral Realism and Explanatory Necessity." In Copp and Zimmerman, *Morality, Reason and Truth*.

————. "Meta-Ethics Naturalized." *Canadian Journal of Philosophy* 10 (1980): 637–62.